BROWNING

PATRI FILIVS

FILIIS PATER

BROWNING

Poetry and Prose

Selected by

SIMON NOWELL-SMITH

HARVARD UNIVERSITY PRESS
Cambridge Massachusetts
1951

Printed and bound in Great Britain
by Butler & Tanner Ltd., Frome and London

Contents

PROSE

ACKNOWLEDGMENTS

No modern editor of Browning can fail to be in the debt of *A Browning Handbook* by William Clyde De Vane (John Murray 1937), that inspired compendium of all earlier commentaries.

Browning's letters are printed by kind permission of Mr. John Murray. The chronological table is adapted, with permission, from the table in Sir Humphrey Milford's *Browning* in the Clarendon English Series, 1941.

To Sir Humphrey Milford and Mr. Frederick Page I owe gratitude for help in elucidating difficulties in the letters.

S. N.-S.

Introduction

A SHORT selection from a poet's work must be limited to what the selector thinks his best, or his most characteristic, poems: short selections from Browning have tended to conform, with honourable variations, to a well-defined pattern. In the more ample space allowed me I have sought to assemble not only the best in Browning's most characteristic kinds—the dramatic lyric and romance, the portrayal of men and women—but something that is good and representative in every kind he tried. The intention is to shew the branches as well as the trunk of the tree. *Pauline* is not a great poem: Browning himself in middle life viewed it with "extreme repugnance" and had no wish for it to be remembered. But without some acquaintance with *Pauline*, as well as with the maturer *Paracelsus*, we cannot measure the extent, or appreciate the nature, of the influence exerted upon Browning by Shelley (we cannot trace the root of our tree); wherefore I have printed more of *Pauline* than anthologists have commonly done; and I have printed it as it first appeared in 1833, instead of in the more easily accessible "definitive" text of 1888, because the understanding of a poet's development, both his thought and his technique, must start with what he wrote at twenty, not with the improvements that occurred to him at seventy-five. For the same reason I have preferred the earliest texts of the later books (except where revision followed hard upon first publication*), and have kept the arrangement of the poems in the original editions. Browning's rearrangements, particularly his shuffling and redealing of *Dramatic Lyrics*, *Dramatic Romances* and *Men and Women* for the collected edition of 1863, have little to commend them.

In his life Browning had two reputations, for wilful obscurity and for deep philosophical and theological wisdom. Neither reputation to-day seems well founded.

* The exceptions are noted in the bibliographical notes that precede each section.

Scholarship has resolved most of the obscurities and biography has rebutted the charge of wilfulness: exuberance and impatience, both enemies of clear expression yet each in its way a virtue, did more to make Browning " difficult" than either intention or any unusual profundity of thought. As for theology, metaphysical or natural, the fact that his poetry once gave strength to those whose faith had otherwise been shaken by Strauss and Renan, or by Darwin and Huxley, does not make a great religious or scientific thinker of him—though it may help to explain what made him a great poet. Therefore in choosing poems that deal with the religious opinions, theological controversies or scientific theories of the age I have given little weight to intellectual consistency, and none to the preferences of his contemporaries. The only two enduring, if disparate, criteria are, as it seems to me: what is poetry, and what throws most light upon Browning. (Browning's views on the origin of species throw more light upon Browning than upon the origin of species.) Thus *Christmas-Eve* has been preferred to *Easter-Day*, and the selected *Parleyings* qualify certainly by the second, if only doubtfully by the first criterion. Yet his most ambitious treatments of belief (with few exceptions) are inevitably here. He would not have been Browning if he had not put the best of his poetry, and of himself, into *Saul*, *Cleon*, *Karshish*, *Bishop Blougram*, *A Death in the Desert*, *Caliban upon Setebos*. If important poems have been omitted, that is because it seemed more just to print these and certain others at their full length—*Mr. Sludge "The Medium"* for instance runs to more than 1500 lines—than to extract from them and from as many more a farrago of uplifting but unrelated "beauties from Browning".

Extraction was unavoidable with the early poems (*Pauline*, *Paracelsus*, *Sordello*), if they were to find room at all. The plays are represented only by lyrics from *Pippa Passes* and *A Blot in the 'Scutcheon*. But the *Dramatic Lyrics* and *Dramatic Romances and Lyrics* of 1842–45 are all here, and all unmutilated; and if the later comparable volumes of shorter poems, from *Men and Women* to *Asolando*, have been subjected to a progressively more rigid selection, in only three instances has a selected poem not been given in full—the song from

James Lee, which Browning himself printed as a separate song in more than one volume of selections; the song from the *Parleying with Charles Avison* ("Roundhead Tune"), which likewise is complete in itself; and a passage from the *Parleying with Francis Furini*, included, as has been suggested, for the light Browning's views on evolution throw upon Browning. There are also two short extracts from the longer narrative poems—a song from *Aristophanes' Apology* ("Thamuris Marching"), and the invocation to the poet's dead wife that closes the first book of *The Ring and the Book*. There is good precedent for detaching both these: without at least the second of them no volume of selections could claim to be representative.

For the longer narrative poems, apart from the two extracts just mentioned, a single book of *The Ring and the Book* does duty. That magnificent verse-novel, published in 1868–9, was followed in the 'seventies by a series of volumes, each containing one long poem—*Balaustion's Adventure*, *Prince Hohenstiel-Schwangau*, *Fifine at the Fair*, *Red Cotton Night-Cap Country*, *Aristophanes' Apology*, *The Inn Album*—not one of which is altogether without interest or altogether without its beauties; not one of which however can hold a candle to the best of *The Ring and the Book*. About that best, opinions have differed; and when Mr. D. C. Somervell wrote, in his shrewd and amusing essay on *The Reputation of Robert Browning*,* that it is a mistake to assume that "about three" of the twelve books contain all of permanent value in the poem, for "only about three can, without serious loss, be omitted", he was evidently not thinking of the poor practical anthologist. There are rather more than 21,000 lines in *The Ring and the Book*, and rather fewer than that number, chosen from all Browning's poetry, in the present selection. Properly speaking no one of the books can be spared, not so much because there are good things in every one (and there are), as because together they form a whole and integrated work of art. But once the principle of selection is accepted it no longer matters whether the best books are three in number or nine. To my mind the four that stand out above

* *Essays and Studies by members of the English Association*, Volume XV, 1929.

the rest are Book VI *Giuseppe Caponsacchi*; Book VII *Pompilia*; Book X *The Pope*; and Book XI *Guido*. Of these the first is perhaps the least important in the structure of the whole, and the last for full effect demands a knowledge of Guido's earlier monologue (Book V). Between *Pompilia* and *The Pope*, the two great climaxes of the novel, I have found no basis for choice except my own liking. I must plead, as throughout the volume, anthologist's prerogative.

To the claim that each of Browning's kinds of poetry is represented one exception must be allowed—if indeed his translations from the Greek tragedians are any kind of poetry. His versions of the *Alcestis* and *Hercules Furens* of Euripides are the least inspired parts of the English poems (*Balaustion's Adventure* and *Aristophanes' Apology*) into which he worked them. His rendering of the *Agamemnon* of Æschylus, designed "to be literal at every cost save that of absolute violence to our language", has an academic fascination for the Greek scholar and translator, but to the reader ignorant of Greek it can only seem perverse if not, in places, meaningless. Only rarely and briefly does some peculiar beauty in the original raise Browning to its own height, and even then bathos awaits his descent. In a famous passage of the *Agamemnon* the chorus thus describes the sacrifice of Iphigenia:

> His ministrants, vows done, the father bade—
> Kid-like, above the altar, swathed in pall,
> Take her—lift high, and have no fear at all,
> Head-downward, and the fair mouth's guard
> And frontage hold,—press hard
> From utterance a curse against the House
> By dint of bit—violence bridling speech.
> And as to ground her saffron-vest she shed,
> She smote the sacrificers all and each
> With arrow sweet and piteous,
> From the eye only sped,—
> Significant of will to use a word,
> Just as in pictures: since, full many a time,
> In her sire's guest-hall, by the well-heaped board
> Had she made music,—lovingly with chime
> Of her chaste voice, that unpolluted thing,
> Honoured the third libation,—paian that should bring
> Good fortune to the sire she loved so well.

Browning wrote little formal prose. A few short passages in *Pippa Passes* and the whole of the second part of *A Soul's Tragedy* are in prose; and there are brief forewords and footnotes in some of the volumes, such as the note in which he explained (*obscurum per obscurius*) what he meant by "Bells and Pomegranates". For the rest, three works have been attributed to him, of which only one was published over his own name in his life.

(i) In 1836 there appeared, among the " Lives of Eminent Statesmen" in Lardner's *Cabinet Cyclopædia,* a biography of Thomas Wentworth, Earl of Strafford, by John Forster. Browning is known to have helped Forster see this book to press, and it may be that he afforded some help in the writing of it. In the following year he published his own *Strafford, an historical tragedy* (in verse), in the preface to which he alluded to Forster's book. In 1892 the Browning Society reprinted the book as *Browning's Prose Life of Strafford,* but there is no conclusive evidence that Browning wrote any part of it.

(ii) In the issue of the *Foreign Quarterly Review* for July 1842, the first number edited by John Forster, there was printed an anonymous article which, purporting to review a new book about Tasso, dealt principally with the life and pretensions of Thomas Chatterton. In 1948 Professor Donald Smalley, of the University of Indiana, reprinted this article as *Browning's Essay on Chatterton.* The only direct evidence of Browning's authorship comes from an entry in the journal of "Michael Field" for 1895, but this is supported by the indirect evidence which Professor Smalley finds in the style and psychology.

(iii) In 1851 Edward Moxon, who until lately had been Browning's publisher, invited him to write an introduction to a volume of unpublished letters of Shelley. Browning wrote the essay printed on pages 671–688 below. He seems not to have seen the "originals" of the letters but to have been furnished—he was in Paris—with manuscript copies or proofs. The volume was no sooner published, early in 1852, than the letters were proved to be forgeries: Moxon withdrew his publication, and later gave the "originals" to the British Museum. Browning's essay, which makes only cursory allusion to the letters, remains an important statement of his appreciation of the poet who most influenced his own early poetry. It was reprinted in his lifetime by the Browning Society in 1881 and by the Shelley Society in 1888. More recently it has been edited by Richard Garnett (1903) and H. F. B. Brett-Smith (1921).

Besides these formal prose writings, acknowledged and supposititious, there have survived a large number of Browning's private letters, of which the most notable are his love letters to Elizabeth Barrett Barrett. The first of these was written on 10 January 1845, four months before he met her; the 284th and last on 18 September 1846, in the brief interval between their secret marriage and their elopement. The whole series, together with the 287 letters from E. B. B. to Browning, was preserved by him and confided to his son with permission to "do with them as you please when I am dead and gone". They were published in 1899. It is curious to recall that this exposure of two poets' hearts was condemned by some critics as indecent, and that even G. K. Chesterton, while he maintained that nothing in the world could be too sacred to be known, regretted that the editor had not suppressed—not indeed what was "ardent and noble" in the letters, but what he found "idle and unmeaning." The selection now offered is designed to be representative alike of the ardent, the noble, the idle and the merely factual: some attempt has been made to elucidate the unmeaning. Similarly the letters to other correspondents have been chosen with the intention of illustrating diverse aspects of Browning's mind. The thread that links them all, whether they are written to friends or strangers, sisters-in-law or men of letters, is the thread of humanity. Their subject is *dramatis personæ*, men and women. There never was for Browning any other subject.

SIMON NOWELL-SMITH

Chronological Table

1812	Robert Browning, born in Camberwell, 7 May, son of Robert Browning and Sarah Anne Wiedemann.
1814	Birth of his sister Sarianna (died 22 April 1903).
1828–9	At London University.
1833	*Pauline*, published March.
1834	Visit to St. Petersburg, spring.
1835	*Paracelsus*, August.
1837	*Strafford*, published 1 May and produced by Macready at Covent Garden on that day.
1838	First visit to Italy, April–July.
1840	*Sordello*, March.
1841	*Bells and Pomegranates* I, *Pippa Passes*, April.
1842	*Bells and Pomegranates* II, *King Victor and King Charles*, 12 March; and III, *Dramatic Lyrics*, 26 November.
1843	*Bells and Pomegranates* IV, *The Return of the Druses*, January; and V, *A Blot in the 'Scutcheon*, published 11 February and produced by Macready at Drury Lane on that day.
1844	*Bells and Pomegranates* VI, *Colombe's Birthday*, 20 April; produced by Phelps at the Haymarket 25 April 1853.
	Revisits Italy, September–December.
1845	First meeting with Elizabeth Barrett, 20 May.
	Bells and Pomegranates VII, *Dramatic Romances and Lyrics*, 6 November.
1846	*Bells and Pomegranates* VIII, *Luria* and *A Soul's Tragedy*, 13 April.
	Marriage with Elizabeth Barrett, 12 September; elopement 19 September. Lives for the next fifteen years mainly in Italy.
1849	*Poems*, two volumes, January.
	Birth of his only son, Robert Wiedemann Barrett ("Pen"), 9 March; death of his mother, 18 March.
1850	*Christmas-Eve and Easter-Day*, 1 April.
1852	Introductory essay to *Letters of Percy Bysshe Shelley*, February.
1855	*Men and Women*, two volumes, 17 November.
1861	Death of Elizabeth Barrett Browning, 29 June. Browning henceforward lives mainly in London with frequent visits to Brittany and some, after 1878, to Italy.
1862	*Selections* (by Forster and Procter, dated 1863), December.
1863	*Poetical Works*, three volumes, August; new edition, March 1865.
1864	*Dramatis Personæ*, 28 May; new edition, September.

1865	*Selection* (by Browning himself, supplementary to the "1863" volume), October.
1866	Death of his father, 13 June. Henceforward Browning and his sister Sarianna live together.
1867	Honorary M.A. of Oxford, 26 June, and honorary Fellow of Balliol College, October.
1868	*Poetical Works*, six volumes, March–July. *The Ring and the Book* Vol. I, 21 November, and Vol. II, 26 December.
1869	*The Ring and the Book* Vol. III, 30 January, and Vol. IV, 27 February. New edition, 1872.
1871	*Balaustion's Adventure*, August; reprinted 1872 and 1881. *Prince Hohenstiel-Schwangau*, December.
1872	*Fifine at the Fair*, June. *Selections* (later called "first series", not identical with either of the earlier selections), December.
1873	*Red Cotton Night-Cap Country*, May.
1875	*Aristophanes' Apology*, 15 April. *The Inn Album*, November.
1876	*Pacchiarotto*, 18 July.
1877	*The Agamemnon of Æschylus*, 15 October.
1878	*La Saisiaz* (inspired by the death of Browning's friend Anne Egerton-Smith 14 September 1877), published 15 May with *The Two Poets of Croisic*.
1879	*Dramatic Idyls*, 28 April; new edition (as "first series"), 1882.
1880	*Selections*, second series, May. *Dramatic Idyls*, second series, July.
1881	Foundation of the Browning Society.
1883	*Jocoseria*, March; reprinted April, May.
1884	*Ferishtah's Fancies*, 21 November; reprinted December 1884, February 1885.
1887	*Parleyings with Certain People of Importance in their Day*, January.
1888–9	*Poetical Works*, sixteen volumes; Vol. XVII (*Asolando*) added 1894.
1889	*Asolando* (dated 1890), 12 December; sixth edition, January 1890. Died in Venice, 12 December; buried in Poets' Corner, Westminster Abbey, 31 December.

POETRY

Pauline

A FRAGMENT OF A CONFESSION

1833

Pauline; a Fragment of a Confession. Plus ne suis ce que j'ai été, Et ne le sçaurois jamais être. Marot. London: Saunders and Otley, Conduit Street. 1833.

Royal 12mo. Pp. 72. Paper boards.

THIS anonymous work was published in March 1833. A few copies were given to the author's friends or sent to reviewers: not one was sold. It is now one of the rarest of nineteenth-century books.

Browning first publicly acknowledged authorship of thc poem when, reluctantly and under threat of piracy, he included it, with some corrections and alterations, in the collected edition of 1868. He revised it more thoroughly for the collection of 1888–9.

The poem consists of 1031 lines. Lines 1–403, 732–830 and 903–end are reprinted here in the text of the first edition. A few necessary corrections of punctuation have been made.

Pauline

PAULINE, mine own, bend o'er me—thy soft breast
Shall pant to mine—bend o'er me—thy sweet eyes,
And loosened hair, and breathing lips, and arms
Drawing me to thee—these build up a screen
To shut me in with thee, and from all fear,
So that I might unlock the sleepless brood
Of fancies from my soul, their lurking place,
Nor doubt that each would pass, ne'er to return
To one so watched, so loved, and so secured.
But what can guard thee but thy naked love?
Ah, dearest! whoso sucks a poisoned wound
Envenoms his own veins,—thou art so good,
So calm—if thou should'st wear a brow less light
For some wild thought which, but for me, were kept
From out thy soul, as from a sacred star.
Yet till I have unlocked them it were vain
To hope to sing; some woe would light on me;
Nature would point at one, whose quivering lip
Was bathed in her enchantments—whose brow burned
Beneath the crown, to which her secrets knelt;
Who learned the spell which can call up the dead,
And then departed, smiling like a fiend
Who has deceived God. If such one should seek
Again her altars, and stand robed and crowned
Amid the faithful: sad confession first,
Remorse and pardon, and old claims renewed,
Ere I can be—as I shall be no more.

I had been spared this shame, if I had sate
By thee for ever, from the first, in place
Of my wild dreams of beauty and of good,
Or with them, as an earnest of their truth.
No thought nor hope, having been shut from thee,

No vague wish unexplained—no wandering aim
Sent back to bind on Fancy's wings, and seek
Some strange fair world, where it might be a law;
But doubting nothing, had been led by thee,
Thro' youth, and saved, as one at length awaked,
Who has slept thro' a peril. Ah! vain, vain!

Thou lovest me—the past is in its grave,
Tho' its ghost haunts us—still this much is ours,
To cast away restraint, lest a worse thing
Wait for us in the darkness. Thou lovest me,
And thou art to receive not love, but faith,
For which thou wilt be mine, and smile, and take
All shapes, and shames, and veil without a fear
That form which music follows like a slave;
And I look to thee, and I trust in thee,
As in a Northern night one looks alway
Unto the East for morn, and spring and joy.
Thou seest then my aimless, hopeless state,
And resting on some few old feelings, won
Back by thy beauty, would'st that I essay
The task, which was to me what now thou art:
And why should I conceal one weakness more?

Thou wilt remember one warm morn, when Winter
Crept aged from the earth, and Spring's first breath
Blew soft from the moist hills—the black-thorn boughs,
So dark in the bare wood, when glistening
In the sunshine were white with coming buds,
Like the bright side of a sorrow—and the banks
Had violets opening from sleep like eyes—
I walked with thee, who knew not a deep shame
Lurked beneath smiles and careless words, which sought
To hide it—till they wandered and were mute;
As we stood listening on a sunny mound
To the wind murmuring in the damp copse,
Like heavy breathings of some hidden thing
Betrayed by sleep—until the feeling rushed
That I was low indeed, yet not so low
As to endure the calmness of thine eyes;

And so I told thee all, while the cool breast
I leaned on altered not its quiet beating;
And long ere words, like a hurt bird's complaint,
Bade me look up and be what I had been,
I felt despair could never live by thee.
Thou wilt remember:—thou art not more dear
Than song was once to me; and I ne'er sung
But as one entering bright halls, where all
Will rise and shout for him. Sure I must own
That I am fallen—having chosen gifts
Distinct from theirs—that I am sad—and fain
Would give up all to be but where I was;
Not high as I had been, if faithful found—
But low and weak, yet full of hope, and sure
Of goodness as of life—that I would lose
All this gay mastery of mind, to sit
Once more with them, trusting in truth and love,
And with an aim—not being what I am.

Oh, Pauline! I am ruined! who believed
That tho' my soul had floated from its sphere
Of wide dominion into the dim orb
Of self—that it was strong and free as ever:—
It has conformed itself to that dim orb,
Reflecting all its shades and shapes, and now
Must stay where it alone can be adored.
I have felt this in dreams—in dreams in which
I seemed the fate from which I fled; I felt
A strange delight in causing my decay;
I was a fiend, in darkness chained for ever
Within some ocean-cave; and ages rolled,
Till thro' the cleft rock, like a moonbeam, came
A white swan to remain with me; and ages
Rolled, yet I tired not of my first joy
In gazing on the peace of its pure wings.
And then I said, "It is most fair to me,
Yet its soft wings must sure have suffered change
From the thick darkness—sure its eyes are dim—
Its silver pinions must be cramped and numbed
With sleeping ages here; it cannot leave me,

For it would seem, in light, beside its kind,
Withered—tho' here to me most beautiful."
And then I was a young witch, whose blue eyes,
As she stood naked by the river springs,
Drew down a god—I watched his radiant form
Growing less radiant—and it gladdened me;
Till one morn, as he sat in the sunshine
Upon my knees, singing to me of heaven,
He turned to look at me, ere I could lose
The grin with which I viewed his perishing.
And he shrieked and departed, and sat long
By his deserted throne—but sunk at last,
Murmuring, as I kissed his lips and curled
Around him, "I am still a god—to thee."
Still I can lay my soul bare in its fall,
For all the wandering and all the weakness
Will be a saddest comment on the song.
And if, that done, I can be young again,
I will give up all gained as willingly
As one gives up a charm which shuts him out
From hope, or part, or care, in human kind.
As life wanes, all its cares, and strife, and toil,
Seem strangely valueless, while the old trees
Which grew by our youth's home—the waving mass
Of climbing plants, heavy with bloom and dew—
The morning swallows with their songs like words,—
All these seem clear and only worth our thoughts.
So aught connected with my early life——
My rude songs or my wild imaginings,
How I look on them—most distinct amid
The fever and the stir of after years!

I ne'er had ventured e'en to hope for this,
Had not the glow I felt at HIS award,
Assured me all was not extinct within.
HIM whom all honor—whose renown springs up
Like sunlight which will visit all the world;
So that e'en they who sneered at him at first,
Come out to it, as some dark spider crawls
From his foul nets, which some lit torch invades,

Yet spinning still new films for his retreat.—
Thou didst smile, poet,—but, can *we* forgive?

Sun-treader—life and light be thine for ever;
Thou art gone from us—years go by—and spring
Gladdens, and the young earth is beautiful,
Yet thy songs come not—other bards arise,
But none like thee—they stand—thy majesties,
Like mighty works which tell some Spirit there
Hath sat regardless of neglect and scorn,
Till, its long task completed, it hath risen
And left us, never to return: and all
Rush in to peer and praise when all in vain.
The air seems bright with thy past presence yet,
But thou art still for me, as thou hast been
When I have stood with thee, as on a throne
With all thy dim creations gathered round
Like mountains,—and I felt of mould like them,
And creatures of my own were mixed with them,
Like things half-lived, catching and giving life.
But thou art still for me, who have adored,
Tho' single, panting but to hear thy name,
Which I believed a spell to me alone,
Scarce deeming thou wert as a star to men—
As one should worship long a sacred spring
Scarce worth a moth's flitting, which long grasses cross,
And one small tree embowers droopingly,
Joying to see some wandering insect won,
To live in its few rushes—or some locust
To pasture on its boughs—or some wild bird
Stoop for its freshness from the trackless air,
And then should find it but the fountain-head,
Long lost, of some great river—washing towns
And towers, and seeing old woods which will live
But by its banks, untrod of human foot,
Which, when the great sun sinks, lie quivering
In light as some thing lieth half of life
Before God's foot—waiting a wondrous change
—Then girt with rocks which seek to turn or stay
Its course in vain, for it does ever spread

Like a sea's arm as it goes rolling on,
Being the pulse of some great country—so
Wert thou to me—and art thou to the world.
And I, perchance, half feel a strange regret,
That I am not what I have been to thee:
Like a girl one has loved long silently,
In her first loveliness, in some retreat,
When first emerged, all gaze and glow to view
Her fresh eyes, and soft hair, and lips which bleed
Like a mountain berry. Doubtless it is sweet
To see her thus adored—but there have been
Moments, when all the world was in his praise,
Sweeter than all the pride of after hours.
Yet, Sun-treader, all hail!—from my heart's heart
I bid thee hail!—e'en in my wildest dreams,
I am proud to feel I would have thrown up all
The wreathes of fame which seemed o'erhanging me,
To have seen thee, for a moment, as thou art.

And if thou livest—if thou lovest, spirit!
Remember me, who set this final seal
To wandering thought—that one so pure as thou
Could never die. Remember me, who flung
All honor from my soul—yet paused and said,
"There is one spark of love remaining yet,
For I have nought in common with him—shapes
Which followed him avoid me, and foul forms
Seek me, which ne'er could fasten on his mind;
And tho' I feel how low I am to him,
Yet I aim not even to catch a tone
Of all the harmonies which he called up,
So one gleam still remains, altho' the last."
Remember me—who praise thee e'en with tears,
For never more shall I walk calm with thee;
Thy sweet imaginings are as an air,
A melody, some wondrous singer sings,
Which, though it haunt men oft in the still eve,
They dream not to essay; yet it no less,
But more is honored. I was thine in shame,
And now when all thy proud renown is out,

I am a watcher, whose eyes have grown dim
With looking for some star—which breaks on him,
Altered, and worn, and weak, and full of tears.

Autumn has come—like Spring returned to us,
Won from her girlishness—like one returned
A friend that was a lover—nor forgets
The first warm love, but full of sober thoughts
Of fading years; whose soft mouth quivers yet
With the old smile—but yet so changed and still!
And here am I the scoffer, who have probed
Life's vanity, won by a word again
Into my old life—for one little word
Of this sweet friend, who lives in loving me,
Lives strangely on my thoughts, and looks, and words,
As fathoms down some nameless ocean thing
Its silent course of quietness and joy.
O dearest, if, indeed, I tell the past,
May'st thou forget it as a sad sick dream;
Or if it linger—my lost soul too soon
Sinks to itself, and whispers, we shall be
But closer linked—two creatures whom the earth
Bears singly—with strange feelings, unrevealed
But to each other; or two lonely things
Created by some Power, whose reign is done,
Having no part in God, or his bright world.
I am to sing; whilst ebbing day dies soft,
As a lean scholar dies, worn o'er his book,
And in the heaven stars steal out one by one,
As hunted men steal to their mountain watch.
I must not think—lest this new impulse die
In which I trust. I have no confidence,
So I will sing on—fast as fancies come—
Rudely—the verse being as the mood it paints.

I strip my mind bare—whose first elements
I shall unveil—not as they struggled forth
In infancy, nor as they now exist,
That I am grown above them, and can rule them,
But in that middle stage, when they were full,

Yet ere I had disposed them to my will;
And then I shall show how these elements
Produced my present state, and what it is.

I am made up of an intensest life,
Of a most clear idea of consciousness
Of self—distinct from all its qualities,
From all affections, passions, feelings, powers;
And thus far it exists, if tracked in all,
But linked in me, to self-supremacy,
Existing as a centre to all things,
Most potent to create, and rule, and call
Upon all things to minister to it;
And to a principle of restlessness
Which would be all, have, see, know, taste, feel, all—
This is myself; and I should thus have been,
Though gifted lower than the meanest soul.

And of my powers, one springs up to save
From utter death a soul with such desires
Confined to clay—which is the only one
Which marks me—an imagination which
Has been an angel to me—coming not
In fitful visions, but beside me ever,
And never failing me; so tho' my mind
Forgets not—not a shred of life forgets—
Yet I can take a secret pride in calling
The dark past up—to quell it regally.

A mind like this must dissipate itself,
But I have always had one lode-star; now,
As I look back, I see that I have wasted,
Or progressed as I looked toward that star—
A need, a trust, a yearning after God,
A feeling I have analysed but late,
But it existed, and was reconciled
With a neglect of all I deemed his laws,
Which yet, when seen in others, I abhorred.
I felt as one beloved, and so shut in
From fear—and thence I date my trust in signs

And omens—for I saw God every where;
And I can only lay it to the fruit
Of a sad after-time that I could doubt
Even his being—having always felt
His presence—never acting from myself,
Still trusting in a hand that leads me through
All danger; and this feeling still has fought
Against my weakest reason and resolves.

And I can love nothing—and this dull truth
Has come the last—but sense supplies a love
Encircling me and mingling with my life.

These make myself—for I have sought in vain
To trace how they were formed by circumstance,
For I still find them—turning my wild youth
Where they alone displayed themselves, converting
All objects to their use—now see their course!

They came to me in my first dawn of life,
Which passed alone with wisest ancient books,
All halo-girt with fancies of my own,
And I myself went with the tale—a god,
Wandering after beauty—or a giant,
Standing vast in the sunset—an old hunter,
Talking with gods—or a high-crested chief,
Sailing with troops of friends to Tenedos;
I tell you, nought has ever been so clear
As the place, the time, the fashion of those lives.
I had not seen a work of lofty art,
Nor woman's beauty, nor sweet nature's face,
Yet, I say, never morn broke clear as those
On the dim clustered isles in the blue sea:
The deep groves, and white temples, and wet caves—
And nothing ever will surprise me now—
Who stood beside the naked Swift-footed,
Who bound my forehead with Proserpine's hair.

An' strange it is, that I who could so dream,
Should e'er have stooped to aim at aught beneath—

Aught low, or painful, but I never doubted;
So as I grew, I rudely shaped my life
To my immediate wants, yet strong beneath
Was a vague sense of powers folded up—
A sense that tho' those shadowy times were past,
Their spirit dwelt in me, and I should rule.

Then came a pause, and long restraint chained down
My soul, till it was changed. I lost myself,
And were it not that I so loathe that time,
I could recall how first I learned to turn
My mind against itself; and the effects,
In deeds for which remorse were vain, as for
The wanderings of delirious dream; yet thence
Came cunning, envy, falsehood, which so long
Have spotted me—at length I was restored,
Yet long the influence remained; and nought
But the still life I led, apart from all,
Which left my soul to seek its old delights,
Could e'er have brought me thus far back to peace.
As peace returned, I sought out some pursuit:
And song rose—no new impulse—but the one
With which all others best could be combined.
My life has not been that of those whose heaven
Was lampless, save where poesy shone out;
But as a clime, where glittering mountain-tops,
And glancing sea, and forests steeped in light,
Give back reflected the far-flashing sun;
For music, (which is earnest of a heaven,
Seeing we know emotions strange by it,
Not else to be revealed,) is as a voice,
A low voice calling Fancy, as a friend,
To the green woods in the gay summer time.
And she fills all the way with dancing shapes,
Which have made painters pale; and they go on
While stars look at them, and winds call to them,
As they leave life's path for the twilight world,
Where the dead gather. This was not at first,
For I scarce knew what I would do. I had
No wish to paint, no yearning—but I sang.

And first I sang, as I in dream have seen
Music wait on a lyrist for some thought,
Yet singing to herself until it came.
I turned to those old times and scenes, where all
That's beautiful had birth for me, and made
Rude verses on them all; and then I paused—
I had done nothing, so I sought to know
What mind had yet achieved. No fear was mine
As I gazed on the works of mighty bards,
In the first joy at finding my own thoughts
Recorded, and my powers exemplified,
And feeling their aspirings were my own.
And then I first explored passion and mind;
And I began afresh; I rather sought
To rival what I wondered at, than form
Creations of my own; so much was light
Lent back by others, yet much was my own.

I paused again—a change was coming on,
I was no more a boy—the past was breaking
Before the coming, and like fever worked.
I first thought on myself—and here my powers
Burst out. I dreamed not of restraint, but gazed
On all things: schemes and systems went and came,
And I was proud (being vainest of the weak),
In wandering o'er them, to seek out some one
To be my own; as one should wander o'er
The white way for a star.

* * * *

Night, and one single ridge of narrow path
Between the sullen river and the woods
Waving and muttering—for the moonless night
Has shaped them into images of life,
Like the upraising of the giant-ghosts,
Looking on earth to know how their sons fare.
Thou art so close by me, the roughest swell
Of wind in the tree-tops hides not the panting
Of thy soft breasts; no—we will pass to morning—
Morning—the rocks, and vallies, and old woods.

How the sun brightens in the mist, and here,—
Half in the air, like creatures of the place,
Trusting the element—living on high boughs
That swing in the wind—look at the golden spray,
Flung from the foam-sheet of the cataract,
Amid the broken rocks—shall we stay here
With the wild hawks?—no, ere the hot noon come
Dive we down—safe;—see this our new retreat
Walled in with a sloped mound of matted shrubs,
Dark, tangled, old and green—still sloping down
To a small pool whose waters lie asleep
Amid the trailing boughs turned water-plants
And tall trees over-arch to keep us in,
Breaking the sunbeams into emerald shafts,
And in the dreamy water one small group
Of two or three strange trees are got together,
Wondering at all around—as strange beasts herd
Together far from their own land—all wildness—
No turf nor moss, for boughs and plants pave all,
And tongues of bank go shelving in the waters,
Where the pale-throated snake reclines his head,
And old grey stones lie making eddies there;
The wild mice cross them dry-shod—deeper in—
Shut thy soft eyes—now look—still deeper in:
This is the very heart of the woods—all round,
Mountain-like, heaped above us; yet even here
One pond of water gleams—far off the river
Sweeps like a sea, barred out from land; but one—
One thin clear sheet has over-leaped and wound
Into this silent depth, which gained, it lies
Still, as but let by sufferance; the trees bend
O'er it as wild men watch a sleeping girl,
And thro' their roots long creeping plants stretch out
Their twined hair, steeped and sparkling; farther on,
Tall rushes and thick flag-knots have combined
To narrow it; so, at length, a silver thread
It winds, all noiselessly, thro' the deep wood,
Till thro' a cleft way, thro' the moss and stone,
It joins its parent-river with a shout.
Up for the glowing day—leave the old woods:

See, they part, like a ruined arch, the sky!
Nothing but sky appears, so close the root
And grass of the hill-top level with the air—
Blue sunny air, where a great cloud floats, laden
With light, like a dead whale that white birds pick,
Floating away in the sun in some north sea.
Air, air—fresh life-blood—thin and searching air—
The clear, dear breath of God, that loveth us:
Where small birds reel and winds take their delight.
Water is beautiful, but not like air.
See, where the solid azure waters lie,
Made as of thickened air, and down below,
The fern-ranks, like a forest spread themselves,
As tho' each pore could feel the element;
Where the quick glancing serpent winds his way—
Float with me there, Pauline, but not like air.
Down the hill—stop—a clump of trees, see, set
On a heap of rocks, which look o'er the far plains,
And envious climbing shrubs would mount to rest,
And peer from their spread boughs. There they wave,
looking
At the muleteers, who whistle as they go
To the merry chime of their morning bells, and all
The little smoking cots, and fields, and banks,
And copses, bright in the sun; my spirit wanders.
Hedge-rows for me—still, living, hedge-rows, where
The bushes close, and clasp above, and keep
Thought in—I am concentrated—I feel;—
But my soul saddens when it looks beyond;
I cannot be immortal, nor taste all.
O God! where does this tend—these struggling aims!
What would I have? what is this "sleep," which seems
To bound all? can there be a "waking" point
Of crowning life? The soul would never rule—
It would be first in all things—it would have
Its utmost pleasure filled,—but that complete
Commanding for commanding sickens it.
The last point that I can trace is, rest beneath
Some better essence than itself—in weakness;
This is "myself"—not what I think should be,

And what is that I hunger for but God?
My God, my God! let me for once look on thee
As tho' nought else existed: we alone.
And as creation crumbles, my soul's spark
Expands till I can say, "Even from myself
I need thee, and I feel thee, and I love thee;
I do not plead my rapture in thy works
For love of thee—or that I feel as one
Who cannot die—but there is that in me
Which turns to thee, which loves, or which should love."

* * * * *

Love me—love me, Pauline, love nought but me;
Leave me not. All these words are wild and weak,
Believe them not, Pauline. I stooped so low
But to behold thee purer by my side,
To show thou art my breath—my life—a last
Resource—an extreme want: never believe
Aught better could so look to thee, nor seek
Again the world of good thoughts left for me.
There were bright troops of undiscovered suns,
Each equal in their radiant course. There were
Clusters of far fair isles, which ocean kept
For his own joy, and his waves broke on them
Without a choice. And there was a dim crowd
Of visions, each a part of the dim whole.
And a star left his peers and came with peace
Upon a storm, and all eyes pined for him.
And one isle harboured a sea-beaten ship,
And the crew wandered in its bowers, and plucked
Its fruits, and gave up all their hopes for home.
And one dream came to a pale poet's sleep,
And he said, "I am singled out by God,
No sin must touch me." I am very weak,
But what I would express is,—Leave me not,
Still sit by me—with beating breast, and hair
Loosened—watching earnest by my side,
Turning my books, or kissing me when I
Look up—like summer wind. Be still to me
A key to music's mystery, when mind fails,

A reason, a solution and a clue.
You see I have thrown off my prescribed rules:
I hope in myself—and hope, and pant, and love—
You'll find me better—know me more than when
You loved me as I was. Smile not; I have
Much yet to gladden you—to dawn on you.

No more of the past—I'll look within no more—
I have too trusted to my own wild wants—
Too trusted to myself—to intuition—
Draining the wine alone in the still night,
And seeing how—as gathering films arose,
As by an inspiration life seemed bare
And grinning in its vanity, and ends
Hard to be dreamed of, stared at me as fixed,
And others suddenly became all foul,
As a fair witch turned an old hag at night.
No more of this—we will go hand in hand,
I will go with thee, even as a child,
Looking no further than thy sweet commands.
And thou hast chosen where this life shall be—
The land which gave me thee shall be our home,
Where nature lies all wild amid her lakes
And snow-swathed mountains, and vast pines all girt
With ropes of snow—where nature lies all bare,
Suffering none to view her but a race
Most stinted and deformed—like the mute dwarfs
Which wait upon a naked Indian queen.
And there (the time being when the heavens are thick
With storms) I'll sit with thee while thou dost sing
Thy native songs, gay as a desert bird
Who crieth as he flies for perfect joy,
Or telling me old stories of dead knights.
Or I will read old lays to thee—how she,
The fair pale sister, went to her chill grave
With power to love, and to be loved, and live.
Or we will go together, like twin gods
Of the infernal world, with scented lamp
Over the dead—to call and to awake—
Over the unshaped images which lie

Within my mind's cave—only leaving all
That tells of the past doubts. So when spring comes,
And sunshine comes again like an old smile,
And the fresh waters, and awakened birds,
And budding woods await us—I shall be
Prepared, and we will go and think again,
And all old loves shall come to us—but changed
As some sweet thought which harsh words veiled before;
Feeling God loves us, and that all that errs,
Is a strange dream which death will dissipate;
And then when I am firm we'll seek again
My own land, and again I will approach
My old designs, and calmly look on all
The works of my past weakness, as one views
Some scene where danger met him long before.
Ah! that such pleasant life should be but dreamed!

But whate'er come of it—and tho' it fade,
And tho' ere the cold morning all be gone
As it will be;—tho' music wait for me,
And fair eyes and bright wine, laughing like sin,
Which steals back softly on a soul half saved;
And I be first to deny all, and despise
This verse, and these intents which seem so fair;
Still this is all my own, this moment's pride,
No less I make an end in perfect joy.
E'en in my brightest time, a lurking fear
Possessed me. I well knew my weak resolves,
I felt the witchery that makes mind sleep
Over its treasures—as one half afraid
To make his riches definite—but now
These feelings shall not utterly be lost,
I shall not know again that nameless care,
Lest leaving all undone in youth, some new
And undreamed end reveal itself too late:
For this song shall remain to tell for ever,
That when I lost all hope of such a change,
Suddenly Beauty rose on me again.
No less I make an end in perfect joy,
For I, having thus again been visited,

Shall doubt not many another bliss awaits,
And tho' this weak soul sink, and darkness come,
Some little word shall light it up again,
And I shall see all clearer and love better;
I shall again go o'er the tracts of thought,
As one who has a right; and I shall live
With poets—calmer—purer still each time,
And beauteous shapes will come to me again,
And unknown secrets will be trusted me,
Which were not mine when wavering—but now
I shall be priest and lover, as of old.

Sun-treader, I believe in God, and truth,
And love; and as one just escaped from death
Would bind himself in bands of friends to feel
He lives indeed—so, I would lean on thee;
Thou must be ever with me—most in gloom
When such shall come—but chiefly when I die,
For I seem dying, as one going in the dark
To fight a giant—and live thou for ever,
And be to all what thou hast been to me—
All in whom this wakes pleasant thoughts of me,
Know my last state is happy—free from doubt,
Or touch of fear. Love me and wish me well!

Paracelsus
1835

Paracelsus. By Robert Browning. London: published by Effingham Wilson, Royal Exchange. MDCCCXXXV.

F'cap 8vo. Pp. xii + 216. Paper boards.

Paracelsus is a dramatic poem in five scenes, comprising some 4150 lines. The passages selected here are Scene I, lines 317–491 and 709–end; two lyrics from Scene IV; and Scene V, lines 320–432 and 583–end. The headings for the two lyrics, *Song* and *Romance*, are taken from the *Selection* of his poems which Browning made in 1865 (Moxon's Miniature Poets).

The text of the first edition of *Paracelsus* appears in many places to be corrupt, and the manuscript in the Victoria and Albert Museum is not always helpful in resolving difficulties. The first of Browning's several revisions was made for the two-volume collected edition of his *Poems* 1849, and some corrections from this have been adopted in the present selection. In three instances, where the sense or the rime-scheme seemed to demand it, whole lines have been borrowed from the 1849 volume and incorporated into the first-edition text: attention is drawn to these in footnotes.

Paracelsus

PARACELSUS ASPIRES

FROM SCENE I—WÜRZBURG, 1507

FESTUS, PARACELSUS, MICHAL

Fest. There is a curse upon the earth; let man
Presume not to serve God apart from such
Appointed channel as he wills shall gather
Imperfect tributes—for that sole obedience
Valued perchance. He seeks not that his altars
Blaze—careless how, so that they do but blaze.—
Though I doubt much if he consent that we
Discover this great secret I know well
You will allege no other comprehends
The work in question save its labourer:
I shall assume the aim improved; and you
That I am implicated in the issue
Not simply as your friend, but as yourself—
As though it were my task that you perform,
And some plague dogg'd my heels till it were done.
Suppose this own'd then; you are born to KNOW.
(You will heed well your answers, for my faith
Shall meet implicitly what they affirm)—
I cannot think you have annex'd to such
Selection aught beyond a steadfast will,
An intense purpose—gifts that would induce
Scorn or neglect of ordinary means
And instruments of success: no destiny
Dispenses with endeavour. Now, dare you search
Your inmost heart, and candidly avow
Whether you have not rather wild desire
For this distinction, than a full assurance
That it exists; or whether you discern
The path to the fulfilment of your purpose
Clear as that purpose—and again, that purpose

Clear as your yearning to be singled out
For its possessor. Dare you answer this?
Par. (*After a pause.*) No, I have nought to fear! who will may know
The secret'st workings of my soul. What though
It be so?—if indeed the strong desire
Eclipse the aim in me?—if splendour break
Upon the outset of my path alone,
And duskest shade succeed? What fairer seal
Shall I require to my authentic mission
Than this fierce energy?—this instinct striving
Because its nature is to strive?—enticed
By the security of no broad course—
Where error is not, but success is sure.
How know I else such glorious fate my own,
But in the restless irresistible force
That works within me? Is it for human will
To institute such impulses?—still less,
To disregard their promptings? What should I
Do, kept among you all; your loves, your cares,
Your life—all to be mine? Be sure that God
Ne'er dooms to waste the strength he deigns impart.
Ask the gier-eagle why she stoops at once
Into the vast and unexplored abyss!
What fullgrown power informs her from the first!
Why she not marvels, strenuously beating
The silent boundless regions of the sky!
Be sure they sleep not whom God needs; nor fear
Their holding light his charge, when every hour
That finds that charge delay'd is a new death.
Thus for the faith in which I trust; and hence
I can abjure so well the secret arts
These pedants strive to learn—the magic they
So reverence. I shall scarcely seek to know
If it exist: too intimate a tie
Connects me with our God. A sullen fiend
To do my bidding—fallen and hateful sprites
To help me—what are these, at best, beside
God every where, sustaining and directing,
So that the earth shall yield her secrets up

And every object shall be charged to strike,
To teach, to gratify, and to suggest?
And I am young, Festus, happy and free!
I can devote myself; I have a life
To give; I, who am singled out for this.
Think, think; the wide east, where old Wisdom sprung;
The bright south, where she dwelt; the populous north,
All are passed o'er—it lights on me. 'Tis time
New hopes should animate the world—new light
Should dawn from new revealings to a race
Weigh'd down so long, forgotten so long; so shall
The heaven reserved for us at last receive
No creatures whom unwonted splendours blind,
But ardent to confront the unclouded blaze
Whose beams not seldom lit their pilgrimage,
Not seldom glorified their life below.

Fest. My words have their old fate and make faint stand
Against your glowing periods; I renounce
All hope of learning further on this head;
And what I next advance holds good as well
With one assured that all these things are true;
For might not such seek out a fast retreat—
After approved example—their to have
Calm converse with the great dead—soul to soul—
Who laid up treasure with the like intent?
To lift himself into their airy place,
And fill out full their unfulfill'd careers,
Unravelling the knots their baffled skill
Pronounced inextricable, but surely left
Far less confused? A fresh eye, a fresh hand,
Might do much at their vigour's waning-point—
Succeeding with new-breathed and untried force—
As at old games a runner snatch'd the torch
From runner still? Such one might well do this.
But you have link'd to this, your enterprize,
An arbitrary and most perplexing scheme
Of seeking it in strange and untried paths;
Rejecting past example, practice, precept—
That so you may stand aidless and alone:

If in this wild rejection you regard
Mankind and their award of fame—'tis clear,
Whate'er you may protest, knowledge is not
Paramount in your love; or for her sake
You would collect all help from every source—
Friend, foe, assistant, rival, all would merge
In the broad class of those who show'd her haunts
And those who show'd them not.

Par. What shall I say?
Festus, from childhood I have been possess'd
By a fire—by a true fire, or faint or fierce,
As from without some master, so it seem'd,
Repress'd or urged its current: this but ill
Expresses what I would convey—but rather
I will believe an angel ruled me thus,
Than that my soul's own workings, own high nature,
So became manifest. I knew not then
What whisper'd in the evening, and spoke out
At midnight. If some mortal, born too soon,
Were laid away in some great trance—the ages
Coming and going all the while—until
His true time's advent, and could then record
The words they spoke who kept watch by his bed,
Then I might tell more of the breath so light
Upon my eyelids, and the fingers light
Among my hair. Youth is confused; yet never
So dull was I but when that spirit pass'd
I turn'd to him, scarce consciously, as turns
A water-snake when fairies cross his sleep:
And having this within me and about me
When Einsiedeln, its hills, and lakes, and plains
Confined me—what oppressive joy was mine
When life grew plain, and I first view'd the throng'd,
The ever-moving, concourse of mankind!
Believe that ere I join'd them—ere I knew
The purpose of the pageant, or the place
Consign'd to me within its ranks—while yet
Wonder was freshest and delight most pure—
'Twas then that least supportable appear'd
A station with the brightest of the crowd;

A portion with the proudest of them all!
And from the tumult in my breast, this only
Could I collect—that I must thenceforth die,
Or elevate myself far, far above
The gorgeous spectacle; what seem'd a longing
To trample on yet save mankind at once—
To make some unexampled sacrifice
In their behalf—to wring some wondrous good
From heaven or earth for them—to perish, winning
Eternal weal in the act: as who should dare
Pluck out the angry thunder from its cloud,
That, all its gather'd flame discharged on him,
No storm might threaten summer's azure weather—
Yet never to be mix'd with them so much
As to have part even in my own work—share
In my own largess. Once the feat achieved,
I would withdraw from their officious praise,
Would gently put aside their profuse thanks,
Like some knight traversing a wilderness,
Who, on his way, may chance to free a tribe
Of desert-people from their dragon-foe;
When all the swarthy race press round to kiss
His feet, and choose him for their king, and yield
Their poor tents, pitch'd among the sand-hills, for
His realm; and he points, smiling, to his scarf,
Heavy with rivel'd gold, his burgonet,
Gay set with twinkling stones—and to the east,
Where these must be display'd . . .

* * * * *

Mich. Stay with us Aureole! cast those hopes away,
And stay with us: an angel warns me, too,
Man should be humble; you are very proud!
And God dethroned has doleful plagues for such!
Warns me to have in dread no quick repulse,
No slow defeat, but a complete success!
You will find all you seek, and perish so!

Par. (*After a pause.*) Are these the barren first fruits
I should fear?
Is love like this the natural lot of all?

How many years of hate might one such hour
O'erbalance? Dearest Michal, dearest Festus,
What shall I say, if not that I desire
Well to deserve that love, and will, dear friends,
In swerving nothing from my high resolves.
See, the great moon! and ere the mottled owls
Were wide awake, I should have made all sure
For my departure that remains to do;
So answer not, while I run lightly o'er
The topics you have urged to-night. It seems
We acquiesce at last in all, save only
If I am like to compass what I seek
In the untried career I chuse; and then,
If that career, making but small account
Of much of life's delight, will offer joys
Sufficient to sustain my soul—for thus
I understand these fond fears just express'd.
And first; the lore you praise and I neglect,
The labours and the precepts of old sages,
I have not slightly disesteem'd. But then
Truth is within ourselves; it takes no rise
From outward things, whate'er you may believe:
There is an inmost centre in us all,
Where truth abides in fulness; and around,
Wall within wall, the gross flesh hems it in,
Perfect and true perception—which is truth;
A baffling and perverting carnal mesh
Which blinds it, and makes error: and, "*to know*"
Rather consists in opening out a way
Whence the imprison'd splendour may dart forth,
Than in effecting entry for the light
Supposed to be without. Watch narrowly
The demonstration of a truth, its birth,
And you shall trace the effluence to its spring
And source within us, where broods radiance vast,
To be elicited ray by ray, as chance
Shall favour: *chance*—for hitherto,
Even as we know not how those beams are born,
As little know we what unlocks their lair;
For men have oft grown old among their books

And died, case-harden'd in their ignorance,
Whose careless youth had promised what long years
Of unremitted labour ne'er perform'd:
While, contrary, it has chanced some idle day,
To autumn loiterers just as fancy-free
As the midges in the sun, has oft brought forth
A truth—produced mysteriously as cape
Of cloud grown out of the invisible mist.
Hence, may not truth be lodged alike in all,
The lowest as the highest? some slight film
The interposing bar which binds a soul?
Some film removed the happy outlet whence
It issues proudly? seeing that the soul
Is deathless (we know well) but oftener coop'd
A prisoner and a thrall, than a throned power;
That it strives weakly in the child, is loosed
In manhood, clogg'd by sickness, back compell'd
By age and waste, set free at last by death:
That not alone when life flows still do truth
And power emerge, but also when strange chance
Affects its current; in unused conjuncture,
Where sickness breaks the body—hunger, watching,
Excess, or languor—oftenest death's approach—
Peril, deep joy, or woe. One man shall crawl
Through life, surrounded with all stirring things,
Unmoved—and he goes mad; and from the wreck
Of what he was, by his wild talk alone,
You first collect how great a spirit he hid.
Seeing all this why should I pine in vain
Attempts to win some day the august form
Of Truth to stand before me, and compel
My dark unvalued frame to change its nature,
And straight become suffused with light—at best
For my sole good—leaving the world to seek
Salvation out as it best may, or follow
The same long thorny course? No, I will learn
How to set free the soul alike in all,
By searching out the laws by which the flesh
Accloys the spirit. We may not be doom'd
To cope with seraphs, but at least the rest

Shall cope with us. Make no more giants, God!
But elevate the race at once! We ask
But to put forth our strength, our human strength,
All starting fairly, all equipp'd alike,
Gifted alike, and eagle-eyed, true-hearted.
See if we cannot beat thy angels yet!
Such is my task. I go to gather this
Mysterious knowledge, here and there dispersed
About the world, long lost or ever-hidden;
And why should I be sad, or lorn of hope?
Why ever make man's good distinct from God's?
Or, finding they are one, why have mistrust?
Who shall succeed if not one pledged like me?
Mine is no mad attempt to build a world
Apart from his, like those who set themselves
To find the nature of the spirit they bore,
And, taught betimes that all their gorgeous dreams
And beauteous fancies, hopes, and aspirations,
Were born only to wither in this life,
Refused to curb or moderate their longings,
Or fit them to this narrow sphere, but chose
To figure and conceive another world
And other frames meet for their vast desires,
And all a dream! Thus was life scorn'd; but life
Shall yet be crown'd: twine amaranth! I am priest!
And all for yielding with a lively spirit
A poor existence—parting with a youth
Like theirs who squander every energy
Convertible to good on painted toys,
Breath-bubbles, gilded dust! And though I spurn
All adventitious aims, from empty praise
To love's award, yet whoso deems such helps
Important and concerns himself for me
May know even these will follow with the rest—
As in the steady rolling Mayne, asleep
Yonder, is mingled and involved a mass
Of schistous particles of ore. And even
My own affections, laid to rest awhile—
Will waken purified, subdued alone
By all I have achieved; till then—till then . . .

Ah! the time-wiling loitering of a page
Through bower and over lawn, till eve shall bring
The stately lady's presence whom he loves—
The broken sleep of the fisher whose rough coat
Enwraps the queenly pearl—these are faint types!
See, see, they look on me—I triumph now!
Tell me, Festus, Michal, but one thing—I have told
All I shall e'er disclose to mortal . . . now,
Do you believe I shall accomplish this?

Fest. I do believe!

Mich. And I, dear Aureole!

Par. Those words shall never fade from out my brain.
'Tis earnest of the end—shall never fade!
Are there not Festus, are there not dear Michal,
Two points in the adventure of the diver:
One—when a beggar he prepares to plunge?
One—when a prince he rises with his pearl?
Festus, I plunge!

SONG

HEAP cassia, sandal-buds, and stripes
    Of labdanum, and aloe-balls
Smear'd with dull nard an Indian wipes
    From out her hair: such balsam falls
    Down sea-side mountain pedestals,
From tall trees where tired winds are fain,
Spent with the vast and howling main,
To treasure half their island-gain;
And strew faint sweetness from some old
    Egyptian's fine worm-eaten shroud,
Which breaks to dust when once unroll'd;
    Or shredded perfume, like a cloud
    From closet long to quiet vow'd,
With moth'd and dropping arras hung,
Mouldering her lute and books among,
As when a queen, long dead, was young.

Song: l. 5 supplied from *Poems* 1849.

ROMANCE

Over the sea our galleys went,
Cleaving prows in order brave,
With speeding wind and a bounding wave—
  A gallant armament:
Each bark built out of a forest-tree,
  Left leafy and rough as first it grew,
And nail'd all over the gaping sides,
Within and without, with black-bull hides,
Seeth'd in fat and suppled in flame,
To bear the playful billows' game;
So each good ship was rude to see,
Rude and bare to outward view,
  But each upbore a stately tent:
Cedar-pales in scented row
Kept out the flakes of dancing brine:
An awning droop'd the mast below,
That neither noon-tide nor star-shine,
Nor moonlight cold which maketh mad,
  Might pierce the regal tenement.
When the sun dawn'd, gay and glad
We set the sail and plied the oar;
But when the night-wind blew like breath,
For joy of one day's voyage more,
We sang together on the wide sea,
Like men at peace on a peaceful shore;
Each sail was loosed to the wind so free,
Each helm made sure by the twilight star,
And in a sleep as calm as death,
We, the voyagers from afar,
  Lay stretch'd—each weary crew
In a circle round its wondrous tent,
Whence gleam'd soft light and curl'd rich scent,
  And with light and perfume, music too:
At morn we started beside the mast,
And still each ship was sailing fast!

Romance: l. 10 supplied from *Poems* 1849.

Now one morn land appeared!—a speck
  Dim trembling betwixt sea and sky—
Not so the isles our voyage must find
  Should meet our longing eye;
But the heaving sea was black behind
Many a night and many a day,
And land, though but a rock, was nigh;
So we broke the cedar pales away,
And let the purple flap in the wind:
  And a statue bright was on every deck!
We shouted, every man of us,
And steer'd right into the harbour thus,
With pomp and pæan glorious.

An hundred shapes of lucid stone!
  All day we built its shrine for each—
A shrine of rock for every one—
Nor paused till in the westering sun
  We sate together on the beach
To sing, because our task was done;
When lo! what shouts and merry songs!
What laughter all the distance stirs!
A loaded raft, and happy throngs
Of gentle islanders!
"Our isles are just at hand," they cried,
  "Like cloudlets faint in even sleeping;
Our temple-gates are open'd wide,
  Our olive-groves thick shade are keeping
For these majestic forms," they cried.
Then we awoke with sudden start
From our deep dream, and knew, too late,
How bare the rock, how desolate,
Which had received our precious freight:
  Yet we called out—"Depart!
Our gifts, once given, must here abide:
  Our work is done; we have no heart
To mar our work," we cried.

PARACELSUS ATTAINS

FROM SCENE V—SALZBURG, 1541

FESTUS, PARACELSUS

Par. Festus, my own friend, you are come at last?
As you say, 'tis an awful enterprise—
But you believe I shall go through with it:
'Tis like you, and I thank you; thank him for me,
Dear Michal! See how bright St. Saviour's spire
Flames in the sunset; all its figures quaint
Gay in the glancing light: you might conceive them
A troop of yellow-vested, white-haired Jews . . .
Fest. Not that blessed time—not our youth's time, dear God!
Par. Ha—stay! true, I forget—all is done since!
And he is come to judge me: how he speaks,
How calm, how well! yes, it is true, all true;
All quackery; all deceit! myself can laugh
The first at it, if you desire: but still
You know the obstacles which taught me tricks
So foreign to my nature—envy, and hate—
Blind opposition—brutal prejudice—
Bald ignorance—what wonder if I sunk
To humour them the way they most approved?
My cheats were never palm'd on such as you,
Dear Festus. I will kneel if you require me,
Impart the meagre knowledge I possess,
Explain its bounded nature, and avow
My insufficiency—whate'er you will:
I give the fight up! let there be an end,
A privacy, an obscure nook for me.
I want to be forgotten even by God!
But if that cannot be, dear Festus, lay me,
When I shall die, within some narrow grave,
Not by itself—for that would be too proud—
But where such graves are thickest; see it look
Nowise distinguish'd from the hillocks round,
So that the peasant at his brother's bed

Shall tread upon my own and know it not;
So we shall all be equal at the last,
Or class'd according to life's natural ranks,
Fathers, sons, brothers, friends—not rich, nor wise,
Nor gifted: lay me thus, then say "He lived
Too much advanced before his brother men:
They kept him still in front; 'twas for their good,
But still a dangerous station. Strange it were
That he should tell God he had never rank'd
With men: so here at least he is a man!"
Fest. That God shall take thee to his breast, dear Spirit,
Unto his breast, be sure! and here on earth
Shall splendour sit upon thy name for ever!
Sun! all the heaven is glad for thee: what care
If lower mountains light their snowy phares
At thine effulgence, yet acknowledge not
The source of day? their theft shall be their bale,
For after ages shall retrack the beams,
And put aside the crowd of busy ones,
And worship thee alone—the master-mind,
The thinker, the explorer, the creator;
And who should sneer at the convulsive throes
With which thy deeds were born would scorn as well
The winding sheet of subterraneous fire
Which, pent and writhing, sends no less at last
Huge islands up amid the simmering sea!
Behold thy might in me! thou hast infused
Thy soul in mine; and I am grand as thou,
Seeing I comprehend thee—I so simple,
Thou so august! I recognize thee first;
I saw thee rise, and I have watch'd thee well,
And though no glance reveal that thou acceptest
My homage—thus no less I proffer it,
And bid thee enter gloriously thy rest!
Par. Festus!
Fest. I am for noble Aureole, God!
I am upon his side, come weal or woe!
His portion shall be mine! He has done well!
I would have sinn'd, had I been strong enough,
As he has sinn'd! Reward him or I waive

Reward! If thou canst find no place for him,
He shall be king elsewhere, and I will be
His slave for ever! . . . There are two of us!
Par. Dear Festus!
Fest. Here, dear Aureole! ever by you!
Par. Nay, speak on, or I dream again. Speak on!
Some story, any thing—only your voice.
I shall dream else. Speak on!
Fest. Thus the Mayne glideth
Where my love abideth;
Sleep's no softer: it proceeds
On through lawns, on through meads,
On and on, whate'er befall,
Meandering and musical,
Though the niggard pasturage
Bears not on its shaven edge
Aught but weeds and waving grasses
To behold it as it passes,
Save here and there a scanty patch
Of primroses, too faint to catch
A weary bee . . .
Par. More, more; say on!
Fest. And scarce it pushes
Its gentle way through strangling rushes,
Where the glossy king-fisher
Flutters when noon-heats are near,
Glad the shelving banks to shun,
Red and steaming in the sun,
Where the shrew-mouse with pale throat
Burrows, and the speckled stoat,
Where the quick sand-pipers flit
In and out the soft and wet
Clay that breeds them, brown as they.
Nought disturbs its quiet way,
Save some lazy stork that springs,
Trailing it with legs and wings,
Whom the shy fox from the hill
Arouses . . .
Par. My heart! they loose my heart, those simple words;

Its darkness passes, which nought else could touch;
Like some dark snake that force may not expel,
Which glideth out to music sweet and low.

* * * * *

Par. Yes, it was in me; I was born for it—
I, Paracelsus: it was mine by right.
Doubtless a searching and impetuous spirit
Might learn from its own motions that some task
Like this awaited it about the world;
Might seek somewhere in this blank life of ours
For fit delights to stay its longings vast;
And, grappling strenuously with Fate, compel her
To fill the creature full whom she dared frame
Hungry for joy; and, bravely tyrannous,
Grow in demand, still craving more and more,
And make the joy conceded prove a pledge
Of further joy to follow—bating nothing
Of its desires, but seizing all pretence
To turn the knowledge and the rapture wrung
From Destiny as an extreme, last boon,
Into occasion for new covetings,
New strifes, new triumphs. Doubtless a strong spirit
Might do all this unaided and alone,
So glorious is our nature, so august
Man's inborn uninstructed impulses—
His naked spirit so majestical!
But it was born in me: I was made so.
Thus much time saved: the feverish appetites,
The tumult of unproved desire, the aimless
Uncertain yearnings, near-sighted ambition,
Distrust, mistake, and all that ends in tears
Were saved me, though the lion heart repines not
At working through such lets its purpose out.
You may be sure I was not all exempt
From human trouble: just so much of doubt
As bade me plant a surer foot upon
The sun-road—kept my eye unruin'd mid
The fierce and flashing splendour—set my heart

Trembling so much as warn'd me I stood there
On sufferance—not to idly gaze, but have
Remembrance of a darkling race; save that,
I stood at first where all aspire at last
To reach—the secret of the world was mine.
I knew, I felt, not as one knows or feels
Aught else; a vast perception unexpress'd,
Uncomprehended by our narrow thought,
But somehow felt and known in every shift
And change in the spirit I bear—nay, dare I say,
In every pore of this fast-fading frame
I felt, I knew what God is, what we are,
What life is—how God tastes an infinite joy
In infinite ways—one everlasting bliss,
From whom all being emanates, all power
Proceeds; in whom is life for evermore,
Yet whom existence in its lowest form
Includes; where dwells enjoyment there is He!
With still a flying point of bliss remote—
A happiness in store afar—a sphere
Of distant glory in full view; thus climbs
Pleasure its heights for ever and for ever!
The centre-fire heaves underneath the earth,
And the earth changes like a human face;
The molten ore bursts up among the rocks—
Winds into the stone's heart—outbranches bright
In hidden mines—spots barren river-beds—
Crumbles into fine sand where sunbeams bask—
God joys therein! The wroth sea's waves are edged
With foam, white as the bitten lip of Hate:
When in the solitary waste strange groups
Of young volcanos come up, cyclops-like,
Staring together with their eyes on flame,
God tastes a pleasure in their uncouth pride!
Then all is still: earth is a wintry clod;
But spring-wind, like a dancing psaltress, passes
Over its breast to waken it; rare verdure
Buds here and there upon rough banks, between
The wither'd tree-roots and the cracks of frost,
Like a smile striving with a wrinkled face;

The grass grows bright, the boughs are swoln with
 blooms,
Like chrysalids impatient for the air;
The shining dorrs are busy; beetles run
Along the furrows, ants make their ado;
Above birds fly in merry flocks—the lark
Soars up and up, shivering for very joy;
Afar the ocean sleeps; white fishing-gulls
Flit where the strand is purple with its tribe
Of nested limpets; savage creatures seek
Their loves in wood and plain; and God renews
His ancient rapture! Thus He dwells in all,
From life's minute beginnings, up at last
To man—the consummation of this scheme
Of being—the completion of this sphere
Of life: whose attributes had here and there
Been scatter'd o'er the visible world before,
Asking to be combin'd—dim fragments meant
To be united in some wondrous whole—
Imperfect qualities throughout creation,
Suggesting some one creature yet to make—
(So would a spirit deem, intent on watching
The purpose of the world from its faint rise
To its mature development)—some point
Whereto those wandering rays should all converge—
Might: neither put forth blindly, nor controll'd
Calmly by perfect knowledge—to be used
At risk—inspir'd or check'd by hope and fear—
Knowledge: not intuition, but the slow
Uncertain fruit of an enhancing toil,
Strengthen'd by love—love: not serenely pure,
But power from weakness, like a chance-sown plant
Which, cast on stubborn soil, puts forth changed buds,
And softer stains, unknown in happier climes:
Love which endures, and doubts, and is oppress'd,
And cherish'd—suffering much, and much sustain'd—
A blind, unfailing, and devoted love:
A half-enlighten'd, often-chequer'd trust:
Anticipations, hints of these and more
Are strewn confusedly everywhere—all seek

An object to possess and stamp their own;
All shape out dimly the forthcoming race,
The heir of hopes too fair to turn out false,
And Man appears at last: so far the seal
Is put on life: one stage of being complete,
One scheme wound up; and from the grand result
A supplementary reflux of light,
Illustrates all the inferior grades, explains
Each back step in the circle: not alone
The clear dawn of those qualities shines out,
But the new glory mixes with the heaven
And earth. Man, once descried, imprints for ever
His presence on all lifeless things—the winds
Are henceforth voices, wailing, or a shout,
A querulous mutter, or a quick gay laugh—
Never a senseless gust now man is born:
The herded pines commune, and have deep thoughts,
A secret they assemble to discuss,
When the sun drops behind their trunks which glare
Like grates of hell: the peerless cup afloat
Of the lake-lily is an urn, some nymph
Swims bearing high above her head: no bird
Whistles unseen, but through the gaps above
That let light in upon the gloomy woods,
A shape peeps from the breezy forest-top,
Arch with small pucker'd mouth and mocking eye:
The morn has enterprise—deep quiet droops
With evening—triumph when the sun takes rest—
Voluptuous transport when the corn-fields ripen
Beneath a warm moon like a happy face:
And this to fill us with regard for man,
Deep apprehension of his passing worth,
Desire to work his proper nature out,
To ascertain his rank and final place,
For all these things tend upward—progress is
The law of life—man is not man as yet:
Nor shall I deem his object served, his end
Attain'd, his genuine strength put fairly out,
While only here and there a star dispels
The darkness—here and there a towering mind

O'erlooks its crawling fellows: when the host
Is out at once to the despair of night;
When all mankind is perfected alike,
Equal in full-blown powers—then, not till then,
Begins the general infancy of man;
For wherefore make account of feverish starts
Of restless members of a dormant whole—
Impatient nerves which quiver while the body
Slumbers as in a grave? O long ago
The brow was twitch'd, the tremulous lids astir,
The peaceful mouth disturb'd—half-utter'd speech
Ruffled the lip; sometimes the teeth were set,
The breath drawn sharp, the strong right-hand clench'd
stronger—
As it would pluck a lion by the maw:
The glorious creature laugh'd out even in sleep!
But when arous'd—each giant-limb awake,
Each sinew strung, the great heart pulsing fast—
He shall start up, and stand on his own earth—
Then shall his long triumphant march begin—
Thence shall his being date; what thus collected
He shall achieve, shall be set down to him!
When all the race is perfected alike
As *man*, that is: all tended to mankind
And, man produced, all has its end thus far;
But in completed man begins anew
A tendency to God. Prognostics told
Man's near approach; so in man's self arise
August anticipations, symbols, types
Of a dim splendour ever on before,
In the eternal circle life pursues:
For men begin to pass their nature's bound,
To have new hopes and cares which fast supplant
Their proper joys and griefs; they grow too great
For narrow creeds of right and wrong, which fade
Before unmeasur'd thirst for good; while peace
Rises within them ever more and more.
Such men are even now upon the earth—
Serene amid the half-form'd creatures round,
Whom they should save and join with them at last:

Such was my task, and I was born to it—
Free, as I said but now, from much that chains
Spirits high-dower'd, but limited and vex'd
By a divided and delusive aim—
A shadow mocking a reality
Whose truth avails not wholly to disperse
The flitting mimic which itself has bred,
And so remains perplex'd and nigh put out
By its fantastic fellow's wavering gleam;
But from the first, the cheat could lure me not:
I never fashion'd out a fancied good
Distinct from man's; a service to be done—
A glory to be minister'd unto,
With powers put forth at man's expense, withdrawn
From labouring in his behalf; a strength
Reserved that might avail him: I ne'er cared
Lest his success run counter to success
Elsewhere: for God is glorified in man,
And to man's glory vow'd I soul and limb.
Yet, constituted thus, and thus endow'd,
I fail'd: I gazed on power till I grew blind.
Power: I could not take my eyes from that—
That only was to be preserved, increased
At any risk; display'd, struck out at once—
The sign, and note, and character of man.
I saw no use in the past: only a scene
Of degradation, ugliness, and tears;
The record of disgraces best forgotten;
A sullen page in human chronicles
To be erased: I saw no cause why man
Should not be all-sufficient even now;
Or why his annals should be forced to tell
That once the tide of light about to break
Upon the world was seal'd within its spring,
Although my own name led the brightness in:
I would have had one day, one moment's space,
Change man's condition, push each slumbering claim
To mastery o'er the elemental world
At once to full maturity: then roll
Oblivion o'er its work, and hide from man

What night had usher'd morn. Not so, dear child
Of after-days, wilt thou reject the Past,
Big with deep warnings of the proper tenure
By which thou hast the earth: for thee the Present
Shall have distinct and trembling beauty, seen
Beside its shadow—whence, in strong relief,
Its features shall stand out: nor yet on thee
Shall burst the Future, as successive zones
Of several wonder open on some spirit
Flying secure and glad from heaven to heaven;
But hope, and fear, and love, shall keep thee man!
All this was hid from me: as one by one
My dreams grew dim, my wide aims circumscribed—
As actual good within my reach decreased,
While obstacles sprung up this way and that,
To keep me from effecting half the sum,
Small as it proved: as objects, mean within
The primal aggregate, remain'd alone
Of all the company, and, even the least,
More than a match for my concentred strength . . .
What wonder if I saw no way to shun
Despair? for power seem'd shut from man for ever.
In this conjuncture, as I prayed to die,
A strange adventure made me know One Sin
Had spotted my career from its uprise;
I saw Aprile—my Aprile there![1]
And as the poor melodious wretch disburthen'd
His heart, and moan'd his weakness in my ear,
I learn'd my own deep error: love's undoing
Taught me the worth of love in man's estate,
And what proportion love should hold with power
In his right constitution: love preceding
Power—with much power always much more love;
Love still too straiten'd in its present means,
And earnest for new power to set it free.
I learn'd this, and supposed the whole was learn'd:
And thus, when men received with stupid wonder
My first revealings—would have worshipp'd me—
And I despised and loathed their proffer'd praise;

[1] Line supplied from *Poems* 1849.

When, with awaken'd eyes, they took revenge
For past credulity in casting shame
On my real knowledge—and I hated them—
It was not strange I saw no good in man,
To overbalance all the wear and waste
Of faculties, display'd in vain, but born
To prosper in some better sphere: and why?
In my own heart love had not been made wise
To trace love's faint beginnings in mankind—
To know even hate is but a mask of love's;
To see a good in evil, and a hope
In ill-success; to sympathize—be proud
Of their half-reasons, faint aspirings, struggles
Dimly for truth—their poorest fallacies,
And prejudice, and fears, and cares, and doubts;
All with a touch of nobleness, for all
Their error, all ambitious, upward tending,
Like plants in mines which never saw the sun,
But dream of him, and guess where he may be,
And do their best to climb and get to him:
All this I knew not, and I fail'd; let men
Regard me, and the poet dead long ago
Who loved too rashly; and shape forth a third,
And better temper'd spirit, warn'd by both;
As from the over-radiant star too mad
To drink the light-springs, beamless thence itself—
And the dark orb which borders the abyss,
Ingulf'd in icy night, might have its course
A temperate and equidistant world:
Meanwhile, I have done well, though not all well.
As yet men cannot do without contempt—
'Tis for their good, and therefore fit awhile
That they reject me, and speak scorn of me;
But after, they will know me well: I stoop
Into a dark tremendous sea of cloud,
But 'tis but for a time; I press God's lamp
Close to my breast—its splendour, soon or late,
Will pierce the gloom: I shall emerge one day.
You understand me? I have said enough?

Fest. Now die, dear Aureole!

Par. Festus, let my hand—
This hand, lie in your own . . . my own true friend!
Aprile! hand in hand with you, Aprile!

Fest. And this was Paracelsus!

Sordello

1840

Sordello. By Robert Browning. London: Edward Moxon, Dover Street. MDCCCXL.

F'cap 8vo. Pp. iv + 256. Paper boards.

Sordello is a narrative poem in six books and comprised, on its appearance in 1840, some 5800 lines. It was first reprinted, in a revised and slightly lengthened form, in the collected *Poems* 1863.

The passage here reprinted from the first edition is Book the First, lines 345–699. This is virtually the same passage as was included, under the heading *Childhood of Sordello*, in the volume of *Selections* made anonymously by John Forster and B. W. Procter (Barry Cornwall), with Browning's sanction, in 1862.

Sordello

CHILDHOOD OF SORDELLO

. . . For he—for he—
"Gate-vein of this hearts' blood of Lombardy"
(If I should falter now)—for he is Thine!
Sordello, thy forerunner, Florentine!
A herald-star I know thou didst absorb
Relentless into the consummate orb
That scared it from its right to roll along
A sempiternal path with dance and song
Fulfilling its allotted period
Serenest of the progeny of God
Who yet resigns it not; his darling stoops
With no quenched lights, desponds with no blank troops
Of disenfranchised brilliances, for, blent
Utterly with thee, its shy element
Like thine upburneth prosperous and clear:
Still, what if I approach the august sphere
Named now with only one name, disentwine
That under current soft and argentine
From its fierce mate in the majestic mass
Leavened as the sea whose fire was mixt with glass
In John's transcendent vision, launch once more
That lustre? Dante, pacer of the shore
Where glutted Hell disgorgeth filthiest gloom,
Unbitten by its whirring sulphur-spume—
Or whence the grieved and obscure waters slope
Into a darkness quieted by hope—
Plucker of amaranths grown beneath God's eye
In gracious twilights where his Chosen lie,
I would do this! if I should falter now—
  In Mantua-territory half is slough
Half pine-tree forest; maples, scarlet-oaks
Breed o'er the river-beds; even Mincio chokes

With sand the summer through; but 'tis morass
In winter up to Mantua walls. There was
(Some thirty years before this evening's coil)
One spot reclaimed from the surrounding spoil,
Goito; just a castle built amid
A few low mountains; firs and larches hid
Their main defiles and rings of vineyard bound
The rest: some captured creature in a pound,
Whose artless wonder quite precludes distress,
Secure beside in its own loveliness,
So peered with airy head, below, above,
The castle at its toils the lapwings love
To glean among at grape-time. Pass within:
A maze of corridors contrived for sin,
Dusk winding-stairs, dim galleries got past,
You gain the inmost chambers, gain at last
A maple-panelled room: that haze which seems
Floating about the panel, if there gleams
A sunbeam over it will turn to gold
And in light-graven characters unfold
The Arab's wisdom everywhere; what shade
Marred them a moment, those slim pillars made,
Cut like a company of palms to prop
The roof, each kissing top entwined with top,
Leaning together; in the carver's mind
Some knot of bacchanals, flushed cheek combined
With straining forehead, shoulders purpled, hair
Diffused between, who in a goat-skin bear
A vintage; graceful sister-palms: but quick
To the main wonder now. A vault, see; thick
Black shade about the ceiling, though fine slits
Across the buttress suffer light by fits
Upon a marvel in the midst: nay, stoop—
A dullish grey-streaked cumbrous font, a group
Round it, each side of it, where'er one sees,
Upholds it—shrinking Caryatides
Of just-tinged marble like Eve's lilied flesh
Beneath her Maker's finger when the fresh
First pulse of life shot brightening the snow:
The font's edge burthens every shoulder, so

They muse upon the ground, eyelids half closed,
Some, with meek arms behind their backs disposed,
Some, crossed above their bosoms, some, to veil
Their eyes, some, propping chin and cheek so pale,
Some, hanging slack an utter helpless length
Dead as a buried vestal whose whole strength
Goes when the grate above shuts heavily;
So dwell these noiseless girls, patient to see,
Like priestesses because of sin impure
Penanced for ever, who resigned endure,
Having that once drunk sweetness to the dregs;
And every eve Sordello's visit begs
Pardon for them: constant as eve he came
To sit beside each in her turn, the same
As one of them, a certain space: and awe
Made a great indistinctness till he saw
Sunset slant cheerful through the buttress chinks,
Gold seven times globed; surely our maiden shrink
And a smile stirs her as if one faint grain
Her load were lightened, one shade less the stain
Obscured her forehead, yet one more bead slipt
From off the rosary whereby the crypt
Keeps count of the contritions of its charge?
Then with a step more light, a heart more large,
He may depart, leave her and every one
To linger out the penance in mute stone.
Ah, but Sordello? 'Tis the tale I mean
To tell you. In this castle may be seen,
On the hill tops, or underneath the vines,
Or southward by the mound of firs and pines
That shuts out Mantua, still in loneliness,
A slender boy in a loose page's dress,
Sordello: do but look on him awhile
Watching ('tis autumn) with an earnest smile
The noisy flock of thievish birds at work
Among the yellowing vineyards; see him lurk
('Tis winter with its sullenest of storms)
Beside that arras-length of broidered forms,
On tiptoe, lifting in both hands a light
Which makes yon warrior's visage flutter bright

—Ecelo, dismal father of the brood,
And Ecelin, close to the girl he wooed
—Auria, and their Child, with all his wives
From Agnes to the Tuscan that survives,
Lady of the castle, Adelaide: his face
—Look, now he turns away! Yourselves shall trace
(The delicate nostril swerving wide and fine,
A sharp and restless lip, so well combine
With that calm brow) a soul fit to receive
Delight at every sense; you can believe
Sordello foremost in the regal class
Nature has broadly severed from her mass
Of men and framed for pleasure as she frames
Some happy lands that have luxurious names
For loose fertility; a footfall there
Suffices to upturn to the warm air
Half-germinating spices, mere decay
Produces richer life, and day by day
New pollen on the lily-petal grows,
And still more labyrinthine buds the rose.
You recognise at once the finer dress
Of flesh that amply lets in loveliness
At eye and ear, while round the rest is furled
(As though she would not trust them with her world)
A veil that shows a sky not near so blue,
And lets but half the sun look fervid through:
How can such love like souls on each full-fraught
Discovery brooding, blind at first to aught
Beyond its beauty; till exceeding love
Becomes an aching weight, and to remove
A curse that haunts such natures—to preclude
Their finding out themselves can work no good
To what they love nor make it very blest
By their endeavour, they are fain invest
The lifeless thing with life from their own soul
Availing it to purpose, to control,
To dwell distinct and have peculiar joy
And separate interests that may employ
That beauty fitly, for its proper sake;
Nor rest they here: fresh births of beauty wake

Fresh homage; every grade of love is past,
With every mode of loveliness; then cast
Inferior idols off their borrowed crown
Before a coming glory: up and down
Runs arrowy fire, while earthly forms combine
To throb the secret forth; a touch divine—
And the scaled eyeball owns the mystic rod:
Visibly through his garden walketh God.
So fare they—Now revert: one character
Denotes them through the progress and the stir;
A need to blend with each external charm,
Bury themselves, the whole heart wide and warm,
In something not themselves; they would belong
To what they worship—stronger and more strong
Thus prodigally fed—that gathers shape
And feature, soon imprisons past escape
The votary framed to love and to submit
Nor ask, as passionate he kneels to it,
Whence grew the idol's empery. So runs
A legend; Light had birth ere moons and suns,
Flowing through space a river and alone,
Till chaos burst and blank the spheres were strown
Hither and thither, foundering and blind,
When into each of them rushed Light—to find
Itself no place, foiled of its radiant chance.
Let such forego their just inheritance!
For there's a class that eagerly looks, too,
On beauty, but, unlike the gentler crew,
Proclaims each new revealment born a twin
With a distinctest consciousness within
Referring still the quality, now first
Revealed, to their own soul; its instinct nursed
In silence, now remembered better, shown
More thoroughly, but not the less their own;
A dream come true; the special exercise
Of any special function that implies
The being fair or good or wise or strong,
Dormant within their nature all along—
Whose fault? So homage other souls direct
Without, turns inward; how should this deject

Thee, soul? they murmur; wherefore strength be quelled
Because, its trivial accidents withheld,
Organs are missed that clog the world, inert,
Wanting a will, to quicken and exert,
Like thine—existence cannot satiate,
Cannot surprise: laugh thou at envious fate,
Who from earth's simplest combination stampt
With individuality—uncrampt
By living its faint elemental life,
Dost soar to heaven's complexest essence, rife
With grandeurs, unaffronted to the last,
Equal to being all.
In truth? Thou hast
Life, then—wilt challenge life for us: thy race
Is vindicated so, obtains its place
In thy ascent, the first of us; whom we
May follow, to the meanest, finally,
With our more bounded wills?
Ah, but to find
A certain mood enervate such a mind,
Counsel it slumber in the solitude
Thus reached nor, stooping, task for mankind's good
Its nature just as life and time accord
(Too narrow an arena to reward
Emprize—the world's occasion worthless since
Not absolutely fitted to evince
Its mastery) or if yet worse befall,
And a desire possess it to put all
That nature forth, forcing our straitened sphere
Contain it; to display completely here
The mastery another life should learn,
Thrusting in time eternity's concern,
So that Sordello. . . . Fool, who spied the mark
Of leprosy upon him, violet dark
Already as he loiters? Born just now—
With the new century—beside the glow
And efflorescence out of barbarism;
Witness a Greek or two from the abysm
That stray through Florence-town with studious air,
Calming the chisel of that Pisan pair . . .

If Nicolo should carve a Christus yet!
While at Sienna is Guidone set,
Forehead on hand; a painful birth must be
Matured ere San Eufemio's sacristy
Or transept gather fruits of one great gaze
At the noon-sun: look you! An orange haze—
The same blue stripe round that—and, i' the midst,
Thy spectral whiteness, mother-maid, who didst
Pursue the dizzy painter!
Woe then worth
Any officious babble letting forth
The leprosy confirmed and ruinous
To spirit lodged in a contracted house!
Go back to the beginning rather; blend
It gently with Sordello's life; the end
Is piteous, you shall see, but much between
Pleasant enough; meantime some pyx to screen
The full-grown pest, some lid to shut upon
The goblin! As they found at Babylon,
(Colleagues mad Lucius and sage Antonine)
Sacking the city, by Apollo's shrine
Its pride, in rummaging the rarities,
A cabinet; be sure, who made the prize
Opened it greedily; and out there curled
Just such another plague, for half the world
Was stung. Crawl in then, hag, and crouch asquat,
Keeping that blotchy bosom thick in spot
Until your time is ripe! The coffer-lid
Is fastened and the coffer safely hid
Under the Loxian's choicest gifts of gold.
Who will may hear Sordello's story told,
And how he never could remember when
He dwelt not at Goito; calmly then
About this secret lodge of Adelaide's
Glided his youth away: beyond the glades
On the fir-forest's border, and the rim
Of the low range of mountain, was for him
No other world: but that appeared his own
To wander through at pleasure and alone.

The castle too seemed empty; far and wide
Might he disport; unless the northern side
Lay under a mysterious interdict—
Slight, just enough remembered to restrict
His roaming to the corridors, the vault
Where those fónt-bearers expiate their fault,
The maple-chamber, and the little nooks
And nests and breezy parapet that looks
Over the woods to Mantua; there he strolled.
Some foreign women-servants, very old,
Tended and crept about him—all his clue
To the world's business and embroiled ado
Distant a dozen hill-tops at the most.
And first a simple sense of life engrossed
Sordello in his drowsy Paradise;
The day's adventures for the day suffice—
Its constant tribute of perceptions strange
With sleep and stir in healthy interchange
Suffice, and leave him for the next at ease
Like the great palmer-worm that strips the trees,
Eats the life out of every luscious plant,
And when September finds them sere or scant
Puts forth two wondrous winglets, alters quite,
And hies him after unforeseen delight;
So fed Sordello, not a shard disheathed;
As ever round each new discovery wreathed
Luxuriantly the fancies infantine
His admiration, bent on making fine
Its novel friend at any risk, would fling
In gay profusion forth: a ficklest king
Confessed those minions! Eager to dispense
So much from his own stock of thought and sense
As might enable each to stand alone
And serve him for a fellow; with his own
Joining the qualities that just before
Had graced some older favourite: so they wore
A fluctuating halo, yesterday
Set flicker and to-morrow filched away;
Those upland objects each of separate name,
Each with an aspect never twice the same,

Waxing and waning as the new-born host
Of fancies, like a single night's hoar-frost,
Gave to familiar things a face grotesque;
Only, preserving through the mad burlesque
A grave regard: conceive; the orpine patch
Blossoming earliest on the log-house-thatch
The day those archers wound along the vines—
Related to the Chief that left their lines
To climb with clinking step the northern stair
Up to the solitary chambers where
Sordello never came. Thus thrall reached thrall;
He o'er-festooning every interval
As the adventurous spider, making light
Of distance, shoots her threads from depth to height,
From barbican to battlement; so flung
Fantasies forth and in their centre swung
Our architect : the breezy morning fresh
Above, and merry; all his waving mesh
Laughing with lucid dew-drops rainbow-edged.
This world of ours by tacid pact is pledged
To laying such a spangled fabric low
Whether by gradual brush or gallant blow:
But its abundant will was balked here: doubt
Rose tardily in one so fenced about
From most that nutures judgment, care and pain:
Judgment, that dull expedient we are fain,
Less favoured, to adopt betimes and force
Stead us, diverted from our natural course
Of joys, contrive some yet amid the dearth,
Vary and render them, it may be, worth
Most we forego: suppose Sordello hence
Selfish enough, without a moral sense
However feeble; what informed the boy
Others desired a portion in his joy?
Or say a ruthful chance broke woof and warp—
A heron's nest beat down by March winds sharp,
A fawn breathless beneath the precipice,
A bird with unsoiled breast and filmless eyes
Warm in the brake—could these undo the trance
Lapping Sordello? Not a circumstance

That makes for you, friend Naddo! Eat fern-seed
And peer beside us and report indeed
If (your word) Genius dawned with throes and stings
And the whole fiery catalogue, while springs,
Summers and winters quietly came and went,
Putting at length that period to content
By right the world should have imposed. . . .

SONGS FROM

Pippa Passes

1841

A Blot in the 'Scutcheon

1843

Bells and Pomegranates. No. I.—Pippa Passes. By Robert Browning, author of "Paracelsus." London: Edward Moxon, Dover Street. MDCCCXLI.

Royal 8vo. Pp. 16. Printed paper wrappers.

Bells and Pomegranates. No. V.—A Blot in the 'Scutcheon. A Tragedy, in three acts. By Robert Browning, author of "Paracelsus." London: Edward Moxon, Dover Street. MDCCCXLIII.

Royal 8vo. Pp. 16. Printed paper wrappers.

BETWEEN 1841 and 1846 Browning published eight pamphlets under the general title *Bells and Pomegranates*. Six contained poetic dramas—I *Pippa Passes* 1841; II *King Victor and King Charles* 1842; IV *The Return of the Druses* 1843; V *A Blot in the 'Scutcheon* 1843; VI *Colombe's Birthday* 1844; and VIII *Luria* and *A Soul's Tragedy* 1846. The third and seventh pamphlets, containing lyrical and narrative poems, are recorded on page 70 below.

Five of the six songs from *Pippa Passes* printed here are given in the text of the first edition ; as also is Mertoun's song from *A Blot in the 'Scutcheon*. An exception has been made of the third of Pippa's songs ("Give her but a least excuse to love me!"), which is given in the revised form, with altered rhythm and a longer stanza, first published in the collected *Poems*, two volumes, 1849.

SONGS FROM

Pippa Passes

AND

A Blot in the 'Scutcheon

PIPPA'S SONGS

I

All service ranks the same with God:
If now, as formerly he trod
Paradise, God's presence fills
Our earth, and each but as God wills
Can work—God's puppets, best and worst,
Are we; there is no last nor first.

Say not, a small event! Why small?
Costs it more pain this thing ye call
A great event should come to pass
Than that? Untwine me, from the mass
Of deeds that make up life, one deed
Power shall fall short in or exceed!

II

The year's at the spring,
And day's at the morn:
Morning's at seven;
The hill-side's dew-pearled:
The lark's on the wing,
The snail's on the thorn;
God's in his heaven—
All's right with the world!

III

Give her but a least excuse to love me!
When—where—
How—can this arm establish her above me,
If fortune fixed her as my lady there,
There already, to eternally reprove me?
("Hist"—said Kate the queen;
But "Oh—" cried the maiden, binding her tresses,
"'Tis only a page that carols unseen
Crumbling your hounds their messes!")

Is she wronged?—To the rescue of her honour,
My heart!
Is she poor?—What costs it to be styled a donour?
Merely an earth's to cleave, a sea's to part!
But that fortune should have thrust all this upon her!
("Nay, list,"—bade Kate the queen;
And still cried the maiden, binding her tresses,
"'Tis only a page that carols unseen
Fitting your hawks their jesses!")

IV

A king lived long ago,
In the morning of the world,
When earth was nigher heaven than now:
And the king's locks curled
Disparting o'er a forehead full
As the milk-white space 'twixt horn and horn
Of some sacrificial bull—
Only calm as a babe new-born:
For he was got to a sleepy mood,
So safe from all decrepitude,
Age with its bane so sure gone by,
(The Gods so loved him while he dreamed,)
That, having lived thus long, there seemed
No need the king should ever die.

Among the rocks his city was:
Before his palace, in the sun,

He sate to see his people pass,
And judge them every one
From its threshold of smooth stone.
They haled him many a valley-thief
Caught in the sheep-pens—robber-chief,
Swarthy and shameless—beggar-cheat—
Spy-prowler—or some pirate found
On the sea-sand left aground;
Sometimes there clung about his feet
With bleeding lip and burning cheek
A woman, bitterest wrong to speak
Of one with sullen, thickset brows:
Sometimes from out the prison-house
The angry priests a pale wretch brought,
Who through some chink had pushed and pressed,
Knees and elbows, belly and breast,
Worm-like into the temple,—caught
He was by the very God
Who ever in the darkness strode
Backward and forward, keeping watch
O'er his brazen bowls, such rogues to catch:
These, all and every one,
The king judged, sitting in the sun.

His councillors, on left and right,
Looked anxious up,—but no surprise
Disturbed the king's old smiling eyes,
Where the very blue had turned to white.
A python passed one day
The silent streets—until he came,
With forky tongue and eyes on flame,
Where the old king judged alway;
But when he saw the sweepy hair,
Girt with a crown of berries rare
The God will hardly give to wear
To the maiden who singeth, dancing bare
In the altar-smoke by the pine-torch lights,
At his wondrous forest rites,—
But which the God's self granted him
For setting free each felon limb

Because of earthly murder done
Faded till other hope was none;—
Seeing this, he did not dare
Approach that threshold in the sun,
Assault the old king smiling there.

V

Over-head the tree-tops meet—
Flowers and grass spring 'neath one's feet—
What are the voices of birds
—Ay, and of beasts,—but words—our words,
Only so much more sweet?
That knowledge with my life begun!
But I had so near made out the sun—
Could count your stars, the Seven and One!
Like the fingers of my hand—
Nay, could all but understand
How and wherefore the moon ranges—
And just when out of her soft fifty changes
No unfamiliar face might overlook me—
Suddenly God took me.

A GIRL'S SONG

You'll love me yet!—and I can tarry
Your love's protracted growing:
June reared that bunch of flowers you carry
From seeds of April's sowing.

I plant a heartfull now—some seed
At least is sure to strike
And yield—what you'll not care, indeed,
To pluck, but, may be, like

To look upon . . . my whole remains,
A grave's one violet:
Your look?—that pays a thousand pains.
What's death?—You'll love me yet!

MERTOUN'S SONG

THERE's a woman like a dew-drop, she's so purer than the purest,
And her noble heart's the noblest, yes, and her sure faith's the surest:
And her eyes are dark and humid, like the depth on depth of lustre
Hid i' the harebell, while her tresses, sunnier than the wild-grape cluster,
Gush in golden-tinted plenty down her neck's rose-misted marble:
Then her voice's music . . . call it the well's bubbling, the bird's warble!

And this woman says, "My days were sunless and my nights were moonless,
Parched the pleasant April herbage, and the lark's heart's outbreak tuneless,
If you loved me not!" And I who—(ah, for words of flame!) adore her!
Who am mad to lay my spirit prostrate palpably before her—
I may enter at her portal soon, as now her lattice takes me,
And by noontide as by midnight make her mine, as hers she makes me!

Dramatic Lyrics

1842

Dramatic Romances and Lyrics

1845

Bells and Pomegranates. No. III.—Dramatic Lyrics. By Robert Browning, author of "Paracelsus." London: Edward Moxon, Dover Street. MDCCCXLII.

Royal 8vo. Pp. 16. Printed paper wrappers.

Bells and Pomegranates. No. VII. Dramatic Romances & Lyrics. By Robert Browning, author of "Paracelsus." London: Edward Moxon, Dover Street. MDCCCXLV.

Royal 8vo. Pp. 24. Printed paper wrappers.

Poems By Robert Browning. In two volumes. Vol. I [II]. A new edition. London: Chapman & Hall, 186, Strand. 1849.

F'cap 8vo. Vol. I, pp. viii + 388; vol. II, pp. viii + 416. Cloth boards.

THE contents of *Bells and Pomegranates* Nos. III and VII were combined under the heading *Dramatic Romances and Lyrics* in the *Poems* of 1849. The order of the poems remained the same (save that three short pieces were omitted), and the principal alterations were in the titles: such familiar titles as *My Last Duchess*, *Porphyria's Lover* and *Home-Thoughts from the Sea* made their first appearance in the collection of 1849. In later collected editions Browning redistributed the poems, with others, under the headings *Dramatic Lyrics*, *Dramatic Romances* and *Men and Women*. "The logic of Browning's re-assignment," as Professor De Vane has remarked, "is not always apparent."

The text, titles and arrangement of 1849 have been followed here. The three omitted pieces have been restored under the combined title given to them in all editions since 1863, *Nationality in Drinks*. One poem, however, *Saul*, has been excluded. In *Bells and Pomegranates* 1845 and in *Poems* 1849 the first part only of *Saul* (sections 1–9) was printed: the complete poem, in nineteen sections, did not appear until 1855, in *Men and Women*. The 1855 text will be found on page 337 below.

Dramatic Lyrics
AND
Romances

CAVALIER TUNES

I—MARCHING ALONG

I

KENTISH Sir Byng stood for his King,
Bidding the crop-headed Parliament swing:
And, pressing a troop unable to stoop
And see the rogues flourish and honest folk droop,
Marched them along, fifty-score strong,
Great-hearted gentlemen, singing this song.

II

God for King Charles! Pym and such carles
To the Devil that prompts 'em their treasonous parles!
Cavaliers, up! Lips from the cup,
Hands from the pasty, nor bite take nor sup
Till you're (*Chorus*) *marching along, fifty-score strong,*
Great-hearted gentlemen, singing this song.

III

Hampden to Hell, and his obsequies' knell
Serve Hazelrig, Fiennes, and young Harry as well!
England, good cheer! Rupert is near!
Kentish and loyalists, keep we not here

(*Cho.*) *Marching along, fifty-score strong,*
Great-hearted gentlemen, singing this song?

IV

Then, God for King Charles! Pym and his snarls
To the Devil that pricks on such pestilent carles!
Hold by the right, you double your might;
So, onward to Nottingham, fresh for the fight,

(*Cho.*) *March we along, fifty-score strong,*
Great-hearted gentlemen, singing this song!

II—GIVE A ROUSE

I

KING CHARLES, and who'll do him right now?
King Charles, and who's ripe for fight now?
Give a rouse: here's, in Hell's despite now,
King Charles!

II

Who gave me the goods that went since?
Who raised me the house that sank once?
Who helped me to gold I spent since?
Who found me in wine you drank once?

(*Cho.*) *King Charles, and who'll do him right now?*
King Charles, and who's ripe for fight now?
Give a rouse: here's, in Hell's despite now,
King Charles!

III

To whom used my boy George quaff else,
By the old fool's side that begot him?
For whom did he cheer and laugh else,
While Noll's damned troopers shot him?

(*Cho.*) *King Charles, and who'll do him right now?*
King Charles, and who's ripe for fight now?
Give a rouse: here's, in Hell's despite now,
King Charles!

III—BOOT AND SADDLE

I

Boot, saddle, to horse, and away!
Rescue my Castle, before the hot day
Brightens to blue from its silvery gray,

(*Cho.*) *Boot, saddle, to horse, and away!*

II

Ride past the suburbs, asleep as you'd say;
Many's the friend there, will listen and pray
"God's luck to gallants that strike up the lay,

(*Cho.*) *Boot, saddle, to horse, and away!*"

III

Forty miles off, like a roebuck at bay,
Flouts Castle Brancepeth the Roundheads' array:
Who laughs, "Good fellows ere this, by my fay,

(*Cho.*) *Boot, saddle, to horse, and away?*"

IV

Who? My wife Gertrude; that, honest and gay,
Laughs when you talk of surrendering, "Nay!
I've better counsellors; what counsel they?

(*Cho.*) *Boot, saddle, to horse, and away!*"

MY LAST DUCHESS

FERRARA

That's my last Duchess painted on the wall,
Looking as if she were alive; I call
That piece a wonder, now: Frà Pandolf's hands
Worked busily a day, and there she stands.

Will't please you sit and look at her? I said
"Frà Pandolf" by design, for never read
Strangers like you that pictured countenance,
The depth and passion of its earnest glance,
But to myself they turned (since none puts by
The curtain I have drawn for you, but I)
And seemed as they would ask me, if they durst,
How such a glance came there; so, not the first
Are you to turn and ask thus. Sir, 'twas not
Her husband's presence only, called that spot
Of joy into the Duchess' cheek: perhaps
Frà Pandolf chanced to say "Her mantle laps
Over my Lady's wrist too much," or "Paint
Must never hope to reproduce the faint
Half-flush that dies along her throat;" such stuff
Was courtesy, she thought, and cause enough
For calling up that spot of joy. She had
A heart . . . how shall I say? . . . too soon made glad,
Too easily impressed; she liked whate'er
She looked on, and her looks went everywhere.
Sir, 'twas all one! My favor at her breast,
The dropping of the daylight in the West,
The bough of cherries some officious fool
Broke in the orchard for her, the white mule
She rode with round the terrace—all and each
Would draw from her alike the approving speech,
Or blush, at least. She thanked men,—good; but thanked
Somehow . . . I know not how . . . as if she ranked
My gift of a nine hundred years old name
With anybody's gift. Who'd stoop to blame
This sort of trifling? Even had you skill
In speech—(which I have not)—to make your will
Quite clear to such an one, and say "Just this
Or that in you disgusts me; here you miss,
Or there exceed the mark"—and if she let
Herself be lessoned so, nor plainly set
Her wits to yours, forsooth, and made excuse,
—E'en then would be some stooping, and I chuse
Never to stoop. Oh, Sir, she smiled, no doubt,
Whene'er I passed her; but who passed without

Much the same smile? This grew; I gave commands;
Then all smiles stopped together. There she stands
As if alive. Will't please you rise? We'll meet
The company below, then. I repeat,
The Count your Master's known munificence
Is ample warrant that no just pretence
Of mine for dowry will be disallowed;
Though his fair daughter's self, as I avowed
At starting, is my object. Nay, we'll go
Together down, Sir! Notice Neptune, tho',
Taming a sea-horse, thought a rarity,
Which Claus of Innsbruck cast in bronze for me.

COUNT GISMOND

AIX IN PROVENCE

I

Christ God, who savest men, save most
  Of men Count Gismond who saved me!
Count Gauthier, when he chose his post,
  Chose time and place and company
To suit it; when he struck at length
My honor 'twas with all his strength.

II

And doubtlessly ere he could draw
  All points to one, he must have schemed!
That miserable morning saw
  Few half so happy as I seemed,
While being dressed in Queen's array
To give our Tourney prize away.

III

I thought they loved me, did me grace
  To please themselves; 'twas all their deed;
God makes, or fair or foul, our face;
  If showing mine so caused to bleed
My cousins' hearts, they should have dropped
A word, and straight the play had stopped.

IV

They, too, so beauteous! Each a queen
  By virtue of her brow and breast;
Not needing to be crowned, I mean,
  As I do. E'en when I was dressed,
Had either of them spoke, instead
Of glancing sideways with still head!

V

But no: they let me laugh, and sing
  My birthday song quite through, adjust
The last rose in my garland, fling
  A last look on the mirror, trust
My arms to each an arm of theirs,
And so descend the castle-stairs—

VI

And come out on the morning troop
  Of merry friends who kissed my cheek,
And called me Queen, and made me stoop
  Under the canopy—(a streak
That pierced it, of the outside sun,
Powdered with gold its gloom's soft dun)—

VII

And they could let me take my state
  And foolish throne amid applause
Of all come there to celebrate
  My Queen's day—Oh, I think the cause
Of much was, they forgot no crowd
Makes up for parents in their shroud!

VIII

Howe'er that be, all eyes were bent
  Upon me, when my cousins cast
Theirs down; 'twas time I should present
  The victor's crown, but . . . there, 'twill last
No long time . . . the old mist again
Blinds me as then it did. How vain!

IX

See! Gismond's at the gate, in talk
With his two boys: I can proceed.
Well, at that moment, who should stalk
Forth boldly (to my face, indeed)
But Gauthier, and he thundered "Stay!"
And all stayed. "Bring no crowns, I say!"

X

"Bring torches! Wind the penance-sheet
About her! Let her shun the chaste,
Or lay herself before their feet!
Shall she, whose body I embraced
A night long, queen it in the day?
For Honor's sake no crowns, I say!"

XI

I? What I answered? As I live,
I never fancied such a thing
As answer possible to give.
What says the body when they spring
Some monstrous torture-engine's whole
Strength on it? No more says the soul.

XII

Till out strode Gismond; then I knew
That I was saved. I never met
His face before, but, at first view,
I felt quite sure that God had set
Himself to Satan; who would spend
A minute's mistrust on the end?

XIII

He strode to Gauthier, in his throat
Gave him the lie, then struck his mouth
With one back-handed blow that wrote
In blood men's verdict there. North, South,
East, West, I looked. The lie was dead,
And damned, and truth stood up instead.

XIV

This glads me most, that I enjoyed
  The heart of the joy, with my content
In watching Gismond unalloyed
  By any doubt of the event:
God took that on him—I was bid
Watch Gismond for my part: I did.

XV

Did I not watch him while he let
  His armourer just brace his greaves,
Rivet his hauberk, on the fret
  The while! His foot . . . my memory leaves
No least stamp out, nor how anon
He pulled his ringing gauntlets on.

XVI

And e'en before the trumpet's sound
  Was finished, prone lay the false Knight,
Prone as his lie, upon the ground:
  Gismond flew at him, used no sleight
Of the sword, but open-breasted drove,
Cleaving till out the truth he clove.

XVII

Which done, he dragged him to my feet
  And said "Here die, but end thy breath
In full confession, lest thou fleet
  From my first, to God's second death!
Say, hast thou lied?" And, "I have lied
To God and her," he said, and died.

XVIII

Then Gismond, kneeling to me, asked
  —What safe my heart holds, tho' no word
Could I repeat now, if I tasked
  My powers for ever, to a third
Dear even as you are. Pass the rest
Until I sank upon his breast.

XIX

Over my head his arm he flung
  Against the world; and scarce I felt
His sword, that dripped by me and swung,
  A little shifted in its belt,—
For he began to say the while
How South our home lay many a mile.

XX

So 'mid the shouting multitude
  We two walked forth to never more
Return. My cousins have pursued
  Their life, untroubled as before
I vexed them. Gauthier's dwelling-place
God lighten! May his soul find grace!

XXI

Our elder boy has got the clear
  Great brow; tho' when his brother's black
Full eye shows scorn, it . . . Gismond here?
  And have you brought my tercel back?
I just was telling Adela
How many birds it struck since May.

INCIDENT OF THE FRENCH CAMP

I

You know, we French stormed Ratisbon:
  A mile or so away
On a little mound, Napoléon
  Stood on our storming-day;
With neck out-thrust, you fancy how,
  Legs wide, arms locked behind,
As if to balance the prone brow
  Oppressive with its mind.

II

Just as perhaps he mused "My plans
  That soar, to earth may fall,
Let once my army-leader Lannes
  Waver at yonder wall,"—
Out 'twixt the battery-smokes there flew
  A rider, bound on bound
Full-galloping; nor bridle drew
  Until he reached the mound.

III

Then off there flung in smiling joy,
  And held himself erect
By just his horse's mane, a boy:
  You hardly could suspect—
(So tight he kept his lips compressed,
  Scarce any blood came thro')
You looked twice ere you saw his breast
  Was all but shot in two.

IV

"Well," cried he, "Emperor, by God's grace
  We've got you Ratisbon!
The Marshal's in the market-place,
  And you'll be there anon
To see your flag-bird flap his vans
  Where I, to heart's desire,
Perched him!" The Chief's eye flashed; his plans
  Soared up again like fire.

V

The Chief's eye flashed; but presently
  Softened itself, as sheathes
A film the mother eagle's eye
  When her bruised eaglet breathes:
"You're wounded!" "Nay," his soldier's pride
  Touched to the quick, he said:
"I'm killed, Sire!" And, his Chief beside,
  Smiling the boy fell dead.

SOLILOQUY OF THE SPANISH CLOISTER

Gr-r-r—there go, my heart's abhorrence!
  Water your damned flower-pots, do!
If hate killed men, Brother Lawrence,
  God's blood, would not mine kill you!
What? your myrtle-bush wants trimming?
  Oh, that rose has prior claims—
Needs its leaden vase filled brimming?
  Hell dry you up with its flames!

II

At the meal we sit together:
  Salve tibi! I must hear
Wise talk of the kind of weather,
  Sort of season, time of year:
Not a plenteous cork-crop: scarcely
  Dare we hope oak-galls, I doubt:
What's the Latin name for "parsley"?
  What's the Greek name for Swine's Snout?

III

Whew! We'll have our platter burnished,
  Laid with care on our own shelf!
With a fire-new spoon we're furnished,
  And a goblet for ourself,
Rinsed like something sacrificial
  Ere 'tis fit to touch our chaps—
Marked with L. for our initial!
  (He, he! There his lily snaps!)

IV

Saint, forsooth! While brown Dolores
  Squats outside the Convent bank,
With Sanchicha, telling stories,
  Steeping tresses in the tank,

Blue-black, lustrous, thick like horsehairs,
—Can't I see his dead eye glow
Bright, as 'twere a Barbary corsair's?
(That is, if he'd let it show!)

V

When he finishes refection,
Knife and fork he never lays
Cross-wise, to my recollection,
As do I, in Jesu's praise.
I, the Trinity illustrate,
Drinking watered orange-pulp—
In three sips the Arian frustrate;
While he drains his at one gulp!

VI

Oh, those melons! If he's able
We're to have a feast; so nice!
One goes to the Abbot's table,
All of us get each a slice.
How go on your flowers? None double?
Not one fruit-sort can you spy?
Strange!—And I, too, at such trouble,
Keep 'em close-nipped on the sly!

VII

There's a great text in Galatians,
Once you trip on it, entails
Twenty-nine distinct damnations,
One sure, if another fails.
If I trip him just a-dying,
Sure of Heaven as sure can be,
Spin him round and send him flying
Off to Hell, a Manichee?

VIII

Or, my scrofulous French novel,
On grey paper with blunt type!
Simply glance at it, you grovel
Hand and foot in Belial's gripe:

If I double down its pages
  At the woeful sixteenth print,
When he gathers his greengages,
  Ope a sieve and slip it in't?

IX

Or, there's Satan!—one might venture
  Pledge one's soul to him, yet leave
Such a flaw in the indenture
  As he'd miss till, past retrieve,
Blasted lay that rose-acacia
  We're so proud of! *Hy, Zy, Hine*...
'St, there's Vespers! *Plena gratiâ*
  Ave, Virgo! Gr-r-r—you swine!

IN A GONDOLA

He sings.

I SEND my heart up to thee, all my heart
  In this my singing!
For the stars help me, and the sea bears part;
  The very night is clinging
Closer to Venice' streets to leave one space
  Above me, whence thy face
May light my joyous heart to thee its dwelling-place.

She speaks.

Say after me, and try to say
My very words, as if each word
Came from you of your own accord,
In your own voice, in your own way:
"This woman's heart, and soul, and brain
Are mine as much as this gold chain
She bids me wear; which" (say again)
"I choose to make by cherishing
A precious thing, or choose to fling
Over the boat-side, ring by ring."
And yet once more say . . . no word more!
Since words are only words. Give o'er!

Unless you call me, all the same,
Familiarly by my pet-name
Which, if the Three should hear you call,
And me reply to, would proclaim
At once our secret to them all:
Ask of me, too, command me, blame—
Do break down the partition-wall
'Twixt us, the daylight world beholds
Curtained in dusk and splendid folds.
What's left but—all of mc to take?
I am the Three's; prevent them, slake
Your thirst! 'Tis said, the Arab sage
In practising with gems can loose
Their subtle spirit in his cruce
And leave but ashes: so, sweet mage,
Leave them my ashes when thy use
Sucks out my soul, thy heritage!

He sings.

1

Past we glide, and past, and past!
  What's that poor Agnese doing
Where they make the shutters fast?
  Grey Zanobi's just a-wooing
To his couch the purchased bride:
  Past we glide!

2

Past we glide, and past, and past!
  Why's the Pucci Palace flaring
Like a beacon to the blast?
  Guests by hundreds—not one caring
If the dear host's neck were wried:
  Past we glide!

She sings.

1

The Moth's kiss, first!
Kiss me as if you made believe
You were not sure, this eve,

How my face, your flower, had pursed
Its petals up; so, here and there
You brush it, till I grow aware
Who wants me, and wide open burst.

2

The Bee's kiss, now!
Kiss me as if you entered gay
My heart at some noonday,
A bud that dares not disallow
The claim, so all is rendered up,
And passively its shattered cup
Over your head to sleep I bow.

He sings.

I

What are we two?
I am a Jew,
And carry thee, farther than friends can pursue,
To a feast of our tribe,
Where they need thee to bribe
The devil that blasts them unless he imbibe
Thy . . . Shatter the vision for ever! And now,
As of old, I am I, Thou art Thou!

2

Say again, what we are?
The sprite of a star,
I lure thee above where the Destinies bar
My plumes their full play
Till a ruddier ray
Than my pale one announce there is withering away
Some . . . Shatter the vision for ever! And now,
As of old, I am I, Thou art Thou!

He muses.

Oh, which were best, to roam or rest?
The land's lap or the water's breast?

To sleep on yellow millet-sheaves,
Or swim in lucid shallows, just
Eluding water-lily leaves,
An inch from Death's black fingers, thrust
To lock you, whom release he must;
Which life were best on Summer eves?

He speaks, musing.

Lie back; could thought of mine improve you?
From this shoulder let there spring
A wing; from this, another wing;
Wings, not legs and feet, shall move you!
Snow-white must they spring, to blend
With your flesh, but I intend
They shall deepen to the end,
Broader, into burning gold,
Till both wings crescent-wise enfold
Your perfect self, from 'neath your feet
To o'er your head, where, lo, they meet
As if a million sword-blades hurled
Defiance from you to the world!

Rescue me thou, the only real !
And scare away this mad Ideal
That came, nor motions to depart!
Thanks! Now, stay ever as thou art!

Still he muses.

1

What if the Three should catch at last
Thy serenader? While there's cast
Paul's cloak about my head, and fast
Gian pinions me, Himself has past
His stylet thro' my back; I reel;
And . . . is it Thou I feel?

2

They trail me, these three godless knaves,
Past every church that sains and saves,

Nor stop till, where the cold sea raves
By Lido's wet accursed graves,
They scoop mine, roll me to its brink,
And . . . on Thy breast I sink!

She replies, musing.

Dip your arm o'er the boat-side, elbow-deep,
As I do: thus: were Death so unlike Sleep,
Caught this way? Death's to fear from flame, or steel,
Or poison doubtless; but from water—feel!

Go find the bottom! Would you stay me? There!
Now pluck a great blade of that ribbon-grass
To plait in where the foolish jewel was,
I flung away: since you have praised my hair,
'Tis proper to be choice in what I wear.

He speaks.

Row home? must we row home? Too surely
Know I where its front's demurely
Over the Giudecca piled;
Window just with window mating,
Door on door exactly waiting,
All's the set face of a child:
But behind it, where's a trace
Of the staidness and reserve,
And formal lines without a curve,
In the same child's playing-face?
No two windows look one way
O'er the small sea-water thread
Below them. Ah, the autumn day
I, passing, saw you overhead!
First, out a cloud of curtain blew,
Then, a sweet cry, and last, came you—
To catch your loory that must needs
Escape just then, of all times then,
To peck a tall plant's fleecy seeds,
And make me happiest of men.
I scarce could breathe to see you reach
So far back o'er the balcony,

(To catch him ere he climbed too high
Above you in the Smyrna peach)
That quick the round smooth cord of gold,
This coiled hair on your head, unrolled,
Fell down you like a gorgeous snake
The Roman girls were wont, of old,
When Rome there was, for coolness' sake
To let lie curling o'er their bosoms.
Dear loory, may his beak retain
Ever its delicate rose stain
As if the wounded lotus-blossoms
Had marked their thief to know again!

Stay longer yet, for others' sake
Than mine! what should your chamber do?
—With all its rarities that ache
In silence while day lasts, but wake
At night-time and their life renew,
Suspended just to pleasure you
—That brought against their will together
These objects, and, while day lasts, weave
Around them such a magic tether
That they look dumb: your harp, believe,
With all the sensitive tight strings
That dare not speak, now to itself
Breathes slumbrously as if some elf
Went in and out the chords, his wings
Make murmur whersoe'er they graze,
As an angel may, between the maze
Of midnight palace-pillars, on
And on, to sow God's plagues have gone
Through guilty glorious Babylon.
And while such murmurs flow, the nymph
Bends o'er the harp-top from her shell,
As the dry limpet for the lymph
Come with a tune he knows so well.
And how your statues' hearts must swell!
And how your pictures must descend
To see each other, friend with friend!
Oh, could you take them by surprise,

You'd find Schidone's eager Duke
Doing the quaintest courtesies
To that prim Saint by Haste-thee-Luke:
And, deeper into her rock den,
Bold Castelfranco's Magdalen
You'd find retreated from the ken
Of that robed counsel-keeping Ser—
As if the Tizian thinks of her,
And is not, rather, gravely bent
On seeing for himself what toys
Are these, his progeny invent,
What litter now the board employs
Whereon he signed a document
That got him murdered! Each enjoys
Its night so well, you cannot break
The sport up, so, indeed must make
More stay with me, for others' sake.

She speaks.

1

To-morrow, if a harp-string, say,
Is used to tie the jasmine back
That overfloods my room with sweets,
Contrive your Zorzi somehow meets
My Zanze: in the ribbon's black,
The Three are watching; keep away.

2

Your gondola—let Zorzi wreathe
A mesh of water-weeds about
Its prow, as if he unaware
Had struck some quay or bridge-foot stair;
That I may throw a paper out
As you and he go underneath.

There's Zanze's vigilant taper; safe are we!
Only one minute more to-night with me?
Resume your past self of a month ago!
Be you the bashful gallant, I will be

The lady with the colder breast than snow:
Now bow you, as becomes, nor touch my hand
More than I touch yours when I step to land,
And say, All thanks, Siora!—
Heart to heart,
And lips to lips! Yet once more, ere we part,
Clasp me, and make me thine, as mine thou art!

He is surprised, and stabbed.

It was ordained to be so, Sweet,—and best
Comes now, beneath thine eyes, and on thy breast.
Still kiss me! Care not for the cowards! Care
Only to put aside thy beauteous hair
My blood will hurt! The Three, I do not scorn
To death, because they never lived: but I
Have lived indeed, and so—(yet one more kiss)—can die!

ARTEMIS PROLOGUIZES

I AM a Goddess of the ambrosial courts,
And save by Here, Queen of Pride, surpassed
By none whose temples whiten this the world.
Thro' Heaven I roll my lucid moon along;
I shed in Hell o'er my pale people peace;
On Earth, I, caring for the creatures, guard
Each pregnant yellow wolf and fox-bitch sleek,
And every feathered mother's callow brood,
And all that love green haunts and loneliness.
Of men, the chaste adore me, hanging crowns
Of poppies red to blackness, bell and stem,
Upon my image at Athenai here;
And this dead Youth, Asclepios bends above,
Was dearest to me. He my buskined step
To follow thro' the wild-wood leafy ways,
And chase the panting stag, or swift with darts
Stop the swift ounce, or lay the leopard low,
Neglected homage to another God:
Whence Aphrodite, by no midnight smoke

Of tapers lulled, in jealousy dispatched
A noisome lust that, as the gadbee stings,
Possessed his stepdame Phaidra for himself
The son of Theseus her great absent spouse.
Hippolutos exclaiming in his rage
Against the miserable Queen, she judged
Life insupportable, and, pricked at heart
An Amazonian stranger's race should dare
To scorn her, perished by the murderous cord:
Yet, ere she perished, blasted in a scroll
The fame of him her swerving made not swerve,
Which Theseus read, returning, and believed,
So exiled, in the blindness of his wrath,
The man without a crime, who, last as first,
Loyal, divulged not to his sire the truth.
Now Theseus from Poseidon had obtained
That of his wishes should be granted Three,
And this he imprecated straight—alive
May ne'er Hippolutos reach other lands!
Poseidon heard, ai ai! And scarce the prince
Had stepped into the fixed boots of the car,
That give the feet a stay against the strength
Of the Henetian horses, and around
His body flung the reins, and urged their speed
Along the rocks and shingles of the shore,
When from the gaping wave a monster flung
His obscene body in the coursers' path!
These, mad with terror as the sea-bull sprawled
Wallowing about their feet, lost care of him
That reared them; and the master-chariot-pole
Snapping beneath their plunges like a reed,
Hippolutos, whose feet were trammeled fast,
Was yet dragged forward by the circling rein
Which either hand directed; nor was quenched
The frenzy of that flight before each trace,
Wheel-spoke and splinter of the woeful car,
Each boulder-stone, sharp stub, and spiny shell,
Huge fish-bone wrecked and wreathed amid the sands
On that detested beach, was bright with blood
And morsels of his flesh: then fell the steeds

Head-foremost, crashing in their mooned fronts,
Shivering with sweat, each white eye horror-fixed.
His people, who had witnessed all afar,
Bore back the ruins of Hippolutos.
But when his sire, too swoln with pride, rejoiced,
(Indomitable as a man foredoomed)
That vast Poseidon had fulfilled his prayer,
I, in a flood of glory visible,
Stood o'er my dying votary, and deed
By deed revealed, as all took place, the truth.
Then Theseus lay the woefullest of men,
And worthily; but ere the death-veils hid
His face, the murdered prince full pardon breathed
To his rash sire. Whereat Athenai wails.
So, I who ne'er forsake my votaries,
Lest in the cross-way none the honey-cake
Should tender, nor pour out the dog's hot life;
Lest at my fain the priests disconsolate
Should dress my image with some faded poor
Few crowns, made favours of, nor dare object
Such slackness to my worshippers who turn
The trusting heart and loaded hand elsewhere,
As they had climbed Oulumpos to report
Of Artemis and nowhere found her throne—
I interposed: and, this eventful night,
While round the funeral pyre the populace
Stood with fierce light on their black robes that blind
Each sobbing head, while yet their hair they clipped
O'er the dead body of their withered prince,
And, in his palace, Theseus prostrated
On the cold hearth, his brow cold as the slab
'Twas bruised on, groaned away the heavy grief—
As the pyre fell, and down the cross logs crashed,
Sending a crowd of sparkles thro' the night,
And the gay fire, elate with mastery,
Towered like a serpent o'er the clotted jars
Of wine, dissolving oils and frankincense,
And splendid gums, like gold,—my potency
Conveyed the perished man to my retreat
In the thrice venerable forest here.

And this white-bearded Sage who squeezes now
The berried plant, is Phoibos' son of fame,
Asclepios, whom my radiant brother taught
The doctrine of each herb and flower and root,
To know their secret'st virtue and express
The saving soul of all—who so has soothed
With lavers the torn brow and murdered cheeks,
Composed the hair and brought its gloss again,
And called the red bloom to the pale skin back,
And laid the strips and jagged ends of flesh
Even once more, and slacked the sinew's knot
Of every tortured limb—that now he lies
As if mere sleep possessed him underneath
These interwoven oaks and pines. Oh, cheer,
Divine presenter of the healing rod
Thy snake, with ardent throat and lulling eye,
Twines his lithe spires around! I say, much cheer!
Proceed thou with thy wisest pharmacics!
And ye, white crowd of woodland sister-nymphs,
Ply, as the Sage directs, these buds and leaves
That strew the turf around the Twain! While I
Await, in fitting silence, the event.

WARING

I

I

WHAT'S become of Waring
Since he gave us all the slip,
Chose land-travel or seafaring,
Boots and chest, or staff and scrip,
Rather than pace up and down
Any longer London-town?

II

Who'd have guessed it from his lip,
Or his brow's accustomed bearing,
On the night he thus took ship,
Or started landward?—little caring

For us, it seems, who supped together,
(Friends of his too, I remember)
And walked home thro' the merry weather,
The snowiest in all December;
I left his arm that night myself
For what's-his-name's, the new prose-poet,
That wrote the book there, on the shelf—
How, forsooth, was I to know it
If Waring meant to glide away
Like a ghost at break of day?
Never looked he half so gay!

III

He was prouder than the Devil:
How he must have cursed our revel!
Ay, and many other meetings,
Indoor visits, outdoor greetings,
As up and down he paced this London,
With no work done, but great works undone,
Where scarce twenty knew his name.
Why not, then, have earlier spoken,
Written, bustled? Who's to blame
If your silence kept unbroken?
"True, but there were sundry jottings,
Stray-leaves, fragments, blurrs and blottings,
Certain first steps were achieved
Already which"—(is that your meaning?)
"Had well borne out whoe'er believed
In more to come!" But who goes gleaning
Hedge-side chance-blades, while full-sheaved
Stand cornfields by him? Pride, o'erweening
Pride alone, puts forth such claims
O'er the day's distinguished names.

IV

Meantime, how much I loved him,
I find out now I've lost him:
I, who cared not if I moved him,
Who could so carelessly accost him,
Henceforth never shall get free

Of his ghostly company,
His eyes that just a little wink
As deep I go into the merit
Of this and that distinguished spirit—
His cheeks' raised colour, soon to sink,
As long I dwell on some stupendous
And tremendous (Heaven defend us!)
Monstr'-inform'-ingens-horrend-ous
Demoniaco-seraphic
Penman's latest piece of graphic.
Nay, my very wrist grows warm
With his dragging weight of arm!
E'en so, swimmingly appears,
Thro' one's after-supper musings,
Some lost Lady of old years,
With her beauteous vain endeavour,
And goodness unrepaid as ever;
The face, accustomed to refusings,
We, puppies that we were . . . Oh never
Surely, nice of conscience, scrupled
Being aught like false, forsooth, to?
Telling aught but honest truth to?
What a sin, had we centupled
Its possessor's grace and sweetness!
No! she heard in its completeness
Truth, for truth's a weighty matter,
And, truth at issue, we can't flatter!
Well, 'tis done with: she's exempt
From damning us thro' such a sally;
And so she glides, as down a valley,
Taking up with her contempt,
Past our reach; and in, the flowers
Shut her unregarded hours.

V

Oh, could I have him back once more,
This Waring, but one half-day more!
Back, with the quiet face of yore,
So hungry, for acknowledgment
Like mine! I'd fool him to his bent!

Feed, should not he, to heart's content?
I'd say, "to only have conceived
Your great works, tho' they ne'er make progress,
Surpasses all we've yet achieved!"
I'd lie so, I should be believed.
I'd make such havoc of the claims
Of the day's distinguished names
To feast him with, as feasts an ogress
Her sharp-toothed golden-crowned child!
Or, as one feasts a creature rarely
Captured here, unreconciled
To capture; and completely gives
Its pettish humours licence, barely
Requiring that it lives.

VI

Ichabod, Ichabod,
The glory is departed!
Travels Waring East away?
Who, of knowledge, by hearsay,
Reports a man upstarted
Somewhere as a God,
Hordes grown European-hearted,
Millions of the wild made tame
On a sudden at his fame?
In Vishnu-land what Avatar?
Or who, in Moscow, toward the Czar,
With the demurest of footfalls
Over the Kremlin's pavement, bright
With serpentine and syenite,
Steps, with five other Generals,
That simultaneously take snuff,
For each to have pretext enough
To kerchiefwise unfurl his sash
Which, softness' self, is yet the stuff
To hold fast where a steel chain snaps,
And leave the grand white neck no gash?
Waring, in Moscow, to those rough
Cold northern natures borne, perhaps,
Like the lambwhite maiden dear

From the circle of mute kings,
Unable to repress the tear,
Each as his sceptre down he flings,
To Dian's fane at Taurica,
Where now a captive priestess, she alway
Mingles her tender grave Hellenic speech
With theirs, tuned to the hailstone-beaten beach,
As pours some pigeon, from the myrrhy lands
Rapt by the whirlblast to fierce Scythian strands
Where breed the swallows, her melodious cry
Amid their barbarous twitter!
In Russia? Never! Spain were fitter!
Ay, most likely 'tis in Spain
That we and Waring meet again—
Now, while he turns down that cool narrow lane
Into the blackness, out of grave Madrid
All fire and shine—abrupt as when there's slid
Its stiff gold blazing pall
From some black coffin-lid.
Or, best of all,
I love to think
The leaving us was just a feint;
Back here to London did he slink;
And now works on without a wink
Of sleep, and we are on the brink
Of something great in fresco-paint:
Some garret's ceiling, walls and floor,
Up and down and o'er and o'er
He splashes, as none splashed before
Since great Caldara Polidore:
Or Music means this land of ours
Some favour yet, to pity won
By Purcell from his Rosy Bowers,—
"Give me my so long promised son,
Let Waring end what I begun!"
Then down he creeps and out he steals
Only when the night conceals
His face—in Kent 'tis cherry-time,
Or, hops are picking; or, at prime
Of March, he wanders as, too happy,

Years ago when he was young,
Some mild eve when woods grew sappy,
And the early moths had sprung
To life from many a trembling sheath
Woven the warm boughs beneath;
While small birds said to themselves
What should soon be actual song,
And young gnats, by tens and twelves,
Made as if they were the throng
That crowd around and carry aloft
The sound they have nursed, so sweet and pure,
Out of a myriad noises soft,
Into a tone that can endure
Amid the noise of a July noon,
When all God's creatures crave their boon,
All at once and all in tune,
And get it, happy as Waring then,
Having first within his ken
What a man might do with men,
And far too glad, in the even-glow,
To mix with your world he meant to take
Into his hand, he told you, so—
And out of it his world to make,
To contract and to expand
As he shut or oped his hand.
Oh, Waring, what's to really be?
A clear stage and a crowd to see!
Some Garrick—say—out shall not he
The heart of Hamlet's mystery pluck ?
Or, where most unclean beasts are rife,
Some Junius—am I right?—shall tuck
His sleeve, and out with flaying-knife!
Some Chatterton shall have the luck
Of calling Rowley into life!
Some one shall somehow run a muck
With this old world, for want of strife
Sound asleep: contrive, contrive
To rouse us, Waring! Who's alive?
Our men scarce seem in earnest now:
Distinguished names!—but 'tis, somehow,

As if they played at being names
Still more distinguished, like the games
Of children. Turn our sport to earnest
With a visage of the sternest!
Bring the real times back, confessed
Still better than our very best!

II

I

"When I last saw Waring . . ."
(How all turned to him who spoke—
You saw Waring? Truth or joke?
In land-travel, or sea-faring?)

II

"We were sailing by Triest,
Where a day or two we harboured:
A sunset was in the West,
When, looking over the vessel's side,
One of our company espied
A sudden speck to larboard.
And, as a sea-duck flies and swims
At once, so came the light craft up,
With its sole lateen sail that trims
And turns (the water round its rims
Dancing, as round a sinking cup)
And by us like a fish it curled,
And drew itself up close beside,
Its great sail on the instant furled,
And o'er its planks, a shrill voice cried,
(A neck as bronzed as a Lascar's)
'Buy wine of us, you English Brig?
Or fruit, tobacco and cigars?
A Pilot for you to Triest?
Without one, look you ne'er so big,
They'll never let you up the bay!
We natives should know best.'
I turned, and 'just those fellows' way,'
Our captain said, 'The 'long-shore thieves
Are laughing at us in their sleeves.'

III

"In truth, the boy leaned laughing back;
And one, half-hidden by his side
Under the furled sail, soon I spied,
With great grass hat, and kerchief black,
Who looked up, with his kingly throat,
Said somewhat, while the other shook
His hair back from his eyes to look
Their longest at us; then the boat,
I know not how, turned sharply round,
Laying her whole side on the sea
As a leaping fish does; from the lee
Into the weather, cut somehow
Her sparkling path beneath our bow;
And so went off, as with a bound,
Into the rose and golden half
Of the sky, to overtake the sun,
And reach the shore, like the sea-calf
Its singing cave; yet I caught one
Glance ere away the boat quite passed,
And neither time nor toil could mar
Those features: so I saw the last
Of Waring!"—You? Oh, never star
Was lost here, but it rose afar!
Look East, where whole new thousands are!
In Vishnu-land what Avatar?

RUDEL TO THE LADY OF TRIPOLI

I

I KNOW a Mount, the gracious Sun perceives
First when he visits, last, too, when he leaves
The world; and, vainly favored, it repays
The day-long glory of his steadfast gaze
By no change of its large calm front of snow.
And underneath the Mount, a Flower I know,
He cannot have perceived, that changes ever
At his approach; and, in the lost endeavour

To live his life, has parted, one by one,
With all a flower's true graces, for the grace
Of being but a foolish mimic sun,
With ray-like florets round a disk-like face.
Men nobly call by many a name the Mount,
As over many a land of theirs its large
Calm front of snow like a triumphal targe
Is reared, and still with old names, fresh ones vie,
Each to its proper praise and own account:
Men call the Flower, the Sunflower, sportively.

II

Oh, Angel of the East, one, one gold look
Across the waters to this twilight nook,
—The far sad waters, Angel, to this nook!

III

Dear Pilgrim, art thou for the East indeed?
Go! Saying ever as thou dost proceed,
That I, French Rudel, choose for my device
A sunflower outspread like a sacrifice
Before its idol. See! These inexpert
And hurried fingers could not fail to hurt
The woven picture; 'tis a woman's skill
Indeed; but nothing baffled me, so, ill
Or well, the work is finished. Say, men feed
On songs I sing, and therefore bask the bees
On my flower's breast as on a platform broad:
But, as the flower's concern is not for these
But solely for the sun, so men applaud
In vain this Rudel, he not looking here
But to the East—the East! Go, say this, Pilgrim dear!

CRISTINA

I

She should never have looked at me,
  If she meant I should not love her!
There are plenty . . . men, you call such,
I suppose . . . she may discover

All her soul to, if she pleases,
 And yet leave much as she found them:
But I'm not so, and she knew it
 When she fixed me, glancing round them.

II

What? To fix me thus meant nothing?
 But I can't tell . . . there's my weakness . . .
What her look said!—no vile cant, sure,
 About "need to strew the bleakness
Of some lone shore with its pearl-seed,
 That the Sea feels"—no "strange yearning
That such souls have, most to lavish
 Where there's chance of least returning."

III

Oh, we're sunk enough here, God knows!
 But not quite so sunk that moments,
Sure tho' seldom, are denied us,
 When the spirit's true endowments
Stand out plainly from its false ones,
 And apprise it if pursuing
Or the right way or the wrong way,
 To its triumph or undoing.

IV

There are flashes struck from midnights,
 There are fire-flames noondays kindle,
Whereby piled-up honors perish,
 Whereby swoln ambitions dwindle,
While just this or that poor impulse,
 Which for once had play unstifled,
Seems the sole work of a life-time
 That away the rest have trifled.

V

Doubt you if, in some such moment,
 As she fixed me, she felt clearly,
Ages past the soul existed,
 Here an age 'tis resting merely,

And hence, fleets again for ages:
  While the true end, sole and single,
It stops here for is, this love-way,
  With some other soul to mingle?

VI

Else it loses what it lived for,
  And eternally must lose it;
Better ends may be in prospect,
  Deeper blisses, if you choose it,
But this life's end and this love-bliss
  Have been lost here. Doubt you whether
This she felt, as, looking at me,
  Mine and her souls rushed together?

VII

Oh, observe! Of course, next moment,
  The world's honors, in derision,
Trampled out the light for ever:
  Never fear but there's provision
Of the Devil's to quench knowledge
  Lest we walk the earth in rapture!
—Making those who catch God's secret
  Just so much more prize their capture.

VIII

Such am I; the secret's mine now!
  She has lost me—I have gained her!
Her soul's mine: and, thus, grown perfect,
  I shall pass my life's remainder,
Life will just hold out the proving
  Both our powers, alone and blended—
And then, come the next life quickly!
  This world's use will have been ended.

MADHOUSE CELLS

I—JOHANNES AGRICOLA IN MEDITATION

There's Heaven above, and night by night,
  I look right through its gorgeous roof;
No sun and moons though e'er so bright
  Avail to stop me; splendor-proof
I keep the broods of stars aloof:
For I intend to get to God,
  For 'tis to God I speed so fast,
For in God's breast, my own abode,
  Those shoals of dazzling glory past,
I lay my spirit down at last.
I lie where I have always lain,
  God smiles as he has always smiled;
Ere suns and moons could wax and wane,
  Ere stars were thundergirt, or piled
The Heavens, God thought on me his child;
Ordained a life for me, arrayed
  Its circumstances, every one
To the minutest; ay, God said
  This head this hand should rest upon
Thus, ere he fashioned star or sun.
And having thus created me,
  Thus rooted me, he bade me grow,
Guiltless for ever, like a tree
  That buds and blooms, nor seeks to know
  The law by which it prospers so:
But sure that thought and word and deed
  All go to swell his love for me,
Me, made because that love had need
  Of something irrevocably
Pledged solely its content to be.
Yes, yes, a tree which must ascend,—
  No poison-gourd foredoomed to stoop!
I have God's warrant, could I blend
  All hideous sins, as in a cup,
To drink the mingled venoms up,

Secure my nature will convert
 The draught to blossoming gladness fast,
While sweet dews turn to the gourd's hurt,
 And bloat, and while they bloat it, blast,
As from the first its lot was cast.
For as I lie, smiled on, full fed
 By unexhausted power to bless,
I gaze below on Hell's fierce bed,
 And those its waves of flame oppress,
Swarming in ghastly wretchedness;
Whose life on earth aspired to be
 One altar-smoke, so pure!—to win
If not love like God's love to me,
 At least to keep his anger in,
And all their striving turned to sin!
 Priest, doctor, hermit, monk grown white
With prayer, the broken-hearted nun,
 The martyr, the wan acolyte,
The incense-swinging child,—undone
Before God fashioned star or sun!
God, whom I praise; how could I praise,
 If such as I might understand,
Make out, and reckon on, his ways,
 And bargain for his love, and stand,
Paying a price, at his right hand?

II—PORPHYRIA'S LOVER

THE rain set early in to-night,
 The sullen wind was soon awake,
It tore the elm-tops down for spite,
 And did its worst to vex the lake,
I listened with heart fit to break;
When glided in Porphyria: straight
 She shut the cold out and the storm,
And kneeled and made the cheerless grate
 Blaze up, and all the cottage warm;
Which done, she rose, and from her form
Withdrew the dripping cloak and shawl,
 And laid her soiled gloves by, untied

Her hat and let the damp hair fall,
  And, last, she sate down by my side
And called me. When no voice replied,
She put my arm about her waist,
  And made her smooth white shoulder bare,
And all her yellow hair displaced,
  And, stooping, made my cheek lie there,
And spread o'er all her yellow hair,
Murmuring how she loved me; she
  Too weak, for all her heart's endeavour,
To set its struggling passion free
  From pride, and vainer ties dissever,
And give herself to me for ever:
But passion sometimes would prevail,
  Nor could to-night's gay feast restrain
A sudden thought of one so pale
  For love of her, and all in vain;
So, she was come through wind and rain.
Be sure I looked up at her eyes
  Proud, very proud; at last I knew
Porphyria worshipped me; surprise
  Made my heart swell, and still it grew
While I debated what to do.
That moment she was mine, mine, fair,
  Perfectly pure and good: I found
A thing to do, and all her hair
  In one long yellow string I wound
Three times her little throat around,
And strangled her. No pain felt she;
  I am quite sure she felt no pain.
As a shut bud that holds a bee
  I warily oped her lids; again
Laughed the blue eyes without a stain.
And I untightened next the tress
  About her neck; her cheek once more
Blushed bright beneath my burning kiss:
  I propped her head up as before,
Only, this time *my* shoulder bore
Her head, which droops upon it still:
  The smiling rosy little head,

So glad it has its utmost will,
  That all it scorned at once is fled,
And I, its love, am gained instead!
Porphyria's love: she guessed not how
  Her darling one wish would be heard.
And thus we sit together now,
  And all night long we have not stirred,
And yet God has not said a word!

THROUGH THE METIDJA TO ABD-EL-KADR

1842

I

As I ride, as I ride,
With a full heart for my guide,
So its tide rocks my side,
As I ride, as I ride,
That, as I were double-eyed,
He, in whom our Tribes confide,
Is descried, ways untried
As I ride, as I ride.

II

As I ride, as I ride
To our Chief and his Allied,
Who dares chide my heart's pride
As I ride, as I ride?
Or are witnesses denied—
Through the desert waste and wide
Do I glide unespied
As I ride, as I ride?

III

As I ride, as I ride,
When an inner voice has cried,
The sands slide, nor abide
(As I ride, as I ride)

O'er each visioned Homicide
That came vaunting (has he lied?)
To reside—where he died,
As I ride, as I ride.

IV

As I ride, as I ride,
Ne'er has spur my swift horse plied,
Yet his hide, streaked and pied,
As I ride, as I ride,
Shows where sweat has sprung and dried,
—Zebra-footed, ostrich-thighed—
How has vied stride with stride
As I ride, as I ride!

V

As I ride, as I ride,
Could I loose what Fate has tied,
Ere I pried, she should hide
As I ride, as I ride,
All that's meant me: satisfied
When the Prophet and the Bride
Stop veins I'd have subside
As I ride, as I ride!

THE PIED PIPER OF HAMELIN

A CHILD'S STORY

I

Hamelin Town's in Brunswick,
By famous Hanover city;
The River Weser, deep and wide,
Washes its wall on the southern side;
A pleasanter spot you never spied;
But, when begins my ditty,
Almost five hundred years ago,
To see the townsfolk suffer so
From vermin, was a pity.

II

Rats!
They fought the dogs, and killed the cats,
And bit the babies in the cradles,
And ate the cheeses out of the vats,
And licked the soup from the cook's own ladles,
Split open the kegs of salted sprats,
Made nests inside men's Sunday hats,
And even spoiled the women's chats,
By drowning their speaking
With shrieking and squeaking
In fifty different sharps and flats.

III

At last the people in a body
To the Town Hall came flocking:
"'Tis clear," cried they, "our Mayor's a noddy;
And as for our Corporation—shocking
To think we buy gowns lined with ermine
For dolts that can't or won't determine
What's best to rid us of our vermin!
You hope, because you're old and obese,
To find in the furry civic robe ease?
Rouse up, Sirs! Give your brains a racking
To find the remedy we're lacking,
Or, sure as fate, we'll send you packing!"
At this the Mayor and Corporation
Quaked with a mighty consternation.

IV

An hour they sate in council,
At length the Mayor broke silence:
"For a guilder I'd my ermine gown sell
I wish I were a mile hence!
It's easy to bid one rack one's brain—
I'm sure my poor head aches again
I've scratched it so, and all in vain.
Oh for a trap, a trap, a trap!"
Just as he said this, what should hap

At the chamber door but a gentle tap?
"Bless us," cried the Mayor, "what's that?"
(With the Corporation as he sat,
Looking little though wondrous fat;
Nor brighter was his eye, nor moister
Than a too-long-opened oyster,
Save when at noon his paunch grew mutinous
For a plate of turtle green and glutinous)
"Only a scraping of shoes on the mat?
Anything like the sound of a rat
Makes my heart go pit-a-pat!"

V

"Come in!"—the Mayor cried, looking bigger:
And in did come the strangest figure!
His queer long coat from heel to head
Was half of yellow and half of red;
And he himself was tall and thin,
With sharp blue eyes, each like a pin,
And light loose hair, yet swarthy skin,
No tuft on cheek nor beard on chin,
But lips where smiles went out and in—
There was no guessing his kith and kin!
And nobody could enough admire
The tall man and his quaint attire:
Quoth one: "It's as my great-grandsire,
Starting up at the Trump of Doom's tone,
Had walked this way from his painted tomb-stone!"

VI

He advanced to the council-table:
And, "Please your honours," said he, "I'm able,
By means of a secret charm, to draw
All creatures living beneath the sun,
That creep, or swim, or fly, or run,
After me so as you never saw!
And I chiefly use my charm
On creatures that do people harm,
The mole, and toad, and newt, and viper;
And people call me the Pied Piper."

(And here they noticed round his neck
A scarf of red and yellow stripe,
To match with his coat of the self same cheque;
And at the scarf's end hung a pipe;
And his fingers, they noticed, were ever straying
As if impatient to be playing
Upon this pipe, as low it dangled
Over his vesture so old-fangled.)
"Yet," said he, "poor piper as I am,
In Tartary I freed the Cham,
Last June, from his huge swarms of gnats;
I eased in Asia the Nizam
Of a monstrous brood of vampyre-bats;
And, as for what your brain bewilders,
If I can rid your town of rats
Will you give me a thousand guilders?"
"One? fifty thousand!"—was the exclamation
Of the astonished Mayor and Corporation.

VII

Into the street the Piper stept,
  Smiling first a little smile,
As if he knew what magic slept
  In his quiet pipe the while;
Then, like a musical adept,
To blow the pipe his lips he wrinkled,
And green and blue his sharp eyes twinkled
Like a candle flame where salt is sprinkled;
And ere three shrill notes the pipe uttered,
You heard as if an army muttered;
And the muttering grew to a grumbling;
And the grumbling grew to a mighty rumbling;
And out of the houses the rats came tumbling:
Great rats, small rats, lean rats, brawny rats,
Brown rats, black rats, grey rats, tawny rats,
Grave old plodders, gay young friskers,
  Fathers, mothers, uncles, cousins,
Cocking tails and pricking whiskers,
  Families by tens and dozens,

Brothers, sisters, husbands, wives—
Followed the Piper for their lives.
From street to street he piped advancing,
And step for step they followed dancing,
Until they came to the river Weser
Wherein all plunged and perished
—Save one who, stout as Julius Cæsar,
Swam across and lived to carry
(As he the manuscript he cherished)
To Rat-land home his commentary,
Which was, "At the first shrill notes of the pipe,
I heard a sound as of scraping tripe,
And putting apples, wondrous ripe,
Into a cider-press's gripe:
And a moving away of pickle-tub-boards,
And a leaving ajar of conserve-cupboards,
And the drawing the corks of train-oil-flasks,
And a breaking the hoops of butter-casks;
And it seemed as if a voice
(Sweeter far than by harp or bý psaltery
Is breathed) called out, Oh rats, rejoice!
The world is grown to one vast drysaltery!
So munch on, crunch on, take your nuncheon,
Breakfast, supper, dinner, luncheon!
And just as a bulky sugar-puncheon,
All ready staved, like a great sun shone
Glorious scarce an inch before me,
Just as methought it said, Come, bore me!
—I found the Weser rolling o'er me."

VIII

You should have heard the Hamelin people
Ringing the bells till they rocked the steeple;
"Go," cried the Mayor, "and get long poles!
Poke out the nests and block up the holes!
Consult with carpenters and builders,
And leave in our town not even a trace
Of the rats!"—when suddenly up the face
Of the Piper perked in the market-place,
With a, "First, if you please, my thousand guilders!"

IX

A thousand guilders! The Mayor looked blue;
So did the Corporation too.
For council dinners made rare havock
With Claret, Moselle, Vin-de-Grave, Hock;
And half the money would replenish
Their cellar's biggest butt with Rhenish.
To pay this sum to a wandering fellow
With a gipsy coat of red and yellow!
"Beside," quoth the Mayor with a knowing wink,
"Our business was done at the river's brink;
We saw with our eyes the vermin sink,
And what's dead can't come to life, I think.
So, friend, we're not the folks to shrink
From the duty of giving you something for drink,
And a matter of money to put in your poke;
But, as for the guilders, what we spoke
Of them, as you very well know, was in joke.
Beside, our losses have made us thrifty;
A thousand guilders! Come, take fifty!"

X

The Piper's face fell, and he cried,
"No trifling! I can't wait, beside!
I've promised to visit by dinner time
Bagdat, and accept the prime
Of the Head Cook's pottage, all he's rich in,
For having left, in the Caliph's kitchen,
Of a nest of scorpions no survivor—
With him I proved no bargain-driver,
With you, don't think I'll bate a stiver!
And folks who put me in a passion
May find me pipe to another fashion."

XI

"How?" cried the Mayor, "d'ye think I'll brook
Being worse treated than a Cook?
Insulted by a lazy ribald
With idle pipe and vesture piebald?

You threaten us, fellow? Do your worst,
Blow your pipe there till you burst!"

XII

Once more he stept into the street;
  And to his lips again
Laid his long pipe of smooth straight cane;
  And ere he blew three notes (such sweet
Soft notes as yet musician's cunning
  Never gave the enraptured air)
There was a rustling, that seemed like a bustling
Of merry crowds justling at pitching and hustling,
Small feet were pattering, wooden shoes clattering,
Little hands clapping, and little tongues chattering,
And, like fowls in a farm-yard when barley is scattering,
Out came the children running.
All the little boys and girls,
With rosy cheeks and flaxen curls,
And sparkling eyes and teeth like pearls,
Tripping and skipping, ran merrily after
The wonderful music with shouting and laughter.

XIII

The Mayor was dumb, and the Council stood
As if they were changed into blocks of wood,
Unable to move a step, or cry
To the children merrily skipping by—
And could only follow with the eye
That joyous crowd at the Piper's back.
But how the Mayor was on the rack,
And the wretched Council's bosoms beat,
As the Piper turned from the High Street
To where the Weser rolled its waters
Right in the way of their sons and daughters!
However he turned from South to West,
And to Koppelberg Hill his steps addressed,
And after him the children pressed;
Great was the joy in every breast.

"He never can cross that mighty top!
He's forced to let the piping drop,
And we shall see our children stop!"
When, lo, as they reached the mountain's side,
A wondrous portal opened wide,
As if a cavern was suddenly hollowed;
And the Piper advanced and the children followed,
And when all were in to the very last,
The door in the mountain side shut fast.
Did I say, all? No! One was lame,
And could not dance the whole of the way;
And in after years, if you would blame
His sadness, he was used to say,—
"It's dull in our town since my playmates left!
I can't forget that I'm bereft
Of all the pleasant sights they see,
Which the Piper also promised me;
For he led us, he said, to a joyous land,
Joining the town and just at hand,
Where waters gushed and fruit-trees grew,
And flowers put forth a fairer hue,
And everything was strange and new;
The sparrows were brighter than peacocks here,
And their dogs outran our fallow deer,
And honey-bees had lost their stings,
And horses were born with eagles' wings;
And just as I became assured
My lame foot would be speedily cured,
The music stopped and I stood still,
And found myself outside the Hill,
Left alone against my will,
To go now limping as before,
And never hear of that country more!"

XIV

Alas, alas for Hamelin!
  There came into many a burgher's pate
  A text which says, that Heaven's Gate
  Opes to the Rich at as easy rate
As the needle's eye takes a camel in!

The Mayor sent East, West, North, and South
To offer the Piper by word of mouth,
  Wherever it was men's lot to find him,
Silver and gold to his heart's content,
If he'd only return the way he went,
  And bring the children behind him.
But when they saw 'twas a lost endeavour,
And Piper and dancers were gone for ever,
They made a decree that lawyers never
  Should think their records dated duly
If, after the day of the month and year,
These words did not as well appear,
"And so long after what happened here
  On the Twenty-second of Júly,
Thirteen hundred and Seventy-six:"
And the better in memory to fix
The place of the Children's last retreat,
They called it, the Pied Piper's Street—
Where any one playing on pipe or tabor
Was sure for the future to lose his labour.
Nor suffered they Hostelry or Tavern
  To shock with mirth a street so solemn;
But opposite the place of the cavern
  They wrote the story on a column,
And on the Great Church Window painted
The same, to make the world acquainted
How their children were stolen away;
And there it stands to this very day.
And I must not omit to say
That in Transylvania there's a tribe
Of alien people that ascribe
The outlandish ways and dress
On which their neighbours lay such stress,
To their fathers and mothers having risen
Out of some subterraneous prison
Into which they were trepanned
Long time ago in a mighty band
Out of Hamelin town in Brunswick land,
But how or why, they don't understand.

XV

So, Willy, let you and me be wipers
Of scores out with all men—especially pipers:
And, whether they pipe us free, from rats or fróm mice,
If we've promised them aught, let us keep our promise.

"HOW THEY BROUGHT THE GOOD NEWS FROM GHENT TO AIX"

16—

I

I SPRANG to the stirrup, and Joris, and he:
I galloped, Dirck galloped, we galloped all three;
"Good speed!" cried the watch, as the gate-bolts undrew;
"Speed!" echoed the wall to us galloping through;
Behind shut the postern, the lights sank to rest,
And into the midnight we galloped abreast.

II

Not a word to each other; we kept the great pace
Neck by neck, stride by stride, never changing our place;
I turned in my saddle and made its girths tight,
Then shortened each stirrup, and set the pique right,
Rebuckled the cheek-strap, chained slacker the bit,
Nor galloped less steadily Roland a whit.

III

'Twas moonset at starting; but while we drew near
Lokeren, the cocks crew and twilight dawned clear;
At Boom, a great yellow star came out to see;
At Düffeld, 'twas morning as plain as could be;
And from Mecheln church-steeple we heard the half-chime,
So Joris broke silence with, "Yet there is time!"

IV

At Aerschot, up leaped of a sudden the sun,
And against him the cattle stood black every one,

To stare thro' the mist at us galloping past,
And I saw my stout galloper Roland at last,
With resolute shoulders, each butting away
The haze, as some bluff river headland its spray.

V

And his low head and crest, just one sharp ear bent back
For my voice, and the other pricked out on his track;
And one eye's black intelligence,—ever that glance
O'er its white edge at me, his own master, askance!
And the thick heavy spume-flakes which aye and anon
His fierce lips shook upwards in galloping on.

VI

By Hasselt, Dirck groaned; and cried Joris, "Stay spur!
Your Roos galloped bravely, the fault's not in her,
We'll remember at Aix"—for one heard the quick wheeze
Of her chest, saw the stretched neck and staggering knees,
And sunk tail, and horrible heave of the flank,
As down on her haunches she shuddered and sank.

VII

So we were left galloping, Joris and I,
Past Looz and past Tongres, no cloud in the sky;
The broad sun above laughed a pitiless laugh,
'Neath our feet broke the brittle bright stubble like chaff;
Till over by Dalhem a dome-spire sprang white,
And "Gallop," gasped Joris, "for Aix is in sight!"

VIII

"How they'll greet us!"—and all in a moment his roan
Rolled neck and croup over, lay dead as a stone;
And there was my Roland to bear the whole weight
Of the news which alone could save Aix from her fate,
With his nostrils like pits full of blood to the brim,
And with circles of red for his eye-sockets' rim.

IX

Then I cast loose my buffcoat, each holster let fall,
Shook off both my jack-boots, let go belt and all,

Stood up in the stirrup, leaned, patted his ear,
Called my Roland his pet-name, my horse without peer;
Clapped my hands, laughed and sang, any noise, bad or
good,
Till at length into Aix Roland galloped and stood.

X

And all I remember is, friends flocking round
As I sate with his head 'twixt my knees on the ground,
And no voice but was praising this Roland of mine,
As I poured down his throat our last measure of wine,
Which (the burgesses voted by common consent)
Was no more than his due who brought good news from
Ghent.

PICTOR IGNOTUS

FLORENCE, 15—

I COULD have painted pictures like that youth's
Ye praise so. How my soul springs up! No bar
Stayed me—ah, thought which saddens while it soothes!—
Never did fate forbid me, star by star,
To outburst on your night with all my gift
Of fires from God: nor would my flesh have shrunk
From seconding my soul, with eyes uplift
And wide to Heaven, or, straight like thunder, sunk
To the centre, of an instant; or around
Turned calmly and inquisitive, to scan
The license and the limit, space and bound,
Allowed to Truth made visible in Man.
And, like that youth ye praise so, all I saw,
Over the canvass could my hand have flung,
Each face obedient to its passion's law,
Each passion clear proclaimed without a tongue;
Whether Hope rose at once in all the blood,
A-tiptoe for the blessing of embrace,
Or Rapture drooped the eyes, as when her brood
Pull down the nesting dove's heart to its place,

Or Confidence lit swift the forehead up,
  And locked the mouth fast, like a castle braved,—
O Human faces, hath it spilt, my cup?
  What did ye give me that I have not saved?
Nor will I say I have not dreamed (how well!)
  Of going—I, in each new picture,—forth,
As, making new hearts beat and bosoms swell,
  To Pope or Kaiser, East, West, South or North,
Bound for the calmly satisfied great State,
  Or glad aspiring little burgh, it went,
Flowers cast upon the car which bore the freight,
  Through old streets named afresh from its event,
Till it reached home, where learned Age should greet
  My face, and Youth, the star not yet distinct
Above his hair, lie learning at my feet!—
  Oh, thus to live, I and my picture, linked
With love about, and praise, till life should end,
  And then not go to Heaven, but linger here,
Here on my earth, earth's every man my friend,—
  The thought grew frightful, 'twas so wildly dear!
But a voice changed it! Glimpses of such sights
  Have scared me, like the revels thro' a door
Of some strange House of Idols at its rites;
  This world seemed not the world it was before!
Mixed with my loving trusting ones there trooped
  . . . Who summoned those cold faces that begun
To press on me and judge me? Tho' I stooped
  Shrinking, as from the soldiery a nun,
They drew me forth, and spite of me . . . enough!
  These buy and sell our pictures, take and give,
Count them for garniture and household-stuff,
  And where they live our pictures needs must live,
And see their faces, listen to their prate,
  Partakers of their daily pettiness,
Discussed of,—"This I love, or this I hate,
  This likes me more, and this affects me less!"
Wherefore I chose my portion. If at whiles
  My heart sinks, as monotonous I paint
These endless cloisters and eternal aisles
  With the same series, Virgin, Babe, and Saint,

With the same cold, calm, beautiful regard,
  At least no merchant traffics in my heart;
The sanctuary's gloom at least shall ward
  Vain tongues from where my pictures stand apart;
Only prayer breaks the silence of the shrine
  While, blackening in the daily candle-smoke,
They moulder on the damp wall's travertine,
  'Mid echoes the light footstep never woke.
So die, my pictures; surely, gently die!
  Oh, youth, men praise so,—holds their praise its worth?
Blown harshly, keeps the trump its golden cry?
  Tastes sweet the water with such specks of earth?

THE ITALIAN IN ENGLAND

THAT second time they hunted me
From hill to plain, from shore to sea,
And Austria, hounding far and wide
Her blood-hounds thro' the country-side,
Breathed hot and instant on my trace,—
I made six days a hiding-place
Of that dry green old aqueduct
Where I and Charles, when boys, have plucked
The fire-flies from the roof above,
Bright creeping thro' the moss they love.
—How long it seems since Charles was lost!
Six days the soldiers crossed and crossed
The country in my very sight;
And when that peril ceased at night,
The sky broke out in red dismay
With signal-fires; well, there I lay
Close covered o'er in my recess,
Up to the neck in ferns and cress,
Thinking on Metternich our friend,
And Charles's miserable end,
And much beside, two days; the third,
Hunger o'ercame me when I heard
The peasants from the village go
To work among the maize; you know,

With us, in Lombardy, they bring
Provisions packed on mules, a string
With little bells that cheer their task,
And casks, and boughs on every cask
To keep the sun's heat from the wine;
These I let pass in jingling line,
And, close on them, dear noisy crew,
The peasants from the village, too;
For at the very rear would troop
Their wives and sisters in a group
To help, I knew; when these had passed,
I threw my glove to strike the last,
Taking the chance: she did not start,
Much less cry out, but stooped apart
One instant, rapidly glanced round,
And saw me beckon from the ground:
A wild bush grows and hides my crypt;
She picked my glove up while she stripped
A branch off, then rejoined the rest
With that; my glove lay in her breast:
Then I drew breath: they disappeared:
It was for Italy I feared.

An hour, and she returned alone
Exactly where my glove was thrown.
Meanwhile came many thoughts; on me
Rested the hopes of Italy;
I had devised a certain tale
Which, when 'twas told her, could not fail
Persuade a peasant of its truth;
I meant to call a freak of youth
This hiding, and give hopes of pay,
And no temptation to betray.
But when I saw that woman's face,
Its calm simplicity of grace,
Our Italy's own attitude
In which she walked thus far, and stood,
Planting each naked foot so firm,
To crush the snake and spare the worm—

At first sight of her eyes, I said,
"I am that man upon whose head
They fix the price, because I hate
The Austrians over us: the State
Will give you gold—oh, gold so much,
If you betray me to their clutch!
And be your death, for aught I know,
If once they find you saved their foe.
Now, you must bring me food and drink,
And also paper, pen, and ink,
And carry safe what I shall write
To Padua, which you'll reach at night
Before the Duomo shuts; go in,
And wait till Tenebræ begin;
Walk to the Third Confessional,
Between the pillar and the wall,
And kneeling whisper *whence comes peace?*
Say it a second time; then cease;
And if the voice inside returns,
From Christ and Freedom; what concerns
The cause of Peace?—for answer, slip
My letter where you placed your lip;
Then come back happy we have done
Our mother service—I, the son,
As you the daughter of our land!"

Three mornings more, she took her stand
In the same place, with the same eyes:
I was no surer of sun-rise
Than of her coming: we conferred
Of her own prospects, and I heard
She had a lover—stout and tall,
She said—then let her eyelids fall,
"He could do much"—as if some doubt
Entered her heart,—then, passing out,
"She could not speak for others—who
Had other thoughts; herself she knew:"
And so she brought me drink and food.
After four days, the scouts pursued

Another path: at last arrived
The help my Paduan friends contrived
To furnish me: she brought the news:
For the first time I could not choose
But kiss her hand and lay my own
Upon her head—"This faith was shown
To Italy, our mother;—she
Uses my hand and blesses thee!"
She followed down to the sea-shore;
I left and never saw her more.

How very long since I have thought
Concerning—much less wished for—aught
Beside the good of Italy
For which I live and mean to die!
I never was in love; and since
Charles proved false, nothing could convince
My inmost heart I had a friend;
However, if I pleased to spend
Real wishes on myself—say, Three—
I know at least what one should be;
I would grasp Metternich until
I felt his red wet throat distil
In blood thro' these two hands: and next,
—Nor much for that am I perplexed—
Charles, perjured traitor, for his part,
Should die slow of a broken heart
Under his new employers: last
—Ah, there, what should I wish? For fast
Do I grow old and out of strength.—
If I resolved to seek at length
My father's house again, how scared
They all would look, and unprepared!
My brothers live in Austria's pay
—Disowned me long ago, men say;
And all my early mates who used
To praise me so—perhaps induced
More than one early step of mine—
Are turning wise; while some opine

"Freedom grows License," some suspect
"Haste breeds Delay," and recollect
They always said, such premature
Beginnings never could endure!
So, with a sullen "All's for best,"
The land seems settling to its rest.
I think, then, I should wish to stand
This evening in that dear, lost land,
Over the sea the thousand miles,
And know if yet that woman smiles
With the calm smile; some little farm
She lives in there, no doubt; what harm
If I sate on the door-side bench,
And, while her spindle made a trench
Fantastically in the dust,
Inquired of all her fortunes—just
Her children's ages and their names,
And what may be the husband's aims
For each of them—I'd talk this out,
And sit there, for an hour about,
Then kiss her hand once more, and lay
Mine on her head, and go my way.

So much for idle wishing—how
It steals the time! To business now!

THE ENGLISHMAN IN ITALY

PIANO DI SORRENTO

Fortù, Fortù, my beloved one,
  Sit here by my side,
On my knees put up both little feet!
  I was sure, if I tried,
I could make you laugh spite of Scirocco:
  Now, open your eyes—
Let me keep you amused till he vanish
  In black from the skies,

With telling my memories over
  As you tell your beads;
All the memories plucked at Sorrento
  —The flowers, or the weeds.

Time for rain! for your long hot dry Autumn
  Had net-worked with brown
The white skin of each grape on the bunches,
  Marked like a quail's crown,
Those creatures you make such account of,
  Whose heads,—specked with white
Over brown like a great spider's back,
  As I told you last night,—
Your mother bites off for her supper;
  Red-ripe as could be,
Pomegranates were chapping and splitting
  In halves on the tree:
And betwixt the loose walls of great flintstone,
  Or in the thick dust
On the path, or straight out of the rock side,
  Wherever could thrust
Some burnt sprig of bold hardy rock-flower
  Its yellow face up,
For the prize were great butterflies fighting,
  Some five for one cup.
So, I guessed, ere I got up this morning,
  What change was in store,
By the quick rustle-down of the quail-nets
  Which woke me before
I could open my shutter, made fast
  With a bough and a stone,
And look thro' the twisted dead vine-twigs,
  Sole lattice that's known!
Quick and sharp rang the rings down the net-poles,
  While, busy beneath,
Your priest and his brother tugged at them,
  The rain in their teeth:
And out upon all the flat house-roofs
  Where split figs lay drying,

The girls took the frails under cover:
  Nor use seemed in trying
To get out the boats and go fishing,
  For, under the cliff,
Fierce the black water frothed o'er the blind-rock.
  No seeing our skiff
Arrive about noon from Amalfi,
  —Our fisher arrive,
And pitch down his basket before us,
  All trembling alive
With pink and grey jellies, your sea-fruit,
  —You touch the strange lumps,
And mouths gape there, eyes open, all manner
  Of horns and of humps,
Which only the fisher looks grave at,
  While round him like imps
Cling screaming the children as naked
  And brown as his shrimps;
Himself too as bare to the middle—
  —You see round his neck
The string and its brass coin suspended,
  That saves him from wreck.
But to-day not a boat reached Salerno,
  So back to a man
Came our friends, with whose help in the vineyards
  Grape-harvest began:
In the vat, half-way up in our house-side,
  Like blood the juice spins,
While your brother all bare-legged is dancing
  Till breathless he grins
Dead-beaten, in effort on effort
  To keep the grapes under,
Since still when he seems all but master,
  In pours the fresh plunder
From girls who keep coming and going
  With basket on shoulder,
And eyes shut against the rain's driving,
  Your girls that are older,—
For under the hedges of aloe,
  And where, on its bed

Of the orchard's black mould, the love-apple
  Lies pulpy and red,
All the young ones are kneeling and filling
  Their laps with the snails
Tempted out by this first rainy weather,—
  Your best of regales,
As to-night will be proved to my sorrow,
  When, supping in state,
We shall feast our grape-gleaners (two dozen,
  Three over one plate)
With lasagne so tempting to swallow
  In slippery ropes,
And gourds fried in great purple slices,
  That colour of popes.
Meantime, see the grape-bunch they've brought you,—
  The rain-water slips
O'er the heavy blue bloom on each globe
  Which the wasp to your lips
Still follows with fretful persistence—
  Nay, taste, while awake,
This half of a curd-white smooth cheese-ball,
  That peels, flake by flake,
Like an onion's, each smoother and whiter;
  Next, sip this weak wine
From the thin green glass flask, with its stopper,
  A leaf of the vine,—
And end with the prickly-pear's red flesh
  That leaves thro' its juice
The stony black seeds on your pearl-teeth
  . . . Scirocco is loose!
Hark! the quick, whistling pelt of the olives
  Which, thick in one's track,
Tempt the stranger to pick up and bite them,
  Tho' not yet half black!
How the old twisted olive trunks shudder!
  The medlars let fall
Their hard fruit, and the brittle great fig-trees
  Snap off, figs and all,—
For here comes the whole of the tempest!
  No refuge, but creep

Back again to my side and my shoulder,
And listen or sleep.

O how will your country show next week,
When all the vine-boughs
Have been stripped of their foliage to pasture
The mules and the cows?
Last eve, I rode over the mountains;
Your brother, my guide,
Soon left me, to feast on the myrtles
That offered, each side,
Their fruit-balls, black, glossy, and luscious,—
Or strip from the sorbs
A treasure, so rosy and wondrous,
Of hairy gold orbs!
But my mule picked his sure, sober path out,
Just stopping to neigh
When he recognised down in the valley
His mates on their way
With the faggots, and barrels of water;
And soon we emerged
From the plain, where the woods could scarce follow;
And still as we urged
Our way, the woods wondered, and left us,
As up still we trudged
Though the wild path grew wilder each instant,
And place was e'en grudged
'Mid the rock-chasms, and piles of loose stones
(Like the loose broken teeth
Of some monster, which climbed there to die
From the ocean beneath)
Place was grudged to the silver-grey fume-weed
That clung to the path,
And dark rosemary, ever a-dying,
That, 'spite the wind's wrath,
So loves the salt rock's face to seaward,—
And lentisks as staunch
To the stone where they root and bear berries,—
And . . . what shows a branch

Coral-coloured, transparent, with circlets
  Of pale seagreen leaves—
Over all trod my mule with the caution
  Of gleaners o'er sheaves,
Still, foot after foot like a lady—
  So, round after round,
He climbed to the top of Calvano,
  And God's own profound
Was above me, and round me the mountains,
  And under, the sea,
And within me, my heart to bear witness
  What was and shall be!
Oh heaven, and the terrible crystal!
  No rampart excludes
Your eye from the life to be lived
  In the blue solitudes!
Oh, those mountains, their infinite movement!
  Still moving with you—
For, ever some new head and breast of them
  Thrusts into view
To observe the intruder—you see it
  If quickly you turn
And, before they escape you, surprise them—
  They grudge you should learn
How the soft plains they look on, lean over,
  And love (they pretend)
—Cower beneath them; the flat sea-pine crouches,
  The wild fruit-trees bend,
E'en the myrtle-leaves curl, shrink and shut—
  All is silent and grave—
'Tis a sensual and timorous beauty—
  How fair, but a slave!
So, I turned to the sea,—and there slumbered
  As greenly as ever
Those isles of the siren, your Galli;
  No ages can sever
The Three, nor enable their sister
  To join them,—half way
On the voyage, she looked at Ulysses—
  No farther to-day;

Tho' the small one, just launched in the wave,
  Watches breast-high and steady
From under the rock, her bold sister
  Swum half-way already.
Fortù, shall we sail there together
  And see from the sides
Quite new rocks show their faces—new haunts
  Where the siren abides?
Shall we sail round and round them, close over
  The rocks, tho' unseen,
That ruffle the gray glassy water
  To glorious green?
Then scramble from splinter to splinter,
  Reach land and explore,
On the largest, the strange square black turret
  With never a door,
Just a loop to admit the quick lizards;
  Then, stand there and hear
The birds' quiet singing, that tells us
  What life is, so clear!
The secret they sang to Ulysses,
  When, ages ago,
He heard and he knew this life's secret,
  I hear and I know!

Ah, see! The sun breaks o'er Calvano—
  He strikes the great gloom
And flutters it o'er the mount's summit
  In airy gold fume!
All is over! Look out, see the gypsy,
  Our tinker and smith,
Has arrived, set up bellows and forge,
  And down-squatted forthwith
To his hammering, under the wall there;
  One eye keeps aloof
The urchins that itch to be putting
  His jews'-harps to proof,
While the other, thro' locks of curled wire,
  Is watching how sleek

Shines the hog, come to share in the windfalls
  —An abbot's own cheek!
All is over! Wake up and come out now,
  And down let us go,
And see the fine things got in order
  At Church for the show
Of the Sacrament, set forth this evening;
  To-morrow's the Feast
Of the Rosary's Virgin, by no means
  Of Virgins the least—
As you'll hear in the off-hand discourse
  Which (all nature, no art)
The Dominican brother, these three weeks,
  Was getting by heart.
Not a post nor a pillar but's dizened
  With red and blue papers;
All the roof waves with ribbons, each altar
  A-blaze with long tapers;
But the great masterpiece is the scaffold
  Rigged glorious to hold
All the fiddlers and fifers and drummers,
  And trumpeters bold,
Not afraid of Bellini nor Auber,
  Who, when the priest's hoarse,
Will strike us up something that's brisk
  For the feast's second course.
And then will the flaxon-wigged Image
  Be carried in pomp
Thro' the plain, while in gallant procession
  The priests mean to stomp.
And all round the glad church lie old bottles
  With gunpowder stopped,
Which will be, when the Image re-enters,
  Religiously popped.
And at night from the crest of Calvano
  Great bonfires will hang,
On the plain will the trumpets join chorus,
  And more poppers bang!
At all events, come—to the garden,
  As far as the wall,

See me tap with a hoe on the plaster
  Till out there shall fall
A scorpion with wide angry nippers!

  . . . "Such trifles"—you say?
Fortù, in my England at home,
  Men meet gravely to-day
And debate, if abolishing Corn-laws
  Is righteous and wise
—If 'tis proper, Scirocco should vanish
  In black from the skies!

THE LOST LEADER

I

Just for a handful of silver he left us,
  Just for a riband to stick in his coat—
Found the one gift of which fortune bereft us,
  Lost all the others she lets us devote;
They, with the gold to give, doled him out silver,
  So much was theirs who so little allowed:
How all our copper had gone for his service!
  Rags—were they purple, his heart had been proud!
We that had loved him so, followed him, honoured him,
  Lived in his mild and magnificent eye,
Learned his great language, caught his clear accents,
  Made him our pattern to live and to die!
Shakespeare was of us, Milton was for us,
  Burns, Shelley, were with us,—they watch from their
    graves!
He alone breaks from the van and the freemen,
  He alone sinks to the rear and the slaves!

II

We shall march prospering,—not thro' his presence;
  Songs may inspirit us,—not from his lyre;
Deeds will be done,—while he boasts his quiescence,
  Still bidding crouch whom the rest bade aspire:

Blot out his name, then,—record one lost soul more,
  One task more declined, one more footpath untrod,
One more triumph for devils, and sorrow for angels,
  One wrong more to man, one more insult to God!
Life's night begins: let him never come back to us!
  There would be doubt, hesitation and pain,
Forced praise on our part—the glimmer of twilight,
  Never glad confident morning again!
Best fight on well, for we taught him,—strike gallantly,
  Aim at our heart ere we pierce through his own;
Then let him receive the new knowledge and wait us,
  Pardoned in Heaven, the first by the throne!

THE LOST MISTRESS

I

All's over, then—does truth sound bitter
  As one at first believes?
Hark, 'tis the sparrows' good-night twitter
  About your cottage eaves!

II

And the leaf-buds on the vine are woolly,
  I noticed that, to-day;
One day more bursts them open fully
  —You know the red turns gray.

III

To-morrow we meet the same then, dearest?
  May I take your hand in mine?
Mere friends are we,—well, friends the merest
  Keep much that I'll resign:

IV

For each glance of that eye so bright and black,
  Though I keep with heart's endeavour,—
Your voice, when you wish the snowdrops back,
  Though it stays in my soul for ever!—

V

—Yet I will but say what mere friends say,
Or only a thought stronger;
I will hold your hand but as long as all may,
Or so very little longer!

HOME-THOUGHTS FROM ABROAD

I

Oh, to be in England
Now that April's there,
And whoever wakes in England
Sees, some morning, unaware,
That the lowest boughs and the brush-wood sheaf
Round the elm-tree bole are in tiny leaf,
While the chaffinch sings on the orchard bough
In England—now!

II

And after April, when May follows,
And the whitethroat builds, and all the swallows—
Hark! where my blossomed pear-tree in the hedge
Leans to the field and scatters on the clover
Blossoms and dewdrops—at the bent spray's edge—
That's the wise thrush; he sings each song twice over,
Lest you should think he never could recapture
The first fine careless rapture!
And though the fields look rough with hoary dew,
All will be gay when noontide wakes anew
The buttercups, the little children's dower,
—Far brighter than this gaudy melon-flower!

HOME-THOUGHTS FROM THE SEA

Nobly, nobly Cape Saint Vincent to the north-west died away;
Sunset ran, one glorious blood-red, reeking into Cadiz Bay;
Bluish mid the burning water, full in face Trafalgar lay;

In the dimmest north-east distance, dawned Gibraltar grand and gray;
"Here and here did England help me,—how can I help England?"—say,
Whoso turns as I, this evening, turn to God to praise and pray,
While Jove's planet rises yonder, silent over Africa.

THE BISHOP ORDERS HIS TOMB AT ST PRAXED'S CHURCH

ROME, 15—

VANITY, saith the preacher, vanity!
Draw round my bed: is Anselm keeping back?
Nephews—sons mine . . . ah God, I know not! Well—
She, men would have to be your mother once,
Old Gandolf envied me, so fair she was!
What's done is done, and she is dead beside,
Dead long ago, and I am Bishop since,
And as she died so must we die ourselves,
And thence ye may perceive the world's a dream.
Life, how and what is it? As here I lie
In this state-chamber, dying by degrees,
Hours and long hours in the dead night, I ask
"Do I live, am I dead?" Peace, peace seems all.
St. Praxed's ever was the church for peace;
And so, about this tomb of mine. I fought
With tooth and nail to save my niche, ye know:
—Old Gandolf cozened me, despite my care;
Shrewd was that snatch from out the corner South
He graced his carrion with, God curse the same!
Yet still my niche is not so cramped but thence
One sees the pulpit o' the epistle-side,
And somewhat of the choir, those silent seats,
And up into the aery dome where live
The angels, and a sunbeam's sure to lurk:
And I shall fill my slab of basalt there,
And 'neath my tabernacle take my rest,

With those nine columns round me, two and two,
The odd one at my feet where Anselm stands:
Peach-blossom marble all, the rare, the ripe
As fresh-poured red wine of a mighty pulse
—Old Gandolf with his paltry onion-stone,
Put me where I may look at him! True peach,
Rosy and flawless: how I earned the prize!
Draw close: that conflagration of my church
—What then? So much was saved if aught were missed!
My sons, ye would not be my death? Go dig
The white-grape vineyard where the oil-press stood,
Drop water gently till the surface sinks,
And if ye find . . . Ah, God I know not, I! . . .
Bedded in store of rotten figleaves soft,
And corded up in a tight olive-frail,
Some lump, ah God, of *lapis lazuli*,
Big as a Jew's head cut off at the nape,
Blue as a vein o'er the Madonna's breast . . .
Sons, all have I bequeathed you, villas, all,
That brave Frascati villa with its bath,
So, let the blue lump poise between my knees,
Like God the Father's globe on both his hands
Ye worship in the Jesu Church so gay,
For Gandolf shall not choose but see and burst!
Swift as a weaver's shuttle fleet our years:
Man goeth to the grave, and where is he?
Did I say basalt for my slab, sons? Black—
'Twas ever antique-black I meant! How else
Shall ye contrast my frieze to come beneath?
The bas-relief in bronze ye promised me,
Those Pans and Nymphs ye wot of, and perchance
Some tripod, thyrsus, with a vase or so,
The Saviour at his sermon on the mount,
St. Praxed in a glory, and one Pan
Ready to twitch the Nymph's last garment off,
And Moses with the tables . . . but I know
Ye mark me not! What do they whisper thee,
Child of my bowels, Anselm? Ah, ye hope
To revel down my villas while I gasp
Bricked o'er with beggar's mouldy travertine

Which Gandolf from his tomb-top chuckles at!
Nay, boys, ye love me—all of jasper, then!
'Tis jasper ye stand pledged to, lest I grieve
My bath must needs be left behind, alas!
One block, pure green as a pistachio-nut,
There's plenty jasper somewhere in the world—
And have I not St. Praxed's ear to pray
Horses for ye, and brown Greek manuscripts,
And mistresses with great smooth marbly limbs?
—That's if ye carve my epitaph aright,
Choice Latin, picked phrase, Tully's every word,
No gaudy ware like Gandolf's second line—
Tully, my masters? Ulpian serves his need!
And then how I shall lie through centuries,
And hear the blessed mutter of the mass,
And see God made and eaten all day long,
And feel the steady candle-flame, and taste
Good strong thick stupifying incense-smoke!
For as I lie here, hours of the dead night,
Dying in state and by such slow degrees,
I fold my arms as if they clasped a crook,
And stretch my feet forth straight as stone can point,
And let the bedclothes for a mortcloth drop
Into great laps and folds of sculptor's-work:
And as yon tapers dwindle, and strange thoughts
Grow, with a certain humming in my ears,
About the life before I lived this life,
And this life too, Popes, Cardinals and Priests,
St. Praxed at his sermon on the mount,
Your tall pale mother with her talking eyes,
And new-found agate urns as fresh as day,
And marble's language, Latin pure, discreet,
—Aha, ELUCESCEBAT quoth our friend?
No Tully, said I, Ulpian at the best!
Evil and brief hath been my pilgrimage.
All *lapis*, all, sons! Else I give the Pope
My villas: will ye ever eat my heart?
Ever your eyes were as a lizard's quick,
They glitter like your mother's for my soul,
Or ye would heighten my impoverished frieze,

Piece out its starved design, and fill my vase
With grapes, and add a vizor and a Term,
And to the tripod ye would tie a lynx
That in his struggle throws the thyrsus down,
To comfort me on my entablature
Whereon I am to lie till I must ask
"Do I live, am I dead?" There, leave me, there!
For ye have stabbed me with ingratitude
To death—ye wish it—God, ye wish it! Stone—
Gritstone, a-crumble! Clammy squares which sweat
As if the corpse they keep were oozing through—
And no more *lapis* to delight the world!
Well, go! I bless ye. Fewer tapers there,
But in a row: and, going, turn your backs
—Ay, like departing altar-ministrants,
And leave me in my church, the church for peace,
That I may watch at leisure if he leers—
Old Gandolf, at me, from his onion-stone,
As still he envied me, so fair she was!

GARDEN-FANCIES

I—THE FLOWER'S NAME

I

HERE's the garden she walked across,
  Arm in my arm, such a short while since:
Hark, now I push its wicket, the moss
  Hinders the hinges and makes them wince!
She must have reached this shrub ere she turned,
  As back with that murmur the wicket swung;
For she laid the poor snail, my chance foot spurned,
  To feed and forget it the leaves among.

II

Down this side of the gravel-walk
  She went while her robe's edge brushed the box:
And here she paused in her gracious talk
  To point me a moth on the milk-white flox.

Roses, ranged in valiant row,
  I will never think that she passed you by!
She loves you noble roses, I know;
  But yonder, see, where the rock-plants lie!

III

This flower she stopped at, finger on lip,
  Stooped over, in doubt, as settling its claim;
Till she gave me, with pride to make no slip,
  Its soft meandering Spanish name.
What a name! was it love, or praise?
  Speech half-asleep, or song half-awake?
I must learn Spanish, one of these days,
  Only for that slow sweet name's sake.

IV

Roses, if I live and do well,
  I may bring her, one of these days,
To fix you fast with as fine a spell,
  Fit you each with his Spanish phrase!
But do not detain me now; for she lingers
  There, like sunshine over the ground,
And ever I see her soft white fingers
  Searching after the bud she found.

V

Flower, you Spaniard, look that you grow not,
  Stay as you are and be loved for ever!
Bud, if I kiss you 'tis that you blow not,
  Mind, the shut pink mouth opens never!
For while thus it pouts, her fingers wrestle,
  Twinkling the audacious leaves between,
Till round they turn and down they nestle—
  Is not the dear mark still to be seen?

VI

Where I find her not, beauties vanish;
  Whither I follow her, beauties flee;
Is there no method to tell her in Spanish
  June's twice June since she breathed it with me?

Come, bud, show me the least of her traces,
  Treasure my lady's lightest foot-fall
—Ah, you may flout and turn up your faces—
  Roses, you are not so fair after all!

II—SIBRANDUS SCHAFNABURGENSIS

I

Plague take all your pedants, say I!
  He who wrote what I hold in my hand,
Centuries back was so good as to die,
  Leaving this rubbish to cumber the land;
This, that was a book in its time,
  Printed on paper and bound in leather,
Last month in the white of a matin-prime
  Just when the birds sang all together.

II

Into the garden I brought it to read,
  And under the arbute and laurustine
Read it, so help me grace in my need,
  From title-page to closing line.
Chapter on chapter did I count,
  As a curious traveller counts Stonehenge;
Added up the mortal amount;
  And then proceeded to my revenge.

III

Yonder's a plum-tree, with a crevice
  An owl would build in, were he but sage;
For a lap of moss, like a fine pont-levis
  In a castle of the middle age,
Joins to a lip of gum, pure amber;
  When he'd be private, there might he spend
Hours alone in his lady's chamber:
  Into this crevice I dropped our friend.

IV

Splash, went he, as under he ducked,
  —I knew at the bottom rain-drippings stagnate;
Next a handful of blossoms I plucked
  To bury him with, my bookshelf's magnate;
Then I went in-doors, brought out a loaf,
  Half a cheese, and a bottle of Chablis;
Lay on the grass and forgot the oaf
  Over a jolly chapter of Rabelais.

V

Now, this morning, betwixt the moss
  And gum that locked our friend in limbo,
A spider had spun his web across,
  And sate in the midst with arms a-kimbo:
So, I took pity, for learning's sake,
  And, *de profundis, accentibus lætis,*
Cantate! quoth I, as I got a rake,
  And up I fished his delectable treatise.

VI

Here you have it, dry in the sun,
  With all the binding all of a blister,
And great blue spots where the ink has run,
  And reddish streaks that wink and glister
O'er the page so beautifully yellow—
  Oh, well have the droppings played their tricks!
Did he guess how toadstools grow, this fellow?
  Here's one stuck in his chapter six!

VII

How did he like it when the live creatures
  Tickled and toused and browsed him all over,
And worm, slug, eft, with serious features,
  Came in, each one, for his right of trover;
When the water-beetle with great blind deaf face
  Made of her eggs the stately deposit,
And the newt borrowed just so much of the preface
  As tiled in the top of his black wife's closet.

VIII

All that life, and fun, and romping,
  All that frisking, and twisting, and coupling,
While slowly our poor friend's leaves were swamping,
  And clasps were cracking, and covers suppling!
As if you had carried sour John Knox
  To the play-house at Paris, Vienna, or Munich,
Fastened him into a front-row box,
  And danced off the Ballet with trousers and tunic.

IX

Come, old Martyr! What, torment enough is it?
  Back to my room shall you take your sweet self!
Good bye, mother-beetle; husband-eft, *sufficit!*
  See the snug niche I have made on my shelf:
A.'s book shall prop you up, B.'s shall cover you,
  Here's C. to be grave with, or D. to be gay,
And with E. on each side, and F. right over you,
  Dry-rot at ease till the Judgment-day!

THE LABORATORY

ANCIEN RÉGIME

I

Now that I, tying thy glass mask tightly,
May gaze thro' these faint smokes curling whitely,
As thou pliest thy trade in this devil's-smithy—
Which is the poison to poison her, prithee?

II

He is with her; and they know that I know
Where they are, what they do: they believe my tears flow
While they laugh, laugh at me, at me fled to the drear
Empty church, to pray God in, for them!—I am here.

III

Grind away, moisten and mash up thy paste,
Pound at thy powder,—I am not in haste!
Better sit thus, and observe thy strange things,
Than go where men wait me and dance at the King's.

IV

That in the mortar—you call it a gum?
Ah, the brave tree whence such gold oozings come!
And yonder soft phial, the exquisite blue,
Sure to taste sweetly,—is that poison too?

V

Had I but all of them, thee and thy treasures,
What a wild crowd of invisible pleasures!
To carry pure death in an earring, a casket,
A signet, a fan-mount, a fillagree-basket!

VI

Soon, at the King's, a mere lozenge to give
And Pauline should have just thirty minutes to live!
But to light a pastile, and Elise, with her head,
And her breast, and her arms, and her hands, should
drop dead!

VII

Quick—is it finished? The colour's too grim!
Why not soft like the phial's, enticing and dim?
Let it brighten her drink, let her turn it and stir,
And try it and taste, ere she fix and prefer!

VIII

What a drop! She's not little, no minion like me—
That's why she ensnared him: this never will free
The soul from those strong, great eyes,—say, "no!"
To that pulse's magnificent come-and-go.

IX

For only last night, as they whispered, I brought
My own eyes to bear on her so, that I thought
Could I keep them one half minute fixed, she would fall,
Shrivelled; she fell not; yet this does it all!

X

Not that I bid you spare her the pain!
Let death be felt and the proof remain;
Brand, burn up, bite into its grace—
He is sure to remember her dying face!

XI

Is it done? Take my mask off! Nay, be not morose,
It kills her, and this prevents seeing it close:
The delicate droplet, my whole fortune's fee—
If it hurts her, beside, can it ever hurt me?

XII

Now, take all my jewels, gorge gold to your fill,
You may kiss me, old man, on my mouth if you will!
But brush this dust off me, lest horror it brings
Ere I know it—next moment I dance at the King's!

THE CONFESSIONAL

SPAIN

I

It is a lie—their Priests, their Pope,
Their Saints, their . . . all they fear or hope
Are lies, and lies—there! thro' my door
And ceiling, there! and walls and floor,
There, lies, they lie, shall still be hurled,
Till spite of them I reach the world!

II

You think Priests just and holy men!
Before they put me in this den,
I was a human creature too,
With flesh and blood like one of you,
A girl that laughed in beauty's pride
Like lilies in your world outside.

III

I had a lover—shame avaunt!
This poor wrenched body, grim and gaunt,
Was kissed all over till it burned,
By lips the truest, love e'er turned
His heart's own tint: one night they kissed
My soul out in a burning mist.

IV

So, next day when the accustomed train
Of things grew round my sense again,
"That is a sin," I said—and slow
With downcast eyes to church I go,
And pass to the confession-chair,
And tell the old mild father there.

V

But when I faulter Beltran's name,
"Ha?" quoth the father; "much I blame
The sin; yet wherefore idly grieve?
Despair not,—strenuously retrieve!
Nay, I will turn this love of thine
To lawful love, almost divine.

VI

"For he is young, and led astray,
This Beltran, and he schemes, men say,
To change the laws of church and state;
So, thine shall be an angel's fate,
Who, ere the thunder breaks, should roll
Its cloud away and save his soul.

VII

"For, when he lies upon thy breast,
Thou mayst demand and be possessed
Of all his plans, and next day steal
To me, and all those plans reveal,
That I and every priest, to purge
His soul, may fast and use the scourge."

VIII

That father's beard was long and white,
With love and truth his brow seemed bright;
I went back, all on fire with joy.
And, that same evening, bade the boy,
Tell me, as lovers should, heart-free,
Something to prove his love of me.

IX

He told me what he would not tell
For hope of heaven or fear of Hell;
And I lay listening in such pride,
And, soon as he had left my side,
Tripped to the church by morning-light
To save his soul in his despite.

X

I told the father all his schemes,
Who were his comrades, what their dreams;
"And now make haste," I said, "to pray
The one spot from his soul away;
To-night he comes, but not the same
Will look!" At night he never came.

XI

Nor next night: on the after-morn,
I went forth with a strength new-born:
The church was empty; something drew
My steps into the street; I knew
It led me to the market-place—
Where, lo,—on high—the father's face!

XII

That horrible black scaffold drest—
The stapled block . . . God sink the rest!
That head strapped back, that blinding vest,
Those knotted hands and naked breast—
Till near one busy hangman pressed—
And—on the neck these arms caressed. . . .

XIII

No part in aught they hope or fear!
No Heaven with them, no Hell,—and here,
No Earth, not so much space as pens
My body in their worst of dens
But shall bear God and Man my cry—
Lies—lies, again—and still, they lie!

THE FLIGHT OF THE DUCHESS

I

You're my friend:
I was the man the Duke spoke to;
I helped the Duchess to cast off his yoke, too;
So, here's the tale from beginning to end,
My friend!

II

Ours is a great wild country:
If you climb to our castle's top,
I don't see where your eye can stop;
For when you've passed the corn-field country,
Where vineyards leave off, flocks are packed,
And sheep-range leads to cattle-tract,
And cattle-tract to open-chase,
And open-chase to the very base
Of the mountain, where, at a funeral pace,
Round about, solemn and slow,
One by one, row after row,
Up and up the pine-trees go,

So, like black priests up, and so
Down the other side again
To another greater, wilder country,
That's one vast red drear burnt-up plain,
Branched thro' and thro' with many a vein
Whence iron's dug, and copper's dealt;
Look right, look left, look straight before,—
Beneath they mine, above they smelt,
Copper-ore and iron-ore,
And forge and furnace mould and melt,
And so on, more and ever more,
Till, at the last, for a bounding belt,
Comes the salt sand hoar of the great sea shore,
—And the whole is our Duke's country!

III

I was born the day this present Duke was—
(And O, says the song, ere I was old!)
In the castle where the other Duke was—
(When I was hopeful and young, not old!)
I in the Kennel, he in the Bower:
We are of like age to an hour.
My father was Huntsman in that day;
Who has not heard my father say
That, when a boar was brought to bay,
Three times, four times out of five,
With his huntspear he'd contrive
To get the killing-place transfixed,
And pin him true, both eyes betwixt?
And that's why the old Duke had rather
Have lost a salt-pit than my father,
And loved to have him ever in call;
That's why my father stood in the hall
When the old Duke brought his infant out
To show the people, and while they passed
The wondrous bantling round about,
Was first to start at the outside blast
As the Kaiser's courier blew his horn,
Just a month after the babe was born.
"And" quoth the Kaiser's courier, "since

The Duke has got an Heir, our Prince
Needs the Duke's self at his side:"
The Duke looked down and seemed to wince,
But he thought of wars o'er the world wide,
Castles a-fire, men on their march,
The toppling tower, the crashing arch;
And up he looked, and awhile he eyed
The row of crests and shields and banners,
Of all achievements after all manners,
And "ay," said the Duke with a surly pride.
The more was his comfort when he died
At next year's end, in a velvet suit,
With a gilt glove on his hand, and his foot
In a silken shoe for a leather boot,
Petticoated like a herald,
In a chamber next to an ante-room,
Where he breathed the breath of page and groom,
What he called stink, and they, perfume:
—They should have set him on red Berold,
Mad with pride, like fire to manage!
They should have got his cheek fresh tannage
Such a day as to-day in the merry sunshine!
Had they stuck on his fist a rough-foot merlin!
(Hark, the wind's on the heath at its game!
Oh for a noble falcon-lanner
To flap each broad wing like a banner,
And turn in the wind, and dance like flame!)
Had they broached a cask of white beer from Berlin!
—Or if you incline to prescribe mere wine—
Put to his lips when they saw him pine,
A cup of our own Moldavia fine,
Cotnar, for instance, green as May sorrel,
And ropy with sweet,—we shall not quarrel.

IV

So, at home, the sick tall yellow Duchess
Was left with the infant in her clutches,
She being the daughter of God knows who:
And now was the time to revisit her tribe,

So, abroad and afar they went, the two,
And let our people rail and gibe
At the empty Hall and extinguished fire,
As loud as we liked, but ever in vain,
Till after long years we had our desire,
And back came the Duke and his mother again.

V

And he came back the pertest little ape
That ever affronted human shape;
Full of his travel, struck at himself—
You'd say, he despised our bluff old ways
—Not he! For in Paris they told the elf
That our rough North land was the Land of Lays,
The one good thing left in evil days;
Since the Mid-Age was the Heroic Time,
And only in wild nooks like ours
Could you taste of it yet as in its prime,
And see true castles, with proper towers,
Young-hearted women, old-minded men,
And manners now as manners were then.
So, all that the old Dukes had been, without knowing it,
This Duke would fain know he was, without being it;
'Twas not for the joy's self, but the joy of his showing it,
Nor for the pride's self, but the pride of our seeing it,
He revived all usages thoroughly worn-out,
The souls of them fumed-forth, the hearts of them torn-
out:
And chief in the chase his neck he perilled,
On a lathy horse, all legs and length,
With blood for bone, all speed, no strength;
—They should have set him on red Berold,
With the red eye slow consuming in fire,
And the thin stiff ear like an abbey spire!

VI

Well, such as he was, he must marry, we heard
And out of a convent, at the word,
Came the Lady, in time of spring.
—Oh, old thoughts they cling, they cling!

That day, I know, with a dozen oaths
I clad myself in thick hunting-clothes
Fit for the chase of urox or buffle
In winter-time when you need to muffle;
But the Duke had a mind we should cut a figure,
And so we saw the Lady arrive:
My friend, I have seen a white crane bigger!
She was the smallest lady alive,
Made, in a piece of Nature's madness,
Too small, almost, for the life and gladness
That over-filled her, as some hive
Out of the bears' reach on the high trees
Is crowded with its safe merry bees:
In truth, she was not hard to please!
Up she looked, down she looked, round at the mead,
Straight at the castle, that's best indeed
To look at from outside the walls:
As for us, styled the "serfs and thralls,"
She as much thanked me as if she had said it,
(With her eyes, do you understand?)
Because I patted her horse while I led it;
And Max, who rode on her other hand,
Said, no bird flew past but she enquired
What its true name was, nor ever seemed tired—
If that was an eagle she saw hover,—
If the green and gray bird on the field was the plover.
When suddenly appeared the Duke,
And as down she sprung, the small foot pointed
On to my hand,—as with a rebuke,
And as if his backbone were not jointed,
The Duke stepped rather aside than forward,
And welcomed her with his grandest smile;
And, mind you, his mother all the while
Chilled in the rear, like a wind to Nor'ward;
And up, like a weary yawn, with its pullies
Went, in a shriek, the rusty portcullis;
And, like a glad sky the north-wind sullies,
The Lady's face stopped its play,
As if her first hair had grown grey—
For such things must begin some one day!

VII

In a day or two she was well again;
As who should say, "You labour in vain!
This is all a jest against God, who meant
I should ever be, as I am, content
And glad in his sight; therefore, glad I will be!"
So, smiling as at first went she.

VIII

She was active, stirring, all fire—
Could not rest, could not tire—
To a stone she had given life!
(I myself loved once, in my day,)
—For a Shepherd's, Miner's, Huntsman's wife,
(I had a wife, I know what I say,)
Never in all the world such an one!
And here was plenty to be done,
And she that could do it, great or small,
She was to do nothing at all.
There was already this man in his post,
This in his station, and that in his office,
And the Duke's plan admitted a wife, at most,
To meet his eye, with the other trophies,
Now outside the Hall, now in it,
To sit thus, stand thus, see and be seen,
At the proper place in the proper minute,
And die away the life between.
And it was amusing enough, each infraction
Of rule (but for after-sadness that came)
To hear the consummate self-satisfaction
With which the young Duke and the old Dame
Would let her advise, and criticise,
And, being a fool, instruct the wise,
And, child-like, parcel out praise or blame:
They bore it all in complacent guise,
As tho' an artificer, after contriving
A wheel-work image as if it were living,
Should find with delight it could motion to strike him!
So found the Duke, and his mother like him,—

The Lady hardly got a rebuff—
That had not been contemptuous enough,
With his cursed smirk, as he nodded applause,
And kept off the old mother-cat's claws.

IX

So, the little Lady grew silent and thin,
   Paling and ever paling,
As the way is with a hid chagrin;
   And the Duke perceived that she was ailing,
And said in his heart, "'Tis done to spite me!
But I shall find in my power to right me!"
Don't swear, friend—the Old One, many a year,
Is in Hell, and the Duke's self . . . you shall hear.

X

Well, early in autumn, at first winter-warning,
When the stag had to break with his foot, of a morning,
A drinking-hole out of the fresh tender ice
That covered the pond till the sun, in a trice,
Loosening it, let out a ripple of gold,
And another and another, and faster and faster,
Till, dimpling to blindness, the wide water rolled:
Then it so chanced that the Duke our master
Asked himself what were the pleasures in season,
And found, since the calendar bade him be hearty,
He should do the Middle Age no treason
In resolving on a hunting-party.
Always provided, old books showed the way of it!
What meant old poets by their strictures?
And when old poets had said their say of it,
How taught old painters in their pictures?
We must revert to the proper channels,
Workings in tapestry, paintings on pannels,
And gather up Woodcraft's authentic traditions:
Here was food for our various ambitions,
As on each case, exactly stated,
—To encourage your dog, now, the properest chirrup,
Or best prayer to St. Hubert on mounting your stirrup—
We of the household took thought and debated.

Blessed was he whose back ached with the jerkin
His sire was wont to do forest-work in;
Blesseder he who nobly sunk "ohs"
And "ahs" while he tugged on his grandsire's trunkhose;
What signified hats if they had no rims on,
Each slouching before and behind like the scallop,
And able to serve at sea for a shallop,
Loaded with lacquer and looped with crimson?
So that the deer now, to make a short rhyme on't,
What with our Venerers, Prickers, and Verderers,
Might hope for real hunters at length, and not murderers,
And oh, the Duke's tailor—he had a hot time on't!

XI

Now you must know, that when the first dizziness
Of flap-hats and buff-coats and jackboots subsided,
The Duke put this question, "The Duke's part provided,
Had not the Duchess some share in the business?"
For out of the mouth of two or three witnesses,
Did he establish all fit-or-unfitnesses:
And, after much laying of heads together,
Somebody's cap got a notable feather
By the announcement with proper unction
That he had discovered the lady's function;
Since ancient authors held this tenet,
"When horns wind a mort and the deer is at siege,
Let the dame of the Castle prick forth on her jennet,
And with water to wash the hands of her liege
In a clean ewer with a fair toweling,
Let her preside at the disemboweling."
Now, my friend, if you had so little religion
As to catch a hawk, some falcon-lanner,
And thrust her broad wings like a banner
Into a coop for a vulgar pigeon;
And if day by day, and week by week,
You cut her claws, and sealed her eyes,
And clipped her wings, and tied her beak,
Would it cause you any great surprise
If when you decided to give her an airing
You found she needed a little preparing?

—I say, should you be such a curmudgeon,
If she clung to the perch, as to take it in dudgeon?
Yet when the Duke to his lady signified,
Just a day before, as he judged most dignified,
In what a pleasure she was to participate,—
And, instead of leaping wide in flashes,
Her eyes just lifted their long lashes,
As if pressed by fatigue even he could not dissipate,
And duly acknowledged the Duke's forethought,
But spoke of her health, if her health were worth aught,
Of the weight by day and the watch by night,
And much wrong now that used to be right,
So, thanking him, declined the hunting,—
Was conduct ever more affronting?
With all the ceremony settled—
With the towel ready, and the sewer
Polishing up his oldest ewer,
And the jennet pitched upon, a piebald,
Black-barred, cream-coated and pink eye-ball'd,—
No wonder if the Duke was nettled!
And when she persisted nevertheless,—
Well, I suppose here's the time to confess
That there ran half round our Lady's chamber
A balcony none of the hardest to clamber;
And that Jacynth the tire-woman, ready in waiting,
Stayed in call outside, what need of relating?
And since Jacynth was like a June rose, why, a fervent
Adorer of Jacynth, of course, was your servant;
And if she had the habit to peep through the casement,
How could I keep at any vast distance?
And so, as I say, on the Lady's persistence,
The Duke, dumb stricken with amazement,
Stood for awhile in a sultry smother,
And then, with a smile that partook of the awful,
Turned her over to his yellow mother
To learn what was decorous and lawful;
And the mother smelt blood with a cat-like instinct,
As her cheek quick whitened thro' all its quince-tinct—
Oh, but the Lady heard the whole truth at once!
What meant she?—Who was she?—Her duty and station,

The wisdom of age and the folly of youth, at once,
Its decent regard and its fitting relation—
In brief, my friend, set all the devils in hell free
And turn them out to carouse in a belfry,
And treat the priests to a fifty-part canon,
And then you may guess how that tongue of hers ran on!
Well, somehow or other it ended at last
And, licking her whiskers, out she passed;
And after her,—making (he hoped) a face
Like Emperor Nero or Sultan Saladin,
Stalked the Duke's self with the austere grace
Of ancient hero or modern paladin,—
From door to staircase—oh, such a solemn
Unbending of the vertebral column!

XII

However, at sunrise our company mustered,
And here was the huntsman bidding unkennel,
And there 'neath his bonnet the pricker blustered,
With feather dank as a bough of wet fennel;
For the court-yard's four walls were filled with fog
You might cut as an axe chops a log.
Like so much wool for colour and bulkiness;
And out rode the Duke in a perfect sulkiness,
Since before breakfast, a man feels but queasily,
And a sinking at the lower abdomen
Begins the day with indifferent omen:
And lo, as he looked around uneasily,
The sun ploughed the fog up and drove it asunder
This way and that from the valley under;
And, looking thro' the court-yard arch,
Down in the valley, what should meet him
But a troop of Gypsies on their march,
No doubt with the annual gifts to greet him.

XIII

Now, in your land, Gypsies reach you, only
After reaching all lands beside;
North they go, south they go, trooping or lonely,
And still, as they travel far and wide,

Catch they and keep now a trace here, a trace there,
That puts you in mind of a place here, a place there:
But with us, I believe they rise out of the ground,
And nowhere else, I take it, are found
With the earth-tint yet so freshly embrowned;
Born, no doubt, like insects which breed on
The very fruit they are meant to feed on:
For the earth—not a use to which they don't turn it,
The ore that grows in the mountain's womb,
Or the sand in the pits like a honeycomb,
They sift and soften it, bake it and burn it—
Whether they weld you, for instance, a snaffle
With side-bars never a brute can baffle;
Or a lock that's a puzzle of wards within wards;
Or, if your colt's fore-foot inclines to curve inwards,
Horseshoes they'll hammer which turn on a swivel
And won't allow the hoof to shrivel;
Then they cast bells like the shell of the winkle,
That keep a stout heart in the ram with their
  tinkle:
But the sand—they pinch and pound it like otters;
Commend me to Gypsy glass-makers and potters!
Glasses they'll blow you, crystal-clear,
Where just a faint cloud of rose shall appear,
As if in pure water you dropped and let die
A bruised black-blooded mulberry;
And that other sort, their crowning pride,
With long white threads distinct inside,
Like the lake-flower's fibrous roots which dangle
Loose such a length and never tangle,
Where the bold sword-lily cuts the clear waters,
And the cup-lily couches with all the white daughters:
Such are the works they put their hand to,
And the uses they turn and twist iron and sand to.
And these made the troop which our Duke saw sally
Towards his castle from out of the valley,
Men and women, like new-hatched spiders,
Come out with the morning to greet our riders;
And up they wound till they reached the ditch,
Whereat all stopped save one, a witch,

That I knew, as she hobbled from the group,
By her gait, directly, and her stoop,
I, whom Jacynth was used to importune
To let that same witch tell us our fortune,
The oldest Gypsy then above ground;
And, so sure as the autumn season came round,
She paid us a visit for profit or pastime,
And every time, as she swore, for the last time.
And presently she was seen to sidle
Up to the Duke till she touched his bridle,
So that the horse of a sudden reared up
As under its nose the old witch peered up
With her worn-out eyes, or rather eye-holes
Of no use now but to gather brine,
And began a kind of level whine
Such as they used to sing to their viols
When their ditties they go grinding
Up and down with nobody minding:
And, then as of old, at the end of the humming
Her usual presents were forthcoming
—A dog-whistle blowing the fiercest of trebles,
(Just a sea-shore stone holding a dozen fine pebbles,)
Or a porcelain mouth-piece to screw on a pipe-end,—
And so she awaited her annual stipend.
But this time, the Duke would scarcely vouchsafe
A word in reply; and in vain she felt
With twitching fingers at her belt
For the purse of sleek pine-martin pelt,
Ready to put what he gave in her pouch safe,—
Till, either to quicken his apprehension,
Or possibly with an after-intention,
She was come, she said, to pay her duty
To the new Duchess, the youthful beauty.
No sooner had she named his Lady,
Than a shine lit up the face so shady,
And its smirk returned with a novel meaning—
For it struck him, the babe just wanted weaning;
If one gave her a taste of what life was and sorrow,
She, foolish to-day, would be wiser to-morrow;
And who so fit a teacher of trouble

As this sordid crone bent well nigh double?
So, glancing at her wolf-skin vesture,
(If such it was, for they grow so hirsute
That their own fleece serves for natural fur suit)
He was contrasting, 'twas plain from his gesture,
The life of the lady so flower-like and delicate
With the loathsome squalor of this helicat.
I, in brief, was the man the Duke beckoned
From out of the throng, and while I drew near
He told the crone, as I since have reckoned
By the way he bent and spoke into her ear
With circumspection and mystery,
The main of the Lady's history,
Her frowardness and ingratitude;
And for all the crone's submissive attitude
I could see round her mouth the loose plaits tightening,
And her brow with assenting intelligence brightening,
As tho' she engaged with hearty good will
Whatever he now might enjoin to fulfil,
And promised the lady a thorough frightening.
And so, just giving her a glimpse
Of a purse, with the air of a man who imps
The wing of the hawk that shall fetch the hernshaw,
He bade me take the gypsy mother
And set her telling some story or other
Of hill or dale, oak-wood or fernshaw,
To while away a weary hour
For the Lady left alone in her bower,
Whose mind and body craved exertion
And yet shrank from all better diversion.

XIV

Then clapping heel to his horse, the mere curvetter,
Out rode the Duke, and after his hollo
Horses and hounds swept, huntsman and servitor,
And back I turned and bade the crone follow.
And what makes me confident what's to be told you
Had all along been of this crone's devising,

Is, that, on looking round sharply, behold you,
There was a novelty quick as surprising:
For first, she had shot up a full head in stature,
And her step kept pace with mine nor faultered,
As if age had foregone its usurpature,
And the ignoble mien was wholly altered,
And the face looked quite of another nature,
And the change reached too, whatever the change meant,
Her shaggy wolf-skin cloak's arrangement,
For where its tatters hung loose like sedges,
Gold coins were glittering on the edges,
Like the band-roll strung with tomans
Which proves the veil a Persian woman's:
And under her brow, like a snail's horns newly
Come out as after the rain he paces,
Two unmistakeable eye-points duly
Live and aware looked out of their places.
So we went and found Jacynth at the entry
Of the Lady's chamber standing sentry;
I told the command and produced my companion,
And Jacynth rejoiced to admit any one,
For since last night, by the same token,
Not a single word had the Lady spoken:
So they went in both to the presence together,
While I in the balcony watched the weather.

XV

And now, what took place at the very first of all,
I cannot tell, as I never could learn it:
Jacynth constantly wished a curse to fall
On that little head of hers and burn it,
If she knew how she came to drop so soundly
Asleep of a sudden and there continue
The whole time sleeping as profoundly
As one of the boars my father would pin you
'Twixt the eyes where the life holds garrison,
—Jacynth forgive me the comparison!
But where I begin my own narration
Is a little after I took my station

To breathe the fresh air from the balcony,
And, having in those days a falcon eye,
To follow the hunt thro' the open country,
From where the bushes thinlier crested
The hillocks, to a plain where's not one tree:—
When, in a moment, my ear was arrested
By—was it singing, or was it saying,
Or a strange musical instrument playing
In the chamber?—and to be certain
I pushed the lattice, pulled the curtain,
And there lay Jacynth asleep,
Yet as if a watch she tried to keep,
In a rosy sleep along the floor
With her head against the door;
While in the midst, on the seat of state,
Like a queen the Gypsy woman sate,
With head and face downbent
On the Lady's head and face intent,
For, coiled at her feet like a child at ease,
The lady sate between her knees
And o'er them the Lady's clasped hands met,
And on those hands her chin was set,
And her upturned face met the face of the crone
Wherein the eyes had grown and grown
As if she could double and quadruple
At pleasure the play of either pupil
—Very like by her hands slow fanning,
As up and down like a gor-crow's flappers
They moved to measure like bell clappers
—I said, is it blessing, is it banning,
Do they applaud you or burlesque you?
Those hands and fingers with no flesh on?
When, just as I thought to spring in to the rescue,
At once I was stopped by the Lady's expression:
For it was life her eyes were drinking
From the crone's wide pair above unwinking,
Life's pure fire received without shrinking,
Into the heart and breast whose heaving
Told you no single drop they were leaving—
Life, that filling her, past redundant

Into her very hair, back swerving
Over each shoulder, loose and abundant,
As her head thrown back showed the white throat curving,
And the very tresses shared in the pleasure,
Moving to the mystic measure,
Bounding as the bosom bounded.
I stopped short, more and more confounded,
As still her cheeks burned and eyes glistened,
As she listened and she listened,—
When all at once a hand detained me,
And the selfsame contagion gained me,
And I kept time to the wondrous chime,
Making out words and prose and rhyme,
Till it seemed that the music furled
Its wings like a task fulfilled, and dropped
From under the words it first had propped,
And left them midway in the world,
And word took word as hand takes hand,
I could hear at last, and understand,
And when I held the unbroken thread,
The Gypsy said:—

"And so at last we find my tribe,
And so I set thee in the midst,
And to one and all of them describe
What thou saidst and what thou didst,
Our long and terrible journey thro',
And all thou art ready to say and do
In the trials that remain:
I trace them the vein and the other vein
That meet on thy brow and part again,
Making our rapid mystic mark;
And I bid my people prove and probe
Each eye's profound and glorious globe
Till they detect the kindred spark
In those depths so dear and dark,
Like the spots that snap, and burst, and flee,
Circling over the midnight sea.
And on that young round cheek of thine
I make them recognise the tinge,

As when of the costly scarlet wine
They drip so much as will impinge
And spread in a thinnest scale afloat
One thick gold drop from the olive's coat
Over a silver plate whose sheen
Still thro' the mixture shall be seen.
For, so I prove thee, to one and all,
Fit, when my people ope their breast,
To see the sign, and hear the call,
And take the vow, and stand the test
Which adds one more child to the rest—
When the breast is bare and the arms are wide,
And the world is left outside.
For there is probation to decree,
And many and long must the trials be
Thou shalt victoriously endure,
If that brow is true and those eyes are sure;
Like a jewel-finder's fierce assay
Of the prize he dug from its mountain tomb,—
Let once the vindicating ray
Leap out amid the anxious gloom,
And steel and fire have done their part
And the prize falls on its finder's heart;
So, trial after trial past,
Wilt thou fall at the very last
Breathless, half in trance
With the thrill of the great deliverance,
Into our arms for evermore;
And thou shalt know, those arms once curled
About thee, what we knew before,
How love is the only good in the world.
Henceforth be loved as heart can love,
Or brain devise, or hand approve!
Stand up, look below,
It is our life at thy feet we throw
To step with into light and joy;
Not a power of life but we'll employ
To satisfy thy nature's want;
Art thou the tree that props the plant,

Or the climbing plant that seeks the tree—
Canst thou help us, must we help thee?
If any two creatures grew into one,
They would do more than the world has done;
Tho' each apart were never so weak,
Yet vainly thro' the world should ye seek
For the knowledge and the might
Which in such union grew their right:
So, to approach, at least, that end,
And blend,—as much as may be, blend
Thee with us or us with thee,
As climbing-plant or propping-tree,
Shall some one deck thee, over and down,
Up and about, with blossoms and leaves?
Fix his heart's fruit for thy garland crown,
Cling with his soul as the gourd-vine cleaves,
Die on thy boughs and disappear
While not a leaf of thine is sere?
Or is the other fate in store,
And art thou fitted to adore,
To give thy wondrous self away,
And take a stronger nature's sway?
I forsee and I could foretell
Thy future portion, sure and well—
But those passionate eyes speak true, speak true,
And let them say what thou shalt do!
Only, be sure thy daily life,
In its peace, or in its strife,
Never shall be unobserved;
We pursue thy whole career,
And hope for it, or doubt, or fear,—
Lo, hast thou kept thy path or swerved,
We are beside thee, in all thy ways,
With our blame, with our praise,
Our shame to feel, our pride to show,
Glad, sorry—but indifferent, no!
Whether it is thy lot to go,
For the good of us all, where the haters meet
In the crowded city's horrible street;

Or thou step alone thro' the morass
Where never sound yet was
Save the dry quick clap of the stork's bill,
For the air is still, and the water still,
When the blue breast of the dipping coot
Dives under, and all again is mute.
So at the last shall come old age,
Decrepit as befits that stage;
How else wouldst thou retire apart
With the hoarded memories of thy heart,
And gather all to the very least
Of the fragments of life's earlier feast,
Let fall through eagerness to find
The crowning dainties yet behind?
Ponder on the entire past
Laid together thus at last,
When the twilight helps to fuse
The first fresh, with the faded hues,
And the outline of the whole,
As round eve's shades their framework roll,
Grandly fronts for once thy soul:
And then as, 'mid the dark, a gleam
Of yet another morning breaks,
And like the hand which ends a dream,
Death, with the might of his sunbeam
Touches the flesh and the soul awakes,
Then—"
Ay, then, indeed, something would happen!
But what? For here her voice changed like a bird's;
There grew more of the music and less of the words;
Had Jacynth only been by me to clap pen
To paper and put you down every syllable,
With those clever clerkly fingers,
All that I've forgotten as well as what lingers
In this old brain of mine that's but ill able
To give you even this poor version
Of the speech I spoil, as it were, with stammering
—More fault of those who had the hammering
Of prosody into me and syntax,
And did it, not with hobnails but tintacks!

But to return from this excursion,—
Just, do you mark, when the song was sweetest,
The peace most deep and the charm completest,
There came, shall I say, a snap—
And the charm vanished!
And my sense returned, so strangely banished,
And, starting as from a nap,
I knew the crone was bewitching my lady,
With Jacynth asleep; and but one spring made I,
Down from the casement, round to the portal,
Another minute and I had entered,
When the door opened, and more than mortal
Stood, with a face where to my mind centred
All beauties I ever saw or shall see,
The Duchess—I stopped as if struck by palsy.
She was so different, happy and beautiful,
I felt at once that all was best,
And that I had nothing to do, for the rest,
But wait her commands, obey and be dutiful.
Not that, in fact, there was any commanding,
—I saw the glory of her eye,
And the brow's height and the breast's expanding,
And I was hers to live or to die.
As for finding what she wanted,
You know God Almighty granted
Such little signs should serve his wild creatures
To tell one another all their desires,
So that each knows what its friend requires,
And does its bidding without teachers.
I preceded her; the crone
Followed silent and alone;
I spoke to her, but she merely jabbered
In the old style; both her eyes had slunk
Back to their pits; her stature shrunk;
In short, the soul in its body sunk
Like a blade sent home to its scabbard.
We descended, I preceding;
Crossed the court with nobody heeding;
All the world was at the chase,
The court-yard like a desert-place,

The stable emptied of its small fry;
I saddle myself the very palfrey
I remember patting while it carried her,
The day she arrived and the Duke married her.
And, do you know, though it's easy deceiving
Oneself in such matters, I can't help believing
The lady had not forgotten it either,
And knew the poor devil so much beneath her
Would have been only too glad for her service
To dance on hot ploughshares like a Turk dervise,
But unable to pay proper duty where owing it
Was reduced to that pitiful method of showing it:
For though the moment I began setting
His saddle on my own nag of Berold's begetting,
(Not that I meant to be obtrusive)
She stopped me, while his rug was shifting,
By a single rapid finger's lifting,
And, with a gesture kind but conclusive,
And a little shake of the head, refused me,—
I say, although she never used me,
Yet when she was mounted, the gypsy behind her,
And I ventured to remind her,
I suppose with a voice of less steadiness
Than usual, for my feeling exceeded me,
—Something to the effect that I was in readiness
Whenever God should please she needed me,—
Then, do you know, her face looked down on me
With a look that placed a crown on me,
And she felt in her bosom,—mark, her bosom—
And, as a flower-tree drops its blossom,
Dropped me—ah, had it been a purse
Of silver, my friend, or gold that's worse,
Why, you see, as soon as I found myself
So understood,—that a true heart so may gain
Such a reward,—I should have gone home again,
Kissed Jacynth, and soberly drowned myself!
It was a little plait of hair
Such as friends in a convent make
To wear, each for the other's sake,—
This, see, which at my breast I wear,

Ever did (rather to Jacynth's grudgment),
And ever shall, till the Day of Judgment.
And then,—and then,—to cut short,—this is idle,
These are feelings it is not good to foster,—
I pushed the gate wide, she shook the bridle,
And the palfrey bounded,—and so we lost her!

XVI

When the liquor's out, why clink the cannakin?
I did think to describe you the panic in
The redoubtable breast of our master the mannikin,
And what was the pitch of his mother's yellowness,
How she turned as a shark to snap the spare-rib
Clean off, sailors say, from a pearl-diving Carib,
When she heard, what she called, the flight of the
feloness—
But it seems such child's play
What they said and did with the lady away!
And to dance on, when we've lost the music,
Always made me—and no doubt makes you—sick.
Nay, to my mind, the world's face looked so stern
As that sweet form disappeared thro' the postern,
She that kept it in constant good humour,
It ought to have stopped; there seemed nothing to do
more.
But the world thought otherwise and went on,
And my head's one that its spite was spent on:
Thirty years are fled since that morning,
And with them all my head's adorning.
Nor did the old Duchess die outright,
As you expect, of suppressed spite,
The natural end of every adder
Not suffered to empty its poison-bladder:
But she and her son agreed, I take it,
That no one should touch on the story to wake it,
For the wound in the Duke's pride rankled fiery,
So they made no search and small inquiry—
And when fresh gypsies have paid us a visit, I've
Noticed the couple were never inquisitive,
But told them they're folks the Duke don't want here,

And bade them make haste and cross the frontier.
Brief, the Duchess was gone and the Duke was glad of it
And the old one was in the young one's stead,
And took, in her place, the household's head,
And a blessed time the household had of it!
And were I not, as a man may say, cautious
How I trench, more than needs, on the nauseous,
I could favour you with sundry touches
Of the paint-smutches with which the Duchess
Heightened the mellowness of her cheek's yellowness
(To get on faster) until at last her
Cheek grew to be one master-plaster
Of mucus and fucus from mere use of ceruse
Till in short she grew from scalp to udder
Just the object to make you shudder!

XVII

You're my friend—
What a thing friendship is, world without end!
How it gives the heart and soul a stir-up,
As if somebody broached you a glorious runlet,
And pured out all lovelily, sparkling, and sunlit,
Our green Moldavia, the streaky syrup,
Cotnar as old as the time of the Druids—
Friendship's as good as that monarch of fluids
To supple a dry brain, fill you its ins-and-outs,—
Gives your Life's hour-glass a shake when the thin sand
    doubts
Whether to run on or stop short, and guarantees
Age is not all made of stark sloth and arrant ease!
I have seen my little Lady once more,
Jacynth, the Gypsy, Berold, and the rest of it,
For to me spoke the Duke, as I told you before;
I always wanted to make a clean breast of it,
And now it is made—why, my heart's-blood, that went
    trickle,
Trickle, but anon, in such muddy dribblets,
Is pumped up brisk now, thro' the main ventricle,
And genially floats me about the giblets!

I'll tell you what I intend to do:
I must see this fellow his sad life thro'
—He is our Duke after all,
And I, as he says, but a serf and thrall;
My father was born here and I inherit
His fame, a chain he bound his son with,—
Could I pay in a lump I should prefer it,
But there's no mine to blow up and get done with,
So I must stay till the end of the chapter:
For, as to our middle-age-manners-adapter,
Be it a thing to be glad on or sorry on,
One day or other, his head in a morion,
And breast in a hauberk, his heels he'll kick up
Slain by some onslaught fierce of hiccup.
And then, when red doth the sword of our Duke rust,
And its leathern sheath lies o'ergrown with a blue crust,
Then, I shall scrape together my earnings;
For, you see, in the Churchyard Jacynth reposes,
And our children all went the way of the roses—
It's a long lane that knows no turnings—
One needs but little tackle to travel in,
So, just one stout cloak shall I indue,
And for a staff, what beats the javelin
With which his boars my father pinned you?
And then, for a purpose you shall hear presently,
Taking some Cotnar, a tight plump skinfull,
I shall go journeying, who but I, pleasantly?
Sorrow is vain and despondency sinful.
What's a man's age? He must hurry more, that's all;
Cram in a day, what his youth took a year to hold;
When we mind labour, then only, we're too old—
What age had Methusalem when he begat Saul?
And at last, as its haven some buffeted ship sees,
(Come all the way from the north-parts with sperm oil)
I shall get safely out of the turmoil
And arrive one day at the land of the gypsies
And find my lady, or hear the last news of her
From some old thief and son of Lucifer,
His forehead chapletted green with wreathy hop,
Sunburned all over like an Æthiop:

And when my Cotnar begins to operate
And the tongue of the rogue to run at a proper rate,
And our wine-skin, tight once, shows each flaccid dent,
I shall drop in with—as if by accident—
"You never knew then, how it all ended,
What fortunes good or bad attended
The little lady your Queen befriended?"
—And when that's told me, what's remaining?
This world's too hard for my explaining—
The same wise judge of matters equine
Who still preferred some slim four-year-old
To the big-boned stock of mighty Berold,
And for strong Cotnar drank French weak wine,
He also must be such a Lady's scorner!
Smooth Jacob still robs homely Esau,
Now up, now down, the world's one see-saw!
—So, I shall find out some snug corner
Under a hedge, like Orson the wood-knight,
Turn myself round and bid the world good night;
And sleep a sound sleep till the trumpet's blowing
Wakes me (unless priests cheat us laymen)
To a world where's to be no further throwing
Pearls before swine that can't value them. Amen!

EARTH'S IMMORTALITIES

FAME

See, as the prettiest graves will do in time,
Our poet's wants the freshness of its prime;
Spite of the sexton's browsing horse, the sods
Have struggled thro' its binding osier-rods;
Headstone and half-sunk footstone lean awry,
Wanting the brick-work promised by and by;
How the minute grey lichens, plate o'er plate,
Have softened down the crisp-cut name and date!

LOVE

So, the year's done with!
(*Love me for ever!*)
All March begun with,
April's endeavour;
May-wreaths that bound me
June needs must sever!
Now snows fall round me,
Quenching June's fever—
(*Love me for ever!*)

SONG

I

Nay but you, who do not love her,
Is she not pure gold, my mistress?
Holds earth aught—speak truth—above her?
Aught like this tress, see, and this tress,
And this last fairest tress of all,
So fair, see, ere I let it fall!

II

Because, you spend your lives in praising;
To praise, you search the wide world over;
So, why not witness, calmly gazing,
If earth holds aught—speak truth—above her?
Above this tress, and this I touch
But cannot praise, I love so much!

THE BOY AND THE ANGEL

Morning, evening, noon, and night,
"Praise God," sang Theocrite.

Then to his poor trade he turned,
By which the daily meal was earned.

Hard he laboured, long and well;
O'er his work the boy's curls fell:

But ever, at each period,
He stopped and sang, "Praise God."

Then back again his curls he threw,
And cheerful turned to work anew.

Said Blaise, the listening monk, "Well done;
I doubt not thou art heard, my son:

"As well as if thy voice to-day
Were praising God, the Pope's great way.

"This Easter Day, the Pope at Rome
Praises God from Peter's dome."

Said Theocrite, "Would God that I
Might praise Him, that great way, and die!"

Night passed, day shone,
And Theocrite was gone.

With God a day endures alway,
A thousand years are but a day.

God said in Heaven, "Nor day nor night
Now brings the voice of my delight."

Then Gabriel, like a rainbow's birth,
Spread his wings and sank to earth;

Entered in flesh, the empty cell,
Lived there, and played the craftsman well:

And morning, evening, noon, and night,
Praised God in place of Theocrite.

And from a boy, to youth he grew:
The man put off the stripling's hue:

The man matured and fell away
Into the season of decay:

And ever o'er the trade he bent,
And ever lived on earth content.

(He did God's will; to him, all one
If on the earth or in the sun.)

God said, "A praise is in mine ear;
There is no doubt in it, no fear:

"So sing old worlds, and so
New worlds that from my footstool go.

"Clearer loves sound other ways:
I miss my little human praise."

Then forth sprang Gabriel's wings, off fell
The flesh disguise, remained the cell.

'Twas Easter Day: he flew to Rome,
And paused above Saint Peter's dome.

In the tiring-room close by
The great outer gallery,

With his holy vestments dight,
Stood the new Pope, Theocrite:

And all his past career
Came back upon him clear,

Since when, a boy, he plied his trade,
Till on his life the sickness weighed;

And in his cell, when death drew near,
An angel in a dream brought cheer:

And rising from the sickness drear
He grew a priest, and now stood here.

To the East with praise he turned,
And on his sight the angel burned.

"I bore thee from thy craftsman's cell,
And set thee here ; I did not well.

"Vainly I left my angel's-sphere,
Vain was thy dream of many a year.

"Thy voice's praise seemed weak; it dropped—
Creation's chorus stopped!

"Go back and praise again
The early way—while I remain.

"With that weak voice of our disdain,
Take up Creation's pausing strain.

"Back to the cell and poor employ:
Become the craftsman and the boy."

Theocrite grew old at home;
A new Pope dwelt in Peter's Dome.

One vanished as the other died:
They sought God side by side.

MEETING AT NIGHT

I

The grey sea and the long black land;
And the yellow half-moon large and low;
And the startled little waves that leap
In fiery ringlets from their sleep,
As I gain the cove with pushing prow,
And quench its speed in the slushy sand.

II

Then a mile of warm sea-scented beach;
Three fields to cross till a farm appears;
A tap at the pane, the quick sharp scratch
And blue spurt of a lighted match,
And a voice less loud, thro' its joys and fears,
Than the two hearts beating each to each!

PARTING AT MORNING

Round the cape of a sudden came the sea,
And the sun looked over the mountain's rim—
And straight was a path of gold for him,
And the need of a world of men for me.

NATIONALITY IN DRINKS

CLARET

I

My heart sank with our Claret-flask,
 Just now, beneath the heavy sedges
That serve this pond's black face for mask;
 And still at yonder broken edges
Of the hole, where up the bubbles glisten,
After my heart I look and listen.

II

Our laughing little flask, compell'd
 Thro' depth to depth more bleak and shady;
As when, both arms beside her held,
 Feet straightened out, some gay French lady
Is caught up from Life's light and motion,
And dropped into Death's silent ocean!

TOKAY

UP jumped Tokay on our table,
Like a pygmy castle-warder,
Dwarfish to see, but stout and able,
Arms and accoutrements all in order;
And fierce he looked north, then, wheeling south,
Blew with his bugle a challenge to Drouth,
Cocked his flap-hat with the tosspot-feather,
Twisted his thumb in his red moustache,
Gingled his huge brass spurs together,
Tightened his waist with its Buda sash,
And then with an impudence nought could abash,
Shrugged his hump-shoulder,
To tell the beholder,
For twenty such knaves he should laugh but the bolder,
And so with his sword-hilt gallantly jutting,
And dexter-hand on his haunch abutting,
Went the little man from Ausbruch, strutting!

BEER

HERE'S to Nelson's memory!
'Tis the second time that I, at sea,
Right off Cape Trafalgar here,
Have drunk it deep in British beer:
Nelson for ever—any time
Am I his to command in prose or rhyme!
Give me of Nelson only a touch,
And I guard it, be it little or much;
Here's one the Captain gives, and so
Down at the word, by George, shall it go!
He says that at Greenwich they show the beholder
Nelson's coat, "still with tar on the shoulder,
For he used to lean with one shoulder digging,
Jigging, as it were, and zig-zag-zigging,
Up against the mizen rigging!"

TIME'S REVENGES

I've a Friend, over the sea;
I like him, but he loves me;
It all grew out of the books I write;
They find such favour in his sight
That he slaughters you with savage looks
Because you don't admire my books:
He does himself though,—and if some vein
Were to snap to-night in this heavy brain,
To-morrow month, if I lived to try,
Round should I just turn quietly,
Or out of the bedclothes stretch my hand
Till I found him, come from his foreign land
To be my nurse in this poor place,
And make me broth, and wash my face,
And light my fire, and, all the while,
Bear with his old good-humoured smile
That I told him "Better have kept away
Than come and kill me, night and day,
With worse than fever's throbs and shoots,
At the creaking of his clumsy boots."
I am as sure that this he would do,
As that Saint Paul's is striking Two:
And I think I had rather . . . woe is me!
—Yes, rather see him than not see,
If lifting a hand would seat him there
Before me in the empty chair
To-night, when my head aches indeed,
And I can neither think, nor read,
And these blue fingers will not hold
The pen; this garret's freezing cold!

And I've a Lady—There he wakes,
The laughing fiend and prince of snakes
Within me, at her name, to pray
Fate send some creature in the way
Of my love for her, to be down-torn
Upthrust and onward borne

So I might prove myself that sea
Of passion which I needs must be!
Call my thoughts false and my fancies quaint,
And my style infirm, and its figures faint,
All the critics say, and more blame yet,
And not one angry word you get!
But, please you, wonder I would put
My cheek beneath that Lady's foot
Rather than trample under mine
The laurels of the Florentine,
And you shall see how the Devil spends
A fire God gave for other ends!
I tell you, I stride up and down
This garret, crowned with love's best crown,
And feasted with love's perfect feast,
To think I kill for her, at least,
Body and soul and peace and fame,
Alike youth's end and manhood's aim,
—So is my spirit, as flesh with sin,
Filled full, eaten out and in
With the face of her, the eyes of her,
The lips and little chin, the stir
Of shadow round her mouth; and she
—I'll tell you,—calmly would decree
That I should roast at a slow fire,
If that would compass her desire
And make her one whom they invite
To the famous ball to-morrow night.

There may be Heaven; there must be Hell;
Meantime, there is our Earth here—well!

THE GLOVE

PETER RONSARD *loquitur*

"Heigho," yawned one day King Francis,
"Distance all value enhances!
When a man's busy, why, leisure
Strikes him as wonderful pleasure,—

'Faith, and at leisure once is he?
Straightway he wants to be busy.
Here we've got peace; and aghast I'm
Caught thinking war the true pastime!
Is there a reason in metre?
Give us your speech, master Peter!"
I who, if mortal dare say so,
Ne'er am at loss with my Naso,
"Sire," I replied, "joys prove cloudlets:
Men are the merest Ixions"—
Here the King whistled aloud, "Let's
. . . Heigho . . . go look at our lions!"
Such are the sorrowful chances
If you talk fine to King Francis.

And so, to the courtyard proceeding,
Our company, Francis was leading,
Increased by new followers tenfold
Before he arrived at the penfold;
Lords, ladies, like clouds which bedizen
At sunset the western horizon.
And Sir De Lorge pressed 'mid the foremost
With the dame he professed to adore most—
Oh, what a face! One by fits eyed
Her, and the horrible pitside;
For the penfold surrounded a hollow
Which led where the eye scarce dared follow,
And shelved to the chamber secluded
Where Bluebeard, the great lion, brooded.
The king hailed his keeper, an Arab
As glossy and black as a scarab,
And bade him make sport and at once stir
Up and out of his den the old monster.
They opened a hole in the wire-work
Across it, and dropped there a firework,
And fled; one's heart's beating redoubled;
A pause, while the pit's mouth was troubled,
The blackness and silence so utter,
By the firework's slow sparkling and sputter;

Then earth in a sudden contortion
Gave out to our gaze her abortion!
Such a brute! Were I friend Clement Marot
(Whose experience of nature's but narrow,
And whose faculties move in no small mist
When he versifies David the Psalmist)
I should study that brute to describe you
Illum Juda Leonem de Tribu!
One's whole blood grew curdling and creepy
To see the black mane, vast and heapy,
The tail in the air stiff and straining,
The wide eyes, nor waxing nor waning,
As over the barrier which bounded
His platform, and us who surrounded
The barrier, they reached and they rested
On the space that might stand him in best stead:
For who knew, he thought, what the amazement,
The eruption of clatter and blaze meant,
And if, in this minute of wonder,
No outlet, 'mid lightning and thunder,
Lay broad, and, his shackles all shivered,
The lion at last was delivered?
Ay, that was the open sky o'erhead!
And you saw by the flash on his forehead,
By the hope in those eyes wide and steady,
He was leagues in the desert already,
Driving the flocks up the mountain,
Or catlike couched hard by the fountain
To waylay the date-gathering negress:
So guarded be entrance or egress.
"How he stands!" quoth the King: "we may well swear,
No novice, we've won our spurs elsewhere,
And so can afford the confession,
We exercise wholesome discretion
In keeping aloof from his threshold;
Once hold you, those jaws want no fresh hold,
Their first would too pleasantly purloin
The visitor's brisket or sirloin:
But who's he would prove so fool-hardy?
Not the best man of Marignan, pardie!"

The sentence no sooner was uttered,
Than over the rails a glove fluttered,
Fell close to the lion, and rested:
The dame 'twas, who flung it and jested
With life so, De Lorge had been wooing
For months past; he sate there pursuing
His suit, weighing out with nonchalance
Fine speeches like gold from a balance.

Sound the trumpet, no true knight's a tarrier!
De Lorge made one leap at the barrier,
Walked straight to the glove,—while the lion
Ne'er moved, kept his far-reaching eye on
The palm-tree-edged desert-spring's sapphire,
And the musky oiled skin of the Kaffir,—
Picked it up, and as calmly retreated,
Leaped back where the lady was seated,
And full in the face of its owner
Flung the glove—

"Your heart's queen, you dethrone her?
So should I"—cried the King—"'twas mere vanity,
Not love, set that task to humanity!"
Lords and ladies alike turned with loathing
From such a proved wolf in sheep's clothing.

Not so, I; for I caught an expression
In her brow's undisturbed self-possession
Amid the Court's scoffing and merriment,—
As if from no pleasing experiment
She rose, yet of pain not much heedful
So long as the process was needful—
As if she had tried in a crucible,
To what "speeches like gold" were reducible,
And, finding the finest prove copper,
Felt the smoke in her face was but proper;
To know what she had *not* to trust to,
Was worth all the ashes, and dust too.
She went out 'mid hooting and laughter;
Clement Marot stayed; I followed after,

And asked, as a grace, what it all meant—
If she wished not the rash deed's recalment?
"For I"—so I spoke—"am a Poet:
Human nature,—behoves that I know it!"

She told me, "Too long had I heard
Of the deed proved alone by the word:
For my love,—what De Lorge would not dare!
With my scorn—what De Lorge could compare!
And the endless descriptions of death
He would brave when my lip formed a breath,
I must reckon as braved, or, of course,
Doubt his word—and moreover, perforce,
For such gifts as no lady could spurn,
Must offer my love in return.
When I looked on your lion, it brought
All the dangers at once to my thought,
Encountered by all sorts of men,
Before he was lodged in his den,—
From the poor slave whose club or bare hands
Dug the trap, set the snare on the sands,
With no King and no Court to applaud,
By no shame, should he shrink, overawed,
Yet to capture the creature made shift,
That his rude boys might laugh at the gift,
To the page who last leaped o'er the fence
Of the pit, on no greater pretence
Than to get back the bonnet he dropped,
Lest his pay for a week should be stopped—
So, wiser I judged it to make
One trial what 'death for my sake'
Really meant, while the power was yet mine,
Than to wait until time should define
Such a phase not so simply as I,
Who took it to mean just 'to die.'
The blow a glove gives is but weak—
Does the mark yet discolour my cheek?
But when the heart suffers a blow,
Will the pain pass so soon, do you know?"

I looked, as away she was sweeping,
And saw a youth eagerly keeping
As close as he dared to the doorway:
No doubt that a noble should more weigh
His life than befits a plebeian;
And yet, had our brute been Nemean—
(I judge by a certain calm fervor
The youth stepped with, forward to serve her)
—He'd have scarce thought you did him the worst
turn
If you whispered "Friend, what you'd get, first earn!"
And when, shortly after, she carried
Her shame from the Court, and they married,
To that marriage some happiness, maugre
The voice of the Court, I dared augur.

For De Lorge, he made women with men vie,
Those in wonder and praise, these in envy;
And in short stood so plain a head taller
That he wooed and won . . . How do you call her?
The beauty, that rose in the sequel
To the King's love, who loved her a week well;
And 'twas noticed he never would honour
De Lorge (who looked daggers upon her)
With the easy commission of stretching
His legs in the service, and fetching
His wife, from her chamber, those straying
Sad gloves she was always mislaying,
While the King took the closet to chat in,—
But of course this adventure came pat in;
And never the King told the story,
How bringing a glove brought such glory,
But the wife smiled—"His nerves are grown firmer—
Mine he brings now and utters no murmur!"

Venienti occurrite morbo!
With which moral I drop my theorbo.

Christmas-Eve

and

Easter-Day

1850

Christmas-Eve and Easter-Day. A Poem. By Robert Browning. London: Chapman & Hall, 186, Strand. 1850.

F'cap 8vo. Pp. iv + 144. Cloth boards.

THE first of the two parts of this volume, *Christmas-Eve*, is reprinted here in full.

Christmas-Eve and Easter-Day

CHRISTMAS-EVE

I

Out of the little chapel I burst
Into the fresh night air again.
I had waited a good five minutes first
In the doorway, to escape the rain
That drove in gusts down the common's centre,
At the edge of which the chapel stands,
Before I plucked up heart to enter:
Heaven knows how many sorts of hands
Reached past me, groping for the latch
Of the inner door that hung on catch,
More obstinate the more they fumbled,
Till, giving way at last with a scold
Of the crazy hinge, in squeezed or tumbled
One sheep more to the rest in fold,
And left me irresolute, standing sentry
In the sheepfold's lath-and-plaster entry,
Four feet long by two feet wide,
Partitioned off from the vast inside—
I blocked up half of it at least.
No remedy; the rain kept driving:
They eyed me much as some wild beast,
That congregation, still arriving,
Some of them by the mainroad, white
A long way past me into the night,
Skirting the common, then diverging;
Not a few suddenly emerging
From the common's self thro' the paling-gaps,—
—They house in the gravel-pits perhaps,

Where the road stops short with its safeguard border
Of lamps, as tired of such disorder;—
But the most turned in yet more abruptly
From a certain squalid knot of alleys,
Where the town's bad blood once slept corruptly,
Which now the little chapel rallies
And leads into day again,—its priestliness
Lending itself to hide their beastliness
So cleverly (thanks in part to the mason),
And putting so cheery a whitewashed face on
Those neophytes too much in lack of it,
That, where you cross the common as I did,
And meet the party thus presided,
"Mount Zion," with Love-lane at the back of it,
They front you as little disconcerted,
As, bound for the hills, her fate averted
And her wicked people made to mind him,
Lot might have marched with Gomorrah behind him.

II

Well, from the road, the lanes or the common,
In came the flock: the fat weary woman,
Panting and bewildered, down-clapping
Her umbrella with a mighty report,
Grounded it by me, wry and flapping,
A wreck of whalebones; then, with a snort,
Like a startled horse, at the interloper
Who humbly knew himself improper,
But could not shrink up small enough,
Round to the door, and in,—the gruff
Hinge's invariable scold
Making your very blood run cold.
Prompt in the wake of her, up-pattered
On broken clogs, the many-tattered
Little old-faced, peaking sister-turned-mother
Of the sickly babe she tried to smother
Somehow up, with its spotted face,
From the cold, on her breast, the one warm place;
She too must stop, wring the poor suds dry
Of a draggled shawl, and add thereby

Her tribute to the door-mat, sopping
Already from my own clothes' dropping,
Which yet she seemed to grudge I should stand on;
Then stooping down to take off her pattens,
She bore them defiantly, in each hand one,
Planted together before her breast
And its babe, as good as a lance in rest.
Close on her heels, the dingy satins
Of a female something, past me flitted,
With lips as much too white, as a streak
Lay far too red on each hollow cheek;
And it seemed the very door-hinge pitied
All that was left of a woman once,
Holding at least its tongue for the nonce.
Then a tall yellow man, like the Penitent Thief,
With his jaw bound up in a handkerchief,
And eyelids screwed together tight,
Led himself in by some inner light.
And, except from him, from each that entered,
I had the same interrogation—
"What, you, the alien, you have ventured
To take with us, elect, your station?
A carer for none of it, a Gallio?"—
Thus, plain as print, I read the glance
At a common prey, in each countenance,
As of huntsman giving his hounds the tallyho:
And, when the door's cry drowned their wonder,
The draught, it always sent in shutting,
Made the flame of the single tallow candle
In the cracked square lanthorn I stood under,
Shoot its blue lip at me, rebutting,
As it were, the luckless cause of scandal:
I verily thought the zealous light
(In the chapel's secret, too!) for spite,
Would shudder itself clean off the wick,
With the airs of a St. John's Candlestick.
There was no standing it much longer.
"Good folks," said I, as resolve grew stronger,
"This way you perform the Grand-Inquisitor,
When the weather sends you a chance visitor?

You are the men, and wisdom shall die with you,
And none of the old Seven Churches vie with you!
But still, despite the pretty perfection
To which you carry your trick of exclusiveness,
And, taking God's word under wise protection,
Correct its tendency to diffusiveness,
Bidding one reach it over hot ploughshares,—
Still, as I say, though you've found salvation,
If I should choose to cry—as now—'Shares!'—
Scc if thc bcst of you bars mc my ration!
Because I prefer for my expounder
Of the laws of the feast, the feast's own Founder:
Mine's the same right with your poorest and sickliest,
Supposing I don the marriage-vestiment;
So, shut your mouth, and open your Testament,
And carve me my portion at your quickliest!"
Accordingly, as a shoemaker's lad
With wizened face in want of soap,
And wet apron wound round his waist like a rope,
After stopping outside, for his cough was bad,
To get the fit over, poor gentle creature,
And so avoid disturbing the preacher,
Passed in, I sent my elbow spikewise
At the shutting door, and entered likewise,—
Received the hinge's accustomed greeting,
Crossed the threshold's magic pentacle,
And found myself in full conventicle,
—To wit, in Zion Chapel Meeting,
On the Christmas-Eve of 'Forty-nine,
Which, calling its flock to their special clover,
Found them assembled and one sheep over,
Whose lot, as the weather pleased, was mine.

III

I very soon had enough of it.
The hot smell and the human noises,
And my neighbour's coat, the greasy cuff of it,
Were a pebble-stone that a child's hand poises,
Compared with the pig-of-lead-like pressure
Of the preaching-man's immense stupidity,

As he poured his doctrine forth, full measure,
To meet his audience's avidity.
You needed not the wit of the Sybil
To guess the cause of it all, in a twinkling—
No sooner had our friend an inkling
Of treasure hid in the Holy Bible,
(Whenever it was the thought first struck him
How Death, at unawares, might duck him
Deeper than the grave, and quench
The gin-shop's light in Hell's grim drench)
Than he handled it so, in fine irreverence,
As to hug the Book of books to pieces:
And, a patchwork of chapters and texts in severance,
Not improved by the private dog's-ears and
 creases,
Having clothed his own soul with, he'd fain see equipt
 yours,—
So tossed you again your Holy Scriptures.
And you picked them up, in a sense, no doubt:
Nay, had but a single face of my neighbours
Appeared to suspect that the preacher's labours
Were help which the world could be saved without,
'Tis odds but I had borne in quiet
A qualm or two at my spiritual diet;
Or, who can tell? had even mustered
Somewhat to urge in behalf of the sermon:
But the flock sate on, divinely flustered,
Sniffing, methought, its dew of Hermon
With such content in every snuffle,
As the devil inside us loves to ruffle.
My old fat woman purred with pleasure,
And thumb round thumb went twirling faster,
While she, to his periods keeping measure,
Maternally devoured the pastor.
The man with the handkerchief, untied it,
Showed us a horrible wen inside it,
Gave his eyelids yet another screwing,
And rocked himself as the woman was doing.
The shoemaker's lad, discreetly choking,
Kept down his cough. 'Twas too provoking!

My gorge rose at the nonsense and stuff of it,
And saying, like Eve when she plucked the apple,
"I wanted a taste, and now there's enough of it,"
I flung out of the little chapel.

IV

There was a lull in the rain, a lull
In the wind too; the moon was risen,
And would have shone out pure and full,
But for the ramparted cloud-prison,
Block on block built up in the west,
For what purpose the wind knows best,
Who changes his mind continually.
And the empty other half of the sky
Seemed in its silence as if it knew
What, any moment, might look through
A chance-gap in that fortress massy:—
Through its fissures you got hints
Of the flying moon, by the shifting tints,
Now, a dull lion-colour, now, brassy
Burning to yellow, and whitest yellow,
Like furnace-smoke just ere the flames bellow,
All a-simmer with intense strain
To let her through,—then blank again,
At the hope of her appearance failing.
Just by the chapel, a break in the railing
Shows a narrow path directly across;
'Tis ever dry walking there, on the moss—
Besides, you go gently all the way uphill:
I stooped under and soon felt better:
My head grew light, my limbs more supple,
As I walked on, glad to have slipt the fetter;
My mind was full of the scene I had left,
That placid flock, that pastor vociferant,
—How this outside was pure and different!
The sermon, now—what a mingled weft
Of good and ill! were either less,
Its fellow had coloured the whole distinctly;
But alas for the excellent earnestness,
And the truths, quite true if stated succinctly,

But as surely false, in their quaint presentment,
However to pastor and flock's contentment!
Say rather, such truths looked false to your eyes,
With his provings and parallels twisted and twined,
Till how could you know them, grown double their
size,
In the natural fog of the good man's mind?
Like yonder spots of our roadside lamps,
Haloed about with the common's damps.
Truth remains true, the fault's in the prover;
The zeal was good, and the aspiration;
And yet, and yet, yet, fifty times over,
Pharaoh received no demonstration
By his Baker's dream of Baskets Three,
Of the doctrine of the Trinity,—
Although, as our preacher thus embellished it,
Apparently his hearers relished it
With so unfeigned a gust—who knows if
They did not prefer our friend to Joseph?
But so it is everywhere, one way with all of them!
These people have really felt, no doubt,
A something, the motion they style the Call of
them;
And this is their method of bringing about,
By a mechanism of words and tones,
(So many texts in so many groans)
A sort of reviving or reproducing,
More or less perfectly, (who can tell?—)
Of the mood itself, that strengthens by using;
And how it happens, I understand well.
A tune was born in my head last week,
Out of the thump-thump and shriek-shriek
Of the train, as I came by it, up from Manchester;
And when, next week, I take it back again,
My head will sing to the engine's clack again,
While it only makes my neighbour's haunches stir,
—Finding no dormant musical sprout
In him, as in me, to be jolted out.
'Tis the taught already that profit by teaching;
He gets no more from the railway's preaching,

Than, from this preacher who does the rail's office, I,
Whom therefore the flock casts a jealous eye on.
Still, why paint over their door "Mount Zion,"
To which all flesh shall come, saith the prophecy?

V

But wherefore be harsh on a single case?
After how many modes, this Christmas-Eve,
Does the selfsame weary thing take place?
The same endeavour to make you believe,
And much with the same effect, no more:
Each method abundantly convincing,
As I say, to those convinced before,
But scarce to be swallowed without wincing,
By the not-as-yet-convinced. For me,
I have my own church equally.
And in *this* church my faith sprang first!
(I said, as I reached the rising ground,
And the wind began again, with a burst
Of rain in my face, and a glad rebound
From the heart beneath, as if, God speeding me,
I entered His church-door, Nature leading me)
—In youth I looked to these very skies,
And probing their immensities,
I found God there, His visible power;
Yet felt in my heart, amid all its sense
Of that power, an equal evidence
That His love, there too, was the nobler dower.
For the loving worm within its clod,
Were diviner than a loveless god
Amid his worlds, I will dare to say.
You know what I mean: God's all, man's nought:
But also, God, whose pleasure brought
Man into being, stands away
As it were, an handbreadth off, to give
Room for the newly-made to live,
And look at Him from a place apart,
And use His gifts of brain and heart,
Given, indeed, but to keep for ever.
Who speaks of man, then, must not sever

Man's very elements from man,
Saying, "But all is God's"—whose plan
Was to create man and then leave him
Able, His own word saith, to grieve Him,
But able to glorify Him too,
As a mere machine could never do,
That prayed or praised, all unaware
Of its fitness for aught but praise and prayer,
Made perfect as a thing of course.
Man, therefore, stands on his own stock
Of love and power as a pin-point rock,
And, looking to God who ordained divorce
Of the rock from His boundless continent,
Sees in His Power made evident,
Only excess by a million fold
O'er the power God gave man in the mould.
For, see: Man's hand, first formed to carry
A few pounds' weight, when taught to marry
Its strength with an engine's, lifts a mountain,
—Advancing in power by one degree;
And why count steps through eternity?
But Love is the ever springing fountain:
Man may enlarge or narrow his bed
For the water's play, but the water head—
How can he multiply or reduce it?
As easy create it, as cause it to cease:
He may profit by it, or abuse it;
But 'tis not a thing to bear increase
As power will: be love less or more
In the heart of man, he keeps it shut
Or opes it wide as he pleases, but
Love's sum remains what it was before
So, gazing up, in my youth, at love
As seen through power, ever above
All modes which make it manifest,
My soul brought all to a single test—
That He, the Eternal First and Last,
Who, in His power, had so surpassed
All man conceives of what is might,—
Whose wisdom, too, showed infinite,

—Would prove as infinitely good;
Would never, my soul understood,
With power to work all love desires,
Bestow e'en less than man requires:
That He who endlessly was teaching,
Above my spirit's utmost reaching,
What love can do in the leaf or stone,
(So that to master this alone,
This done in the stone or leaf for me,
I must go on learning endlessly)
Would never need that I, in turn,
Should point him out a defect unheeded,
And show that God had yet to learn
What the meanest human creature needed,—
—Not life, to wit, for a few short years,
Tracking His way through doubts and fears,
While the stupid earth on which I stay
Suffers no change, but passive adds
Its myriad years to myriads,
Though I, He gave it to, decay,
Seeing death come and choose about me,
And my dearest ones depart without me.
No! love which, on earth, amid all the shows of it,
Has ever been seen the sole good of life in it,
The love, ever growing there, spite of the strife in it,
Shall arise, made perfect, from death's repose of it!
And I shall behold Thee, face to face,
O God, and in Thy light retrace
How in all I loved here, still wast Thou!
Whom pressing to, then, as I fain would now,
I shall find as able to satiate
The love, Thy gift, as my spirit's wonder
Thou art able to quicken and sublimate,
With this sky of Thine, that I now walk under,
And glory in Thee as thus I gaze,
—Thus, thus! oh, let men keep their ways
Of seeking Thee in a narrow shrine—
Be this my way! And this *is* mine!

VI

For lo, what think you? suddenly
The rain and the wind ceased, and the sky
Received at once the full fruition
Of the moon's consummate apparition.
The black cloud-barricade was riven,
Ruined beneath her feet, and driven
Deep in the west; while, bare and breathless,
North and south and east lay ready
For a glorious Thing, that, dauntless, deathless,
Sprang across them, and stood steady.
'Twas a moon-rainbow, vast and perfect,
From heaven to heaven extending, perfect
As the mother-moon's self, full in face.
It rose, distinctly at the base
With its seven proper colours chorded,
Which still, in the rising, were compressed,
Until at last they cöalesced,
And supreme the spectral creature lorded
In a triumph of whitest white,—
Above which intervened the night.
But above night too, like the next,
The second of a wondrous sequence,
Reaching in rare and rarer frequence,
Till the heaven of heavens be circumflext,
Another rainbow rose, a mightier,
Fainter, flushier, and flightier,—
Rapture dying along its verge!
Oh, whose foot shall I see emerge,
WHOSE, from the straining topmost dark,
On to the keystone of that arc?

VII

This sight was shown me, there and then,—
Me, one out of a world of men,
Singled forth, as the chance might hap
To another, if in a thunderclap
Where I heard noise, and you saw flame,
Some one man knew God called his name.

For me, I think I said, "Appear!
Good were it to be ever here.
If Thou wilt, let me build to Thee
Service-tabernacles Three,
Where, for ever in Thy presence,
In ecstatic acquiescence,
Far alike from thriftless learning
And ignorance's undiscerning,
I may worship and remain!"
Thus, at the show above me, gazing
With upturned eyes, I felt my brain
Glutted with the glory, blazing
Throughout its whole mass, over and under,
Until at length it burst asunder,
And out of it bodily there streamed
The too-much glory, as it seemed,
Passing from out me to the ground,
Then palely serpentining round
Into the dark with mazy error.

VIII

All at once I looked up with terror.
He was there.
He Himself with His human air,
On the narrow pathway, just before:
I saw the back of Him, no more—
He had left the chapel, then, as I.
I forgot all about the sky.
No face: only the sight
Of a sweepy Garment, vast and white,
With a hem that I could recognise.
I felt terror, no surprise:
My mind filled with the cataract,
At one bound, of the mighty fact.
I remembered, He did say
Doubtless, that, to this world's end,
Where two or three should meet and pray,
He would be in the midst, their Friend:
Certainly He was there with them.

And my pulses leaped for joy
Of the golden thought without alloy,
That I saw His very Vesture's hem.
Then rushed the blood back, cold and clear
With a fresh enhancing shiver of fear,
And I hastened, cried out while I pressed
To the salvation of the Vest,
"But not so, Lord! It cannot be
That Thou, indeed, art leaving me—
Me, that have despised Thy friends.
Did my heart make no amends?
Thou art the Love of God—above
His Power, didst hear me place His Love,
And that was leaving the world for Thee!
Therefore Thou must not turn from me
As if I had chosen the other part.
Folly and pride o'ercame my heart.
Our best is bad, nor bears Thy test;
Still it should be our very best.
I thought it best that Thou, the Spirit,
Be worshipped in spirit and in truth,
And in beauty, as even we require it—
Not in the forms burlesque, uncouth,
I left but now, as scarcely fitted
For Thee: I knew not what I pitied:
But, all I felt there, right or wrong,
What is it to Thee, who curest sinning?
Am I not weak as Thou art strong?
I have looked to Thee from the beginning,
Straight up to Thee through all the world
Which, like an idle scroll, lay furled
To nothingness on either side:
And since the time Thou wast descried,
Spite of the weak heart, so have I
Lived ever, and so fain would die,
Living and dying, Thee before!
But if Thou leavest me—"

IX

Less or more,
I suppose that I spoke thus.
When,—have mercy, Lord, on us!
The whole Face turned upon me full.
And I spread myself beneath it,
As when the bleacher spreads, to seethe it
In the cleansing sun, his wool,—
Steeps in the flood of noontide whiteness
Some defiled, discoloured web—
So lay I, saturate with brightness.
And when the flood appeared to ebb,
Lo, I was walking, light and swift,
With my senses settling fast and steadying,
But my body caught up in the whirl and drift
Of the Vesture's amplitude, still eddying
On, just before me, still to be followed,
As it carried me after with its motion:
What shall I say?—as a path were hollowed
And a man went weltering through the ocean,
Sucked along in the flying wake
Of the luminous water-snake.
Darkness and cold were cloven, as through
I passed, upborne yet walking too.
And I turned to myself at intervals,—
"So He said, and so it befals.
God who registers the cup
Of mere cold water, for His sake
To a disciple rendered up,
Disdains not His own thirst to slake
At the poorest love was ever offered:
And because it was my heart I proffered,
With true love trembling at the brim,
He suffers me to follow Him
For ever, my own way,—dispensed
From seeking to be influenced
By all the less immediate ways
That earth, in worships manifold,
Adopts to reach, by prayer and praise,
The Garment's hem, which, lo, I hold!"

X

And so we crossed the world and stopped.
For where am I, in city or plain,
Since I am 'ware of the world again?
And what is this that rises propped
With pillars of prodigious girth?
Is it really on the earth,
This miraculous Dome of God?
Has the angel's measuring-rod
Which numbered cubits, gem from gem,
'Twixt the gates of the New Jerusalem,
Meted it out,—and what he meted,
Have the sons of men completed?
—Binding, ever as he bade,
Columns in this colonnade
With arms wide open to embrace
The entry of the human race
To the breast of . . . what is it, yon building,
Ablaze in front, all paint and gilding,
With marble for brick, and stones of price
For garniture of the edifice?
Now I see: it is no dream:
It stands there and it does not seem;
For ever, in pictures, thus it looks,
And thus I have read of it in books,
Often in England, leagues away,
And wondered how those fountains play,
Growing up eternally
Each to a musical water-tree,
Whose blossoms drop, a glittering boon,
Before my eyes, in the light of the moon,
To the granite layers underneath.
Liar and dreamer in your teeth!
I, the sinner that speak to you,
Was in Rome this night, and stood, and knew
Both this and more! For see, for see,
The dark is rent, mine eye is free
To pierce the crust of the outer wall,
And I view inside, and all there, all,

As the swarming hollow of a hive,
The whole Basilica alive!
Men in the chancel, body, and nave,
Men on the pillars' architrave,
Men on the statues, men on the tombs
With popes and kings in their porphyry wombs,
All famishing in expectation
Of the main-altar's consummation.
For see, for see, the rapturous moment
Approaches, and earth's best endowment
Blends with heaven's: the taper-fires
Pant up, the winding brazen spires
Heave loftier yet the baldachin;
The incense-gaspings, long kept in,
Suspire in clouds; the organ blatant
Holds his breath and grovels latent,
As if God's hushing finger grazed him,
(Like Behemoth when He praised him)
At the silver bell's shrill tinkling,
Quick cold drops of terror sprinkling
On the sudden pavement strewed
With faces of the multitude.
Earth breaks up, time drops away,
In flows heaven, with its new day
Of endless life, when He who trod,
Very Man and very God,
This earth in weakness, shame and pain,
Dying the death whose signs remain
Up yonder on the accursed tree,—
Shall come again, no more to be
Of captivity the thrall,
But the one God, all in all,
King of kings, and Lord of lords,
As His servant John received the words,
"I died, and live for evermore!"

XI

Yet I was left outside the door.
Why sate I there on the threshold-stone,
Left till He returns, alone

Save for the Garment's extreme fold
Abandoned still to bless my hold?—
My reason, to my doubt, replied,
As if a book were opened wide,
And at a certain page I traced
Every record undefaced,
Added by successive years,—
The harvestings of truth's stray ears
Singly gleaned, and in one sheaf
Bound together for belief.
Yes, I said—that He will go
And sit with these in turn, I know.
Their faith's heart beats, though her head swims
Too giddily to guide her limbs,
Disabled by their palsy-stroke
From propping me. Though Rome's gross yoke
Drops off, no more to be endured,
Her teaching is not so obscured
By errors and perversities,
That no truth shines athwart the lies:
And He, whose eye detects a spark
Even where, to man's, the whole seems dark,
May well see flame where each beholder
Acknowledges the embers smoulder.
But I, a mere man, fear to quit
The clue God gave me as most fit
To guide my footsteps through life's maze,
Because Himself discerns all ways
Open to reach Him: I, a man
He gave to mark where faith began
To swerve aside, till from its summit
Judgment drops her damning plummet,
Pronouncing such a fatal space
Departed from the Founder's base:
He will not bid me enter too,
But rather sit, as now I do,
Awaiting His return outside.
—'Twas thus my reason straight replied,
And joyously I turned, and pressed
The Garment's skirt upon my breast,

Until, afresh its light suffusing me,
My heart cried,—what has been abusing me
That I should wait here lonely and coldly,
Instead of rising, entering boldly,
Baring truth's face, and letting drift
Her veils of lies as they choose to shift?
Do these men praise Him? I will raise
My voice up to their point of praise!
I see the error; but above
The scope of error, see the love.—
Oh, love of those first Christian days!
—Fanned so soon into a blaze,
From the spark preserved by the trampled sect,
That the antique sovereign Intellect
Which then sate ruling in the world,
Like a change in dreams, was hurled
From the throne he reigned upon:
—You looked up, and he was gone!
Gone, his glory of the pen!
—Love, with Greece and Rome in ken,
Bade her scribes abhor the trick
Of poetry and rhetoric,
And exult, with hearts set free,
In blessed imbecility
Scrawled, perchance, on some torn sheet,
Leaving Livy incomplete.
Gone, his pride of sculptor, painter!
—Love, while able to acquaint her
With the thousand statues yet
Fresh from chisel, pictures wet
From brush, she saw on every side,
Chose rather with an infant's pride
To frame those portents which impart
Such unction to true Christian Art.
Gone, Music too! The air was stirred
By happy wings: Terpander's bird
(That, when the cold came, fled away)
Would tarry not the wintry day,—
As more-enduring sculpture must,
Till a filthy saint rebuked the gust

With which he chanced to get a sight
Of some dear naked Aphrodite
He glanced a thought above the toes of,
By breaking zealously her nose off.
Love, surely, from that music's lingering,
Might have filched her organ-fingering,
Nor chose rather to set prayings
To hog-grunts, praises to horse-neighings.
Love was the startling thing, the new;
Love was the all-sufficient too;
And seeing that, you see the rest.
As a babe can find its mother's breast
As well in darkness as in light,
Love shut our eyes, and all seemed right.
True, the world's eyes are open now:
—Less need for me to disallow
Some few that keep Love's zone unbuckled,
Peevish as ever to be suckled,
Lulled by the same old baby-prattle
With intermixture of the rattle,
When she would have them creep, stand steady
Upon their feet, or walk already,
Not to speak of trying to climb.
I will be wise another time,
And not desire a wall between us,
When next I see a church-roof cover
So many species of one genus,
All with foreheads bearing *Lover*
Written above the earnest eyes of them;
All with breasts that beat for beauty,
Whether sublimed, to the surprise of them,
In noble daring, steadfast duty,
The heroic in passion, or in action,—
Or, lowered for the senses' satisfaction,
To the mere outside of human creatures,
Mere perfect form and faultless features.
What! with all Rome here, whence to levy
Such contributions to their appetite,
With women and men in a gorgeous bevy,
They take, as it were, a padlock, and clap it tight

On their southern eyes, restrained from feeding
On the glories of their ancient reading,
On the beauties of their modern singing,
On the wonders of the builder's bringing,
On the majesties of Art around them,—
And, all these loves, late struggling incessant,
When faith has at last united and bound them,
They offer up to God for a present!
Why, I will, on the whole, be rather proud of it,—
And, only taking the act in reference
To the other recipients who might have allowed of it,
I will rejoice that God had the preference!

XII

So I summed up my new resolves:
Too much love there can never be.
And where the intellect devolves
Its function on love exclusively,
I, as one who possesses both,
Will accept the provision, nothing loth,
—Will feast my love, then depart elsewhere,
That my intellect may find its share.
And ponder, O soul, the while thou departest,
And see thou applaud the great heart of the artist,
Who, examining the capabilities
Of the block of marble he has to fashion
Into a type of thought or passion,—
Not always, using obvious facilities,
Shapes it, as any artist can,
Into a perfect symmetrical man,
Complete from head to foot of the life-size,
Such as old Adam stood in his wife's eyes,—
But, now and then, bravely aspires to consummate
A Colossus by no means so easy to come at,
And uses the whole of his block for the bust,
Leaving the minds of the public to finish it,
Since cut it ruefully short he must:
On the face alone he expends his devotion;
He rather would mar than resolve to diminish it,
—Saying, "Applaud me for this grand notion

Of what a face may be! As for completing it
In breast and body and limbs, do *that*, you!"
All hail! I fancy how, happily meeting it,
A trunk and legs would perfect the statue,
Could man carve so as to answer volition.
And how much nobler than petty cavils,
A hope to find, in my spirit-travels,
Some artist of another ambition,
Who having a block to carve, no bigger,
Has spent his power on the opposite quest,
And believed to begin at the feet was best—
For so may I see, ere I die, the whole figure!

XIII

No sooner said than out in the night!
And still as we swept through storm and night,
My heart beat lighter and more light:
And lo, as before, I was walking swift,
With my senses settling fast and steadying,
But my body caught up in the whirl and drift
Of the Vesture's amplitude, still eddying
On just before me, still to be followed,
As it carried me after with its motion,
—What shall I say?—as a path were hollowed,
And a man went weltering through the ocean,
Sucked along in the flying wake
Of the luminous water-snake.

XIV

Alone! I am left alone once more—
(Save for the Garment's extreme fold
Abandoned still to bless my hold)
Alone, beside the entrance-door
Of a sort of temple,—perhaps a college,
—Like nothing I ever saw before
At home in England, to my knowledge.
The tall, old, quaint, irregular town!
It may be . . . though *which*, I can't affirm . . . any
Of the famous middle-age towns of Germany;
And this flight of stairs where I sit down,

Is it Halle, Weimar, Cassel, or Frankfort,
Or Göttingen, that I have to thank for't?
It may be Göttingen,—most likely.
Through the open door I catch obliquely
Glimpses of a lecture-hall;
And not a bad assembly neither—
Ranged decent and symmetrical
On benches, waiting what's to see there;
Which, holding still by the Vesture's hem,
I also resolve to see with them,
Cautious this time how I suffer to slip
The chance of joining in fellowship
With any that call themselves His friends,
As these folks do, I have a notion.
But hist—a buzzing and emotion!
All settle themselves, the while ascends
By the creaking rail to the lecture-desk,
Step by step, deliberate
Because of his cranium's over-freight,
Three parts sublime to one grotesque,
If I have proved an accurate guesser,
The hawk-nosed, high-cheek-boned Professor.
I felt at once as if there ran
A shoot of love from my heart to the man—
That sallow, virgin-minded, studious
Martyr to mild enthusiasm,
As he uttered a kind of cough-preludious
That woke my sympathetic spasm,
(Beside some spitting that made me sorry)
And stood, surveying his auditory
With a wan pure look, well nigh celestial,—
—Those blue eyes had survived so much!
While, under the foot they could not smutch,
Lay all the fleshly and the bestial.
Over he bowed, and arranged his notes,
Till the auditory's clearing of throats
Was done with, died into silence;
And, when each glance was upward sent,
Each bearded mouth composed intent,
And a pin might be heard drop half a mile hence,—

He pushed back higher his spectacles,
Let the eyes stream out like lamps from cells,
And giving his head of hair—a hake
Of undressed tow, for color and quantity—
One rapid and impatient shake,
(As our own young England adjusts a jaunty tie
When about to impart, on mature digestion,
Some thrilling view of the surplice-question)
—The Professor's grave voice, sweet though hoarse,
Broke into his Christmas-Eve's discourse.

XV

And he began it by observing
How reason dictated that men
Should rectify the natural swerving,
By a reversion, now and then,
To the well-heads of knowledge, few
And far away, whence rolling grew
The life-stream wide whereat we drink,
Commingled, as we needs must think,
With waters alien to the source:
To do which, aimed this Eve's discourse.
Since, where could be a fitter time
For tracing backward to its prime,
This Christianity, this lake,
This reservoir, whereat we slake,
From one or other bank, our thirst?
So he proposed inquiring first
Into the various sources whence
This Myth of Christ is derivable;
Demanding from the evidence,
(Since plainly no such life was liveable)
How these phenomena should class?
Whether 'twere best opine Christ was,
Or never was at all, or whether
He was and was not, both together—
It matters little for the name,
So the Idea be left the same:
Only, for practical purpose' sake,
'Twas obviously as well to take

The popular story,—understanding
How the ineptitude of the time,
And the penman's prejudice, expanding
Fact into fable fit for the clime,
Had, by slow and sure degrees, translated it
Into this myth, this Individuum,—
Which, when reason had strained and abated it
Of foreign matter, gave, for residuum,
A Man!—a right true man, however,
Whose work was worthy a man's endeavour!
Work, that gave warrant almost sufficient
To his disciples, for rather believing
He was just omnipotent and omniscient,
As it gives to us, for as frankly receiving
His word, their tradition,—which, though it meant
Something entirely different
From all that those who only heard it,
In their simplicity thought and averred it,
Had yet a meaning quite as respectable:
For, among other doctrines delectable,
Was he not surely the first to insist on,
The natural sovereignty of our race?—
Here the lecturer came to a pausing-place.
And while his cough, like a drouthy piston,
Tried to dislodge the husk that grew to him,
I seized the occasion of bidding adieu to him,
The Vesture still within my hand.

XVI

I could interpret its command.
This time He would not bid me enter
The exhausted air-bell of the Critic.
Truth's atmosphere may grow mephitic
When Papist struggles with Dissenter,
Impregnating its pristine clarity,
—One, by his daily fare's vulgarity,
Its gust of broken meat and garlic;
—One, by his soul's too-much presuming,
To turn the frankincense's fuming
And vapours of the candle starlike

Into the cloud her wings she buoys on:
And each, that sets the pure air seething,
Poisoning it for healthy breathing—
But the Critic leaves no air to poison;
Pumps out by a ruthless ingenuity
Atom by atom, and leaves you—vacuity.
Thus much of Christ, does he reject?
And what retain? His intellect?
What is it I must reverence duly?
Poor intellect for worship, truly,
Which tells me simply what was told
(If mere morality, bereft
Of the God in Christ, be all that's left)
Elsewhere by voices manifold;
With this advantage, that the stater
Made nowise the important stumble
Of adding, he, the sage and humble,
Was also one with the Creator.
You urge Christ's followers' simplicity:
But how does shifting blame, evade it?
Have wisdom's words no more felicity?
The stumbling-block, His speech—who laid it?
How comes it that for one found able
To sift the truth of it from fable,
Millions believe it to the letter?
Christ's goodness, then—does that fare better?
Strange goodness, which upon the score
Of being goodness, the mere due
Of man to fellow-man, much more
To God,—should take another view
Of its possessor's privilege,
And bid him rule his race! You pledge
Your fealty to such rule? What, all—
From Heavenly John and Attic Paul,
And that brave weather-battered Peter
Whose stout faith only stood completer
For buffets, sinning to be pardoned,
As the more his hands hauled nets, they hardened,—
All, down to you, the man of men,
Professing here at Göttingen,

Compose Christ's flock! So, you and I
Are sheep of a good man! and why?
The goodness,—how did he acquire it?
Was it self-gained, did God inspire it?
Choose which; then tell me, on what ground
Should its possessor dare propound
His claim to rise o'er us an inch?
Were goodness all some man's invention,
Who arbitrarily made mention
What we should follow, and where flinch,—
What qualities might take the style
Of right and wrong,—and had such guessing
Met with as general acquiescing
As graced the Alphabet erewhile,
When A got leave an Ox to be,
No Camel (quoth the Jews) like G,—
For thus inventing thing and title
Worship were that man's fit requital.
But if the common conscience must
Be ultimately judge, adjust
Its apt name to each quality
Already known,—I would decree
Worship for such mere demonstration
And simple work of nomenclature,
Only the day I praised, not Nature,
But Harvey, for the circulation.
I would praise such a Christ, with pride
And joy, that he, as none beside,
Had taught us how to keep the mind
God gave him, as God gave his kind,
Freer than they from fleshly taint!
I would call such a Christ our Saint,
As I declare our Poet, him
Whose insight makes all others dim:
A thousand poets pried at life,
And only one amid the strife
Rose to be Shakespeare! Each shall take
His crown, I'd say, for the world's sake—
Though some objected—"Had we seen
The heart and head of each, what screen

Was broken there to give them light,
While in ourselves it shuts the sight,
We should no more admire, perchance,
That these found truth out at a glance,
Than marvel how the bat discerns
Some pitch-dark cavern's fifty turns,
Led by a finer tact, a gift
He boasts, which other birds must shift
Without, and grope as best they can."
No, freely I would praise the man,—
Nor one whit more, if he contended
That gift of his, from God, descended.
Ah, friend, what gift of man's does not?
No nearer Something, by a jot,
Rise an infinity of Nothings
Than one: take Euclid for your teacher:
Distinguish kinds: do crownings, clothings,
Make that Creator which was creature?
Multiply gifts upon his head,
And what, when all's done, shall be said
But . . . the more gifted he, I ween!
That one's made Christ, another, Pilate,
And This might be all That has been,—
So what is there to frown or smile at?
What is left for us, save, in growth
Of soul, to rise up, far past both,
From the gift looking to the Giver,
And from the cistern to the River,
And from the finite to Infinity,
And from man's dust to God's divinity?

XVII

Take all in a word: the Truth in God's breast
Lies trace for trace upon ours impressed:
Though He is so bright and we so dim,
We are made in His image to witness Him;
And were no eye in us to tell,
Instructed by no inner sense,
The light of Heaven from the dark of Hell,
That light would want its evidence,—

Though Justice, Good and Truth were still
Divine, if, by some demon's will,
Hatred and wrong had been proclaimed
Law through the worlds, and Right misnamed.
No mere exposition of morality
Made or in part or in totality,
Should win you to give it worship, therefore:
And, if no better proof you will care for,
—Whom do you count the worst man upon earth?
Be sure, he knows, in his conscience, more
Of what Right is, than arrives at birth
In the best man's acts that we bow before:
This last *knows* better—true; but my fact is,
'Tis one thing to know, and another to practise;
And thence I conclude that the real God-function
Is to furnish a motive and injunction
For practising what we know already.
And such an injunction and such a motive
As the God in Christ, do you waive, and "heady
High minded," hang your tablet-votive
Outside the fane on a finger-post?
Morality to the uttermost,
Supreme in Christ as we all confess,
Why need *we* prove would avail no jot
To make Him God, if God He were not?
What is the point where Himself lays stress?
Does the precept run "Believe in Good,
In Justice, Truth, now understood
For the first time?"—or, "Believe in Me,
Who lived and died, yet essentially
Am Lord of Life?" Whoever can take
The same to his heart and for mere love's sake
Conceive of the love,—that man obtains
A new truth; no conviction gains
Of an old one only, made intense
By a fresh appeal to his faded sense.

XVIII

Can it be that He stays inside?
Is the Vesture left me to commune with?

Could my soul find aught to sing in tune with
Even at this lecture, if she tried?
Oh, let me at lowest sympathise
With the lurking drop of blood that lies
In the desiccated brain's white roots
Without a throb for Christ's attributes,
As the Lecturer makes his special boast!
If love's dead there, it has left a ghost.
Admire we, how from heart to brain
(Though to say so strike the doctors dumb)
One instinct rises and falls again,
Restoring the equilibrium.
And how when the Critic had done his best,
And the Pearl of Price, at reason's test,
Lay dust and ashes levigable
On the Professor's lecture-table;
When we looked for the inference and monition
That our faith, reduced to such a condition,
Be swept forthwith to its natural dust-hole,—
He bids us, when we least expect it,
Take back our faith,—if it be not just whole,
Yet a pearl indeed, as his tests affect it,
Which fact pays the damage done rewardingly,
So, prize we our dust and ashes accordingly!
"Go home and venerate the Myth
I thus have experimented with—
This Man, continue to adore him
Rather than all who went before him,
And all who ever followed after!"—
Surely for this I may praise you, my brother!
Will you take the praise in tears or laughter?
That's one point gained: can I compass another?
Unlearned love was safe from spurning—
Can't we respect your loveless learning?
Let us at least give Learning honor!
What laurels had we showered upon her,
Girding her loins up to perturb
Our theory of the Middle Verb;
Or Turklike brandishing a scimetar
O'er anapæsts in comic-trimeter;

Or curing the halt and maimed Iketides,
While we lounged on at our indebted ease:
Instead of which, a tricksy demon
Sets her at Titus or Philemon!
When Ignorance wags his ears of leather
And hates God's word, 'tis altogether;
Nor leaves he his congenial thistles
To go and browze on Paul's Epistles.
—And you, the audience, who might ravage
The world wide, enviably savage
Nor heed the cry of the retriever,
More than Herr Heine (before his fever),—
I do not tell a lie so arrant
As say my passion's wings are furled up,
And, without the plainest Heavenly warrant,
I were ready and glad to give this world up—
But still, when you rub the brow meticulous,
And ponder the profit of turning holy
If not for God's, for your own sake solely,
—God forbid I should find you ridiculous!
Deduce from this lecture all that eases you,
Nay, call yourselves, if the calling pleases you,
"Christians,"—abhor the Deist's pravity,—
Go on, you shall no more move my gravity,
Than, when I see boys ride a-cockhorse,
I find it in my heart to embarrass them
By hinting that their stick's a mock horse,
And they really carry what they say carries them.

XIX

So sate I talking with my mind.
I did not long to leave the door
And find a new church, as before,
But rather was quiet and inclined
To prolong and enjoy the gentle resting
From further tracking and trying and testing.
This tolerance is a genial mood!
(Said I, and a little pause ensued).
One trims the bark 'twixt shoal and shelf,
And sees, each side, the good effects of it,

A value for religion's self,
A carelessness about the sects of it.
Let me enjoy my own conviction,
Not watch my neighbour's faith with fretfulness,
Still spying there some dereliction
Of truth, perversity, forgetfulness!
Better a mild indifferentism,
To teach that all our faiths (though duller
His shines through a dull spirit's prism)
Originally had one colour—
Sending me on a pilgrimage
Through ancient and through modern times
To many peoples, various climes,
Where I may see Saint, Savage, Sage
Fuse their respective creeds in one
Before the general Father's throne!

XX

. . . 'Twas the horrible storm began afresh!
The black night caught me in his mesh,
Whirled me up, and flung me prone.
I was left on the college-step alone.
I looked, and far there, ever fleeting
Far, far away, the receding gesture,
And looming of the lessening Vesture,
Swept forward from my stupid hand,
While I watched my foolish heart expand
In the lazy glow of benevolence,
O'er the various modes of man's belief.
I sprang up with fear's vehemence.
—Needs must there be one way, our chief
Best way of worship: let me strive
To find it, and when found, contrive
My fellows also take their share.
This constitutes my earthly care:
God's is above it and distinct!
For I, a man, with men am linked,
And not a brute with brutes; no gain
That I experience, must remain

Unshared: but should my best endeavour
To share it, fail—subsisteth ever
God's care above, and I exult
That God, by God's own ways occult,
May—doth, I will believe—bring back
All wanderers to a single track!
Meantime, I can but testify
God's care for me—no more, can I—
It is but for myself I *know*.
The world rolls witnessing around me
Only to leave me as it found me;
Men cry there, but my ear is slow.
Their races flourish or decay
—What boots it, while yon lucid way
Loaded with stars, divides the vault?
How soon my soul repairs its fault
When, sharpening senses' hebetude,
She turns on my own life! So viewed,
No mere mote's-breadth but teems immense
With witnessings of providence:
And woe to me if when I look
Upon that record, the sole book
Unsealed to me, I take no heed
Of any warning that I read!
Have I been sure, this Christmas-Eve,
God's own hand did the rainbow weave,
Whereby the truth from heaven slid
Into my soul?—I cannot bid
The world admit He stooped to heal
My soul, as if in a thunder-peal
Where one heard noise, and one saw flame,
I only knew He named my name.
And what is the world to me, for sorrow
Or joy in its censures, when to-morrow
It drops the remark, with just-turned head
Then, on again—That man is dead?
Yes,—but for me—my name called,—drawn
As a conscript's lot from the lap's black yawn,
He has dipt into on a battle-dawn:

Bid out of life by a nod, a glance,—
Stumbling, mute-mazed, at nature's chance,—
With a rapid finger circled round,
Fixed to the first poor inch of ground,
To fight from, where his foot was found;
Whose ear but a minute since lay free
To the wide camp's buzz and gossipry—
Summoned, a solitary man,
To end his life where his life began,
From the safe glad rear, to the dreadful van!
Soul of mine, hadst thou caught and held
By the hem of the Vesture . . .

XXI

And I caught
At the flying Robe, and unrepelled
Was lapped again in its folds full-fraught
With warmth and wonder and delight,
God's mercy being infinite.
And scarce had the words escaped my tongue,
When, at a passionate bound, I sprung
Out of the wandering world of rain,
Into the little chapel again.

XXII

How else was I found there, bolt upright
On my bench, as if I had never left it?
—Never flung out on the common at night
Nor met the storm and wedge-like cleft it,
Seen the raree-show of Peter's successor,
Or the laboratory of the Professor!
For the Vision, *that* was true, I wist,
True as that heaven and earth exist.
There sate my friend, the yellow and tall,
With his neck and its wen in the selfsame place;
Yet my nearest neighbour's cheek showed gall,
She had slid away a contemptuous space:
And the old fat woman, late so placable,
Eyed me with symptoms, hardly mistakeable,

Of her milk of kindness turning rancid:
In short a spectator might have fancied
That I had nodded betrayed by a slumber,
Yet kept my seat, a warning ghastly,
Through the heads of the sermon, nine in number,
To wake up now at the tenth and lastly.
But again, could such a disgrace have happened?
Each friend at my elbow had surely nudged it;
And, as for the sermon, where did my nap end?
Unless I heard it, could I have judged it?
Could I report as I do at the close,
First, the preacher speaks through his nose:
Second, his gesture is too emphatic:
Thirdly, to waive what's pedagogic,
The subject-matter itself lacks logic:
Fourthly, the English is ungrammatic.
Great news! the preacher is found no Pascal,
Whom, if I pleased, I might to the task call
Of making square to a finite eye
The circle of infinity,
And find so all-but-just-succeeding!
Great news! the sermon proves no reading
Where bee-like in the flowers I may bury me,
Like Taylor's, the immortal Jeremy!
And now that I know the very worst of him,
What was it I thought to obtain at first of him?
Ha! Is God mocked, as He asks?
Shall I take on me to change His tasks,
And dare, despatched to a river-head
For a simple draught of the element,
Neglect the thing for which He sent,
And return with another thing instead?—
Saying . . . "Because the water found
Welling up from underground,
Is mingled with the taints of earth,
While Thou, I know, dost laugh at dearth,
And couldest, at a word, convulse
The world with the leap of its river-pulse,—
Therefore I turned from the oozings muddy,
And bring thee a chalice I found, instead:

See the brave veins in the breccia ruddy!
One would suppose that the marble bled.
What matters the water? A hope I have nursed,
That the waterless cup will quench my thirst."
—Better have knelt at the poorest stream
That trickles in pain from the straitest rift!
For the less or the more is all God's gift,
Who blocks up or breaks wide the granite-seam.
And here, is there water or not, to drink?
I, then, in ignorance and weakness,
Taking God's help, have attained to think
My heart does best to receive in meekness
This mode of worship, as most to His mind,
Where earthly aids being cast behind,
His All in All appears serene,
With the thinnest human veil between,
Letting the mystic Lamps, the Seven,
The many motions of His spirit,
Pass, as they list, to earth from Heaven.
For the preacher's merit or demerit,
It were to be wished the flaws were fewer
In the earthen vessel, holding treasure,
Which lies as safe in a golden ewer;
But the main thing is, does it hold good measure?
Heaven soon sets right all other matters!—
Ask, else, these ruins of humanity,
This flesh worn out to rags and tatters,
This soul at struggle with insanity,
Who thence take comfort, can I doubt,
Which an empire gained, were a loss without.
May it be mine! And let us hope
That no worse blessing befal the Pope,
Turn'd sick at last of the day's buffoonery,
Of his posturings and his petticoatings,
Beside the Bourbon bully's gloatings
In the bloody orgies of drunk poltroonery!
Nor may the Professor forego its peace
At Göttingen, presently, when, in the dusk
Of his life, if his cough, as I fear, should increase,
Prophesied of by that horrible husk;

And when, thicker and thicker, the darkness fills
The world through his misty spectacles,
And he gropes for something more substantial
Than a fable, myth, or personification,
May Christ do for him, what no mere man shall,
And stand confessed as the God of salvation!
Meantime, in the still recurring fear
Lest myself, at unawares, be found,
While attacking the choice of my neighbours round,
Without my own made—I choose here!
The giving out of the hymn reclaims me;
I have done!—And if any blames me,
Thinking that merely to touch in brevity
The topics I dwell on, were unlawful,—
Or, worse, that I trench, with undue levity,
On the bounds of the Holy and the awful,
I praise the heart, and pity the head of him,
And refer myself to THEE, instead of him;
Who head and heart alike discernest,
Looking below light speech we utter,
When the frothy spume and frequent sputter
Prove that the soul's depths boil in earnest!
May the truth shine out, stand ever before us!
I put up pencil and join chorus
To Hepzibah Tune, without further apology,
The last five verses of the third section
Of the seventeenth hymn in Whitfield's Collection,
To conclude with the doxology.

Men and Women

1855

Men and Women. By Robert Browning. In two volumes. Vol. I [II]. London: Chapman and Hall, 193, Piccadilly. 1855.

F'cap 8vo. Vol. I, pp. iv + 260; Vol. II, pp. iv + 244. Cloth boards.

The two volumes of *Men and Women* contained fifty poems and one play. Of the poems, the first nine sections of *Saul* had been included among the *Dramatic Romances and Lyrics* of 1845; and *The Twins* had been printed in a pamphlet—

> Two Poems by Elizabeth Barrett and Robert Browning. London: Chapman & Hall, 193, Piccadilly. 1854.
>
> Crown 8vo. Pp. 16. Printed paper wrappers.

(Pamphlet issues of *Cleon* and *The Statue and the Bust*, purporting to have been published by Edward Moxon in 1855, are known to have been printed at least some twenty-five years later.)

In the later collected editions of his works Browning redistributed the fifty poems into sections headed *Dramatic Lyrics, Dramatic Romances* and *Men and Women*: the play, *In a Balcony*, formed a section by itself.

The following pieces are omitted from the present selection: *A Lovers' Quarrel, Mesmerism, A Pretty Woman, How it strikes a Contemporary, Master Hugues of Saxe-Gotha, Before, After, In Three Days, Old Pictures in Florence, In a Balcony, Protus, Holy-Cross Day, The Guardian-Angel, The Heretic's Tragedy*. The remaining poems are given in the text of the first edition, with evident errors corrected. In *Transcendentalism*, line 22, the correction "German Bœhme", made by Browning in 1868, has been preferred to the "Swedish Bœhme" of the first edition. In *One Word More*, stanza 15, line 8, the reading of 1872 and later

> Karshish, Cleon, Norbert and the fifty

has been preferred. The allusion is to the characters in *An Epistle of Karshish, Cleon* and *In a Balcony*. The earlier editions printed "Karshook" for "Karshish"—Karshook being a character in another poem, written at about the same period but not included either in *Men and Women* or in any collected edition during Browning's life.

Men and Women

LOVE AMONG THE RUINS

1

Where the quiet-coloured end of evening smiles
Miles and miles
On the solitary pastures where our sheep
Half-asleep
Tinkle homeward thro' the twilight, stray or stop
As they crop—

2

Was the site once of a city great and gay,
(So they say)
Of our country's very capital, its prince
Ages since
Held his court in, gathered councils, wielding far
Peace or war.

3

Now—the country does not even boast a tree,
As you see,
To distinguish slopes of verdure, certain rills
From the hills
Intersect and give a name to, (else they run
Into one)

4

Where the domed and daring palace shot its spires
Up like fires
O'er the hundred-gated circuit of a wall
Bounding all,
Made of marble, men might march on nor be prest,
Twelve abreast.

5

And such plenty and perfection, see, of grass
Never was!
Such a carpet as, this summer-time, o'erspreads
And embeds
Every vestige of the city, guessed alone,
Stock or stone—

6

Where a multitude of men breathed joy and woe
Long ago;
Lust of glory pricked their hearts up, dread of shame
Struck them tame;
And that glory and that shame alike, the gold
Bought and sold.

7

Now,—the single little turret that remains
On the plains,
By the caper overrooted, by the gourd
Overscored,
While the patching houseleek's head of blossom winks
Through the chinks—

8

Marks the basement whence a tower in ancient time
Sprang sublime,
And a burning ring all round, the chariots traced
As they raced,
And the monarch and his minions and his dames
Viewed the games.

9

And I know, while thus the quiet-coloured eve
Smiles to leave
To their folding, all our many-tinkling fleece
In such peace,
And the slopes and rills in undistinguished grey
Melt away—

10

That a girl with eager eyes and yellow hair
Waits me there
In the turret, whence the charioteers caught soul
For the goal,
When the king looked, where she looks now, breathless, dumb
Till I come.

11

But he looked upon the city, every side,
Far and wide,
All the mountains topped with temples, all the glades'
Colonnades,
All the causeys, bridges, aqueducts,—and then,
All the men!

12

When I do come, she will speak not, she will stand,
Either hand
On my shoulder, give her eyes the first embrace
Of my face,
Ere we rush, ere we extinguish sight and speech
Each on each.

13

In one year they sent a million fighters forth
South and north,
And they built their gods a brazen pillar high
As the sky,
Yet reserved a thousand chariots in full force—
Gold, of course.

14

Oh, heart! oh, blood that freezes, blood that burns!
Earth's returns
For whole centuries of folly, noise and sin!
Shut them in,
With their triumphs and their glories and the rest.
Love is best!

EVELYN HOPE

1

Beautiful Evelyn Hope is dead
  Sit and watch by her side an hour.
That is her book-shelf, this her bed;
  She plucked that piece of geranium-flower,
Beginning to die too, in the glass.
  Little has yet been changed, I think—
The shutters are shut, no light may pass
  Save two long rays thro' the hinge's chink.

2

Sixteen years old when she died!
  Perhaps she had scarcely heard my name—
It was not her time to love: beside,
  Her life had many a hope and aim,
Duties enough and little cares,
  And now was quiet, now astir—
Till God's hand beckoned unawares,
  And the sweet white brow is all of her.

3

Is it too late then, Evelyn Hope?
  What, your soul was pure and true,
The good stars met in your horoscope,
  Made you of spirit, fire and dew—
And just because I was thrice as old,
  And our paths in the world diverged so wide,
Each was nought to each, must I be told?
  We were fellow mortals, nought beside?

4

No, indeed! for God above
  Is great to grant, as mighty to make,
And creates the love to reward the love,—
  I claim you still, for my own love's sake!

Delayed it may be for more lives yet,
  Through worlds I shall traverse, not a few—
Much is to learn and much to forget
  Ere the time be come for taking you.

5

But the time will come,—at last it will,
  When, Evelyn Hope, what meant, I shall say,
In the lower earth, in the years long still,
  That body and soul so pure and gay?
Why your hair was amber, I shall divine,
  And your mouth of your own geranium's red—
And what you would do with me, in fine,
  In the new life come in the old one's stead.

6

I have lived, I shall say, so much since then,
  Given up myself so many times,
Gained me the gains of various men,
  Ransacked the ages, spoiled the climes;
Yet one thing, one, in my soul's full scope,
  Either I missed or itself missed me—
And I want and find you, Evelyn Hope!
  What is the issue? let us see!

7

I loved you, Evelyn, all the while;
  My heart seemed full as it could hold—
There was place and to spare for the frank young smile
  And the red young mouth and the hair's young gold.
So, hush,—I will give you this leaf to keep—
  See, I shut it inside the sweet cold hand.
There, that is our secret! go to sleep;
  You will wake, and remember, and understand

UP AT A VILLA—DOWN IN THE CITY

AS DISTINGUISHED BY AN ITALIAN PERSON OF QUALITY

I

Had I but plenty of money, money enough and to spare,
The house for me, no doubt, were a house in the city-square.
Ah, such a life, such a life, as one leads at the window there!

2

Something to see, by Bacchus, something to hear, at least!
There, the whole day long, one's life is a perfect feast;
While up at a villa one lives, I maintain it, no more than a beast.

3

Well now, look at our villa! stuck like the horn of a bull
Just on a mountain's edge as bare as the creature's skull,
Save a mere shag of a bush with hardly a leaf to pull!
—I scratch my own, sometimes, to see if the hair's turned wool.

4

But the city, oh the city—the square with the houses! Why?
They are stone-faced, white as a curd, there's something to take the eye!
Houses in four straight lines, not a single front awry!
You watch who crosses and gossips, who saunters, who hurries by:
Green blinds, as a matter of course, to draw when the sun gets high;
And the shops with fanciful signs which are painted properly.

5

What of a villa? Though winter be over in March by rights,
'Tis May perhaps ere the snow shall have withered well off the heights:
You've the brown ploughed land before, where the oxen steam and wheeze,
And the hills over-smoked behind by the faint grey olive trees.

6

Is it better in May, I ask you? you've summer all at once;
In a day he leaps complete with a few strong April suns!
'Mid the sharp short emerald wheat, scarce risen three fingers well,
The wild tulip, at end of its tube, blows out its great red bell,
Like a thin clear bubble of blood, for the children to pick and sell.

7

Is it ever hot in the square? There's a fountain to spout and splash!
In the shade it sings and springs; in the shine such foam-bows flash
On the horses with curling fish-tails, that prance and paddle and pash
Round the lady atop in the conch—fifty gazers do not abash,
Though all that she wears is some weeds round her waist in a sort of sash!

8

All the year long at the villa, nothing's to see though you linger,
Except yon cypress that points like Death's lean lifted fore-finger.
Some think fireflies pretty, when they mix in the corn and mingle,
Or thrid the stinking hemp till the stalks of it seem a-tingle.

Late August or early September, the stunning cicala is shrill,
And the bees keep their tiresome whine round the resinous firs on the hill.
Enough of the seasons,—I spare you the months of the fever and chill.

9

Ere opening your eyes in the city, the blessed church-bells begin:
No sooner the bells leave off, than the diligence rattles in:
You get the pick of the news, and it costs you never a pin.
By and by there's the travelling doctor gives pills, lets blood, draws teeth;
Or the Pulcinello-trumpet breaks up the market beneath.
At the post-office such a scene-picture—the new play, piping hot!
And a notice how, only this morning, three liberal thieves were shot.
Above it, behold the archbishop's most fatherly of rebukes,
And beneath, with his crown and his lion, some little new law of the Duke's!
Or a sonnet with flowery marge, to the Reverend Don So-and-so
Who is Dante, Boccaccio, Petrarca, Saint Jerome, and Cicero,
"And moreover," (the sonnet goes rhyming) "the skirts of St. Paul has reached,
Having preached us those six Lent-lectures more unctuous than ever he preached."
Noon strikes,—here sweeps the procession! our Lady borne smiling and smart
With a pink gauze gown all spangles, and seven swords stuck in her heart!
Bang, *whang*, *whang*, goes the drum, *tootle-te-tootle* the fife;
No keeping one's haunches still: it's the greatest pleasure in life.

10

But bless you, it's dear—it's dear! fowls, wine, at double the rate.
They have clapped a new tax upon salt, and what oil pays passing the gate
It's a horror to think of. And so, the villa for me, not the city!
Beggars can scarcely be choosers—but still—ah, the pity, the pity!
Look, two and two go the priests, then the monks with cowls and sandals,
And the penitents dressed in white shirts, a-holding the yellow candles.
One, he carries a flag up straight, and another a cross with handles,
And the Duke's guard brings up the rear, for the better prevention of scandals.
Bang, whang, whang, goes the drum, *tootle-te-tootle* the fife.
Oh, a day in the city-square, there is no such pleasure in life!

A WOMAN'S LAST WORD

1

Let's contend no more, Love,
Strive nor weep—
All be as before, Love,
—Only sleep!

2

What so wild as words are?
—I and thou
In debate, as birds are,
Hawk on bough!

3

See the creature stalking
While we speak—
Hush and hide the talking,
Cheek on cheek!

4

What so false as truth is,
  False to thee?
Where the serpent's tooth is,
  Shun the tree—

5

Where the apple reddens
  Never pry—
Lest we lose our Edens,
  Eve and I!

6

Be a god and hold me
  With a charm—
Be a man and fold me
  With thine arm!

7

Teach me, only teach, Love!
  As I ought
I will speak thy speech, Love,
  Think thy thought—

8

Meet, if thou require it,
  Both demands,
Laying flesh and spirit
  In thy hands!

9

That shall be to-morrow
  Not to-night:
I must bury sorrow
  Out of sight.

10

—Must a little weep, Love,
  —Foolish me!
And so fall asleep, Love,
  Loved by thee.

FRA LIPPO LIPPI

I AM poor brother Lippo, by your leave!
You need not clap your torches to my face.
Zooks, what's to blame? you think you see a monk!
What, it's past midnight, and you go the rounds,
And here you catch me at an alley's end
Where sportive ladies leave their doors ajar.
The Carmine's my cloister: hunt it up,
Do,—harry out, if you must show your zeal,
Whatever rat, there, haps on his wrong hole,
And nip each softling of a wee white mouse,
Weke, weke, that's crept to keep him company!
Aha, you know your betters? Then, you'll take
Your hand away that's fiddling on my throat,
And please to know me likewise. Who am I?
Why, one, sir, who is lodging with a friend
Three streets off—he's a certain . . . how d'ye call?
Master—a . . . Cosimo of the Medici,
In the house that caps the corner. Boh! you were best!
Remember and tell me, the day you're hanged,
How you affected such a gullet's-gripe!
But you, sir, it concerns you that your knaves
Pick up a manner nor discredit you.
Zooks, are we pilchards, that they sweep the streets
And count fair prize what comes into their net?
He's Judas to a tittle, that man is!
Just such a face! why, sir, you make amends.
Lord, I'm not angry! Bid your hangdogs go
Drink out this quarter-florin to the health
Of the munificent House that harbours me
(And many more beside, lads! more beside!)
And all's come square again. I'd like his face—
His, elbowing on his comrade in the door
With the pike and lantern,—for the slave that holds
John Baptist's head a-dangle by the hair
With one hand ("look you, now," as who should say)
And his weapon in the other, yet unwiped!
It's not your chance to have a bit of chalk,

A wood-coal or the like? or you should see!
Yes, I'm the painter, since you style me so.
What, brother Lippo's doings, up and down,
You know them and they take you? like enough!
I saw the proper twinkle in your eye—
'Tell you I liked your looks at very first.
Let's sit and set things straight now, hip to haunch.
Here's spring come, and the nights one makes up bands
To roam the town and sing out carnival,
And I've been three weeks shut within my mew,
A-painting for the great man, saints and saints
And saints again. I could not paint all night—
Ouf! I leaned out of window for fresh air.
There came a hurry of feet and little feet,
A sweep of lute-strings, laughs, and whifts of song,—
Flower o' the broom,
Take away love, and our earth is a tomb!
Flower o' the quince,
I let Lisa go, and what good's in life since?
Flower o' the thyme—and so on. Round they went.
Scarce had they turned the corner when a titter,
Like the skipping of rabbits by moonlight,—three slim shapes—
And a face that looked up . . . zooks, sir, flesh and blood,
That's all I'm made of! Into shreds it went,
Curtain and counterpane and coverlet,
All the bed furniture—a dozen knots,
There was a ladder! down I let myself,
Hands and feet, scrambling somehow, and so dropped,
And after them. I came up with the fun
Hard by St. Laurence, hail fellow, well met,—
Flower o' the rose,
If I've been merry, what matter who knows?
And so as I was stealing back again
To get to bed and have a bit of sleep
Ere I rise up to-morrow and go work
On Jerome knocking at his poor old breast
With his great round stone to subdue the flesh,
You snap me of the sudden. Ah, I see!
Though your eye twinkles still, you shake your head—

Mine's shaved,—a monk, you say—the sting's in that!
If Master Cosimo announced himself,
Mum's the word naturally; but a monk!
Come, what am I a beast for? tell us, now!
I was a baby when my mother died
And father died and left me in the street.
I starved there, God knows how, a year or two
On fig-skins, melon-parings, rinds and shucks,
Refuse and rubbish. One fine frosty day
My stomach being empty as your hat,
The wind doubled me up and down I went.
Old Aunt Lapaccia trussed me with one hand,
(Its fellow was a stinger as I knew)
And so along the wall, over the bridge,
By the straight cut to the convent. Six words, there,
While I stood munching my first bread that month:
"So, boy, you're minded," quoth the good fat father
Wiping his own mouth, 'twas refection-time,—
"To quit this very miserable world?
Will you renounce" . . . The mouthful of bread? thought I;
By no means! Brief, they made a monk of me;
I did renounce the world, its pride and greed,
Palace, farm, villa, shop and banking-house,
Trash, such as these poor devils of Medici
Have given their hearts to—all at eight years old.
Well, sir, I found in time, you may be sure,
'Twas not for nothing—the good bellyful,
The warm serge and the rope that goes all round,
And day-long blessed idleness beside!
"Let's see what the urchin's fit for"—that came next.
Not overmuch their way, I must confess.
Such a to-do! they tried me with their books.
Lord, they'd have taught me Latin in pure waste!
Flower o' the clove,
All the Latin I construe is, "*amo*" *I love!*
But, mind you, when a boy starves in the streets
Eight years together, as my fortune was,
Watching folk's faces to know who will fling
The bit of half-stripped grape-bunch he desires,

And who will curse or kick him for his pains—
Which gentleman processional and fine,
Holding a candle to the Sacrament
Will wink and let him lift a plate and catch
The droppings of the wax to sell again,
Or holla for the Eight and have him whipped,—
How say I?—nay, which dog bites, which lets drop
His bone from the heap of offal in the street!
—The soul and sense of him grow sharp alike,
He learns the look of things, and none the less
For admonitions from the hunger-pinch.
I had a store of such remarks, be sure,
Which, after I found leisure, turned to use:
I drew men's faces on my copy-books,
Scrawled them within the antiphonary's marge,
Joined legs and arms to the long music-notes,
Found nose and eyes and chin for A.s and B.s,
And made a string of pictures of the world
Betwixt the ins and outs of verb and noun,
On the wall, the bench, the door. The monks looked
    black.
"Nay," quoth the Prior, "turn him out, d'ye say?
In no wise. Lose a crow and catch a lark.
What if at last we get our man of parts,
We Carmelites, like those Camaldolese
And Preaching Friars, to do our church up fine
And put the front on it that ought to be!"
And hereupon they bade me daub away.
Thank you! my head being crammed, their walls a blank,
Never was such prompt disemburdening.
First, every sort of monk, the black and white,
I drew them, fat and lean: then, folks at church,
From good old gossips waiting to confess
Their cribs of barrel-droppings, candle-ends,—
To the breathless fellow at the altar-foot,
Fresh from his murder, safe and sitting there
With the little children round him in a row
Of admiration, half for his beard and half
For that white anger of his victim's son
Shaking a fist at him with one fierce arm,

Signing himself with the other because of Christ
(Whose sad face on the cross sees only this
After the passion of a thousand years)
Till some poor girl, her apron o'er her head
Which the intense eyes looked through, came at eve
On tip-toe, said a word, dropped in a loaf,
Her pair of ear-rings and a bunch of flowers
The brute took growling, prayed, and then was gone.
I painted all, then cried, "'tis ask and have—
Choose, for more's ready!"—laid the ladder flat,
And showed my covered bit of cloister-wall.
The monks closed in a circle and praised loud
Till checked, (taught what to see and not to see,
Being simple bodies) "that's the very man!
Look at the boy who stoops to pat the dog!
That woman's like the Prior's niece who comes
To care about his asthma: it's the life!"
But there my triumph's straw-fire flared and funked—
Their betters took their turn to see and say:
The Prior and the learned pulled a face
And stopped all that in no time. "How? what's here?
Quite from the mark of painting, bless us all!
Faces, arms, legs and bodies like the true
As much as pea and pea! it's devil's-game!
Your business is not to catch men with show,
With homage to the perishable clay,
But lift them over it, ignore it all,
Make them forget there's such a thing as flesh.
Your business is to paint the souls of men—
Man's soul, and it's a fire, smoke . . . no it's not . . .
It's vapour done up like a new-born babe—
(In that shape when you die it leaves your mouth)
It's . . . well, what matters talking, it's the soul!
Give us no more of body than shows soul.
Here's Giotto, with his Saint a-praising God!
That sets you praising,—why not stop with him?
Why put all thoughts of praise out of our heads
With wonder at lines, colours, and what not?
Paint the soul, never mind the legs and arms!
Rub all out, try at it a second time.

Oh, that white smallish female with the breasts,
She's just my niece . . . Herodias, I would say,—
Who went and danced and got men's heads cut off—
Have it all out!" Now, is this sense, I ask?
A fine way to paint soul, by painting body
So ill, the eye can't stop there, must go further
And can't fare worse! Thus, yellow does for white
When what you put for yellow's simply black,
And any sort of meaning looks intense
When all beside itself means and looks nought.
Why can't a painter lift each foot in turn,
Left foot and right foot, go a double step,
Make his flesh liker and his soul more like,
Both in their order? Take the prettiest face,
The Prior's niece . . . patron-saint—is it so pretty
You can't discover if it means hope, fear,
Sorrow or joy? won't beauty go with these?
Suppose I've made her eyes all right and blue,
Can't I take breath and try to add life's flash,
And then add soul and heighten them threefold?
Or say there's beauty with no soul at all—
(I never saw it—put the case the same—)
If you get simple beauty and nought else,
You get about the best thing God invents,—
That's somewhat. And you'll find the soul you have missed,
Within yourself when you return Him thanks!
"Rub all out!" well, well, there's my life, in short,
And so the thing has gone on ever since.
I'm grown a man no doubt, I've broken bounds—
You should not take a fellow eight years old
And make him swear to never kiss the girls—
I'm my own master, paint now as I please—
Having a friend, you see, in the Corner-house!
Lord, it's fast holding by the rings in front—
Those great rings serve more purposes than just
To plant a flag in, or tie up a horse!
And yet the old schooling sticks—the old grave eyes
Are peeping o'er my shoulder as I work,
The heads shake still—"It's Art's decline, my son!

You're not of the true painters, great and old:
Brother Angelico's the man, you'll find:
Brother Lorenzo stands his single peer.
Fag on at flesh, you'll never make the third!"
Flower o' the pine,
You keep your mistr . . . manners, and I'll stick to mine!
I'm not the third, then: bless us, they must know!
Don't you think they're the likeliest to know,
They, with their Latin? so I swallow my rage,
Clench my teeth, suck my lips in tight, and paint
To please them—sometimes do, and sometimes don't,
For, doing most, there's pretty sure to come
A turn—some warm eve finds me at my saints—
A laugh, a cry, the business of the world—
(*Flower o' the peach,*
Death for us all, and his own life for each!)
And my whole soul revolves, the cup runs o'er,
The world and life's too big to pass for a dream,
And I do these wild things in sheer despite,
And play the fooleries you catch me at,
In pure rage! the old mill-horse, out at grass
After hard years, throws up his stiff heels so,
Although the miller does not preach to him
The only good of grass is to make chaff.
What would men have? Do they like grass or no—
May they or mayn't they? all I want's the thing
Settled for ever one way: as it is,
You tell too many lies and hurt yourself.
You don't like what you only like too much,
You do like what, if given you at your word,
You find abundantly detestable.
For me, I think I speak as I was taught—
I always see the Garden and God there
A-making man's wife—and, my lesson learned,
The value and significance of flesh,
I can't unlearn ten minutes afterward.

You understand me: I'm a beast, I know.
But see, now—why, I see as certainly
As that the morning-star's about to shine,

What will hap some day. We've a youngster here
Comes to our convent, studies what I do,
Slouches and stares and lets no atom drop—
His name is Guidi—he'll not mind the monks—
They call him Hulking Tom, he lets them talk—
He picks my practice up—he'll paint apace,
I hope so—though I never live so long,
I know what's sure to follow. You be judge!
You speak no Latin more than I, belike—
However, you're my man, you've seen the world
—The beauty and the wonder and the power,
The shapes of things, their colours, lights and shades,
Changes, surprises,—and God made it all!
—For what? do you feel thankful, ay or no,
For this fair town's face, yonder river's line,
The mountain round it and the sky above,
Much more the figures of man, woman, child,
These are the frame to? What's it all about?
To be passed o'er, despised? or dwelt upon,
Wondered at? oh, this last of course, you say.
But why not do as well as say,—paint these
Just as they are, careless what comes of it?
God's works—paint anyone, and count it crime
To let a truth slip. Don't object, "His works
Are here already—nature is complete:
Suppose you reproduce her—(which you can't)
There's no advantage! you must beat her, then."
For, don't you mark, we're made so that we love
First when we see them painted, things we have passed
Perhaps a hundred times nor cared to see;
And so they are better, painted—better to us,
Which is the same thing. Art was given for that—
God uses us to help each other so,
Lending our minds out. Have you noticed, now,
Your cullion's hanging face? A bit of chalk,
And trust me but you should, though! How much more,
If I drew higher things with the same truth!
That were to take the Prior's pulpit-place,
Interpret God to all of you! oh, oh,
It makes me mad to see what men shall do

And we in our graves! This world's no blot for us,
Nor blank—it means intensely, and means good:
To find its meaning is my meat and drink.
"Ay, but you don't so instigate to prayer"
Strikes in the Prior! "when your meaning's plain
It does not say to folks—remember matins—
Or, mind you fast next Friday." Why, for this
What need of art at all? A skull and bones,
Two bits of stick nailed cross-wise, or, what's best,
A bell to chime the hour with, does as well.
I painted a St. Laurence six months since
At Prato, splashed the fresco in fine style.
"How looks my painting, now the scaffold's down?"
I ask a brother: "Hugely," he returns—
"Already not one phiz of your three slaves
That turn the Deacon off his toasted side,
But's scratched and prodded to our heart's content,
The pious people have so eased their own
When coming to say prayers there in a rage.
We get on fast to see the bricks beneath.
Expect another job this time next year,
For pity and religion grow i' the crowd—
Your painting serves its purpose!" Hang the fools!

—That is—you'll not mistake an idle word
Spoke in a huff by a poor monk, God wot,
Tasting the air this spicy night which turns
The unaccustomed head like Chianti wine!
Oh, the church knows! don't misreport me, now!
It's natural a poor monk out of bounds
Should have his apt word to excuse himself:
And hearken how I plot to make amends.
I have bethought me: I shall paint a piece
. . . There's for you! Give me six months, then go, see
Something in Sant' Ambrogio's . . . (bless the nuns!
They want a cast of my office) I shall paint
God in the midst, Madonna and her babe,
Ringed by a bowery, flowery angel-brood,
Lilies and vestments and white faces, sweet
As puff on puff of grated orris-root

When ladies crowd to church at midsummer.
And then in the front, of course a saint or two—
Saint John, because he saves the Florentines,
Saint Ambrose, who puts down in black and white
The convent's friends and gives them a long day,
And Job, I must have him there past mistake,
The man of Uz, (and Us without the z,
Painters who need his patience.) Well, all these
Secured at their devotions, up shall come
Out of a corner when you least expect,
As one by a dark stair into a great light,
Music and talking, who but Lippo! I!—
Mazed, motionless and moon-struck—I'm the man!
Back I shrink—what is this I see and hear?
I, caught up with my monk's things by mistake,
My old serge gown and rope that goes all round,
I, in this presence, this pure company!
Where's a hole, where's a corner for escape?
Then steps a sweet angelic slip of a thing
Forward, puts out a soft palm—"Not so fast!"
—Addresses the celestial presence, "nay—
He made you and devised you, after all,
Though he's none of you! Could Saint John there, draw—
His camel-hair make up a painting-brush?
We come to brother Lippo for all that,
Iste perfecit opus!" So, all smile—
I shuffle sideways with my blushing face
Under the cover of a hundred wings
Thrown like a spread of kirtles when you're gay
And play hot cockles, all the doors being shut,
Till, wholly unexpected, in there pops
The hothead husband! Thus I scuttle off
To some safe bench behind, not letting go
The palm of her, the little lily thing
That spoke the good word for me in the nick,
Like the Prior's niece . . . Saint Lucy, I would say.
And so all's saved for me, and for the church
A pretty picture gained. Go, six months hence!
Your hand, sir, and good bye: no lights, no lights!

The street's hushed, and I know my own way back—
Don't fear me! There's the grey beginning. Zooks!

A TOCCATA OF GALUPPI'S

I

OH, Galuppi, Baldassaro, this is very sad to find!
I can hardly misconceive you; it would prove me deaf and blind;
But although I give you credit, 'tis with such a heavy mind!

2

Here you come with your old music, and here's all the good it brings.
What, they lived once thus at Venice, where the merchants were the kings,
Where St. Mark's is, where the Doges used to wed the sea with rings?

3

Ay, because the sea's the street there; and 'tis arched by . . . what you call
. . . Shylock's bridge with houses on it, where they kept the carnival!
I was never out of England—it's as if I saw it all!

4

Did young people take their pleasure when the sea was warm in May?
Balls and masks begun at midnight, burning ever to mid-day,
When they made up fresh adventures for the morrow, do you say?

5

Was a lady such a lady, cheeks so round and lips so red,—
On her neck the small face buoyant, like a bell-flower on its bed,
O'er the breast's superb abundance where a man might base his head?

6

Well (and it was graceful of them) they'd break talk off and afford
—She, to bite her mask's black velvet, he to finger on his sword,
While you sat and played Toccatas, stately at the clavichord?

7

What? Those lesser thirds so plaintive, sixths diminished, sigh on sigh,
Told them something? Those suspensions, those solutions—"Must we die?"
Those commiserating sevenths—"Life might last! we can but try!"

8

"Were you happy?"—"Yes."—"And are you still as happy?"—"Yes—And you?"
—"Then more kisses"—"Did *I* stop them, when a million seemed so few?"
Hark—the dominant's persistence, till it must be answered to!

9

So an octave struck the answer. Oh, they praised you, I dare say!
"Brave Galuppi! that was music! good alike at grave and gay!
I can always leave off talking, when I hear a master play."

10

Then they left you for their pleasure: till in due time, one by one,
Some with lives that came to nothing, some with deeds as well undone,
Death came tacitly and took them where they never see the sun.

11

But when I sit down to reason,—think to take my stand nor
swerve
Till I triumph o'er a secret wrung from nature's close
reserve,
In you come with your cold music, till I creep thro' every
nerve.

12

Yes, you, like a ghostly cricket, creaking where a house was
burned—
"Dust and ashes, dead and done with, Venice spent what
Venice earned!
The soul, doubtless, is immortal—where a soul can be discerned.

13

"Yours for instance, you know physics, something of
geology,
Mathematics are your pastime; souls shall rise in their
degree;
Butterflies may dread extinction,—you'll not die, it cannot
be!

14

"As for Venice and its people, merely born to bloom and
drop,
Here on earth they bore their fruitage, mirth and folly were
the crop.
What of soul was left, I wonder, when the kissing had to
stop?

15

"Dust and ashes!" So you creak it, and I want the heart to
scold.
Dear dead women, with such hair, too—what's become of
all the gold
Used to hang and brush their bosoms? I feel chilly and
grown old.

BY THE FIRE-SIDE

1

How well I know what I mean to do
  When the long dark Autumn evenings come,
And where, my soul, is thy pleasant hue?
  With the music of all thy voices, dumb
In life's November too!

2

I shall be found by the fire, suppose,
  O'er a great wise book as beseemeth age,
While the shutters flap as the cross-wind blows,
  And I turn the page, and I turn the page,
Not verse now, only prose!

3

Till the young ones whisper, finger on lip,
  "There he is at it, deep in Greek—
Now or never, then, out we slip
  To cut from the hazels by the creek
A mainmast for our ship."

4

I shall be at it indeed, my friends!
  Greek puts already on either side
Such a branch-work forth, as soon extends
  To a vista opening far and wide,
And I pass out where it ends.

5

The outside-frame like your hazel-trees—
  But the inside-archway narrows fast,
And a rarer sort succeeds to these,
  And we slope to Italy at last
And youth, by green degrees.

6

I follow wherever I am led,
  Knowing so well the leader's hand—
Oh, woman-country, wooed, not wed,
  Loved all the more by earth's male-lands,
Laid to their hearts instead!

7

Look at the ruined chapel again
  Half way up in the Alpine gorge.
Is that a tower, I point you plain,
  Or is it a mill or an iron forge
Breaks solitude in vain?

8

A turn, and we stand in the heart of things;
  The woods are round us, heaped and dim;
From slab to slab how it slips and springs,
  The thread of water single and slim,
Thro' the ravage some torrent brings!

9

Does it feed the little lake below?
  That speck of white just on its marge
Is Pella; see, in the evening glow
  How sharp the silver spear-heads charge
When Alp meets Heaven in snow.

10

On our other side is the straight-up rock;
  And a path is kept 'twixt the gorge and it
By boulder-stones where lichens mock
  The marks on a moth, and small ferns fit
Their teeth to the polished block.

11

Oh, the sense of the yellow mountain flowers,
  And the thorny balls, each three in one,
The chestnuts throw on our path in showers,
  For the drop of the woodland fruit's begun
These early November hours—

12

That crimson the creeper's leaf across
Like a splash of blood, intense, abrupt,
O'er a shield, else gold from rim to boss,
And lay it for show on the fairy-cupped
Elf-needled mat of moss,

13

By the rose-flesh mushrooms, undivulged
Last evening—nay, in to-day's first dew
Yon sudden coral nipple bulged
Where a freaked, fawn-coloured, flaky crew
Of toad-stools peep indulged.

14

And yonder, at foot of the fronting ridge
That takes the turn to a range beyond,
Is the chapel reached by the one-arched bridge
Where the water is stopped in a stagnant pond
Danced over by the midge.

15

The chapel and bridge are of stone alike,
Blackish grey and mostly wet;
Cut hemp-stalks steep in the narrow dyke.
See here again, how the lichens fret
And the roots of the ivy strike!

16

Poor little place, where its one priest comes
On a festa-day, if he comes at all,
To the dozen folk from their scattered homes,
Gathered within that precinct small
By the dozen ways one roams

17

To drop from the charcoal-burners' huts,
Or climb from the hemp-dressers' low shed,
Leave the grange where the woodman stores his nuts,
Or the wattled cote where the fowlers spread
Their gear on the rock's bare juts.

18

It has some pretension too, this front,
  With its bit of fresco half-moon-wise
Set over the porch, art's early wont—
  'Tis John in the Desert, I surmise,
But has borne the weather's brunt—

19

Not from the fault of the builder, though,
  For a pent-house properly projects
Where three carved beams make a certain show,
  Dating—good thought of our architect's—
'Five, six, nine, he lets you know.

20

And all day long a bird sings there,
  And a stray sheep drinks at the pond at times:
The place is silent and aware;
  It has had its scenes, its joys and crimes,
But that is its own affair.

21

My perfect wife, my Leonor,
  Oh, heart my own, oh, eyes, mine too,
Whom else could I dare look backward for,
  With whom beside should I dare pursue
The path grey heads abhor?

22

For it leads to a crag's sheer edge with them;
  Youth, flowery all the way, there stops—
Not they; age threatens and they contemn,
  Till they reach the gulf wherein youth drops,
One inch from our life's safe hem!

23

With me, youth led—I will speak now,
  No longer watch you as you sit
Reading by fire-light, that great brow
  And the spirit-small hand propping it
Mutely—my heart knows how—

24

When, if I think but deep enough,
You are wont to answer, prompt as rhyme;
And you, too, find without a rebuff
The response your soul seeks many a time
Piercing its fine flesh-stuff—

25

My own, confirm me! If I tread
This path back, is it not in pride
To think how little I dreamed it led
To an age so blest that by its side
Youth seems the waste instead!

26

My own, see where the years conduct!
At first, 'twas something our two souls
Should mix as mists do: each is sucked
Into each now; on, the new stream rolls,
Whatever rocks obstruct.

27

Think, when our one soul understands
The great Word which makes all things new—
When earth breaks up and Heaven expands—
How will the change strike me and you
In the House not made with hands?

28

Oh, I must feel your brain prompt mine,
Your heart anticipate my heart,
You must be just before, in fine,
See and make me see, for your part,
New depths of the Divine!

29

But who could have expected this,
When we two drew together first
Just for the obvious human bliss,
To satisfy life's daily thirst
With a thing men seldom miss?

30

Come back with me to the first of all,
  Let us lean and love it over again—
Let us now forget and then recall,
  Break the rosary in a pearly rain,
And gather what we let fall!

31

What did I say?—that a small bird sings
  All day long, save when a brown pair
Of hawks from the wood float with wide wings
  Strained to a bell: 'gainst the noon-day glare
You count the streaks and rings.

32

But at afternoon or almost eve
  'Tis better; then the silence grows
To that degree, you half believe
  It must get rid of what it knows,
Its bosom does so heave.

33

Hither we walked, then, side by side,
  Arm in arm and cheek to cheek,
And still I questioned or replied,
  While my heart, convulsed to really speak,
Lay choking in its pride.

34

Silent the crumbling bridge we cross,
  And pity and praise the chapel sweet,
And care about the fresco's loss,
  And wish for our souls a like retreat,
And wonder at the moss.

35

Stoop and kneel on the settle under—
  Look through the window's grated square:
Nothing to see! for fear of plunder,
  The cross is down and the altar bare,
As if thieves don't fear thunder.

36

We stoop and look in through the grate,
  See the little porch and rustic door,
Read duly the dead builder's date,
  Then cross the bridge we crossed before,
Take the path again—but wait!

37

Oh moment, one and infinite!
  The water slips o'er stock and stone;
The west is tender, hardly bright.
  How grey at once is the evening grown—
One star, the chrysolite!

38

We two stood there with never a third,
  But each by each, as each knew well.
The sights we saw and the sounds we heard,
  The lights and the shades made up a spell
Till the trouble grew and stirred.

39

Oh, the little more, and how much it is!
  And the little less, and what worlds away!
How a sound shall quicken content to bliss,
  Or a breath suspend the blood's best play,
And life be a proof of this!

40

Had she willed it, still had stood the screen
  So slight, so sure, 'twixt my love and her.
I could fix her face with a guard between,
  And find her soul as when friends confer,
Friends—lovers that might have been.

41

For my heart had a touch of the woodland time,
  Wanting to sleep now over its best.
Shake the whole tree in the summer-prime,
  But bring to the last leaf no such test.
"Hold the last fast!" says the rhyme.

42

For a chance to make your little much,
  To gain a lover and lose a friend,
Venture the tree and a myriad such,
  When nothing you mar but the year can mend!
But a last leaf—fear to touch.

43

Yet should it unfasten itself and fall
  Eddying down till it find your face
At some slight wind—(best chance of all!)
  Be your heart henceforth its dwelling-place
You trembled to forestal!

44

Worth how well, those dark grey eyes,
  —That hair so dark and dear, how worth
That a man should strive and agonise,
  And taste a very hell on earth
For the hope of such a prize!

45

Oh, you might have turned and tried a man,
  Set him a space to weary and wear,
And prove which suited more your plan,
  His best of hope or his worst despair,
Yet end as he began.

46

But you spared me this, like the heart you are,
  And filled my empty heart at a word.
If you join two lives, there is oft a scar,
  They are one and one, with a shadowy third;
One near one is too far.

47

A moment after, and hands unseen
  Were hanging the night around us fast.
But we knew that a bar was broken between
  Life and life; we were mixed at last
In spite of the mortal screen.

48

The forests had done it; there they stood—
 We caught for a second the powers at play:
They had mingled us so, for once and for good,
 Their work was done—we might go or stay,
They relapsed to their ancient mood.

49

How the world is made for each of us!
 How all we perceive and know in it
Tends to some moment's product thus,
 When a soul declares itself—to wit,
By its fruit—the thing it does!

50

Be Hate that fruit or Love that fruit,
 It forwards the General Deed of Man,
And each of the Many helps to recruit
 The life of the race by a general plan,
Each living his own, to boot.

51

I am named and known by that hour's feat,
 There took my station and degree.
So grew my own small life complete
 As nature obtained her best of me—
One born to love you, sweet!

52

And to watch you sink by the fire-side now
 Back again, as you mutely sit
Musing by fire-light, that great brow
 And the spirit-small hand propping it
Yonder, my heart knows how!

53

So the earth has gained by one man more,
 And the gain of earth must be Heaven's gain too,
And the whole is well worth thinking o'er
 When the autumn comes: which I mean to do
One day, as I said before.

ANY WIFE TO ANY HUSBAND

1

My love, this is the bitterest, that thou
Who art all truth and who dost love me now
As thine eyes say, as thy voice breaks to say—
Should'st love so truly and could'st love me still
A whole long life through, had but love its will,
Would death that leads me from thee brook delay!

2

I have but to be by thee, and thy hand
Would never let mine go, thy heart withstand
The beating of my heart to reach its place.
When should I look for thee and feel thee gone?
When cry for the old comfort and find none?
Never, I know! Thy soul is in thy face.

3

Oh, I should fade—'tis willed so! might I save,
Gladly I would, whatever beauty gave
Joy to thy sense, for that was precious too.
It is not to be granted. But the soul
Whence the love comes, all ravage leaves that whole;
Vainly the flesh fades—soul makes all things new.

4

And 'twould not be because my eye grew dim
Thou could'st not find the love there, thanks to Him
Who never is dishonoured in the spark
He gave us from his fire of fires, and bade
Remember whence it sprang nor be afraid
While that burns on, though all the rest grow dark.

5

So, how thou would'st be perfect, white and clean
Outside as inside, soul and soul's demesne
Alike, this body given to show it by!
Oh, three-parts through the worst of life's abyss,
What plaudits from the next world after this,
Could'st thou repeat a stroke and gain the sky!

6

And is it not the bitterer to think
That, disengage our hands and thou wilt sink
  Although thy love was love in very deed?
I know that nature! Pass a festive day
Thou dost not throw its relic-flower away
  Nor bid its music's loitering echo speed.

7

Thou let'st the stranger's glove lie where it fell;
If old things remain old things all is well,
  For thou art grateful as becomes man best:
And hadst thou only heard me play one tune,
Or viewed me from a window, not so soon
  With thee would such things fade as with the rest.

8

I seem to see! we meet and part: 'tis brief:
The book I opened keeps a folded leaf,
  The very chair I sat on, breaks the rank;
That is a portrait of me on the wall—
Three lines, my face comes at so slight a call;
  And for all this, one little hour's to thank.

9

But now, because the hour through years was fixed,
Because our inmost beings met and mixed,
  Because thou once hast loved me—wilt thou dare
Say to thy soul and Who may list beside,
"Therefore she is immortally my bride,
  Chance cannot change that love, nor time impair.

10

"So, what if in the dusk of life that's left,
I, a tired traveller, of my sun bereft,
  Look from my path when, mimicking the same,
The fire-fly glimpses past me, come and gone?
—Where was it till the sunset? where anon
  It will be at the sunrise! what's to blame?"

11

Is it so helpful to thee? canst thou take
The mimic up, nor, for the true thing's sake,
  Put gently by such efforts at a beam?
Is the remainder of the way so long
Thou need'st the little solace, thou the strong?
  Watch out thy watch, let weak ones doze and dream!

12

"—Ah, but the fresher faces! Is it true,"
Thou'lt ask, "some eyes are beautiful and new?
  Some hair,—how can one choose but grasp such wealth?
And if a man would press his lips to lips
Fresh as the wilding hedge-rose-cup there slips
  The dew-drop out of, must it be by stealth?

13

"It cannot change the love kept still for Her,
Much more than, such a picture to prefer
  Passing a day with, to a room's bare side.
The painted form takes nothing she possessed,
Yet while the Titian's Venus lies at rest
  A man looks. Once more, what is there to chide?"

14

So must I see, from where I sit and watch,
My own self sell myself, my hand attach
  Its warrant to the very thefts from me—
Thy singleness of soul that made me proud,
Thy purity of heart I loved aloud,
  Thy man's truth I was bold to bid God see!

15

Love so, then, if thou wilt! Give all thou canst
Away to the new faces—disentranced—
  (Say it and think it) obdurate no more,
Re-issue looks and words from the old mint—
Pass them afresh, no matter whose the print
  Image and superscription once they bore!

16

Re-coin thyself and give it them to spend,—
It all comes to the same thing at the end,
  Since mine thou wast, mine art, and mine shalt be,
Faithful or faithless, sealing up the sum
Or lavish of my treasure, thou must come
  Back to the heart's place here I keep for thee!

17

Only, why should it be with stain at all?
Why must I, 'twixt the leaves of coronal,
  Put any kiss of pardon on thy brow?
Why need the other women know so much
And talk together, "Such the look and such
  The smile he used to love with, then as now!"

18

Might I die last and shew thee! Should I find
Such hardship in the few years left behind,
  If free to take and light my lamp, and go
Into thy tomb, and shut the door and sit
Seeing thy face on those four sides of it
  The better that they are so blank, I know!

19

Why, time was what I wanted, to turn o'er
Within my mind each look, get more and more
  By heart each word, too much to learn at first,
And join thee all the fitter for the pause
'Neath the low door-way's lintel. That were cause
  For lingering, though thou calledst, if I durst!

20

And yet thou art the nobler of us two.
What dare I dream of, that thou canst not do,
  Outstripping my ten small steps with one stride?
I'll say then, here's a trial and a task—
Is it to bear?—if easy, I'll not ask—
  Though love fail, I can trust on in thy pride.

21

Pride?—when those eyes forestal the life behind
The death I have to go through!—when I find,
Now that I want thy help most, all of thee!
What did I fear? Thy love shall hold me fast
Until the little minute's sleep is past
And I wake saved.—And yet, it will not be!

AN EPISTLE

CONTAINING THE STRANGE MEDICAL EXPERIENCE OF KARSHISH THE ARAB PHYSICIAN

Karshish, the picker-up of learning's crumbs,
The not-incurious in God's handiwork
(This man's-flesh He hath admirably made,
Blown like a bubble, kneaded like a paste,
To coop up and keep down on earth a space
That puff of vapour from His mouth, man's soul)
—To Abid, all-sagacious in our art,
Breeder in me of what poor skill I boast,
Like me inquisitive how pricks and cracks
Befall the flesh through too much stress and strain,
Whereby the wily vapour fain would slip
Back and rejoin its source before the term,—
And aptest in contrivance, under God,
To baffle it by deftly stopping such:—
The vagrant Scholar to his Sage at home
Sends greeting (health and knowledge, fame with peace)
Three samples of true snake-stone—rarer still,
One of the other sort, the melon-shaped,
(But fitter, pounded fine, for charms than drugs)
And writeth now the twenty-second time.

My journeyings were brought to Jericho,
Thus I resume. Who studious in our art
Shall count a little labour unrepaid?
I have shed sweat enough, left flesh and bone

On many a flinty furlong of this land.
Also the country-side is all on fire
With rumours of a marching hitherward—
Some say Vespasian cometh, some, his son.
A black lynx snarled and pricked a tufted ear;
Lust of my blood inflamed his yellow balls:
I cried and threw my staff and he was gone.
Twice have the robbers stripped and beaten me,
And once a town declared me for a spy,
But at the end, I reach Jerusalem,
Since this poor covert where I pass the night,
This Bethany, lies scarce the distance thence
A man with plague-sores at the third degree
Runs till he drops down dead. Thou laughest here!
'Sooth, it elates me, thus reposed and safe,
To void the stuffing of my travel-scrip
And share with thee whatever Jewry yields.
A viscid choler is observable
In tertians, I was nearly bold to say,
And falling-sickness hath a happier cure
Than our school wots of: there's a spider here
Weaves no web, watches on the ledge of tombs,
Sprinkled with mottles on an ash-grey back;
Take five and drop them . . . but who knows his mind,
The Syrian run-a-gate I trust this to?
His service payeth me a sublimate
Blown up his nose to help the ailing eye.
Best wait: I reach Jerusalem at morn,
There set in order my experiences,
Gather what most deserves and give thee all—
Or I might add, Judea's gum-tragacanth
Scales off in purer flakes, shines clearer-grained,
Cracks 'twixt the pestle and the porphyry,
In fine exceeds our produce. Scalp-disease
Confounds me, crossing so with leprosy—
Thou hadst admired one sort I gained at Zoar—
But zeal outruns discretion. Here I end.

Yet stay: my Syrian blinketh gratefully,
Protesteth his devotion is my price—

Suppose I write what harms not, though he steal?
I half resolve to tell thee, yet I blush,
What set me off a-writing first of all.
An itch I had, a sting to write, a tang!
For, be it this town's barrenness—or else
The Man had something in the look of him—
His case has struck me far more than 'tis worth.
So, pardon if—(lest presently I lose
In the great press of novelty at hand
The care and pains this somehow stole from me)
I bid thee take the thing while fresh in mind,
Almost in sight—for, wilt thou have the truth?
The very man is gone from me but now,
Whose ailment is the subject of discourse.
Thus then, and let thy better wit help all.

'Tis but a case of mania—subinduced
By epilepsy, at the turning-point
Of trance prolonged unduly some three days,
When by the exhibition of some drug
Or spell, exorcisation, stroke of art
Unknown to me and which 'twere well to know,
The evil thing out-breaking all at once
Left the man whole and sound of body indeed,—
But, flinging, so to speak, life's gates too wide,
Making a clear house of it too suddenly,
The first conceit that entered pleased to write
Whatever it was minded on the wall
So plainly at that vantage, as it were,
(First come, first served) that nothing subsequent
Attaineth to erase the fancy-scrawls
Which the returned and new-established soul
Hath gotten now so thoroughly by heart
That henceforth she will read or these or none.
And first—the man's own firm conviction rests
That he was dead (in fact they buried him)
That he was dead and then restored to life
By a Nazarene physician of his tribe:
—'Sayeth, the same bade "Rise," and he did rise.
"Such cases are diurnal," thou wilt cry.

Not so this figment!—not, that such a fume,
Instead of giving way to time and health,
Should eat itself into the life of life,
As saffron tingeth flesh, blood, bones and all!
For see, how he takes up the after-life.
The man—it is one Lazarus a Jew,
Sanguine, proportioned, fifty years of age,
The body's habit wholly laudable,
As much, indeed, beyond the common health
As he were made and put aside to shew.
Think, could we penetrate by any drug
And bathe the wearied soul and worried flesh,
And bring it clear and fair, by three days sleep!
Whence has the man the balm that brightens all?
This grown man eyes the world now like a child.
Some elders of his tribe, I should premise,
Led in their friend, obedient as a sheep,
To bear my inquisition. While they spoke,
Now sharply, now with sorrow,—told the case,—
He listened not except I spoke to him,
But folded his two hands and let them talk,
Watching the flies that buzzed: and yet no fool.
And that's a sample how his years must go.
Look if a beggar, in fixed middle-life,
Should find a treasure, can he use the same
With straitened habits and with tastes starved small,
And take at once to his impoverished brain
The sudden element that changes things,
—That sets the undreamed-of rapture at his hand,
And puts the cheap old joy in the scorned dust?
Is he not such an one as moves to mirth—
Warily parsimonious, when's no need,
Wasteful as drunkenness at undue times?
All prudent counsel as to what befits
The golden mean, is lost on such an one.
The man's fantastic will is the man's law.
So here—we'll call the treasure knowledge, say—
Increased beyond the fleshly faculty—
Heaven opened to a soul while yet on earth,
Earth forced on a soul's use while seeing Heaven.

The man is witless of the size, the sum,
The value in proportion of all things,
Or whether it be little or be much.
Discourse to him of prodigious armaments
Assembled to besiege his city now,
And of the passing of a mule with gourds—
'Tis one! Then take it on the other side,
Speak of some trifling fact—he will gaze rapt
With stupor as its very littleness—
(Far as I see) as if in that indeed
He caught prodigious import, whole results;
And so will turn to us the bystanders
In ever the same stupor (note this point)
That we too see not with his opened eyes!
Wonder and doubt come wrongly into play,
Preposterously, at cross purposes.
Should his child sicken unto death,—why, look
For scarce abatement of his cheerfulness,
Or pretermission of his daily craft—
While a word, gesture, glance, from that same child
At play or in the school or laid asleep,
Will start him to an agony of fear,
Exasperation, just as like! demand
The reason why—"'tis but a word," object—
"A gesture"—he regards thee as our lord
Who lived there in the pyramid alone,
Looked at us, dost thou mind, when being young
We both would unadvisedly recite
Some charm's beginning, from that book of his,
Able to bid the sun throb wide and burst
All into stars, as suns grown old are wont.
Thou and the child have each a veil alike
Thrown o'er your heads from under which ye both
Stretch your blind hands and trifle with a match
Over a mine of Greek fire, did ye know!
He holds on firmly to some thread of life—
(It is the life to lead perforcedly)
Which runs across some vast distracting orb
Of glory on either side that meagre thread,
Which, conscious of, he must not enter yet—

The spiritual life around the earthly life!
The law of that is known to him as this—
His heart and brain move there, his feet stay here.
So is the man perplext with impulses
Sudden to start off crosswise, not straight on,
Proclaiming what is Right and Wrong across—
And not along—this black thread through the blaze—
"It should be " balked by "here it cannot be."
And oft the man's soul springs into his face
As if he saw again and heard again
His sage that bade him "Rise" and he did rise.
Something—a word, a tick of the blood within
Admonishes—then back he sinks at once
To ashes, that was very fire before,
In sedulous recurrence to his trade
Whereby he earneth him the daily bread—
And studiously the humbler for that pride,
Professedly the faultier that he knows
God's secret, while he holds the thread of life.
Indeed the especial marking of the man
Is prone submission to the Heavenly will—
Seeing it, what it is, and why it is.
'Sayeth, he will wait patient to the last
For that same death which will restore his being
To equilibrium, body loosening soul
Divorced even now by premature full growth:
He will live, nay, it pleaseth him to live
So long as God please, and just how God please.
He even seeketh not to please God more
(Which meaneth, otherwise) than as God please.
Hence I perceive not he affects to preach
The doctrine of his sect whate'er it be—
Make proselytes as madmen thirst to do.
How can he give his neighbour the real ground,
His own conviction? ardent as he is—
Call his great truth a lie, why still the old
"Be it as God please" reassureth him.
I probed the sore as thy disciple should—
"How, beast," said I, "this stolid carelessness
Sufficeth thee, when Rome is on her march

To stamp out like a little spark thy town,
Thy tribe, thy crazy tale and thee at once?"
He merely looked with his large eyes on me.
The man is apathetic, you deduce?
Contrariwise he loves both old and young,
Able and weak—affects the very brutes
And birds—how say I? flowers of the field—
As a wise workman recognises tools
In a master's workshop, loving what they make.
Thus is the man as harmless as a lamb:
Only impatient, let him do his best,
At ignorance and carelessness and sin——
An indignation which is promptly curbed.
As when in certain travels I have feigned
To be an ignoramus in our art
According to some preconceived design,
And happened to hear the land's practitioners
Steeped in conceit sublimed by ignorance,
Prattle fantastically on disease,
Its cause and cure—and I must hold my peace!

Thou wilt object—why have I not ere this
Sought out the sage himself, the Nazarene
Who wrought this cure, enquiring at the source,
Conferring with the frankness that befits?
Alas! it grieveth me, the learned leech
Perished in a tumult many years ago,
Accused,—our learning's fate,—of wizardry,
Rebellion, to the setting up a rule
And creed prodigious as described to me.
His death which happened when the earthquake fell
(Prefiguring, as soon appeared, the loss
To occult learning in our lord the sage
That lived there in the pyramid alone)
Was wrought by the mad people—that's their wont—
On vain recourse, as I conjecture it,
To his tried virtue, for miraculous help—
How could he stop the earthquake? That's their way!
The other imputations must be lies:
But take one—though I loathe to give it thee,

In mere respect to any good man's fame!
(And after all our patient Lazarus
Is stark mad—should we count on what he says?
Perhaps not—though in writing to a leech
'Tis well to keep back nothing of a case.)
This man so cured regards the curer then,
As—God forgive me—who but God himself,
Creator and Sustainer of the world,
That came and dwelt in flesh on it awhile!
—'Sayeth that such an One was born and lived,
Taught, healed the sick, broke bread at his own house,
Then died, with Lazarus by, for aught I know,
And yet was . . . what I said nor choose repeat,
And must have so avouched himself, in fact,
In hearing of this very Lazarus
Who saith—but why all this of what he saith?
Why write of trivial matters, things of price
Calling at every moment for remark?
I noticed on the margin of a pool
Blue-flowering borage, the Aleppo sort,
Aboundeth, very nitrous. It is strange!

Thy pardon for this long and tedious case,
Which, now that I review it, needs must seem
Unduly dwelt on, prolixly set forth.
Nor I myself discern in what is writ
Good cause for the peculiar interest
And awe indeed this man has touched me with.
Perhaps the journey's end, the weariness
Had wrought upon me first. I met him thus—
I crossed a ridge of short sharp broken hills
Like an old lion's cheek-teeth. Out there came
A moon made like a face with certain spots
Multiform, manifold, and menacing:
Then a wind rose behind me. So we met
In this old sleepy town at unaware,
The man and I. I send thee what is writ.
Regard it as a chance, a matter risked
To this ambiguous Syrian—he may lose,
Or steal, or give it thee with equal good.

Jerusalem's repose shall make amends
For time this letter wastes, thy time and mine,
Till when, once more thy pardon and farewell!

The very God! think, Abib; dost thou think?
So, the All-Great, were the All-Loving too—
So, through the thunder comes a human voice
Saying, "O heart I made, a heart beats here!
Face, my hands fashioned, see it in myself.
Thou hast no power nor may'st conceive of mine,
But love I gave thee, with Myself to love,
And thou must love me who have died for thee!"
The madman saith He said so: it is strange.

A SERENADE AT THE VILLA

1

THAT was I, you heard last night
When there rose no moon at all,
Nor, to pierce the strained and tight
Tent of heaven, a planet small:
Life was dead, and so was light.

2

Not a twinkle from the fly,
Not a glimmer from the worm.
When the crickets stopped their cry,
When the owls forbore a term,
You heard music; that was I.

3

Earth turned in her sleep with pain,
Sultrily suspired for proof:
In at heaven and out again,
Lightning!—where it broke the roof,
Bloodlike, some few drops of rain.

4

What they could my words expressed,
  O my love, my all, my one!
Singing helped the verses best,
  And when singing's best was done,
To my lute I left the rest.

5

So wore night; the east was grey,
  White the broad-faced hemlock flowers;
Soon would come another day;
  Ere its first of heavy hours
Found me, I had past away.

6

What became of all the hopes,
  Words and song and lute as well?
Say, this struck you—"When life gropes
  Feebly for the path where fell
Light last on the evening slopes,

7

"One friend in that path shall be
  To secure my steps from wrong;
One to count night day for me,
  Patient through the watches long,
Serving most with none to see."

8

Never say—as something bodes—
  "So the worst has yet a worse!
When life halts 'neath double loads,
  Better the task-master's curse
Than such music on the roads!

9

"When no moon succeeds the sun,
  Nor can pierce the midnight's tent
Any star, the smallest one,
  While some drops, where lightning went,
Show the final storm begun—

10

"When the fire-fly hides its spot,
When the garden-voices fail
In the darkness thick and hot,—
Shall another voice avail,
That shape be where those are not?

11

"Has some plague a longer lease
Proffering its help uncouth?
Can't one even die in peace?
As one shuts one's eyes on youth,
Is that face the last one sees?"

12

Oh, how dark your villa was,
Windows fast and obdurate!
How the garden grudged me grass
Where I stood—the iron gate
Ground its teeth to let me pass!

MY STAR

All that I know
Of a certain star,
Is, it can throw
(Like the angled spar)
Now a dart of red,
Now a dart of blue,
Till my friends have said
They would fain see, too,
My star that dartles the red and the blue!
Then it stops like a bird,—like a flower, hangs furled;
They must solace themselves with the Saturn above it.
What matter to me if their star is a world?
Mine has opened its soul to me; therefore I love it.

INSTANS TYRANNUS

I

Of the million or two, more or less,
I rule and possess,
One man, for some cause undefined,
Was least to my mind.

2

I struck him, he grovelled of course—
For, what was his force?
I pinned him to earth with my weight
And persistence of hate—
And he lay, would not moan, would not curse,
As if lots might be worse.

3

"Were the object less mean, would he stand
At the swing of my hand!
For obscurity helps him and blots
The hole where he squats."
So I set my five wits on the stretch
To inveigle the wretch.
All in vain! gold and jewels I threw,
Still he couched there perdue.
I tempted his blood and his flesh,
Hid in roses my mesh,
Choicest cates and the flagon's best spilth—
Still he kept to his filth!

4

Had he kith now or kin, were access
To his heart, if I press—
Just a son or a mother to seize—
No such booty as these!
Were it simply a friend to pursue
'Mid my million or two,
Who could pay me in person or pelf
What he owes me himself.

No! I could not but smile through my chafe—
For the fellow lay safe
As his mates do, the midge and the nit,
—Through minuteness, to wit.

5

Then a humor more great took its place
At the thought of his face,
The droop, the low cares of the mouth,
The trouble uncouth
'Twixt the brows, all that air one is fain
To put out of its pain—
And, no, I admonished myself,
"Is one mocked by an elf,
Is one baffled by toad or by rat?
The gravamen's in that!
How the lion, who crouches to suit
His back to my foot,
Would admire that I stand in debate!
But the Small is the Great
If it vexes you,—that is the thing!
Toad or rat vex the King?
Though I waste half my realm to unearth
Toad or rat, 'tis well worth!"

6

So I soberly laid my last plan
To extinguish the man.
Round his creep-hole,—with never a break
Ran my fires for his sake;
Over-head, did my thunders combine
With my under-ground mine:
Till I looked from my labor content
To enjoy the event.

7

When sudden . . . how think ye, the end?
Did I say "without friend?"
Say rather, from marge to blue marge
The whole sky grew his targe

With the sun's self for visible boss,
While an Arm ran across
Which the earth heaved beneath like a breast
Where the wretch was safe prest!
Do you see? just my vengeance complete,
The man sprang to his feet,
Stood erect, caught at God's skirts, and prayed!
—So, *I* was afraid!

"CHILDE ROLAND TO THE DARK TOWER CAME"

See Edgar's Song in "Lear"

I

My first thought was, he lied in every word,
That hoary cripple, with malicious eye
Askance to watch the working of his lie
On mine, and mouth scarce able to afford
Suppression of the glee that pursed and scored
Its edge at one more victim gained thereby.

2

What else should he be set for, with his staff?
What, save to waylay with his lies, ensnare
All travellers that might find him posted there,
And ask the road? I guessed what skull-like laugh
Would break, what crutch 'gin write my epitaph
For pastime in the dusty thoroughfare,

3

If at his counsel I should turn aside
Into that ominous tract which, all agree,
Hides the Dark Tower. Yet acquiescingly
I did turn as he pointed; neither pride
Nor hope rekindling at the end descried,
So much as gladness that some end should be.

4

For, what with my whole world-wide wandering,
  What with my search drawn out thro' years, my hope
  Dwindled into a ghost not fit to cope
With that obstreperous joy success would bring,—
I hardly tried now to rebuke the spring
  My heart made, finding failure in its scope.

5

As when a sick man very near to death
  Seems dead indeed, and feels begin and end
  The tears and takes the farewell of each friend,
And hears one bid the other go, draw breath
Freelier outside, ("since all is o'er," he saith,
  "And the blow fall'n no grieving can amend")

6

While some discuss if near the other graves
  Be room enough for this, and when a day
  Suits best for carrying the corpse away,
With care about the banners, scarves and staves,—
And still the man hears all, and only craves
  He may not shame such tender love and stay.

7

Thus, I had so long suffered in this quest,
  Heard failure prophesied so oft, been writ
  So many times among "The Band"—to wit,
The knights who to the Dark Tower's search addressed
Their steps—that just to fail as they, seemed best,
  And all the doubt was now—should I be fit.

8

So, quiet as despair, I turned from him,
  That hateful cripple, out of his highway
  Into the path he pointed. All the day
Had been a dreary one at best, and dim
Was settling to its close, yet shot one grim
  Red leer to see the plain catch its estray.

9

For mark! no sooner was I fairly found
  Pledged to the plain, after a pace or two,
  Than pausing to throw backward a last view
To the safe road, 'twas gone! grey plain all round!
Nothing but plain to the horizon's bound.
  I might go on; nought else remained to do.

10

So on I went. I think I never saw
  Such starved ignoble nature; nothing throve:
  For flowers—as well expect a cedar grove!
But cockle, spurge, according to their law
Might propagate their kind, with none to awe,
  You'd think: a burr had been a treasure-trove.

11

No! penury, inertness, and grimace,
  In some strange sort, were the land's portion. "See
  Or shut your eyes"—said Nature peevishly—
"It nothing skills: I cannot help my case:
The Judgment's fire alone can cure this place,
  Calcine its clods and set my prisoners free."

12

If there pushed any ragged thistle-stalk
  Above its mates, the head was chopped—the bents
  Were jealous else. What made those holes and rents
In the dock's harsh swarth leaves—bruised as to baulk
All hope of greenness? 'tis a brute must walk
  Pashing their life out, with a brute's intents.

13

As for the grass, it grew as scant as hair
  In leprosy—thin dry blades pricked the mud
  Which underneath looked kneaded up with blood.
One stiff blind horse, his every bone a-stare,
Stood stupified, however he came there—
  Thrust out past service from the devil's stud!

14

Alive? he might be dead for all I know,
With that red gaunt and colloped neck a-strain,
And shut eyes underneath the rusty mane.
Seldom went such grotesqueness with such woe:
I never saw a brute I hated so—
He must be wicked to deserve such pain.

15

I shut my eyes and turned them on my heart.
As a man calls for wine before he fights,
I asked one draught of earlier, happier sights
Ere fitly I could hope to play my part.
Think first, fight afterwards—the soldier's art:
One taste of the old times sets all to rights!

16

Not it! I fancied Cuthbert's reddening face
Beneath its garniture of curly gold,
Dear fellow, till I almost felt him fold
An arm in mine to fix me to the place,
That way he used. Alas! one night's disgrace!
Out went my heart's new fire and left it cold.

17

Giles, then, the soul of honour—there he stands
Frank as ten years ago when knighted first.
What honest men should dare (he said) he durst.
Good—but the scene shifts—faugh! what hangman's hands
Pin to his breast a parchment? his own bands
Read it. Poor traitor, spit upon and curst!

18

Better this present than a past like that—
Back therefore to my darkening path again.
No sound, no sight as far as eye could strain.
Will the night send a howlet or a bat?
I asked: when something on the dismal flat
Came to arrest my thoughts and change their train.

19

A sudden little river crossed my path
  As unexpected as a serpent comes.
  No sluggish tide congenial to the glooms—
This, as it frothed by, might have been a bath
For the fiend's glowing hoof—to see the wrath
  Of its black eddy bespate with flakes and spumes.

20

So petty yet so spiteful! all along,
  Low scrubby alders kneeled down over it;
  Drenched willows flung them headlong in a fit
Of mute despair, a suicidal throng:
The river which had done them all the wrong,
  Whate'er that was, rolled by, deterred no whit.

21

Which, while I forded,—good saints, how I feared
  To set my foot upon a dead man's cheek,
  Each step, or feel the spear I thrust to seek
For hollows, tangled in his hair or beard!
—It may have been a water-rat I speared,
  But, ugh! it sounded like a baby's shriek.

22

Glad was I when I reached the other bank.
  Now for a better country. Vain presage!
  Who were the strugglers, what war did they wage
Whose savage trample thus could pad the dank
Soil to a plash? toads in a poisoned tank,
  Or wild cats in a red-hot iron cage—

23

The fight must so have seemed in that fell cirque.
  What kept them there, with all the plain to choose?
  No foot-print leading to that horrid mews,
None out of it: mad brewage set to work
Their brains, no doubt, like galley-slaves the Turk
  Pits for his pastime, Christians against Jews.

24

And more than that—a furlong on—why, there!
What bad use was that engine for, that wheel,
Or brake, not wheel—that harrow fit to reel
Men's bodies out like silk? with all the air
Of Tophet's tool, on earth left unaware,
Or brought to sharpen its rusty teeth of steel.

25

Then came a bit of stubbed ground, once a wood,
Next a marsh, it would seem, and now mere earth
Desperate and done with; (so a fool finds mirth,
Makes a thing and then mars it, till his mood
Changes and off he goes!) within a rood
Bog, clay and rubble, sand and stark black dearth.

26

Now blotches rankling, coloured gay and grim,
Now patches where some leanness of the soil's
Broke into moss or substances like boils;
Then came some palsied oak, a cleft in him
Like a distorted mouth that splits its rim
Gaping at death, and dies while it recoils.

27

And just as far as ever from the end!
Nought in the distance but the evening, nought
To point my footstep further! At the thought,
A great black bird, Apollyon's bosom-friend,
Sailed past, nor beat his wide wing dragon-penned
That brushed my cap—perchance the guide I sought.

28

For looking up, aware I somehow grew,
'Spite of the dusk, the plain had given place
All round to mountains—with such name to grace
Mere ugly heights and heaps now stol'n in view.
How thus they had surprised me,—solve it, you!
How to get from them was no plainer case.

29

Yet half I seemed to recognise some trick
Of mischief happened to me, God knows when—
In a bad dream perhaps. Here ended, then,
Progress this way. When, in the very nick
Of giving up, one time more, came a click
As when a trap shuts—you're inside the den!

30

Burningly it came on me all at once,
This was the place! those two hills on the right
Crouched like two bulls locked horn in horn in fight
While to the left, a tall scalped mountain . . . Dunce,
Fool, to be dozing at the very nonce,
After a life spent training for the sight!

31

What in the midst lay but the Tower itself?
The round squat turret, blind as the fool's heart,
Built of brown stone, without a counterpart
In the whole world. The tempest's mocking elf
Points to the shipman thus the unseen shelf
He strikes on, only when the timbers start.

32

Not see? because of night perhaps?—Why, day
Came back again for that! before it left,
The dying sunset kindled through a cleft:
The hills, like giants at a hunting, lay—
Chin upon hand, to see the game at bay,—
"Now stab and end the creature—to the heft!"

33

Not hear? when noise was everywhere? it tolled
Increasing like a bell. Names in my ears,
Of all the lost adventurers my peers,—
How such a one was strong, and such was bold,
And such was fortunate, yet each of old
Lost, lost! one moment knelled the woe of years.

34

There they stood, ranged along the hill-sides—met
To view the last of me, a living frame
For one more picture! in a sheet of flame
I saw them and I knew them all. And yet
Dauntless the slug-horn to my lips I set
And blew. "*Childe Roland to the Dark Tower came.*"

RESPECTABILITY

I

Dear, had the world in its caprice
Deigned to proclaim "I know you both,
Have recognised your plighted troth,
Am sponsor for you—live in peace!"—
How many precious months and years
Of youth had passed, that speed so fast,
Before we found it out at last,
The world, and what it fears?

2

How much of priceless life were spent
With men that every virtue decks,
And women models of their sex,
Society's true ornament,—
Ere we dared wander, nights like this,
Thro' wind and rain, and watch the Seine,
And feel the Boulevart break again
To warmth and light and bliss?

3

I know! the world proscribes not love;
Allows my finger to caress
Your lip's contour and downiness,
Provided it supply a glove.
The world's good word!—the Institute!
Guizot receives Montalembert!
Eh? down the court three lampions flare—
Put forward your best foot!

A LIGHT WOMAN

1

So far as our story approaches the end,
Which do you pity the most of us three?—
My friend, or the mistress of my friend
With her wanton eyes, or me?

2

My friend was already too good to lose,
And seemed in the way of improvement yet,
When she crossed his path with her hunting-noose
And over him drew her net.

3

When I saw him tangled in her toils,
A shame, said I, if she adds just him
To her nine-and-ninety other spoils,
The hundredth, for a whim!

4

And before my friend be wholly hers,
How easy to prove to him, I said,
An eagle's the game her pride prefers,
Though she snaps at the wren instead!

5

So I gave her eyes my own eyes to take,
My hand sought hers as in earnest need,
And round she turned for my noble sake,
And gave me herself indeed.

6

The eagle am I, with my fame in the world,
The wren is he, with his maiden face.
—You look away and your lip is curled?
Patience, a moment's space!

7

For see—my friend goes shaking and white;
He eyes me as the basilisk:
I have turned, it appears, his day to night,
Eclipsing his sun's disc.

8

And I did it, he thinks, as a very thief:
"Though I love her—that he comprehends—
One should master one's passions, (love, in chief)
And be loyal to one's friends!"

9

And she,—she lies in my hand as tame
As a pear hung basking over a wall;
Just a touch to try and off it came;
'Tis mine,—can I let it fall?

10

With no mind to eat it, that's the worst!
Were it thrown in the road, would the case assist?
'Twas quenching a dozen blue-flies' thirst
When I gave its stalk a twist.

11

And I,—what I seem to my friend, you see—
What I soon shall seem to his love, you guess.
What I seem to myself, do you ask of me?
No hero, I confess.

12

'Tis an awkward thing to play with souls,
And matter enough to save one's own.
Yet think of my friend, and the burning coals
He played with for bits of stone!

13

One likes to show the truth for the truth;
That the woman was light is very true:
But suppose she says,—never mind that youth—
What wrong have I done to you?

14

Well, any how, here the story stays,
So far at least as I understand;
And, Robert Browning, you writer of plays,
Here's a subject made to your hand!

THE STATUE AND THE BUST

THERE's a palace in Florence, the world knows well,
And a statue watches it from the square,
And this story of both do the townsmen tell.

Ages ago, a lady there,
At the farthest window facing the east
Asked, "Who rides by with the royal air?"

The brides-maids' prattle around her ceased;
She leaned forth, one on either hand;
They saw how the blush of the bride increased—

They felt by its beats her heart expand—
As one at each ear and both in a breath
Whispered, "The Great-Duke Ferdinand."

That selfsame instant, underneath,
The Duke rode past in his idle way,
Empty and fine like a swordless sheath.

Gay he rode, with a friend as gay,
Till he threw his head back—"Who is she?"
—"A Bride the Riccardi brings home to-day."

Hair in heaps laid heavily
Over a pale brow spirit-pure—
Carved like the heart of the coal-black tree,

Crisped like a war-steed's encolure—
Which vainly sought to dissemble her eyes
Of the blackest black our eyes endure.

And lo, a blade for a knight's emprise
Filled the fine empty sheath of a man,—
The Duke grew straightway brave and wise.

He looked at her, as a lover can;
She looked at him, as one who awakes,—
The past was a sleep, and her life began.

As love so ordered for both their sakes,
A feast was held that selfsame night
In the pile which the mighty shadow makes.

(For Via Larga is three-parts light,
But the Palace overshadows one,
Because of a crime which may God requite!

To Florence and God the wrong was done,
Through the first republic's murder there
By Cosimo and his cursed son.)

The Duke (with the statue's face in the square)
Turned in the midst of his multitude
At the bright approach of the bridal pair.

Face to face the lovers stood
A single minute and no more,
While the bridegroom bent as a man subdued—

Bowed till his bonnet brushed the floor—
For the Duke on the lady a kiss conferred,
As the courtly custom was of yore.

In a minute can lovers exchange a word?
If a word did pass, which I do not think,
Only one out of the thousand heard.

That was the bridegroom. At day's brink
He and his bride were alone at last
In a bed-chamber by a taper's blink.

Calmly he said that her lot was cast,
That the door she had passed was shut on her
Till the final catafalk repassed.

The world meanwhile, its noise and stir,
Through a certain window facing the east
She might watch like a convent's chronicler.

Since passing the door might lead to a feast,
And a feast might lead to so much beside,
He, of many evils, chose the least.

"Freely I choose too," said the bride—
"Your window and its world suffice."
So replied the tongue, while the heart replied—

"If I spend the night with that devil twice,
May his window serve as my loop of hell
Whence a damned soul looks on Paradise!

"I fly to the Duke who loves me well,
Sit by his side and laugh at sorrow
Ere I count another ave-bell.

"'Tis only the coat of a page to borrow,
And tie my hair in a horse-boy's trim,
And I save my soul—but not to-morrow"—

(She checked herself and her eye grew dim)—
"My father tarries to bless my state:
I must keep it one day more for him.

"Is one day more so long to wait?
Moreover the Duke rides past, I know—
We shall see each other, sure as fate."

She turned on her side and slept. Just so!
So we resolve on a thing and sleep.
So did the lady, ages ago.

That night the Duke said, "Dear or cheap
As the cost of this cup of bliss may prove
To body or soul, I will drain it deep."

And on the morrow, bold with love,
He beckoned the bridegroom (close on call,
As his duty bade, by the Duke's alcove)

And smiled "'Twas a very funeral
Your lady will think, this feast of ours,—
A shame to efface, whate'er befall!

"What if we break from the Arno bowers,
And let Petraja, cool and green,
Cure last night's fault with this morning's flowers?"

The bridegroom, not a thought to be seen
On his steady brow and quiet mouth,
Said, "Too much favour for me so mean!

"Alas! my lady leaves the south.
Each wind that comes from the Apennine
Is a menace to her tender youth.

"No way exists, the wise opine,
If she quits her palace twice this year,
To avert the flower of life's decline."

Quoth the Duke, "A sage and a kindly fear.
Moreover Petraja is cold this spring—
Be our feast to-night as usual here!"

And then to himself—"Which night shall bring
Thy bride to her lover's embraces, fool—
Or I am the fool, and thou art his king!

"Yet my passion must wait a night, nor cool—
For to-night the Envoy arrives from France
Whose heart I unlock with thyself, my tool.

"I need thee still and might miss perchance.
To-day is not wholly lost, beside,
With its hope of my lady's countenance—

"For I ride—what should I do but ride?
And passing her palace, if I list,
May glance at its window—well betide!"

So said, so done: nor the lady missed
One ray that broke from the ardent brow,
Nor a curl of the lips where the spirit kissed.

Be sure that each renewed the vow,
No morrow's sun should arise and set
And leave them then as it left them now.

But next day passed, and next day yet,
With still fresh cause to wait one more
Ere each leaped over the parapet.

And still, as love's brief morning wore,
With a gentle start, half smile, half sigh,
They found love not as it seemed before.

They thought it would work infallibly,
But not in despite of heaven and earth—
The rose would blow when the storm passed by.

Meantime they could profit in winter's dearth
By winter's fruits that supplant the rose;
The world and its ways have a certain worth!

And to press a point while these oppose
Were a simple policy—best wait,
And lose no friends and gain no foes.

Meanwhile, worse fates than a lover's fate,
Who daily may ride and lean and look
Where his lady watches behind the grate!

And she—she watched the square like a book
Holding one picture and only one,
Which daily to find she undertook.

When the picture was reached the book was done,
And she turned from it all night to scheme
Of tearing it out for herself next sun.

Weeks grew months, years—gleam by gleam
The glory dropped from youth and love,
And both perceived they had dreamed a dream,

Which hovered as dreams do, still above,—
But who can take a dream for truth?
Oh, hide our eyes from the next remove!

One day as the lady saw her youth
Depart, and the silver thread that streaked
Her hair, and, worn by the serpent's tooth,

The brow so puckered, the chin so peaked,—
And wondered who the woman was,
So hollow-eyed and haggard-cheeked,

Fronting her silent in the glass—
"Summon here," she suddenly said,
"Before the rest of my old self pass,

"Him, the Carver, a hand to aid,
Who moulds the clay no love will change,
And fixes a beauty never to fade.

"Let Robbia's craft so apt and strange
Arrest the remains of young and fair,
And rivet them while the seasons range.

"Make me a face on the window there
Waiting as ever, mute the while,
My love to pass below in the square!

"And let me think that it may beguile
Dreary days which the dead must spend
Down in their darkness under the aisle—

"To say,—'What matters at the end?
I did no more while my heart was warm,
Than does that image, my pale-faced friend.'

"Where is the use of the lip's red charm,
The heaven of hair, the pride of the brow,
And the blood that blues the inside arm—

"Unless we turn, as the soul knows how,
The earthly gift to an end divine?
A lady of clay is as good, I trow."

But long ere Robbia's cornice, fine
With flowers and fruits which leaves enlace,
Was set where now is the empty shrine—

(With, leaning out of a bright blue space,
As a ghost might from a chink of sky,
The passionate pale lady's face—

Eyeing ever with earnest eye
And quick-turned neck at its breathless stretch,
Some one who ever passes by—)

The Duke sighed like the simplest wretch
In Florence, "So, my dream escapes!
Will its record stay?" And he bade them fetch

Some subtle fashioner of shapes—
"Can the soul, the will, die out of a man
Ere his body find the grave that gapes?

"John of Douay shall work my plan,
Mould me on horseback here aloft,
Alive—(the subtle artisan!)

"In the very square I cross so oft!
That men may admire, when future suns
Shall touch the eyes to a purpose soft,

"While the mouth and the brow are brave in bronze—
Admire and say, 'When he was alive,
How he would take his pleasure once!'

"And it shall go hard but I contrive
To listen meanwhile and laugh in my tomb
At indolence which aspires to strive."

So! while these wait the trump of doom,
How do their spirits pass, I wonder,
Nights and days in the narrow room?

Still, I suppose, they sit and ponder
What a gift life was, ages ago,
Six steps out of the chapel yonder.

Surely they see not God, I know,
Nor all that chivalry of His,
The soldier-saints who, row on row,

Burn upward each to his point of bliss—
Since, the end of life being manifest,
He had cut his way thro' the world to this.

I hear your reproach—"But delay was best,
For their end was a crime!"—Oh, a crime will do
As well, I reply, to serve for a test,

As a virtue golden through and through,
Sufficient to vindicate itself
And prove its worth at a moment's view.

Must a game be played for the sake of pelf?
Where a button goes, 'twere an epigram
To offer the stamp of the very Guelph.

The true has no value beyond the sham.
As well the counter as coin, I submit,
When your table's a hat, and your prize, a dram.

Stake your counter as boldly every whit,
Venture as truly, use the same skill,
Do your best, whether winning or losing it,

If you choose to play—is my principle!
Let a man contend to the uttermost
For his life's set prize, be it what it will!

The counter our lovers staked was lost
As surely as if it were lawful coin:
And the sin I impute to each frustrate ghost

Was, the unlit lamp and the ungirt loin,
Though the end in sight was a crime, I say.
You of the virtue, (we issue join)
How strive you? *De te, fabula!*

LOVE IN A LIFE

1

Room after room,
I hunt the house through
We inhabit together.
Heart, fear nothing, for, heart, thou shalt find her,
Next time, herself!—not the trouble behind her
Left in the curtain, the couch's perfume!
As she brushed it, the cornice-wreath blossomed anew,—
Yon looking-glass gleamed at the wave of her feather.

2

Yet the day wears,
And door succeeds door;
I try the fresh fortune—
Range the wide house from the wing to the centre.
Still the same chance! she goes out as I enter.

Spend my whole day in the quest,—who cares?
But 'tis twilight, you see,—with such suites to explore,
Such closets to search, such alcoves to importune!

LIFE IN A LOVE

Escape me?
Never—
Beloved!
While I am I, and you are you,
So long as the world contains us both,
Me the loving and you the loth,
While the one eludes, must the other pursue.
My life is a fault at last, I fear—
It seems too much like a fate, indeed!
Though I do my best I shall scarce succeed—
But what if I fail of my purpose here?
It is but to keep the nerves at strain,
To dry one's eyes and laugh at a fall,
And baffled, get up to begin again,—
So the chace takes up one's life, that's all.
While, look but once from your farthest bound,
At me so deep in the dust and dark,
No sooner the old hope drops to ground
Than a new one, straight to the self-same mark,
I shape me—
Ever
Removed!

THE LAST RIDE TOGETHER

I

I said—Then, dearest, since 'tis so,
Since now at length my fate I know,
Since nothing all my love avails,
Since all my life seemed meant for, fails,
Since this was written and needs must be—
My whole heart rises up to bless
Your name in pride and thankfulness!

Take back the hope you gave,—I claim
Only a memory of the same,
—And this beside, if you will not blame,
  Your leave for one more last ride with me.

2

My mistress bent that brow of hers,
Those deep dark eyes where pride demurs
When pity would be softening through,
Fixed me a breathing-while or two
  With life or death in the balance—Right!
The blood replenished me again:
My last thought was at least not vain.
I and my mistress, side by side
Shall be together, breathe and ride,
So one day more am I deified.
  Who knows but the world may end to-night?

3

Hush! if you saw some western cloud
All billowy-bosomed, over-bowed
By many benedictions—sun's
And moon's and evening-star's at once—
  And so, you, looking and loving best,
Conscious grew, your passion drew
Cloud, sunset, moonrise, star-shine too
Down on you, near and yet more near,
Till flesh must fade for heaven was here!—
Thus leant she and lingered—joy and fear!
  Thus lay she a moment on my breast.

4

Then we began to ride. My soul
Smoothed itself out, a long-cramped scroll
Freshening and fluttering in the wind.
Past hopes already lay behind.
  What need to strive with a life awry?
Had I said that, had I done this,
So might I gain, so might I miss.

Might she have loved me? just as well
She might have hated,—who can tell?
Where had I been now if the worst befell?
  And here we are riding, she and I.

5

Fail I alone, in words and deeds?
Why, all men strive and who succeeds?
We rode; it seemed my spirit flew,
Saw other regions, cities new,
  As the world rushed by on either side.
I thought, All labour, yet no less
Bear up beneath their unsuccess.
Look at the end of work, contrast
The petty Done the Undone vast,
This present of theirs with the hopeful past!
  I hoped she would love me. Here we ride.

6

What hand and brain went ever paired?
What heart alike conceived and dared?
What act proved all its thought had been?
What will but felt the fleshly screen?
  We ride and I see her bosom heave.
There's many a crown for who can reach.
Ten lines, a statesman's life in each!
The flag stuck on a heap of bones,
A soldier's doing! what atones?
They scratch his name on the Abbey-stones.
  My riding is better, by their leave.

7

What does it all mean, poet? well,
Your brain's beat into rhythm—you tell
What we felt only; you expressed
You hold things beautiful the best,
  And pace them in rhyme so, side by side.
'Tis something, nay 'tis much—but then,
Have you yourself what's best for men?

Are you—poor, sick, old ere your time—
Nearer one whit your own sublime
Than we who never have turned a rhyme?
 Sing, riding's a joy! For me, I ride.

8

And you, great sculptor—so you gave
A score of years to art, her slave,
And that's your Venus—whence we turn
To yonder girl that fords the burn!
 You acquiesce and shall I repine?
What, man of music, you, grown grey
With notes and nothing else to say,
Is this your sole praise from a friend,
"Greatly his opera's strains intend,
But in music we know how fashions end!"
 I gave my youth—but we ride, in fine.

9

Who knows what's fit for us? Had fate
Proposed bliss here should sublimate
My being; had I signed the bond—
Still one must lead some life beyond,
 —Have a bliss to die with, dim-descried.
This foot once planted on the goal,
This glory-garland round my soul,
Could I descry such? Try and test!
I sink back shuddering from the quest—
Earth being so good, would Heaven seem best?
 Now, Heaven and she are beyond this ride.

10

And yet—she has not spoke so long!
What if Heaven be, that, fair and strong
At life's best, with our eyes upturned
Whither life's flower is first discerned,
 We, fixed so, ever should so abide?
What if we still ride on, we two,
With life for ever old yet new,

Changed not in kind but in degree,
The instant made eternity,—
And Heaven just prove that I and she
  Ride, ride together, for ever ride?

THE PATRIOT

AN OLD STORY

1

It was roses, roses, all the way,
  With myrtle mixed in my path like mad.
The house-roofs seemed to heave and sway,
  The church-spires flamed, such flags they had,
A year ago on this very day!

2

The air broke into a mist with bells,
  The old walls rocked with the crowds and cries.
Had I said, "Good folks, mere noise repels—
  But give me your sun from yonder skies!"
They had answered, "And afterward, what else?"

3

Alack, it was I who leaped at the sun,
  To give it my loving friends to keep.
Nought man could do, have I left undone
  And you see my harvest, what I reap
This very day, now a year is run.

4

There's nobody on the house-tops now—
  Just a palsied few at the windows set—
For the best of the sight is, all allow,
  At the Shambles' Gate—or, better yet,
By the very scaffold's foot, I trow.

5

I go in the rain, and, more than needs,
  A rope cuts both my wrists behind,
And I think, by the feel, my forehead bleeds,
  For they fling, whoever has a mind,
Stones at me for my year's misdeeds.

6

Thus I entered Brescia, and thus I go!
  In such triumphs, people have dropped down dead.
"Thou, paid by the World,—what dost thou owe
  Me?" God might have questioned: but now instead
'Tis God shall requite! I am safer so.

BISHOP BLOUGRAM'S APOLOGY

  No more wine? then we'll push back chairs and talk.
A final glass for me, tho': cool, i'faith!
We ought to have our Abbey back, you see.
It's different, preaching in basilicas,
And doing duty in some masterpiece
Like this of brother Pugin's, bless his heart!
I doubt if they're half baked, those chalk rosettes,
Ciphers and stucco-twiddlings everywhere;
It's just like breathing in a lime-kiln: eh?
These hot long ceremonies of our church
Cost us a little—oh, they pay the price,
You take me—amply pay it! Now, we'll talk.

  So, you despise me, Mr. Gigadibs.
No deprecation,—nay, I beg you, sir!
Beside 'tis our engagement: don't you know,
I promised, if you'd watch a dinner out,
We'd see truth dawn together?—truth that peeps
Over the glass's edge when dinner's done,
And body gets its sop and holds its noise
And leaves soul free a little. Now's the time—
'Tis break of day! You do despise me then.
And if I say, "despise me,"—never fear—

I know you do not in a certain sense—
Not in my arm-chair for example: here,
I well imagine you respect my place
(Status, *entourage*, worldly circumstance)
Quite to its value—very much indeed
—Are up to the protesting eyes of you
In pride at being seated here for once—
You'll turn it to such capital account!
When somebody, through years and years to come,
Hints of the bishop,—names me—that's enough—
"Blougram? I knew him"—(into it you slide)
"Dined with him once, a Corpus Christi Day,
All alone, we two—he's a clever man—
And after dinner,—why, the wine you know,—
Oh, there was wine, and good!—what with the wine . . .
'Faith, we began upon all sorts of talk!
He's no bad fellow, Blougram—he had seen
Something of mine he relished—some review—
He's quite above their humbug in his heart,
Half-said as much, indeed—the thing's his trade—
I warrant, Blougram's sceptical at times—
How otherwise? I liked him, I confess!"
Che ch'é, my dear sir, as we say at Rome,
Don't you protest now! It's fair give and take;
You have had your turn and spoken your home-truths—
The hand's mine now, and here you follow suit.

Thus much conceded, still the first fact stays—
You do despise me; your ideal of life
Is not the bishop's—you would not be I—
You would like better to be Goethe, now,
Or Buonaparte—or, bless me, lower still,
Count D'Orsay,—so you did what you preferred,
Spoke as you thought, and, as you cannot help,
Believed or disbelieved, no matter what,
So long as on that point, whate'er it was,
You loosed your mind, were whole and sole yourself.
—That, my ideal never can include,
Upon that element of truth and worth
Never be based! for say they make me Pope

(They can't—suppose it for our argument)
Why, there I'm at my tether's end—I've reached
My height, and not a height which pleases you.
An unbelieving Pope won't do, you say.
It's like those eerie stories nurses tell,
Of how some actor played Death on a stage
With pasteboard crown, sham orb, and tinselled dart,
And called himself the monarch of the world,
Then going in the tire-room afterward
Because the play was done, to shift himself,
Got touched upon the sleeve familiarly
The moment he had shut the closet door
By Death himself. Thus God might touch a Pope
At unawares, ask what his baubles mean,
And whose part he presumed to play just now?
Best be yourself, imperial, plain and true!

So, drawing comfortable breath again,
You weigh and find whatever more or less
I boast of my ideal realised
Is nothing in the balance when opposed
To your ideal, your grand simple life,
Of which you will not realise one jot.
I am much, you are nothing; you would be all,
I would be merely much—you beat me there.

No, friend, you do not beat me,—hearken why.
The common problem, yours, mine, every one's,
Is not to fancy what were fair in life
Provided it could be,—but, finding first
What may be, then find how to make it fair
Up to our means—a very different thing!
No abstract intellectual plan of life
Quite irrespective of life's plainest laws,
But one, a man, who is man and nothing more,
May lead within a world which (by your leave)
Is Rome or London—not Fool's-paradise.
Embellish Rome, idealise away,
Make Paradise of London if you can,
You're welcome, nay, you're wise.

A simile!
We mortals cross the ocean of this world
Each in his average cabin of a life—
The best's not big, the worst yields elbow-room.
Now for our six months' voyage—how prepare?
You come on shipboard with a landsman's list
Of things he calls convenient—so they are!
An India screen is pretty furniture,
A piano-forte is a fine resource,
All Balzac's novels occupy one shelf,
The new edition fifty volumes long;
And little Greek books with the funny type
They get up well at Leipsic fill the next—
Go on! slabbed marble, what a bath it makes!
And Parma's pride, the Jerome, let us add!
'Twere pleasant could Correggio's fleeting glow
Hang full in face of one where'er one roams,
Since he more than the others brings with him
Italy's self,—the marvellous Modenese!
Yet 'twas not on your list before, perhaps.
—Alas! friend, here's the agent . . . is't the name?
The captain, or whoever's master here—
You see him screw his face up; what's his cry
Ere you set foot on shipboard? "Six feet square!"
If you won't understand what six feet mean,
Compute and purchase stores accordingly—
And if in pique because he overhauls
Your Jerome, piano and bath, you come on board
Bare—why you cut a figure at the first
While sympathetic landsmen see you off;
Not afterwards, when, long ere half seas o'er,
You peep up from your utterly naked boards
Into some snug and well-appointed berth
Like mine, for instance (try the cooler jug—
Put back the other, but don't jog the ice)
And mortified you mutter "Well and good—
He sits enjoying his sea-furniture—
'Tis stout and proper, and there's store of it,
Though I've the better notion, all agree,
Of fitting rooms up! hang the carpenter,

Neat ship-shape fixings and contrivances—
I would have brought my Jerome, frame and all!"
And meantime you bring nothing: never mind—
You've proved your artist-nature: what you don't,
You might bring, so despise me, as I say.

Now come, let's backward to the starting place.
See my way: we're two college friends, suppose—
Prepare together for our voyage, then,
Each note and check the other in his work,—
Here's mine, a bishop's outfit; criticise!
What's wrong? why won't you be a bishop too?

Why, first, you don't believe, you don't and can't,
(Not statedly, that is, and fixedly
And absolutely and exclusively)
In any revelation called divine.
No dogmas nail your faith—and what remains
But say so, like the honest man you are?
First, therefore, overhaul theology!
Nay, I too, not a fool, you please to think,
Must find believing every whit as hard,
And if I do not frankly say as much,
The ugly consequence is clear enough.

Now, wait, my friend; well, I do not believe—
If you'll accept no faith that is not fixed,
Absolute and exclusive, as you say.
(You're wrong—I mean to prove it in due time)
Meanwhile, I know where difficulties lie
I could not, cannot solve, nor ever shall,
So give up hope accordingly to solve—
(To you, and over the wine). Our dogmas then
With both of us, tho' in unlike degree,
Missing full credence—overboard with them!
I mean to meet you on your own premise—
Good, there go mine in company with yours!

And now what are we? unbelievers both,
Calm and complete, determinately fixed

To-day, to-morrow, and for ever, pray?
You'll guarantee me that? Not so, I think.
In no-wise! all we've gained is, that belief,
As unbelief before, shakes us by fits,
Confounds us like its predecessor. Where's
The gain? how can we guard our unbelief,
Make it bear fruit to us?—the problem here.
Just when we are safest, there's a sunset-touch,
A fancy from a flower-bell, some one's death,
A chorus-ending from Euripides,—
And that's enough for fifty hopes and fears
As old and new at once as Nature's self,
To rap and knock and enter in our soul,
Take hands and dance there, a fantastic ring,
Round the ancient idol, on his base again,—
The grand Perhaps! we look on helplessly,—
There the old misgivings, crooked questions are—
This good God,—what he could do, if he would,
Would, if he could—then must have done long since:
If so, when, where, and how? some way must be,—
Once feel about, and soon or late you hit
Some sense, in which it might be, after all.
Why not, "The Way, the Truth, the Life?"

—That way
Over the mountain, which who stands upon
Is apt to doubt if it's indeed a road;
While if he views it from the waste itself,
Up goes the line there, plain from base to brow,
Not vague, mistakeable! what's a break or two
Seen from the unbroken desert either side?
And then (to bring in fresh philosophy)
What if the breaks themselves should prove at last
The most consummate of contrivances
To train a man's eye, teach him what is faith,—
And so we stumble at truth's very test?
What have we gained then by our unbelief
But a life of doubt diversified by faith,
For one of faith diversified by doubt.
We called the chess-board white,—we call it black.

"Well," you rejoin, "the end's no worse, at least,
We've reason for both colours on the board.
Why not confess, then, where I drop the faith
And you the doubt, that I'm as right as you?"

Because, friend, in the next place, this being so,
And both things even,—faith and unbelief
Left to a man's choice,—we'll proceed a step,
Returning to our image, which I like.

A man's choice, yes—but a cabin-passenger's—
The man made for the special life of the world—
Do you forget him? I remember though!
Consult our ship's conditions and you find
One and but one choice suitable to all,
The choice that you unluckily prefer
Turning things topsy-turvy—they or it
Going to the ground. Belief or unbelief
Bears upon life, determines its whole course,
Begins at its beginning. See the world
Such as it is,—you made it not, nor I;
I mean to take it as it is,—and you
Not so you'll take it,—though you get nought else.
I know the special kind of life I like,
What suits the most my idiosyncrasy,
Brings out the best of me and bears me fruit
In power, peace, pleasantness, and length of days.
I find that positive belief does this
For me, and unbelief, no whit of this.
—For you, it does, however—that we'll try!
'Tis clear, I cannot lead my life, at least
Induce the world to let me peaceably,
Without declaring at the outset, "Friends,
I absolutely and peremptorily
Believe!"—I say faith is my waking life.
One sleeps, indeed, and dreams at intervals,
We know, but waking's the main point with us,
And my provision's for life's waking part.
Accordingly, I use heart, head and hands
All day, I build, scheme, study and make friends;

And when night overtakes me, down I lie,
Sleep, dream a little, and get done with it,
The sooner the better, to begin afresh.
What's midnight's doubt before the dayspring's faith?
You, the philosopher, that disbelieve,
That recognise the night, give dreams their weight—
To be consistent you should keep your bed,
Abstain from healthy acts that prove you a man,
For fear you drowse perhaps at unawares!
And certainly at night you'll sleep and dream,
Live through the day and bustle as you please.
And so you live to sleep as I to wake,
To unbelieve as I to still believe?
Well, and the common sense of the world calls you
Bed-ridden,—and its good things come to me.
Its estimation, which is half the fight,
That's the first cabin-comfort I secure—
The next . . . but you perceive with half an eye!
Come, come, it's best believing, if we can—
You can't but own that.

Next, concede again—
If once we choose belief, on all accounts
We can't be too decisive in our faith,
Conclusive and exclusive in its terms,
To suit the world which gives us the good things.
In every man's career are certain points
Whereon he dares not be indifferent;
The world detects him clearly, if he is,
As baffled at the game, and losing life.
He may care little or he may care much
For riches, honour, pleasure, work, repose,
Since various theories of life and life's
Success are extant which might easily
Comport with either estimate of these,
And whoso chooses wealth or poverty,
Labour or quiet, is not judged a fool
Because his fellows would choose otherwise.
We let him choose upon his own account
So long as he's consistent with his choice.

But certain points, left wholly to himself,
When once a man has arbitrated on,
We say he must succeed there or go hang.
Thus, he should wed the woman he loves most
Or needs most, whatsoe'er the love or need—
For he can't wed twice. Then, he must avouch
Or follow, at the least, sufficiently,
The form of faith his conscience holds the best,
Whate'er the process of conviction was.
For nothing can compensate his mistake
On such a point, the man himself being judge—
He cannot wed twice, nor twice lose his soul.

Well now—there's one great form of Christian faith
I happened to be born in—which to teach
Was given me as I grew up, on all hands,
As best and readiest means of living by;
The same on examination being proved
The most pronounced moreover, fixed, precise
And absolute form of faith in the whole world—
Accordingly, most potent of all forms
For working on the world. Observe, my friend,
Such as you know me, I am free to say,
In these hard latter days which hamper one,
Myself, by no immoderate exercise
Of intellect and learning, and the tact
To let external forces work for me,
Bid the street's stones be bread and they are bread,
Bid Peter's creed, or, rather, Hildebrand's,
Exalt me o'er my fellows in the world
And make my life an ease and joy and pride,
It does so,—which for me's a great point gained,
Who have a soul and body that exact
A comfortable care in many ways.
There's power in me and will to dominate
Which I must exercise, they hurt me else:
In many ways I need mankind's respect,
Obedience, and the love that's born of fear:
While at the same time, there's a taste I have,
A toy of soul, a titillating thing,

Refuses to digest these dainties crude.
The naked life is gross till clothed upon:
I must take what men offer, with a grace
As though I would not, could I help it, take!
A uniform to wear though over-rich—
Something imposed on me, no choice of mine;
No fancy-dress worn for pure fashion's sake
And despicable therefore! now men kneel
And kiss my hand—of course the Church's hand.
Thus I am made, thus life is best for me,
And thus that it should be I have procured;
And thus it could not be another way,
I venture to imagine.

You'll reply—
So far my choice, no doubt, is a success;
But were I made of better elements,
With nobler instincts, purer tastes, like you,
I hardly would account the thing success
Though it do all for me I say.

But, friend,
We speak of what is—not of what might be,
And how 'twere better if 'twere otherwise.
I am the man you see here plain enough—
Grant I'm a beast, why beasts must lead beasts' lives!
Suppose I own at once to tail and claws—
The tailless man exceeds me; but being tailed
I'll lash out lion-fashion, and leave apes
To dock their stump and dress their haunches up.
My business is not to remake myself,
But make the absolute best of what God made.
Or—our first simile—though you proved me doomed
To a viler berth still, to the steerage-hole,
The sheep-pen or the pig-stye, I should strive
To make what use of each were possible;
And as this cabin gets upholstery,
That hutch should rustle with sufficient straw.

But, friend, I don't acknowledge quite so fast
I fail of all your manhood's lofty tastes

Enumerated so complacently,
On the mere ground that you forsooth can find
In this particular life I choose to lead
No fit provision for them. Can you not?
Say you, my fault is I address myself
To grosser estimators than I need,
And that's no way of holding up the soul—
Which, nobler, needs men's praise perhaps, yet knows
One wise man's verdict outweighs all the fools',—
Would like the two, but, forced to choose, takes that?
I pine among my million imbeciles
(You think) aware some dozen men of sense
Eye me and know me, whether I believe
In the last winking Virgin, as I vow,
And am a fool, or disbelieve in her
And am a knave,—approve in neither case,
Withhold their voices though I look their way:
Like Verdi when, at his worst opera's end
(The thing they gave at Florence,—what's its name?)
While the mad houseful's plaudits near out-bang
His orchestra of salt-box, tongs and bones,
He looks through all the roaring and the wreaths
Where sits Rossini patient in his stall.

Nay, friend, I meet you with an answer here—
For even your prime men who appraise their kind
Are men still, catch a thing within a thing,
See more in a truth than the truth's simple self,
Confuse themselves. You see lads walk the street
Sixty the minute; what's to note in that?
You see one lad o'erstride a chimney-stack;
Him you must watch—he's sure to fall, yet stands!
Our interest's on the dangerous edge of things.
The honest thief, the tender murderer,
The superstitious atheist, demireps
That love and save their souls in new French books—
We watch while these in equilibrium keep
The giddy line midway: one step aside,
They're classed and done with. I, then, keep the line
Before your sages,—just the men to shrink

From the gross weights, coarse scales, and labels broad
You offer their refinement. Fool or knave?
Why needs a bishop be a fool or knave
When there's a thousand diamond weights between?
So I enlist them. Your picked Twelve, you'll find,
Profess themselves indignant, scandalised
At thus being held unable to explain
How a superior man who disbelieves
May not believe as well: that's Schelling's way!
It's through my coming in the tail of time,
Nicking the minute with a happy tact.
Had I been born three hundred years ago
They'd say, "What's strange? Blougram of course
    believes;"
And, seventy years since, "disbelieves of course."
But now, "He may believe; and yet, and yet
How can he?"—All eyes turn with interest.
Whereas, step off the line on either side—
You, for example, clever to a fault,
The rough and ready man that write apace,
Read somewhat seldomer, think perhaps even less—
You disbelieve! Who wonders and who cares?
Lord So-and-So—his coat bedropt with wax,
All Peter's chains about his waist, his back
Brave with the needlework of Noodledom,
Believes! Again, who wonders and who cares?
But I, the man of sense and learning too,
The able to think yet act, the this, the that,
I, to believe at this late time of day!
Enough; you see, I need not fear contempt.

—Except it's yours! admire me as these may,
You don't. But what at least do you admire?
Present your own perfections, your ideal,
Your pattern man for a minute—oh, make haste!
Is it Napoleon you would have us grow?
Concede the means; allow his head and hand,
(A large concession, clever as you are)
Good!—In our common primal element
Of unbelief (we can't believe, you know—

We're still at that admission, recollect)
Where do you find—apart from, towering-o'er
The secondary temporary aims
Which satisfy the gross tastes you despise—
Where do you find his star?—his crazy trust
God knows through what or in what? it's alive
And shines and leads him and that's all we want.
Have we aught in our sober night shall point
Such ends as his were, and direct the means
Of working out our purpose straight as his,
Nor bring a moment's trouble on success
With after-care to justify the same?
—Be a Napoleon and yet disbelieve!
Why, the man's mad, friend, take his light away.
What's the vague good of the world for which you'd
dare
With comfort to yourself blow millions up?
We neither of us see it! we do see
The blown-up millions—spatter of their brains
And writhing of their bowels and so forth,
In that bewildering entanglement
Of horrible eventualities
Past calculation to the end of time!
Can I mistake for some clear word of God
(Which were my ample warrant for it all)
His puff of hazy instincts, idle talk,
"The state, that's I," quack-nonsense about kings,
And (when one beats the man to his last hold)
The vague idea of setting things to rights,
Policing people efficaciously,
More to their profit, most of all to his own;
The whole to end that dismallest of ends
By an Austrian marriage, cant to us the church,
And resurrection of the old *régime*.
Would I, who hope to live a dozen years,
Fight Austerlitz for reasons such and such?
No: for, concede me but the merest chance
Doubt may be wrong—there's judgment, life to come!
With just that chance, I dare not. Doubt proves right?
This present life is all? you offer me

Its dozen noisy years with not a chance
That wedding an Arch-Duchess, wearing lace,
And getting called by divers new-coined names,
Will drive off ugly thoughts and let me dine,
Sleep, read and chat in quiet as I like!
Therefore, I will not.

Take another case;
Fit up the cabin yet another way.
What say you to the poet's? shall we write
Hamlets, Othellos—make the world our own,
Without a risk to run of either sort?
I can't!—to put the strongest reason first.
"But try," you urge, "the trying shall suffice:
The aim, if reached or not, makes great the life.
Try to be Shakspeare, leave the rest to fate!"
Spare my self knowledge—there's no fooling me!
If I prefer remaining my poor self,
I say so not in self-dispraise but praise.
If I'm a Shakspeare, let the well alone—
Why should I try to be what now I am?
If I'm no Shakspeare, as too probable,—
His power and consciousness and self-delight
And all we want in common, shall I find—
Trying for ever? while on points of taste
Wherewith, to speak it humbly, he and I
Are dowered alike—I'll ask you, I or he,
Which in our two lives realises most?
Much, he imagined—somewhat, I possess.
He had the imagination; stick to that!
Let him say "In the face of my soul's works
Your world is worthless and I touch it not
Lest I should wrong them"—I withdraw my plea.
But does he say so? look upon his life!
Himself, who only can, gives judgment there.
He leaves his towers and gorgeous palaces
To build the trimmest house in Stratford town;
Saves money, spends it, owns the worth of things,
Giulio Romano's pictures, Dowland's lute;
Enjoys a show, respects the puppets, too,

And none more, had he seen its entry once,
Than "Pandulph, of fair Milan cardinal."
Why then should I who play that personage,
The very Pandulph Shakspeare's fancy made,
Be told that had the poet chanced to start
From where I stand now (some degree like mine
Being just the goal he ran his race to reach)
He would have run the whole race back, forsooth,
And left being Pandulph, to begin write plays?
Ah, the earth's best can be but the earth's best!
Did Shakspeare live, he could but sit at home
And get himself in dreams the Vatican,
Greek busts, Venetian paintings, Roman walls,
And English books, none equal to his own,
Which I read, bound in gold, (he never did).
—Terni and Naples' bay and Gothard's top—
Eh, friend? I could not fancy one of these—
But, as I pour this claret, there they are—
I've gained them—crossed St. Gothard last July
With ten mules to the carriage and a bed
Slung inside; is my hap the worse for that?
We want the same things, Shakspeare and myself,
And what I want, I have: he, gifted more,
Could fancy he too had it when he liked,
But not so thoroughly that if fate allowed
He would not have it also in my sense.
We play one game. I send the ball aloft
No less adroitly that of fifty strokes
Scarce five go o'er the wall so wide and high
Which sends them back to me: I wish and get.
He struck balls higher and with better skill,
But at a poor fence level with his head,
And hit—his Stratford house, a coat of arms,
Successful dealings in his grain and wool,—
While I receive heaven's incense in my nose
And style myself the cousin of Queen Bess.
Ask him, if this life's all, who wins the game?

Believe—and our whole argument breaks up.
Enthusiasm's the best thing, I repeat;

Only, we can't command it; fire and life
Are all, dead matter's nothing, we agree:
And be it a mad dream or God's very breath,
The fact's the same,—belief's fire once in us,
Makes of all else mere stuff to show itself.
We penetrate our life with such a glow
As fire lends wood and iron—this turns steel,
That burns to ash—all's one, fire proves its power
For good or ill, since men call flare success.
But paint a fire, it will not therefore burn.
Light one in me, I'll find it food enough!
Why, to be Luther—that's a life to lead,
Incomparably better than my own.
He comes, reclaims God's earth for God, he says,
Sets up God's rule again by simple means,
Re-opens a shut book, and all is done.
He flared out in the flaring of mankind;
Such Luther's luck was—how shall such be mine?
If he succeeded, nothing's left to do:
And if he did not altogether—well,
Strauss is the next advance. All Strauss should be
I might be also. But to what result?
He looks upon no future: Luther did.
What can I gain on the denying side?
Ice makes no conflagration. State the facts,
Read the text right, emancipate the world—
The emancipated world enjoys itself
With scarce a thank-you—Blougram told it first
It could not owe a farthing,—not to him
More than St. Paul! 'twould press its pay, you think?
Then add there's still that plaguey hundredth chance
Strauss may be wrong. And so a risk is run—
For what gain? not for Luther's, who secured
A real heaven in his heart throughout his life,
Supposing death a little altered things!

"Ay, but since really I lack faith," you cry,
"I run the same risk really on all sides,
In cool indifference as bold unbelief.
As well be Strauss as swing 'twixt Paul and him.

It's not worth having, such imperfect faith,
Nor more available to do faith's work
Than unbelief like yours. Whole faith, or none!"

Softly, my friend! I must dispute that point.
Once own the use of faith, I'll find you faith.
We're back on Christian ground. You call for faith:
I show you doubt, to prove that faith exists.
The more of doubt, the stronger faith, I say,
If faith o'ercomes doubt. How I know it does?
By life and man's free will, God gave for that!
To mould life as we choose it, shows our choice:
That's our one act, the previous work's His own.
You criticise the soil? it reared this tree—
This broad life and whatever fruit it bears!
What matter though I doubt at every pore,
Head-doubts, heart-doubts, doubts at my fingers' ends,
Doubts in the trivial work of every day,
Doubts at the very bases of my soul
In the grand moments when she probes herself—
If finally I have a life to show,
The thing I did, brought out in evidence
Against the thing done to me underground
By Hell and all its brood, for aught I know?
I say, whence sprang this? shows it faith or doubt?
All's doubt in me; where's break of faith in this?
It is the idea, the feeling and the love
God means mankind should strive for and show forth,
Whatever be the process to that end,—
And not historic knowledge, logic sound,
And metaphysical acumen, sure!
"What think ye of Christ," friend? when all's done and said,
You like this Christianity or not?
It may be false, but will you wish it true?
Has it your vote to be so if it can?
Trust you an instinct silenced long ago
That will break silence and enjoin you love
What mortified philosophy is hoarse,
And all in vain, with bidding you despise?

If you desire faith—then you've faith enough.
What else seeks God—nay, what else seek ourselves?
You form a notion of me, we'll suppose,
On hearsay; it's a favourable one:
"But still," (you add) "there was no such good man,
Because of contradictions in the facts.
One proves, for instance, he was born in Rome,
This Blougram—yet throughout the tales of him
I see he figures as an Englishman."
Well, the two things are reconcileable.
But would I rather you discovered that,
Subjoining—"Still, what matter though they be?
Blougram concerns me nought, born here or there."

Pure faith indeed—you know not what you ask!
Naked belief in God the Omnipotent,
Omniscient, Omnipresent, sears too much
The sense of conscious creatures to be borne.
It were the seeing him, no flesh shall dare.
Some think, Creation's meant to show him forth:
I say, it's meant to hide him all it can,
And that's what all the blessed Evil's for.
Its use in time is to environ us,
Our breath, our drop of dew, with shield enough
Against that sight till we can bear its stress.
Under a vertical sun, the exposed brain
And lidless eye and disemprisoned heart
Less certainly would wither up at once
Than mind, confronted with the truth of Him.
But time and earth case-harden us to live;
The feeblest sense is trusted most; the child
Feels God a moment, ichors o'er the place,
Plays on and grows to be a man like us.
With me, faith means perpetual unbelief
Kept quiet like the snake 'neath Michael's foot
Who stands calm just because he feels it writhe.
Or, if that's too ambitious,—here's my box—
I need the excitation of a pinch
Threatening the torpor of the inside-nose
Nigh on the imminent sneeze that never comes.

"Leave it in peace" advise the simple folk—
Make it aware of peace by itching-fits,
Say I—let doubt occasion still more faith!

You'll say, once all believed, man, woman, child,
In that dear middle-age these noodles praise.
How you'd exult if I could put you back
Six hundred years, blot out cosmogony,
Geology, ethnology, what not,
(Greek endings with the little passing-bell
That signifies some faith's about to die)
And set you square with Genesis again,—
When such a traveller told you his last news,
He saw the ark a-top of Ararat
But did not climb there since 'twas getting dusk
And robber-bands infest the mountain's foot!
How should you feel, I ask, in such an age,
How act? As other people felt and did;
With soul more blank than this decanter's knob,
Believe—and yet lie, kill, rob, fornicate
Full in belief's face, like the beast you'd be!

No, when the fight begins within himself,
A man's worth something. God stoops o'er his head,
Satan looks up between his feet—both tug—
He's left, himself, in the middle: the soul wakes
And grows. Prolong that battle through his life!
Never leave growing till the life to come!
Here, we've got callous to the Virgin's winks
That used to puzzle people wholesomely—
Men have outgrown the shame of being fools.
What are the laws of Nature, not to bend
If the Church bid them, brother Newman asks.
Up with the Immaculate Conception, then—
On to the rack with faith—is my advice!
Will not that hurry us upon our knees
Knocking our breasts, "It can't be—yet it shall!
Who am I, the worm, to argue with my Pope?
Low things confound the high things!" and so forth.
That's better than acquitting God with grace

As some folks do. He's tried—no case is proved,
Philosophy is lenient—He may go!

You'll say—the old system's not so obsolete
But men believe still: ay, but who and where?
King Bomba's lazzaroni foster yet
The sacred flame, so Antonelli writes;
But even of these, what ragamuffin-saint
Believes God watches him continually,
As he believes in fire that it will burn,
Or rain that it will drench him? Break fire's law,
Sin against rain, although the penalty
Be just a singe or soaking? No, he smiles;
Those laws are laws that can enforce themselves.

The sum of all is—yes, my doubt is great,
My faith's the greater—then my faith's enough.
I have read much, thought much, experienced much,
Yet would die rather than avow my fear
The Naples' liquefaction may be false,
When set to happen by the palace-clock
According to the clouds or dinner-time.
I hear you recommend, I might at least
Eliminate, decrassify my faith
Since I adopt it; keeping what I must
And leaving what I can—such points as this!
I won't—that is, I can't throw one away.
Supposing there's no truth in what I said
About the need of trials to man's faith,
Still, when you bid me purify the same,
To such a process I discern no end,
Clearing off one excrescence to see two;
There's ever a next in size, now grown as big,
That meets the knife—I cut and cut again!
First cut the Liquefaction, what comes last
But Fichte's clever cut at God himself?
Experimentalize on sacred things?
I trust nor hand nor eye nor heart nor brain
To stop betimes: they all get drunk alike.
The first step, I am master not to take.

You'd find the cutting-process to your taste
As much as leaving growths of lies unpruned,
Nor see more danger in it, you retort.
Your taste's worth mine; but my taste proves more
wise
When we consider that the steadfast hold
On the extreme end of the chain of faith
Gives all the advantage, makes the difference,
With the rough purblind mass we seek to rule.
We are their lords, or they are free of us
Just as we tighten or relax that hold.
So, other matters equal, we'll revert
To the first problem—which if solved my way
And thrown into the balance turns the scale—
How we may lead a comfortable life,
How suit our luggage to the cabin's size.

Of course you are remarking all this time
How narrowly and grossly I view life,
Respect the creature-comforts, care to rule
The masses, and regard complacently
"The cabin," in our old phrase! Well, I do.
I act for, talk for, live for this world now,
As this world calls for action, life and talk—
No prejudice to what next world may prove,
Whose new laws and requirements my best pledge
To observe then, is that I observe these now,
Doing hereafter what I do meanwhile.
Let us concede (gratuitously though)
Next life relieves the soul of body, yields
Pure spiritual enjoyments: well, my friend,
Why lose this life in the meantime, since its use
May be to make the next life more intense?

Do you know, I have often had a dream
(Work it up in your next month's article)
Of man's poor spirit in its progress still
Losing true life for ever and a day
Through ever trying to be and ever being
In the evolution of successive spheres,

Before its actual sphere and place of life,
Halfway into the next, which having reached,
It shoots with corresponding foolery
Halfway into the next still, on and off!
As when a traveller, bound from north to south,
Scouts fur in Russia—what's its use in France?
In France spurns flannel—where's its need in Spain?
In Spain drops cloth—too cumbrous for Algiers!
Linen goes next, and last the skin itself,
A superfluity at Timbuctoo.
When, through his journey, was the fool at ease?
I'm at ease now, friend—worldly in this world
I take and like its way of life; I think
My brothers who administer the means
Live better for my comfort—that's good too;
And God, if he pronounce upon it all,
Approves my service, which is better still.
If He keep silence,—why for you or me
Or that brute-beast pulled-up in to-day's "Times,"
What odds is't, save to ourselves, what life we lead?

You meet me at this issue—you declare,
All special-pleading done with, truth is truth,
And justifies itself by undreamed ways.
You don't fear but it's better, if we doubt,
To say so, acting up to our truth perceived
However feebly. Do then,—act away!
'Tis there I'm on the watch for you! How one acts
Is, both of us agree, our chief concern:
And how you'll act is what I fain would see
If, like the candid person you appear,
You dare to make the most of your life's scheme
As I of mine, live up to its full law
Since there's no higher law that counterchecks.
Put natural religion to the test
You've just demolished the revealed with—quick,
Down to the root of all that checks your will,
All prohibition to lie, kill, and thieve
Or even to be an atheistic priest!
Suppose a pricking to incontinence—

Philosophers deduce you chastity
Or shame, from just the fact that at the first
Whoso embraced a woman in the plain,
Threw club down, and forewent his brains beside,
So stood a ready victim in the reach
Of any brother-savage club in hand—
Hence saw the use of going out of sight
In wood or cave to prosecute his loves—
I read this in a French book t'other day.
Does law so analyzed coerce you much?
Oh, men spin clouds of fuzz where matters end,
But you who reach where the first thread begins,
You'll soon cut that!—which means you can, but won't
Through certain instincts, blind, unreasoned-out,
You dare not set aside, you can't tell why,
But there they are, and so you let them rule.
Then, friend, you seem as much a slave as I,
A liar, conscious coward and hypocrite,
Without the good the slave expects to get,
Suppose he has a master after all!
You own your instincts—why what else do I,
Who want, am made for, and must have a God
Ere I can be aught, do aught?—no mere name
Want, but the true thing with what proves its truth,
To wit, a relation from that thing to me,
Touching from head to foot—which touch I feel,
And with it take the rest, this life of ours!
I live my life here; yours you dare not live.

Not as I state it, who (you please subjoin)
Disfigure such a life and call it names,
While, in your mind, remains another way
For simple men: knowledge and power have rights,
But ignorance and weakness have rights too.
There needs no crucial effort to find truth
If here or there or anywhere about—
We ought to turn each side, try hard and see,
And if we can't, be glad we've earned at least
The right, by one laborious proof the more,
To graze in peace earth's pleasant pasturage.

Men are not gods, but, properly, are brutes.
Something we may see, all we cannot see—
What need of lying? I say, I see all,
And swear to each detail the most minute
In what I think a man's face—you, mere cloud:
I swear I hear him speak and see him wink,
For fear, if once I drop the emphasis,
Mankind may doubt if there's a cloud at all.
You take the simpler life—ready to see,
Willing to see—for no cloud's worth a face—
And leaving quiet what no strength can move,
And which, who bids you move? who has the right?
I bid you; but you are God's sheep, not mine—
"*Pastor est tui Dominus.*" You find
In these the pleasant pastures of this life
Much you may eat without the least offence,
Much you don't eat because your maw objects,
Much you would eat but that your fellow-flock
Open great eyes at you and even butt,
And thereupon you like your friends so much
You cannot please yourself, offending them—
Though when they seem exorbitantly sheep,
You weigh your pleasure with their butts and kicks
And strike the balance. Sometimes certain fears
Restrain you—real checks since you find them so—
Sometimes you please yourself and nothing checks;
And thus you graze through life with not one lie,
And like it best.

But do you, in truth's name?
If so, you beat—which means—you are not I—
Who needs must make earth mine and feed my fill
Not simply unbutted at, unbickered with,
But motioned to the velvet of the sward
By those obsequious wethers' very selves.
Look at me, sir; my age is double yours.
At yours, I knew beforehand, so enjoyed,
What now I should be—as, permit the word,
I pretty well imagine your whole range
And stretch of tether twenty years to come.

We both have minds and bodies much alike.
In truth's name, don't you want my bishopric,
My daily bread, my influence and my state?
You're young, I'm old, you must be old one day;
Will you find then, as I do hour by hour,
Women their lovers kneel to, that cut curls
From your fat lap-dog's ears to grace a brooch—
Dukes, that petition just to kiss your ring—
With much beside you know or may conceive?
Suppose we die to-night: well, here am I,
Such were my gains, life bore this fruit to me,
While writing all the same my articles
On music, poetry, the fictile vase
Found at Albano, or Anacreon's Greek.
But you—the highest honour in your life,
The thing you'll crown yourself with, all your days,
Is—dining here and drinking this last glass
I pour you out in sign of amity
Before we part for ever. Of your power
And social influence, worldly worth in short,
Judge what's my estimation by the fact—
I do not condescend to enjoin, beseech,
Hint secresy on one of all these words!
You're shrewd and know that should you publish it
The world would brand the lie—my enemies first,
Who'd sneer—"the bishop's an arch-hypocrite,
And knave perhaps, but not so frank a fool."
Whereas I should not dare for both my ears
Breathe one such syllable, smile one such smile,
Before my chaplain who reflects myself—
My shade's so much more potent than your flesh.
What's your reward, self-abnegating friend?
Stood you confessed of those exceptional
And privileged great natures that dwarf mine—
A zealot with a mad ideal in reach,
A poet just about to print his ode,
A statesman with a scheme to stop this war,
An artist whose religion is his art,
I should have nothing to object! such men
Carry the fire, all things grow warm to them,

Their drugget's worth my purple, they beat me.
But you,—you're just as little those as I—
You, Gigadibs, who, thirty years of age,
Write statedly for Blackwood's Magazine,
Believe you see two points in Hamlet's soul
Unseized by the Germans yet—which view you'll
print—
Meantime the best you have to show being still
That lively lightsome article we took
Almost for the true Dickens,—what's the name?
"The Slum and Cellar—or Whitechapel life
Limned after dark!" it made me laugh, I know,
And pleased a month and brought you in ten pounds.
—Success I recognise and compliment,
And therefore give you, if you please, three words
(The card and pencil-scratch is quite enough)
Which whether here, in Dublin, or New York,
Will get you, prompt as at my eyebrow's wink,
Such terms as never you aspired to get
In all our own reviews and some not ours.
Go write your lively sketches—be the first
"Blougram, or The Eccentric Confidence"—
Or better simply say, "The Outward-bound."
Why, men as soon would throw it in my teeth
As copy and quote the infamy chalked broad
About me on the church-door opposite.
You will not wait for that experience though,
I fancy, howsoever you decide,
To discontinue—not detesting, not
Defaming, but at least—despising me!

Over his wine so smiled and talked his hour
Sylvester Blougram, styled *in partibus*
Episcopus, nec non—(the deuce knows what
It's changed to by our novel hierarchy)
With Gigadibs the literary man,
Who played with spoons, explored his plate's design,
And ranged the olive stones about its edge,
While the great bishop rolled him out his mind.

For Blougram, he believed, say, half he spoke.
The other portion, as he shaped it thus
For argumentatory purposes,
He felt his foe was foolish to dispute.
Some arbitrary accidental thoughts
That crossed his mind, amusing because new,
He chose to represent as fixtures there,
Invariable convictions (such they seemed
Beside his interlocutor's loose cards
Flung daily down, and not the same way twice)
While certain hell-deep instincts, man's weak tongue
Is never bold to utter in their truth
Because styled hell-deep ('tis an old mistake
To place hell at the bottom of the earth)
He ignored these,—not having in readiness
Their nomenclature and philosophy:
He said true things, but called them by wrong names.
"On the whole," he thought, "I justify myself
On every point where cavillers like this
Oppugn my life: he tries one kind of fence—
I close—he's worsted, that's enough for him;
He's on the ground! if the ground should break away
I take my stand on, there's a firmer yet
Beneath it, both of us may sink and reach.
His ground was over mine and broke the first.
So let him sit with me this many a year!"

He did not sit five minutes. Just a week
Sufficed his sudden healthy vehemence.
(Something had struck him in the "Outward-bound"
Another way than Blougram's purpose was)
And having bought, not cabin-furniture
But settler's-implements (enough for three)
And started for Australia—there, I hope,
By this time he has tested his first plough,
And studied his last chapter of St. John.

MEMORABILIA

I

Ah, did you once see Shelley plain,
And did he stop and speak to you?
And did you speak to him again?
How strange it seems, and new!

2

But you were living before that,
And you are living after,
And the memory I started at—
My starting moves your laughter!

3

I crossed a moor with a name of its own
And a use in the world no doubt,
Yet a hand's-breadth of it shines alone
'Mid the blank miles round about—

4

For there I picked up on the heather
And there I put inside my breast
A moulted feather, an eagle-feather—
Well, I forget the rest.

ANDREA DEL SARTO

CALLED "THE FAULTLESS PAINTER"

But do not let us quarrel any more,
No, my Lucrezia; bear with me for once:
Sit down and all shall happen as you wish.
You turn your face, but does it bring your heart?
I'll work then for your friend's friend, never fear,
Treat his own subject after his own way,
Fix his own time, accept too his own price,
And shut the money into this small hand
When next it takes mine. Will it? tenderly?

Oh, I'll content him,—but to-morrow, Love!
I often am much wearier than you think,
This evening more than usual, and it seems
As if—forgive now—should you let me sit
Here by the window with your hand in mine
And look a half hour forth on Fiesole,
Both of one mind, as married people use,
Quietly, quietly, the evening through,
I might get up to-morrow to my work
Cheerful and fresh as ever. Let us try.
To-morrow how you shall be glad for this!
Your soft hand is a woman of itself,
And mine the man's bared breast she curls inside.
Don't count the time lost, either; you must serve
For each of the five pictures we require—
It saves a model. So! keep looking so—
My serpentining beauty, rounds on rounds!
—How could you ever prick those perfect ears,
Even to put the pearl there! oh, so sweet—
My face, my moon, my everybody's moon,
Which everybody looks on and calls his,
And, I suppose, is looked on by in turn,
While she looks—no one's: very dear, no less!
You smile? why, there's my picture ready made.
There's what we painters call our harmony!
A common greyness silvers everything,—
All in a twilight, you and I alike
—You, at the point of your first pride in me
(That's gone you know),—but I, at every point;
My youth, my hope, my art, being all toned down
To yonder sober pleasant Fiesole.
There's the bell clinking from the chapel-top;
That length of convent-wall across the way
Holds the trees safer, huddled more inside;
The last monk leaves the garden; days decrease
And autumn grows, autumn in everything.
Eh? the whole seems to fall into a shape
As if I saw alike my work and self
And all that I was born to be and do,
A twilight-piece. Love, we are in God's hand.

How strange now, looks the life he makes us lead!
So free we seem, so fettered fast we are;
I feel he laid the fetter: let it lie!
This chamber for example—turn your head—
All that's behind us! you don't understand
Nor care to understand about my art,
But you can hear at least when people speak;
And that cartoon, the second from the door
—It is the thing, Love! so such things should be—
Behold Madonna, I am bold to say.
I can do with my pencil what I know,
What I see, what at bottom of my heart
I wish for, if I ever wish so deep—
Do easily, too—when I say perfectly
I do not boast, perhaps: yourself are judge
Who listened to the Legate's talk last week,
And just as much they used to say in France.
At any rate 'tis easy, all of it,
No sketches first, no studies, that's long past—
I do what many dream of all their lives
—Dream? strive to do, and agonise to do,
And fail in doing. I could count twenty such
On twice your fingers, and not leave this town,
Who strive—you don't know how the others strive
To paint a little thing like that you smeared
Carelessly passing with your robes afloat,
Yet do much less, so much less, some one says,
(I know his name, no matter) so much less!
Well, less is more, Lucrezia! I am judged.
There burns a truer light of God in them,
In their vexed, beating, stuffed and stopped-up brain,
Heart, or whate'er else, than goes on to prompt
This low-pulsed forthright craftsman's hand of mine.
Their works drop groundward, but themselves, I know,
Reach many a time a heaven that's shut to me,
Enter and take their place there sure enough,
Though they come back and cannot tell the world.
My works are nearer heaven, but I sit here.
The sudden blood of these men! at a word—
Praise them, it boils, or blame them, it boils too.

I, painting from myself and to myself,
Know what I do, am unmoved by men's blame
Or their praise either. Somebody remarks
Morello's outline there is wrongly traced,
His hue mistaken—what of that? or else,
Rightly traced and well ordered—what of that?
Ah, but a man's reach should exceed his grasp,
Or what's a Heaven for? all is silver-grey
Placid and perfect with my art—the worse!
I know both what I want and what might gain—
And yet how profitless to know, to sigh
"Had I been two, another and myself,
Our head would have o'erlooked the world!" No doubt.
Yonder's a work, now, of that famous youth
The Urbinate who died five years ago.
('Tis copied, George Vasari sent it me).
Well, I can fancy how he did it all,
Pouring his soul, with kings and popes to see,
Reaching that Heaven might so replenish him,
Above and through his art—for it gives way;
That arm is wrongly put—and there again—
A fault to pardon in the drawing's lines,
Its body, so to speak! its soul is right,
He means right—that, a child may understand.
Still, what an arm! and I could alter it.
But all the play, the insight and the stretch—
Out of me! out of me! And wherefore out?
Had you enjoined them on me, given me soul,
We might have risen to Rafael, I and you.
Nay, Love, you did give all I asked, I think—
More than I merit, yes, by many times.
But had you—oh, with the same perfect brow,
And perfect eyes, and more than perfect mouth,
And the low voice my soul hears, as a bird
The fowler's pipe, and follows to the snare—
Had you, with these the same, but brought a mind!
Some women do so. Had the mouth there urged
"God and the glory! never care for gain.
The present by the future, what is that?
Live for fame, side by side with Angelo—

Rafael is waiting. Up to God all three!"
I might have done it for you. So it seems—
Perhaps not. All is as God over-rules.
Beside, incentives come from the soul's self;
The rest avail not. Why do I need you?
What wife had Rafael, or has Angelo?
In this world, who can do a thing, will not—
And who would do it, cannot, I perceive;
Yet the will's somewhat—somewhat, too, the power—
And thus we half-men struggle. At the end,
God, I conclude, compensates, punishes.
'Tis safer for me, if the award be strict,
That I am something underrated here,
Poor this long while, despised, to speak the truth.
I dared not, do you know, leave home all day,
For fear of chancing on the Paris lords.
The best is when they pass and look aside;
But they speak sometimes; I must bear it all.
Well may they speak! That Francis, that first time,
And that long festal year at Fontainebleau!
I surely then could sometimes leave the ground,
Put on the glory, Rafael's daily wear,
In that humane great monarch's golden look,—
One finger in his beard or twisted curl
Over his mouth's good mark that made the smile,
One arm about my shoulder, round my neck,
The jingle of his gold chain in my ear,
I painting proudly with his breath on me,
All his court round him, seeing with his eyes,
Such frank French eyes, and such a fire of souls
Profuse, my hand kept plying by those hearts,—
And, best of all, this, this, this face beyond,
This in the back-ground, waiting on my work,
To crown the issue with a last reward!
A good time, was it not, my kingly days?
And had you not grown restless—but I know—
'Tis done and past; 'twas right, my instinct said;
Too live the life grew, golden and not grey—
And I'm the weak-eyed bat no sun should tempt
Out of the grange whose four walls make his world.

How could it end in any other way?
You called me, and I came home to your heart.
The triumph was to have ended there—then if
I reached it ere the triumph, what is lost?
Let my hands frame your face in your hair's gold,
You beautiful Lucrezia that are mine!
"Rafael did this, Andrea painted that—
The Roman's is the better when you pray,
But still the other's Virgin was his wife—"
Men will excuse me. I am glad to judge
Both pictures in your presence; clearer grows
My better fortune, I resolve to think.
For, do you know, Lucrezia, as God lives,
Said one day Angelo, his very self,
To Rafael . . . I have known it all these years . . .
(When the young man was flaming out his thoughts
Upon a palace-wall for Rome to see,
Too lifted up in heart because of it)
"Friend, there's a certain sorry little scrub
Goes up and down our Florence, none cares how,
Who, were he set to plan and execute
As you are pricked on by your popes and kings,
Would bring the sweat into that brow of yours!"
To Rafael's!—And indeed the arm is wrong.
I hardly dare—yet, only you to see,
Give the chalk here—quick, thus the line should go!
Ay, but the soul! he's Rafael! rub it out!
Still, all I care for, if he spoke the truth,
(What he? why, who but Michael Angelo?
Do you forget already words like those?)
If really there was such a chance, so lost,
Is, whether you're—not grateful—but more pleased.
Well, let me think so. And you smile indeed!
This hour has been an hour! Another smile?
If you would sit thus by me every night
I should work better, do you comprehend?
I mean that I should earn more, give you more.
See, it is settled dusk now; there's a star;
Morello's gone, the watch-lights shew the wall,
The cue-owls speak the name we call them by.

Come from the window, Love,—come in, at last,
Inside the melancholy little house
We built to be so gay with. God is just.
King Francis may forgive me. Oft at nights
When I look up from painting, eyes tired out,
The walls become illumined, brick from brick
Distinct, instead of mortar fierce bright gold,
That gold of his I did cement them with!
Let us but love each other. Must you go?
That Cousin here again? he waits outside?
Must see you—you, and not with me? Those loans!
More gaming debts to pay? you smiled for that?
Well, let smiles buy me! have you more to spend?
While hand and eye and something of a heart
Are left me, work's my ware, and what's it worth?
I'll pay my fancy. Only let me sit
The grey remainder of the evening out,
Idle, you call it, and muse perfectly
How I could paint were I but back in France,
One picture, just one more—the Virgin's face,
Not your's this time! I want you at my side
To hear them—that is, Michael Angelo—
Judge all I do and tell you of its worth.
Will you? To-morrow, satisfy your friend.
I take the subjects for his corridor,
Finish the portrait out of hand—there, there,
And throw him in another thing or two
If he demurs; the whole should prove enough
To pay for this same Cousin's freak. Beside,
What's better and what's all I care about,
Get you the thirteen scudi for the ruff.
Love, does that please you? Ah, but what does he,
The Cousin! what does he to please you more?

I am grown peaceful as old age to-night.
I regret little, I would change still less.
Since there my past life lies, why alter it?
The very wrong to Francis! it is true
I took his coin, was tempted and complied,
And built this house and sinned, and all is said.

My father and my mother died of want.
Well, had I riches of my own? you see
How one gets rich! Let each one bear his lot.
They were born poor, lived poor, and poor they died:
And I have laboured somewhat in my time
And not been paid profusely. Some good son
Paint my two hundred pictures—let him try!
No doubt, there's something strikes a balance. Yes,
You loved me quite enough, it seems to-night.
This must suffice me here. What would one have?
In heaven, perhaps, new chances, one more chance—
Four great walls in the New Jerusalem
Meted on each side by the angel's reed,
For Leonard, Rafael, Angelo and me
To cover—the three first without a wife,
While I have mine! So—still they overcome
Because there's still Lucrezia,—as I choose.

Again the Cousin's whistle! Go, my Love.

IN A YEAR

I

Never any more
While I live,
Need I hope to see his face
As before.
Once his love grown chill,
Mine may strive—
Bitterly we re-embrace,
Single still.

2

Was it something said,
Something done,
Vexed him? was it touch of hand,
Turn of head?

Strange! that very way
  Love begun.
I as little understand
  Love's decay.

3

When I sewed or drew,
  I recall
How he looked as if I sang,
  —Sweetly too.
If I spoke a word,
  First of all
Up his cheek the color sprang,
  Then he heard.

4

Sitting by my side,
  At my feet,
So he breathed the air I breathed,
  Satisfied!
I, too, at love's brim
  Touched the sweet:
I would die if death bequeathed
  Sweet to him.

5

"Speak, I love thee best!"
  He exclaimed.
"Let thy love my own foretell,—"
  I confessed:
"Clasp my heart on thine
  Now unblamed,
Since upon thy soul as well
  Hangeth mine!"

6

Was it wrong to own,
  Being truth?
Why should all the giving prove
  His alone?

I had wealth and ease,
  Beauty, youth—
Since my lover gave me love,
  I gave these.

7

That was all I meant,
  —To be just,
And the passion I had raised
  To content.
Since he chose to change
  Gold for dust,
If I gave him what he praised
  Was it strange?

8

Would he loved me yet,
  On and on,
While I found some way undreamed
  —Paid my debt!
Gave more life and more,
  Till, all gone,
He should smile "She never seemed
  Mine before.

9

"What—she felt the while,
  Must I think?
Love's so different with us men,"
  He should smile.
"Dying for my sake—
  White and pink!
Can't we touch these bubbles then
  But they break?"

10

Dear, the pang is brief.
  Do thy part,
Have thy pleasure. How perplext
  Grows belief!

Well, this cold clay clod
Was man's heart.
Crumble it—and what comes next?
Is it God?

SAUL

I

SAID Abner, "At last thou art come! Ere I tell, ere thou speak,
Kiss my cheek, wish me well!" Then I wished it, and did kiss his cheek.
And he, "Since the King, O my friend, for thy countenance sent,
Neither drunken nor eaten have we; nor until from his tent
Thou return with the joyful assurance the King liveth yet,
Shall our lip with the honey be bright, with the water be wet.
For out of the black mid-tent's silence, a space of three days,
Not a sound hath escaped to thy servants, of prayer or of praise,
To betoken that Saul and the Spirit have ended their strife,
And that, faint in his triumph, the monarch sinks back upon life.

2

Yet now my heart leaps, O beloved! God's child, with his dew
On thy gracious gold hair, and those lilies still living and blue
Just broken to twine round thy harp-strings, as if no wild heat
Were now raging to torture the desert!"

3

Then I, as was meet,
Knelt down to the God of my fathers, and rose on my feet,
And ran o'er the sand burnt to powder. The tent was unlooped;
I pulled up the spear that obstructed, and under I stooped;

Hands and knees on the slippery grass-patch, all withered and gone,
That extends to the second enclosure, I groped my way on
Till I felt where the foldskirts fly open. Then once more I prayed,
And opened the foldskirts and entered, and was not afraid,
But spoke, "Here is David, thy servant!" And no voice replied.
At the first I saw nought but the blackness; but soon I descried
A something more black than the blackness—the vast, the upright
Main prop which sustains the pavilion: and slow into sight
Grew a figure against it, gigantic and blackest of all;—
Then a sunbeam, that burst thro' the tent-roof,—showed Saul.

4

He stood as erect as that tent-prop; both arms stretched out wide
On the great cross-support in the centre, that goes to each side:
He relaxed not a muscle, but hung there,—as, caught in his pangs
And waiting his change the king-serpent all heavily hangs,
Far away from his kind, in the pine, till deliverance come
With the spring-time,—so agonized Saul, drear and stark, blind and dumb.

5

Then I tuned my harp,—took off the lilies we twine round its chords
Lest they snap 'neath the stress of the noontide—those sunbeams like swords!
And I first played the tune all our sheep know, as, one after one,
So docile they come to the pen-door, till folding be done.

They are white and untorn by the bushes, for lo, they have
fed
Where the long grasses stifle the water within the stream's
bed;
And now one after one seeks its lodging, as star follows star
Into eve and the blue far above us,—so blue and so far!

6

—Then the tune, for which quails on the cornland will each
leave his mate
To fly after the player; then, what makes the crickets elate,
Till for boldness they fight one another: and then, what has
weight
To set the quick jerboa a-musing outside his sand house—
There are none such as he for a wonder, half bird and half
mouse!—
God made all the creatures and gave them our love and
our fear,
To give sign, we and they are his children, one family here.

7

Then I played the help-tune of our reapers, their wine-song,
when hand
Grasps at hand, eye lights eye in good friendship, and great
hearts expand
And grow one in the sense of this world's life.—And then,
the last song
When the dead man is praised on his journey—"Bear, bear
him along
With his few faults shut up like dead flowerets! are balm-
seeds not here
To console us? The land has none left, such as he on the
bier.
Oh, would we might keep thee, my brother!"—And then,
the glad chaunt
Of the marriage,—first go the young maidens, next, she
whom we vaunt
As the beauty, the pride of our dwelling.—And then, the
great march
Wherein man runs to man to assist him and buttress an arch

Nought can break; who shall harm them, our friends?—
Then, the chorus intoned
As the Levites go up to the altar in glory enthroned . . .
But I stopped here—for here in the darkness, Saul groaned.

8

And I paused, held my breath in such silence, and listened apart;
And the tent shook, for mighty Saul shuddered,—and sparkles 'gan dart
From the jewels that woke in his turban at once with a start—
All its lordly male-sapphires, and rubies courageous at heart.
So the head—but the body still moved not, still hung there erect.
And I bent once again to my playing, pursued it unchecked,
As I sang,—

9

"Oh, our manhood's prime vigour! no spirit feels waste,
Not a muscle is stopped in its playing, nor sinew unbraced.
Oh, the wild joys of living! the leaping from rock up to rock—
The strong rending of boughs from the fir-tree,—the cool silver shock
Of the plunge in a pool's living water,—the hunt of the bear,
And the sultriness shewing the lion is couched in his lair.
And the meal—the rich dates—yellowed over with gold dust divine,
And the locust's-flesh steeped in the pitcher; the full draught of wine,
And the sleep in the dried river-channel where bullrushes tell
That the water was wont to go warbling so softly and well.
How good is man's life, the mere living! how fit to employ
All the heart and the soul and the senses, for ever in joy!
Hast thou loved the white locks of thy father, whose sword thou didst guard

When he trusted thee forth with the armies, for glorious reward?
Didst thou see the thin hands of thy mother, held up as men sung
The low song of the nearly-departed, and heard her faint tongue
Joining in while it could to the witness, 'Let one more attest,
I have lived, seen God's hand thro' a lifetime, and all was for best . . .'
Then they sung thro' their tears in strong triumph, not much,—but the rest.
And thy brothers, the help and the contest, the working whence grew
Such result as from seething grape-bundles, the spirit strained true!
And the friends of thy boyhood—that boyhood of wonder and hope,
Present promise, and wealth of the future beyond the eye's scope,—
Till lo, thou art grown to a monarch; a people is thine;
And all gifts which the world offers singly, on one head combine!
On one head, all the beauty and strength, love and rage, like the throe
That, a-work in the rock, helps its labour, and lets the gold go:
High ambition and deeds which surpass it, fame crowning it,—all
Brought to blaze on the head of one creature—King Saul!"

10

And lo, with that leap of my spirit, heart, hand, harp and voice,
Each lifting Saul's name out of sorrow, each bidding rejoice
Saul's fame in the light it was made for—as when, dare I say,
The Lord's army in rapture of service, strains through its array,
And upsoareth the cherubim-chariot—"Saul!" cried I, and stopped,

And waited the thing that should follow. Then Saul, who hung propt
By the tent's cross-support in the centre, was struck by his name.
Have ye seen when Spring's arrowy summons goes right to the aim,
And some mountain, the last to withstand her, that held, (he alone,
While the vale laughed in freedom and flowers) on a broad bust of stone
A year's snow bound about for a breastplate,—leaves grasp of the sheet?
Fold on fold all at once it crowds thunderously down to his feet,
And there fronts you, stark, black but alive yet, your mountain of old,
With his rents, the successive bequeathings of ages untold—
Yea, each harm got in fighting your battles, each furrow and scar
Of his head thrust 'twixt you and the tempest—all hail, there they are!
Now again to be softened with verdure, again hold the nest
Of the dove, tempt the goat and its young to the green on its crest
For their food in the ardours of summer! One long shudder thrilled
All the tent till the very air tingled, then sank and was stilled,
At the King's self left standing before me, released and aware.
What was gone, what remained? all to traverse 'twixt hope and despair—
Death was past, life not come—so he waited. Awhile his right hand
Held the brow, helped the eyes left too vacant forthwith to remand
To their place what new objects should enter: 'twas Saul as before.
I looked up and dared gaze at those eyes, nor was hurt any more

Than by slow pallid sunsets in autumn, ye watch from the
shore
At their sad level gaze o'er the ocean—a sun's slow decline
Over hills which, resolved in stern silence, o'erlap and
entwine
Base with base to knit strength more intense: so, arm folded
in arm
O'er the chest whose slow heavings subsided.

11

What spell or what charm,
(For, awhile there was trouble within me) what next should
I urge
To sustain him where song had restored him?—Song filled
to the verge
His cup with the wine of this life, pressing all that it yields
Of mere fruitage, the strength and the beauty! Beyond, on
what fields,
Glean a vintage more potent and perfect to brighten the eye
And bring blood to the lip, and commend them the cup
they put by?
He saith, "It is good;" still he drinks not—he lets me praise
life,
Gives assent, yet would die for his own part.

12

Then fancies grew rife
Which had come long ago on the pastures, when round me
the sheep
Fed in silence—above, the one eagle wheeled slow as in
sleep,
And I lay in my hollow, and mused on the world that might
lie
'Neath his ken, though I saw but the strip 'twixt the hill
and the sky:
And I laughed—"Since my days are ordained to be passed
with my flocks,
Let me people at least with my fancies, the plains and the
rocks,
Dream the life I am never to mix with, and image the show

Of mankind as they live in those fashions I hardly shall
know!
Schemes of life, its best rules and right uses, the courage
that gains,
And the prudence that keeps what men strive for." And
now these old trains
Of vague thought came again; I grew surer; so once more
the string
Of my harp made response to my spirit, as thus—

13

"Yea, my king,"
I began—"thou dost well in rejecting mere comforts that
spring
From the mere mortal life held in common by man and by
brute:
In our flesh grows the branch of this life, in our soul it bears
fruit.
Thou hast marked the slow rise of the tree,—how its stem
trembled first
Till it passed the kid's lip, the stag's antler; then safely
outburst
The fan-branches all round; and thou mindedst when these
too, in turn
Broke a-bloom and the palm-tree seemed perfect; yet more
was to learn,
Ev'n the good that comes in with the palm-fruit. Our dates
shall we slight,
When their juice brings a cure for all sorrow? or care for
the plight
Of the palm's self whose slow growth produced them? Not
so! stem and branch
Shall decay, nor be known in their place, while the palm-
wine shall staunch
Every wound of man's spirit in winter. I pour thee such
wine.
Leave the flesh to the fate it was fit for! the spirit be thine!
By the spirit, when age shall o'ercome thee, thou still shalt
enjoy

More indeed, than at first when inconscious, the life of a
boy.
Crush that life, and behold its wine running! each deed
thou hast done
Dies, revives, goes to work in the world; until e'en as the
sun
Looking down on the earth, though clouds spoil him,
though tempests efface,
Can find nothing his own deed produced not, must every
where trace
The results of his past summer-prime,—so, each ray of thy
will,
Every flash of thy passion and prowess, long over, shall
thrill
Thy whole people the countless, with ardour, till they too
give forth
A like cheer to their sons, who in turn, fill the south and
the north
With the radiance thy deed was the germ of. Carouse in the
past.
But the license of age has its limit; thou diest at last.
As the lion when age dims his eye-ball, the rose at her
height,
So with man—so his power and his beauty for ever take
flight.
No! again a long draught of my soul-wine! look forth o'er
the years—
Thou hast done now with eyes for the actual; begin with
the seer's!
Is Saul dead? in the depth of the vale make his tomb—bid
arise
A grey mountain of marble heaped four-square, till built to
the skies.
Let it mark where the great First King slumbers—whose
fame would ye know?
Up above see the rock's naked face, where the record shall
go
In great characters cut by the scribe,—Such was Saul, so he
did;
With the sages directing the work, by the populace chid,—

For not half, they'll affirm, is comprised there! Which fault to amend,
In the grove with his kind grows the cedar, whereon they shall spend
(See, in tablets 'tis level before them) their praise, and record
With the gold of the graver, Saul's story,—the statesman's great word
Side by side with the poet's sweet comment. The river's a-wave
With smooth paper-reeds grazing each other when prophet winds rave:
So the pen gives unborn generations their due and their part
In thy being! Then, first of the mighty, thank God that thou art."

14

And behold while I sang . . . But O Thou who didst grant me that day,
And before it not seldom hast granted, thy help to essay,
Carry on and complete an adventure,—my Shield and my Sword
In that act where my soul was thy servant, thy word was my word,—
Still be with me, who then at the summit of human endeavour
And scaling the highest man's thought could, gazed hopeless as ever
On the new stretch of Heaven above me—till, Mighty to save,
Just one lift of thy hand cleared that distance—God's throne from man's grave!
Let me tell out my tale to its ending—my voice to my heart,
Which can scarce dare believe in what marvels that night I took part,
As this morning I gather the fragments, alone with my sheep,
And still fear lest the terrible glory evanish like sleep!

For I wake in the grey dewy covert, while Hebron upheaves
The dawn struggling with night on his shoulder, and Kidron retrieves
Slow the damage of yesterday's sunshine.

15

I say then,—my song
While I sang thus, asuring the monarch, and ever more strong
Made a proffer of good to console him—he slowly resumed
His old motions and habitudes kingly. The right hand replumed
His black locks to their wonted composure, adjusted the swathes
Of his turban, and see—the huge sweat that his countenance bathes,
He wipes off with the robe; and he girds now his loins as of yore,
And feels slow for the armlets of price, with the clasp set before.
He is Saul, ye remember in glory,—ere error had bent
The broad brow from the daily communion; and still, though much spent
Be the life and the bearing that front you, the same, God did choose,
To receive what a man may waste, desecrate, never quite lose.
So sank he along by the tent-prop, till, stayed by the pile
Of his armour and war-cloak and garments, he leaned there awhile,
And so sat out my singing,—one arm round the tent-prop, to raise
His bent head, and the other hung slack—till I touched on the praise
I foresaw from all men in all times, to the man patient there,
And thus ended, the harp falling forward. Then first I was 'ware
That he sat, as I say, with my head just above his vast knees
Which were thrust out on each side around me, like oak-roots which please

To encircle a lamb when it slumbers. I looked up to know
If the best I could do had brought solace: he spoke not, but slow
Lifted up the hand slack at his side, till he laid it with care
Soft and grave, but in mild settled will, on my brow: thro' my hair
The large fingers were pushed, and he bent back my head, with kind power—
All my face back, intent to peruse it, as men do a flower.
Thus held he me there with his great eyes that scrutinised mine—
And oh, all my heart how it loved him! but where was the sign?
I yearned—"Could I help thee, my father, inventing a bliss,
I would add to that life of the past, both the future and this.
I would give thee new life altogether, as good, ages hence,
As this moment,—had love but the warrant, love's heart to dispense!"

16

Then the truth came upon me. No harp more—no song more! out-broke—

17

"I have gone the whole round of Creation: I saw and I spoke!
I, a work of God's hand for that purpose, received in my brain
And pronounced on the rest of his handwork—returned him again
His creation's approval or censure: I spoke as I saw.
I report, as a man may of God's work—all's love, yet all's law!
Now I lay down the judgeship he lent me. Each faculty tasked
To perceive him, has gained an abyss, where a dew-drop was asked.
Have I knowledge? confounded it shrivels at wisdom laid bare.

Have I forethought? how purblind, how blank, to the
Infinite care!
Do I task any faculty highest, to image success?
I but open my eyes,—and perfection, no more and no less,
In the kind I imagined, full-fronts me, and God is seen God
In the star, in the stone, in the flesh, in the soul and the
clod.
And thus looking within and around me, I ever renew
(With that stoop of the soul which in bending upraises it
too)
The submission of Man's nothing-perfect to God's All-
Complete,
As by each new obeisance in spirit, I climb to his feet!
Yet with all this abounding experience, this Deity known,
I shall dare to discover some province, some gift of my own.
There's one faculty pleasant to exercise, hard to hoodwink,
I am fain to keep still in abeyance, (I laugh as I think)
Lest, insisting to claim and parade in it, wot ye, I worst
E'en the Giver in one gift.—Behold! I could love if I durst!
But I sink the pretension as fearing a man may o'ertake
God's own speed in the one way of love: I abstain, for love's
sake!
—What, my soul? see thus far and no farther? when doors
great and small,
Nine-and-ninety flew ope at our touch, should the
hundredth appal?
In the least things, have faith, yet distrust in the greatest of
all?
Do I find love so full in my nature, God's ultimate gift,
That I doubt his own love can compete with it? here, the
parts shift?
Here, the creature surpass the Creator, the end, what
Began?—
Would I fain in my impotent yearning do all for this man,
And dare doubt He alone shall not help him, who yet alone
can?
Would it ever have entered my mind, the bare will, much
less power,
To bestow on this Saul what I sang of, the marvellous
dower

Of the life he was gifted and filled with? to make such a soul,
Such a body, and then such an earth for insphering the whole?
And doth it not enter my mind (as my warm tears attest)
These good things being given, to go on, and give one more, the best?
Ay, to save and redeem and restore him, maintain at the height
This perfection,—succeed with life's dayspring, death's minute of night?
Interpose at the difficult minute, snatch Saul, the mistake,
Saul, the failure, the ruin he seems now,—and bid him awake
From the dream, the probation, the prelude, to find himself set
Clear and safe in new light and new life,—a new harmony yet
To be run, and continued, and ended—who knows?—or endure!
The man taught enough by life's dream, of the rest to make sure.
By the pain-throb, triumphantly winning intensified bliss,
And the next world's reward and repose, by the struggle in this.

18

"I believe it! 'tis Thou, God, that givest, 'tis I who receive:
In the first is the last, in thy will is my power to believe.
All's one gift: thou canst grant it moreover, as prompt to my prayer
As I breathe out this breath, as I open these arms to the air.
From thy will, stream the worlds, life and nature, thy dread Sabaoth:
I will?—the mere atoms despise me! and why am I not loth
To look that, even that in the face too? why is it I dare
Think but lightly of such impuissance? what stops my despair?
This;—'tis not what man Does which exalts him, but what man Would do!
See the king—I would help him but cannot, the wishes fall through.

Could I wrestle to raise him from sorrow, grow poor to
enrich,
To fill up his life, starve my own out, I would—knowing
which,
I know that my service is perfect.—Oh, speak through me
now!
Would I suffer for him that I love? So wilt Thou—so wilt
Thou!
So shall crown thee the topmost, ineffablest, uttermost
Crown—
And thy love fill infinitude wholly, nor leave up nor down
One spot for the creature to stand in! It is by no breath,
Turn of eye, wave of hand, that Salvation joins issue with
death!
As thy Love is discovered almighty, almighty be proved
Thy power, that exists with and for it, of Being beloved!
He who did most, shall bear most; the strongest shall stand
the most weak.
'Tis the weakness in strength that I cry for! my flesh, that I
seek
In the Godhead! I seek and I find it. O Saul, it shall be
A Face like my face that received thee: a Man like to me,
Thou shalt love and be loved by, for ever! a Hand like this
hand
Shall throw open the gates of new life to thee! See the
Christ stand!"

19

I know not too well how I found my way home in the night.
There were witnesses, cohorts about me, to left and to right,
Angels, powers, the unuttered, unseen, the alive—the
aware—
I repressed, I got through them as hardly, as strugglingly
there,
As a runner beset by the populace famished for news—
Life or death. The whole earth was awakened, hell loosed
with her crews;
And the stars of night beat with emotion, and tingled and
shot
Out in fire the strong pain of pent knowledge: but I fainted
not.

For the Hand still impelled me at once and supported—suppressed
All the tumult, and quenched it with quiet, and holy behest,
Till the rapture was shut in itself, and the earth sank to rest.
Anon at the dawn, all that trouble had withered from earth—
Not so much, but I saw it die out in the day's tender birth;
In the gathered intensity brought to the grey of the hills;
In the shuddering forests' new awe; in the sudden wind-thrills;
In the startled wild beasts that bore off, each with eye sidling still
Tho' averted, in wonder and dread; and the birds stiff and chill
That rose heavily, as I approached them, made stupid with awe!
E'en the serpent that slid away silent,—he felt the new Law.
The same stared in the white humid faces upturned by the flowers;
The same worked in the heart of the cedar, and moved the vine-bowers.
And the little brooks witnessing murmured, persistent and low,
With their obstinate, all but hushed voices—E'en so! it is so.

"DE GUSTIBUS——"

I

Your ghost will walk, you lover of trees,
(If loves remain)
In an English lane,
By a cornfield-side a-flutter with poppies.
Hark, those two in the hazel coppice—
A boy and a girl, if the good fates please,
Making love, say,—
The happier they!

Draw yourself up from the light of the moon,
And let them pass, as they will too soon,
With the beanflowers' boon,
And the blackbird's tune,
And May, and June!

2

What I love best in all the world,
Is, a castle, precipice-encurled,
In a gash of the wind-grieved Apennine.
Or look for me, old fellow of mine,
(If I get my head from out the mouth
O' the grave, and loose my spirit's bands,
And come again to the land of lands)—
In a sea-side house to the farther south,
Where the baked cicalas die of drouth,
And one sharp tree ('tis a cypress) stands,
By the many hundred years red-rusted,
Rough iron-spiked, ripe fruit-o'ercrusted,
My sentinel to guard the sands
To the water's edge. For, what expands
Without the house, but the great opaque
Blue breadth of sea, and not a break?
While, in the house, for ever crumbles
Some fragment of the frescoed walls,
From blisters where a scorpion sprawls.
A girl bare-footed brings and tumbles
Down on the pavement, green-flesh melons,
And says there's news to-day—the king
Was shot at, touched in the liver-wing,
Goes with his Bourbon arm in a sling.
—She hopes they have not caught the felons.
Italy, my Italy!
Queen Mary's saying serves for me—
(When fortune's malice
Lost her, Calais.)
Open my heart and you will see
Graved inside of it, "Italy."
Such lovers old are I and she;
So it always was, so it still shall be!

WOMEN AND ROSES

I

I DREAM of a red-rose tree.
And which of its roses three
Is the dearest rose to me?

2

Round and round, like a dance of snow
In a dazzling drift, as its guardians, go
Floating the women faded for ages,
Sculptured in stone, on the poet's pages.
Then follow the women fresh and gay,
Living and loving and loved to-day.
Last, in the rear, flee the multitude of maidens,
Beauties unborn. And all, to one cadence,
They circle their rose on my rose tree.

3

Dear rose, thy term is reached.
Thy leaf hangs loose and bleached:
Bees pass it unimpeached.

4

Stay then, stoop, since I cannot climb,
You, great shapes of the antique time!
How shall I fix you, fire you, freeze you,
Break my heart at your feet to please you?
Oh! to possess, and be possessed!
Hearts that beat 'neath each pallid breast!
But once of love, the poesy, the passion,
Drink once and die!—In vain, the same fashion,
They circle their rose on my rose tree.

5

Dear rose, thy joy's undimmed;
Thy cup is ruby-rimmed,
Thy cup's heart nectar-brimmed.

6

Deep as drops from a statue's plinth
The bee sucked in by the hyacinth,
So will I bury me while burning,
Quench like him at a plunge my yearning,
Eyes in your eyes, lips on your lips!
Fold me fast where the cincture slips,
Prison all my soul in eternities of pleasure!
Girdle me once! But no—in their old measure
They circle their rose on my rose tree.

7

Dear rose without a thorn,
Thy bud's the babe unborn:
First streak of a new morn.

8

Wings, lend wings for the cold, the clear!
What's far conquers what is near.
Roses will bloom nor want beholders,
Sprung from the dust where our own flesh moulders.
What shall arrive with the cycle's change?
A novel grace and a beauty strange.
I will make an Eve, be the artist that began her,
Shaped her to his mind!—Alas! in like manner
They circle their rose on my rose tree.

CLEON

"As certain also of your own poets have said"—

CLEON the poet, (from the sprinkled isles,
Lily on lily, that o'erlace the sea,
And laugh their pride when the light wave lisps
"Greece")—
To Protos in his Tyranny: much health!

They give thy letter to me, even now:
I read and seem as if I heard thee speak.

The master of thy galley still unlades
Gift after gift; they block my court at last
And pile themselves along its portico
Royal with sunset, like a thought of thee:
And one white she-slave from the group dispersed
Of black and white slaves, (like the chequer-work
Pavement, at once my nation's work and gift,
Now covered with this settle-down of doves)
One lyric woman, in her crocus vest
Woven of sea-wools, with her two white hands
Commends to me the strainer and the cup
Thy lip hath bettered ere it blesses mine.

Well-counselled, king, in thy munificence!
For so shall men remark, in such an act
Of love for him whose song gives life its joy,
Thy recognition of the use of life;
Nor call thy spirit barely adequate
To help on life in straight ways, broad enough
For vulgar souls, by ruling and the rest.
Thou, in the daily building of thy tower,
Whether in fierce and sudden spasms of toil,
Or through dim lulls of unapparent growth,
Or when the general work 'mid good acclaim
Climbed with the eye to cheer the architect,
Didst ne'er engage in work for mere work's sake—
Hadst ever in thy heart the luring hope
Of some eventual rest a-top of it,
Whence, all the tumult of the building hushed,
Thou first of men mightst look out to the east.
The vulgar saw thy tower; thou sawest the sun.
For this, I promise on thy festival
To pour libation, looking o'er the sea,
Making this slave narrate thy fortunes, speak
Thy great words, and describe thy royal face—
Wishing thee wholly where Zeus lives the most
Within the eventual element of calm.

Thy letter's first requirement meets me here.
It is as thou hast heard : in one short life

I, Cleon, have effected all those things
Thou wonderingly dost enumerate.
That epos on thy hundred plates of gold
Is mine,—and also mine the little chaunt,
So sure to rise from every fishing-bark
When, lights at prow, the seamen haul their nets.
The image of the sun-god on the phare
Men turn from the sun's self to see, is mine;
The Pœcile, o'er-storied its whole length,
As thou didst hear, with painting, is mine too.
I know the true proportions of a man
And woman also, not observed before;
And I have written three books on the soul,
Proving absurd all written hitherto,
And putting us to ignorance again.
For music,—why, I have combined the moods,
Inventing one. In brief, all arts are mine;
Thus much the people know and recognise,
Throughout our seventeen islands. Marvel not.
We of these latter days, with greater mind
Than our forerunners, since more composite,
Look not so great (beside their simple way)
To a judge who only sees one way at once,
One mind-point, and no other at a time,—
Compares the small part of a man of us
With some whole man of the heroic age,
Great in his way,—not ours, nor meant for ours,
And ours is greater, had we skill to know.
Yet, what we call this life of men on earth,
This sequence of the soul's achievements here,
Being, as I find much reason to conceive,
Intended to be viewed eventually
As a great whole, not analysed to parts,
But each part having reference to all,—
How shall a certain part, pronounced complete,
Endure effacement by another part?
Was the thing done?—Then what's to do again?
See, in the chequered pavement opposite,
Suppose the artist made a perfect rhomb,
And next a lozenge, then a trapezoid—

He did not overlay them, superimpose
The new upon the old and blot it out,
But laid them on a level in his work,
Making at last a picture; there it lies.
So, first the perfect separate forms were made,
The portions of mankind—and after, so,
Occurred the combination of the same.
Or where had been a progress, otherwise?
Mankind, made up of all the single men,—
In such a synthesis the labour ends.
Now, mark me—those divine men of old time
Have reached, thou sayest well, each at one point
The outside verge that rounds our faculty;
And where they reached, who can do more than reach?
It takes but little water just to touch
At some one point the inside of a sphere,
And, as we turn the sphere, touch all the rest
In due succession: but the finer air
Which not so palpably nor obviously,
Though no less universally, can touch
The whole circumference of that emptied sphere,
Fills it more fully than the water did;
Holds thrice the weight of water in itself
Resolved into a subtler element.
And yet the vulgar call the sphere first full
Up to the visible height—and after, void;
Not knowing air's more hidden properties.
And thus our soul, misknown, cries out to Zeus
To vindicate his purpose in its life—
Why stay we on the earth unless to grow?
Long since, I imaged, wrote the fiction out,
That he or other God descended here
And, once for all, showed simultaneously
What, in its nature, never can be shown
Piecemeal or in succession;—showed, I say,
The worth both absolute and relative
Of all His children from the birth of time,
His instruments for all appointed work.
I now go on to image,—might we hear
The judgment which should give the due to each,

Shew where the labour lay and where the ease,
And prove Zeus' self, the latent, everywhere!
This is a dream. But no dream, let us hope,
That years and days, the summers and the springs
Follow each other with unwaning powers—
The grapes which dye thy wine, are richer far
Through culture, than the wild wealth of the rock;
The suave plum than the savage-tasted drupe;
The pastured honey-bee drops choicer sweet;
The flowers turn double, and the leaves turn flowers;
That young and tender crescent-moon, thy slave,
Sleeping upon her robe as if on clouds,
Refines upon the women of my youth.
What, and the soul alone deteriorates?
I have not chanted verse like Homer's, no—
Nor swept string like Terpander, no—nor carved
And painted men like Phidias and his friend:
I am not great as they are, point by point:
But I have entered into sympathy
With these four, running these into one soul,
Who, separate, ignored each others' arts.
Say, is it nothing that I know them all?
The wild flower was the larger—I have dashed
Rose-blood upon its petals, pricked its cup's
Honey with wine, and driven its seed to fruit,
And show a better flower if not so large.
I stand, myself. Refer this to the gods
Whose gift alone it is! which, shall I dare
(All pride apart) upon the absurd pretext
That such a gift by chance lay in my hand,
Discourse of lightly or depreciate?
It might have fallen to another's hand—what then?
I pass too surely—let at least truth stay!

And next, of what thou followest on to ask.
This being with me as I declare, O king,
My works, in all these varicoloured kinds,
So done by me, accepted so by men—
Thou askest if (my soul thus in men's hearts)
I must not be accounted to attain

The very crown and proper end of life.
Inquiring thence how, now life closeth up,
I face death with success in my right hand:
Whether I fear death less than dost thyself
The fortunate of men. "For" (writest thou)
"Thou leavest much behind, while I leave nought:
Thy life stays in the poems men shall sing,
The pictures men shall study; while my life,
Complete and whole now in its power and joy,
Dies altogether with my brain and arm,
Is lost indeed; since,—what survives myself?
The brazen statue that o'erlooks my grave,
Set on the promontory which I named.
And that—some supple courtier of my heir
Shall use its robed and sceptred arm, perhaps,
To fix the rope to, which best drags it down.
I go, then: triumph thou, who dost not go!"

Nay, thou art worthy of hearing my whole mind.
Is this apparent, when thou turn'st to muse
Upon the scheme of earth and man in chief,
That admiration grows as knowledge grows?
That imperfection means perfection hid,
Reserved in part, to grace the after-time?
If, in the morning of philosophy,
Ere aught had been recorded, aught perceived,
Thou, with the light now in thee, couldst have looked
On all earth's tenantry, from worm to bird,
Ere man had yet appeared upon the stage—
Thou wouldst have seen them perfect, and deduced
The perfectness of others yet unseen.
Conceding which,—had Zeus then questioned thee
"Wilt thou go on a step, improve on this,
Do more for visible creatures than is done?"
Thou wouldst have answered, "Ay, by making each
Grow conscious in himself—by that alone.
All's perfect else: the shell sucks fast the rock,
The fish strikes through the sea, the snake both swims
And slides; the birds take flight, forth range the beasts,
Till life's mechanics can no further go—

And all this joy in natural life, is put,
Like fire from off Thy finger into each,
So exquisitely perfect is the same.
But 'tis pure fire—and they mere matter are;
It has them, not they it: and so I choose,
For man, Thy last premeditated work
(If I might add a glory to this scheme)
That a third thing should stand apart from both,
A quality arise within the soul,
Which, intro-active, made to supervise
And feel the force it has, may view itself,
And so be happy." Man might live at first
The animal life: but is there nothing more?
In due time, let him critically learn
How he lives; and, the more he gets to know
Of his own life's adaptabilities,
The more joy-giving will his life become.
The man who hath this quality, is best.

But thou, king, hadst more reasonably said:
"Let progress end at once,—man make no step
Beyond the natural man, the better beast,
Using his senses, not the sense of sense."
In man there's failure, only since he left
The lower and inconscious forms of life.
We called it an advance, the rendering plain
A spirit might grow conscious of that life,
And, by new lore so added to the old,
Take each step higher over the brute's head.
This grew the only life, the pleasure-house,
Watch-tower and treasure-fortress of the soul,
Which whole surrounding flats of natural life
Seemed only fit to yield subsistence to;
A tower that crowns a country. But alas!
The soul now climbs it just to perish there,
For thence we have discovered ('tis no dream—
We know this, which we had not else perceived)
That there's a world of capability
For joy, spread round about us, meant for us,
Inviting us; and still the soul craves all,

And still the flesh replies, "Take no jot more
Than ere you climbed the tower to look abroad!
Nay, so much less, as that fatigue has brought
Deduction to it." We struggle—fain to enlarge
Our bounded physical recipiency,
Increase our power, supply fresh oil to life,
Repair the waste of age and sickness. No,
It skills not: life's inadequate to joy,
As the soul sees joy, tempting life to take.
They praise a fountain in my garden here
Wherein a Naiad sends the water-spurt
Thin from her tube; she smiles to see it rise.
What if I told her, it is just a thread
From that great river which the hills shut up,
And mock her with my leave to take the same?
The artificer has given her one small tube
Past power to widen or exchange—what boots
To know she might spout oceans if she could ?
She cannot lift beyond her first straight thread.
And so a man can use but a man's joy
While he sees God's. Is it, for Zeus to boast
"See, man, how happy I live, and despair—
That I may be still happier—for thy use!"
If this were so, we could not thank our Lord,
As hearts beat on to doing: 'tis not so—
Malice it is not. Is it carelessness?
Still, no. If care—where is the sign, I ask—
And get no answer: and agree in sum,
O king, with thy profound discouragement,
Who seest the wider but to sigh the more.
Most progress is most failure! thou sayest well.

The last point now:—thou dost except a case—
Holding joy not impossible to one
With artist-gifts—to such a man as I—
Who leave behind me living works indeed;
For, such a poem, such a painting lives.
What? dost thou verily trip upon a word,
Confound the accurate view of what joy is
(Caught somewhat clearer by my eyes than thine)

With feeling joy? confound the knowing how
And showing how to live (my faculty)
With actually living?—Otherwise
Where is the artist's vantage o'er the king?
Because in my great epos I display
How divers men young, strong, fair, wise, can act—
Is this as though I acted? if I paint,
Carve the young Phœbus, am I therefore young?
Methinks I'm older that I bowed myself
The many years of pain that taught me art!
Indeed, to know is something, and to prove
How all this beauty might be enjoyed, is more:
But, knowing nought, to enjoy is something too.
Yon rower with the moulded muscles there
Lowering the sail, is nearer it than I.
I can write love-odes—thy fair slave's an ode.
I get to sing of love, when grown too grey
For being beloved: she turns to that young man
The muscles all a-ripple on his back.
I know the joy of kingship: well—thou art king!

"But," sayest thou—(and I marvel, I repeat,
To find thee tripping on a mere word) "what
Thou writest, paintest, stays: that does not die:
Sappho survives, because we sing her songs,
And Æschylus, because we read his plays!"
Why, if they live still, let them come and take
Thy slave in my despite—drink from thy cup—
Speak in my place. Thou diest while I survive?
Say rather that my fate is deadlier still,—
In this, that every day my sense of joy
Grows more acute, my soul (intensified
In power and insight) more enlarged, more keen;
While every day my hairs fall more and more,
My hand shakes, and the heavy years increase—
The horror quickening still from year to year,
The consummation coming past escape
When I shall know most, and yet least enjoy—
When all my works wherein I prove my worth,
Being present still to mock me in men's mouths,

Alive still, in the phrase of such as thou,
I, I, the feeling, thinking, acting man,
The man who loved his life so over much,
Shall sleep in my urn. It is so horrible,
I dare at times imagine to my need
Some future state revealed to us by Zeus,
Unlimited in capability
For joy, as this is in desire for joy,
To seek which, the joy-hunger forces us.
That, stung by straitness of our life, made strait
On purpose to make sweet the life at large—
Freed by the throbbing impulse we call death
We burst there as the worm into the fly,
Who, while a worm still, wants his wings. But, no!
Zeus has not yet revealed it; and, alas!
He must have done so—were it possible!

Live long and happy, and in that thought die,
Glad for what was. Farewell. And for the rest,
I cannot tell thy messenger aright
Where to deliver what he bears of thine
To one called Paulus—we have heard his fame
Indeed, if Christus be not one with him—
I know not, nor am troubled much to know.
Thou canst not think a mere barbarian Jew,
As Paulus proves to be, one circumcised,
Hath access to a secret shut from us?
Thou wrongest our philosophy, O king,
In stooping to inquire of such an one,
As if his answer could impose at all.
He writeth, doth he? well, and he may write.
Oh, the Jew findeth scholars! certain slaves
Who touched on this same isle, preached him and Christ;
And (as I gathered from a bystander)
Their doctrines could be held by no sane man.

THE TWINS

"Give" and "It-shall-be-given-unto-you"

1

GRAND rough old Martin Luther
Bloomed fables—flowers on furze,
The better the uncouther:
Do roses stick like burrs?

2

A beggar asked an alms
One day at an abbey-door,
Said Luther; but, seized with qualms,
The Abbot replied, "We're poor!"

3

"Poor, who had plenty once,
When gifts fell thick as rain:
But they give us nought, for the nonce,
And how should we give again?"

4

Then the beggar, "See your sins!
Of old, unless I err,
Ye had brothers for inmates, twins,
Date and Dabitur."

5

"While Date was in good case
Dabitur flourished too:
For Dabitur's lenten face,
No wonder if Date rue."

6

"Would ye retrieve the one?
Try and make plump the other!
When Date's penance is done,
Dabitur helps his brother."

7

"Only, beware relapse!"
  The Abbot hung his head.
This beggar might be, perhaps,
  An angel, Luther said.

POPULARITY

1

Stand still, true poet that you are,
  I know you; let me try and draw you.
Some night you'll fail us. When afar
  You rise, remember one man saw you,
Knew you, and named a star.

2

My star, God's glow-worm! Why extend
  That loving hand of His which leads you,
Yet locks you safe from end to end
  Of this dark world, unless He needs you—
Just saves your light to spend?

3

His clenched Hand shall unclose at last
  I know, and let out all the beauty.
My poet holds the future fast,
  Accepts the coming ages' duty,
Their present for this past.

4

That day, the earth's feast-master's brow
  Shall clear, to God the chalice raising;
"Others give best at first, but Thou
  For ever set'st our table praising,—
Keep'st the good wine till now."

5

Meantime, I'll draw you as you stand,
  With few or none to watch and wonder.
I'll say—a fisher (on the sand
  By Tyre the Old) his ocean-plunder,
A netful, brought to land.

6

Who has not heard how Tyrian shells
  Enclosed the blue, that dye of dyes
Whereof one drop worked miracles,
  And coloured like Astarte's eyes
Raw silk the merchant sells?

7

And each bystander of them all
  Could criticise, and quote tradition
How depths of blue sublimed some pall,
  To get which, pricked a king's ambition;
Worth sceptre, crown and ball.

8

Yet there's the dye,—in that rough mesh,
  The sea has only just o'er-whispered!
Live whelks, the lip's-beard dripping fresh,
  As if they still the water's lisp heard
Through foam the rock-weeds thresh.

9

Enough to furnish Solomon
  Such hangings for his cedar-house,
That when gold-robed he took the throne
  In that abyss of blue, the Spouse
Might swear his presence shone

10

Most like the centre-spike of gold
  Which burns deep in the blue-bell's womb,
What time, with ardours manifold,
  The bee goes singing to her groom,
Drunken and overbold.

11

Mere conchs! not fit for warp or woof!
  Till art comes,—comes to pound and squeeze
And clarify,—refines to proof
  The liquor filtered by degrees,
While the world stands aloof.

12

And there's the extract, flasked and fine,
  And priced, and saleable at last!
And Hobbs, Nobbs, Stokes and Nokes combine
  To paint the future from the past,
Put blue into their line.

13

Hobbs hints blue,—straight he turtle eats.
  Nobbs prints blue,—claret crowns his cup.
Nokes outdares Stokes in azure feats,—
  Both gorge. Who fished the murex up?
What porridge had John Keats?

TWO IN THE CAMPAGNA

1

I WONDER do you feel to-day
  As I have felt, since, hand in hand,
We sat down on the grass, to stray
  In spirit better through the land,
This morn of Rome and May?

2

For me, I touched a thought, I know,
  Has tantalised me many times,
(Like turns of thread the spiders throw
  Mocking across our path) for rhymes
To catch at and let go.

3

Help me to hold it: first it left
  The yellowing fennel, run to seed
There, branching from the brickwork's cleft,
  Some old tomb's ruin: yonder weed
Took up the floating weft,

4

Where one small orange cup amassed
  Five beetles,—blind and green they grope
Among the honey-meal,—and last
  Everywhere on the grassy slope
I traced it. Hold it fast!

5

The champaign with its endless fleece
  Of feathery grasses everywhere!
Silence and passion, joy and peace,
  An everlasting wash of air—
Rome's ghost since her decease.

6

Such life there, through such lengths of hours,
  Such miracles performed in play,
Such primal naked forms of flowers,
  Such letting Nature have her way
While Heaven looks from its towers.

7

How say you? Let us, O my dove,
  Let us be unashamed of soul,
As earth lies bare to heaven above.
  How is it under our control
To love or not to love?

8

I would that you were all to me,
  You that are just so much, no more—
Nor yours, nor mine,—nor slave nor free!
  Where does the fault lie? what the core
Of the wound, since wound must be?

9

I would I could adopt your will,
See with your eyes, and set my heart
Beating by yours, and drink my fill
At your soul's springs,—your part, my part
In life, for good and ill.

10

No. I yearn upward—touch you close,
Then stand away. I kiss your cheek,
Catch your soul's warmth,—I pluck the rose
And love it more than tongue can speak—
Then the good minute goes.

11

Already how am I so far
Out of that minute? Must I go
Still like the thistle-ball, no bar,
Onward, whenever light winds blow,
Fixed by no friendly star?

12

Just when I seemed about to learn!
Where is the thread now? Off again!
The old trick! Only I discern—
Infinite passion and the pain
Of finite hearts that yearn.

A GRAMMARIAN'S FUNERAL

Time—Shortly after the revival of learning in Europe

Let us begin and carry up this corpse,
Singing together.
Leave we the common crofts, the vulgar thorpes,
Each in its tether
Sleeping safe on the bosom of the plain,
Cared-for till cock-crow.
Look out if yonder's not the day again
Rimming the rock-row!

That's the appropriate country—there, man's thought,
    Rarer, intenser,
Self-gathered for an outbreak, as it ought,
    Chafes in the censer!
Leave we the unlettered plain its herd and crop;
    Seek we sepulture
On a tall mountain, citied to the top,
    Crowded with culture!
All the peaks soar, but one the rest excels;
    Clouds overcome it;
No, yonder sparkle is the citadel's
    Circling its summit!
Thither our path lies—wind we up the heights—
    Wait ye the warning?
Our low life was the level's and the night's;
    He's for the morning!
Step to a tune, square chests, erect the head,
    'Ware the beholders!
This is our master, famous, calm, and dead,
    Borne on our shoulders.

Sleep, crop and herd! sleep, darkling thorpe and croft,
    Safe from the weather!
He, whom we convoy to his grave aloft,
    Singing together,
He was a man born with thy face and throat,
    Lyric Apollo!
Long he lived nameless: how should spring take note
    Winter would follow?
Till lo, the little touch, and youth was gone!
    Cramped and diminished,
Moaned he, "New measures, other feet anon!
    My dance is finished"?
No, that's the world's way! (keep the mountain-side,
    Make for the city.)
He knew the signal, and stepped on with pride
    Over men's pity;
Left play for work, and grappled with the world
    Bent on escaping:

"What's in the scroll," quoth he, "thou keepest furled?
    Shew me their shaping,
Theirs, who most studied man, the bard and sage,—
    Give!"—So he gowned him,
Straight got by heart that book to its last page:
    Learned, we found him!
Yea, but we found him bald too—eyes like lead,
    Accents uncertain:
"Time to taste life," another would have said,
    "Up with the curtain!"
This man said rather, "Actual life comes next?
    Patience a moment!
Grant I have mastered learning's crabbed text,
    Still, there's the comment.
Let me know all. Prate not of most or least,
    Painful or easy:
Even to the crumbs I'd fain eat up the feast,
    Ay, nor feel queasy!"
Oh, such a life as he resolved to live,
    When he had learned it,
When he had gathered all books had to give;
    Sooner, he spurned it!
Image the whole, then execute the parts—
    Fancy the fabric
Quite, ere you build, ere steel strike fire from quartz,
    Ere mortar dab brick!

(Here's the town-gate reached: there's the market-place
    Gaping before us.)
Yea, this in him was the peculiar grace
    (Hearten our chorus)
Still before living he'd learn how to live—
    No end to learning.
Earn the means first—God surely will contrive
    Use for our earning.
Others mistrust and say—"But time escapes,—
    Live now or never!"
He said, "What's Time? leave Now for dogs and apes!
    Man has For ever."

Back to his book then: deeper drooped his head;
    Calculus racked him:
Leaden before, his eyes grew dross of lead;
    Tussis attacked him.
"Now, Master, take a little rest!"—not he!
    (Caution redoubled!
Step two a-breast, the way winds narrowly.)
    Not a whit troubled,
Back to his studies, fresher than at first,
    Fierce as a dragon
He, (soul-hydroptic with a sacred thirst)
    Sucked at the flagon.
Oh, if we draw a circle premature,
    Heedless of far gain,
Greedy for quick returns of profit, sure,
    Bad is our bargain!
Was it not great? did not he throw on God,
    (He loves the burthen)—
God's task to make the heavenly period
    Perfect the earthen?
Did not he magnify the mind, shew clear
    Just what it all meant?
He would not discount life, as fools do here,
    Paid by instalment!
He ventured neck or nothing—heaven's success
    Found, or earth's failure:
"Wilt thou trust death or not?" he answered "Yes.
    Hence with life's pale lure!"
That low man seeks a little thing to do,
    Sees it and does it:
This high man, with a great thing to pursue,
    Dies ere he knows it.
That low man goes on adding one to one,
    His hundred's soon hit:
This high man, aiming at a million,
    Misses an unit.
That, has the world here—should he need the next,
    Let the world mind him!
This, throws himself on God, and unperplext
    Seeking shall find Him.

So, with the throttling hands of Death at strife,
    Ground he at grammar;
Still, thro' the rattle, parts of speech were rife.
    While he could stammer
He settled *Hoti's* business—let it be!—
    Properly based *Oun*—
Gave us the doctrine of the enclitic *De*,
    Dead from the waist down.
Well, here's the platform, here's the proper place.
    Hail to your purlieus
All ye highfliers of the feathered race,
    Swallows and curlews!
Here's the top-peak! the multitude below
    Live, for they can there.
This man decided not to Live but Know—
    Bury this man there?
Here—here's his place, where meteors shoot, clouds form,
    Lightnings are loosened,
Stars come and go! let joy break with the storm—
    Peace let the dew send!
Lofty designs must close in like effects:
    Loftily lying,
Leave him—still loftier than the world suspects,
    Living and dying.

ONE WAY OF LOVE

I

ALL June I bound the rose in sheaves.
Now, rose by rose, I strip the leaves,
And strew them where Pauline may pass.
She will not turn aside? Alas!
Let them lie. Suppose they die?
The chance was they might take her eye.

2

How many a month I strove to suit
These stubborn fingers to the lute!

To-day I venture all I know.
She will not hear my music? So!
Break the string—fold music's wing.
Suppose Pauline had bade me sing!

3

My whole life long I learned to love.
This hour my utmost art I prove
And speak my passion.—Heaven or hell?
She will not give me heaven? 'Tis well!
Lose who may—I still can say,
Those who win heaven, blest are they.

ANOTHER WAY OF LOVE

I

June was not over,
Though past the full,
And the best of her roses
Had yet to blow,
When a man I know
(But shall not discover,
Since ears are dull,
And time discloses)
Turned him and said with a man's true air,
Half sighing a smile in a yawn, as 'twere,—
"If I tire of your June, will she greatly care?"

2

Well, Dear, in-doors with you!
True, serene deadness
Tries a man's temper.
What's in the blossom
June wears on her bosom?
Can it clear scores with you?
Sweetness and redness,
Eadem semper!
Go, let me care for it greatly or slightly!
If June mends her bowers now, your hand left unsightly
By plucking their roses,—my June will do rightly.

3

And after, for pastime,
  If June be refulgent
With flowers in completeness,
  All petals, no prickles,
  Delicious as trickles
Of wine poured at mass-time,—
  And choose One indulgent
To redness and sweetness:
Or if, with experience of man and of spider,
She use my June-lightning, the strong insect-ridder,
To stop the fresh spinning,—why, June will consider.

"TRANSCENDENTALISM"

A POEM IN TWELVE BOOKS

Stop playing, poet! may a brother speak?
'Tis you speak, that's your error. Song's our art:
Whereas you please to speak these naked thoughts
Instead of draping them in sights and sounds.
—True thoughts, good thoughts, thoughts fit to treasure up!
But why such long prolusion and display,
Such turning and adjustment of the harp,
And taking it upon your breast at length,
Only to speak dry words across its strings?
Stark-naked thought is in request enough—
Speak prose and holloa it till Europe hears!
The six-foot Swiss tube, braced about with bark,
Which helps the hunter's voice from Alp to Alp—
Exchange our harp for that,—who hinders you?

But here's your fault; grown men want thought, you think;
Thought's what they mean by verse, and seek in verse:
Boys seek for images and melody,
Men must have reason—so you aim at men.
Quite otherwise! Objects throng our youth, 'tis true,
We see and hear and do not wonder much.

If you could tell us what they mean, indeed!
As German Bœhme never cared for plants
Until it happed, a-walking in the fields,
He noticed all at once that plants could speak,
Nay, turned with loosened tongue to talk with him.
That day the daisy had an eye indeed—
Colloquised with the cowslip on such themes!
We find them extant yet in Jacob's prose.
But by the time youth slips a stage or two
While reading prose in that tough book he wrote,
(Collating, and emendating the same
And settling on the sense most to our mind)
We shut the clasps and find life's summer past.
Then, who helps more, pray, to repair our loss—
Another Bœhme with a tougher book
And subtler meanings of what roses say,—
Or some stout Mage like him of Halberstadt,
John, who made things Bœhme wrote thoughts about?
He with a "look you!" vents a brace of rhymes,
And in there breaks the sudden rose herself,
Over us, under, round us every side,
Nay, in and out the tables and the chairs
And musty volumes, Bœhme's book and all,—
Buries us with a glory, young once more,
Pouring heaven into this shut house of life.

So come, the harp back to your heart again!
You are a poem, though your poem's naught.
The best of all you did before, believe,
Was your own boy's-face o'er the finer chords
Bent, following the cherub at the top
That points to God with his paired half-moon wings.

MISCONCEPTIONS

I

This is a spray the Bird clung to,
Making it blossom with pleasure,
Ere the high tree-top she sprung to,
Fit for her nest and her treasure.

Oh, what a hope beyond measure
Was the poor spray's, which the flying feet hung to,—
So to be singled out, built in, and sung to!

2

This is a heart the Queen leant on,
Thrilled in a minute erratic,
Ere the true bosom she bent on,
Meet for love's regal dalmatic.
Oh, what a fancy ecstatic
Was the poor heart's, ere the wanderer went on—
Love to be saved for it, proffered to, spent on!

ONE WORD MORE

TO E.B.B.

1

THERE they are, my fifty men and women
Naming me the fifty poems finished!
Take them, Love, the book and me together.
Where the heart lies, let the brain lie also.

2

Rafael made a century of sonnets,
Made and wrote them in a certain volume
Dinted with the silver-pointed pencil
Else he only used to draw Madonnas:
These, the world might view—but One, the volume.
Who that one, you ask? Your heart instructs you.
Did she live and love it all her life-time?
Did she drop, his lady of the sonnets,
Die, and let it drop beside her pillow
Where it lay in place of Rafael's glory,
Rafael's cheek so duteous and so loving—
Cheek, the world was wont to hail a painter's,
Rafael's cheek, her love had turned a poet's?

3

You and I would rather read that volume,
(Taken to his beating bosom by it)
Lean and list the bosom-beats of Rafael,
Would we not? than wonder at Madonnas—
Her, San Sisto names, and Her, Foligno,
Her, that visits Florence in a vision,
Her, that's left with lilies in the Louvre—
Seen by us and all the world in circle.

4

You and I will never read that volume.
Guido Reni, like his own eye's apple
Guarded long the treasure-book and loved it.
Guido Reni dying, all Bologna
Cried, and the world with it, "Ours—the treasure!"
Suddenly, as rare things will, it vanished.

5

Dante once prepared to paint an angel:
Whom to please? You whisper "Beatrice."
While he mused and traced it and retraced it,
(Peradventure with a pen corroded
Still by drops of that hot ink he dipped for,
When, his left-hand i' the hair o' the wicked,
Back he held the brow and pricked its stigma,
Bit into the live man's flesh for parchment,
Loosed him, laughed to see the writing rankle,
Let the wretch go festering thro' Florence)—
Dante, who loved well because he hated,
Hated wickedness that hinders loving,
Dante standing, studying his angel,—
In there broke the folk of his Inferno.
Says he—"Certain people of importance"
(Such he gave his daily, dreadful line to)
Entered and would seize, forsooth, the poet.
Says the poet—"Then I stopped my painting."

6

You and I would rather see that angel,
Painted by the tenderness of Dante,
Would we not?—than read a fresh Inferno.

7

You and I will never see that picture.
While he mused on love and Beatrice,
While he softened o'er his outlined angel,
In they broke, those "people of importance:"
We and Bice bear the loss forever.

8

What of Rafael's sonnets, Dante's picture?

9

This: no artist lives and loves that longs not
Once, and only once, and for One only,
(Ah, the prize!) to find his love a language
Fit and fair and simple and sufficient—
Using nature that's an art to others,
Not, this one time, art that's turned his nature.
Ay, of all the artists living, loving,
None but would forego his proper dowry,—
Does he paint? he fain would write a poem,—
Does he write? he fain would paint a picture,
Put to proof art alien to the artist's,
Once, and only once, and for One only,
So to be the man and leave the artist,
Save the man's joy, miss the artist's sorrow.

10

Wherefore? Heaven's gift takes earth's abatement!
He who smites the rock and spreads the water,
Bidding drink and live a crowd beneath him,
Even he, the minute makes immortal,
Proves, perchance, his mortal in the minute,
Desecrates, belike, the deed in doing.
While he smites, how can he but remember,

So he smote before, in such a peril,
When they stood and mocked—"Shall smiting help us?"
When they drank and sneered—"A stroke is easy!"
When they wiped their mouths and went their journey,
Throwing him for thanks—"But drought was pleasant."
Thus old memories mar the actual triumph;
Thus the doing savours of disrelish;
Thus achievement lacks a gracious somewhat;
O'er-importuned brows becloud the mandate,
Carelessness or consciousness, the gesture.
For he bears an ancient wrong about him,
Sees and knows again those phalanxed faces,
Hears, yet one time more, the 'customed prelude—
"How should'st thou, of all men, smite, and save us?"
Guesses what is like to prove the sequel—
"Egypt's flesh-pots—nay, the drought was better."

11

Oh, the crowd must have emphatic warrant!
Theirs, the Sinai-forehead's cloven brilliance,
Right-arm's rod-sweep, tongue's imperial fiat.
Never dares the man put off the prophet.

12

Did he love one face from out the thousands,
(Were she Jethro's daughter, white and wifely,
Were she but the Æthiopian bondslave,)
He would envy yon dumb patient camel,
Keeping a reserve of scanty water
Meant to save his own life in the desert;
Ready in the desert to deliver
(Kneeling down to let his breast be opened)
Hoard and life together for his mistress.

13

I shall never, in the years remaining,
Paint you pictures, no, nor carve you statues,
Make you music that should all-express me;
So it seems: I stand on my attainment.
This of verse alone, one life allows me;

Verse and nothing else have I to give you.
Other heights in other lives, God willing—
All the gifts from all the heights, your own, Love!

14

Yet a semblance of resource avails us—
Shade so finely touched, love's sense must seize it.
Take these lines, look lovingly and nearly,
Lines I write the first time and the last time.
He who works in fresco, steals a hair-brush,
Curbs the liberal hand, subservient proudly,
Cramps his spirit, crowds its all in little,
Makes a strange art of an art familiar,
Fills his lady's missal-marge with flowerets.
He who blows thro' bronze, may breathe thro' silver,
Fitly serenade a slumbrous princess.
He who writes, may write for once, as I do.

15

Love, you saw me gather men and women,
Live or dead or fashioned by my fancy,
Enter each and all, and use their service,
Speak from every mouth,—the speech, a poem.
Hardly shall I tell my joys and sorrows,
Hopes and fears, belief and disbelieving:
I am mine and yours—the rest be all men's,
Karshish, Cleon, Norbert and the fifty.
Let me speak this once in my true person,
Not as Lippo, Roland or Andrea,
Though the fruit of speech be just this sentence—
Pray you, look on these my men and women,
Take and keep my fifty poems finished;
Where my heart lies, let my brain lie also!
Poor the speech; be how I speak, for all things.

16

Not but that you know me! Lo, the moon's self!
Here in London, yonder late in Florence,
Still we find her face, the thrice-transfigured.
Curving on a sky imbrued with colour,

Drifted over Fiesole by twilight,
Came she, our new crescent of a hair's-breadth.
Full she flared it, lamping Samminiato,
Rounder 'twixt the cypresses and rounder,
Perfect till the nightingales applauded.
Now, a piece of her old self, impoverished,
Hard to greet, she traverses the houseroofs,
Hurries with unhandsome thrift of silver,
Goes dispiritedly,—glad to finish.

17

What, there's nothing in the moon note-worthy?
Nay—for if that moon could love a mortal,
Use, to charm him (so to fit a fancy)
All her magic ('tis the old sweet mythos)
She would turn a new side to her mortal,
Side unseen of herdsman, huntsman, steersman—
Blank to Zoroaster on his terrace,
Blind to Galileo on his turret,
Dumb to Homer, dumb to Keats—him, even!
Think, the wonder of the moonstruck mortal—
When she turns round, comes again in heaven,
Opens out anew for worse or better!
Proves she like some portent of an ice-berg
Swimming full upon the ship it founders,
Hungry with huge teeth of splintered crystals?
Proves she as the paved-work of a sapphire
Seen by Moses when he climbed the mountain?
Moses, Aaron, Nadab and Abihu
Climbed and saw the very God, the Highest,
Stand upon the paved-work of a sapphire.
Like the bodied heaven in his clearness
Shone the stone, the sapphire of that paved-work,
When they ate and drank and saw God also!

18

What were seen? None knows, none ever shall know.
Only this is sure—the sight were other,
Not the moon's same side, born late in Florence,
Dying now impoverished here in London.

God be thanked, the meanest of his creatures
Boasts two soul-sides, one to face the world with,
One to show a woman when he loves her.

19

This I say of me, but think of you, Love!
This to you—yourself my moon of poets!
Ah, but that's the world's side—there's the wonder—
Thus they see you, praise you, think they know you.
There, in turn I stand with them and praise you,
Out of my own self, I dare to phrase it.
But the best is when I glide from out them,
Cross a step or two of dubious twilight,
Come out on the other side, the novel
Silent silver lights and darks undreamed of,
Where I hush and bless myself with silence.

20

Oh, their Rafael of the dear Madonnas,
Oh, their Dante of the dread Inferno,
Wrote one song—and in my brain I sing it,
Drew one angel—borne, see, on my bosom!

Dramatis Personæ

1864

Dramatis Personæ. By Robert Browning. London: Chapman and Hall, 193 Piccadilly. 1864.

Crown 8vo. Pp. vi + 252. Cloth boards.

[The same: second edition, 1864.]

THE first edition of *Dramatis Personæ* was published in May 1864; the second in the following September. In the interval Browning had added three stanzas to *Gold Hair* and had made a number of small changes in several other poems. (A pamphlet issue of *Gold Hair*, purporting to have been printed by W. Clowes & Sons in 1864, may be presumed to be a forgery.)

The text of the second edition is followed here, with evident errors corrected. Of the first poem in the volume, *James Lee* (later renamed *James Lee's Wife*), one only of the nine sections is included. Four whole poems are omitted—*The Worst of It, Dîs Aliter Visum, Too Late* and the *Epilogue*.

Dramatis Personæ

From JAMES LEE

AMONG THE ROCKS

I

Oh, good gigantic smile o' the brown old earth,
  This autumn morning! How he sets his bones
To bask i' the sun, and thrusts out knees and feet
For the ripple to run over in its mirth;
  Listening the while, where on the heap of stones
The white breast of the sea-lark twitters sweet.

2

That is the doctrine, simple, ancient, true;
  Such is life's trial, as old earth smiles and knows.
If you loved only what were worth your love,
Love were clear again, and wholly well for you:
  Make the low nature better by your throes!
Give earth yourself, go up for gain above!

GOLD HAIR

A STORY OF PORNIC

I

Oh, the beautiful girl, too white,
  Who lived at Pornic, down by the sea,
Just where the sea and the Loire unite!
  And a boasted name in Brittany
She bore, which I will not write.

2

Too white, for the flower of life is red;
  Her flesh was the soft, seraphic screen
Of a soul that is meant (her parents said)
  To just see earth, and hardly be seen,
And blossom in Heaven instead.

3

Yet earth saw one thing, one how fair!
  One grace that grew to its full on earth:
Smiles might be sparse on her cheek so spare,
  And her waist want half a girdle's girth,
But she had her great gold hair.

4

Hair, such a wonder of flix and floss,
  Freshness and fragrance—floods of it, too!
Gold, did I say? Nay, gold's mere dross:
  Here, Life smiled, "Think what I meant to do!"
And Love sighed, "Fancy my loss!"

5

So, when she died, it was scarce more strange
  Than that, when some delicate evening dies,
And you follow its spent sun's pallid range,
  There's a shoot of colour startles the skies
With sudden, violent change,—

6

That, while the breath was nearly to seek,
  As they put the little cross to her lips,
She changed; a spot came out on her cheek,
  A spark from her eye in mid-eclipse,
And she broke forth, "I must speak!"

7

"Not my hair!" made the girl her moan—
  "All the rest is gone or to go;
But the last, last grace, my all, my own,
  Let it stay in the grave, that the ghosts may know!
Leave my poor gold hair alone!"

8

The passion thus vented, dead lay she;
  Her parents sobbed their worst on that,
All friends joined in, nor observed degree:
  For indeed the hair was to wonder at,
As it spread—not flowing free,

9

But curled around her brow, like a crown,
  And coiled beside her cheeks, like a cap,
And calmed about her neck—ay, down
  To her breast, pressed flat, without a gap
I' the gold, it reached her gown.

10

All kissed that face, like a silver wedge
  Mid the yellow wealth, nor disturbed its hair;
E'en the priest allowed death's privilege,
  As he planted the crucifix with care
On her breast, 'twixt edge and edge.

11

And thus was she buried, inviolate
  Of body and soul, in the very space
By the altar; keeping saintly state
  In Pornic church, for her pride of race,
Pure life, and piteous fate.

12

And in after-time would your fresh tear fall,
  Though your mouth might twitch with a dubious smile,
As they told you of gold both robe and pall,
  How she prayed them leave it alone awhile,
So it never was touched at all.

13

Years flew; this legend grew at last
  The life of the lady; all she had done,
All been, in the memories fading fast
  Of lover and friend, was summed in one
Sentence survivors passed:

14

To wit, she was meant for Heaven, not earth;
  Had turned an angel before the time:
Yet, since she was mortal, in such dearth
  Of frailty, all you could count a crime
Was—she knew her gold hair's worth.

15

At little pleasant Pornic church,
  It chanced, the pavement wanted repair,
Was taken to pieces: left in the lurch,
  A certain sacred space lay bare,
And the boys began research.

16

'Twas the space where our sires would lay a saint,
  A benefactor,—a bishop, suppose,
A baron with armour-adornments quaint,
  A dame with chased ring and jewelled rose,
Things sanctity saves from taint;

17

So we come to find them in after-days
  When the corpse is presumed to have done with
    gauds
Of use to the living, in many ways:
  For the boys get pelf, and the town applauds,
And the church deserves the praise.

18

They grubbed with a will: and at length—*O cor*
  Humanum, pectora cæca, and the rest!—
They found—no gauds they were prying for,
  No ring, no rose, but—who would have guessed?—
A double Louis-d'or!

19

Here was a case for the priest: he heard,
  Marked, inwardly digested, laid
Finger on nose, smiled, "A little bird
  Chirps in my ear:" then, "Bring a spade,
Dig deeper!"—he gave the word.

20

And lo, when they came to the coffin-lid,
  Or the rotten planks which composed it once,
Why, there lay the girl's skull wedged amid
  A mint of money, it served for the nonce
To hold in its hair-heaps hid!

21

Hid there? Why? Could the girl be wont
  (She, the stainless soul) to treasure up
Money, earth's trash and Heaven's affront?
  Had a spider found out the communion-cup,
Was a toad in the christening-font?

22

Truth is truth: too true it was.
  Gold! She hoarded and hugged it first,
Longed for it, leaned o'er it, loved it—alas—
  Till the humour grew to a head and burst,
And she cried, at the final pass,—

23

"Talk not of God, my heart is stone!
  Nor lover nor friend—be gold for both!
Gold I lack; and, my all, my own,
  It shall hide in my hair. I scarce die loth,
If they let my hair alone!"

24

Louis-d'ors, some six times five,
  And duly double, every piece.
Now, do you see? With the priest to shrive,
  With parents preventing her soul's release
By kisses that kept alive,—

25

With Heaven's gold gates about to ope,
With friends' praise, gold-like, lingering still,
An instinct had bidden the girl's hand grope
For gold, the true sort—"Gold in Heaven, if you will;
But I keep earth's too, I hope."

26

Enough! The priest took the grave's grim yield:
The parents, they eyed that price of sin
As if *thirty pieces* lay revealed
On the place *to bury strangers in*,
The hideous Potter's Field.

27

But the priest bethought him: " 'Milk that's spilt'
—You know the adage! Watch and pray!
Saints tumble to earth with so slight a tilt!
It would build a new altar; that, we may!"
And the altar therewith was built.

28

Why I deliver this horrible verse?
As the text of a sermon, which now I preach:
Evil or good may be better or worse
In the human heart, but the mixture of each
Is a marvel and a curse.

29

The candid incline to surmise of late
That the Christian faith may be false, I find;
For our Essays-and-Reviews' debate
Begins to tell on the public mind,
And Colenso's words have weight:

30

I still, to suppose it true, for my part,
    See reasons and reasons; this, to begin:
'Tis the faith that launched point-blank her dart
    At the head of a lie—taught Original Sin,
The Corruption of Man's Heart.

ABT VOGLER

AFTER HE HAS BEEN EXTEMPORIZING UPON THE MUSICAL INSTRUMENT OF HIS INVENTION

I

Would that the structure brave, the manifold music I build,
    Bidding my organ obey, calling its keys to their work,
Claiming each slave of the sound, at a touch, as when Solomon willed
    Armies of angels that soar, legions of demons that lurk,
Man, brute, reptile, fly,—alien of end and of aim,
    Adverse, each from the other heaven-high, hell-deep removed,—
Should rush into sight at once as he named the ineffable Name,
    And pile him a palace straight, to pleasure the princess he loved!

2

Would it might tarry like his, the beautiful building of mine,
    This which my keys in a crowd pressed and importuned to raise!
Ah, one and all, how they helped, would dispart now and now combine,
    Zealous to hasten the work, heighten their master his praise!
And one would bury his brow with a blind plunge down to hell,
    Burrow awhile and build, broad on the roots of things,
Then up again swim into sight, having based me my palace well,
    Founded it, fearless of flame, flat on the nether springs.

3

And another would mount and march, like the excellent minion he was,
Ay, another and yet another, one crowd but with many a crest,
Raising my rampired walls of gold as transparent as glass,
Eager to do and die, yield each his place to the rest:
For higher still and higher (as a runner tips with fire,
When a great illumination surprises a festal night—
Outlining round and round Rome's dome from space to spire)
Up, the pinnacled glory reached, and the pride of my soul was in sight.

4

In sight? Not half! for it seemed, it was certain, to match man's birth,
Nature in turn conceived, obeying an impulse as I;
And the emulous heaven yearned down, made effort to reach the earth,
As the earth had done her best, in my passion, to scale the sky:
Novel splendours burst forth, grew familiar and dwelt with mine,
Not a point nor peak but found and fixed its wandering star;
Meteor-moons, balls of blaze: and they did not pale nor pine,
For earth had attained to heaven, there was no more near nor far.

5

Nay more; for there wanted not who walked in the glare and glow,
Presences plain in the place; or, fresh from the Protoplast,
Furnished for ages to come, when a kindlier wind should blow,
Lured now to begin and live, in a house to their liking at last;

Or else the wonderful Dead who have passed through the body and gone,
But were back once more to breathe in an old world worth their new:
What never had been, was now; what was, as it shall be anon;
And what is,—shall I say, matched both? for I was made perfect too.

6

All through my keys that gave their sounds to a wish of my soul,
All through my soul that praised as its wish flowed visibly forth,
All through music and me! For think, had I painted the whole,
Why, there it had stood, to see, nor the process so wonder-worth:
Had I written the same, made verse—still, effect proceeds from cause,
Ye know why the forms are fair, ye hear how the tale is told;
It is all triumphant art, but art in obedience to laws,
Painter and poet are proud in the artist-list enrolled:—

7

But here is the finger of God, a flash of the will that can,
Existent behind all laws, that made them and, lo, they are!
And I know not if, save in this, such gift be allowed to man,
That out of three sounds he frame, not a fourth sound, but a star.
Consider it well: each tone of our scale in itself is nought;
It is everywhere in the world—loud, soft, and all is said:
Give it to me to use! I mix it with two in my thought;
And, there! Ye have heard and seen: consider and bow the head!

8

Well, it is gone at last, the palace of music I reared;
  Gone! and the good tears start, the praises that come too slow;
For one is assured at first, one scarce can say that he feared,
  That he even gave it a thought, the gone thing was to go.
Never to be again! But many more of the kind
  As good, nay, better perchance: is this your comfort to me?
To me, who must be saved because I cling with my mind
  To the same, same self, same love, same God: ay, what was, shall be.

9

Therefore to whom turn I but to Thee, the ineffable Name?
  Builder and maker, Thou, of houses not made with hands!
What, have fear of change from Thee who art ever the same?
  Doubt that Thy power can fill the heart that Thy power expands?
There shall never be one lost good! What was, shall live as before;
  The evil is null, is nought, is silence implying sound;
What was good, shall be good, with, for evil, so much good more;
  On the earth the broken arcs; in the heaven, a perfect round.

10

All we have willed or hoped or dreamed of good, shall exist;
  Not its semblance, but itself; no beauty, nor good, nor power
Whose voice has gone forth, but each survives for the melodist
  When eternity affirms the conception of an hour.
The high that proved too high, the heroic for earth too hard,
  The passion that left the ground to lose itself in the sky,
Are music sent up to God by the lover and the bard;
  Enough that He heard it once: we shall hear it by-and-by.

11

And what is our failure here but a triumph's evidence
For the fulness of the days? Have we withered or agonized?
Why else was the pause prolonged but that singing might issue thence?
Why rushed the discords in, but that harmony should be prized?
Sorrow is hard to bear, and doubt is slow to clear,
Each sufferer says his say, his scheme of the weal and woe:
But God has a few of us whom He whispers in the ear;
The rest may reason and welcome: 'tis we musicians know.

12

Well, it is earth with me; silence resumes her reign:
I will be patient and proud, and soberly acquiesce.
Give me the keys. I feel for the common chord again,
Sliding by semitones, till I sink to the minor,—yes,
And I blunt it into a ninth, and I stand on alien ground,
Surveying a while the heights I rolled from into the deep;
Which, hark, I have dared and done, for my resting-place is found,
The C Major of this life: so, now I will try to sleep.

RABBI BEN EZRA

I

Grow old along with me!
The best is yet to be,
The last of life, for which the first was made:
Our times are in His hand
Who saith "A whole I planned,
Youth shows but half; trust God: see all, nor be afraid!"

2

Not that, amassing flowers,
Youth sighed "Which rose make ours,
Which lily leave and then as best recall?"
Not that, admiring stars,
It yearned "Nor Jove, nor Mars;
Mine be some figured flame which blends,
transcends them all!"

3

Not for such hopes and fears
Annulling youth's brief years,
Do I remonstrate: folly wide the mark!
Rather I prize the doubt
Low kinds exist without,
Finished and finite clods, untroubled by a spark.

4

Poor vaunt of life indeed,
Were man but formed to feed
On joy, to solely seek and find and feast:
Such feasting ended, then
As sure an end to men;
Irks care the crop-full bird? Frets doubt the
maw-crammed beast?

5

Rejoice we are allied
To That which doth provide
And not partake, effect and not receive!
A spark disturbs our clod;
Nearer we hold of God
Who gives, than of His tribes that take, I must
believe.

6

Then, welcome each rebuff
That turns earth's smoothness rough,
Each sting that bids nor sit nor stand but go!

Be our joys three-parts pain!
Strive, and hold cheap the strain;
Learn, nor account the pang; dare, never grudge the throe!

7

For thence,—a paradox
Which comforts while it mocks,—
Shall life succeed in that it seems to fail:
What I aspired to be,
And was not, comforts me:
A brute I might have been, but would not sink i' the scale.

8

What is he but a brute
Whose flesh hath soul to suit,
Whose spirit works lest arms and legs want play?
To man, propose this test—
Thy body at its best,
How far can that project thy soul on its lone way?

9

Yet gifts should prove their use:
I own the Past profuse
Of power each side, perfection every turn:
Eyes, ears took in their dole,
Brain treasured up the whole;
Should not the heart beat once "How good to live and learn?"

10

Not once beat "Praise be Thine!
I see the whole design,
I, who saw Power, see now Love perfect too:
Perfect I call Thy plan:
Thanks that I was a man!
Maker, remake, complete,—I trust what Thou shalt do!"

11

For pleasant is this flesh;
Our soul, in its rose-mesh
Pulled ever to the earth, still yearns for rest:
Would we some prize might hold
To match those manifold
Possessions of the brute,—gain most, as we did
best!

12

Let us not always say
"Spite of this flesh to-day
I strove, made head, gained ground upon the
whole!"
As the bird wings and sings,
Let us cry "All good things
Are ours, nor soul helps flesh more, now, than
flesh helps soul!"

13

Therefore I summon age
To grant youth's heritage,
Life's struggle having so far reached its term:
Thence shall I pass, approved
A man, for aye removed
From the developed brute; a God though in the
germ.

14

And I shall thereupon
Take rest, ere I be gone
Once more on my adventure brave and new:
Fearless and unperplexed,
When I wage battle next,
What weapons to select, what armour to indue.

15

Youth ended, I shall try
My gain or loss thereby;
Be the fire ashes, what survives is gold:

And I shall weigh the same,
Give life its praise or blame:
Young, all lay in dispute; I shall know, being
old.

16

For note, when evening shuts,
A certain moment cuts
The deed off, calls the glory from the grey:
A whisper from the west
Shoots—"Add this to the rest,
Take it and try its worth: here dies another
day."

17

So, still within this life,
Though lifted o'er its strife,
Let me discern, compare, pronounce at last,
"This rage was right i' the main,
That acquiescence vain:
The Future I may face now I have proved the
Past."

18

For more is not reserved
To man, with soul just nerved
To act to-morrow what he learns to-day:
Here, work enough to watch
The Master work, and catch
Hints of the proper craft, tricks of the tool's true
play.

19

As it was better, youth
Should strive, through acts uncouth,
Toward making, than repose on aught found
made;
So, better, age, exempt
From strife, should know, than tempt
Further. Thou waitedst age; wait death nor be
afraid!

20

Enough now, if the Right
And Good and Infinite
Be named here, as thou callest thy hand thine own,
With knowledge absolute,
Subject to no dispute
From fools that crowded youth, nor let thee feel alone.

21

Be there, for once and all,
Severed great minds from small,
Announced to each his station in the Past!
Was I, the world arraigned,
Were they, my soul disdained,
Right? Let age speak the truth and give us peace at last!

22

Now, who shall arbitrate?
Ten men love what I hate,
Shun what I follow, slight what I receive;
Ten, who in ears and eyes
Match me: we all surmise,
They, this thing, and I, that: whom shall my soul believe?

23

Not on the vulgar mass
Called "work," must sentence pass,
Things done, that took the eye and had the price;
O'er which, from level stand,
The low world laid its hand,
Found straightway to its mind, could value in a trice:

24

But all, the world's coarse thumb
And finger failed to plumb,
So passed in making up the main account;
All instincts immature,
All purposes unsure,
That weighed not as his work, yet swelled the
man's amount:

25

Thoughts hardly to be packed
Into a narrow act,
Fancies that broke through language and
escaped;
All I could never be,
All, men ignored in me,
This, I was worth to God, whose wheel the
pitcher shaped.

26

Ay, note that Potter's wheel,
That metaphor! and feel
Why time spins fast, why passive lies our clay,—
Thou, to whom fools propound,
When the wine makes its round,
"Since life fleets, all is change; the Past gone,
seize to-day!"

27

Fool! All that is, at all,
Lasts ever, past recall;
Earth changes, but thy soul and God stand sure:
What entered into thee,
That was, is, and shall be:
Time's wheel runs back or stops; Potter and clay
endure.

28

He fixed thee mid this dance
Of plastic circumstance,
This Present, thou, forsooth, wouldst fain arrest:
Machinery just meant
To give thy soul its bent,
Try thee and turn thee forth, sufficiently
impressed.

29

What though the earlier grooves
Which ran the laughing loves
Around thy base, no longer pause and press?
What though, about thy rim,
Scull-things in order grim
Grow out, in graver mood, obey the sterner
stress?

30

Look not thou down but up!
To uses of a cup,
The festal board, lamp's flash and trumpet's
peal,
The new wine's foaming flow,
The Master's lips a-glow!
Thou, heaven's consummate cup, what needst
thou with earth's wheel?

31

But I need, now as then,
Thee, God, who mouldest men;
And since, not even while the whirl was worst,
Did I,—to the wheel of life
With shapes and colours rife,
Bound dizzily,—mistake my end, to slake Thy
thirst:

32

So, take and use Thy work!
Amend what flaws may lurk,
What strain o' the stuff, what warpings past the aim!
My times be in Thy hand!
Perfect the cup as planned!
Let age approve of youth, and death complete the same!

A DEATH IN THE DESERT

[SUPPOSED of Pamphylax the Antiochene:
It is a parchment, of my rolls the fifth,
Hath three skins glued together, is all Greek,
And goeth from *Epsilon* down to *Mu*:
Lies second in the surnamed Chosen Chest,
Stained and conserved with juice of terebinth,
Covered with cloth of hair, and lettered *Xi*,
From Xanthus, my wife's uncle, now at peace:
Mu and *Epsilon* stand for my own name,
I may not write it, but I make a cross
To show I wait His coming, with the rest,
And leave off here: beginneth Pamphylax.]

I said, "If one should wet his lips with wine,
And slip the broadest plantain-leaf we find,
Or else the lappet of a linen robe,
Into the water-vessel, lay it right,
And cool his forehead just above the eyes,
The while a brother, kneeling either side,
Should chafe each hand and try to make it warm, --
He is not so far gone but he might speak."

This did not happen in the outer cave,
Nor in the secret chamber of the rock,
Where, sixty days since the decree was out,
We had him, bedded on a camel-skin,

And waited for his dying all the while;
But in the midmost grotto: since noon's light
Reached there a little, and we would not lose
The last of what might happen on his face.

I at the head, and Xanthus at the feet,
With Valens and the Boy, had lifted him,
And brought him from the chamber in the depths,
And laid him in the light where we might see:
For certain smiles began about his mouth,
And his lids moved, presageful of the end.

Beyond, and half way up the mouth o' the cave,
The Bactrian convert, having his desire,
Kept watch, and made pretence to graze a goat
That gave us milk, on rags of various herb,
Plantain and quitch, the rocks' shade keeps alive:
So that if any thief or soldier passed,
(Because the persecution was aware)
Yielding the goat up promptly with his life,
Such man might pass on, joyful at a prize,
Nor care to pry into the cool o' the cave.
Outside was all noon and the burning blue.

"Here is wine," answered Xanthus,—dropped a drop;
I stooped and placed the lap of cloth aright,
Then chafed his right hand, and the Boy his left:
But Valens had bethought him, and produced
And broke a ball of nard, and made perfume.
Only, he did—not so much wake, as—turn
And smile a little, as a sleeper does
If any dear one call him, touch his face—
And smiles and loves, but will not be disturbed.

Then Xanthus said a prayer, but still he slept:
It is the Xanthus that escaped to Rome,
Was burned, and could not write the chronicle.

Then the Boy sprang up from his knees, and ran,
Stung by the splendour of a sudden thought,
And fetched the seventh plate of graven lead
Out of the secret chamber, found a place,
Pressing with finger on the deeper dints,
And spoke, as 'twere his mouth proclaiming first,
"I am the Resurrection and the Life."

Whereat he opened his eyes wide at once,
And sat up of himself, and looked at us;
And thenceforth nobody pronounced a word:
Only, outside, the Bactrian cried his cry
Like the lone desert-bird that wears the ruff,
As signal we were safe, from time to time.

First he said, "If a friend declared to me,
This my son Valens, this my other son,
Were James and Peter,—nay, declared as well
This lad was very John,—I could believe!
—Could, for a moment, doubtlessly believe:
So is myself withdrawn into my depths,
The soul retreated from the perished brain
Whence it was wont to feel and use the world
Through these dull members, done with long ago.
Yet I myself remain; I feel myself:
And there is nothing lost. Let be, awhile!"

[This is the doctrine he was wont to teach,
How divers persons witness in each man,
Three souls which make up one soul: first, to wit,
A soul of each and all the bodily parts,
Seated therein, which works, and is what Does,
And has the use of earth, and ends the man
Downward: but, tending upward for advice,
Grows into, and again is grown into
By the next soul, which, seated in the brain,
Useth the first with its collected use,
And feeleth, thinketh, willeth,—is what Knows:
Which, duly tending upward in its turn,
Grows into, and again is grown into

By the last soul, that uses both the first,
Subsisting whether they assist or no,
And, constituting man's self, is what Is—
And leans upon the former, makes it play,
As that played off the first: and, tending up,
Holds, is upheld by, God, and ends the man
Upward in that dread point of intercourse,
Nor needs a place, for it returns to Him.
What Does, what Knows, what Is; three souls, one
man.
I give the glossa of Theotypas.]

And then, "A stick, once fire from end to end;
Now, ashes save the tip that holds a spark!
Yet, blow the spark, it runs back, spreads itself
A little where the fire was: thus I urge
The soul that served me, till it task once more
What ashes of my brain have kept their shape,
And these make effort on the last o' the flesh,
Trying to taste again the truth of things—"
(He smiled)—"their very superficial truth;
As that ye are my sons, that it is long
Since James and Peter had release by death,
And I am only he, your brother John,
Who saw and heard, and could remember all.
Remember all! It is not much to say.
What if the truth broke on me from above
As once and oft-times? Such might hap again:
Doubtlessly He might stand in presence here,
With head wool-white, eyes flame, and feet like brass,
The sword and the seven stars, as I have seen—
I who now shudder only and surmise
'How did your brother bear that sight and live?'

"If I live yet, it is for good, more love
Through me to men: be nought but ashes here
That keep awhile my semblance, who was John,—
Still, when they scatter, there is left on earth
No one alive who knew (consider this!)
—Saw with his eyes and handled with his hands

That which was from the first, the Word of Life.
How will it be when none more saith 'I saw'?

"Such ever was love's way: to rise, it stoops.
Since I, whom Christ's mouth taught, was bidden
 teach,
I went, for many years, about the world,
Saying 'It was so; so I heard and saw,'
Speaking as the case asked: and men believed.
Afterward came the message to myself
In Patmos isle; I was not bidden teach,
But simply listen, take a book and write,
Nor set down other than the given word,
With nothing left to my arbitrament
To choose or change: I wrote, and men believed.
Then, for my time grew brief, no message more,
No call to write again, I found a way,
And, reasoning from my knowledge, merely taught
Men should, for love's sake, in love's strength, believe;
Or I would pen a letter to a friend
And urge the same as friend, nor less nor more:
Friends said I reasoned rightly, and believed.
But at the last, why, I seemed left alive
Like a sea-jelly weak on Patmos strand,
To tell dry sea-beach gazers how I fared
When there was mid-sea, and the mighty things;
Left to repeat, 'I saw, I heard, I knew,'
And go all over the old ground again,
With Antichrist already in the world,
And many Antichrists, who answered prompt
'Am I not Jasper as thyself art John?
Nay, young, whereas through age thou mayest forget:
Wherefore, explain, or how shall we believe?'
I never thought to call down fire on such,
Or, as in wonderful and early days,
Pick up the scorpion, tread the serpent dumb;
But patient stated much of the Lord's life
Forgotten or misdelivered, and let it work:
Since much that at the first, in deed and word,
Lay simply and sufficiently exposed,

Had grown (or else my soul was grown to match,
Fed through such years, familiar with such light,
Guarded and guided still to see and speak)
Of new significance and fresh result;
What first were guessed as points, I now knew stars,
And named them in the Gospel I have writ.
For men said, 'It is getting long ago:'
'Where is the promise of His coming?'—asked
These young ones in their strength, as loth to wait,
Of me who, when their sires were born, was old.
I, for I loved them, answered, joyfully,
Since I was there, and helpful in my age;
And, in the main, I think such men believed.
Finally, thus endeavouring, I fell sick,
Ye brought me here, and I supposed the end,
And went to sleep with one thought that, at least,
Though the whole earth should lie in wickedness,
We had the truth, might leave the rest to God.
Yet now I wake in such decrepitude
As I had slidden down and fallen afar,
Past even the presence of my former self,
Grasping the while for stay at facts which snap,
Till I am found away from my own world,
Feeling for foot-hold through a blank profound,
Along with unborn people in strange lands,
Who say—I hear said or conceive they say—
'Was John at all, and did he say he saw?
Assure us, ere we ask what he might see!'

"And how shall I assure them? Can they share
—They, who have flesh, a veil of youth and strength
About each spirit, that needs must bide its time,
Living and learning still as years assist
Which wear the thickness thin, and let man see—
With me who hardly am withheld at all,
But shudderingly, scarce a shred between,
Lie bare to the universal prick of light?
Is it for nothing we grow old and weak,
We whom God loves? When pain ends, gain ends too.
To me, that story—ay, that Life and Death

Of which I wrote 'it was'—to me, it is;
—Is, here and now: I apprehend nought else.
Is not God now i' the world His power first made?
Is not His love at issue still with sin,
Closed with and cast and conquered, crucified
Visibly when a wrong is done on earth?
Love, wrong, and pain, what see I else around?
Yea, and the Resurrection and Uprise
To the right hand of the throne—what is it beside,
When such truth, breaking bounds, o'erfloods my soul,
And, as I saw the sin and death, even so
See I the need yet transiency of both,
The good and glory consummated thence?
I saw the Power; I see the Love, once weak,
Resume the Power: and in this word 'I see,'
Lo, there is recognized the Spirit of both
That, moving o'er the spirit of man, unblinds
His eye and bids him look. These are, I see;
But ye, the children, His beloved ones too,
Ye need,—as I should use an optic glass
I wondered at erewhile, somewhere i' the world,
It had been given a crafty smith to make;
A tube, he turned on objects brought too close,
Lying confusedly insubordinate
For the unassisted eye to master once:
Look through his tube, at distance now they lay,
Become succinct, distinct, so small, so clear!
Just thus, ye needs must apprehend what truth
I see, reduced to plain historic fact,
Diminished into clearness, proved a point
And far away: ye would withdraw your sense
From out eternity, strain it upon time,
Then stand before that fact, that Life and Death,
Stay there at gaze, till it dispart, dispread,
As though a star should open out, all sides,
And grow the world on you, as it is my world.

"For life, with all it yields of joy and woe,
And hope and fear,—believe the aged friend,—

Is just our chance o' the prize of learning love,
How love might be, hath been indeed, and is;
And that we hold thenceforth to the uttermost
Such prize despite the envy of the world,
And, having gained truth, keep truth: that is all.
But see the double way wherein we are led,
How the soul learns diversely from the flesh!
With flesh, that hath so little time to stay,
And yields mere basement for the soul's emprise,
Expect prompt teaching. Helpful was the light,
And warmth was cherishing and food was choice
To every man's flesh, thousand years ago,
As now to yours and mine; the body sprang
At once to the height, and stayed: but the soul,—no!
Since sages who, this noontide, meditate
In Rome or Athens, may descry some point
Of the eternal power, hid yestereve;
And as thereby the power's whole mass extends,
So much extends the æther floating o'er,
The love that tops the might, the Christ in God.
Then, as new lessons shall be learned in these
Till earth's work stop and useless time run out,
So duly, daily, needs provision be
For keeping the soul's prowess possible,
Building new barriers as the old decay,
Saving us from evasion of life's proof,
Putting the question ever, 'Does God love,
And will ye hold that truth against the world?'
Ye know there needs no second proof with good
Gained for our flesh from any earthly source:
We might go freezing, ages,—give us fire,
Thereafter we judge fire at its full worth,
And guard it safe through every chance, ye know!
That fable of Prometheus and his theft,
How mortals gained Jove's fiery flower, grows old
(I have been used to hear the pagans own)
And out of mind; but fire, howe'er its birth,
Here is it, precious to the sophist now
Who laughs the myth of Æschylus to scorn,
As precious to those satyrs of his play,

Who touched it in gay wonder at the thing.
While were it so with the soul,—this gift of truth
Once grasped, were this our soul's gain safe, and sure
To prosper as the body's gain is wont,—
Why, man's probation would conclude, his earth
Crumble; for he both reasons and decides,
Weighs first, then chooses: will he give up fire
For gold or purple once he knows its worth?
Could he give Christ up were His worth as plain?
Therefore, I say, to test man, shift the proofs,
Nor may he grasp that fact like other fact,
And straightway in his life acknowledge it,
As, say, the indubitable bliss of fire.
Sigh ye, 'It had been easier once than now?'
To give you answer I am left alive;
Look at me who was present from the first!
Ye know what things I saw; then came a test,
My first, befitting me who so had seen:
'Forsake the Christ thou sawest transfigured, Him
Who trod the sea and brought the dead to life?
What should wring this from thee?'—ye laugh and
ask.
What wrung it? Even a torchlight and a noise,
The sudden Roman faces, violent hands,
And fear of what the Jews might do! Just that,
And, it is written, 'I forsook and fled':
There was my trial, and it ended thus.
Ay, but my soul had gained its truth, could grow:
Another year or two,—what little child,
What tender woman that had seen no least
Of all my sights, but barely heard them told,
Who did not clasp the cross with a light laugh,
Or wrap the burning robe round, thanking God?
Well, was truth safe for ever, then? Not so.
Already had begun the silent work
Whereby truth, deadened of its absolute blaze,
Might need love's eye to pierce the o'erstretched
doubt:
Teachers were busy, whispering 'All is true
As the aged ones report; but youth can reach

Where age gropes dimly, weak with stir and strain,
And the full doctrine slumbers till to-day.'
Thus, what the Roman's lowered spear was found,
A bar to me who touched and handled truth,
Now proved the glozing of some new shrewd tongue,
This Ebion, this Cerinthus or their mates,
Till imminent was the outcry 'Save us Christ!'
Whereon I stated much of the Lord's life
Forgotten or misdelivered, and let it work.
Such work done, as it will be, what comes next?
What do I hear say, or conceive men say,
'Was John at all, and did he say he saw?
Assure us, ere we ask what he might see!'

"Is this indeed a burthen for late days,
And may I help to bear it with you all,
Using my weakness which becomes your strength?
For if a babe were born inside this grot,
Grew to a boy here, heard us praise the sun,
Yet had but yon sole glimmer in light's place,—
One loving him and wishful he should learn,
Would much rejoice himself was blinded first
Month by month here, so made to understand
How eyes, born darkling, apprehend amiss:
I think I could explain to such a child
There was more glow outside than gleams he caught,
Ay, nor need urge 'I saw it, so believe!'
It is a heavy burthen you shall bear
In latter days, new lands, or old grown strange,
Left without me, which must be very soon.
What is the doubt, my brothers? Quick with it!
I see you stand conversing, each new face,
Either in fields, of yellow summer eves,
On islets yet unnamed amid the sea;
Or pace for shelter 'neath a portico
Out of the crowd in some enormous town
Where now the larks sing in a solitude;
Or muse upon blank heaps of stone and sand
Idly conjectured to be Ephesus:
And no one asks his fellow any more

'Where is the promise of His coming?' but
'Was He revealed in any of His lives,
As Power, as Love, as Influencing Soul?'

"Quick, for time presses, tell the whole mind out,
And let us ask and answer and be saved!
My book speaks on, because it cannot pass;
One listens quietly, nor scoffs but pleads
'Here is a tale of things done ages since;
What truth was ever told the second day?
Wonders, that would prove doctrine, go for nought.
Remains the doctrine, love; well, we must love,
And what we love most, power and love in one,
Let us acknowledge on the record here,
Accepting these in Christ: must Christ then be?
Has He been? Did not we ourselves make Him?
Our mind receives but what it holds, no more.
First of the love, then; we acknowledge Christ—
A proof we comprehend His love, a proof
We had such love already in ourselves,
Knew first what else we should not recognize.
'Tis mere projection from man's inmost mind,
And, what he loves, thus falls reflected back,
Becomes accounted somewhat out of him;
He throws it up in air, it drops down earth's,
With shape, name, story added, man's old way.
How prove you Christ came otherwise at least?
Next try the power: He made and rules the world:
Certes there is a world once made, now ruled,
Unless things have been ever as we see.
Our sires declared a charioteer's yoked steeds
Brought the sun up the east and down the west,
Which only of itself now rises, sets,
As if a hand impelled it and a will,—
Thus they long thought, they who had will and
    hands:
But the new question's whisper is distinct,
Wherefore must all force needs be like ourselves?
We have the hands, the will; what made and drives
The sun is force, is law, is named, not known,

While will and love we do know; marks of these,
Eye-witnesses attest, so books declare—
As that, to punish or reward our race,
The sun at undue times arose or set
Or else stood still: what do not men affirm?
But earth requires as urgently reward
Or punishment to-day as years ago,
And none expects the sun will interpose:
Therefore it was mere passion and mistake,
Or erring zeal for right, which changed the truth.
Go back, far, farther, to the birth of things;
Ever the will, the intelligence, the love,
Man's!—which he gives, supposing he but finds,
As late he gave head, body, hands and feet,
To help these in what forms he called his gods.
First, Jove's brow, Juno's eyes were swept away,
But Jove's wrath, Juno's pride continued long;
As last, will, power, and love discarded these,
So law in turns discards power, love, and will.
What proveth God is otherwise at least?
All else, projection from the mind of man!'

"Nay, do not give me wine, for I am strong,
But place my gospel where I put my hands.

"I say that man was made to grow, not stop;
That help, he needed once, and needs no more,
Having grown up but an inch by, is withdrawn:
For he hath new needs, and new helps to these.
This imports solely, man should mount on each
New height in view; the help whereby he mounts,
The ladder-rung his foot has left, may fall,
Since all things suffer change save God the Truth.
Man apprehends Him newly at each stage
Whereat earth's ladder drops, its service done;
And nothing shall prove twice what once was proved.
You stick a garden-plot with ordered twigs
To show inside lie germs of herbs unborn,
And check the careless step would spoil their birth;
But when herbs wave, the guardian twigs may go,

Since should ye doubt of virtues, question kinds,
It is no longer for old twigs ye look,
Which proved once underneath lay store of seed,
But to the herb's self, by what light ye boast,
For what fruit's signs are. This book's fruit is plain,
Nor miracles need prove it any more.
Doth the fruit show? Then miracles bade 'ware
At first of root and stem, saved both till now
From trampling ox, rough boar and wanton goat.
What? Was man made a wheelwork to wind up,
And be discharged, and straight wound up anew?
No!—grown, his growth lasts; taught, he ne'er forgets:
May learn a thousand things, not twice the same.

"This might be pagan teaching: now hear mine.

"I say, that as the babe, you feed awhile,
Becomes a boy and fit to feed himself,
So, minds at first must be spoon-fed with truth:
When they can eat, babe's nurture is withdrawn.
I fed the babe whether it would or no:
I bid the boy or feed himself or starve.
I cried once, 'That ye may believe in Christ,
Behold this blind man shall receive his sight!'
I cry now, 'Urgest thou, *for I am shrewd*
And smile at stories how John's word could cure—
Repeat that miracle and take my faith?'
I say, that miracle was duly wrought
When, save for it, no faith was possible.
Whether a change were wrought i' the shows o' the world,
Whether the change came from our minds which see
Of the shows o' the world so much as and no more
Than God wills for His purpose,—(what do I
See now, suppose you, there where you see rock
Round us?)—I know not; such was the effect,
So faith grew, making void more miracles
Because too much: they would compel, not help.
I say, the acknowledgment of God in Christ

Accepted by thy reason, solves for thee
All questions in the earth and out of it,
And has so far advanced thee to be wise.
Wouldst thou unprove this to re-prove the proved?
In life's mere minute, with power to use that proof,
Leave knowledge and revert to how it sprung?
Thou hast it; use it and forthwith, or die!

"For I say, this is death and the sole death,
When a man's loss comes to him from his gain,
Darkness from light, from knowledge ignorance,
And lack of love from love made manifest;
A lamp's death when, replete with oil, it chokes;
A stomach's when, surcharged with food, it starves.
With ignorance was surety of a cure.
When man, appalled at nature, questioned first
'What if there lurk a might behind this might?'
He needed satisfaction God could give,
And did give, as ye have the written word:
But when he finds might still redouble might,
Yet asks, 'Since all is might, what use of will?'
—Will, the one source of might,—he being man
With a man's will and a man's might, to teach
In little how the two combine in large,—
That man has turned round on himself and stands,
Which in the course of nature is, to die.

"And when man questioned, 'What if there be love
Behind the will and might, as real as they?'—
He needed satisfaction God could give,
And did give, as ye have the written word:
But when, beholding that love everywhere,
He reasons, 'Since such love is everywhere,
And since ourselves can love and would be loved,
We ourselves make the love, and Christ was not,'—
How shall ye help this man who knows himself,
That he must love and would be loved again,
Yet, owning his own love that proveth Christ,
Rejecteth Christ through very need of Him?
The lamp o'erswims with oil, the stomach flags
Loaded with nurture, and that man's soul dies.

"If he rejoin, 'But this was all the while
A trick; the fault was, first of all, in thee,
Thy story of the places, names and dates,
Where, when and how the ultimate truth had rise,
—Thy prior truth, at last discovered none,
Whence now the second suffers detriment.
What good of giving knowledge if, because
Of the manner of the gift, its profit fail?
And why refuse what modicum of help
Had stopped the after-doubt, impossible
I' the face of truth—truth absolute, uniform?
Why must I hit of this and miss of that,
Distinguish just as I be weak or strong,
And not ask of thee and have answer prompt,
Was this once, was it not once?—then and now
And evermore, plain truth from man to man.
Is John's procedure just the heathen bard's?
Put question of his famous play again
How for the ephemerals' sake, Jove's fire was filched,
And carried in a cane and brought to earth:
The fact is in the fable, cry the wise,
Mortals obtained the boon, so much is fact,
Though fire be spirit and produced on earth.
As with the Titan's, so now with thy tale:
Why breed in us perplexity, mistake,
Nor tell the whole truth in the proper words?'

"I answer, Have ye yet to argue out
The very primal thesis, plainest law,
—Man is not God but hath God's end to serve,
A master to obey, a course to take,
Somewhat to cast off, somewhat to become?
Grant this, then man must pass from old to new,
From vain to real, from mistake to fact,
From what once seemed good, to what now proves best.
How could man have progression otherwise?
Before the point was mooted 'What is God?'
No savage man inquired 'What am myself?'
Much less replied, 'First, last, and best of things.'

Man takes that title now if he believes
Might can exist with neither will nor love,
In God's case—what he names now Nature's Law—
While in himself he recognizes love
No less than might and will: and rightly takes.
Since if man prove the sole existent thing
Where these combine, whatever their degree,
However weak the might or will or love,
So they be found there, put in evidence,—
He is as surely higher in the scale
Than any might with neither love nor will,
As life, apparent in the poorest midge,
When the faint dust-speck flits, ye guess its wing,
Is marvellous beyond dead Atlas' self:
I give such to the midge for resting-place!
Thus, man proves best and highest—God, in fine,
And thus the victory leads but to defeat,
The gain to loss, best rise to the worst fall,
His life becomes impossible, which is death.

"But if, appealing thence, he cower, avouch
He is mere man, and in humility
Neither may know God nor mistake himself;
I point to the immediate consequence
And say, by such confession straight he falls
Into man's place, a thing nor God nor beast,
Made to know that he can know and not more:
Lower than God who knows all and can all,
Higher than beasts which know and can so far
As each beast's limit, perfect to an end,
Nor conscious that they know, nor craving more;
While man knows partly but conceives beside,
Creeps ever on from fancies to the fact,
And in this striving, this converting air
Into a solid he may grasp and use,
Finds progress, man's distinctive mark alone,
Not God's, and not the beasts': God is, they are,
Man partly is and wholly hopes to be.
Such progress could no more attend his soul
Were all it struggles after found at first

And guesses changed to knowledge absolute,
Than motion wait his body, were all else
Than it the solid earth on every side,
Where now through space he moves from rest to rest.
Man, therefore, thus conditioned, must expect
He could not, what he knows now, know at first;
What he considers that he knows to-day,
Come but to-morrow, he will find misknown;
Getting increase of knowledge, since he learns
Because he lives, which is to be a man,
Set to instruct himself by his past self:
First, like the brute, obliged by facts to learn,
Next, as man may, obliged by his own mind,
Bent, habit, nature, knowledge turned to law.
God's gift was that man should conceive of truth
And yearn to gain it, catching at mistake,
As midway help till he reach fact indeed.
The statuary ere he mould a shape
Boasts a like gift, the shape's idea, and next
The aspiration to produce the same;
So, taking clay, he calls his shape thereout,
Cries ever 'Now I have the thing I see':
Yet all the while goes changing what was wrought,
From falsehood like the truth, to truth itself.
How were it had he cried 'I see no face,
No breast, no feet i' the ineffectual clay?'
Rather commend him that he clapped his hands,
And laughed 'It is my shape and lives again!'
Enjoyed the falsehood, touched it on to truth,
Until yourselves applaud the flesh indeed
In what is still flesh-imitating clay.
Right in you, right in him, such way be man's!
God only makes the live shape at a jet.
Will ye renounce this pact of creatureship?
The pattern on the Mount subsists no more,
Seemed awhile, then returned to nothingness;
But copies, Moses strove to make thereby,
Serve still and are replaced as time requires:
By these, make newest vessels, reach the type!
If ye demur, this judgment on your head,

Never to reach the ultimate, angels' law,
Indulging every instinct of the soul
There where law, life, joy, impulse are one thing!

"Such is the burthen of the latest time.
I have survived to hear it with my ears,
Answer it with my lips: does this suffice?
For if there be a further woe than such,
Wherein my brothers struggling need a hand,
So long as any pulse is left in mine,
May I be absent even longer yet,
Plucking the blind ones back from the abyss,
Though I should tarry a new hundred years!"

But he was dead: 'twas about noon, the day
Somewhat declining: we five buried him
That eve, and then, dividing, went five ways,
And I, disguised, returned to Ephesus.

By this, the cave's mouth must be filled with sand.
Valens is lost, I know not of his trace;
The Bactrian was but a wild, childish man,
And could not write nor speak, but only loved:
So, lest the memory of this go quite,
Seeing that I to-morrow fight the beasts,
I tell the same to Phœbas, whom believe!
For many look again to find that face,
Beloved John's to whom I ministered,
Somewhere in life about the world; they err:
Either mistaking what was darkly spoke
At ending of his book, as he relates,
Or misconceiving somewhat of this speech
Scattered from mouth to mouth, as I suppose.
Believe ye will not see him any more
About the world with his divine regard!
For all was as I say, and now the man
Lies as he lay once, breast to breast with God.

[Cerinthus read and mused; one added this:

"If Christ, as thou affirmest, be of men
Mere man, the first and best but nothing more,—
Account Him, for reward of what He was,
Now and for ever, wretchedest of all.
For see; Himself conceived of life as love,
Conceived of love as what must enter in,
Fill up, make one with His each soul He loved:
Thus much for man's joy, all men's joy for Him.
Well, He is gone, thou sayest, to fit reward.
But by this time are many souls set free,
And very many still retained alive:
Nay, should His coming be delayed awhile,
Say, ten years longer (twelve years, some compute)
See if, for every finger of thy hands,
There be not found, that day the world shall end,
Hundreds of souls, each holding by Christ's word
That He will grow incorporate with all,
With me as Pamphylax, with him as John,
Groom for each bride! Can a mere man do this?
Yet Christ saith, this He lived and died to do.
Call Christ, then, the illimitable God,
Or lost!"

But 'twas Cerinthus that is lost.]

CALIBAN UPON SETEBOS

OR NATURAL THEOLOGY IN THE ISLAND

"Thou thoughtest that I was altogether such an one as thyself"

['WILL sprawl, now that the heat of day is best,
Flat on his belly in the pit's much mire,
With elbows wide, fists clenched to prop his chin;
And, while he kicks both feet in the cool slush,
And feels about his spine small eft-things course,
Run in and out each arm, and make him laugh;
And while above his head a pompion-plant,
Coating the cave-top as a brow its eye,
Creeps down to touch and tickle hair and beard,

And now a flower drops with a bee inside,
And now a fruit to snap at, catch and crunch:
He looks out o'er yon sea which sunbeams cross
And recross till they weave a spider-web,
(Meshes of fire, some great fish breaks at times)
And talks to his own self, howe'er he please,
Touching that other, whom his dam called God.
Because to talk about Him, vexes—ha,
Could He but know! and time to vex is now,
When talk is safer than in winter-time.
Moreover Prosper and Miranda sleep
In confidence he drudges at their task,
And it is good to cheat the pair, and gibe,
Letting the rank tongue blossom into speech.]

Setebos, Setebos, and Setebos!
'Thinketh, He dwelleth i' the cold o' the moon.

'Thinketh He made it, with the sun to match,
But not the stars; the stars came otherwise;
Only made clouds, winds, meteors, such as that:
Also this isle, what lives and grows thereon,
And snaky sea which rounds and ends the same.

'Thinketh, it came of being ill at ease:
He hated that He cannot change His cold,
Nor cure its ache. 'Hath spied an icy fish
That longed to 'scape the rock-stream where she lived,
And thaw herself within the lukewarm brine
O' the lazy sea her stream thrusts far amid,
A crystal spike 'twixt two warm walls of wave;
Only she ever sickened, found repulse
At the other kind of water, not her life,
(Green-dense and dim-delicious, bred o' the sun)
Flounced back from bliss she was not born to breathe,
And in her old bounds buried her despair,
Hating and loving warmth alike: so He.

'Thinketh, He made thereat the sun, this isle,
Trees and the fowls here, beast and creeping thing.

Yon otter, sleek-wet, black, lithe as a leech;
Yon auk, one fire-eye in a ball of foam,
That floats and feeds; a certain badger brown
He hath watched hunt with that slant white-wedge eye
By moonlight; and the pie with the long tongue
That pricks deep into oakwarts for a worm,
And says a plain word when she finds her prize,
But will not eat the ants; the ants themselves
That build a wall of seeds and settled stalks
About their hole—He made all these and more,
Made all we see, and us, in spite: how else?
He could not, Himself, make a second self
To be His mate; as well have made Himself.
He would not make what He mislikes or slights,
An eyesore to Him, or not worth His pains:
But did, in envy, listlessness or sport,
Make what Himself would fain, in a manner, be—
Weaker in most points, stronger in a few,
Worthy, and yet mere playthings all the while,
Things He admires and mocks too,—that is it.
Because, so brave, so better though they be,
It nothing skills if He begin to plague.
Look now, I melt a gourd-fruit into mash,
Add honeycomb and pods, I have perceived,
Which bite like finches when they bill and kiss,—
Then, when froth rises bladdery, drink up all,
Quick, quick, till maggots scamper through my brain;
And throw me on my back i' the seeded thyme,
And wanton, wishing I were born a bird.
Put case, unable to be what I wish,
I yet could make a live bird out of clay:
Would not I take clay, pinch my Caliban
Able to fly?—for, there, see, he hath wings,
And great comb like the hoopoe's to admire,
And there, a sting to do his foes offence,
There, and I will that he begin to live,
Fly to yon rock-top, nip me off the horns
Of grigs high up that make the merry din,
Saucy through their veined wings, and mind me not.
In which feat, if his leg snapped, brittle clay,

And he lay stupid-like,—why, I should laugh;
And if he, spying me, should fall to weep,
Beseech me to be good, repair his wrong,
Bid his poor leg smart less or grow again,—
Well, as the chance were, this might take or else
Not take my fancy: I might hear his cry,
And give the manikin three legs for his one,
Or pluck the other off, leave him like an egg,
And lessoned he was mine and merely clay.
Were this no pleasure, lying in the thyme,
Drinking the mash, with brain become alive,
Making and marring clay at will? So He.

'Thinketh, such shows nor right nor wrong in Him,
Nor kind, nor cruel: He is strong and Lord.
'Am strong myself compared to yonder crabs
That march now from the mountain to the sea;
'Let twenty pass, and stone the twenty-first,
Loving not, hating not, just choosing so.
'Say, the first straggler that boasts purple spots
Shall join the file, one pincer twisted off;
'Say, this bruised fellow shall receive a worm,
And two worms he whose nippers end in red;
As it likes me each time, I do: so He.

Well then, 'supposeth He is good i' the main,
Placable if His mind and ways were guessed,
But rougher than His handiwork, be sure!
Oh, He hath made things worthier than Himself,
And envieth that, so helped, such things do more
Than He who made them! What consoles but this?
That they, unless through Him, do nought at all,
And must submit: what other use in things?
'Hath cut a pipe of pithless elder-joint
That, blown through, gives exact the scream o' the jay
When from her wing you twitch the feathers blue:
Sound this, and little birds that hate the jay
Flock within stone's throw, glad their foe is hurt:
Put case such pipe could prattle and boast forsooth
"I catch the birds, I am the crafty thing,

I make the cry my maker cannot make
With his great round mouth; he must blow through
mine!"
Would not I smash it with my foot? So He.

But wherefore rough, why cold and ill at ease?
Aha, that is a question! Ask, for that,
What knows,—the something over Setebos
That made Him, or He, may be, found and fought,
Worsted, drove off and did to nothing, perchance.
There may be something quiet o'er His head,
Out of His reach, that feels nor joy nor grief,
Since both derive from weakness in some way.
I joy because the quails come; would not joy
Could I bring quails here when I have a mind:
This Quiet, all it hath a mind to, doth.
'Esteemeth stars the outposts of its couch,
But never spends much thought nor care that way.
It may look up, work up,—the worse for those
It works on! 'Careth but for Setebos
The many-handed as a cuttle-fish,
Who, making Himself feared through what He does,
Looks up, first, and perceives He cannot soar
To what is quiet and hath happy life;
Next looks down here, and out of very spite
Makes this a bauble-world to ape yon real,
These good things to match those as hips do grapes.
'Tis solace making baubles, ay, and sport.
Himself peeped late, eyed Prosper at his books
Careless and lofty, lord now of the isle:
Vexed, 'stitched a book of broad leaves, arrow-shaped,
Wrote thereon, he knows what, prodigious words;
Has peeled a wand and called it by a name;
Weareth at whiles for an enchanter's robe
The eyed skin of a supple oncelot;
And hath an ounce sleeker than youngling mole,
A four-legged serpent he makes cower and couch,
Now snarl, now hold its breath and mind his eye,
And saith she is Miranda and my wife:

'Keeps for his Ariel a tall pouch-bill crane
He bids go wade for fish, and straight disgorge;
Also a sea-beast, lumpish, which he snared,
Blinded the eyes of, and brought somewhat tame,
And split its toe-webs, and now pens the drudge
In a hole o' the rock and calls him Caliban;
A bitter heart, that bides its time and bites.
'Plays thus at being Prosper in a way,
Taketh his mirth with make-believes: so He.

His dam held that the Quiet made all things
Which Setebos vexed only: 'holds not so.
Who made them weak, meant weakness He might vex.
Had He meant other, while His hand was in,
Why not make horny eyes no thorn could prick,
Or plate my scalp with bone against the snow,
Or overscale my flesh 'neath joint and joint,
Like an orc's armour? Ay,—so spoil His sport!
He is the One now: only He doth all.

'Saith, He may like, perchance, what profits Him.
Ay, himself loves what does him good; but why?
'Gets good no otherwise. This blinded beast
Loves whoso places flesh-meat on his nose,
But, had he eyes, would want no help, but hate
Or love, just as it liked him: He hath eyes.
Also it pleaseth Setebos to work,
Use all His hands, and exercise much craft,
By no means for the love of what is worked.
'Tasteth, himself, no finer good i' the world
When all goes right, in this safe summer-time,
And he wants little, hungers, aches not much,
Than trying what to do with wit and strength.
'Falls to make something: 'piled yon pile of turfs,
And squared and stuck there squares of soft white chalk,
And, with a fish-tooth, scratched a moon on each,
And set up endwise certain spikes of tree,
And crowned the whole with a sloth's skull a-top,
Found dead i' the woods, too hard for one to kill.

No use at all i' the work, for work's sole sake;
'Shall some day knock it down again: so He.

'Saith He is terrible: watch His feats in proof!
One hurricane will spoil six good months' hope.
He hath a spite against me, that I know,
Just as He favours Prosper, who knows why?
So it is, all the same, as well I find.
'Wove wattles half the winter, fenced them firm
With stone and stake to stop she-tortoises
Crawling to lay their eggs here: well, one wave,
Feeling the foot of Him upon its neck,
Gaped as a snake does, lolled out its large tongue,
And licked the whole labour flat: so much for spite.
'Saw a ball flame down late (yonder it lies)
Where, half an hour before, I slept i' the shade:
Often they scatter sparkles: there is force!
'Dug up a newt He may have envied once
And turned to stone, shut up inside a stone.
Please Him and hinder this?—What Prosper does?
Aha, if He would tell me how! Not He!
There is the sport: discover how or die!
All need not die, for of the things o' the isle
Some flee afar, some dive, some run up trees;
Those at His mercy,—why, they please Him most
When . . . when . . .well, never try the same way twice!
Repeat what act has pleased, He may grow wroth.
You must not know His ways, and play Him off,
Sure of the issue. 'Doth the like himself:
'Spareth a squirrel that it nothing fears
But steals the nut from underneath my thumb,
And when I threat, bites stoutly in defence:
'Spareth an urchin that, contrariwise,
Curls up into a ball, pretending death
For fright at my approach: the two ways please.
But what would move my choler more than this,
That either creature counted on its life
To-morrow and next day and all days to come,
Saying forsooth in the inmost of its heart,
"Because he did so yesterday with me,

And otherwise with such another brute,
So must he do henceforth and always."—Ay?
'Would teach the reasoning couple what "must" means!
'Doth as he likes, or wherefore Lord? So He.

'Conceiveth all things will continue thus,
And we shall have to live in fear of Him
So long as He lives, keeps His strength: no change,
If He have done His best, make no new world
To please Him more, so leave off watching this,—
If He surprise not even the Quiet's self
Some strange day,—or, suppose, grow into it
As grubs grow butterflies: else, here are we,
And there is He, and nowhere help at all.

'Believeth with the life, the pain shall stop.
His dam held different, that after death
He both plagued enemies and feasted friends:
Idly! He doth His worst in this our life,
Giving just respite lest we die through pain,
Saving last pain for worst,—with which, an end.
Meanwhile, the best way to escape His ire
Is, not to seem too happy. Sees, himself,
Yonder two flies, with purple films and pink,
Bask on the pompion-bell above: kills both.
'Sees two black painful beetles roll their ball
On head and tail as if to save their lives:
Moves them the stick away they strive to clear.

Even so, 'would have Him misconceive, suppose
This Caliban strives hard and ails no less,
And always, above all else, envies Him.
Wherefore he mainly dances on dark nights,
Moans in the sun, gets under holes to laugh,
And never speaks his mind save housed as now:
Outside, 'groans, curses. If He caught me here,
O'erheard this speech, and asked "What chucklest at?"
'Would, to appease Him, cut a finger off,
Or of my three kid yearlings burn the best,
Or let the toothsome apples rot on tree,

Or push my tame beast for the orc to taste:
While myself lit a fire, and made a song
And sung it, "*What I hate, be consecrate*
To celebrate Thee and Thy state, no mate
For Thee; what see for envy in poor me?"
Hoping the while, since evils sometimes mend,
Warts rub away, and sores are cured with slime,
That some strange day, will either the Quiet catch
And conquer Setebos, or likelier He
Decrepit may doze, doze, as good as die.

[What, what? A curtain o'er the world at once!
Crickets stop hissing; not a bird—or, yes,
There scuds His raven that hath told Him all!
It was fool's play, this prattling! Ha! The wind
Shoulders the pillared dust, death's house o' the move,
And fast invading fires begin! White blaze—
A tree's head snaps—and there, there, there, there, there,
His thunder follows! Fool to gibe at Him!
Lo! 'Lieth flat and loveth Setebos!
'Maketh his teeth meet through his upper lip,
Will let those quails fly, will not eat this month
One little mess of whelks, so he may 'scape!]

CONFESSIONS

I

WHAT is he buzzing in my ears?
  "Now that I come to die,
Do I view the world as a vale of tears?"
  Ah, reverend sir, not I!

2

What I viewed there once, what I view again,
  Where the physic bottles stand
On the table's edge,—is a suburb lane,
  With a wall to my bedside hand.

3

That lane sloped, much as the bottles do,
  From a house you could descry
O'er the garden-wall: is the curtain blue
  Or green to a healthy eye?

4

To mine, it serves for the old June weather
  Blue above lane and wall;
And that farthest bottle labelled "Ether"
  Is the house o'er-topping all.

5

At a terrace, somewhat near its stopper,
  There watched for me, one June,
A girl: I know, sir, it's improper,
  My poor mind's out of tune.

6

Only, there was a way . . . you crept
  Close by the side, to dodge
Eyes in the house, two eyes except:
  They styled their house "The Lodge."

7

What right had a lounger up their lane?
  But, by creeping very close,
With the good wall's help,—their eyes might
    strain
  And stretch themselves to Oes,

8

Yet never catch her and me together,
  As she left the attic, there,
By the rim of the bottle labelled "Ether,"
  And stole from stair to stair,

9

And stood by the rose-wreathed gate. Alas,
We loved, sir—used to meet:
How sad and bad and mad it was—
But then, how it was sweet!

MAY AND DEATH

1

I WISH that when you died last May,
Charles, there had died along with you
Three parts of spring's delightful things;
Ay, and, for me, the fourth part too.

2

A foolish thought, and worse, perhaps!
There must be many a pair of friends
Who, arm in arm, deserve the warm
Moon-births and the long evening-ends.

3

So, for their sakes, be May still May!
Let their new time, as mine of old,
Do all it did for me: I bid
Sweet sights and sounds throng manifold.

4

Only, one little sight, one plant,
Woods have in May, that starts up green
Save a sole streak which, so to speak,
Is spring's blood, spilt its leaves between,—

5

That, they might spare; a certain wood
Might miss the plant; their loss were small:
But I,—whene'er the leaf grows there,
Its drop comes from my heart, that's all.

PROSPICE

Fear death?—to feel the fog in my throat,
  The mist in my face,
When the snows begin, and the blasts denote
  I am nearing the place,
The power of the night, the press of the storm,
  The post of the foe;
Where he stands, the Arch Fear in a visible form,
  Yet the strong man must go:
For the journey is done and the summit attained,
  And the barriers fall,
Though a battle's to fight ere the guerdon be gained,
  The reward of it all.
I was ever a fighter, so—one fight more,
  The best and the last!
I would hate that death bandaged my eyes, and forbore,
  And bade me creep past.
No! let me taste the whole of it, fare like my peers
  The heroes of old,
Bear the brunt, in a minute pay glad life's arrears
  Of pain, darkness and cold.
For sudden the worst turns the best to the brave,
  The black minute's at end,
And the elements' rage, the fiend-voices that rave,
  Shall dwindle, shall blend,
Shall change, shall become first a peace, then a joy,
  Then a light, then thy breast,
O thou soul of my soul! I shall clasp thee again,
  And with God be the rest!

YOUTH AND ART

I

It once might have been, once only:
  We lodged in a street together,
You, a sparrow on the housetop lonely,
  I, a lone she-bird of his feather.

2

Your trade was with sticks and clay,
  You thumbed, thrust, patted and polished,
Then laughed "They will see some day
  Smith made, and Gibson demolished."

3

My business was song, song, song;
  I chirped, cheeped, trilled and twittered,
"Kate Brown's on the boards ere long,
  And Grisi's existence embittered!"

4

I earned no more by a warble
  Than you by a sketch in plaster;
You wanted a piece of marble,
  I needed a music-master.

5

We studied hard in our styles,
  Chipped each at a crust like Hindoos,
For air, looked out on the tiles,
  For fun, watched each other's windows.

6

You lounged, like a boy of the South,
  Cap and blouse—nay, a bit of beard too;
Or you got it, rubbing your mouth
  With fingers the clay adhered to.

7

And I—soon managed to find
  Weak points in the flower-fence facing,
Was forced to put up a blind
  And be safe in my corset-lacing.

8

No harm! It was not my fault
  If you never turned your eyes' tail up,
As I shook upon E *in alt.*,
  Or ran the chromatic scale up:

9

For spring bade the sparrows pair,
  And the boys and girls gave guesses,
And stalls in our street looked rare
  With bulrush and watercresses.

10

Why did not you pinch a flower
  In a pellet of clay and fling it?
Why did not I put a power
  Of thanks in a look, or sing it?

11

I did look, sharp as a lynx,
  (And yet the memory rankles)
When models arrived, some minx
  Tripped up-stairs, she and her ankles.

12

But I think I gave you as good!
  "That foreign fellow,—who can know
How she pays, in a playful mood,
  For his tuning her that piano?"

13

Could you say so, and never say
  "Suppose we join hands and fortunes,
And I fetch her from over the way,
  Her, piano, and long tunes and short tunes?"

14

No, no: you would not be rash,
  Nor I rasher and something over:
You've to settle yet Gibson's hash,
  And Grisi yet lives in clover.

15

But you meet the Prince at the Board,
  I'm queen myself at *bals-paré*,
I've married a rich old lord,
  And you're dubbed knight and an R.A.

16

Each life's unfulfilled, you see;
It hangs still, patchy and scrappy:
We have not sighed deep, laughed free,
Starved, feasted, despaired,—been happy.

17

And nobody calls you a dunce,
And people suppose me clever:
This could but have happened once,
And we missed it, lost it for ever.

A FACE

If one could have that little head of hers
Painted upon a background of pale gold,
Such as the Tuscan's early art prefers!
No shade encroaching on the matchless mould
Of those two lips, which should be opening soft
In the pure profile; not as when she laughs,
For that spoils all: but rather as if aloft
Yon hyacinth, she loves so, leaned its staff's
Burthen of honey-coloured buds to kiss
And capture 'twixt the lips apart for this.
Then her lithe neck, three fingers might surround,
How it should waver on the pale gold ground
Up to the fruit-shaped, perfect chin it lifts!
I know, Correggio loves to mass, in rifts
Of heaven, his angel faces, orb on orb
Breaking its outline, burning shades absorb:
But these are only massed there, I should think,
Waiting to see some wonder momently
Grow out, stand full, fade slow against the sky
(That's the pale ground you'd see this sweet face by),
All heaven, meanwhile, condensed into one eye
Which fears to lose the wonder, should it wink.

A LIKENESS

Some people hang portraits up
In a room where they dine or sup:
And the wife clinks tea-things under,
And her cousin, he stirs his cup,
Asks, "Who was the lady, I wonder?"
"'Tis a daub John bought at a sale,"
Quoth the wife,—looks black as thunder:
"What a shade beneath her nose!
Snuff-taking, I suppose,—"
Adds the cousin, while John's corns ail.

Or else, there's no wife in the case,
But the portrait's queen of the place,
Alone mid the other spoils
Of youth,—masks, gloves and foils,
And pipe-sticks, rose, cherry-tree, jasmine,
And the long whip, the tandem-lasher,
And the cast from a fist ("not, alas! mine,
But my master's, the Tipton Slasher")
And the cards where pistol-balls mark ace,
And a satin shoe used for cigar-case,
And the chamois-horns ("shot in the Chablais")
And prints—Rarey drumming on Cruiser,
And Sayers, our champion, the bruiser,
And the little edition of Rabelais:
Where a friend, with both hands in his pockets,
May saunter up close to examine it,
And remark a good deal of Jane Lamb in it,
"But the eyes are half out of their sockets;
That hair's not so bad, where the gloss is,
But they've made the girl's nose a proboscis:
Jane Lamb, that we danced with at Vichy!
What, is not she Jane? Then, who is she?"

All that I own is a print,
An etching, a mezzotint;
'Tis a study, a fancy, a fiction,
Yet a fact (take my conviction)

Because it has more than a hint
Of a certain face, I never
Saw elsewhere touch or trace of
In women I've seen the face of:
Just an etching, and, so far, clever.

I keep my prints, an imbroglio,
Fifty in one portfolio.
When somebody tries my claret,
We turn round chairs to the fire,
Chirp over days in a garret,
Chuckle o'er increase of salary,
Taste the good fruits of our leisure,
Talk about pencil and lyre,
And the National Portrait Gallery:
Then I exhibit my treasure.
After we've turned over twenty,
And the debt of wonder my crony owes
Is paid to my Marc Antonios,
He stops me—"*Festina lentè!*
What's that sweet thing there, the etching?"
How my waistcoat-strings want stretching,
How my cheeks grow red as tomatos,
How my heart leaps! But hearts, after leaps, ache.

"By the by, you must take, for a keepsake,
That other, you praised, of Volpato's."
The fool! would he try a flight further and say
He never saw, never before to-day,
What was able to take his breath away,
A face to lose youth for, to occupy age
With the dream of, meet death with,—why, I'll not
  engage
But that, half in a rapture and half in a rage,
I should toss him the thing's self—"'Tis only a
  duplicate,
A thing of no value! Take it, I supplicate!"

MR SLUDGE "THE MEDIUM"

Now, don't sir! Don't expose me! Just this once!
This was the first and only time, I'll swear,—
Look at me,—see, I kneel,—the only time,
I swear, I ever cheated,—yes, by the soul
Of Her who hears—(your sainted mother, sir!)
All, except this last accident, was truth—
This little kind of slip!—and even this,
It was your own wine, sir, the good champagne,
(I took it for Catawba,—you're so kind)
Which put the folly in my head!

"Get up?"
You still inflict on me that terrible face?
You show no mercy?—Not for Her dear sake,
The sainted spirit's, whose soft breath even now
Blows on my cheek—(don't you feel something, sir?)
You'll tell?

Go tell, then! Who the devil cares
What such a rowdy chooses to . . .

Aie—aie—aie!
Please, sir! your thumbs are through my windpipe, sir!
Ch—ch!

Well, sir, I hope you've done it now!
Oh Lord! I little thought, sir, yesterday,
When your departed mother spoke those words
Of peace through me, and moved you, sir, so much,
You gave me—(very kind it was of you)
These shirt-studs—(better take them back again,
Please, sir!)—yes, little did I think so soon
A trifle of trick, all through a glass too much
Of his own champagne, would change my best of friends
Into an angry gentleman!

Though, 'twas wrong.
I don't contest the point; your anger's just:

Whatever put such folly in my head,
I know 'twas wicked of me. There's a thick,
Dusk, undeveloped spirit (I've observed)
Owes me a grudge—a negro's, I should say,
Or else an Irish emigrant's; yourself
Explained the case so well last Sunday, sir,
When we had summoned Franklin to clear up
A point about those shares in the telegraph:
Ay, and he swore . . . or might it be Tom Paine? . . .
Thumping the table close by where I crouched,
He'd do me soon a mischief: that's come true!

Why, now your face clears! I was sure it would!
Then, this one time . . . don't take your hand away,
Through yours I surely kiss your mother's hand . . .
You'll promise to forgive me?—or, at least,
Tell nobody of this? Consider, sir!
What harm can mercy do? Would but the shade
Of the venerable dead-one just vouchsafe
A rap or tip! What bit of paper's here?
Suppose we take a pencil, let her write,
Make the least sign, she urges on her child
Forgiveness? There now! Eh? Oh! 'Twas your foot,
And not a natural creak, sir?

Answer, then!
Once, twice, thrice . . . see, I'm waiting to say "thrice!"
All to no use? No sort of hope for me?
It's all to post to Greeley's newspaper?

What? If I told you all about the tricks?
Upon my soul!—the whole truth, and nought else,
And how there's been some falsehood—for your part,
Will you engage to pay my passage out,
And hold your tongue until I'm safe on board?
England's the place, not Boston—no offence!
I see what makes you hesitate: don't fear!
I mean to change my trade and cheat no more,
Yes, this time really it's upon my soul!
Be my salvation!—under Heaven, of course.

I'll tell some queer things. Sixty Vs must do.
A trifle, though, to start with! We'll refer
The question to this table?

How you're changed!
Then split the difference; thirty more, we'll say.
Ay, but you leave my presents! Else I'll swear
'Twas all through those: you wanted yours again,
So, picked a quarrel with me, to get them back!
Tread on a worm, it turns, sir! If I turn,
Your fault! 'Tis you'll have forced me! Who's obliged
To give up life yet try no self-defence?
At all events, I'll run the risk. Eh?

Done!
May I sit, sir? This dear old table, now!
Please, sir, a parting egg-nogg and cigar!
I've been so happy with you! Nice stuffed chairs,
And sympathetic sideboards; what an end
To all the instructive evenings! (It's alight.)
Well, nothing lasts, as Bacon came and said!
Here goes,—but keep your temper, or I'll scream!

Fol-lol-the-rido-liddle-iddle-ol!
You see, sir, it's your own fault more than mine;
It's all your fault, you curious gentlefolk!
You're prigs,—excuse me,—like to look so spry,
So clever, while you cling by half a claw
To the perch whereon you puff yourselves at roost,
Such piece of self-conceit as serves for perch
Because you chose it, so it must be safe.
Oh, otherwise you're sharp enough! You spy
Who slips, who slides, who holds by help of wing,
Wanting real foothold,—who can't keep upright
On the other perch, your neighbour chose, not you:
There's no outwitting you respecting him!
For instance, men love money—that, you know—
And what men do to gain it: well, suppose
A poor lad, say a help's son in your house,
Listening at keyholes, hears the company

Talk grand of dollars, V-notes, and so forth,
How hard they are to get, how good to hold,
How much they buy,—if, suddenly, in pops he—
"*I*'ve got a V-note!"—what do you say to him?
What's your first word which follows your last kick?
"Where did you steal it, rascal?" That's because
He finds you, fain would fool you, off your perch,
Not on the special piece of nonsense, sir,
Elected your parade-ground: let him try
Lies to the end of the list,—"He picked it up,
His cousin died and left it him by will,
The President flung it to him, riding by,
An actress trucked it for a curl of his hair,
He dreamed of luck and found his shoe enriched,
He dug up clay, and out of clay made gold"—
How would you treat such possibilities?
Would not you, prompt, investigate the case
With cow-hide? "Lies, lies, lies," you'd shout: and why?
Which of the stories might not prove mere truth!
This last, perhaps, that clay was turned to coin!
Let's see, now, give him me to speak for him!
How many of your rare philosophers,
In plaguy books I've had to dip into,
Believed gold could be made thus, saw it made
And made it? Oh, with such philosophers
You're on your best behaviour! While the lad—
With him, in a trice, you settle likelihoods,
Nor doubt a moment how he got his prize:
In his case, you hear, judge and execute,
All in a breath: so would most men of sense.

But let the same lad hear you talk as grand
At the same keyhole, you and company,
Of signs and wonders, the invisible world;
How wisdom scouts our vulgar unbelief
More than our vulgarest credulity;
How good men have desired to see a ghost,
What Johnson used to say, what Wesley did,
Mother Goose thought, and fiddle-diddle-dee:—
If he then break in with, "Sir, *I* saw a ghost!"

Ah, the ways change! He finds you perched and prim;
It's a conceit of yours that ghosts may be:
There's no talk now of cow-hide. "Tell it out!
Don't fear us! Take your time and recollect!
Sit down first: try a glass of wine, my boy!
And, David, (is not that your Christian name?)
Of all things, should this happen twice—it may—
Be sure, while fresh in mind, you let us know!"
Does the boy blunder, blurt out this, blab that,
Break down in the other, as beginners will?
All's candour, all's considerateness—"No haste!
Pause and collect yourself! We understand!
That's the bad memory, or the natural shock,
Or the unexplained *phenomena!*"

Egad,
The boy takes heart of grace; finds, never fear,
The readiest way to ope your own heart wide,
Show—what I call your peacock-perch, pet post
To strut, and spread the tail, and squawk upon!
"Just as you thought, much as you might expect!
There be more things in heaven and earth, Horatio," . . .
And so on. Shall not David take the hint,
Grow bolder, stroke you down at quickened rate?
If he ruffle a feather, it's "Gently, patiently!
Manifestations are so weak at first!
Doubting, moreover, kills them, cuts all short,
Cures with a vengeance!"

There, sir, that's your style!
You and your boy—such pains bestowed on him,
Or any headpiece of the average worth,
To teach, say, Greek, would perfect him apace,
Make him a Person ("Porson?" thank you, sir!)
Much more, proficient in the art of lies.
You never leave the lesson! Fire alight,
Catch you permitting it to die! You've friends;
There's no withholding knowledge,—least from those
Apt to look elsewhere for their souls' supply:
Why should not you parade your lawful prize?

Who finds a picture, digs a medal up,
Hits on a first edition,—he henceforth
Gives it his name, grows notable: how much more,
Who ferrets out a "medium?" "David's yours,
You highly-favoured man? Then, pity souls
Less privileged! Allow us share your luck!"
So, David holds the circle, rules the roast,
Narrates the vision, peeps in the glass ball,
Sets to the spirit-writing, hears the raps,
As the case may be.

Now mark! To be precise—
Though I say, "lies" all these, at this first stage,
'Tis just for science' sake: I call such grubs
By the name of what they'll turn to, dragonflies.
Strictly, it's what good people style untruth;
But yet, so far, not quite the full-grown thing:
It's fancying, fable-making, nonsense-work—
What never meant to be so very bad—
The knack of story-telling, brightening up
Each dull old bit of fact that drops its shine.
One does see somewhat when one shuts one's eyes,
If only spots and streaks; tables do tip
In the oddest way of themselves: and pens, good Lord,
Who knows if you drive them or they drive you?
'Tis but a foot in the water and out again;
Not that duck-under which decides your dive.
Note this, for it's important: listen why.

I'll prove, you push on David till he dives
And ends the shivering. Here's your circle, now:
Two-thirds of them, with heads like you their host,
Turn up their eyes, and cry, as you expect,
"Lord, who'd have thought it!" But there's always one
Looks wise, compassionately smiles, submits
"Of your veracity no kind of doubt,
But—do you feel so certain of that boy's?
Really, I wonder! I confess myself
More chary of my faith!" That's galling, sir!
What, he the investigator, he the sage,

When all's done? Then, you just have shut your eyes,
Opened your mouth, and gulped down David whole,
You! Terrible were such catastrophe!
So, evidence is redoubled, doubled again,
And doubled besides; once more, "He heard, we heard,
You and they heard, your mother and your wife,
Your children and the stranger in your gates:
Did they or did they not?" So much for him,
The black sheep, guest without the wedding-garb,
And doubting Thomas! Now's your turn to crow:
"He's kind to think you such a fool: Sludge cheats?
Leave you alone to take precautions!"

Straight
The rest join chorus. Thomas stands abashed,
Sips silent some such beverage as this,
Considers if it be harder, shutting eyes
And gulping David in good fellowship,
Than going elsewhere, getting, in exchange,
With no egg-nogg to lubricate the food,
Some just as tough a morsel. Over the way,
Holds Captain Sparks his court: is it better there?
Have not you hunting-stories, scalping-scenes,
And Mexican War exploits to swallow plump
If you'd be free of the stove-side, rocking-chair,
And trio of affable daughters?

Doubt succumbs!
Victory! All your circle's yours again!
Out of the clubbing of submissive wits,
David's performance rounds, each chink gets patched,
Every protrusion of a point's filed fine,
All's fit to set a-rolling round the world,
And then return to David finally,
Lies seven-feet-thick about his first half-inch.
Here's a choice birth of the supernatural,
Poor David's pledged to! You've employed no tool
That laws exclaim at, save the devil's own,
Yet screwed him into henceforth gulling you
To the top of your bent,—all out of one half-lie!

You hold, if there's one half or a hundredth part
Of a lie, that's his fault,—his be the penalty!
I dare say! You'd prove firmer in his place?
You'd find the courage,—that first flurry over,
That mild bit of romancing-work at end,—
To interpose with "It gets serious, this;
Must stop here. Sir, I saw no ghost at all.
Inform your friends I made . . . well, fools of them,
And found you ready made. I've lived in clover
These three weeks: take it out in kicks of me!"
I doubt it! Ask your conscience! Let me know,
Twelve months hence, with how few embellishments
You've told almighty Boston of this passage
Of arms between us, your first taste of the foil
From Sludge who could not fence, sir! Sludge, your boy!
I lied, sir,—there! I got up from my gorge
On offal in the gutter, and preferred
Your canvass-backs: I took their carver's size,
Measured his modicum of intelligence,
Tickled him on the cockles of his heart
With a raven feather, and next week found myself
Sweet and clean, dining daintily, dizened smart,
Set on a stool buttressed by ladies' knees,
Every soft smiler calling me her pet,
Encouraging my story to uncoil
And creep out from its hole, inch after inch,
"How last night, I no sooner snug in bed,
Tucked up, just as they left me,—than came raps !
While a light whisked" . . . "Shaped somewhat like a
star?"
"Well, like some sort of stars, ma'am."—"So we thought!
And any voice? Not yet? Try hard, next time,
If you can't hear a voice; we think you may:
At least, the Pennsylvanian 'mediums' did."
Oh, next time comes the voice! "Just as we hoped!"
Are not the hopers proud now, pleased, profuse
Of the natural acknowledgment?

Of course!
So, off we push, illy-oh-yo, trim the boat,

On we sweep with a cataract ahead,
We're midway to the Horse-shoe: stop, who can,
The dance of bubbles gay about our prow!
Experiences become worth waiting for,
Spirits now speak up, tell their inmost mind,
And compliment the "medium" properly,
Concern themselves about his Sunday coat,
See rings on his hand with pleasure. Ask yourself
How you'd receive a course of treats like these!
Why, take the quietest hack and stall him up,
Cram him with corn a month, then out with him
Among his mates on a bright April morn,
With the turf to tread; see if you find or no
A caper in him, if he bucks or bolts!
Much more a youth whose fancies sprout as rank
As toadstool-clump from melon-bed. 'Tis soon,
"Sirrah, you spirit, come, go, fetch and carry,
Read, write, rap, rub-a-dub, and hang yourself!"
I'm spared all further trouble; all's arranged;
Your circle does my business; I may rave
Like an epileptic dervish in the books,
Foam, fling myself flat, rend my clothes to shreds;
No matter: lovers, friends and countrymen
Will lay down spiritual laws, read wrong things right
By the rule of reverse. If Francis Verulam
Styles himself Bacon, spells the name beside
With a *y* and a *k*, says he drew breath in York,
Gave up the ghost in Wales when Cromwell reigned,
(As, sir, we somewhat fear he was apt to say,
Before I found the useful book that knows)
Why, what harm's done? The circle smiles apace,
"It was not Bacon, after all, do you see!
We understand; the trick's but natural:
Such spirits' individuality
Is hard to put in evidence: they incline
To gibe and jeer, these undeveloped sorts.
You see, their world's much like a jail broke loose,
While this of ours remains shut, bolted, barred,
With a single window to it. Sludge, our friend,
Serves as this window, whether thin or thick,

Or stained or stainless; he's the medium-pane
Through which, to see us and be seen, they peep:
They crowd each other, hustle for a chance,
Tread on their neighbour's kibes, play tricks enough!
Does Bacon, tired of waiting, swerve aside?
Up in his place jumps Barnum—'I'm your man,
I'll answer you for Bacon!' Try once more!"

Or else it's—"What's a 'medium'? He's a means,
Good, bad, indifferent, still the only means
Spirits can speak by; he may misconceive,
Stutter and stammer,—he's their Sludge and drudge,
Take him or leave him; they must hold their peace,
Or else, put up with having knowledge strained
To half-expression through his ignorance.
Suppose, the spirit Beethoven wants to shed
New music he's brimfull of; why, he turns
The handle of this organ, grinds with Sludge,
And what he poured in at the mouth o' the mill
As a Thirty-third Sonata, (fancy now!)
Comes from the hopper as bran-new Sludge, nought else,
The Shakers' Hymn in G, with a natural F,
Or the 'Stars and Stripes' set to consecutive fourths."

Sir, where's the scrape you did not help me through,
You that are wise? And for the fools, the folk
Who came to see,—the guests, (observe that word!)
Pray do you find guests criticize your wine,
Your furniture, your grammar, or your nose?
Then, why your "medium?" What's the difference?
Prove your madeira red-ink and gamboge,—
Your Sludge, a cheat—then, somebody's a goose
For vaunting both as genuine. "Guests!" Don't fear!
They'll make a wry face, nor too much of that,
And leave you in your glory.

"No, sometimes
They doubt and say as much!" Ay, doubt they do!
And what's the consequence? "Of course they doubt"—
(You triumph) "that explains the hitch at once!
Doubt posed our 'medium,' puddled his pure mind;

He gave them back their rubbish: pitch chaff in,
Could flour come out o' the honest mill?" So, prompt
Applaud the faithful: cases flock in point,
"How, when a mocker willed a 'medium' once
Should name a spirit James whose name was George,
'James' cried the 'medium,'—'twas the test of truth!"
In short, a hit proves much, a miss proves more.
Does this convince? The better: does it fail?
Time for the double-shotted broadside, then—
The grand means, last resource. Look black and big!
"You style us idiots, therefore—why stop short?
Accomplices in rascality: this we hear
In our own house, from our invited guest
Found brave enough to outrage a poor boy
Exposed by our good faith! Have you been heard?
Now, then, hear us; one man's not quite worth twelve.
You see a cheat? Here's some twelve see an ass:
Excuse me if I calculate: good day!"
Out slinks the sceptic, all the laughs explode,
Sludge waves his hat in triumph!

Or—he don't.

There's something in real truth (explain who can!)
One casts a wistful eye at, like the horse
Who mopes beneath stuffed hay-racks and won't munch
Because he spies a corn-bag: hang that truth,
It spoils all dainties proffered in its place!
I've felt at times when, cockered, cossetted
And coddled by the aforesaid company,
Bidden enjoy their bullying,—never fear,
But o'er their shoulders spit at the flying man,—
I've felt a child; only, a fractious child
That, dandled soft by nurse, aunt, grandmother,
Who keep him from the kennel, sun and wind,
Good fun and wholesome mud,—enjoined be sweet,
And comely and superior,—eyes askance
The ragged sons of the gutter at their game,
Fain would be down with them i' the thick of the filth,
Making dirt-pies, laughing free, speaking plain,
And calling granny the grey old cat she is.

I've felt a spite, I say, at you, at them,
Huggings and humbug—gnashed my teeth to mark
A decent dog pass! It's too bad, I say,
Ruining a soul so!

But what's "so," what's fixed,
Where may one stop? Nowhere! The cheating's nursed
Out of the lying, softly and surely spun
To just your length, sir! I'd stop soon enough:
But you're for progress. "All old, nothing new?
Only the usual talking through the mouth,
Or writing by the hand? I own, I thought
This would develop, grow demonstrable,
Make doubt absurd, give figures we might see,
Flowers we might touch. There's no one doubts you,
Sludge!
You dream the dreams, you see the spiritual sights,
The speeches come in your head, beyond dispute.
Still, for the sceptics' sake, to stop all mouths,
We want some outward manifestation!—well,
The Pennsylvanians gained such; why not Sludge?
He may improve with time!"

Ay, that he may!
He sees his lot: there's no avoiding fate.
'Tis a trifle at first. "Eh, David? Did you hear?
You jogged the table, your foot caused the squeak,
This time you're . . . joking, are you not, my boy?"
"N-n-no!"—and I'm done for, bought and sold hence-
forth.
The old good easy jog-trot way, the . . . eh?
The . . . not so very false, as falsehood goes,
The spinning out and drawing fine, you know,—
Really mere novel-writing of a sort,
Acting, or improvising, make-believe,
Surely not downright cheatery! Any how,
'Tis done with and my lot cast; Cheat's my name:
The fatal dash of brandy in your tea
Has settled what you'll have the souchong's smack:
The caddy gives way to the dram-bottle.

Then, it's so cruel easy! Oh, those tricks
That can't be tricks, those feats by sleight of hand,
Clearly no common conjuror's!—no, indeed!
A conjuror? Choose me any craft in the world
A man puts hand to; and with six months' pains,
I'll play you twenty tricks miraculous
To people untaught the trade: have you seen glass blown,
Pipes pierced? Why, just this biscuit that I chip,
Did you ever watch a baker toss one flat
To the oven? Try and do it! Take my word,
Practise but half as much, while limbs are lithe,
To turn, shove, tilt a table, crack your joints,
Manage your feet, dispose your hands aright,
Work wires that twitch the curtains, play the glove
At end of your slipper, then put out the lights
And . . . there, there, all you want you'll get, I hope!
I found it slip, easy as an old shoe.

Now, lights on table again! I've done my part,
You take my place while I give thanks and rest.
"Well, Judge Humgruffin, what's your verdict, sir?
You, hardest head in the United States,—
Did you detect a cheat here? Wait! Let's see!
Just an experiment first, for candour's sake!
I'll try and cheat you, Judge! The table tilts:
Is it I that move it? Write! I'll press your hand:
Cry when I push, or guide your pencil, Judge!"
Sludge still triumphant! "That a rap, indeed?
That, the real writing? Very like a whale!
Then, if, sir, you—a most distinguished man,
And, were the Judge not here, I'd say, . . . no matter!
Well, sir, if you fail, you can't take us in,—
There's little fear that Sludge will!"

Won't he, ma'am?
But what if our distinguished host, like Sludge,
Bade God bear witness that he played no trick,
While you believed that what produced the raps
Was just a certain child who died, you know,
And whose last breath you thought your lips had felt?

Eh? That's a capital point, ma'am: Sludge begins
At your entreaty with your dearest dead,
The little voice set lisping once again,
The tiny hand made feel for yours once more,
The poor lost image brought back, plain as dreams,
Which image, if a word had chanced recall,
The customary cloud would cross your eyes,
Your heart return the old tick, pay its pang!
A right mood for investigation, this!
One's at one's ease with Saul and Jonathan,
Pompey and Cæsar: but one's own lost child . . .
I wonder, when you heard the first clod drop
From the spadeful at the grave-side, felt you free
To investigate who twitched your funeral scarf
Or brushed your flounces? Then, it came of course,
You should be stunned and stupid; then, (how else?)
Your breath stopped with your blood, your brain struck work.
But now, such causes fail of such effects,
All's changed,—the little voice begins afresh,
Yet you, calm, consequent, can test and try
And touch the truth. "Tests? Didn't the creature tell
Its nurse's name, and say it lived six years,
And rode a rocking-horse? Enough of tests!
Sludge never could learn that!"

He could not, eh?
You compliment him. "Could not?" Speak for yourself!
I'd like to know the man I ever saw
Once,—never mind where, how, why, when,—once saw,
Of whom I do not keep some matter in mind
He'd swear I "could not" know, sagacious soul!
What? Do you live in this world's blow of blacks,
Palaver, gossipry, a single hour
Nor find one smut has settled on your nose,
Of a smut's worth, no more, no less?—one fact
Out of the drift of facts, whereby you learn
What some one was, somewhere, somewhen, somewhy?
You don't tell folk—"See what has stuck to me!
Judge Humgruffin, our most distinguished man,

Your uncle was a tailor, and your wife
Thought to have married Miggs, missed him, hit you!"—
Do you, sir, though you see him twice a-week?
"No," you reply, "what use retailing it?
Why should I?" But, you see, one day you *should*,
Because one day there's much use,—when this fact
Brings you the Judge upon both gouty knees
Before the supernatural; proves that Sludge
Knows, as you say, a thing he "could not" know:
Will not Sludge thenceforth keep an outstretched face,
The way the wind drives?

"Could not!" Look you now,
I'll tell you a story! There's a whiskered chap,
A foreigner, that teaches music here
And gets his bread,—knowing no better way:
He says, the fellow who informed of him
And made him fly his country and fall West,
Was a hunchback cobbler, sat, stitched soles and sang,
In some outlandish place, the city Rome,
In a cellar by their Broadway, all day long;
Never asked questions, stopped to listen or look,
Nor lifted nose from lapstone; let the world
Roll round his three-legged stool, and news run in
The ears he hardly seemed to keep pricked up.
Well, that man went on Sundays, touched his pay,
And took his praise from government, you see;
For something like two dollars every week,
He'd engage tell you some one little thing
Of some one man, which led to many more,
(Because one truth leads right to the world's end,)
And make you that man's master—when he dined
And on what dish, where walked to keep his health
And to what street. His trade was, throwing thus
His sense out, like an anteater's long tongue,
Soft, innocent, warm, moist, impassible,
And when 'twas crusted o'er with creatures—slick,
Their juice enriched his palate. "Could not Sludge!"

I'll go yet a step further, and maintain,

Once the imposture plunged its proper depth
In the rotten of your natures, all of you,—
(If one's not mad nor drunk, and hardly then)
It's impossible to cheat—that's, be found out!
Go tell your brotherhood this first slip of mine,
All to-day's tale, how you detected Sludge,
Behaved unpleasantly, till he was fain confess,
And so has come to grief! You'll find, I think,
Why Sludge still snaps his fingers in your face.
There now, you've told them! What's their prompt reply?
"Sir, did that youth confess he had cheated me,
I'd disbelieve him. He may cheat at times;
That's in the 'medium'-nature, thus they're made,
Vain and vindictive, cowards, prone to scratch.
And so all cats are; still, a cat's the beast
You coax the strange electric sparks from out,
By rubbing back its fur; not so a dog,
Nor lion, nor lamb: 'tis the cat's nature, sir!
Why not the dog's? Ask God, who made them beasts!
D'ye think the sound, the nicely-balanced man
(Like me"—aside)—"like you yourself,"—(aloud)
"—He's stuff to make a 'medium?' Bless your soul,
'Tis these hysteric, hybrid half-and-halfs,
Equivocal, worthless vermin yield the fire!
We must take such as we find them, 'ware their tricks,
Wanting their service. Sir, Sludge took in you—
How, I can't say, not being there to watch:
He was tried, was tempted by your easiness,—
He did not take in me!"

Thank you for Sludge!
I'm to be grateful to such patrons, eh,
When what you hear's my best word? 'Tis a challenge;
"Snap at all strangers, you half-tamed prairie-dog,
So you cower duly at your keeper's nod!
Cat, show what claws were made for, muffling them
Only to me! Cheat others if you can,
Me, if you dare!" And, my wise sir, I dared—
Did cheat you first, made you cheat others next,
And had the help of your vaunted manliness

To bully the incredulous. You used me?
Have not I used you, taken full revenge,
Persuaded folk they knew not their own name,
And straight they'd own the error! Who was the fool
When, to an awe-struck, wide-eyed, open-mouthed
Circle of sages, Sludge would introduce
Milton composing baby-rhymes, and Locke
Reasoning in gibberish, Homer writing Greek
In noughts and crosses, Asaph setting psalms
To crotchet and quaver? I've made a spirit squeak
In sham voice for a minute, then outbroke
Bold in my own, defying the imbeciles—
Have copied some ghost's pothooks, half a page,
Then ended with my own scrawl undisguised.
"All right! The ghost was merely using Sludge,
Suiting itself from his imperfect stock!"
Don't talk of gratitude to me! For what?
For being treated as a showman's ape,
Encouraged to be wicked and make sport,
Fret or sulk, grin or whimper, any mood
So long as the ape be in it and no man—
Because a nut pays every mood alike.
Curse your superior, superintending sort,
Who, since you hate smoke, send up boys that climb
To cure your chimney, bid a "medium" lie
To sweep you truth down! Curse your women too,
Your insolent wives and daughters, that fire up
Or faint away if a male hand squeeze theirs,
Yet, to encourage Sludge, may play with Sludge
As only a "medium," only the kind of thing
They must humour, fondle . . . oh, to misconceive
Were too preposterous! But I've paid them out!
They've had their wish—called for the naked truth,
And in she tripped, sat down and bade them stare:
They had to blush a little and forgive!
"The fact is, children talk so; in next world
All our conventions are reversed,—perhaps
Made light of: something like old prints, my dear!
The Judge has one, he brought from Italy,
A metropolis in the background,—o'er a bridge,

A team of trotting roadsters,—cheerful groups
Of wayside travellers, peasants at their work,
And, full in front, quite unconcerned, why not?
Three nymphs conversing with a cavalier,
And never a rag among them: 'fine,' folk cry—
And heavenly manners seem not much unlike!
Let Sludge go on; we'll fancy it's in print!"
If such as came for wool, sir, went home shorn,
Where is the wrong I did them? 'Twas their choice;
They tried the adventure, ran the risk, tossed up
And lost, as some one's sure to do in games;
They fancied I was made to lose,—smoked glass
Useful to spy the sun through, spare their eyes:
And had I proved a red-hot iron plate
They thought to pierce, and, for their pains, grew
blind,
Whose were the fault but theirs? While, as things go,
Their loss amounts to gain, the more's the shame!
They've had their peep into the spirit-world,
And all this world may know it! They've fed fat
Their self-conceit which else had starved: what chance
Save this, of cackling o'er a golden egg
And compassing distinction from the flock,
Friends of a feather? Well, they paid for it,
And not prodigiously; the price o' the play,
Not counting certain pleasant interludes,
Was scarce a vulgar play's worth. When you buy
The actor's talent, do you dare propose
For his soul beside? Whereas, my soul you buy!
Sludge acts Macbeth, obliged to be Macbeth,
Or you will not hear his first word! Just go through
That slight formality, swear himself's the Thane,
And thenceforth he may strut and fret his hour,
Spout, spawl, or spin his target, no one cares!
Why hadn't I leave to play tricks, Sludge as Sludge?
Enough of it all! I've wiped out scores with you—
Vented your fustian, let myself be streaked
Like a tom-fool with your ochre and carmine,
Worn patchwork your respectable fingers sewed
To metamorphose somebody,—yes, I've earned

My wages, swallowed down my bread of shame,
And shake the crumbs off—where but in your face?

As for religion—why, I served it, sir!
I'll stick to that! With my *phenomena*
I laid the atheist sprawling on his back,
And propped Saint Paul up, or, at least, Swedenborg!
In fact, it's just the proper way to baulk
These troublesome fellows—liars, one and all,
Are not these sceptics? Well, to baffle them,
No use in being squeamish: lie yourself!
Erect your buttress just as wide o' the line,
Your side, as they've built up the wall on theirs;
Where both meet, midway in a point, is truth,
High overhead: so, take your room, pile bricks,
Lie! Oh, there's titillation in all shame!
What snow may lose in white, it gains in rose:
Miss Stokes turns—Rahab,—nor a bad exchange!
Glory be on her, for the good she wrought,
Breeding belief anew 'neath ribs of death,
Brow-beating now the unabashed before,
Ridding us of their whole life's gathered straws
By a live coal from the altar! Why, of old,
Great men spent years and years in writing books
To prove we've souls, and hardly proved it then:
Miss Stokes with her live coal, for you and me!
Surely, to this good issue, all was fair—
Not only fondling Sludge, but, even suppose
He let escape some spice of knavery,—well,
In wisely being blind to it! Don't you praise
Nelson for setting spy-glass to blind eye
And saying . . . what was it—that he could not see
The signal he was bothered with? Ay, indeed!

I'll go beyond: there's a real love of a lie,
Liars find ready-made for lies they make,
As hand for glove, or tongue for sugar-plum.
At best, 'tis never pure and full belief;
Those furthest in the quagmire,—don't suppose
They strayed there with no warning, got no chance

Of a filth-speck in their face, which they clenched teeth,
Bent brow against! Be sure they had their doubts,
And fears, and fairest challenges to try
The floor o' the seeming solid sand! But no!
Their faith was pledged, acquaintance too apprised,
All but the last step ventured, kerchiefs waved,
And Sludge called "pet:" 'twas easier marching on
To the promised land; join those who, Thursday next,
Meant to meet Shakespeare; better follow Sludge—
Prudent, oh sure!—on the alert, how else?
But making for the mid-bog, all the same!
To hear your outcries, one would think I caught
Miss Stokes by the scruff o' the neck, and pitched her flat,
Foolish-face-foremost! Hear these simpletons,
That's all I beg, before my work's begun,
Before I've touched them with my finger-tip!
Thus they await me (do but listen, now!
It's reasoning, this is,—I can't imitate
The baby voice, though) "In so many tales
Must be some truth, truth though a pin-point big,
Yet, some: a single man's deceived, perhaps—
Hardly, a thousand: to suppose one cheat
Can gull all these, were more miraculous far
Than aught we should confess a miracle"—
And so on. Then the Judge sums up—(it's rare)—
Bids you respect the authorities that leap
To the judgment-seat at once,—why, don't you note
The limpid nature, the unblemished life,
The spotless honour, indisputable sense
Of the first upstart with his story? What—
Outrage a boy on whom you ne'er till now
Set eyes, because he finds raps trouble him?

Fools, these are: ay, and how of their opposites
Who never did, at bottom of their hearts,
Believe for a moment?—Men emasculate,
Blank of belief, who played, as eunuchs use,
With superstition safely,—cold of blood,
Who saw what made for them in the mystery,

Took their occasion, and supported Sludge
—As proselytes? No, thank you, far too shrewd!
—But promisers of fair play, encouragers
Of the claimant; who in candour needs must hoist
Sludge up on Mars' Hill, get speech out of Sludge
To carry off, criticize, and cant about!
Didn't Athens treat Saint Paul so?—at any rate,
It's "a new thing," philosophy fumbles at.
Then there's the other picker out of pearl
From dung heaps,—ay, your literary man,
Who draws on his kid gloves to deal with Sludge
Daintily and discreetly,—shakes a dust
Of the doctrine, flavours thence, he well knows how,
The narrative or the novel,—half-believes,
All for the book's sake, and the public's stare,
And the cash that's God's sole solid in this world!
Look at him! Try to be too bold, too gross
For the master! Not you! He's the man for muck;
Shovel it forth, full-splash, he'll smooth your brown
Into artistic richness, never fear!
Find him the crude stuff; when you recognize
Your lie again, you'll doff your hat to it,
Dressed out for company! "For company,"
I say, since there's the relish of success:
Let all pay due respect, call the lie truth,
Save the soft silent smirking gentleman
Who ushered in the stranger: you must sigh
"How melancholy, he, the only one,
Fails to perceive the bearing of the truth
Himself gave birth to!"—There's the triumph's smack!
That man would choose to see the whole world roll
I' the slime o' the slough, so he might touch the tip
Of his brush with what I call the best of browns—
Tint ghost-tales, spirit-stories, past the power
Of the outworn umber and bistre!

Yet I think
There's a more hateful form of foolery—
The social sage's, Solomon of saloons
And philosophic diner-out, the fribble

Who wants a doctrine for a chopping-block
To try the edge of his faculty upon,
Prove how much common sense he'll hack and hew
In the critical minute 'twixt the soup and fish!
These were my patrons: these, and the like of them
Who, rising in my soul now, sicken it,—
These I have injured! Gratitude to these?
The gratitude, forsooth, of a prostitute
To the greenhorn and the bully—friends of hers,
From the wag that wants the queer jokes for his club,
To the snuff-box-decorator, honest man,
Who just was at his wits' end where to find
So genial a Pasiphae! All and each
Pay, compliment, protect from the police,
And how she hates them for their pains, like me!
So much for my remorse at thanklessness
Toward a deserving public!

But, for God?
Ay, that's a question! Well, sir, since you press—
(How you do teaze the whole thing out of me!
I don't mean you, you know, when I say "them:"
Hate you, indeed! But that Miss Stokes, that Judge!
Enough, enough—with sugar: thank you, sir!)
Now for it, then! Will you believe me, though?
You've heard what I confess; I don't unsay
A single word: I cheated when I could,
Rapped with my toe-joints, set sham hands at work,
Wrote down names weak in sympathetic ink,
Rubbed odic lights with ends of phosphor-match,
And all the rest; believe that: believe this,
By the same token, though it seem to set
The crooked straight again, unsay the said,
Stick up what I've thrown down; I can't help that:
It's truth! I somehow vomit truth to-day.
This trade of mine—I don't know, can't be sure
But there was something in it, tricks and all!
Really, I want to light up my own mind.
They were tricks,—true, but what I mean to add
Is also true. First,—don't it strike you, sir?

Go back to the beginning,—the first fact
We're taught is, there's a world beside this world,
With spirits, not mankind, for tenantry;
That much within that world once sojourned here,
That all upon this world will travel there,
And therefore that we, bodily here below,
Must have exactly such an interest
In learning what may be the ways o' the world
Above us, as the disembodied folk
Have (by all analogic likelihood)
In watching how things go in the old world
With us, their sons, successors, and what not.
Oh, yes, with added powers probably,
Fit for the novel state,—old loves grown pure,
Old interests understood aright,—they watch!
Eyes to see, ears to hear, and hands to help,
Proportionate to advancement: they're ahead,
That's all—do what we do, but noblier done—
Use plate, whereas we eat our meals off delf,
(To use a figure.)

Concede that, and I ask
Next, what may be the mode of intercourse
Between us men here, and those once-men there?
First comes the Bible's speech; then, history
With the supernatural element,—you know—
All that we sucked in with our mother's milk,
Grew up with, got inside of us at last,
Till it's found bone of bone and flesh of flesh.
See now, we start with the miraculous,
And know it used to be, at all events:
What's the first step we take, and can't but take,
In arguing from the known to the obscure?
Why this: "What was before, may be to-day.
Since Samuel's ghost appeared to Saul,—of course
My brother's spirit may appear to me."
Go tell your teacher that! What's his reply?
What brings a shade of doubt for the first time
O'er his brow late so luminous with faith?
"Such things have been," says he, "and there's no doubt

Such things may be: but I advise mistrust
Of eyes, ears, stomach, and, more than all, your brain,
Unless it be of your great-grandmother,
Whenever they propose a ghost to you!"
The end is, there's a composition struck;
'Tis settled, we've some way of intercourse
Just as in Saul's time; only, different:
How, when and where, precisely,—find it out!
I want to know, then, what's so natural
As that a person born into this world
And seized on by such teaching, should begin
With firm expectancy and a frank look-out
For his own allotment, his especial share
In the secret,—his particular ghost, in fine?
I mean, a person born to look that way,
Since natures differ: take the painter-sort,
One man lives fifty years in ignorance
Whether grass be green or red,—"No kind of eye
For colour," say you; while another picks
And puts away even pebbles, when a child,
Because of bluish spots and pinky veins—
"Give him forthwith a paint-box!" Just the same
Was I born . . . "medium," you won't let me say,—
Well, seer of the supernatural
Everywhen, everyhow and everywhere,—
Will that do?

I and all such boys of course
Started with the same stock of bible-truth;
Only,—what in the rest you style their sense,
Instinct, blind reasoning but imperative,
This, betimes, taught them the old world had one law
And ours another: "New world, new laws," cried
they:
"None but old laws, seen everywhere at work,"
Cried I, and by their help explained my life
The Jews' way, still a working way to me.
Ghosts made the noises, fairies waved the lights,
Or Santaclaus slid down on New Year's Eve
And stuffed with cakes the stocking at my bed,

Changed the worn shoes, rubbed clean the fingered slate
Of the sum that came to grief the day before.

This could not last long: soon enough I found
Who had worked wonders thus, and to what end:
But did I find all easy, like my mates?
Henceforth no supernatural any more?
Not a whit: what projects the billiard-balls?
"A cue," you answer: "Yes, a cue," said I;
"But what hand, off the cushion, moved the cue?
What unseen agency, outside the world,
Prompted its puppets to do this and that,
Put cakes and shoes and slates into their mind,
These mothers and aunts, nay even schoolmasters?"
Thus high I sprang, and there have settled since.
Just so I reason, in sober earnest still,
About the greater godsends, what you call
The serious gains and losses of my life.
What do I know or care about your world
Which either is or seems to be? This snap
Of my fingers, sir! My care is for myself;
Myself am whole and sole reality
Inside a raree-show and a market-mob
Gathered about it: that's the use of things.
'Tis easy saying they serve vast purposes,
Advantage their grand selves: be it true or false,
Each thing may have two uses. What's a star?
A world, or a world's sun: doesn't it serve
As taper also, time-piece, weather-glass,
And almanac? Are stars not set for signs
When we should shear our sheep, sow corn, prune trees?
The Bible says so.

Well, I add one use
To all the acknowledged uses, and declare
If I spy Charles's Wain at twelve to-night,
It warns me, "Go, nor lose another day,
And have your hair cut, Sludge!" You laugh: and why?
Were such a sign too hard for God to give?
No: but Sludge seems too little for such grace:

Thank you, sir! So you think, so does not Sludge!
When you and good men gape at Providence,
Go into history and bid us mark
Not merely powder-plots prevented, crowns
Kept on kings' heads by miracle enough,
But private mercies—oh, you've told me, sir,
Of such interpositions! How yourself
Once, missing on a memorable day
Your handkerchief—just setting out, you know,—
You must return to fetch it, lost the train,
And saved your precious self from what befell
The thirty-three whom Providence forgot.
You tell, and ask me what I think of this?
Well, sir, I think then, since you needs must know,
What matter had you and Boston city to boot
Sailed skyward, like burnt onion-peelings? Much
To you, no doubt: for me—undoubtedly
The cutting of my hair concerns me more,
Because, however sad the truth may seem,
Sludge is of all-importance to himself.
You set apart that day in every year
For special thanksgiving, were a heathen else:
Well, I who cannot boast the like escape,
Suppose I said "I don't thank Providence
For my part, owing it no gratitude?"
"Nay, but you owe as much"—you'd tutor me,
"You, every man alive, for blessings gained
In every hour of the day, could you but know!
I saw my crowning mercy: all have such,
Could they but see!" Well, sir, why don't they see?
"Because they won't look,—or perhaps, they can't."
Then, sir, suppose I can, and will, and do
Look, microscopically as is right,
Into each hour with its infinitude
Of influences at work to profit Sludge?
For that's the case: I've sharpened up my sight
To spy a providence in the fire's going out,
The kettle's boiling, the dime's sticking fast
Despite the hole i' the pocket. Call such facts
Fancies, too petty a work for Providence,

And those same thanks which you exact from me,
Prove too prodigious payment: thanks for what,
If nothing guards and guides us little men?
No, no, sir! You must put away your pride,
Resolve to let Sludge into partnership!
I live by signs and omens: looked at the roof
Where the pigeons settle—"If the further bird,
The white, takes wing first, I'll confess when thrashed;
Not, if the blue does"—so I said to myself
Last week, lest you should take me by surprise:
Off flapped the white,—and I'm confessing, sir!
Perhaps 'tis Providence's whim and way
With only me, in the world: how can you tell?
"Because unlikely!" Was it likelier, now,
That this our one out of all worlds beside,
The what-d'you-call-'em millions, should be just
Precisely chosen to make Adam for,
And the rest o' the tale? Yet the tale's true, you know:
Such undeserving clod was graced so once;
Why not graced likewise undeserving Sludge?
Are we merit-mongers, flaunt we filthy rags?
All you can bring against my privilege
Is, that another way was taken with you,—
Which I don't question. It's pure grace, my luck.
I'm broken to the way of nods and winks,
And need no formal summoning. You've a help;
Halloa his name or whistle, clap your hands,
Stamp with your foot or pull the bell: all's one,
He understands you want him, here he comes.
Just so, I come at the knocking: you, sir, wait
The tongue of the bell, nor stir before you catch
Reason's clear tingle, nature's clapper brisk,
Or that traditional peal was wont to cheer
Your mother's face turned heavenward: short of these
There's no authentic intimation, eh?
Well, when you hear, you'll answer them, start up
And stride into the presence, top of toe,
And there find Sludge beforehand, Sludge that sprung
At noise o' the knuckle on the partition-wall!
I think myself the more religious man.

Religion's all or nothing; it's no mere smile
Of contentment, sigh of aspiration, sir—
No quality of the finelier-tempered clay
Like its whiteness or its lightness; rather, stuff
Of the very stuff, life of life, self of self.
I tell you, men won't notice; when they do,
They'll understand. I notice nothing else,
I'm eyes, ears, mouth of me, one gaze and gape,
Nothing eludes me, everything's a hint,
Handle and help. It's all absurd, and yet
There's something in it all, I know: how much?
No answer! What does that prove? Man's still man,
Still meant for a poor blundering piece of work
When all's done; but, if somewhat's done, like this,
Or not done, is the case the same? Suppose
I blunder in my guess at the true sense
Of the knuckle-summons, nine time out of ten,—
What if the tenth guess happen to be right?
If the tenth shovel-load of powdered quartz
Yield me the nugget? I gather, crush, sift all,
Pass o'er the failure, pounce on the success.
To give you a notion, now—(let who wins, laugh!)
When first I see a man, what do I first?
Why, count the letters which make up his name,
And as their number chances, even or odd,
Arrive at my conclusion, trim my course:
Hiram H. Horsefall is your honoured name,
And haven't I found a patron, sir, in you?
"Shall I cheat this stranger?" I take apple-pips,
Stick one in either *canthus* of my eye,
And if the left drops first—(your left, sir, stuck)
I'm warned, I let the trick alone this time.
You, sir, who smile, superior to such trash,
You judge of character by other rules:
Don't your rules sometimes fail you? Pray, what rule
Have you judged Sludge by hitherto?

Oh, be sure,

You, everybody blunders, just as I,
In simpler things than these by far! For see:

I knew two farmers,—one, a wiseacre,
Who studied seasons, rummaged almanacs,
Quoted the dew-point, registered the frost,
And then declared, for outcome of his pains,
Next summer must be dampish: 'twas a drought.
His neighbour prophesied such drought would fall,
Saved hay and corn, made cent. per cent. thereby,
And proved a sage indeed: how came his lore?
Because one brindled heifer, late in March,
Stiffened her tail of evenings, and somehow
He got into his head that drought was meant!
I don't expect all men can do as much:
Such kissing goes by favour. You must take
A certain turn of mind for this,—a twist
I' the flesh, as well. Be lazily alive,
Open-mouthed, like my friend the anteater,
Letting all nature's loosely-guarded motes
Settle and, slick, be swallowed! Think yourself
The one i' the world, the one for whom the world
Was made, expect it tickling at your mouth!
Then will the swarm of busy buzzing flies,
Clouds of coincidence, break egg-shell, thrive,
Breed, multiply, and bring you food enough.

I can't pretend to mind your smiling, sir!
Oh, what you mean is this! Such intimate way,
Close converse, frank exchange of offices,
Strict sympathy of the immeasurably great
With the infinitely small, betokened here
By a course of signs and omens, raps and sparks,—
How does it suit the dread traditional text
Of the "Great and Terrible Name?" Shall the Heaven of
Heavens
Stoop to such child's-play?

Please sir, go with me
A moment, and I'll try to answer you.
The "*Magnum et terribile*" (is that right?)
Well, folk began with this in the early day;
And all the acts they recognized in proof

Were thunders, lightnings, earthquakes, whirlwinds, dealt
Indisputably on men whose death they caused.
There, and there only, folk saw Providence
At work,—and seeing it, 'twas right enough
All heads should tremble, hands wring hands amain,
And knees knock hard together at the breath
Of the Name's first letter; why, the Jews, I'm told,
Won't write it down, no, to this very hour,
Nor speak aloud: you know best if 't be so.
Each ague-fit of fear at end, they crept
(Because somehow people once born must live)
Out of the sound, sight, swing and sway of the Name,
Into a corner, the dark rest of the world,
And safe space where as yet no fear had reached;
'Twas there they looked about them, breathed again,
And felt indeed at home, as we might say.
The current of common things, the daily life,
This had their due contempt; no Name pursued
Man from the mountain-top where fires abide,
To his particular mouse-hole at its foot
Where he ate, drank, digested, lived in short:
Such was man's vulgar business, far too small
To be worth thunder: "small," folk kept on, "small,"
With much complacency in those great days!
A mote of sand, you know, a blade of grass—
What was so despicable as mere grass,
Except perhaps the life of the worm or fly
Which fed there? These were "small" and men were
 great.
Well, sir, the old way's altered somewhat since,
And the world wears another aspect now:
Somebody turns our spyglass round, or else
Puts a new lens in it: grass, worm, fly grow big:
We find great things are made of little things,
And little things go lessening till at last
Comes God behind them. Talk of mountains now?
We talk of mould that heaps the mountain, mites
That throng the mould, and God that makes the mites.
The Name comes close behind a stomach-cyst,
The simplest of creations, just a sac

That's mouth, heart, legs and belly at once, yet lives
And feels, and could do neither, we conclude,
If simplified still further one degree:
The small becomes the dreadful and immense!
Lightning, forsooth? No word more upon that!
A tin-foil bottle, a strip of greasy silk,
With a bit of wire and knob of brass, and there's
Your dollar's-worth of lightning! But the cyst—
The life of the least of the little things?

No, no!
Preachers and teachers try another tack,
Come near the truth this time: they put aside
Thunder and lightning: "That's mistake," they cry,
"Thunderbolts fall for neither fright nor sport,
But do appreciable good, like tides,
Changes of the wind, and other natural facts—
'Good' meaning good to man, his body or soul.
Mediate, immediate, all things minister
To man,—that's settled: be our future text
'We are His children!' " So, they now harangue
About the intention, the contrivance, all
That keeps up an incessant play of love,—
See the Bridgewater book.

Amen to it!
Well, sir, I put this question: I'm a child?
I lose no time, but take you at your word:
How shall I act a child's part properly?
Your sainted mother, sir,—used you to live
With such a thought as this a-worrying you?
"She has it in her power to throttle me,
Or stab or poison: she may turn me out,
Or lock me in,—nor stop at this, to-day,
But cut me off to-morrow from the estate
I look for"—(long may you enjoy it, sir!)
"In brief, she may unchild the child I am."
You never had such crotchets? Nor have I!
Who, frank confessing childship from the first,

Cannot both fear and take my ease at once,
So, don't fear,—know what might be, well enough,
But know too, child-like, that it will not be,
At least in my case, mine, the son and heir
Of the kingdom, as yourself proclaim my style.
But do you fancy I stop short at this?
Wonder if suit and service, sons and heirs
Needs must expect, I dare pretend to find?
If, looking for signs proper to such an one,
I straight perceive them irresistible?
Concede that homage is a son's plain right,
And, never mind the nods and raps and winks,
'Tis the pure obvious supernatural
Steps forward, does its duty: why, of course!
I have presentiments; my dreams come true:
I fancy a friend stands whistling all in white
Blithe as a boblink, and he's dead I learn.
I take dislike to a dog my favourite long,
And sell him; he goes mad next week and snaps.
I guess that stranger will turn up to-day
I have not seen these three years; there's his knock.
I wager "sixty peaches on that tree!"—
That I pick up a dollar in my walk,
That your wife's brother's cousin's name was George—
And win on all points. Oh, you wince at this?
You'd fain distinguish between gift and gift,
Washington's oracle and Sludge's itch
O' the elbow when at whist he ought to trump?
With Sludge it's too absurd? *Fine, draw the line*
Somewhere, but, sir, your somewhere is not mine!

Bless us, I'm turning poet! It's time to end.
How you have drawn me out, sir! All I ask
Is—am I heir or not heir? If I'm he,
Then, sir, remember, that same personage
(To judge by what we read in the newspaper)
Requires, besides one nobleman in gold
To carry up and down his coronet,
Another servant, probably a duke,
To hold egg-nogg in readiness: why want

Attendance, sir, when helps in his father's house
Abound, I'd like to know?

Enough of talk!

My fault is that I tell too plain a truth.
Why, which of those who say they disbelieve,
Your clever people, but has dreamed his dream,
Caught his coincidence, stumbled on his fact
He can't explain, (he'll tell you smilingly)
Which he's too much of a philosopher
To count as supernatural, indeed,
So calls a puzzle and problem, proud of it:
Bidding you still be on your guard, you know,
Because one fact don't make a system stand,
Nor prove this an occasional escape
Of spirit beneath the matter: that's the way!
Just so wild Indians picked up, piece by piece,
The fact in California, the fine gold
That underlay the gravel—hoarded these,
But never made a system stand, nor dug!
So wise men hold out in each hollowed palm
A handful of experience, sparkling fact
They can't explain; and since their rest of life
Is all explainable, what proof in this?
Whereas I take the fact, the grain of gold,
And fling away the dirty rest of life,
And add this grain to the grain each fool has found
Of the million other such philosophers,—
Till I see gold, all gold and only gold,
Truth questionless though unexplainable,
And the miraculous proved the commonplace!
The other fools believed in mud, no doubt—
Failed to know gold they saw: was that so strange?
Are all men born to play Bach's fiddle-fugues,
"Time" with the foil in carte, jump their own height,
Cut the mutton with the broadsword, skate a five,
Make the red hazard with the cue, clip nails
While swimming, in five minutes row a mile,
Pull themselves three feet up with the left arm,
Do sums of fifty figures in their head,

And so on, by the scores of instances?
The Sludge with luck, who sees the spiritual facts,
His fellows strive and fail to see, may rank
With these, and share the advantage!

Ay, but share
The drawback! Think it over by yourself;
I have not heart, sir, and the fire's gone grey.
Defect somewhere compensates for success,
Everyone knows that! Oh, we're equals, sir!
The big-legged fellow has a little arm
And a less brain, though big legs win the race:
Do you suppose I 'scape the common lot?
Say, I was born with flesh so sensitive,
Soul so alert, that, practice helping both,
I guess what's going on outside the veil,
Just as a prisoned crane feels pairing-time
In the islands where his kind are, so must fall
To capering by himself some shiny night,
As if your back-yard were a plot of spice—
Thus am I 'ware of the spirit-world : while you,
Blind as a beetle that way,—for amends,
Why, you can double fist and floor me, sir!
Ride that hot, hardmouthed, horrid horse of yours,
Laugh while it lightens, play with the great dog,
Speak your mind though it vex some friend to hear,
Never brag, never bluster, never blush,—
In short, you've pluck, when I'm a coward—there!
I know it, I can't help it,—folly or no,
I'm paralyzed, my hand's no more a hand,
Nor my head, a head, in danger: you can smile
And change the pipe in your cheek. Your gift's not mine.
Would you swap for mine? No! but you'd add my gift
To yours: I dare say! I too sigh at times,
Wish I were stouter, could tell truth nor flinch,
Kept cool when threatened, did not mind so much
Being dressed gaily, making strangers stare,
Eating nice things; when I'd amuse myself,
I shut my eyes and fancy in my brain
I'm—now the President, now, Jenny Lind,

Now, Emerson, now, the Benicia Boy—
With all the civilized world a-wondering
And worshipping! I know it's folly and worse:
I feel such tricks sap, honeycomb the soul,
But I can't cure myself—despond, despair,
And then, hey, presto, there's a turn of the wheel,
Under comes uppermost, fate makes full amends;
Sludge knows and sees and hears a hundred things
You all are blind to,—I've my taste of truth,
Likewise my touch of falsehood,—vice no doubt,
But you've your vices also: I'm content.

What, sir? You won't shake hands? "Because I cheat!
You've found me out in cheating!" That's enough
To make an apostle swear! Why, when I cheat,
Mean to cheat, do cheat, and am caught in the act,
Are you, or rather, am I sure of the fact?
(There's verse again, but I'm inspired somehow.)
Well, then, I'm not sure! I may be, perhaps,
Free as a babe from cheating: how it began,
My gift,—no matter; what 'tis got to be
In the end now, that's the question : answer that!
Had I seen, perhaps, what hand was holding mine,
Leading me whither, I had died of fright,
So, I was made believe I led myself.
If I should lay a six-inch plank from roof
To roof, you would not cross the street, one step,
Even at your mother's summons: but, being shrewd,
If I paste paper on each side of the plank
And swear 'tis solid pavement, why, you'll cross
Humming a tune the while, in ignorance
Beacon Street stretches a hundred feet below:
I walked thus, took the paper-cheat for stone.
Some impulse made me set a thing on the move
Which, started once, ran really by itself;
Beer flows thus, suck the siphon; toss the kite,
It takes the wind and floats of its own force.
Don't let truth's lump rot stagnant for the lack
Of a timely helpful lie to leaven it!
Put a chalk-egg beneath the clucking hen,

She'll lay a real one, laudably deceived,
Daily for weeks to come. I've told my lie,
And seen truth follow, marvels none of mine;
All was not cheating, sir, I'm positive!
I don't know if I move your hand sometimes
When the spontaneous writing spreads so far,
If my knee lifts the table all that height,
Why the inkstand don't fall off the desk a-tilt,
Why the accordion plays a prettier waltz
Than I can pick out on the piano-forte,
Why I speak so much more than I first intend,
Describe so many things I never saw.
I tell you, sir, in one sense, I believe
Nothing at all,—that everybody can,
Will, and does cheat: but in another sense
I'm ready to believe my very self—
That every cheat's inspired, and every lie
Quick with a germ of truth.

You ask perhaps
Why I should condescend to trick at all
If I know a way without it? This is why!
There's a strange secret sweet self-sacrifice
In any desecration of one's soul
To a worthy end,—isn't it Herodotus
(I wish I could read Latin!) who describes
The single gift of the land's virginity,
Demanded in those old Egyptian rites,
(I've but a hazy notion—help me, sir!)
For one purpose in the world, one day in a life,
One hour in the day—thereafter, purity,
And a veil thrown o'er the past for evermore!
Well now, they understood a many things
Down by Nile city, or wherever it was!
I've always vowed, after the minute's lie,
And the good end's gain,—truth should be mine hence-
forth.
This goes to the root of the matter, sir,—this plain
Plump fact: accept it and unlock with it
The wards of many a puzzle!

Or, finally,
Why should I set so fine a gloss on things?
What need I care? I cheat in self-defence,
And there's my answer to a world of cheats!
Cheat? To be sure, sir! What's the world worth else?
Who takes it as he finds, and thanks his stars?
Don't it want trimming, turning, furbishing up
And polishing over? Your so-styled great men,
Do they accept one truth as truth is found,
Or try their skill at tinkering? What's your world?
Here are you born, who are, I'll say at once,
One of the luckiest whether in head and heart,
Body and soul, or all that helps the same.
Well, now, look back: what faculty of yours
Came to its full, had ample justice done
By growing when rain fell, biding its time,
Solidifying growth when earth was dead,
Spiring up, broadening wide, in seasons due?
Never! You shot up and frost nipped you off,
Settled to sleep when sunshine bade you sprout;
One faculty thwarted its fellow: at the end,
All you boast is, "I had proved a topping tree
In other climes"—yet this was the right clime
Had you foreknown the seasons. Young, you've force
Wasted like well-streams: old,—oh, then indeed,
Behold a labyrinth of hydraulic pipes
Through which you'd play off wondrous waterwork;
Only, no water left to feed their play!
Young,—you've a hope, an aim, a love; it's tossed
And crossed and lost: you struggle on, some spark
Shut in your heart against the puffs around,
Through cold and pain; these in due time subside,
Now then for age's triumph, the hoarded light
You mean to loose on the altered face of things,—
Up with it on the tripod! It's extinct.
Spend your life's remnant asking, which was best,
Light smothered up that never peeped forth once,
Or the cold cresset with full leave to shine?
Well, accept this too,—seek the fruit of it
Not in enjoyment, proved a dream on earth,

But knowledge, useful for a second chance,
Another life,—you've lost this world—you've gained
Its knowledge for the next.—What knowledge, sir,
Except that you know nothing? Nay, you doubt
Whether 'twere better have made you man or brute,
If aught be true, if good and evil clash.
No foul, no fair, no inside, no outside,
There's your world!

Give it me! I slap it brisk
With harlequin's pasteboard sceptre: what's it now?
Changed like a rock-flat, rough with rusty weed,
At first wash-over of the returning wave!
All the dry, dead, impracticable stuff
Starts into life and light again; this world
Pervaded by the influx from the next.
I cheat, and what's the happy consequence?
You find full justice straightway dealt you out,
Each want supplied, each ignorance set at ease,
Each folly fooled. No life-long labour now
As the price of worse than nothing! No mere film
Holding you chained in iron, as it seems,
Against the outstretch of your very arms
And legs in the sunshine moralists forbid!
What would you have? Just speak and, there, you see!
You're supplemented, made a whole at last,
Bacon advises, Shakespeare writes you songs,
And Mary Queen of Scots embraces you.
Thus it goes on, not quite like life perhaps,
But so near, that the very difference piques,
Shows that e'en better than this best will be—
This passing entertainment in a hut
Whose bare walls take your taste since, one stage more,
And you arrive at the palace: all half real,
And you, to suit it, less than real beside,
In a dream, lethargic kind of death in life,
That helps the interchange of natures, flesh
Transfused by souls, and such souls! Oh, 'tis choice!
And if at whiles the bubble, blown too thin,
Seem nigh on bursting,—if you nearly see

The real world through the false,—what *do* you see?
Is the old so ruined? You find you're in a flock
Of the youthful, earnest, passionate—genius, beauty,
Rank and wealth also, if you care for these,
And all depose their natural rights, hail you,
(That's me, sir) as their mate and yoke-fellow,
Participate in Sludgehood—nay, grow mine,
I veritably possess them—banish doubt,
And reticence and modesty alike!
Why, here's the Golden Age, old Paradise
Or new Eutopia! Here is life indeed,
And the world well won now, yours for the first time!

And all this might be, may be, and with good help
Of a little lying shall be: so, Sludge lies!
Why, he's at worst your poet who sings how Greeks
That never were, in Troy which never was,
Did this or the other impossible great thing!
He's Lowell—it's a world, you smile and say,
Of his own invention—wondrous Longfellow,
Surprising Hawthorne! Sludge does more than they,
And acts the books they write: the more's his praise!

But why do I mount to poets? Take plain prose—
Dealers in common sense, set these at work,
What can they do without their helpful lies?
Each states the law and fact and face of the thing
Just as he'd have them, finds what he thinks fit,
Is blind to what missuits him, just records
What makes his case out, quite ignores the rest.
It's a History of the World, the Lizard Age,
The Early Indians, the Old Country War,
Jerome Napoleon, whatsoever you please,
All as the author wants it. Such a scribe
You pay and praise for putting life in stones,
Fire into fog, making the past your world.
There's plenty of "How did you contrive to grasp
The thread which led you through this labyrinth?
How build such solid fabric out of air?
How on so slight foundation found this tale,

Biography, narrative?" or, in other words,
"How many lies did it require to make
The portly truth you here present us with?"
"Oh," quoth the penman, purring at your praise,
"'Tis fancy all; no particle of fact:
I was poor and threadbare when I wrote that book
'Bliss in the Golden City.' I, at Thebes?
We writers paint out of our heads, you see!"
"Ah, the more wonderful the gift in you,
The more creativeness and godlike craft!"
But I, do I present you with my piece,
It's "What, Sludge? When my sainted mother spoke
The verses Lady Jane Grey last composed
About the rosy bower in the seventh heaven
Where she and Queen Elizabeth keep house,—
You made the raps? 'Twas your invention that?
Cur, slave and devil!"—eight fingers and two thumbs
Stuck in my throat!

Well, if the marks seem gone,
'Tis because stiffish cock-tail, taken in time,
Is better for a bruise than arnica.

There, sir! I bear no malice: 'tisn't in me.
I know I acted wrongly: still, I've tried
What I could say in my excuse,—to show
The devil's not all devil . . . I don't pretend,
An angel, much less such a gentleman
As you, sir! And I've lost you, lost myself,
Lost all, l-l-l-. . . .

No—are you in earnest, sir?
O, yours, sir, is an angel's part! I know
What prejudice must be, what the common course
Men take to soothe their ruffled self-conceit:
Only you rise superior to it all!
No, sir, it don't hurt much; it's speaking long
That makes me choke a little: the marks will go!
What? Twenty V-notes more, and outfit too,
And not a word to Greeley? One—one kiss

Of the hand that saves me! You'll not let me speak,
I well know, and I've lost the right, too true!
But I must say, sir, if She hears (she does)
Your sainted . . . Well, sir,—be it so! That's, I think,
My bed-room candle. Good night! Bl-l-less you sir!

R-r-r, you brute-beast and blackguard! Cowardly scamp!
I only wish I dared burn down the house
And spoil your sniggering! Oh, what, you're the man?
You're satisfied at last? You've found out Sludge?
We'll see that presently: my turn, sir, next!
I too can tell my story: brute,—do you hear?—
You throttled your sainted mother, that old hag,
In just such a fit of passion: no, it was . . .
To get this house of hers, and many a note
Like these . . . I'll pocket them, however . . . five,
Ten, fifteen . . . ay, you gave her throat the twist,
Or else you poisoned her! Confound the cuss!
Where was my head? I ought to have prophesied
He'll die in a year and join her: that's the way.

I don't know where my head is: what had I done?
How did it all go? I said he poisoned her,
And hoped he'd have grace given him to repent,
Whereon he picked this quarrel, bullied me
And called me cheat: I thrashed him,—who could help?
He howled for mercy, prayed me on his knees
To cut and run and save him from disgrace:
I do so, and once off, he slanders me.
An end of him! Begin elsewhere anew!
Boston's a hole, the herring-pond is wide,
V-notes are something, liberty still more.
Beside, is he the only fool in the world?

APPARENT FAILURE

"We shall soon lose a celebrated building." *Paris Newspaper.*

I

No, for I'll save it! Seven years since,
I passed through Paris, stopped a day
To see the baptism of your Prince;
Saw, made my bow, and went my way:
Walking the heat and headache off,
I took the Seine-side, you surmise,
Thought of the Congress, Gortschakoff,
Cavour's appeal and Buol's replies,
So sauntered till—what met my eyes?

2

Only the Doric little Morgue!
The dead-house where you show your drowned:
Petrarch's Vaucluse makes proud the Sorgue,
Your Morgue has made the Seine renowned.
One pays one's debt in such a case;
I plucked up heart and entered,—stalked,
Keeping a tolerable face
Compared with some whose cheeks were chalked:
Let them! No Briton's to be baulked!

3

First came the silent gazers; next
A screen of glass, we're thankful for;
Last, the sight's self, the sermon's text,
The three men who did most abhor
Their life in Paris yesterday,
So killed themselves: and now, enthroned
Each on his copper couch, they lay
Fronting me, waiting to be owned.
I thought, and think, their sin's atoned.

4

Poor men, God made, and all for that!
The reverence struck me; o'er each head
Religiously was hung its hat,
Each coat dripped by the owner's bed,

Sacred from touch: each had his berth,
  His bounds, his proper place of rest,
Who last night tenanted on earth
  Some arch, where twelve such slept abreast,—
Unless the plain asphalte seemed best.

5

How did it happen, my poor boy?
  You wanted to be Buonaparte
And have the Tuileries for toy,
  And could not, so it broke your heart?
You, old one by his side, I judge,
  Were, red as blood, a socialist,
A leveller! Does the Empire grudge
  You've gained what no Republic missed?
Be quiet, and unclench your fist!

6

And this—why, he was red in vain,
  Or black,—poor fellow that is blue!
What fancy was it, turned your brain?
  Oh, women were the prize for you!
Money gets women, cards and dice
  Get money, and ill-luck gets just
The copper couch and one clear nice
  Cool squirt of water o'er your bust,
The right thing to extinguish lust!

7

It's wiser being good than bad;
  It's safer being meek than fierce:
It's fitter being sane than mad.
  My own hope is, a sun will pierce
The thickest cloud earth ever stretched;
  That, after Last, returns the First,
Though a wide compass round be fetched;
  That what began best, can't end worst,
Nor what God blessed once, prove accurst.

The Ring and the Book

1868–1869

The Ring and the Book. By Robert Browning, M.A., Honorary Fellow of Balliol College, Oxford. In four volumes. Vol. I. Smith, Elder and Co., London. 1868. [Vol. II, 1868; Vols. III and IV, 1869.]

F'cap 8vo. Vol. I, pp. iv + 248; Vol. II, pp. iv + 252; Vol. III, pp. iv + 252; Vol. IV, pp. iv + 236. Cloth boards.

The Ring and the Book is a poem in twelve books, comprising more than 21,000 lines. It is the story of the murder by Count Guido Franceschini of his wife Pompilia, and of his trial and death. In Book I the poet describes the sources of his information and in Book XII he winds up the threads. The intervening books tell the story ten times over, each from a different point of view—(II) the gossip of Half-Rome favourable to Guido; (III) the gossip of the Other Half-Rome favourable to Pompilia; a more judicious account (IV) by Tertium Quid, a nobleman representing "the finer sense o' the city"; (V) Guido's speech in his own defence; (VI) the evidence of Giuseppe Caponsacchi, the "soldier-saint" and hero of the story; (VII) Pompilia's deathbed story of her life; the arguments of counsel for the defence (VIII) and for the prosecution (IX); the summing-up by the Pope (X); and Guido's final self-revelation on the eve of his execution (XI).

The first passage printed here, the conclusion of Book I, is an invocation to the spirit of the poet's wife: the title has been supplied by the editor. Book VII is given in full.

The Ring and the Book

INVOCATION TO E. B. B.

O LYRIC Love, half-angel and half-bird
And all a wonder and a wild desire,—
Boldest of hearts that ever braved the sun,
Took sanctuary within the holier blue,
And sang a kindred soul out to his face,—
Yet human at the red-ripe of the heart—
When the first summons from the darkling earth
Reached thee amid thy chambers, blanched their blue,
And bared them of the glory—to drop down,
To toil for man, to suffer or to die,—
This is the same voice: can thy soul know change?
Hail then, and hearken from the realms of help!
Never may I commence my song, my due
To God who best taught song by gift of thee,
Except with bent head and beseeching hand—
That still, despite the distance and the dark,
What was, again may be; some interchange
Of grace, some splendour once thy very thought,
Some benediction anciently thy smile:
—Never conclude, but raising hand and head
Thither where eyes, that cannot reach, yet yearn
For all hope, all sustainment, all reward,
Their utmost up and on,—so blessing back
In those thy realms of help, that heaven thy home,
Some whiteness which, I judge, thy face makes proud,
Some wanness where, I think, thy foot may fall!

POMPILIA

I AM just seventeen years and five months old,
And, if I lived one day more, three full weeks;
'Tis writ so in the church's register,
Lorenzo in Lucina, all my names
At length, so many names for one poor child,
—Francesca Camilla Vittoria Angela
Pompilia Comparini,—laughable!
Also 'tis writ that I was married there
Four years ago; and they will add, I hope,
When they insert my death, a word or two,—
Omitting all about the mode of death,—
This, in its place, this which one cares to know,
That I had been a mother of a son
Exactly two weeks. It will be through grace
O' the Curate, not through any claim I have;
Because the boy was born at, so baptized
Close to, the Villa, in the proper church:
A pretty church, I say no word against,
Yet stranger-like,—while this Lorenzo seems
My own particular place, I always say.
I used to wonder, when I stood scarce high
As the bed here, what the marble lion meant,
With half his body rushing from the wall,
Eating the figure of a prostrate man—
(To the right, it is, of entry by the door)
An ominous sign to one baptized like me,
Married, and to be buried there, I hope.
And they should add, to have my life complete,
He is a boy and Gaetan by name—
Gaetano, for a reason,—if the friar
Don Celestine will ask this grace for me
Of Curate Ottoboni: he it was
Baptized me: he remembers my whole life
As I do his grey hair.

All these few things
I know are true,—will you remember them?
Because time flies. The surgeon cared for me,

To count my wounds,—twenty-two dagger-wounds,
Five deadly, but I do not suffer much—
Or too much pain,—and am to die to-night.

Oh how good God is that my babe was born,
—Better than born, baptized and hid away
Before this happened, safe from being hurt!
That had been sin God could not well forgive:
He was too young to smile and save himself.
When they took, two days after he was born,
My babe away from me to be baptized
And hidden awhile, for fear his foe should find,—
The country-woman, used to nursing babes,
Said "Why take on so? where is the great loss?
These next three weeks he will but sleep and feed,
Only begin to smile at the month's end;
He would not know you, if you kept him here,
Sooner than that; so, spend three merry weeks
Snug in the Villa, getting strong and stout,
And then I bring him back to be your own,
And both of you may steal to—we know where!"
The month—there wants of it two weeks this day!
Still, I half fancied when I heard the knock
At the Villa in the dusk, it might prove she—
Come to say "Since he smiles before the time,
Why should I cheat you out of one good hour?
Back I have brought him; speak to him and judge!"
Now I shall never see him; what is worse,
When he grows up and gets to be my age,
He will seem hardly more than a great boy;
And if he asks "What was my mother like?"
People may answer "Like girls of seventeen"—
And how can he but think of this and that,
Lucias, Marias, Sofias, who titter or blush
When he regards them as such boys may do?
Therefore I wish some one will please to say
I looked already old though I was young;
Do I not . . . say, if you are by to speak . . .
Look nearer twenty? No more like, at least,
Girls who look arch or redden when boys laugh,

Than the poor Virgin that I used to know
At our street-corner in a lonely niche,—
The babe, that sat upon her knees, broke off,—
Thin white glazed clay, you pitied her the more:
She, not the gay ones, always got my rose.

How happy those are who know how to write!
Such could write what their son should read in time,
Had they a whole day to live out like me.
Also my name is not a common name,
"Pompilia," and may help to keep apart
A little the thing I am from what girls are.
But then how far away, how hard to find
Will anything about me have become,
Even if the boy bethink himself and ask!
No father that he ever knew at all,
Nor ever had—no, never had, I say!
That is the truth,—nor any mother left,
Out of the little two weeks that she lived,
Fit for such memory as might assist:
As good too as no family, no name,
Not even poor old Pietro's name, nor hers,
Poor kind unwise Violante, since it seems
They must not be my parents any more.
That is why something put it in my head
To call the boy "Gaetano"—no old name
For sorrow's sake; I looked up to the sky
And took a new saint to begin anew.
One who has only been made saint—how long?
Twenty-five years: so, carefuller, perhaps,
To guard a namesake than those old saints grow,
Tired out by this time,—see my own five saints!

On second thoughts, I hope he will regard
The history of me as what someone dreamed,
And get to disbelieve it at the last:
Since to myself it dwindles fast to that,
Sheer dreaming and impossibility,—
Just in four days too! All the seventeen years,
Not once did a suspicion visit me

How very different a lot is mine
From any other woman's in the world.
The reason must be, 'twas by step and step
It got to grow so terrible and strange:
These strange woes stole on tiptoe, as it were,
Into my neighbourhood and privacy,
Sat down where I sat, laid them where I lay;
And I was found familiarized with fear,
When friends broke in, held up a torch and cried
"Why, you Pompilia in the cavern thus,
How comes that arm of yours about a wolf?
And the soft length,—lies in and out your feet
And laps you round the knee,—a snake it is!"
And so on.

Well, and they are right enough,
By the torch they hold up now: for first, observe,
I never had a father,—no, nor yet
A mother: my own boy can say at least
"I had a mother whom I kept two weeks!"
Not I, who little used to doubt . . . *I* doubt
Good Pietro, kind Violante, gave me birth?
They loved me always as I love my babe
(—Nearly so, that is—quite so could not be—)
Did for me all I meant to do for him,
Till one surprising day, three years ago,
They both declared, at Rome, before some judge
In some court where the people flocked to hear,
That really I had never been their child,
Was a mere castaway, the careless crime
Of an unknown man, the crime and care too much
Of a woman known too well,—little to these,
Therefore, of whom I was the flesh and blood:
What then to Pietro and Violante, both
No more my relatives than you or you?
Nothing to them! You know what they declared.

So with my husband,—just such a surprise,
Such a mistake, in that relationship!
Everyone says that husbands love their wives,

Guard them and guide them, give them happiness;
'Tis duty, law, pleasure, religion: well,
You see how much of this comes true in mine!
People indeed would fain have somehow proved
He was no husband: but he did not hear,
Or would not wait, and so has killed us all.
Then there is . . . only let me name one more!
There is the friend,—men will not ask about,
But tell untruths of, and give nicknames to,
And think my lover, most surprise of all!
Do only hear, it is the priest they mean,
Giuseppe Caponsacchi: a priest—love,
And love me! Well, yet people think he did.
I am married, he has taken priestly vows,
They know that, and yet go on, say, the same,
"Yes, how he loves you!" "That was love"—they say,
When anything is answered that they ask:
Or else "No wonder you love him"—they say.
Then they shake heads, pity much, scarcely blame—
As if we neither of us lacked excuse,
And anyhow are punished to the full,
And downright love atones for everything!
Nay, I heard read-out in the public court
Before the judge, in presence of my friends,
Letters 'twas said the priest had sent to me,
And other letters sent him by myself,
We being lovers!

Listen what this is like!
When I was a mere child, my mother . . . that's
Violante, you must let me call her so
Nor waste time, trying to unlearn the word, . . .
She brought a neighbour's child of my own age
To play with me of rainy afternoons;
And, since there hung a tapestry on the wall,
We two agreed to find each other out
Among the figures. "Tisbe, that is you,
With half-moon on your hair-knot, spear in hand,
Flying, but no wings, only the great scarf
Blown to a bluish rainbow at your back:

Call off your hound and leave the stag alone!"
"—And there are you, Pompilia, such green leaves
Flourishing out of your five finger-ends,
And all the rest of you so brown and rough:
Why is it you are turned a sort of tree?"
You know the figures never were ourselves
Though we nicknamed them so. Thus, all my life,—
As well what was, as what, like this, was not,—
Looks old, fantastic and impossible:
I touch a fairy thing that fades and fades.
—Even to my babe! I thought, when he was born,
Something began for once that would not end,
Nor change into a laugh at me, but stay
For evermore, eternally quite mine.
Well, so he is,—but yet they bore him off,
The third day, lest my husband should lay traps
And catch him, and by means of him catch me.
Since they have saved him so, it was well done:
Yet thence comes such confusion of what was
With what will be,—that late seems long ago,
And, what years should bring round, already come,
Till even he withdraws into a dream
As the rest do: I fancy him grown great,
Strong, stern, a tall young man who tutors me,
Frowns with the others "Poor imprudent child!
Why did you venture out of the safe street?
Why go so far from help to that lone house?
Why open at the whisper and the knock?"

Six days ago when it was New Year's-day,
We bent above the fire and talked of him,
What he should do when he was grown and great.
Violante, Pietro, each had given the arm
I leant on, to walk by, from couch to chair
And fireside,—laughed, as I lay safe at last,
"Pompilia's march from bed to board is made,
Pompilia back again and with a babe,
Shall one day lend his arm and help her walk!"
Then we all wished each other more New Years.
Pietro began to scheme—"Our cause is gained;

The law is stronger than a wicked man:
Let him henceforth go his way, leave us ours!
We will avoid the city, tempt no more
The greedy ones by feasting and parade,—
Live at the other villa, we know where,
Still farther off, and we can watch the babe
Grow fast in the good air; and wood is cheap
And wine sincere outside the city gate.
I still have two or three old friends will grope
Their way along the mere half-mile of road,
With staff and lantern on a moonless night
When one needs talk: they'll find me, never fear,
And I'll find them a flask of the old sort yet!"
Violante said "You chatter like a crow:
Pompilia tires o' the tattle, and shall to-bed:
Do not too much the first day,—somewhat more
To-morrow, and, the next, begin the cape
And hood and coat! I have spun wool enough."
Oh what a happy friendly eve was that!

And, next day, about noon, out Pietro went—
He was so happy and would talk so much,
Until Violante pushed and laughed him forth
Sight-seeing in the cold,—"So much to see
I' the churches! Swathe your throat three times!" she
cried,
"And, above all, beware the slippery ways,
And bring us all the news by supper-time!"
He came back late, laid by cloak, staff and hat,
Powdered so thick with snow it made us laugh,
Rolled a great log upon the ash o' the hearth,
And bade Violante treat us to a flask,
Because he had obeyed her faithfully,
Gone sight-see through the seven, and found no
church
To his mind like San Giovanni—"There's the fold,
And all the sheep together, big as cats!
And such a shepherd, half the size of life,
Starts up and hears the angel"—when, at the door,
A tap: we started up: you know the rest.

Pietro at least had done no harm, I know;
Nor even Violante, so much harm as makes
Such revenge lawful. Certainly she erred—
Did wrong, how shall I dare say otherwise?—
In telling that first falsehood, buying me
From my poor faulty mother at a price,
To pass off upon Pietro as his child:
If one should take my babe, give him a name,
Say he was not Gaetano and my own,
But that some other woman made his mouth
And hands and feet,—how very false were that!
No good could come of that; and all harm did.
Yet if a stranger were to represent
"Needs must you either give your babe to me
And let me call him mine for ever more,
Or let your husband get him"—ah, my God,
That were a trial I refuse to face!
Well, just so here: it proved wrong but seemed right
To poor Violante—for there lay, she said,
My poor real dying mother in her rags,
Who put me from her with the life and all,
Poverty, pain, shame and disease at once,
To die the easier by what price I fetched—
Also (I hope) because I should be spared
Sorrow and sin,—why may not that have helped?
My father,—he was no one, any one,—
The worse, the likelier,—call him,—he who came,
Was wicked for his pleasure, went his way,
And left no trace to track by; there remained
Nothing but me, the unnecessary life,
To catch up or let fall,—and yet a thing
She could make happy, be made happy with,
This poor Violante,—who would frown thereat?

Well, God, you see! God plants us where we grow.
It is not that, because a bud is born
At a wild briar's end, full i' the wild beast's way,
We ought to pluck and put it out of reach
On the oak-tree top,—say, "There the bud belongs!"
She thought, moreover, real lies were—lies told

For harm's sake; whereas this had good at heart,
Good for my mother, good for me, and good
For Pietro who was meant to love a babe,
And needed one to make his life of use,
Receive his house and land when he should die.
Wrong, wrong, and always wrong! how plainly
    wrong!
For see, this fault kept pricking, as faults do,
All the same at her heart,—this falsehood hatched,
She could not let it go nor keep it fast.
She told me so,—the first time I was found
Locked in her arms once more after the pain,
When the nuns let me leave them and go home,
And both of us cried all the cares away,—
This it was set her on to make amends,
This brought about the marriage—simply this!
Do let me speak for her you blame so much!
When Paul, my husband's brother, found me out,
Heard there was wealth for who should marry me,
So, came and made a speech to ask my hand
For Guido,—she, instead of piercing straight
Through the pretence to the ignoble truth,
Fancied she saw God's very finger point,
Designate just the time for planting me,
(The wild briar-slip she plucked to love and wear)
In soil where I could strike real root, and grow,
And get to be the thing I called myself:
For, wife and husband are one flesh, God says,
And I, whose parents seemed such and were none,
Should in a husband have a husband now,
Find nothing, this time, but was what it seemed,
—All truth and no confusion any more.
I know she meant all good to me, all pain
To herself,—since how could it be aught but pain,
To give me up, so, from her very breast,
The wilding flower-tree-branch that, all those years,
She had got used to feel for and find fixed?
She meant well: has it been so ill i' the main?
That is but fair to ask: one cannot judge
Of what has been the ill or well of life,

The day that one is dying—sorrows change
Into not altogether sorrow-like;
I do see strangeness but scarce misery,
Now it is over, and no danger more.
My child is safe; there seems not so much pain.
It comes, most like, that I am just absolved,
Purged of the past, the foul in me, washed fair,—
One cannot both have and not have, you know,—
Being right now, I am happy and colour things.
Yes, every body that leaves life sees all
Softened and bettered: so with other sights:
To me at least was never evening yet
But seemed far beautifuller than its day,
For past is past.
There was a fancy came,
When somewhere, in the journey with my friend,
We stepped into a hovel to get food;
And there began a yelp here, a bark there,—
Misunderstanding creatures that were wroth
And vexed themselves and us till we retired.
The hovel is life: no matter what dogs bit
Or cats scratched in the hovel I break from,
All outside is lone field, moon and such peace—
Flowing in, filling up as with a sea
Whereon comes Someone, walks fast on the white,
Jesus Christ's self, Don Celestine declares,
To meet me and calm all things back again.

Beside, up to my marriage, thirteen years
Were, each day, happy as the day was long:
This may have made the change too terrible.
I know that when Violante told me first
The cavalier,—she meant to bring next morn,
Whom I must also let take, kiss my hand,—
Would be at San Lorenzo the same eve
And marry me,—which over, we should go
Home both of us without him as before,
And, till she bade speak, I must hold my tongue,
Such being the correct way with girl-brides,

From whom one word would make a father blush,—
I know, I say, that when she told me this,
—Well, I no more saw sense in what she said
Than a lamb does in people clipping wool;
Only lay down and let myself be clipped.
And when next day the cavalier who came
(Tisbe had told me that the slim young man
With wings at head, and wings at feet, and sword
Threatening a monster, in our tapestry,
Would eat a girl else,—was a cavalier)
When he proved Guido Franceschini,—old
And nothing like so tall as I myself,
Hook-nosed and yellow in a bush of beard,
Much like a thing I saw on a boy's wrist,
He called an owl and used for catching birds,—
And when he took my hand and made a smile—
Why, the uncomfortableness of it all
Seemed hardly more important in the case
Than,—when one gives you, say, a coin to spend,—
Its newness or its oldness; if the piece
Weigh properly and buy you what you wish,
No matter whether you get grime or glare!
Men take the coin, return you grapes and figs.
Here, marriage was the coin, a dirty piece
Would purchase me the praise of those I loved:
About what else should I concern myself?

So, hardly knowing what a husband meant,
I supposed this or any man would serve,
No whit the worse for being so uncouth:
For I was ill once and a doctor came
With a great ugly hat, no plume thereto,
Black jerkin and black buckles and black sword,
And white sharp beard over the ruff in front,
And oh so lean, so sour-faced and austere!—
Who felt my pulse, made me put out my tongue,
Then oped a phial, dripped a drop or two
Of a black bitter something,—I was cured!
What mattered the fierce beard or the grim face?
It was the physic beautified the man,

Master Malpichi,—never met his match
In Rome, they said,—so ugly all the same!

However, I was hurried through a storm,
Next dark eve of December's deadest day—
How it rained!—through our street and the Lion's-mouth
And the bit of Corso,—cloaked round, covered close,
I was like something strange or contraband,—
Into blank San Lorenzo, up the aisle,
My mother keeping hold of me so tight,
I fancied we were come to see a corpse
Before the altar which she pulled me toward.
There we found waiting an unpleasant priest
Who proved the brother, not our parish friend,
But one with mischief-making mouth and eye,
Paul, whom I know since to my cost. And then
I heard the heavy church-door lock out help
Behind us: for the customary warmth,
Two tapers shivered on the altar. "Quick—
Lose no time!"—cried the priest. And straightway down
From . . . what's behind the altar where he hid—
Hawk-nose and yellowness and bush and all,
Stepped Guido, caught my hand, and there was I
O' the chancel, and the priest had opened book,
Read here and there, made me say that and this,
And after, told me I was now a wife,
Honoured indeed, since Christ thus weds the Church,
And therefore turned he water into wine,
To show I should obey my spouse like Christ.
Then the two slipped aside and talked apart,
And I, silent and scared, got down again
And joined my mother who was weeping now.
Nobody seemed to mind us any more,
And both of us on tiptoe found our way
To the door which was unlocked by this, and wide.
When we were in the street, the rain had stopped,
All things looked better. At our own house-door,
Violante whispered "No one syllable

To Pietro! Girl-brides never breathe a word!"
"—Well treated to a wetting, draggle-tails!"
Laughed Pietro as he opened—"Very near
You made me brave the gutter's roaring sea
To carry off from roost old dove and young,
Trussed up in church, the cote, by me, the kite!
What do these priests mean, praying folk to death
On stormy afternoons, with Christmas close
To wash our sins off nor require the rain?"
Violante gave my hand a timely squeeze,
Madonna saved me from immodest speech,
I kissed him and was quiet, being a bride.

When I saw nothing more, the next three weeks,
Of Guido—"Nor the Church sees Christ" thought I:
"Nothing is changed however, wine is wine
And water only water in our house.
Nor did I see that ugly doctor since
The cure of the illness: just as I was cured,
I am married,—neither scarecrow will return."

Three weeks, I chuckled—"How would Giulia stare
And Tecla smile and Tisbe laugh outright,
Were it not impudent for brides to talk!"—
Until one morning, as I sat and sang
At the broidery-frame alone i' the chamber,—loud
Voices, two, three together, sobbings too,
And my name, "Guido," "Paolo," flung like stones
From each to the other! In I ran to see.
There stood the very Guido and the priest
With sly face,—formal but nowise afraid,—
While Pietro seemed all red and angry, scarce
Able to stutter out his wrath in words;
And this it was that made my mother sob,
As he reproached her—"You have murdered us,
Me and yourself and this our child beside!"
Then Guido interposed "Murdered or not,
Be it enough your child is now my wife!
I claim and come to take her." Paul put in,
"Consider—kinsman, dare I term you so?—

What is the good of your sagacity
Except to counsel in a strait like this?
I guarantee the parties man and wife
Whether you like or loathe it, bless or ban.
May spilt milk be put back within the bowl—
The done thing, undone? You, it is, we look
For counsel to, you fitliest will advise!
Since milk, though spilt and spoilt, does marble good,
Better we down on knees and scrub the floor,
Than sigh, 'the waste would make a syllabub!'
Help us so turn disaster to account,
So predispose the groom, he needs shall grace
The bride with favour from the very first,
Not begin marriage an embittered man!"
He smiled,—the game so wholly in his hands!
While fast and faster sobbed Violante—"Ay,
All of us murdered, past averting now!
O my sin, O my secret!" and such like.

Then I began to half surmise the truth;
Something had happened, low, mean, underhand,
False, and my mother was to blame, and I
To pity, whom all spoke of, none addressed:
I was the chattel that had caused a crime.
I stood mute,—those who tangled must untie
The embroilment. Pietro cried "Withdraw, my child!
She is not helpful to the sacrifice
At this stage,—do you want the victim by
While you discuss the value of her blood?
For her sake, I consent to hear you talk:
Go, child, and pray God help the innocent!"

I did go and was praying God, when came
Violante, with eyes swollen and red enough,
But movement on her mouth for make-believe
Matters were somehow getting right again.
She bade me sit down by her side and hear.
"You are too young and cannot understand,
Nor did your father understand at first.

I wished to benefit all three of us,
And when he failed to take my meaning,—why,
I tried to have my way at unaware—
Obtained him the advantage he refused.
As if I put before him wholesome food
Instead of broken victual,—he finds change
I' the viands, never cares to reason why,
But falls to blaming me, would fling the plate
From window, scandalize the neighbourhood,
Even while he smacks his lips,—men's way, my child!
But either you have prayed him unperverse
Or I have talked him back into his wits:
And Paolo was a help in time of need,—
Guido, not much—my child, the way of men!
A priest is more a woman than a man,
And Paul did wonders to persuade. In short,
Yes, he was wrong, your father sees and says;
My scheme was worth attempting: and bears fruit,
Gives you a husband and a noble name,
A palace and no end of pleasant things.
What do you care about a handsome youth?
They are so volatile, and teaze their wives!
This is the kind of man to keep the house.
We lose no daughter,—gain a son, that's all:
For 'tis arranged we never separate,
Nor miss, in our grey time of life, the tints
Of you that colour eve to match with morn.
In good or ill, we share and share alike,
And cast our lots into a common lap,
And all three die together as we lived!
Only, at Arezzo,—that's a Tuscan town,
Not so large as this noisy Rome, no doubt,
But older far and finer much, say folks,—
In a great palace where you will be queen,
Know the Archbishop and the Governor,
And we see homage done you ere we die.
Therefore, be good and pardon!"—"Pardon what?
You know things, I am very ignorant:
All is right if you only will not cry!"

And so an end! Because a blank begins
From when, at the word, she kissed me hard and hot,
And took me back to where my father leaned
Opposite Guido—who stood eyeing him,
As eyes the butcher the cast panting ox
That feels his fate is come, nor struggles more,—
While Paul looked archly on, pricked brow at whiles
With the pen-point as to punish triumph there,—
And said "Count Guido, take your lawful wife
Until death part you!"

All since is one blank,
Over and ended; a terrific dream.
It is the good of dreams—so soon they go!
Wake in a horror of heart-beats, you may—
Cry, "The dread thing will never from my thoughts!"
Still, a few daylight doses of plain life,
Cock-crow and sparrow-chirp, or bleat and bell
Of goats that trot by, tinkling, to be milked;
And when you rub your eyes awake and wide,
Where is the harm o' the horror? Gone! So here.
I know I wake,—but from what? Blank, I say!
This is the note of evil: for good lasts.
Even when Don Celestine bade "Search and find!
For your soul's sake, remember what is past,
The better to forgive it,"—all in vain!
What was fast getting indistinct before,
Vanished outright. By special grace perhaps,
Between that first calm and this last, four years
Vanish,—one quarter of my life, you know.
I am held up, amid the nothingness,
By one or two truths only—thence I hang,
And there I live,—the rest is death or dream,
All but those points of my support. I think
Of what I saw at Rome once in the Square
O' the Spaniards, opposite the Spanish House:
There was a foreigner had trained a goat,
A shuddering white woman of a beast,
To climb up, stand straight on a pile of sticks
Put close, which gave the creature room enough:

When she was settled there he, one by one,
Took away all the sticks, left just the four
Whereon the little hoofs did really rest,
There she kept firm, all underneath was air.
So, what I hold by, are my prayer to God,
My hope, that came in answer to the prayer,
Some hand would interpose and save me—hand
Which proved to be my friend's hand: and,—best bliss,—
That fancy which began so faint at first,
That thrill of dawn's suffusion through my dark,
Which I perceive was promise of my child,
The light his unborn face sent long before,—
God's way of breaking the good news to flesh.
That is all left now of those four bad years.
Don Celestine urged "But remember more!
Other men's faults may help me find your own.
I need the cruelty exposed, explained,
Or how can I advise you to forgive?"
He thought I could not properly forgive
Unless I ceased forgetting,—which is true:
For, bringing back reluctantly to mind
My husband's treatment of me,—by a light
That's later than my life-time, I review
And comprehend much and imagine more,
And have but little to forgive at last.
For now,—be fair and say,—is it not true
He was ill-used and cheated of his hope
To get enriched by marriage? Marriage gave
Me and no money, broke the compact so:
He had a right to ask me on those terms,
As Pietro and Violante to declare
They would not give me: so the bargain stood:
They broke it, and he felt himself aggrieved,
Became unkind with me to punish them.
They said 'twas he began deception first,
Nor, in one point whereto he pledged himself,
Kept promise: what of that, suppose it were?
Echoes die off, scarcely reverberate
For ever,—why should ill keep echoing ill,

And never let our ears have done with noise?
Then my poor parents took the violent way
To thwart him,—he must needs retaliate,—wrong,
Wrong, and all wrong,—better say, all blind!
As I myself was, that is sure, who else
Had understood the mystery: for his wife
Was bound in some sort to help somehow there.
It seems as if I might have interposed,
Blunted the edge of their resentment so,
Since he vexed me because they first vexed him;
"I will entreat them to desist, submit,
Give him the money and be poor in peace,—
Certainly not go tell the world: perhaps
He will grow quiet with his gains."

Yes, say
Something to this effect and you do well!
But then you have to see first: I was blind.
That is the fruit of all such wormy ways,
The indirect, the unapproved of God:
You cannot find their author's end and aim,
Not even to substitute your good for bad,
Your open for the irregular; you stand
Stupefied, profitless, as cow or sheep
That miss a man's mind; anger him just twice
By trial at repairing the first fault.
Thus, when he blamed me, "You are a coquette,
A lure-owl posturing to attract birds,
You look love-lures at theatre and church,
In walk, at window!"—that, I knew, was false:
But why he charged me falsely, whither sought
To drive me by such charge,—how could I know?
So, unaware, I only made things worse.
I tried to soothe him by abjuring walk,
Window, church, theatre, for good and all,
As if he had been in earnest: that, you know,
Was nothing like the object of his charge.
Yes, when I got my maid to supplicate
The priest, whose name she read when she would read

Those feigned false letters I was forced to hear
Though I could read no word of,—he should cease
Writing,—nay, if he minded prayer of mine,
Cease from so much as even pass the street
Whereon our house looked,—in my ignorance
I was just thwarting Guido's true intent;
Which was, to bring about a wicked change
Of sport to earnest, tempt a thoughtless man
To write indeed, and pass the house, and more,
Till both of us were taken in a crime.
He ought not to have wished me thus act lies,
Simulate folly,—but,—wrong or right, the wish,—
I failed to apprehend its drift. How plain
It follows,—if I fell into such fault,
He also may have overreached the mark,
Made mistake, by perversity of brain,
In the whole sad strange plot, this same intrigue
To make me and my friend unself ourselves,
Be other man and woman than we were!
Think it out, you who have the time! for me,—
I cannot say less; more I will not say.
Leave it to God to cover and undo!
Only, my dulness should not prove too much!
—Not prove that in a certain other point
Wherein my husband blamed me,—and you blame,
If I interpret smiles and shakes of head,—
I was dull too. Oh, if I dared but speak!
Must I speak? I am blamed that I forwent
A way to make my husband's favour come.
That is true: I was firm, withstood, refused . . .
—Women as you are, how can I find the words?

I felt there was just one thing Guido claimed
I had no right to give nor he to take;
We being in estrangement, soul from soul:
Till, when I sought help, the Archbishop smiled,
Inquiring into privacies of life,
—Said I was blameable—(he stands for God)
Nowise entitled to exemption there.
Then I obeyed,—as surely had obeyed

Were the injunction "Since your husband bids,
Swallow the burning coal he proffers you!"
But I did wrong, and he gave wrong advice
Though he were thrice Archbishop,—that, I know!—
Now I have got to die and see things clear.
Remember I was barely twelve years old—
A child at marriage: I was let alone
For weeks, I told you, lived my child-life still
Even at Arezzo, when I woke and found
First . . . but I need not think of that again—
Over and ended! Try and take the sense
Of what I signify, if it must be so.
After the first, my husband, for hate's sake,
Said one eve, when the simpler cruelty
Seemed somewhat dull at edge and fit to bear,
"We have been man and wife six months almost:
How long is this your comedy to last?
Go this night to my chamber, not your own!"
At which word, I did rush—most true the charge—
And gain the Archbishop's house—he stands for
God—
And fall upon my knees and clasp his feet,
Praying him hinder what my estranged soul
Refused to bear, though patient of the rest:
"Place me within a convent," I implored—
"Let me henceforward lead the virgin life
You praise in Her you bid me imitate!"
What did he answer? "Folly of ignorance!
Know, daughter, circumstances make or mar
Virginity,—'tis virtue or 'tis vice.
That which was glory in the Mother of God
Had been, for instance, damnable in Eve
Created to be mother of mankind.
Had Eve, in answer to her Maker's speech
'Be fruitful, multiply, replenish earth'—
Pouted 'But I choose rather to remain
Single'—why, she had spared herself forthwith
Further probation by the apple and snake,
Been pushed straight out of Paradise! For see—
If motherhood be qualified impure,

I catch you making God command Eve sin!
—A blasphemy so like these Molinists',
I must suspect you dip into their books."
Then he pursued "'Twas in your covenant!"

No! There my husband never used deceit.
He never did by speech nor act imply
"Because of our souls' yearning that we meet
And mix in soul through flesh, which yours and mine
Wear and impress, and make their visible selves,
—All which means, for the love of you and me,
Let us become one flesh, being one soul!"
He only stipulated for the wealth;
Honest so far. But when he spoke as plain—
Dreadfully honest also—"Since our souls
Stand each from each, a whole world's width between,
Give me the fleshy vesture I can reach
And rend and leave just fit for hell to burn!"—
Why, in God's name, for Guido's soul's own sake
Imperilled by polluting mine,—I say,
I did resist; would I had overcome!

My heart died out at the Archbishop's smile;
—It seemed so stale and worn a way o' the world,
As though 'twere nature frowning—"Here is Spring,
The sun shines as he shone at Adam's fall,
The earth requires that warmth reach everywhere:
What, must your patch of snow be saved forsooth
Because you rather fancy snow than flowers?"
Something in this style he began with me.
Last he said, savagely for a good man,
"This explains why you call your husband harsh,
Harsh to you, harsh to whom you love. God's Bread!
The poor Count has to manage a mere child
Whose parents leave untaught the simplest things
Their duty was and privilege to teach,—
Goodwives' instruction, gossips' lore: they laugh
And leave the Count the task,—or leave it me!"
Then I resolved to tell a frightful thing.

"I am not ignorant,—know what I say,
Declaring this is sought for hate, not love.
Sir, you may hear things like almighty God.
I tell you that my housemate, yes—the priest
My husband's brother, Canon Girolamo—
Has taught me what depraved and misnamed love
Means, and what outward signs denote the sin,
For he solicits me and says he loves,
The idle young priest with nought else to do.
My husband sees this, knows this, and lets be.
Is it your counsel I bear this beside?"
"—More scandal, and against a priest this time!
What, 'tis the Canon now?"—less snappishly—
"Rise up, my child, for such a child you are,
The rod were too advanced a punishment!
Let's try the honeyed cake. A parable!
'Without a parable spake He not to them.'
There was a ripe round long black toothsome fruit,
Even a flower-fig, the prime boast of May:
And, to the tree, said . . . either the spirit o' the fig,
Or, if we bring in men, the gardener,
Archbishop of the orchard—had I time
To try o' the two which fits in best: indeed
It might be the Creator's self, but then
The tree should bear an apple, I suppose,—
Well, anyhow, one with authority said
'Ripe fig, burst skin, regale the fig-pecker—
The bird whereof thou art a perquisite!'
'Nay,' with a flounce, replied the restif fig,
'I much prefer to keep my pulp myself:
He may go breakfastless and dinnerless,
Supperless of one crimson seed, for me!'
So, back she flopped into her bunch of leaves.
He flew off, left her,—did the natural lord,—
And lo, three hundred thousand bees and wasps
Found her out, feasted on her to the shuck:
Such gain the fig's that gave its bird no bite!
The moral,—fools elude their proper lot,
Tempt other fools, get ruined all alike.
Therefore go home, embrace your husband quick!

Which if his Canon brother chance to see,
He will the sooner back to book again."

So, home I did go; so, the worst befell:
So, I had proof the Archbishop was just man,
And hardly that, and certainly no more.
For, miserable consequence to me,
My husband's hatred waxed nor waned at all,
His brother's boldness grew effrontery soon,
And my last stay and comfort in myself
Was forced from me: henceforth I looked to God
Only, nor cared my desecrated soul
Should have fair walls, gay windows for the world.
God's glimmer, that came through the ruin-top,
Was witness why all lights were quenched inside:
Henceforth I asked God counsel, not mankind.

So, when I made the effort, saved myself,
They said—"No care to save appearance here!
How cynic,—when, how wanton, were enough!"
—Adding, it all came of my mother's life—
My own real mother, whom I never knew,
Who did wrong (if she needs must have done wrong)
Through being all her life, not my four years,
At mercy of the hateful,—every beast
O' the field was wont to break that fountain-fence,
Trample the silver into mud so murk
Heaven could not find itself reflected there,—
Now they cry "Out on her, who, plashy pool,
Bequeathed turbidity and bitterness
To the daughter-stream where Guido dipt and drank!"

Well, since she had to bear this brand—let me!
The rather do I understand her now,—
From my experience of what hate calls love,—
Much love might be in what their love called hate.
If she sold . . . what they call, sold . . . me her child—
I shall believe she hoped in her poor heart
That I at least might try be good and pure,

Begin to live untempted, not go doomed
And done with ere once found in fault, as she.
Oh and, my mother, it all came to this?
Why should I trust those that speak ill of you,
When I mistrust who speaks even well of them?
Why, since all bound to do me good, did harm,
May not you, seeming as you harmed me most,
Have meant to do most good—and feed your child
From bramble-bush, whom not one orchard-tree
But drew-back bough from, nor let one fruit fall?
This it was for you sacrificed your babe?
Gained just this, giving your heart's hope away
As I might give mine, loving it as you,
If . . . but that never could be asked of me!

There, enough! I have my support again,
Again the knowledge that my babe was, is,
Will be mine only. Him, by death, I give
Outright to God, without a further care,—
But not to any parent in the world,—
So to be safe: why is it we repine?
What guardianship were safer could we choose?
All human plans and projects come to nought,
My life, and what I know of other lives,
Prove that: no plan nor project! God shall care!

And now you are not tired? How patient then
All of you,—Oh yes, patient this long while
Listening, and understanding, I am sure!
Four days ago, when I was sound and well
And like to live, no one would understand.
People were kind, but smiled "And what of him,
Your friend, whose tonsure the rich dark-brown
 hides?
There, there!—your lover, do we dream he was?
A priest too—never were such naughtiness!
Still, he thinks many a long think, never fear,
After the shy pale lady,—lay so light
For a moment in his arms, the lucky one!"
And so on: wherefore should I blame you much?

So we are made, such difference in minds,
Such difference too in eyes that see the minds!
That man, you misinterpret and misprise—
The glory of his nature, I had thought,
Shot itself out in white light, blazed the truth
Through every atom of his act with me:
Yet where I point you, through the crystal shrine,
Purity in quintessence, one dew-drop,
You all descry a spider in the midst.
One says, "The head of it is plain to see,"
And one, "They are the feet by which I judge,"
All say, "Those films were spun by nothing else."

Then, I must lay my babe away with God,
Nor think of him again, for gratitude.
Yes, my last breath shall wholly spend itself
In one attempt more to disperse the stain,
The mist from other breath fond mouths have made,
About a lustrous and pellucid soul:
So that, when I am gone but sorrow stays,
And people need assurance in their doubt
If God yet have a servant, man a friend,
The weak a saviour and the vile a foe,—
Let him be present, by the name invoked,
Giuseppe-Maria Caponsacchi!

There,
Strength comes already with the utterance!
I will remember once more for his sake
The sorrow: for he lives and is belied.
Could he be here, how he would speak for me!

I had been miserable three drear years
In that dread palace and lay passive now,
When I first learned there could be such a man.
Thus it fell: I was at a public play,
In the last days of Carnival last March,
Brought there I knew not why, but now know well.
My husband put me where I sat, in front;

Then crouched down, breathed cold through me
from behind,
Stationed i' the shadow,—none in front could see,—
I, it was, faced the stranger-throng beneath,
The crowd with upturned faces, eyes one stare,
Voices one buzz. I looked but to the stage,
Whereon two lovers sang and interchanged
"True life is only love, love only bliss:
I love thee—thee I love!" then they embraced.
I looked thence to the ceiling and the walls,—
Over the crowd, those voices and those eyes,—
My thoughts went through the roof and out, to
Rome
On wings of music, waft of measured words,—
Set me down there, a happy child again,
Sure that to-morrow would be festa-day,
Hearing my parents praise past festas more,
And seeing they were old if I was young,
Yet wondering why they still would end discourse
With "We must soon go, you abide your time,
And,—might we haply see the proper friend
Throw his arm over you and make you safe!"

Sudden I saw him; into my lap there fell
A foolish twist of comfits, broke my dream
And brought me from the air and laid me low,
As ruined as the soaring bee that's reached
(So Pietro told me at the Villa once)
By the dust-handful. There the comfits lay:
I looked to see who flung them, and I faced
This Caponsacchi, looking up in turn.
Ere I could reason out why, I felt sure,
Whoever flung them, his was not the hand,—
Up rose the round face and good-natured grin
Of him who, in effect, had played the prank,
From covert close beside the earnest face,—
Fat waggish Conti, friend of all the world.
He was my husband's cousin, privileged
To throw the thing: the other, silent, grave,
Solemn almost, saw me, as I saw him.

There is a psalm Don Celestine recites,
"Had I a dove's wings, how I fain would flee!"
The psalm runs not "I hope, I pray for wings,"—
Not "If wings fall from heaven, I fix them fast,"—
Simply "How good it were to fly and rest,
Have hope now, and one day expect content!
How well to do what I shall never do!"
So I said "Had there been a man like that,
To lift me with his strength out of all strife
Into the calm, how I could fly and rest!
I have a keeper in the garden here
Whose sole employment is to strike me low
If ever I, for solace, seek the sun.
Life means with me successful feigning death,
Lying stone-like, eluding notice so,
Forgoing here the turf and there the sky.
Suppose that man had been instead of this!"

Presently Conti laughed into my ear,
—Had tripped up to the raised place where I sat—
"Cousin, I flung them brutishly and hard!
Because you must be hurt, to look austere
As Caponsacchi yonder, my tall friend
A-gazing now. Ah, Guido, you so close?
Keep on your knees, do! Beg her to forgive!
My cornet battered like a cannon-ball.
Good bye, I'm gone!"—nor waited the reply.

That night at supper, out my husband broke,
"Why was that throwing, that buffoonery?
Do you think I am your dupe? What man would dare
Throw comfits in a stranger lady's lap?
'Twas knowledge of you bred such insolence
In Caponsacchi; he dared shoot the bolt,
Using that Conti for his stalking-horse.
How could you see him this once and no more,
When he is always haunting hereabout
At the street-corner or the palace-side,
Publishing my shame and your impudence?
You are a wanton,—I a dupe, you think?

O Christ, what hinders that I kill her quick?"
Whereat he drew his sword and feigned a thrust.

All this, now,—being not so strange to me,
Used to such misconception day by day
And broken-in to bear,—I bore, this time,
More quietly than woman should perhaps:
Repeated the mere truth and held my tongue.

Then he said, "Since you play the ignorant,
I shall instruct you. This amour,—commenced
Or finished or midway in act, all's one,—
'Tis the town-talk; so my revenge shall be.
Does he presume because he is a priest?
I warn him that the sword I wear shall pink
His lily-scented cassock through and through,
Next time I catch him underneath your eaves!"

But he had threatened with the sword so oft
And, after all, not kept his promise. All
I said was, "Let God save the innocent!
Moreover, death is far from a bad fate.
I shall go pray for you and me, not him;
And then I look to sleep, come death or, worse,
Life." So, I slept.

There may have elapsed a week,
When Margherita,—called my waiting-maid,
Whom it is said my husband found too fair—
Who stood and heard the charge and the reply,
Who never once would let the matter rest
From that night forward, but rang changes still
On this the thrust and that the shame, and how
Good cause for jealousy cures jealous fools,
And what a paragon was this same priest
She talked about until I stopped my ears,—
She said, "A week is gone; you comb your hair,
Then go mope in a corner, cheek on palm,
Till night comes round again,—so, waste a week
As if your husband menaced you in sport.

Have not I some acquaintance with his tricks?
Oh no, he did not stab the serving-man
Who made and sang the rhymes about me once!
For why? They sent him to the wars next day.
Nor poisoned he the foreigner, my friend,
Who wagered on the whiteness of my breast,—
The swarth skins of our city in dispute:
For, though he paid me proper compliment,
The Count well knew he was besotted with
Somebody else, a skin as black as ink,
(As all the town knew save my foreigner)
He found and wedded presently,—'Why need
Better revenge?'—the Count asked. But what's
    here?
A priest, that does not fight, and cannot wed,
Yet must be dealt with! If the Count took fire
For the poor pastime of a minute,—me—
What were the conflagration for yourself,
Countess and lady-wife and all the rest?
The priest will perish; you will grieve too late:
So shall the city-ladies' handsomest
Frankest and liberalest gentleman
Die for you, to appease a scurvy dog
Hanging's too good for. Is there no escape?
Were it not simple Christian charity
To warn the priest be on his guard,—save him
Assured death, save yourself from causing it?
I meet him in the street. Give me a glove,
A ring to show for token! Mum's the word!"

I answered, "If you were, as styled, my maid,
I would command you: as you are, you say,
My husband's intimate,—assist his wife
Who can do nothing but entreat 'Be still!'
Even if you speak truth and a crime is planned,
Leave help to God as I am forced to do!
There is no other course, or we should craze,
Seeing such evil with no human cure.
Reflect that God, who makes the storm desist,
Can make an angry violent heart subside.

Why should we venture teach Him governance?
Never address me on this subject more!"

Next night she said, "But I went, all the same,
—Ay, saw your Caponsacchi in his house,
And come back stuffed with news I must outpour.
I told him, 'Sir, my mistress is a stone:
Why should you harm her for no good you get?
For you do harm her—prowl about our place
With the Count never distant half the street,
Lurking at every corner, would you look!
'Tis certain she has witched you with a spell.
Are there not other beauties at your beck?
We all know, Donna This and Monna That
Die for a glance of yours, yet here you gaze!
Go make them grateful, leave the stone its cold!'
And he—oh, he turned first white and then red,
And then—'To her behest I bow myself,
Whom I love with my body and my soul:
Only, a word i' the bowing! See, I write
One little word, no harm to see or hear!
Then, fear no further!' This is what he wrote.
I know you cannot read,—therefore, let me!
'*My idol!*' " . . .

But I took it from her hand
And tore it into shreds. "Why join the rest
Who harm me? Have I ever done you wrong?
People have told me 'tis you wrong myself:
Let it suffice I either feel no wrong
Or else forgive it,—yet you turn my foe!
The others hunt me and you throw a noose!"

She muttered, "Have your wilful way!" I slept.

Whereupon . . . no, I leave my husband out!
It is not to do him more hurt, I speak.
Let it suffice, when misery was most,
One day, I swooned and got a respite so.
She stooped as I was slowly coming to,

This Margherita, ever on my trace,
And whispered—"Caponsacchi!"

If I drowned,
But woke afloat i' the wave with upturned eyes,
And found their first sight was a star! I turned—
For the first time, I let her have her will,
Heard passively,—"The imposthume at such head,
One touch, one lancet-puncture would relieve,—
And still no glance the good physician's way
Who rids you of the torment in a trice!
Still he writes letters you refuse to hear.
He may prevent your husband, kill himself,
So desperate and all foredone is he!
Just hear the pretty verse he made to-day!
A sonnet from Mirtillo. '*Peerless fair* . . .'
All poetry is difficult to read,
—The sense of it is, anyhow, he seeks
Leave to contrive you an escape from hell,
And for that purpose asks an interview.
I can write, I can grant it in your name,
Or, what is better, lead you to his house.
Your husband dashes you against the stones;
This man would place each fragment in a shrine:
You hate him, love your husband!"

I returned,
"It is not true I love my husband,—no,
Nor hate this man. I listen while you speak,
—Assured that what you say is false, the same:
Much as when once, to me a little child,
A rough gaunt man in rags, with eyes on fire,
A crowd of boys and idlers at his heels,
Rushed as I crossed the Square, and held my head
In his two hands, 'Here's she will let me speak!
You little girl, whose eyes do good to mine,
I am the Pope, am Sextus, now the Sixth;
And that Twelfth Innocent, proclaimed to-day,
Is Lucifer disguised in human flesh!
The angels, met in conclave, crowned me!'—thus

He gibbered and I listened; but I knew
All was delusion, ere folks interposed
'Unfasten him, the maniac!' Thus I know
All your report of Caponsacchi false,
Folly or dreaming; I have seen so much
By that adventure at the spectacle,
The face I fronted that one first, last time:
He would belie it by such words and thoughts.
Therefore while you profess to show him me,
I ever see his own face. Get you gone!"

"—That will I, nor once open mouth again,—
No, by Saint Joseph and the Holy Ghost!
On your head be the damage, so adieu!"

And so more days, more deeds I must forget,
Till . . . what a strange thing now is to declare!
Since I say anything, say all if true!
And how my life seems lengthened as to serve!
It may be idle or inopportune,
But, true?—why, what was all I said but truth,
Even when I found that such as are untrue
Could only take the truth in through a lie?
Now—I am speaking truth to the Truth's self:
God will lend credit to my words this time.

It had got half through April. I arose
One vivid daybreak,—who had gone to bed
In the old way my wont those last three years,
Careless until, the cup drained, I should die.
The last sound in my ear, the over-night,
Had been a something let drop on the sly
In prattle by Margherita, "Soon enough
Gaieties end, now Easter's past: a week,
And the Archbishop gets him back to Rome,—
Everyone leaves the town for Rome, this Spring,—
Even Caponsacchi, out of heart and hope,
Resigns himself and follows with the flock."
I heard this drop and drop like rain outside
Fast-falling through the darkness while she spoke:

So had I heard with like indifference,
"And Michael's pair of wings will arrive first
At Rome to introduce the company,
Will bear him from our picture where he fights
Satan,—expect to have that dragon loose
And never a defender!"—my sole thought
Being still, as night came, "Done, another day!
How good to sleep and so get nearer death!"—
When, what, first thing at daybreak, pierced the sleep
With a summons to me? Up I sprang alive,
Light in me, light without me, everywhere
Change! A broad yellow sun-beam was let fall
From heaven to earth,—a sudden drawbridge lay,
Along which marched a myriad merry motes,
Mocking the flies that crossed them and recrossed
In rival dance, companions new-born too.
On the house-eaves, a dripping shag of weed
Shook diamonds on each dull grey lattice-square,
As first one, then another bird leapt by,
And light was off, and lo was back again,
Always with one voice,—where are two such joys?—
The blessed building-sparrow! I stepped forth,
Stood on the terrace,—o'er the roofs, such sky!
My heart sang, "I too am to go away,
I too have something I must care about,
Carry away with me to Rome, to Rome!
The bird brings hither sticks and hairs and wool,
And nowhere else i' the world; what fly breaks rank,
Falls out of the procession that befits,
From window here to window there, with all
The world to choose,—so well he knows his course?
I have my purpose and my motive too,
My march to Rome, like any bird or fly!
Had I been dead! How right to be alive!
Last night I almost prayed for leave to die,
Wished Guido all his pleasure with the sword
Or the poison,—poison, sword, was but a trick,
Harmless, may God forgive him the poor jest!
My life is charmed, will last till I reach Rome!
Yesterday, but for the sin,—ah, nameless be

The deed I could have dared against myself!
Now—see if I will touch an unripe fruit,
And risk the health I want to have and use!
Not to live, now, would be the wickedness,—
For life means to make haste and go to Rome
And leave Arezzo, leave all woes at once!"

Now, understand here, by no means mistake!
Long ago had I tried to leave that house
When it seemed such procedure would stop sin;
And still failed more the more I tried—at first
The Archbishop, as I told you,—next, our lord
The Governor,—indeed I found my way,
I went to the great palace where he rules,
Though I knew well 'twas he who,—when I gave
A jewel or two, themselves had given me,
Back to my parents,—since they wanted bread,
They who had never let me want a nosegay,—he
Spoke of the jail for felons, if they kept
What was first theirs, then mine, so doubly theirs,
Though all the while my husband's most of all!
I knew well who had spoke the word wrought this:
Yet, being in extremity, I fled
To the Governor, as I say,—scarce opened lip
When—the cold cruel snicker close behind—
Guido was on my trace, already there,
Exchanging nod and wink for shrug and smile,
And I—pushed back to him and, for my pains,
Paid with . . . but why remember what is past?
I sought out a poor friar the people call
The Roman, and confessed my sin which came
Of their sin,—that fact could not be repressed,—
The frightfulness of my despair in God:
And, feeling, through the grate, his horror shake,
Implored him, "Write for me who cannot write,
Apprise my parents, make them rescue me!
You bid me be courageous and trust God:
Do you in turn dare somewhat, trust and write
'Dear friends, who used to be my parents once,
And now declare you have no part in me,

This is some riddle I want wit to solve,
Since you must love me with no difference.
Even suppose you altered,—there's your hate,
To ask for: hate of you two dearest ones
I shall find liker love than love found here,
If husbands love their wives. Take me away
And hate me as you do the gnats and fleas,
Even the scorpions! How I shall rejoice!'
Write that and save me!" And he promised—wrote
Or did not write; things never changed at all:
He was not like the Augustinian here!
Last, in a desperation I appealed
To friends, whoever wished me better days,
To Guillichini, that's of kin,—"What, I—
Travel to Rome with you? A flying gout
Bids me deny my heart and mind my leg!"
Then I tried Conti, used to brave—laugh back
The louring thunder when his cousin scowled
At me protected by his presence: "You—
Who well know what you cannot save me from,—
Carry me off! What frightens you, a priest?"
He shook his head, looked grave—"Above my
strength!
Guido has claws that scratch, shows feline teeth;
A formidabler foe than I dare fret:
Give me a dog to deal with, twice the size!
Of course I am a priest and Canon too,
But . . . by the bye . . . though both, not quite so bold
As he, my fellow-Canon, brother-priest,
The personage in such ill odour here
Because of the reports—pure birth o' the brain—
Our Caponsacchi, he's your true Saint George
To slay the monster, set the Princess free,
And have the whole High-Altar to himself:
I always think so when I see that piece
I' the Pieve, that's his church and mine, you know:
Though you drop eyes at mention of his name!"

That name had got to take a half-grotesque
Half-ominous, wholly enigmatic sense,

Like any bye-word, broken bit of song
Born with a meaning, changed by mouth and mouth
That mix it in a sneer or smile, as chance
Bids, till it now means nought but ugliness
And perhaps shame.

—All this intends to say,
That, over-night, the notion of escape
Had seemed distemper, dreaming; and the name,—
Not the man, but the name of him, thus made
Into a mockery and disgrace,—why, she
Who uttered it persistently, had laughed,
"I name his name, and there you start and wince
As criminal from the red tongs' touch!"—yet now,
Now, as I stood letting morn bathe me bright,
Choosing which butterfly should bear my news,—
The white, the brown one, or that tinier blue,—
The Margherita, I detested so,
In she came—"The fine day, the good Spring time!
What, up and out at window? That is best.
No thought of Caponsacchi?—who stood there
All night on one leg, like the sentry crane,
Under the pelting of your water-spout—
Looked last look at your lattice ere he leave
Our city, bury his dead hope at Rome?
Ay, go to looking-glass and make you fine,
While he may die ere touch one least loose hair
You drag at with the comb in such a rage!"

I turned—"Tell Caponsacchi he may come!"

"Tell him to come? Ah, but, for charity,
A truce to fooling! Come? What,—come this eve?
Peter and Paul! But I see through the trick—
Yes, come, and take a flower-pot on his head
Flung from your terrace! No joke, sincere truth?"

How plainly I perceived hell flash and fade
O' the face of her,—the doubt that first paled joy,
Then, final reassurance I indeed

Was caught now, never to be free again!
What did I care?—who felt myself of force
To play with the silk, and spurn the horsehair-
springe.

"But—do you know that I have bade him come,
And in your own name? I presumed so much,
Knowing the thing you needed in your heart.
But somehow—what had I to show in proof?
He would not come: half-promised, that was all,
And wrote the letters you refused to read.
What is the message that shall move him now?"

"After the Ave Maria, at first dark,
I will be standing on the terrace, say!
I would I had a good long lock of hair
Should prove I was not lying! Never mind!"

Off she went—"May he not refuse, that's all—
Fearing a trick!"

I answered, "He will come."
And, all day, I sent prayer like incense up
To God the strong, God the beneficent,
God ever mindful in all strife and strait,
Who, for our own good, makes the need extreme,
Till at the last He puts forth might and saves.
An old rhyme came into my head and rang
Of how a virgin, for the faith of God,
Hid herself, from the Paynims that pursued,
In a cave's heart; until a thunderstone,
Wrapped in a flame, revealed the couch and prey:
And they laughed—"Thanks to lightning, ours at
last!"
And she cried "Wrath of God, assert His love!
Servant of God, thou fire, befriend His child!"
And lo, the fire she grasped at, fixed its flash,
Lay in her hand a calm cold dreadful sword
She brandished till pursuers strewed the ground,
So did the souls within them die away,

As o'er the prostrate bodies, sworded, safe,
She walked forth to the solitudes and Christ:
So should I grasp the lightning and be saved!

And still, as the day wore, the trouble grew
Whereby I guessed there would be born a star,
Until at an intense throe of the dusk,
I started up, was pushed, I dare to say,
Out on the terrace, leaned and looked at last
Where the deliverer waited me: the same
Silent and solemn face, I first descried
At the spectacle, confronted mine once more.

So was that minute twice vouchsafed me, so
The manhood, wasted then, was still at watch
To save me yet a second time: no change
Here, though all else changed in the changing world!

I spoke on the instant, as my duty bade,
In some such sense as this, whatever the phrase.

"Friend, foolish words were borne from you to me;
Your soul behind them is the pure strong wind,
Not dust and feathers which its breath may bear:
These to the witless seem the wind itself,
Since proving thus the first of it they feel.
If by mischance you blew offence my way,
The straws are dropt, the wind desists no whit,
And how such strays were caught up in the street
And took a motion from you, why inquire?
I speak to the strong soul, no weak disguise.
If it be truth,—why should I doubt it truth?—
You serve God specially, as priests are bound,
And care about me, stranger as I am,
So far as wish my good,—that miracle
I take to intimate He wills you serve
By saving me,—what else can He direct?
Here is the service. Since a long while now,
I am in course of being put to death:
While death concerned nothing but me, I bowed

The head and bade, in heart, my husband strike.
Now I imperil something more, it seems,
Something that's trulier me than this myself,
Something I trust in God and you to save.
You go to Rome, they tell me: take me there,
Put me back with my people!"

He replied—
The first word I heard ever from his lips,
All himself in it,—an eternity
Of speech, to match the immeasurable depths
O' the soul that then broke silence—"I am yours."

So did the star rise, soon to lead my step,
Lead on, nor pause before it should stand still
Above the House o' the Babe,—my babe to be,
That knew me first and thus made me know him,
That had his right of life and claim on mine,
And would not let me die till he was born,
But pricked me at the heart to save us both,
Saying "Have you the will? Leave God the way!"
And the way was Caponsacchi—"mine," thank God!
He was mine, he is mine, he will be mine.

No pause i' the leading and the light! I know,
Next night there was a cloud came, and not he:
But I prayed through the darkness till it broke
And let him shine. The second night, he came.

"The plan is rash; the project desperate:
In such a flight needs must I risk your life,
Give food for falsehood, folly or mistake,
Ground for your husband's rancour and revenge"—
So he began again, with the same face.
I felt that, the same loyalty—one star
Turning now red that was so white before—
One service apprehended newly: just
A word of mine and there the white was back!

"No, friend, for you will take me! 'Tis yourself
Risk all, not I,—who let you, for I trust

In the compensating great God: enough!
I know you: when is it that you will come?"

"To-morrow at the day's dawn." Then I heard
What I should do: how to prepare for flight
And where to fly.

That night my husband bade
"—You, whom I loathe, beware you break my sleep
This whole night! Couch beside me like the corpse
I would you were!" The rest you know, I think—
How I found Caponsacchi and escaped.

And this man, men call sinner? Jesus Christ!
Of whom men said, with mouths Thyself mad'st once,
"He hath a devil"—say he was Thy saint,
My Caponsacchi! Shield and show—unshroud
In Thine own time the glory of the soul
If aught obscure,—if ink-spot, from vile pens
Scribbling a charge against him—(I was glad
Then, for the first time, that I could not write)—
Flirted his way, have flecked the blaze!

For me,
'Tis otherwise: let men take, sift my thoughts
—Thoughts I throw like the flax for sun to bleach!
I did think, do think, in the thought shall die,
That to have Caponsacchi for my guide,
Ever the face upturned to mine, the hand
Holding my hand across the world,—a sense
That reads, as only such can read, the mark
God sets on woman, signifying so
She should—shall peradventure—be divine;
Yet 'ware, the while, how weakness mars the print
And makes confusion, leaves the thing men see,
—Not this man,—who from his own soul, re-writes
The obliterated charter,—love and strength
Mending what's marred: "So kneels a votarist,
Weeds some poor waste traditionary plot

Where shrine once was, where temple yet may be,
Purging the place but worshipping the while,
By faith and not by sight, sight clearest so,—
Such way the saints work,"—says Don Celestine.
But I, not privileged to see a saint
Of old when such walked earth with crown and palm,
If I call "saint" what saints call something else—
The saints must bear with me, impute the fault
To a soul i' the bud, so starved by ignorance,
Stinted of warmth, it will not blow this year
Nor recognize the orb which Spring-flowers know.
But if meanwhile some insect with a heart
Worth floods of lazy music, spendthrift joy—
Some fire-fly renounced Spring for my dwarfed cup,
Crept close to me with lustre for the dark,
Comfort against the cold,—what though excess
Of comfort should miscall the creature—sun?
What did the sun to hinder while harsh hands
Petal by petal, crude and colourless,
Tore me? This one heart brought me all the Spring!

Is all told? There's the journey: and where's time
To tell you how that heart burst out in shine?
Yet certain points do press on me too hard.
Each place must have a name, though I forget:
How strange it was—there where the plain begins
And the small river mitigates its flow—
When eve was fading fast, and my soul sank,
And he divined what surge of bitterness,
In overtaking me, would float me back
Whence I was carried by the striding day—
So,—"This grey place was famous once," said he—
And he began that legend of the place
As if in answer to the unspoken fear,
And told me all about a brave man dead,
Which lifted me and let my soul go on!
How did he know too,—at that town's approach
By the rock-side,—that in coming near the signs
Of life, the house-roofs and the church and tower,
I saw the old boundary and wall o' the world

Rise plain as ever round me, hard and cold,
As if the broken circlet joined again,
Tightened itself about me with no break,—
As if the town would turn Arezzo's self,—
The husband there,—the friends my enemies,
All ranged against me, not an avenue
I try, but would be blocked and drive me back
On him,—this other, . . . oh the heart in that!
Did not he find, bring, put into my arms
A new-born babe?—and I saw faces beam
Of the young mother proud to teach me joy,
And gossips round expecting my surprise
At the sudden hole through earth that lets in heaven.
I could believe himself by his strong will
Had woven around me what I thought the world
We went along in, every circumstance,
Towns, flowers and faces, all things helped so well!
For, through the journey, was it natural
Such comfort should arise from first to last?
As I look back, all is one milky way;
Still bettered more, the more remembered, so
Do new stars bud while I but search for old,
And fill all gaps i' the glory, and grow him—
Him I now see make the shine everywhere.
Even at the last when the bewildered flesh,
The cloud of weariness about my soul
Clogging too heavily, sucked down all sense,—
Still its last voice was, "He will watch and care;
Let the strength go, I am content: he stays!"
I doubt not he did stay and care for all—
From that sick minute when the head swam round,
And the eyes looked their last and died on him,
As in his arms he caught me and, you say,
Carried me in, that tragical red eve,
And laid me where I next returned to life
In the other red of morning, two red plates
That crushed together, crushed the time between,
And are since then a solid fire to me,—
When in, my dreadful husband and the world
Broke,—and I saw him, master, by hell's right,

And saw my angel helplessly held back
By guards that helped the malice—the lamb prone,
The serpent towering and triumphant—then
Came all the strength back in a sudden swell,
I did for once see right, do right, give tongue
The adequate protest: for a worm must turn
If it would have its wrong observed by God.
I did spring up, attempt to thrust aside
That ice-block 'twixt the sun and me, lay low
The neutralizer of all good and truth.
If I sinned so,—never obey voice more
O' the Just and Terrible, who bids us—"Bear!"
Not—"Stand by, bear to see my angels bear!"
I am clear it was on impulse to serve God
Not save myself,—no—nor my child unborn!
Had I else waited patiently till now?—
Who saw my old kind parents, silly-sooth
And too much trustful, for their worst of faults,
Cheated, brow-beaten, stripped and starved, cast out
Into the kennel: I remonstrated,
Then sank to silence, for,—their woes at end,
Themselves gone,—only I was left to plague.
If only I was threatened and belied,
What matter? I could bear it and did bear;
It was a comfort, still one lot for all:
They were not persecuted for my sake
And I, estranged, the single happy one.
But when at last, all by myself I stood
Obeying the clear voice which bade me rise,
Not for my own sake but my babe unborn,
And take the angel's hand was sent to help—
And found the old adversary athwart the path—
Not my hand simply struck from the angel's, but
The very angel's self made foul i' the face
By the fiend who struck there,—that I would not bear,
That only I resisted! So, my first
And last resistance was invincible.
Prayers move God; threats, and nothing else, move men!

I must have prayed a man as he were God
When I implored the Governor to right
My parents' wrongs: the answer was a smile.
The Archbishop,—did I clasp his feet enough,
Hide my face hotly on them, while I told
More than I dared make my own mother know?
The profit was—compassion and a jest.
This time, the foolish prayers were done with, right
Used might, and solemnized the sport at once.
All was against the combat: vantage, mine?
The runaway avowed, the accomplice-wife,
In company with the plan-contriving priest?
Yet, shame thus rank and patent, I struck, bare,
At foe from head to foot in magic mail,
And off it withered, cobweb-armoury
Against the lightning! 'Twas truth singed the lies
And saved me, not the vain sword nor weak speech!

You see, I will not have the service fail!
I say, the angel saved me: I am safe!
Others may want and wish, I wish nor want
One point o' the circle plainer, where I stand
Traced round about with white to front the world.
What of the calumny I came across,
What o' the way to the end?—the end crowns all.
The judges judged aright i' the main, gave me
The uttermost of my heart's desire, a truce
From torture and Arezzo, balm for hurt
With the quiet nuns,—God recompense the good!
Who said and sang away the ugly past.
And, when my final fortune was revealed,
What safety while, amid my parents' arms,
My babe was given me! Yes, he saved my babe:
It would not have peeped forth, the bird-like thing,
Through that Arezzo noise and trouble: back
Had it returned nor ever let me see!
But the sweet peace cured all, and let me live
And give my bird the life among the leaves
God meant him! Weeks and months of quietude,
I could lie in such peace and learn so much—

Begin the task, I see how needful now,
Of understanding somewhat of my past,—
Know life a little, I should leave so soon.
Therefore, because this man restored my soul,
All has been right; I have gained my gain, enjoyed
As well as suffered,—nay, got foretaste too
Of better life beginning where this ends—
All through the breathing-while allowed me thus,
Which let good premonitions reach my soul
Unthwarted, and benignant influence flow
And interpenetrate and change my heart,
Uncrossed by what was wicked,—nay, unkind.
For, as the weakness of my time drew nigh,
Nobody did me one disservice more,
Spoke coldly or looked strangely, broke the love
I lay in the arms of, till my boy was born,
Born all in love, with nought to spoil the bliss
A whole long fortnight: in a life like mine
A fortnight filled with bliss is long and much.
All women are not mothers of a boy,
Though they live twice the length of my whole life,
And, as they fancy, happily all the same.
There I lay, then, all my great fortnight long,
As if it would continue, broaden out
Happily more and more, and lead to heaven:
Christmas before me,—was not that a chance?
I never realized God's birth before—
How he grew likest God in being born.
This time I felt like Mary, had my babe
Lying a little on my breast like hers.
So all went on till, just four days ago—
The night and the tap.

O it shall be success
To the whole of our poor family! My friends
. . . Nay, father and mother,—give me back my word!
They have been rudely stripped of life, disgraced
Like children who must needs go clothed too fine,
Carry the garb of Carnival in Lent:

If they too much affected frippery,
They have been punished and submit themselves,
Say no word: all is over, they see God
Who will not be extreme to mark their fault
Or He had granted respite: they are safe.

For that most woeful man my husband once,
Who, needing respite, still draws vital breath,
I—pardon him? So far as lies in me,
I give him for his good the life he takes,
Praying the world will therefore acquiesce.
Let him make God amends,—none, none to me
Who thank him rather that, whereas strange fate
Mockingly styled him husband and me wife,
Himself this way at least pronounced divorce,
Blotted the marriage-bond: this blood of mine
Flies forth exultingly at any door,
Washes the parchment white, and thanks the blow.
We shall not meet in this world nor the next,
But where will God be absent? In His face
Is light, but in His shadow healing too:
Let Guido touch the shadow and be healed!
And as my presence was importunate,—
My earthly good, temptation and a snare,—
Nothing about me but drew somehow down
His hate upon me,—somewhat so excused
Therefore, since hate was thus the truth of him,—
May my evanishment for evermore
Help further to relieve the heart that cast
Such object of its natural loathing forth!
So he was made; he nowise made himself:
I could not love him, but his mother did.
His soul has never lain beside my soul;
But for the unresisting body,—thanks!
He burned that garment spotted by the flesh!
Whatever he touched is rightly ruined: plague
It caught, and disinfection it had craved
Still but for Guido; I am saved through him
So as by fire; to him—thanks and farewell!

Even for my babe, my boy, there's safety thence—
From the sudden death of me, I mean: we poor
Weak souls, how we endeavour to be strong!
I was already using up my life,—
This portion, now, should do him such a good,
This other go to keep off such an ill!
The great life; see, a breath and it is gone!
So is detached, so left all by itself
The little life, the fact which means so much.
Shall not God stoop the kindlier to His work,
His marvel of creation, foot would crush,
Now that the hand He trusted to receive
And hold it, lets the treasure fall perforce?
The better; He shall have in orphanage
His own way all the clearlier: if my babe
Outlive the hour—and he has lived two weeks—
It is through God who knows I am not by.
Who is it makes the soft gold hair turn black,
And sets the tongue, might lie so long at rest,
Trying to talk? Let us leave God alone!
Why should I doubt He will explain in time
What I feel now, but fail to find the words?
My babe nor was, nor is, nor yet shall be
Count Guido Franceschini's child at all—
Only his mother's, born of love not hate!
So shall I have my rights in after-time.
It seems absurd, impossible to-day;
So seems so much else not explained but known.

Ah! Friends, I thank and bless you every one!
No more now: I withdraw from earth and man
To my own soul, compose myself for God.

Well, and there is more! Yes, my end of breath
Shall bear away my soul in being true!
He is still here, not outside with the world,
Here, here, I have him in his rightful place!
'Tis now, when I am most upon the move,
I feel for what I verily find—again
The face, again the eyes, again, through all,

The heart and its immeasurable love
Of my one friend, my only, all my own,
Who put his breast between the spears and me.
Ever with Caponsacchi! Otherwise
Here alone would be failure, loss to me—
How much more loss to him, with life debarred
From giving life, love locked from love's display,
The day-star stopped its task that makes night morn!
O lover of my life, O soldier-saint,
No work begun shall ever pause for death!
Love will be helpful to me more and more
I' the coming course, the new path I must tread,
My weak hand in thy strong hand, strong for that!
Tell him that if I seem without him now,
That's the world's insight! Oh, he understands!
He is at Civita—do I once doubt
The world again is holding us apart?
He had been here, displayed in my behalf
The broad brow that reverberates the truth,
And flashed the word God gave him, back to man!
I know where the free soul is flown! My fate
Will have been hard for even him to bear:
Let it confirm him in the trust of God,
Showing how holily he dared the deed!
And, for the rest,—say, from the deed, no touch
Of harm came, but all good, all happiness,
Not one faint fleck of failure! Why explain?
What I see, oh, he sees and how much more!
Tell him,—I know not wherefore the true word
Should fade and fall unuttered at the last—
It was the name of him I sprang to meet
When came the knock, the summons and the end.
"My great heart, my strong hand are back again!"
I would have sprung to these, beckoning across
Murder and hell gigantic and distinct
O' the threshold, posted to exclude me heaven:
He is ordained to call and I to come!
Do not the dead wear flowers when dressed for God?
Say,—I am all in flowers from head to foot!
Say,—not one flower of all he said and did,

Might seem to flit unnoticed, fade unknown,
But dropped a seed has grown a balsam-tree
Whereof the blossoming perfumes the place
At this supreme of moments! He is a priest;
He cannot marry therefore, which is right:
I think he would not marry if he could.
Marriage on earth seems such a counterfeit,
Mere imitation of the inimitable:
In heaven we have the real and true and sure.
'Tis there they neither marry nor are given
In marriage but are as the angels: right,
Oh how right that is, how like Jesus Christ
To say that! Marriage-making for the earth,
With gold so much,—birth, power, repute so much,
Or beauty, youth so much, in lack of these!
Be as the angels rather, who, apart,
Know themselves into one, are found at length
Married, but marry never, no, nor give
In marriage; they are man and wife at once
When the true time is: here we have to wait
Not so long neither! Could we by a wish
Have what we will and get the future now,
Would we wish ought done undone in the past?
So, let him wait God's instant men call years;
Meantime hold hard by truth and his great soul,
Do out the duty! Through such souls alone
God stooping shows sufficient of His light
For us i' the dark to rise by. And I rise.

Miscellaneous Poems

1870–1889

Fifine at the Fair. By Robert Browning. London: Smith, Elder and Co., 15, Waterloo Place. 1872.

F'cap 8vo. Pp. xii + 172. Cloth boards.

THE prologue (*Amphibian*) and epilogue (*The Householder*) are printed here.

Aristophanes' Apology including a transcript from Euripides being the last adventure of Balaustion. By Robert Browning. London: Smith, Elder, & Co., 15 Waterloo Place. 1875

F'cap 8vo. Pp. viii + 368. Cloth boards.

THE song *Thamuris Marching* has been selected from this volume.

Ferishtah's Fancies. By Robert Browning. London: Smith, Elder, & Co., 15 Waterloo Place. 1884

F'cap 8vo. Pp. viii + 152. Cloth boards.

EACH of the twelve philosophical narratives in blank verse contained in this volume is succeeded by a lyric. Those lyrics are here printed, together with the epilogue.

The remaining poems in this section, though published in Browning's lifetime, were not collected by him into any volume.

Helen's Tower, written for the Marquis of Dufferin in 1870 and privately printed by him, was first published in the *Pall Mall Gazette* on 28 December 1883.

Why I am a Liberal appeared in a book of that name compiled by Andrew Reid, 1885.

The lines *To Edward FitzGerald*, first printed in the *Athenaeum* on 13 July 1889, were occasioned by the publication, in *Letters and Literary Remains of Edward FitzGerald* (edited by W. Aldis Wright, Vol. I, p. 280), of a letter containing the words "Mrs. Browning's Death is rather a relief to me, I must say: no more Aurora Leighs, thank God!"

Miscellaneous Poems

AMPHIBIAN

1

THE fancy I had to-day,
  Fancy which turned a fear!
I swam far out in the bay,
  Since waves laughed warm and clear.

2

I lay and looked at the sun,
  The noon-sun looked at me:
Between us two, no one
  Live creature, that I could see.

3

Yes! There came floating by
  Me, who lay floating too,
Such a strange butterfly!
  Creature as dear as new:

4

Because the membraned wings
  So wonderful, so wide,
So sun-suffused, were things
  Like soul and nought beside.

5

A handbreadth over head!
  All of the sea my own,
It owned the sky instead;
  Both of us were alone.

6

I never shall join its flight,
  For, nought buoys flesh in air.
If it touch the sea—good night!
  Death sure and swift waits there.

7

Can the insect feel the better
  For watching the uncouth play
Of limbs that slip the fetter,
  Pretend as they were not clay?

8

Undoubtedly I rejoice
  That the air comports so well
With a creature which had the choice
  Of the land once. Who can tell?

9

What if a certain soul
  Which early slipped its sheath,
And has for its home the whole
  Of heaven, thus look beneath,

10

Thus watch one who, in the world,
  Both lives and likes life's way,
Nor wishes the wings unfurled
  That sleep in the worm, they say?

11

But sometimes when the weather
  Is blue, and warm waves tempt
To free oneself of tether,
  And try a life exempt

12

From worldly noise and dust,
  In the sphere which overbrims
With passion and thought,—why, just
  Unable to fly, one swims!

13

By passion and thought upborne,
One smiles to oneself—"They fare
Scarce better, they need not scorn
Our sea, who live in the air!"

14

Emancipate through passion
And thought, with sea for sky,
We substitute, in a fashion,
For heaven—poetry:

15

Which sea, to all intent,
Gives flesh such noon-disport
As a finer element
Affords the spirit-sort.

16

Whatever they are, we seem:
Imagine the thing they know;
All deeds they do, we dream;
Can heaven be else but so?

17

And meantime, yonder streak
Meets the horizon's verge;
That is the land, to seek
If we tire or dread the surge:

18

Land the solid and safe—
To welcome again (confess!)
When, high and dry, we chafe
The body, and don the dress.

19

Does she look, pity, wonder
At one who mimics flight,
Swims—heaven above, sea under,
Yet always earth in sight?

THE HOUSEHOLDER

I

SAVAGE I was sitting in my house, late, lone:
  Dreary, weary with the long day's work:
Head of me, heart of me, stupid as a stone:
  Tongue-tied now, now blaspheming like a Turk;
When, in a moment, just a knock, call, cry,
  Half a pang and all a rapture, there again were we!—
"What, and is it really you again?" quoth I:
  "I again, what else did you expect?" quoth She.

2

"Never mind, hie away from this old house—
  Every crumbling brick embrowned with sin and shame
Quick, in its corners ere certain shapes arouse!
  Let them—every devil of the night—lay claim,
Make and mend, or rap and rend, for me! Goodbye!
  God be their guard from disturbance at their glee,
Till, crash, comes down the carcass in a heap!" quoth I:
  "Nay, but there's a decency required!" quoth She.

3

"Ah, but if you knew how time has dragged, days, nights!
  All the neighbour-talk with man and maid—such men!
All the fuss and trouble of street-sounds, window-sights:
  All the worry of flapping door and echoing roof; and then,
All the fancies . . . Who were they had leave, dared try
  Darker arts that almost struck despair in me?
If you knew but how I dwelt down here!" quoth I:
  "And was I so better off up there?" quoth She.

4

"Help and get it over! *Re-united to his wife*
  (How draw up the paper lets the parish people know?)
Lies M. or N., departed from this life,
  Day the this or that, month and year the so and so.

What i' the way of final flourish? Prose, verse? Try!
Affliction sore, long time he bore, or, what is it to be?
Till God did please to grant him ease. Do end!" quoth I:
"I end with—Love is all and Death is nought!" quoth
She.

THAMURIS MARCHING

THAMURIS marching,—lyre and song of Thrace—
(Perpend the first, the worst of woes that were
Allotted lyre and song, ye poet-race!)

Thamuris from Oichalia, feasted there
By kingly Eurutos of late, now bound
For Dorion at the uprise broad and bare

Of Mount Pangaios, (ore with earth enwound
Glittered beneath his footstep)—marching gay
And glad, Thessalia through, came, robed and crowned,

From triumph on to triumph, mid a ray
Of early morn,—came, saw and knew the spot
Assigned him for his worst of woes, that day.

Balura—happier while its name was not—
Met him, but nowise menaced; slipt aside
Obsequious river, to pursue its lot

Of solacing the valley—say, some wide
Thick busy human cluster, house and home,
Embanked for peace, or thrift that thanks the tide.

Thamuris, marching, laughed "Each flake of foam"
(As sparklingly the ripple raced him by)
"Mocks slower clouds adrift in the blue dome!"

For Autumn was the season; red the sky
Held morn's conclusive signet of the sun
To break the mists up, bid them blaze and die.

Morn had the mastery as one by one
All pomps produced themselves along the tract
From earth's far ending to near heaven begun.

Was there a ravaged tree? it laughed compact
With gold, a leaf-ball crisp, high-brandished now,
Tempting to onset frost which late attacked.

Was there a wizened shrub, a starveling bough,
A fleecy thistle filched from by the wind,
A weed, Pan's trampling hoof would disallow?

Each, with a glory and a rapture twined
About it, joined the rush of air and light
And force: the world was of one joyous mind.

Say not the birds flew! they forebore their right—
Swam, revelling onward in the roll of things.
Say not the beasts' mirth bounded! that was flight—

How could the creatures leap, no lift of wings?
Such earth's community of purpose, such
The ease of earth's fulfilled imaginings,—

So did the near and far appear to touch
I' the moment's transport,—that an interchange
Of function, far with near, seemed scarce too much.

And had the rooted plant aspired to range
With the snake's license, while the insect yearned
To glow fixed as the flower, it were not strange—

No more than if the fluttery tree-top turned
To actual music, sang itself aloft;
Or if the wind, impassioned chantress, earned

The right to soar embodied in some soft
Fine form all fit for cloud-companionship,
And, blissful, once touch beauty chased so oft.

Thamuris, marching, let no fancy slip
Born of the fiery transport; lyre and song
Were his, to smite with hand and launch from lip—

Peerless recorded, since the list grew long
Of poets (saith Homeros) free to stand
Pedestaled mid the Muses' temple-throng,

A statued service, laureled, lyre in hand,
(Ay, for we see them)—Thamuris of Thrace
Predominating foremost of the band.

Therefore the morn-ray that enriched his face,
If it gave lambent chill, took flame again
From flush of pride; he saw, he knew the place.

What wind arrived with all the rhythms from plain,
Hill, dale, and that rough wildwood interspersed?
Compounding these to one consummate strain,

It reached him, music; but his own outburst
Of victory concluded the account,
And that grew song which was mere music erst.

"Be my Parnassos, thou Pangaian mount!
And turn thee, river, nameless hitherto!
Famed shalt thou vie with famed Pieria's fount!

"Here I await the end of this ado:
Which wins—Earth's poet or the Heavenly Muse. . . ."

From FERISHTAH'S FANCIES

I

Round us the wild creatures, overhead the trees,
Underfoot the moss-tracks,—life and love with these!
I to wear a fawn-skin, thou to dress in flowers:
All the long lone Summer-day, that greenwood life of ours!

Rich-pavilioned, rather,—still the world without,—
Inside—gold-roofed silk-walled silence round about!
Queen it thou on purple,—I, at watch and ward
Couched beneath the columns, gaze, thy slave, love's guard!

So, for us no world? Let throngs press thee to me!
Up and down amid men, heart by heart fare we!
Welcome squalid vesture, harsh voice, hateful face!
God is soul, souls I and thou: with souls should souls have place.

2

Wish no word unspoken, want no look away!
What if words were but mistake, and looks—too sudden, say!
Be unjust for once, Love! Bear it—well I may!

Do me justice always? Bid my heart—their shrine—
Render back its store of gifts, old looks and words of thine
—Oh, so all unjust—the less deserved, the more divine?

3

You groped your way across my room i' the dear dark dead of night;
At each fresh step a stumble was: but, once your lamp alight,
Easy and plain you walked again: so soon all wrong grew right!

What lay on floor to trip your foot? Each object, late awry,
Looked fitly placed, or proved offence to footing free—for why?
The lamp showed all, discordant late, grown simple symmetry.

Be love your light and trust your guide, with these explore my heart!
No obstacle to trip you then, strike hands and souls apart!
Since rooms and hearts are furnished so,—light shows you,—needs love start?

4

Man I am and man would be, Love—merest man and nothing more.
Bid me seem no other! Eagles boast of pinions—let them soar!
I may put forth angel's plumage, once unmanned, but not before.

Now on earth, to stand suffices,—nay, if kneeling serves, to kneel:
Here you front me, here I find the all of heaven that earth can feel:
Sense looks straight,—not over, under,—perfect sees beyond appeal.

Good you are and wise, full circle: what to me were more outside?
Wiser wisdom, better goodness? Ah, such want the angel's wide
Sense to take and hold and keep them! Mine at least has never tried.

5

Fire is in the flint: true, once a spark escapes,
Fire forgets the kinship, soars till fancy shapes
Some befitting cradle where the babe had birth—
Wholly heaven's the product, unallied to earth.
Splendours recognized as perfect in the star!—
In our flint their home was, housed as now they are.

6

So, the head aches and the limbs are faint!
Flesh is a burthen—even to you!
Can I force a smile with a fancy quaint?
Why are my ailments none or few?

In the soul of me sits sluggishness:
Body so strong and will so weak!
The slave stands fit for the labour—yes,
But the master's mandate is still to seek.

You, now—what if the outside clay
  Helped, not hindered the inside flame?
My dim to-morrow—your plain to-day,
  Yours the achievement, mine the aim?

So were it rightly, so shall it be!
  Only, while earth we pace together
For the purpose apportioned you and me,
  Closer we tread for a common tether.

You shall sigh "Wait for his sluggish soul!
  Shame he should lag, not lamed as I!"
May not I smile "Ungained her goal:
  Body may reach her—bye and bye?"

7

When I vexed you and you chid me,
  And I owned my fault and turned
My cheek the way you bid me,
  And confessed the blow well earned,—

My comfort all the while was
  —Fault was faulty—near, not quite!
Do you wonder why the smile was?
  O'erpunished wrong grew right.

But faults you ne'er suspected,
  Nay, praised, no faults at all,—
Those would you had detected—
  Crushed eggs whence snakes could crawl!

8

Once I saw a chemist take a pinch of powder
—Simple dust it seemed—and half-unstop a phial:
—Out dropped harmless dew. "Mixed nothings make"—quoth he—
"Something!" So they did: a thunderclap, but louder—
Lightning-flash, but fiercer—put spectators' nerves to trial:
Sure enough, we learned what was, imagined what might be.

Had I no experience how a lip's mere tremble,
Look's half hesitation, cheek's just change of colour,
These effect a heartquake,—how should I conceive
What a heaven there may be? Let it but resemble
Earth myself have known! No bliss that's finer, fuller,
Only—bliss that lasts, they say, and fain would I believe.

9

Verse-making was least of my virtues: I viewed with despair
Wealth that never yet was but might be—all that verse-making were
If the life would but lengthen to wish, let the mind be laid bare.
So I said "To do little is bad, to do nothing is worse"—
And made verse.

Love-making,—how simple a matter! No depths to explore,
No heights in a life to ascend! No disheartening Before,
No affrighting Hereafter,—love now will be love evermore.
So I felt "To keep silence were folly:"—all language above,
I made love.

10

Not with my Soul, Love!—bid no Soul like mine
Lap thee around nor leave the poor Sense room!
Soul,—travel-worn, toil-weary,—would confine
Along with Soul, Soul's gains from glow and gloom,
Captures from soarings high and divings deep.
Spoil-laden Soul, how should such memories sleep?
Take Sense, too—let me love entire and whole—
Not with my Soul!

Eyes shall meet eyes and find no eyes between,
Lips feed on lips, no other lips to fear!
No past, no future—so thine arms but screen
The present from surprise! not there, 'tis here—
Not then, 'tis now:—back, memories that intrude!
Make, Love, the universe our solitude,
And, over all the rest, oblivion roll—
Sense quenching Soul!

11

Ask not one least word of praise!
  Words declare your eyes are bright?
What then meant that summer day's
Silence spent in one long gaze?
  Was my silence wrong or right?

Words of praise were all to seek!
  Face of you and form of you,
Did they find the praise so weak
When my lips just touched your cheek—
  Touch which let my soul come through?

12

"Why from the world" Ferishtah smiled "should thanks
  Go to this work of mine? If worthy praise,
Praised let it be and welcome: as verse ranks,
  So rate my verse: if good therein outweighs
  Aught faulty judged, judge justly! Justice says:
Be just to fact, or blaming or approving:
But—generous? No, nor loving!

"Loving! what claim to love has work of mine?
  Concede my life were emptied of its gains
To furnish forth and fill work's strict confine,
  Who works so for the world's sake—he complains
  With cause when hate, not love, rewards his pains.
I looked beyond the world for truth and beauty:
Sought, found and did my duty."

EPILOGUE

OH, Love—no, Love! All the noise below, Love,
Groanings all and moanings—none of Life I lose!
All of Life's a cry just of weariness and woe, Love—
"Hear at least, thou happy one!" How can I, Love, but choose?

Only, when I do hear, sudden circle round me
—Much as when the moon's might frees a space from cloud—
Iridescent splendours: gloom—would else confound me—
Barriered off and banished far—bright-edged the blackest shroud!

Thronging through the cloud-rift, whose are they, the faces
Faint revealed yet sure divined, the famous ones of old?
"What"—they smile—"our names, our deeds so soon erases
Time upon his tablet where Life's glory lies enrolled?

"Was it for mere fool's-play, make-believe and mumming,
So we battled it like men, not boylike sulked or whined?
Each of us heard clang God's 'Come!' and each was coming:
Soldiers all, to forward-face, not sneaks to lag behind!

"How of the field's fortune? That concerned our Leader!
Led, we struck our stroke nor cared for doings left and right:
Each as on his sole head, failer or succeeder,
Lay the blame or lit the praise: no care for cowards: fight!"

Then the cloud-rift broadens, spanning earth that's under,
Wide our world displays its worth, man's strife and strife's success:
All the good and beauty, wonder crowning wonder,
Till my heart and soul applaud perfection, nothing less.

Only, at heart's utmost joy and triumph, terror
Sudden turns the blood to ice: a chill wind disencharms
All the late enchantment! What if all be error—
If the halo irised round my head were, Love, thine arms?

HELEN'S TOWER

Who hears of Helen's Tower may dream perchance
  How the Greek beauty from the Scæan gate
  Gazed on old friends unanimous in hate,
Death-doom'd because of her fair countenance.
Hearts would leap otherwise at thy advance,
  Lady, to whom this tower is consecrate!
  Like hers, thy face once made all eyes elate,
Yet, unlike hers, was bless'd by every glance.

The Tower of Hate is outworn, far and strange:
  A transitory shame of long ago,
  It dies into the sand from which it sprang;
But thine, Love's rock-built Tower, shall fear no change:
  God's self laid stable earth's foundations so,
  When all the morning stars together sang.

WHY I AM A LIBERAL

"Why?" Because all I haply can and do,
  All that I am now, all I hope to be,—
  Whence comes it save from fortune setting free
Body and soul the purpose to pursue
God traced for both? If fetters, not a few,
  Of prejudice, convention, fall from me,
  These shall I bid men—each in his degree
Also God-guided—bear, and gaily too?

But little do or can the best of us:
  That little is achieved through Liberty.
Who then dares hold—emancipated thus—
  His fellow shall continue bound? Not I,
Who live, love, labour freely, nor discuss
  A brother's right to freedom. That is "Why."

TO EDWARD FITZGERALD

I CHANCED upon a new book yesterday:
I opened it, and where my finger lay
'Twixt page and uncut page these words I read
—Some six or seven at most—and learned thereby
That you, FitzGerald, whom by ear and eye
She never knew, "thanked God my wife was dead."

Ay, dead! and were yourself alive, good Fitz,
How to return you thanks would task my wits:
Kicking you seems the common lot of curs—
While more appropriate greeting lends you grace:
Surely to spit there glorifies your face—
Spitting—from lips once sanctified by Hers.

Pacchiarotto

AND OTHER POEMS

1876

La Saisiaz:

THE TWO POETS OF CROISIC

1878

Pacchiarotto and how he worked in distemper: with other poems. By Robert Browning. London: Smith, Elder, & Co., 15 Waterloo Place. 1876.

F'cap 8vo. Pp. viii + 244. Cloth boards.

La Saisiaz: The Two Poets of Croisic: By Robert Browning. London: Smith, Elder, & Co., 15 Waterloo Place. 1878.

F'cap 8vo. Pp. viii + 204. Cloth boards.

ALL but two of the following poems are chosen from among the nineteen in the *Pacchiarotto* volume of 1876.

Pisgah-Sights—III ("Good, to forgive") first appeared, with no title, as a prologue to *La Saisiaz* in the 1878 volume. The justification of its present placing and title is to be found in *Selections from the poetical works of Robert Browning*, second series, 1880—a selection arranged by Browning himself.

A Tale (" What a pretty tale you told me ") first appeared, with no title, as an epilogue to *The Two Poets of Croisic* in the 1878 volume. Browning titled it *A Tale* in his *Selections*, second series, of 1880.

Pacchiarotto

HOUSE

I

SHALL I sonnet-sing you about myself?
  Do I live in a house you would like to see?
Is it scant of gear, has it store of pelf?
  "Unlock my heart with a sonnet-key?"

2

Invite the world, as my betters have done?
  "Take notice: this building remains on view,
Its suites of reception every one,
  Its private apartment and bedroom too;

3

"For a ticket, apply to the Publisher."
  No: thanking the public, I must decline.
A peep through my window, if folk prefer;
  But, please you, no foot over threshold of mine!

4

I have mixed with a crowd and heard free talk
  In a foreign land where an earthquake chanced
And a house stood gaping, nought to baulk
  Man's eye wherever he gazed or glanced.

5

The whole of the frontage shaven sheer,
  The inside gaped: exposed to day,
Right and wrong and common and queer,
  Bare, as the palm of your hand, it lay.

6

The owner? Oh, he had been crushed, no doubt!
  "Odd tables and chairs for a man of wealth!
What a parcel of musty old books about!
  He smoked,—no wonder he lost his health!

7

"I doubt if he bathed before he dressed.
  A brasier?—the pagan, he burned perfumes!
You see it is proved, what the neighbours guessed:
  His wife and himself had separate rooms."

8

Friends, the goodman of the house at least
  Kept house to himself till an earthquake came:
'Tis the fall of its frontage permits you feast
  On the inside arrangement you praise or blame.

9

Outside should suffice for evidence:
  And whoso desires to penetrate
Deeper, must dive by the spirit-sense—
  No optics like yours, at any rate!

10

"Hoity toity! A street to explore,
  Your house the exception! '*With this same key*
Shakespeare unlocked his heart,' once more!"
  Did Shakespeare? If so, the less Shakespeare he!

SHOP

I

So, friend, your shop was all your house!
  Its front, astonishing the street,
Invited view from man and mouse
  To what diversity of treat
  Behind its glass—the single sheet!

2

What gimcracks, genuine Japanese:
  Gape-jaw and goggle-eye, the frog;
Dragons, owls, monkeys, beetles, geese;
  Some crush-nosed human-hearted dog:
  Queer names, too, such a catalogue!

3

I thought "And he who owns the wealth
  Which blocks the window's vastitude,
—Ah, could I peep at him by stealth
  Behind his ware, pass shop, intrude
  On house itself, what scenes were viewed!

4

"If wide and showy thus the shop,
  What must the habitation prove?
The true house with no name a-top—
  The mansion, distant one remove,
  Once get him off his traffic-groove!

5

"Pictures he likes, or books perhaps;
  And as for buying most and best,
Commend me to these city chaps!
  Or else he's social, takes his rest
  On Sundays, with a Lord for guest.

6

"Some suburb-palace, parked about
  And gated grandly, built last year:
The four-mile walk to keep off gout;
  Or big seat sold by bankrupt peer:
  But then he takes the rail, that's clear.

7

"Or, stop! I wager, taste selects
  Some out o' the way, some all-unknown
Retreat: the neighbourhood suspects
  Little that he who rambles lone
  Makes Rothschild tremble on his throne!"

8

Nowise! Nor Mayfair residence
  Fit to receive and entertain,—
Nor Hampstead villa's kind defence
  From noise and crowd, from dust and drain,—
  Nor country-box was soul's domain!

9

Nowise! At back of all that spread
  Of merchandize, woe's me, I find
A hole i' the wall where, heels by head,
  The owner couched, his ware behind,
  —In cupboard suited to his mind.

10

For why? He saw no use of life
  But, while he drove a roaring trade,
To chuckle "Customers are rife!"
  To chafe "So much hard cash outlaid
  Yet zero in my profits made!

11

"This novelty costs pains, but—takes?
  Cumbers my counter! Stock no more!
This article, no such great shakes,
  Fizzes like wild fire? Underscore
  The cheap thing—thousands to the fore!"

12

'Twas lodging best to live most nigh
  (Cramp, coffinlike as crib might be)
Receipt of Custom; ear and eye
  Wanted no outworld: "Hear and see
  The bustle in the shop!" quoth he.

13

My fancy of a merchant-prince
  Was different. Through his wares we groped
Our darkling way to—not to mince
  The matter—no black den where moped
  The master if we interloped!

14

Shop was shop only: household-stuff?
  What did he want with comforts there?
"Walls, ceiling, floor, stay blank and rough,
  So goods on sale show rich and rare!
  '*Sell and scud home*' be shop's affair!"

15

What might he deal in? Gems, suppose!
  Since somehow business must be done
At cost of trouble,—see, he throws
  You choice of jewels, everyone,
  Good, better, best, star, moon and sun!

16

Which lies within your power of purse?
  This ruby that would tip aright
Solomon's sceptre? Oh, your nurse
  Wants simply coral, the delight
  Of teething baby,—stuff to bite!

17

Howe'er your choice fell, straight you took
  Your purchase, prompt your money rang
On counter,—scarce the man forsook
  His study of the "Times," just swang
  Till-ward his hand that stopped the clang,—

18

Then off made buyer with a prize,
  Then seller to his "Times" returned,
And so did day wear, wear, till eyes
  Brightened apace, for rest was earned:
  He locked door long ere candle burned.

19

And whither went he? Ask himself,
  Not me! To change of scene, I think.
Once sold the ware and pursed the pelf,
  Chaffer was scarce his meat and drink,
  Nor all his music—money-chink.

20

Because a man has shop to mind
In time and place, since flesh must live,
Needs spirit lack all life behind,
All stray thoughts, fancies fugitive,
All loves except what trade can give?

21

I want to know a butcher paints,
A baker rhymes for his pursuit,
Candlestick-maker much acquaints
His soul with song, or, haply mute,
Blows out his brains upon the flute!

22

But—shop each day and all day long!
Friend, your good angel slept, your star
Suffered eclipse, fate did you wrong!
From where these sorts of treasures are,
There should our hearts be—Christ, how far!

PISGAH-SIGHTS—I

1

OVER the ball of it,
Peering and prying,
How I see all of it,
Life there, outlying!
Roughness and smoothness,
Shine and defilement,
Grace and uncouthness:
One reconcilement.

2

Orbed as appointed,
Sister with brother
Joins, ne'er disjointed
One from the other.

All's lend-and-borrow;
  Good, see, wants evil,
Joy demands sorrow,
  Angel weds devil!

3

"Which things must—*why* be?"
  Vain our endeavour!
So shall things aye be
  As they were ever.
"Such things should *so* be!"
  Sage our desistence!
Rough-smooth let globe be,
  Mixed—man's existence!

4

Man—wise and foolish,
  Lover and scorner,
Docile and mulish—
  Keep each his corner!
Honey yet gall of it!
  There's the life lying,
And I see all of it,
  Only, I'm dying!

PISGAH-SIGHTS—II

I

COULD I but live again,
  Twice my life over,
Would I once strive again?
  Would not I cover
Quietly all of it—
  Greed and ambition—
So, from the pall of it,
  Pass to fruition?

2

"Soft!" I'd say, "Soul mine!
  Three-score and ten years,
Let the blind mole mine
  Digging out deniers!
Let the dazed hawk soar,
  Claim the sun's rights too!
Turf 'tis thy walk's o'er,
  Foliage thy flight's to."

3

Only a learner,
  Quick one or slow one,
Just a discerner,
  I would teach no one.
I am earth's native:
  No rearranging it!
I be creative,
  Chopping and changing it?

4

March, men, my fellows!
  Those who, above me,
(Distance so mellows)
  Fancy you love me:
Those who, below me,
  (Distance makes great so)
Free to forego me,
  Fancy you hate so!

5

Praising, reviling,
  Worst head and best head,
Past me defiling,
  Never arrested,
Wanters, abounders,
  March, in gay mixture,
Men, my surrounders!
  I am the fixture.

6

So shall I fear thee,
  Mightiness yonder!
Mock-sun—more near thee,
  What is to wonder?
So shall I love thee,
  Down in the dark,—lest
Glowworm I prove thee,
  Star that now sparklest!

PISGAH-SIGHTS—III

1

Good, to forgive;
  Best, to forget!
  Living, we fret;
Dying, we live.
Fretless and free,
  Soul, clap thy pinion!
  Earth have dominion,
Body, o'er thee!

2

Wander at will,
  Day after day,—
  Wander away,
Wandering still—
Soul that canst soar!
  Body may slumber:
  Body shall cumber
Soul-flight no more.

3

Waft of soul's wing!
  What lies above?
  Sunshine and Love,
Skyblue and Spring!

Body hides—where?
  Ferns of all feather,
  Mosses and heather,
Yours be the care!

FEARS AND SCRUPLES

1

HERE'S my case. Of old I used to love him,
  This same unseen friend, before I knew:
Dream there was none like him, none above him,—
  Wake to hope and trust my dream was true.

2

Loved I not his letters full of beauty?
  Not his actions famous far and wide?
Absent, he would know I vowed him duty,
  Present, he would find me at his side.

3

Pleasant fancy! for I had but letters,
  Only knew of actions by hearsay:
He himself was busied with my betters;
  What of that? My turn must come some day.

4

"Some day" proving—no day! Here's the puzzle.
  Passed and passed my turn is. Why complain?
He's so busied! If I could but muzzle
  People's foolish mouths that give me pain!

5

"Letters?" (hear them!) "You a judge of writing?
  Ask the experts!—How they shake the head
O'er these characters, your friend's inditing—
  Call them forgery from A. to Z.!

6

"Actions? Where's your certain proof" (they bother)
"He, of all you find so great and good,
He, he only, claims this, that, the other
Action—claimed by men, a multitude?"

7

I can simply wish I might refute you,
Wish my friend would,—by a word, a wink,—
Bid me stop that foolish mouth,—you brute you!
He keeps absent,—why, I cannot think.

8

Never mind! Though foolishness may flout me,
One thing's sure enough: 'tis neither frost,
No, nor fire, shall freeze or burn from out me
Thanks for truth—though falsehood, gained—
though lost.

9

All my days, I'll go the softlier, sadlier,
For that dream's sake! How forget the thrill
Through and through me as I thought "The gladlier
Lives my friend because I love him still!"

10

Ah, but there's a menace someone utters!
"What and if your friend at home play tricks?
Peep at hide-and-seek behind the shutters?
Mean your eyes should pierce through solid bricks?

11

"What and if he, frowning, wake you, dreamy?
Lay on you the blame that bricks—conceal?
Say '*At least I saw who did not see me,*
Does see now, and presently shall feel'?"

12

"Why, that makes your friend a monster!" say you:
"Had his house no window? At first nod,
Would you not have hailed him?" Hush, I pray you!
What if this friend happen to be—God?

APPEARANCES

I

And so you found that poor room dull,
Dark, hardly to your taste, my dear?
Its features seemed unbeautiful:
But this I know—'twas there, not here,
You plighted troth to me, the word
Which—ask that poor room how it heard!

2

And this rich room obtains your praise
Unqualified,—so bright, so fair,
So all whereat perfection stays?
Ay, but remember—here, not there,
The other word was spoken!—Ask
This rich room how you dropped the mask!

ST MARTIN'S SUMMER

I

No protesting, dearest!
Hardly kisses even!
Don't we both know how it ends?
How the greenest leaf turns serest,
Bluest outbreak—blankest heaven,
Lovers—friends?

2

You would build a mansion,
  I would weave a bower
    —Want the heart for enterprise.
Walls admit of no expansion:
  Trellis-work may haply flower
    Twice the size.

3

What makes glad Life's Winter?
  New buds, old blooms after.
    Sad the sighing "How suspect
Beams would ere mid-Autumn splinter,
  Rooftree scarce support a rafter,
    Walls lie wrecked?"

4

You are young, my princess!
  I am hardly older:
    Yet—I steal a glance behind!
Dare I tell you what convinces
  Timid me that you, if bolder,
    Bold—are blind?

5

Where we plan our dwelling
  Glooms a graveyard surely!
    Headstone, footstone moss may drape,—
Name, date, violets hide from spelling,—
  But, though corpses rot obscurely,
    Ghosts escape.

6

Ghosts! O breathing Beauty,
  Give my frank word pardon!
    What if I—somehow, somewhere—
Pledged my soul to endless duty
  Many a time and oft—Be hard on
    Love—laid there?

7

Nay, blame grief that's fickle,
  Time that proves a traitor,
    Chance, change, all that purpose warps,—
Death who spares to thrust the sickle
  Laid Love low, through flowers which later
    Shroud the corpse!

8

And you, my winsome lady,
  Whisper me with like frankness!
    Lies nothing buried long ago?
Are yon—which shimmer mid the shady
  Where moss and violet run to rankness—
    Tombs or no?

9

Who taxes you with murder?
  My hands are clean—or nearly!
    Love being mortal needs must pass.
Repentance? Nothing were absurder.
  Enough: we felt Love's loss severely;
    Though now—alas!

10

Love's corpse lies quiet therefore,
  Only Love's ghost plays truant,
    And warns us have in wholesome awe
Durable mansionry; that's wherefore
  I weave but trellis-work, pursuant
    —Life, to law.

11

The solid, not the fragile,
  Tempts rain and hail and thunder.
    If bower stand firm at Autumn's close,
Beyond my hope,—why, boughs were agile,
  If bower fall flat, we scarce need wonder
    Wreathing—rose!

12

So, truce to the protesting,
So, muffled be the kisses!
For, would we but avow the truth,
Sober is genuine joy. No jesting!
Ask else Penelope, Ulysses—
Old in youth!

13

For why should ghosts feel angered?
Let all their interference
Be faint march-music in the air!
"Up! Join the rear of us the vanguard!
Up, lovers, dead to all appearance,
Laggard pair!"

14

The while you clasp me closer,
The while I press you deeper,
As safe we chuckle,—under breath,
Yet all the slyer, the jocoser,—
"So, life can boast its day, like leap-year,
Stolen from death!"

15

Ah me—the sudden terror!
Hence quick—avaunt, avoid me,
You cheat, the ghostly flesh-disguised!
Nay, all the ghosts in one! Strange error!
So, 'twas Death's self that clipped and coyed me,
Loved—and lied!

16

Ay, dead loves are the potent!
Like any cloud they used you,
Mere semblance you, but substance they!
Build we no mansion, weave we no tent!
Mere flesh—their spirit interfused you!
Hence, I say!

17

All theirs, none yours the glamour!
Theirs each low word that won me,
Soft look that found me Love's, and left
What else but you—the tears and clamour
That's all your very own! Undone me—
Ghost-bereft!

HERVÉ RIEL

I

On the sea and at the Hogue, sixteen hundred ninety-two,
Did the English fight the French,—woe to France!
And, the thirty-first of May, helter-skelter thro' the blue,
Like a crowd of frightened porpoises a shoal of sharks pursue,
Came crowding ship on ship to St. Malo on the Rance,
With the English fleet in view.

2

'Twas the squadron that escaped, with the victor in full chase;
First and foremost of the drove, in his great ship, Damfreville;
Close on him fled, great and small,
Twenty-two good ships in all;
And they signalled to the place
"Help the winners of a race!
Get us guidance, give us harbour, take us quick—or, quicker still,
Here's the English can and will!"

3

Then the pilots of the place put out brisk and leapt on board;
"Why, what hope or chance have ships like these to pass?" laughed they:

"Rocks to starboard, rocks to port, all the passage scarred
and scored,
Shall the '*Formidable*' here with her twelve and eighty guns
Think to make the river-mouth by the single narrow way,
Trust to enter where 'tis ticklish for a craft of twenty tons,
And with flow at full beside?
Now, 'tis slackest ebb of tide.
Reach the mooring? Rather say,
While rock stands or water runs,
Not a ship will leave the bay!"

4

Then was called a council straight,
Brief and bitter the debate:
"Here's the English at our heels; would you have them
take in tow
All that's left us of the fleet, linked together stern and
bow,
For a prize to Plymouth Sound?
Better run the ships aground!"
(Ended Damfreville his speech).
"Not a minute more to wait!
Let the Captains all and each
Shove ashore, then blow up, burn the vessels on the
beach!
France must undergo her fate.

5

"Give the word!" But no such word
Was ever spoke or heard;
For up stood, for out stepped, for in struck amid all these
—A Captain? A Lieutenant? A Mate—first, second, third?
No such man of mark, and meet
With his betters to compete!
But a simple Breton sailor pressed by Tourville for the
fleet,
A poor coasting-pilot he, Hervé Riel the Croisickese.

6

And "What mockery or malice have we here?" cries Hervé Riel:
"Are you mad, you Malouins? Are you cowards, fools, or rogues?
Talk to me of rocks and shoals, me who took the soundings, tell
On my fingers every bank, every shallow, every swell
'Twixt the offing here and Grève where the river disembogues?
Are you bought by English gold? Is it love the lying's for?
Morn and eve, night and day,
Have I piloted your bay,
Entered free and anchored fast at the foot of Solidor.
Burn the fleet and ruin France? That were worse than fifty Hogues!
Sirs, they know I speak the truth! Sirs, believe me there's a way!
Only let me lead the line,
Have the biggest ship to steer,
Get this '*Formidable*' clear,
Make the others follow mine,
And I lead them, most and least, by a passage I know well,
Right to Solidor past Grève,
And there lay them safe and sound;
And if one ship misbehave,—
—Keel so much as grate the ground,
Why, I've nothing but my life,—here's my head!" cries Hervé Riel.

7

Not a minute more to wait.
"Steer us in, then, small and great!
Take the helm, lead the line, save the squadron!" cried its chief.
Captains, give the sailor place!
He is Admiral, in brief.
Still the north-wind, by God's grace!
See the noble fellow's face

As the big ship, with a bound,
Clears the entry like a hound,
Keeps the passage as its inch of way were the wide sea's profound!
See, safe thro' shoal and rock,
How they follow in a flock,
Not a ship that misbehaves, not a keel that grates the ground,
Not a spar that comes to grief!
The peril, see, is past.
All are harboured to the last,
And just as Hervé Riel hollas "Anchor!"—sure as fate,
Up the English come, too late!

8

So, the storm subsides to calm:
They see the green trees wave
On the heights o'erlooking Grève.
Hearts that bled are stanched with balm.
"Just our rapture to enhance,
Let the English rake the bay,
Gnash their teeth and glare askance
As they cannonade away!
'Neath rampired Solidor pleasant riding on the Rance!"
How hope succeeds despair on each Captain's countenance!
Out burst all with one accord,
"This is Paradise for Hell!
Let France, let France's King
Thank the man that did the thing!"
What a shout, and all one word,
"Hervé Riel!"
As he stepped in front once more,
Not a symptom of surprise
In the frank blue Breton eyes,
Just the same man as before.

9

Then said Damfreville, "My friend,
I must speak out at the end,
Though I find the speaking hard.

Praise is deeper than the lips:
You have saved the King his ships,
You must name your own reward.
'Faith, our sun was near eclipse!
Demand whate'er you will,
France remains your debtor still.
Ask to heart's content and have! or my name's not Damfreville."

10

Then a beam of fun outbroke
On the bearded mouth that spoke,
As the honest heart laughed through
Those frank eyes of Breton blue:
"Since I needs must say my say,
Since on board the duty's done,
And from Malo Roads to Croisic Point, what is it but a run?—
Since 'tis ask and have, I may—
Since the others go ashore—
Come! A good whole holiday!
Leave to go and see my wife, whom I call the Belle Aurore!"
That he asked and that he got,—nothing more.

11

Name and deed alike are lost:
Not a pillar nor a post
In his Croisic keeps alive the feat as it befell;
Not a head in white and black
On a single fishing-smack,
In memory of the man but for whom had gone to wrack
All that France saved from the fight whence England bore the bell.
Go to Paris: rank on rank
Search the heroes flung pell-mell
On the Louvre, face and flank!
You shall look long enough ere you come to Hervé Riel.
So, for better and for worse,
Hervé Riel, accept my verse!

In my verse, Hervé Riel, do thou once more
Save the squadron, honour France, love thy wife the Belle
Aurore!

A TALE

I

What a pretty tale you told me
Once upon a time
—Said you found it somewhere (scold me!)
Was it prose or was it rhyme,
Greek or Latin? Greek, you said,
While your shoulder propped my head.

2

Anyhow there's no forgetting
This much if no more,
That a poet (pray, no petting!)
Yes, a bard, sir, famed of yore,
Went where suchlike used to go,
Singing for a prize, you know.

3

Well, he had to sing, nor merely
Sing but play the lyre;
Playing was important clearly
Quite as singing: I desire,
Sir, you keep the fact in mind
For a purpose that's behind.

4

There stood he, while deep attention
Held the judges round,
—Judges able, I should mention,
To detect the slightest sound
Sung or played amiss: such ears
Had old judges, it appears!

5

None the less he sang out boldly,
  Played in time and tune,
Till the judges, weighing coldly
  Each note's worth, seemed, late or soon,
Sure to smile "In vain one tries
Picking faults out: take the prize!"

6

When, a mischief! Were they seven
  Strings the lyre possessed?
Oh, and afterwards eleven,
  Thank you! Well, sir,—who had guessed
Such ill luck in store?—it happed
One of those same seven strings snapped.

7

All was lost, then! No! a cricket
  (What "cicada"? Pooh!)
—Some mad thing that left its thicket
  For mere love of music—flew
With its little heart on fire,
Lighted on the crippled lyre.

8

So that when (Ah joy!) our singer
  For his truant string
Feels with disconcerted finger,
  What does cricket else but fling
Fiery heart forth, sound the note
Wanted by the throbbing throat?

9

Ay and, ever to the ending,
  Cricket chirps at need,
Executes the hand's intending,
  Promptly, perfectly,—indeed
Saves the singer from defeat
With her chirrup low and sweet.

10

Till, at ending, all the judges
  Cry with one assent
"Take the prize—a prize who grudges
  Such a voice and instrument?
Why, we took your lyre for harp,
So it shrilled us forth F sharp!"

11

Did the conqueror spurn the creature,
  Once its service done?
That's no such uncommon feature
  In the case when Music's son
Finds his Lotte's power too spent
For aiding soul-development.

12

No! This other, on returning
  Homeward, prize in hand,
Satisfied his bosom's yearning:
  (Sir, I hope you understand!)
—Said "Some record there must be
Of this cricket's help to me!"

13

So, he made himself a statue:
  Marble stood, life-size;
On the lyre, he pointed at you,
  Perched his partner in the prize;
Never more apart you found
Her, he throned, from him, she crowned.

14

That's the tale: its application?
  Somebody I know
Hopes one day for reputation
  Through his poetry that's—Oh,
All so learned and so wise
And deserving of a prize!

15

If he gains one, will some ticket,
  When his statue's built,
Tell the gazer "'Twas a cricket
  Helped my crippled lyre, whose lilt
Sweet and low, when strength usurped
Softness' place i' the scale, she chirped?

16

"For as victory was nighest,
  While I sang and played,—
With my lyre at lowest, highest,
  Right alike,—one string that made
'Love' sound soft was snapt in twain,
Never to be heard again,—

17

"Had not a kind cricket fluttered,
  Perched upon the place
Vacant left, and duly uttered
  'Love, Love, Love,' whene'er the bass
Asked the treble to atone
For its somewhat sombre drone."

18

But you don't know music! Wherefore
  Keep on casting pearls
To a—poet? All I care for
  Is—to tell him that a girl's
"Love" comes aptly in when gruff
Grows his singing. (There, enough!)

Dramatic Idyls

FIRST SERIES

1879

SECOND SERIES

1880

Dramatic Idyls. By Robert Browning. London: Smith, Elder, & Co., 15 Waterloo Place. 1879

F'cap 8vo. Pp. vi + 146. Cloth boards.

Dramatic Idyls. Second Series. By Robert Browning. London: Smith, Elder, & Co., 15 Waterloo Place. 1880

F'cap 8vo. Pp. viii + 152. Cloth boards.

EACH volume contained six idyls, the second volume also a prologue and an epilogue. The prologue is here moved to the front of the selection. The poems selected are, with one partial exception, reprinted from the first editions.

The rime-scheme of *Pheidippides* (*a b c d d c a b*) was all Browning's own. In the first edition he inadvertently departed from it in stanzas 8, 10 and 11. These three stanzas are here printed as finally revised by Browning.

Dramatic Idyls

PROLOGUE

"You are sick, that's sure"—they say:
"Sick of what?"—they disagree.
"'Tis the brain"—thinks Doctor A.,
"'Tis the heart"—holds Doctor B.,
"The liver—my life I'd lay!"
"The lungs!" "The lights!"
Ah me!
So ignorant of man's whole
Of bodily organs plain to see—
So sage and certain, frank and free,
About what's under lock and key—
Man's soul!

PHEIDIPPIDES

Χαίρετε, νικῶμεν

First I salute this soil of the blessed, river and rock!
Gods of my birthplace, demons and heroes, honor to all!
Then I name thee, claim thee for our patron, co-equal in praise
—Ay, with Zeus the Defender, with Her of the ægis and spear!
Also, ye of the bow and the buskin, praised be your peer,
Now, henceforth and forever,—O latest to whom I upraise
Hand and heart and voice! For Athens, leave pasture and flock!
Present to help, potent to save, Pan—patron I call!

Archons of Athens, topped by the tettix, see, I return!
See, 'tis myself here standing alive, no spectre that speaks!

Crowned with the myrtle, did you command me, Athens and you,
"Run, Pheidippides, run and race, reach Sparta for aid!
Persia has come, we are here, where is She?" Your command I obeyed,
Ran and raced: like stubble, some field which a fire runs through,
Was the space between city and city: two days, two nights did I burn
Over the hills, under the dales, down pits and up peaks.

Into their midst I broke: breath served but for "Persia has come!
Persia bids Athens proffer slaves'-tribute, water and earth;
Razed to the ground is Eretria—but Athens, shall Athens sink,
Drop into dust and die—the flower of Hellas utterly die,
Die, with the wide world spitting at Sparta, the stupid, the stander-by?
Answer me quick, what help, what hand do you stretch o'er destruction's brink?
How,—when? No care for my limbs!—there's lightning in all and some—
Fresh and fit your message to bear, once lips give it birth!"

O my Athens—Sparta love thee? Did Sparta respond?
Every face of her leered in a furrow of envy, mistrust,
Malice,—each eye of her gave me its glitter of gratified hate!
Gravely they turned to take counsel, to cast for excuses. I stood
Quivering,—the limbs of me fretting as fire frets, an inch from dry wood:
"Persia has come, Athens asks aid, and still they debate?
Thunder, thou Zeus! Athene, are Spartans a quarry beyond
Swing of thy spear? Phoibos and Artemis, clang them 'Ye must'!"

No bolt launched from Olumpos! Lo, their answer at last!
"Has Persia come,—does Athens ask aid,—may Sparta befriend?

Nowise precipitate judgment—too weighty the issue at
stake!
Count we no time lost time which lags through respect to
the Gods!
Ponder that precept of old, 'No warfare, whatever the odds
In your favour, so long as the moon, half-orbed, is unable to
take
Full-circle her state in the sky!' Already she rounds to it
fast:
Athens must wait, patient as we—who judgment suspend."

Athens,—except for that sparkle,—thy name, I had
mouldered to ash!
That sent a blaze through my blood; off, off and away was
I back,
—Not one word to waste, one look to lose on the false and
the vile!
Yet "O Gods of my land!" I cried, as each hillock and
plain,
Wood and stream, I knew, I named, rushing past them
again,
"Have ye kept faith, proved mindful of honors we paid you
erewhile?
Vain was the filleted victim, the fulsome libation! Too rash
Love in its choice, paid you so largely service so slack!

"Oak and olive and bay,—I bid you cease to enwreathe
Brows made bold by your leaf! Fade at the Persian's foot,
You that, our patrons were pledged, should never adorn a
slave!
Rather I hail thee, Parnes,—trust to thy wild waste tract!
Treeless, herbless, lifeless mountain! What matter if slacked
My speed may hardly be, for homage to crag and to cave
No deity deigns to drape with verdure,—at least I can
breathe,
Fear in thee no fraud from the blind, no lie from the mute!"

Such my cry as, rapid, I ran over Parnes' ridge;
Gully and gap I clambered and cleared till, sudden, a bar
Jutted, a stoppage of stone against me, blocking the way.

Right! for I minded the hollow to traverse, the fissure
across:
"Where I could enter, there I depart by! Night in the fosse?
Athens to aid? Though the dive were through Erebos, thus
I obey—
Out of the day dive, into the day as bravely arise! No bridge
Better!"—when—ha! what was it I came on, of wonders
that are?

There, in the cool of a cleft, sat he—majestical Pan!
Ivy drooped wanton, kissed his head, moss cushioned his
hoof:
All the great God was good in the eyes grave-kindly—the
curl
Carved on the bearded cheek, amused at a mortal's awe,
As, under the human trunk, the goat-thighs grand I saw.
"Halt, Pheidippides!"—halt I did, my brain of a whirl:
"Hither to me! Why pale in my presence?" he gracious
began:
"How is it,—Athens, only in Hellas, holds me aloof?

"Athens, she only, rears me no fane, makes me no feast!
Wherefore? Than I what godship to Athens more helpful
of old?
Ay, and still, and forever her friend! Test Pan, trust me!
Go, bid Athens take heart, laugh Persia to scorn, have faith
In the temples and tombs! Go, say to Athens, 'The Goat-
God saith:
When Persia—so much as strews not the soil—is cast in the
sea,
Then praise Pan who fought in the ranks with your most
and least,
Goat-thigh to greaved-thigh, made one cause with the free
and the bold!'

"Say Pan saith: 'Let this, foreshowing the place, be the
pledge!' "
(Gay, the liberal hand held out this herbage I bear
—Fennel—I grasped it a-tremble with dew—whatever it
bode)

"While, as for thee . . ." But enough! He was gone. If I ran hitherto—
Be sure that, the rest of my journey, I ran no longer, but flew.
Parnes to Athens—earth no more, the air was my road:
Here am I back. Praise Pan, we stand no more on the razor's edge!
Pan for Athens, Pan for me! I too have a guerdon rare!

Then Miltiades spoke. "And thee, best runner of Greece,
Whose limbs did duty indeed,—what gift is promised thyself?
Tell it us straightway,—Athens the mother demands of her son!"
Rosily blushed the youth: he paused: but, lifting at length
His eyes from the ground, it seemed as he gathered the rest of his strength
Into the utterance—"Pan spoke thus: 'For what thou hast done
Count on a worthy reward! Henceforth be allowed thee release
From the racer's toil, no vulgar reward in praise or in pelf!'

"I am bold to believe, Pan means reward the most to my mind!
Fight I shall, with our foremost, wherever this fennel may grow,—
Pound—Pan helping us—Persia to dust, and, under the deep,
Whelm her away for ever; and then,—no Athens to save,—
Marry a certain maid, I know keeps faith to the brave,—
Hie to my house and home: and, when my children shall creep
Close to my knees,—recount how the God was awful yet kind,
Promised their sire reward to the full—rewarding him—so!"

Unforeseeing one! Yes, he fought on the Marathon day.
So, when Persia was dust, all cried "To Akropolis!
Run, Pheidippides, one race more! the meed is thy due!
'Athens is saved, thank Pan,' go shout!" He flung down his shield,
Ran like fire once more: and the space 'twixt the Fennel-field
And Athens was stubble again, a field which a fire runs through,
Till in he broke: "Rejoice, we conquer!" Like wine through clay,
Joy in his blood bursting his heart, he died—the bliss!

So, to this day, when friend meets friend, the word of salute
Is still "Rejoice!"—his word which brought rejoicing indeed.
So is Pheidippides happy for ever,—the noble strong man
Who could race like a God, bear the face of a God, whom a God loved so well;
He saw the land saved he had helped to save, and was suffered to tell
Such tidings, yet never decline, but, gloriously as he began,
So to end gloriously—once to shout, thereafter be mute:
"Athens is saved!"—Pheidippides dies in the shout for his meed.

NED BRATTS

'Twas Bedford Special Assize, one daft Midsummer's Day:
A broiling blasting June,—was never its like, men say.
Corn stood sheaf-ripe already, and trees looked yellow as that;
Ponds drained dust-dry, the cattle lay foaming around each flat.
Inside town, dogs went mad, and folk kept bibbing beer
While the parsons prayed for rain. 'Twas horrible, yes—but queer:
Queer—for the sun laughed gay, yet nobody moved a hand
To work one stroke at his trade: as given to understand

That all was come to a stop, work and such worldly ways,
And the world's old self about to end in a merry blaze.
Midsummer's Day moreover was the first of Bedford Fair;
So, Bedford Town's tag-rag and bobtail lay bowsing there.

But the Court House, Quality crammed: through doors ope, windows wide,
High on the Bench you saw sit Lordships side by side.
There frowned Chief Justice Jukes, fumed learned Brother Small,
And fretted their fellow Judge: like threshers, one and all,
Of a reek with laying down the law in a furnace. Why?
Because their lungs breathed flame—the regular crowd forbye—
From gentry pouring in—quite a nosegay, to be sure!
How else could they pass the time, six mortal hours endure
Till night should extinguish day, when matters might haply mend?
Meanwhile no bad resource was—watching begin and end
Some trial for life and death, in a brisk five minutes' space,
And betting which knave would 'scape, which hang, from his sort of face.

So, their Lordships toiled and moiled, and a deal of work was done
(I warrant) to justify the mirth of the crazy sun,
As this and t'other lout, struck dumb at the sudden show
Of red robes and white wigs, boggled nor answered "Boh!"
When asked why he, Tom Styles, should not—because Jack Nokes
Had stolen the horse—be hanged: for Judges must have their jokes,
And louts must make allowance—let's say, for some blue fly
Which punctured a dewy scalp where the frizzles stuck awry—
Else Tom had fleered scot-free, so nearly over and done
Was the main of the job. Full-measure, the gentles enjoyed their fun,

As a twenty-five were tried, rank puritans caught at prayer
In a cow-house and laid by the heels,—have at 'em, devil may care!—
And ten were prescribed the whip, and ten a brand on the cheek,
And five a slit of the nose—just leaving enough to tweak.

Well, things at jolly high-tide, amusement steeped in fire,
While noon smote fierce the roof's red tiles to heart's desire,
The Court a-simmer with smoke, one ferment of oozy flesh,
One spirituous humming musk mount-mounting until its mesh
Entoiled all heads in a fluster, and Serjeant Postlethwayte
—Dashing the wig oblique as he mopped his oily pate—
Cried "Silence, or I grow grease! No loophole lets in air?
Jurymen,—Guilty, Death! Gainsay me if you dare!"
—Things at this pitch, I say,—what hubbub without the doors?
What laughs, shrieks, hoots and yells, what rudest of uproars?

Bounce through the barrier throng a bulk comes rolling vast!
Thumps, kicks,—no manner of use!—spite of them rolls at last
Into the midst a ball which, bursting, brings to view
Publican Black Ned Bratts and Tabby his big wife too:
Both in a muck-sweat, both . . . were never such eyes uplift
At the sight of yawning hell, such nostrils—snouts that sniffed
Sulphur, such mouths a-gape ready to swallow flame!
Horrified, hideous, frank fiend-faces! yet, all the same,
Mixed with a certain . . . eh? how shall I dare style—mirth
The desperate grin of the guess that, could they break from earth,
Heaven was above, and hell might rage in impotence
Below the saved, the saved!

"Confound you! (no offence)!
Out of our way,—push, wife! Yonder their Worships be!"

Ned Bratts has reached the bar, and "Hey, my Lords," roars he,
"A Jury of life and death, Judges the prime of the land,
Constables, javelineers,—all met, if I understand,
To decide so knotty a point as whether 'twas Jack or Joan
Robbed the henroost, pinched the pig, hit the King's Arms with a stone,
Dropped the baby down the well, left the tithesman in the lurch,
Or, three whole Sundays running, not once attended church!
What a pother—do these deserve the parish-stocks or whip,
More or less brow to brand, much or little nose to snip,—
When, in our Public, plain stand we—that's we stand here,
I and my Tab, brass-bold, brick-built of beef and beer,
—Do not we, slut? Step forth and show your beauty, jade!
Wife of my bosom—that's the word now! What a trade
We drove! None said us nay: nobody loved his life
So little as wag a tongue against us,—did they, wife?
Yet they knew us all the while, in their hearts, for what we are
—Worst couple, rogue and quean, unhanged—search near and far!
Eh, Tab? The pedlar, now—o'er his noggin—who warned a mate
To cut and run, nor risk his pack where its loss of weight
Was the least to dread,—aha, how we two laughed a-good
As, stealing round the midden, he came on where I stood
With billet poised and raised,—you, ready with the rope,—
Ah, but that's past, that's sin repented of, we hope!
Men knew us for that same, yet safe and sound stood we!
The lily-livered knaves knew too (I've baulked a d——)
Our keeping the 'Pied Bull' was just a mere pretence:
Too slow make food, drink, lodging, the pounds from out the pence!
There's not a stoppage has chanced to travel, this ten long year,
No break into hall or grange, no lifting of nag or steer,
Not a single roguery, from the cutting of a purse
To the cutting of a throat, but paid us toll. Od's curse!

When Gipsy Smouch made bold to cheat us of our due,
—Eh, Tab? the Squire's strong-box we helped the rascal to—
I think he pulled a face, next Sessions' swinging-time!
He danced the jig that needs no floor,—and, here's the prime,
'Twas Scroggs that houghed the mare! Ay, those were busy days!

"Well, there we flourished brave, like scripture-trees called bays,
Faring high, drinking hard, in money up to head
—Not to say, boots and shoes, when . . . Zounds, I nearly said—
Lord, to unlearn one's language! How shall we labour, wife?
Have you, fast hold, the Book? Grasp, grip it, for your life!
See, sirs, here's life, salvation! Here's—hold but out my breath—
When did I speak so long without once swearing? 'Sdeath,
No, nor unhelped by ale since man and boy! And yet
All yesterday I had to keep my whistle wet
While reading Tab this Book: book? don't say 'book'—they're plays,
Songs, ballads and the like: here's no such strawy blaze,
But sky wide ope, sun, moon, and seven stars out full-flare!
Tab, help and tell! I'm hoarse. A mug! or—no, a prayer!
Dip for one out of the Book! Who wrote it in the Jail
—He plied his pen unhelped by beer, sirs, I'll be bail!

"I've got my second wind. In trundles she—that's Tab.
'Why, Gammer, what's come now, that—bobbing like a crab
On Yule-tide bowl—your head's a-work and both your eyes
Break loose? Afeard, you fool? As if the dead can rise!
Say—Bagman Dick was found last May with fuddling-cap
Stuffed in his mouth: to choke's a natural mishap!'
'Gaffer, be—blessed,' cries she, 'and Bagman Dick as well!
I, you, and he are damned: this Public is our hell:

We live in fire: live coals don't feel!—once quenched, they learn—
Cinders do, to what dust they moulder while they burn!'

" 'If you don't speak straight out,' says I—belike I swore—
'A knobstick, well you know the taste of, shall, once more,
Teach you to talk, my maid!' She ups with such a face,
Heart sunk inside me. 'Well, pad on, my prate-apace!'

" 'I've been about those laces we need for . . . never mind!
If henceforth they tie hands, 'tis mine they'll have to bind.
You know who makes them best—the Tinker in our cage,
Pulled-up for gospelling, twelve years ago: no age
To try another trade,—yet, so he scorned to take
Money he did not earn, he taught himself the make
Of laces, tagged and tough—Dick Bagman found them so!
Good customers were we! Well, last week, you must know
His girl,—the blind young chit, who hawks about his wares,—
She takes it in her head to come no more—such airs
These hussies have! Yet, since we need a stoutish lace,—
"I'll to the jail-bird father, abuse her to his face!"
So, first I filled a jug to give me heart, and then,
Primed to the proper pitch, I posted to their den—
Patmore—they style their prison! I tip the turnkey, catch
My heart up, fix my face, and fearless lift the latch—
Both arms a-kimbo, in bounce with a good round oath
Ready for rapping out: no "Lawks" nor "By my troth!"

" 'There sat my man, the father. He looked up: what one feels
When heart that leapt to mouth drops down again to heels!
He raised his hand . . . Hast seen, when drinking out the night,
And in, the day, earth grow another something quite
Under the sun's first stare? I stood a very stone.

" ' "Woman!" (a fiery tear he put in every tone),

"How should my child frequent your house where lust is
sport,
Violence—trade? Too true! I trust no vague report.
Her angel's hand, which stops the sight of sin, leaves clear
The other gate of sense, lets outrage through the ear.
What has she heard!—which, heard shall never be again.
Better lack food than feast, a Dives in the—wain
Or reign or train—of Charles!" (His language was not ours:
'Tis my belief, God spoke: no tinker has such powers).
"Bread, only bread they bring—my laces: if we broke
Your lump of leavened sin, the loaf's first crumb would
choke!"

" 'Down on my marrow-bones! Then all at once rose he:
His brown hair burst a-spread, his eyes were suns to see:
Up went his hands: "Through flesh, I reach, I read thy soul!
So may some stricken tree look blasted, bough and bole,
Champed by the fire-tooth, charred without, and yet, thrice-
bound
With drериment about, within may life be found,
A prisoned power to branch and blossom as before,
Could but the gardener cleave the cloister, reach the core,
Loosen the vital sap: yet where shall help be found?
Who says 'How save it?'—nor 'Why cumbers it the ground?'
Woman, that tree art thou! All sloughed about with scurf,
Thy stag-horns fright the sky, thy snake-roots sting the turf!
Drunkenness, wantonness, theft, murder gnash and gnarl
Thine outward, case thy soul with coating like the marle
Satan stamps flat upon each head beneath his hoof!
And how deliver such? The strong men keep aloof,
Lover and friend stand far, the mocking ones pass by,
Tophet gapes wide for prey: lost soul, despair and die!
What then? 'Look unto me and be ye saved!' saith God:
'I strike the rock, outstreats the life-stream at my rod![1]
Be your sins scarlet, wool shall they seem like,—although
As crimson red, yet turn white as the driven snow!' "

[1] They did not eat
His flesh, nor suck those oils which thence outstreat.
Donne's *Progress of the Soul,* line 344. [R. B.]

" 'There, there, there! All I seem to somehow understand
Is—that, if I reached home, 'twas through the guiding hand
Of his blind girl which led and led me through the streets
And out of town and up to door again. What greets
First thing my eye, as limbs recover from their swoon?
A book—this Book she gave at parting. "Father's boon—
The Book he wrote: it reads as if he spoke himself:
He cannot preach in bonds, so,—take it down from shelf
When you want counsel,—think you hear his very voice!"

" 'Wicked dear Husband, first despair and then rejoice!
Dear wicked Husband, waste no tick of moment more,
Be saved like me, bald trunk! There's greenness yet at core,
Sap under slough! Read, read!'

"Let me take breath, my lords!
I'd like to know, are these—hers, mine, or Bunyan's words?
I'm 'wildered—scarce with drink,—nowise with drink alone!
You'll say, with heat: but heat's no stuff to split a stone
Like this black boulder—this flint heart of mine: the Book—
That dealt the crashing blow! Sirs, here's the fist that shook
His beard till Wrestler Jem howled like a just-lugged bear!
You had brained me with a feather: at once I grew aware
Christmas was meant for me. A burden at your back,
Good Master Christmas? Nay,—yours was that Joseph's sack,
—Or whose it was,—which held the cup,—compared with mine!
Robbery loads my loins, perjury cracks my chine,
Adultery . . . nay, Tab, you pitched me as I flung!
One word, I'll up with fist . . . No, sweet spouse, hold your tongue!

"I'm hasting to the end. The Book, sirs—take and read!
You have my history in a nutshell,—ay, indeed!
It must off, my burden! See,—slack straps and into pit,
Roll, reach the bottom, rest, rot there—a plague on it!
For a mountain's sure to fall and bury Bedford Town,
'Destruction'—that's the name, and fire shall burn it down!

O 'scape the wrath in time! Time's now, if not too late.
How can I pilgrimage up to the wicket-gate?
Next comes Despond the slough: not that I fear to pull
Through mud, and dry my clothes at brave House Beautiful—
But it's late in the day, I reckon: had I left years ago
Town, wife, and children dear . . . Well, Christmas did, you know!—
Soon I had met in the valley and tried my cudgel's strength
On the enemy horned and winged, a-straddle across its length!
Have at his horns, thwick—thwack: they snap, see! Hoof and hoof—
Bang, break the fetlock-bones! For love's sake, keep aloof
Angels! I'm man and match,—this cudgel for my flail,—
To thresh him, hoofs and horns, bat's wing and serpent's tail!
A chance gone by! But then, what else does Hopeful ding
Into the deafest ear except—hope, hope's the thing?
Too late i' the day for me to thrid the windings: but
There's still a way to win the race by death's short cut!
Did Master Faithful need climb the Delightful Mounts?
No, straight to Vanity Fair,—a fair, by all accounts,
Such as is held outside,—lords, ladies, grand and gay,—
Says he in the face of them, just what you hear me say.
And the Judges brought him in guilty,and brought him out
To die in the market-place—St. Peter's Green's about
The same thing: there they flogged, flayed, buffeted, lanced with knives,
Pricked him with swords,—I'll swear, he'd full a cat's nine lives,—
So to his end at last came Faithful,—ha, ha, he!
Who holds the highest card? for there stands hid, you see,
Behind the rabble-rout, a chariot, pair and all:
He's in, he's off, he's up, through clouds, at trumpet-call,
Carried the nearest way to Heaven-gate! Odds my life—
Has nobody a sword to spare? not even a knife?
Then hang me, draw and quarter! Tab—do the same by her!
O Master Worldly-Wiseman . . . that's Master Interpreter,

Take the will, not the deed! Our gibbet's handy, close:
Forestall Last Judgment-Day! Be kindly, not morose!
There wants no earthly judge-and-jurying: here we stand—
Sentence our guilty selves: so, hang us out of hand!
Make haste for pity's sake! A single moment's loss
Means—Satan's lord once more: his whisper shoots across
All singing in my heart, all praying in my brain,
'It comes of heat and beer!'—hark how he guffaws plain!
'To-morrow you'll wake bright, and, in a safe skin, hug
Your sound selves, Tab and you, over a foaming jug!
You've had such qualms before, time out of mind!' He's
right!
Did not we kick and cuff and curse away, that night
When home we blindly reeled, and left poor humpback Joe
I' the lurch to pay for what . . . somebody did, you know!
Both of us maundered then 'Lame humpback,—never more
Will he come limping, drain his tankard at our door!
He'll swing, while—somebody . . .' Says Tab, 'No, for I'll
peach!'
'I'm for you, Tab,' cries I, 'there's rope enough for each!'
So blubbered we, and bussed, and went to bed upon
The grace of Tab's good thought: by morning, all was gone!
We laughed—'What's life to him, a cripple of no account?'
Oh, waves increase around—I feel them mount and mount!
Hang us! To-morrow brings Tom Bearward with his bears:
One new black-muzzled brute beats Sackerson, he swears:
(Sackerson, for my money!) And, baiting o'er, the Brawl
They lead on Turner's Patch,—lads, lasses, up tails all,—
I'm i' the thick o' the throng! That means the Iron Cage,
—Means the Lost Man inside! Where's hope for such as
wage
War against light? Light's left, light's here, I hold light still,
So does Tab—make but haste to hang us both! You will?"

I promise, when he stopped you might have heard a mouse
Squeak, such a death-like hush sealed up the old Mote
House.
But when the mass of man sank meek upon his knees,
While Tab, alongside, wheezed a hoarse "Do hang us,
please!"

Why, then the waters rose, no eye but ran with tears,
Hearts heaved, heads thumped, until, paying all past arrears
Of pity and sorrow, at last a regular scream outbroke
Of triumph, joy and praise.

My Lord Chief Justice spoke,
First mopping brow and cheek, where still, for one that budged,
Another bead broke fresh: "What Judge, that ever judged
Since first the world began, judged such a case as this?
Why, Master Bratts, long since, folk smelt you out, I wis!
I had my doubts, i' faith, each time you played the fox
Convicting geese of crime in yonder witness-box—
Yea, much did I misdoubt, the thief that stole her eggs
Was hardly goosey's self at Reynard's game, i' feggs!
Yet thus much was to praise—you spoke to point, direct—
Swore you heard, saw the theft: no jury could suspect—
Dared to suspect,—I'll say,—a spot in white so clear:
Goosey was throttled, true: but thereof godly fear
Came of example set, much as our laws intend;
And, though a fox confessed, you proved the Judge's friend.
What if I had my doubts? Suppose I gave them breath,
Brought you to bar: what work to do, ere 'Guilty, Death'
Had paid our pains! What heaps of witnesses to drag
From holes and corners, paid from out the County's bag!
Trial three dog-days long! *Amicus Curiæ*—that's
Your title, no dispute—truth-telling Master Bratts!
Thank you, too, Mistress Tab! Why doubt one word you say?
Hanging you both deserve, hanged both shall be this day!
The tinker needs must be a proper man. I've heard
He lies in Jail long since: if Quality's good word
Warrants me letting loose,—some householder, I mean—
Freeholder, better still,—I don't say but—between
Now and next Sessions . . . Well! Consider of his case,
I promise to, at least: we owe him so much grace.
Not that—no, God forbid!—I lean to think, as you,
The grace that such repent is any jail-bird's due:
I rather see the fruit of twelve years' pious reign—
Astræa Redux, Charles restored his rights again!

—Of which, another time! I somehow feel a peace
Stealing across the world. May deeds like this increase!
So, Master Sheriff, stay that sentence I pronounced
On those two dozen odd: deserving to be trounced
Soundly, and yet . . . well, well, at all events despatch
This pair of—shall I say, sinner-saints?—ere we catch
Their jail-distemper too. Stop tears, or I'll indite
All weeping Bedfordshire for turning Bunyanite!"

So, happily hanged were they,—why lengthen out my tale?—
Where Bunyan's Statue stands facing where stood his Jail.

MULÉYKEH

If a stranger passed the tent of Hóseyn, he cried "A churl's!"
Or haply "God help the man who has neither salt nor bread!"
—"Nay," would a friend exclaim, "he needs nor pity nor scorn
More than who spends small thought on the shore-sands picking pearls,
—Holds but in light esteem the seed-sort, bears instead
On his breast a moon-like prize, some orb which of night makes morn.

"What if no flocks and herds enrich the son of Sinán?
They went when his tribe was mulct, ten thousand camels the due,
Blood-value paid perforce for a murder done of old.
'God gave them, let them go! But never since time began,
Muléykeh, peerless mare, owned master the match of you,
And you are my prize, my Pearl: I laugh at men's land and gold!'

"So in the pride of his soul laughs Hóseyn—and right, I say.
Do the ten steeds run a race of glory? Outstripping all,
Ever Muléykeh stands first steed at the victor's staff.
Who started, the owner's hope, gets shamed and named, that day,

'Silence,' or, last but one, is 'The Cuffed,' as we use to call
Whom the paddock's lord thrusts forth. Right, Hóseyn, I say, to laugh!"

"Boasts he Muléykeh the Pearl?" the stranger replies: "Be sure
On him I waste nor scorn nor pity, but lavish both
On Duhl the son of Sheybán, who withers away in heart
For envy of Hóseyn's luck. Such sickness admits no cure.
A certain poet has sung, and sealed the same with an oath,
'For the vulgar—flocks and herds! The Pearl is a prize apart.' "

Lo, Duhl the son of Sheybán comes riding to Hóseyn's tent,
And he casts his saddle down, and enters and "Peace" bids he.
"You are poor, I know the cause: my plenty shall mend the wrong.
'Tis said of your Pearl—the price of a hundred camels spent
In her purchase were scarce ill paid: such prudence is far from me
Who proffer a thousand. Speak! Long parley may last too long."

Said Hóseyn "You feed young beasts a many, of famous breed,
Slit-eared, unblemished, fat, true offspring of Múzennem:
There stumbles no weak-eyed she in the line as it climbs the hill.
But I love Muléykeh's face: her forefront whitens indeed
Like a yellowish wave's cream-crest. Your camels—go gaze on them!
Her fetlock is foam-splashed too. Myself am the richer still."

A year goes by: lo, back to the tent again rides Duhl.
"You are open-hearted, ay—moist-handed, a very prince.
Why should I speak of sale? Be the mare your simple gift!
My son is pined to death for her beauty: my wife prompts 'Fool,

Beg for his sake the Pearl! Be God the rewarder, since
God pays debts seven for one: who squanders on Him shows
thrift.' "

Said Hóseyn "God gives each man one life, like a lamp, then gives
That lamp due measure of oil: lamp lighted—hold high, wave wide
Its comfort for others to share! once quench it, what help is left?
The oil of your lamp is your son: I shine while Muléykeh lives.
Would I beg your son to cheer my dark if Muléykeh died?
It is life against life: what good avails to the life-bereft?"

Another year, and—hist! What craft is it Duhl designs?
He alights not at the door of the tent as he did last time,
But, creeping behind, he gropes his stealthy way by the trench
Half-round till he finds the flap in the folding, for night combines
With the robber—and such is he: Duhl, covetous up to crime,
Must wring from Hóseyn's grasp the Pearl, by whatever the wrench.

"He was hunger-bitten, I heard: I tempted with half my store,
And a gibe was all my thanks. Is he generous like Spring dew?
Account the fault to me who chaffered with such an one!
He has killed, to feast chance comers, the creature he rode: nay, more—
For a couple of singing-girls his robe has he torn in two:
I will beg! Yet I nowise gained by the tale of my wife and son.

"I swear by the Holy House, my head will I never wash
Till I filch his Pearl away. Fair dealing I tried, then guile,

And now I resort to force. He said we must live or die:
Let him die, then,—let me live! Be bold—but not too rash!
I have found me a peeping-place: breast, bury your breathing while
I explore for myself! Now, breathe! He deceived me not, the spy!

"As he said—there lies in peace Hóseyn—how happy! Beside
Stands tethered the Pearl: thrice winds her headstall about his wrist:
'Tis therefore he sleeps so sound—the moon through the roof reveals.
And, loose on his left, stands too that other, known far and wide,
Buhéyseh, her sister born: fleet is she yet ever missed
The winning tail's fire-flash a-stream past the thunderous heels.

"'No less she stands saddled and bridled, this second, in case some thief
Should enter and seize and fly with the first, as I mean to do.
What then? The Pearl is the Pearl: once mount her we both escape."
Through the skirt-fold in glides Duhl,—so a serpent disturbs no leaf
In a bush as he parts the twigs entwining a nest: clean through,
He is noiselessly at his work: as he planned, he performs the rape.

He has set the tent-door wide, has buckled the girth, has clipped
The headstall away from the wrist he leaves thrice bound as before,
He springs on the Pearl, is launched on the desert like bolt from bow.
Up starts our plundered man: from his breast though the heart be ripped,

Yet his mind has the mastery: behold, in a minute more,
He is out and off and away on Buhéyseh, whose worth we know!

And Hóseyn—his blood turns flame, he has learned long since to ride,
And Buhéyseh does her part,—they gain—they are gaining fast
On the fugitive pair, and Duhl has Ed-Dárraj to cross and quit,
And to reach the ridge El-Sabán,—no safety till that be spied!
And Buhéyseh is, bound by bound, but a horse-length off at last,
For the Pearl has missed the tap of the heel, the touch of the bit.

She shortens her stride, she chafes at her rider the strange and queer:
Buhéyseh is mad with hope—beat sister she shall and must,
Though Duhl, of the hand and heel so clumsy, she has to thank.
She is near now, nose by tail—they are neck by croup—joy! fear!
What folly makes Hóseyn shout "Dog Duhl, Damned son of the Dust,
Touch the right ear and press with your foot my Pearl's left flank!"

And Duhl was wise at the word, and Muléykeh as prompt perceived
Who was urging redoubled pace, and to hear him was to obey,
And a leap indeed gave she, and evanished for ever more.
And Hóseyn looked one long last look as who, all bereaved,
Looks, fain to follow the dead so far as the living may:
Then he turned Buhéyseh's neck slow homeward, weeping sore.

And, lo, in the sunrise, still sat Hóseyn upon the ground
Weeping: and neighbours came, the tribesmen of Bénu-Asád
In the vale of green Er-Rass, and they questioned him of his grief;
And he told from first to last how, serpent-like, Duhl had wound
His way to the nest, and how Duhl rode like an ape, so bad!
And how Buhéyseh did wonders, yet Pearl remained with the thief.

And they jeered him, one and all: "Poor Hóseyn is crazed past hope!
How else had he wrought himself his ruin, in fortune's spite?
To have simply held the tongue were a task for a boy or girl,
And here were Muléykeh again, the eyed like an antelope,
The child of his heart by day, the wife of his breast by night!"—
"And the beaten in speed!" wept Hóseyn: "You never have loved my Pearl."

PAN AND LUNA

Si credere dignum est.—*Georgic.* iii. 390.

O WORTHY of belief I hold it was,
Virgil, your legend in those strange three lines!
No question, that adventure came to pass
One black night in Arcadia: yes, the pines,
Mountains and vallies mingling made one mass
Of black with void black heaven: the earth's confines,
The sky's embrace,—below, above, around,
All hardened into black without a bound.

Fill up a swart stone chalice to the brim
With fresh-squeezed yet fast-thickening poppy-juice:
See how the sluggish jelly, late a-swim,
Turns marble to the touch of who would loose

The solid smooth, grown jet from rim to rim,
By turning round the bowl! So night can fuse
Earth with her all-comprising sky. No less,
Light, the least spark, shows air and emptiness.

And thus it proved when—diving into space,
Stript of all vapour, from each web of mist
Utterly film-free—entered on her race
The naked Moon, full-orbed antagonist
Of night and dark, night's dowry: peak to base,
Upstarted mountains, and each valley, kissed
To sudden life, lay silver-bright: in air
Flew she revealed, Maid-Moon with limbs all bare.

Still as she fled, each depth—where refuge seemed—
Opening a lone pale chamber, left distinct
Those limbs: mid still-retreating blue, she teemed
Herself with whiteness,—virginal, uncinct
By any halo save what finely gleamed
To outline not disguise her: heaven was linked
In one accord with earth to quaff the joy,
Drain beauty to the dregs without alloy.

Whereof she grew aware. What help? When, lo,
A succourable cloud with sleep lay dense:
Some pine-tree-top had caught it sailing slow,
And tethered for a prize: in evidence
Captive lay fleece on fleece of piled-up snow
Drowsily patient: flake-heaped how or whence,
The structure of that succourable cloud,
What matter? Shamed she plunged into its shroud.

Orbed—so the woman-figure poets call
Because of rounds on rounds—that apple-shaped
Head which its hair binds close into a ball
Each side the curving ears—that pure undraped
Pout of the sister paps—that . . . Once for all,
Say—her consummate circle thus escaped
With its innumerous circlets, sank absorbed,
Safe in the cloud—O naked Moon full-orbed!

But what means this? The downy swathes combine,
Conglobe, the smothery coy-caressing stuff
Curdles about her! Vain each twist and twine
Those lithe limbs try, encroached on by a fluff
Fitting as close as fits the dented spine
Its flexile ivory outside-flesh: enough!
The plumy drifts contract, condense, constringe,
Till she is swallowed by the feathery springe.

As when a pearl slips lost in the thin foam
Churned on a sea-shore, and, o'er-frothed, conceits
Herself safe-housed in Amphitrite's dome,—
If, through the bladdery wave-worked yeast, she
meets
What most she loathes and leaps from,—elf from
gnome
No gladlier,—finds that safest of retreats
Bubbles about a treacherous hand wide ope
To grasp her—(divers who pick pearls so grope)—

So lay this Maid-Moon clasped around and caught
By rough red Pan, the god of all that tract:
He it was schemed the snare thus subtly wrought
With simulated earth-breath,—wool-tufts packed
Into a billowy wrappage. Sheep far-sought
For spotless shearings yield such: take the fact
As learned Virgil gives it,—how the breed
Whitens itself for ever: yes, indeed!

If one fore-father ram, though pure as chalk
From tinge on fleece, should still display a tongue
Black 'neath the beast's moist palate, prompt men
baulk
The propagating plague: he gets no young:
They rather slay him,—sell his hide to caulk
Ships with, first steeped in pitch,—nor hands are
wrung
In sorrow for his fate: protected thus,
The purity we love is gained for us.

So did Girl-Moon, by just her attribute
Of unmatched modesty betrayed, lie trapped,
Bruised to the breast of Pan, half god half brute,
Raked by his bristly boar-sward while he lapped
—Never say, kissed her! that were to pollute
Love's language—which moreover proves unapt
To tell how she recoiled—as who finds thorns
Where she sought flowers—when, feeling, she touched
—horns!

Then—does the legend say?—first moon-eclipse
Happened, first swooning-fit which puzzled sore
The early sages? Is that why she dips
Into the dark, a minute and no more,
Only so long as serves her while she rips
The cloud's womb through and, faultless as before,
Pursues her way? No lesson for a maid
Left she, a maid herself thus trapped, betrayed?

Ha, Virgil? Tell the rest, you! "To the deep
Of his domain the wildwood, Pan forthwith
Called her, and so she followed"—in her sleep,
Surely?—"by no means spurning him." The myth
Explain who may! Let all else go, I keep
—As of a ruin just a monolith—
Thus much, one verse of five words, each a boon:
Arcadia, night, a cloud, Pan, and the moon.

EPILOGUE

"Touch him ne'er so lightly, into song he broke:
Soil so quick-receptive,—not one feather-seed,
Not one flower-dust fell but straight its fall awoke
Vitalizing virtue: song would song succeed
Sudden as spontaneous—prove a poet-soul!"

Indeed?

Rock's the song-soil rather, surface hard and bare:
Sun and dew their mildness, storm and frost their rage
Vainly both expend,—few flowers awaken there:
Quiet in its cleft broods—what the after age
Knows and names a pine, a nation's heritage.

Jocoseria

1883

Jocoseria. By Robert Browning. London: Smith, Elder, & Co., 15 Waterloo Place. 1883.

F'cap 8vo. Pp. viii + 148. Cloth boards.

THIS volume contained ten poems, of which four are here reprinted from the first edition. The only notable alteration made by Browning for the collected edition of 1888–9 was in the prologue, l. 4, where "spot" was changed to "blot".

Jocoseria

PROLOGUE

WANTING is—what?
Summer redundant,
Blueness abundant,
—Where is the spot?
Beamy the world, yet a blank all the same,
—Framework which waits for a picture to frame:
What of the leafage, what of the flower?
Roses embowering with nought they embower!
Come then, complete incompletion, O comer,
Pant through the blueness, perfect the summer!
Breathe but one breath
Rose-beauty above,
And all that was death
Grows life, grows love,
Grows love!

CRISTINA AND MONALDESCHI

AH, but how each loved each, Marquis!
Here's the gallery they trod
Both together, he her god,
She his idol,—lend your rod,
Chamberlain!—ay, there they are—"*Quis
Separabit?*"—plain those two
Touching words come into view,
Apposite for me and you!

Since they witness to incessant
Love like ours: King Francis, he—
Diane the adored one, she—
Prototypes of you and me.

Everywhere is carved her Crescent
  With his Salamander-sign—
  Flame-fed creature: flame benign
  To itself or, if malign,

Only to the meddling curious,
  —So be warned, Sir! Where's my head?
  How it wanders! What I said
  Merely meant—the creature, fed
Thus on flame, was scarce injurious
  Save to fools who woke its ire,
  Thinking fit to play with fire.
  'Tis the Crescent you admire?

Then, be Diane! I'll be Francis,
  Crescents change,—true!—wax and wane,
  Woman-like: male hearts retain
  Heat nor, once warm, cool again.
So, we figure—such our chance is—
  I as man and you as . . . What?
  Take offence? My Love forgot
  He plays woman, I do not?

I—the woman? See my habit,
  Ask my people! Anyhow,
  Be we what we may, one vow
  Binds us, male or female. Now,—
Stand, Sir! Read! "*Quis separabit?*"
  Half a mile of pictured way
  Past these palace-walls to-day
  Traversed, this I came to say.

You must needs begin to love me;
  First I hated, then, at best,
  —Have it so!—I acquiesced;
  Pure compassion did the rest.
From below thus raised above me,
  Would you, step by step, descend,
  Pity me, become my friend,
  Like me, like less, loathe at end?

That's the ladder's round you rose by!
  That—my own foot kicked away,
  Having raised you: let it stay,
  Serve you for retreating? Nay.
Close to me you climbed: as close by,
  Keep your station, though the peak
  Reached proves somewhat bare and bleak!
  Woman's strong if man is weak.

Keep here, loving me forever!
  Love's look, gesture, speech, I claim;
  Act love, lie love, all the same—
  Play as earnest were our game!
Lonely I stood long: 'twas clever
  When you climbed, before men's eyes,
  Spurned the earth and scaled the skies,
  Gained my peak and grasped your prize.

Here you stood, then, to men's wonder;
  Here you tire of standing? Kneel!
  Cure what giddiness you feel,
  This way! Do your senses reel?
Not unlikely! What rolls under?
  Yawning death in yon abyss
  Where the waters whirl and hiss
  Round more frightful peaks than this.

Should my buffet dash you thither . . .
  But be sage! No watery grave
  Needs await you: seeming brave
  Kneel on safe, dear timid slave!
You surmised, when you climbed hither,
  Just as easy were retreat
  Should you tire, conceive unmeet
  Longer patience at my feet?

Me as standing, you as stooping,—
  Who arranged for each the pose?
  Lest men think us friends turned foes,
  Keep the attitude you chose!

Men are used to this same grouping—
I and you like statues seen.
You and I, no third between,
Kneel and stand! That makes the scene.

Mar it—and one buffet . . . Pardon!
Needless warmth—wise words in waste!
'Twas prostration that replaced
Kneeling, then? A proof of taste.
Crouch, not kneel, while I mount guard on
Prostrate love—become no waif,
No estray to waves that chafe
Disappointed—love so safe!

Waves that chafe? The idlest fancy!
Peaks that scare? I think we know
Walls enclose our sculpture: so
Grouped, we pose in Fontainebleau.
Up now! Wherefore hesitancy?
Arm in arm and cheek by cheek,
Laugh with me at waves and peak!
Silent still? Why, pictures speak.

See, where Juno strikes Ixion,
Primatice speaks plainly! Pooh—
Rather, Florentine Le Roux!
I've lost head for who is who—
So it swims and wanders! Fie on
What still proves me female! Here,
By the staircase!—for we near
That dark "Gallery of the Deer."

Look me in the eyes once! Steady!
Are you faithful now as erst
On that eve when we two first
Vowed at Avon, blessed and cursed
Faith and falsehood? Pale already?
Forward! Must my hand compel
Entrance—this way? Exit—well,
Somehow, somewhere. Who can tell?

What if to the self-same place in
  Rustic Avon, at the door
  Of the village church once more,
  Where a tombstone paves the floor
By that holy-water basin
  You appealed to—"As, below,
  This stone hides its corpse, e'en so
  I your secrets hide"? What ho!

Friends, my four! You, Priest, confess him!
  I have judged the culprit there:
  Execute my sentence! Care
  For no mail such cowards wear!
Done, Priest? Then, absolve and bless him!
  Now—you three, stab thick and fast,
  Deep and deeper! Dead at last?
  Thanks, friends—Father, thanks! Aghast?

What one word of his confession
  Would you tell me, though I lured
  With that royal crown abjured
  Just because its bars immured
Love too much? Love burst compression,
  Fled free, finally confessed
  All its secrets to that breast
  Whence . . . let Avon tell the rest!

IXION

High in the dome, suspended, of Hell, sad triumph, behold us!
  Here the revenge of a God, there the amends of a Man.
Whirling forever in torment, flesh once mortal, immortal
  Made—for a purpose of hate—able to die and revive,
Pays to the uttermost pang, then, newly for payment replenished,
  Doles out—old yet young—agonies ever afresh;

Whence the result above me: torment is bridged by a rainbow,—
  Tears, sweat, blood,—each spasm, ghastly once, glorified now.
Wrung, by the rush of the wheel ordained my place of reposing,
  Off in a sparklike spray,—flesh become vapour thro' pain,—
Flies the bestowment of Zeus, soul's vaunted bodily vesture,
  Made that his feats observed gain the approval of Man,—
Flesh that he fashioned with sense of the earth and the sky and the ocean,
  Framed should pierce to the star, fitted to pore on the plant,—
All, for a purpose of hate, re-framed, re-fashioned, re-fitted
  Till, consummate at length,—lo, the employment of sense!
Pain's mere minister now to the soul, once pledged to her pleasure—
  Soul, if untrammeled by flesh, unapprehensive of pain!
Body, professed soul's slave, which serving beguiled and betrayed her,
  Made things false seem true, cheated thro' eye and thro' ear,
Lured thus heart and brain to believe in the lying reported,—
  Spurn but the traitrous slave, uttermost atom, away,
What should obstruct soul's rush on the real, the only apparent?
  Say I have erred,—how else? Was I Ixion or Zeus?
Foiled by my senses I dreamed; I doubtless awaken in wonder:
  This proves shine, that—shade? Good was the evil that seemed?
Shall I, with sight thus gained, by torture be taught I was blind once?
  Sisuphos, teaches thy stone—Tantalos, teaches thy thirst
Aught which unaided sense, purged pure, less plainly demonstrates?

No, for the past was dream: now that the dreamers awake,
Sisuphos scouts low fraud, and to Tantalos treason is folly.
Ask of myself, whose form melts on the murderous wheel,
What is the sin which throe and throe prove sin to the sinner!
Say the false charge was true,—thus do I expiate, say,
Arrogant thought, word, deed,—mere man who conceited me godlike,
Sat beside Zeus, my friend—knelt before Heré, my love!
What were the need but of pitying power to touch and disperse it,
Film-work—eye's and ear's—all the distraction of sense?
How should the soul not see, not hear,—perceive and as plainly
Render, in thought, word, deed, back again truth—not a lie?
"Ay, but the pain is to punish thee!" Zeus, once more for a pastime,
Play the familiar, the frank! Speak and have speech in return!
I was of Thessaly king, there ruled and a people obeyed me:
Mine to establish the law, theirs to obey it or die:
Wherefore? Because of the good to the people, because of the honour
Thence accruing to me, king, the king's law was supreme.
What of the weakling, the ignorant criminal? Not who, excuseless,
Breaking my law braved death, knowing his deed and its due—
Nay, but the feeble and foolish, the poor transgressor, of purpose
No whit more than a tree, born to erectness of bole,
Palm or plane or pine, we laud if lofty, columnar—
Loathe, if athwart, askew,—leave to the axe and the flame!
Where is the vision may penetrate earth and beholding acknowledge
Just one pebble at root ruined the straightness of stem?

Whose fine vigilance follows the sapling, accounts for the failure,
—Here blew wind, so it bent: there the snow lodged, so it broke?
Also the tooth of the beast, bird's bill, mere bite of the insect
Gnawed, gnarled, warped their worst: passive it lay to offence.
King—I was man, no more: what I recognised faulty I punished,
Laying it prone: be sure, more than a man had I proved,
Watch and ward o'er the sapling at birthtime had saved it, nor simply
Owned the distortion's excuse,—hindered it wholly: nay, more—
Even a man, as I sat in my place to do judgment, and pallid
Criminals passing to doom shuddered away at my foot,
Could I have probed thro' the face to the heart, read plain a repentance,
Crime confessed fools' play, virtue ascribed to the wise,
Had I not stayed the consignment to doom, not dealt the renewed ones
Life to retraverse the past, light to retrieve the misdeed?
Thus had I done, and thus to have done much more it behoves thee,
Zeus who madest man—flawless or faulty, thy work!
What if the charge were true, as thou mouthest,—Ixion the cherished
Minion of Zeus grew vain, vied with the godships and fell,
Forfeit thro' arrogance? Stranger! I clothed, with the grace of our human,
Inhumanity—gods, natures I likened to ours.
Man among men I had borne me till gods forsooth must regard me
—Nay, must approve, applaud, claim as a comrade at last.
Summoned to enter their circle, I sat—their equal, how other?
Love should be absolute love, faith is in fulness or nought.

"I am thy friend, be mine!" smiled Zeus: "If Heré attract thee,"
  Blushed the imperial cheek, "then—as thy heart may suggest!"
Faith in me sprang to the faith, my love hailed love as its fellow,
  "Zeus, we are friends—how fast! Heré, my heart for thy heart!"
Then broke smile into fury of frown, and the thunder of "Hence, fool!"
  Then thro' the kiss laughed scorn "Limbs or a cloud was to clasp?"
Then from Olumpos to Erebos, then from the rapture to torment,
  Then from the fellow of gods—misery's mate, to the man!
—Man henceforth and forever, who lent from the glow of his nature
  Warmth to the cold, with light coloured the black and the blank.
So did a man conceive of your passion, you passion-protesters!
  So did he trust, so love—being the truth of your lie!
You to aspire to be Man! Man made you who vainly would ape him:
  You are the hollowness, he—filling you, falsifies void.
Even as—witness the emblem, Hell's sad triumph suspended,
  Born of my tears, sweat, blood—bursting to vapour above—
Arching my torment, an iris ghostlike startles the darkness,
  Cold white—jewelry quenched—justifies, glorifies pain.
Strive, my kind, though strife endure thro' endless obstruction,
  Stage after stage, each rise marred by as certain a fall!
Baffled forever—yet never so baffled but, e'en in the baffling,
  When Man's strength proves weak, checked in the body or soul—
Whatsoever the medium, flesh or essence,—Ixion's

Made for a purpose of hate,—clothing the entity Thou,
—Medium whence that entity strives for the Not-Thou beyond it,
Fire elemental, free, frame unencumbered, the All,—
Never so baffled but—when, on the verge of an alien existence,
Heartened to press, by pangs burst to the infinite Pure,
Nothing is reached but the ancient weakness still that arrests strength,
Circumambient still, still the poor human array,
Pride and revenge and hate and cruelty—all it has burst through,
Thought to escape,—fresh formed, found in the fashion it fled,—
Never so baffled but—when Man pays the price of endeavour,
Thunderstruck, downthrust, Tartaros-doomed to the wheel,—
Then, ay, then, from the tears and sweat and blood of his torment,
E'en from the triumph of Hell, up let him look and rejoice!
What is the influence, high o'er Hell, that turns to a rapture
Pain—and despair's murk mists blends in a rainbow of hope?
What is beyond the obstruction, stage by stage tho' it baffle?
Back must I fall, confess "Ever the weakness I fled"?
No, for beyond, far, far is a Purity all-unobstructed!
Zeus was Zeus—not Man: wrecked by his weakness, I whirl.
Out of the wreck I rise—past Zeus to the Potency o'er him!
I—to have hailed him my friend! I—to have clasped her —my love!
Pallid birth of my pain,—where light, where light is, aspiring
Thither I rise, whilst thou—Zeus, keep the godship and sink!

NEVER THE TIME AND THE PLACE

Never the time and the place
  And the loved one all together!
This path—how soft to pace!
  This May—what magic weather!
Where is the loved one's face?
In a dream that loved one's face meets mine,
  But the house is narrow, the place is bleak
Where, outside, rain and wind combine
  With a furtive ear, if I strive to speak,
  With a hostile eye at my flushing cheek,
With a malice that marks each word, each sign!
O enemy sly and serpentine,
  Uncoil thee from the waking man!
    Do I hold the Past
    Thus firm and fast
  Yet doubt if the Future hold I can?
This path so soft to pace shall lead
Thro' the magic of May to herself indeed!
Or narrow if needs the house must be,
Outside are the storms and strangers: we—
Oh, close, safe, warm sleep I and she,
—I and she!

Parleyings

WITH CERTAIN PEOPLE OF IMPORTANCE IN THEIR DAY

1887

Parleyings with Certain People of Importance in Their Day: to wit: Bernard de Mandeville, Daniel Bartoli, Christopher Smart, George Bubb Dodington, Francis Furini, Gerard de Lairesse, and Charles Avison. Introduced by a dialogue between Apollo and the Fates; concluded by another between John Fust and his Friends. By Robert Browning. London: Smith, Elder, & Co., 15 Waterloo Place. 1887.

F'cap 8vo. Pp. viii + 272. Cloth boards.

THE first and third "parleyings" are reprinted here, together with sections VIII–X (renumbered I–III) of the fifth and the song that closes the parleying with Charles Avison. The headings *Furini Sermonizes* and *Roundhead Tune* have been supplied by the editor.

Parleyings

WITH BERNARD DE MANDEVILLE

I

Ay, this same midnight, by this chair of mine,
Come and review thy counsels: art thou still
Staunch to their teaching?—not as fools opine
Its purport might be, but as subtler skill
Could, through turbidity, the loaded line
Of logic casting, sound deep, deeper, till
It touched a quietude and reached a shrine
And recognized harmoniously combine
Evil with good, and hailed truth's triumph—thine,
Sage dead long since, Bernard de Mandeville!

II

Only, 'tis no fresh knowledge that I crave,
Fuller truth yet, new gainings from the grave;
Here we alive must needs deal fairly, turn
To what account Man may Man's portion, learn
Man's proper play with truth in part, before
Entrusted with the whole. I ask no more
Than smiling witness that I do my best
With doubtful doctrine: afterward the rest!
So, silent face me while I think and speak!
A full disclosure? Such would outrage law.
Law deals the same with soul and body: seek
Full truth my soul may, when some babe, I saw
A new-born weakling, starts up strong—not weak—
Man every whit, absolved from earning awe,
Pride, rapture, if the soul attains to wreak
Its will on flesh, at last can thrust, lift, draw,
As mind bids muscle—mind which long has striven,
Painfully urging body's impotence

To effort whereby—once law's barrier riven,
Life's rule abolished—body might dispense
With infancy's probation, straight be given
—Not by foiled darings, fond attempts back-driven,
Fine faults of growth, brave sins which saint when
shriven—
To stand full-statured in magnificence.

III

No: as with body so deals law with soul
That's stung to strength through weakness, strives for good
Through evil,—earth its race-ground, heaven its goal,
Presumably: so far I understood
Thy teaching long ago. But what means this
—Objected by a mouth which yesterday
Was magisterial in antithesis
To half the truths we hold, or trust we may,
Though tremblingly the while? "No sign"—groaned he—
"No stirring of God's finger to denote
He wills that right should have supremacy
On earth, not wrong! How helpful could we quote
But one poor instance when he interposed
Promptly and surely and beyond mistake
Between oppression and its victim, closed
Accounts with sin for once, and bade us wake
From our long dream that justice bears no sword,
Or else forgets whereto its sharpness serves!
So might we safely mock at what unnerves
Faith now, be spared the sapping fear's increase
That haply evil's strife with good shall cease
Never on earth. Nay, after earth, comes peace
Born out of life-long battle? Man's lip curves
With scorn: there, also, what if justice swerves
From dealing doom, sets free by no swift stroke
Right fettered here by wrong, but leaves life's yoke—
Death should loose man from—fresh laid, past release?"

IV

Bernard de Mandeville, confute for me
This parlous friend who captured or set free

Thunderbolts at his pleasure, yet would draw
Back, panic-stricken by some puny straw
Thy gold-rimmed amber-headed cane had whisked
Out of his pathway if the object risked
Encounter, 'scaped thy kick from buckled shoe!
As when folk heard thee in old days pooh-pooh
Addison's tye-wig preachment, grant this friend—
(Whose groan I hear, with guffaugh at the end
Disposing of mock-melancholy)—grant
His bilious mood one potion, ministrant
Of homely wisdom, healthy wit! For, hear!
"With power and will, let preference appear
By intervention ever and aye, help good
When evil's mastery is understood
In some plain outrage, and triumphant wrong
Tramples weak right to nothingness: nay, long
Ere such sad consummation brings despair
To right's adherents, ah, what help it were
If wrong lay strangled in the birth—each head
Of the hatched monster promptly crushed, instead
Of spared to gather venom! We require
No great experience that the inch-long worm,
Free of our heel, would grow to vomit fire,
And one day plague the world in dragon form.
So should wrong merely peep abroad to meet
Wrong's due quietus, leave our world's way safe
For honest walking."

V

Sage, once more repeat
Instruction! 'Tis a sore to soothe not chafe.
Ah, Fabulist, what luck, could I contrive
To coax from thee another "Grumbling Hive"!
My friend himself wrote fables short and sweet:
Ask him—"Suppose the Gardener of Man's ground
Plants for a purpose, side by side with good,
Evil—(and that He does so—look around!
What does the field show?)—were it understood
That purposely the noxious plant was found
Vexing the virtuous, poison close to food,

If, at first stealing-forth of life in stalk
And leaflet-promise, quick His spud should baulk
Evil from budding foliage, bearing fruit?
Such timely treatment of the offending root
Might strike the simple as wise husbandry,
But swift sure extirpation scarce would suit
Shrewder observers. Seed once sown thrives: why
Frustrate its product, miss the quality
Which sower binds himself to count upon?
Had seed fulfilled the destined purpose, gone
Unhindered up to harvest—what know I
But proof were gained that every growth of good
Sprang consequent on evil's neighbourhood?"
So said your shrewdness: true—so did not say
That other sort of theorists who held
Mere unintelligence prepared the way
For either seed's unsprouting: you repelled
Their notion that both kinds could sow themselves.
True! but admit 'tis understanding delves
And drops each germ, what else but folly thwarts
The doer's settled purpose? Let the sage
Concede a use to evil, though there starts
Full many a burgeon thence, to disengage
With thumb and finger lest it spoil the yield
Too much of good's main tribute! But our main
Tough-tendoned mandrake-monster—purge the field
Of him for once and all? It follows plain
Who set him there to grow beholds repealed
His primal law: His ordinance proves vain:
And what beseems a king who cannot reign,
But to drop sceptre valid arm should wield?

VI

"Still there's a parable"—retorts my friend—
"Shows agriculture with a difference!
What of the crop and weeds which solely blend
Because, once planted, none may pluck them thence?
The Gardener contrived thus? Vain pretence!
An enemy it was who unawares
Ruined the wheat by interspersing tares.

Where's our desiderated forethought? Where's
Knowledge, where power and will in evidence?
'Tis Man's-play merely! Craft foils rectitude,
Malignity defeats beneficence.
And grant, at very last of all, the feud
'Twixt good and evil ends, strange thoughts intrude
Though good be garnered safely and good's foe
Bundled for burning. Thoughts steal: Even so—
Why grant tares leave to thus o'ertop, o'ertower
Their field-mate, boast the stalk and flaunt the flower,
Triumph one sunny minute? Knowledge, power
And will thus worked? Man's fancy makes the fault!
Man, with the narrow mind, must cram inside
His finite God's infinitude,—earth's vault
He bids comprise the heavenly far and wide,
Since Man may claim a right to understand
What passes understanding. So, succinct
And trimly set in order, to be scanned
And scrutinised, lo—the divine lies linked
Fast to the human, free to move as moves
Its proper match: awhile they keep the grooves,
Discreetly side by side together pace,
Till sudden comes a stumble incident
Likely enough to Man's weak-footed race,
And he discovers—wings in rudiment,
Such as he boasts, which full-grown, free-distent
Would lift him skyward, fail of flight while pent
Within humanity's restricted space.
Abjure each fond attempt to represent
The formless, the illimitable! Trace
No outline, try no hint of human face
Or form or hand!"

VII

Friend, here's a tracing meant
To help a guess at truth you never knew.
Bend but those eyes now, using mind's eye too,
And note—sufficient for all purposes—
The ground-plan—map you long have yearned for—yes,
Made out in markings—more what artist can?—

Goethe's Estate in Weimar,—just a plan!
A. is the House, and B. the Garden-gate,
And C. the Grass-plot—you've the whole estate
Letter by letter, down to Y. the Pond,
And Z. the Pig-stye. Do you look beyond
The algebraic signs, and captious say
"Is A. the House? But where's the Roof to A.,
Where's Door, where's Window? Needs must House have
such!"
Ay, that were folly. Why so very much
More foolish than our mortal purblind way
Of seeking in the symbol no mere point
To guide our gaze through what were else inane,
But things—their solid selves? "Is, joint by joint,
Orion man-like,—as these dots explain
His constellation? Flesh composed of suns—
How can such be?" exclaim the simple ones.
Look through the sign to the thing signified—
Shown nowise, point by point at best descried,
Each an orb's topmost sparkle: all beside
Its shine is shadow: turn the orb one jot—
Up flies the new flash to reveal 'twas not
The whole sphere late flamboyant in your ken!

VIII

"What need of symbolizing? Fitlier men
Would take on tongue facts—few and faint and far,
Still facts not fancies: quite enough they are,
That Power, that Knowledge, and that Will,—add then
Immensity, Eternity: these jar
Nowise with our permitted thought and speech.
Why human attributes?"
A myth may teach:
Only, who better would expound it thus
Must be Euripides not Æschylus.

IX

Boundingly up through Night's wall dense and dark,
Embattled crags and clouds, out-broke the Sun
Above the conscious earth, and one by one

Her heights and depths absorbed to the last spark
His fluid glory, from the far fine ridge
Of mountain-granite which, transformed to gold,
Laughed first the thanks back, to the vale's dusk fold
On fold of vapour-swathing, like a bridge
Shattered beneath some giant's stamp. Night wist
Her work done and betook herself in mist
To marsh and hollow there to bide her time
Blindly in acquiescence. Everywhere
Did earth acknowledge Sun's embrace sublime
Thrilling her to the heart of things: since there
No ore ran liquid, no spar branched anew,
No arrowy crystal gleamed, but straightway grew
Glad through the inrush—glad nor more nor less
Than, 'neath his gaze, forest and wilderness,
Hill, dale, land, sea, the wh olevast stretch and spread,
The universal world of creatures bred
By Sun's munificence, alike gave praise—
All creatures but one only: gaze for gaze,
Joyless and thankless, who—all scowling can—
Protests against the innumerous praises? Man,
Sullen and silent.
Stand thou forth then, state
Thy wrong, thou sole aggrieved—disconsolate—
While every beast, bird, reptile, insect, gay
And glad acknowledges the bounteous day!

x

Man speaks now: "What avails Sun's earth-felt thrill
To me? Sun penetrates the ore, the plant—
They feel and grow: perchance with subtler skill
He interfuses fly, worm, brute, until
Each favoured object pays life's ministrant
By pressing, in obedience to his will,
Up to completion of the task prescribed,
So stands and stays a type. Myself imbibed
Such influence also, stood and stand complete—
The perfect Man,—head, body, hands and feet,
True to the pattern: but does that suffice?
How of my superadded mind which needs

—Not to be, simply, but to do, and pleads
For—more than knowledge that by some device
Sun quickens matter: mind is nobly fain
To realize the marvel, make—for sense
As mind—the unseen visible, condense
—Myself—Sun's all-pervading influence
So as to serve the needs of mind, explain
What now perplexes. Let the oak increase
His corrugated strength on strength, the palm
Lift joint by joint her fan-fruit, ball and balm,—
Let the coiled serpent bask in bloated peace,—
The eagle, like some skyey derelict,
Drift in the blue, suspended, glorying,—
The lion lord it by the desert-spring,—
What know or care they of the power which pricked
Nothingness to perfection? I, instead,
When all-developed still am found a thing
All-incomplete: for what though flesh had force
Transcending theirs—hands able to unring
The tightened snake's coil, eyes that could outcourse
The eagle's soaring, voice whereat the king
Of carnage couched discrowned? Mind seeks to see,
Touch, understand, by mind inside of me,
The outside mind—whose quickening I attain
To recognize—I only. All in vain
Would mind address itself to render plain
The nature of the essence. Drag what lurks
Behind the operation—that which works
Latently everywhere by outward proof—
Drag that mind forth to face mine? No! aloof
I solely crave that one of all the beams
Which do Sun's work in darkness, at my will
Should operate—myself for once have skill
To realize the energy which streams
Flooding the universe. Above, around,
Beneath—why mocks that mind my own thus found
Simply of service, when the world grows dark,
To half-surmise—were Sun's use understood,
I might demonstrate him supplying food,
Warmth, life, no less the while? To grant one spark

Myself may deal with—make it thaw my blood
And prompt my steps, were truer to the mark
Of mind's requirement than a half-surmise
That somehow secretly is operant
A power all matter feels, mind only tries
To comprehend! Once more—no idle vaunt
'Man comprehends the Sun's self!' Mysteries
At source why probe into? Enough: display,
Make demonstrable, how, by night as day,
Earth's centre and sky's outspan, all's informed
Equally by Sun's efflux!—source from whence
If just one spark I drew, full evidence
Were mine of fire ineffably enthroned—
Sun's self made palpable to Man!"

XI

Thus moaned
Man till Prometheus helped him,—as we learn,—
Offered an artifice whereby he drew
Sun's rays into a focus,—plain and true,
The very Sun in little: made fire burn
And henceforth do Man service—glass-conglobed
Though to a pin-point circle—all the same
Comprising the Sun's self, but Sun disrobed
Of that else-unconceived essential flame
Borne by no naked sight. Shall mind's eye strive
Achingly to companion as it may
The supersubtle effluence, and contrive
To follow beam and beam upon their way
Hand-breadth by hand-breadth, till sense faint—confessed
Frustrate, eluded by unknown unguessed
Infinitude of action? Idle quest!
Rather ask aid from optics. Sense, descry
The spectrum—mind, infer immensity!
Little? In little, light, warmth, life are blessed—
Which, in the large, who sees to bless? Not I
More than yourself: so, good my friend, keep still
Trustful with—me? with thee, sage Mandeville!

WITH CHRISTOPHER SMART

I

It seems as if . . . or did the actual chance
Startle me and perplex? Let truth be said!
How might this happen? Dreaming, blindfold led
By visionary hand, did soul's advance
Precede my body's, gain inheritance
Of fact by fancy—so that when I read
At length with waking eyes your Song, instead
Of mere bewilderment, with me first glance
Was but full recognition that in trance
Or merely thought's adventure some old day
Of dim and done-with boyishness, or—well,
Why might it not have been, the miracle
Broke on me as I took my sober way
Through veritable regions of our earth
And made discovery, many a wondrous one?

II

Anyhow, fact or fancy, such its birth:
I was exploring some huge house, had gone
Through room and room complacently, no dearth
Anywhere of the signs of decent taste,
Adequate culture: wealth had run to waste
Nowise, nor penury was proved by stint:
All showed the Golden Mean without a hint
Of brave extravagance that breaks the rule.
The master of the mansion was no fool
Assuredly, no genius just as sure!
Safe mediocrity had scorned the lure
Of now too much and now too little cost,
And satisfied me sight was never lost
Of moderate design's accomplishment
In calm completeness. On and on I went,
With no more hope than fear of what came next,
Till lo, I push a door, sudden uplift
A hanging, enter, chance upon a shift
Indeed of scene! So—thus it is thou deck'st,
High heaven, our low earth's brick-and-mortar work?

III

It was the Chapel. That a star, from murk
Which hid, should flashingly emerge at last,
Were small surprise: but from broad day I passed
Into a presence that turned shine to shade.
There fronted me the Rafael Mother-Maid,
Never to whom knelt votarist in shrine
By Nature's bounty helped, by Art's divine
More varied—beauty with magnificence—
Than this: from floor to roof one evidence
Of how far earth may rival heaven. No niche
Where glory was not prisoned to enrich
Man's gaze with gold and gems, no space but glowed
With colour, gleamed with carving—hues which owed
Their outburst to a brush the painter fed
With rainbow-substance—rare shapes never wed
To actual flesh and blood, which, brain-born once,
Became the sculptor's dowry, Art's response
To earth's despair. And all seemed old yet new:
Youth,—in the marble's curve, the canvas' hue,
Apparent,—wanted not the crowning thrill
Of age the consecrator. Hands long still
Had worked here—could it be, what lent them skill
Retained a power to supervise, protect,
Enforce new lessons with the old, connect
Our life with theirs? No merely modern touch
Told me that here the artist, doing much,
Elsewhere did more, perchance does better, lives—
So needs must learn.

IV

Well, these provocatives
Having fulfilled their office, forth I went
Big with anticipation—well nigh fear—
Of what next room and next for startled eyes
Might have in store, surprise beyond surprise.
Next room and next and next—what followed here?
Why, nothing! not one object to arrest
My passage—everywhere too manifest

The previous decent null and void of best
And worst, mere ordinary right and fit,
Calm commonplace which neither missed, nor hit
Inch-high, inch-low, the placid mark proposed.

V

Armed with this instance, have I diagnosed
Your case, my Christopher? The man was sound
And sane at starting: all at once the ground
Gave way beneath his step, a certain smoke
Curled up and caught him, or perhaps down broke
A fireball wrapping flesh and spirit both
In conflagration. Then—as heaven were loth
To linger—let earth understand too well
How heaven at need can operate—off fell
The flame-robe, and the untransfigured man
Resumed sobriety,—as he began,
So did he end nor alter pace, not he!

VI

Now, what I fain would know is—could it be
That he—whoe'er he was that furnished forth
The Chapel, making thus, from South to North,
Rafael touch Leighton, Michelagnolo
Join Watts, was found but once combining so
The elder and the younger, taking stand
On Art's supreme,—or that yourself who sang
A Song where flute-breath silvers trumpet-clang,
And stations you for once on either hand
With Milton and with Keats, empowered to claim
Affinity on just one point—(or blame
Or praise my judgment, thus it fronts you full)—
How came it you resume the void and null,
Subside to insignificance,—live, die
—Proved plainly two mere mortals who drew nigh
One moment—that, to Art's best hierarchy,
This, to the superhuman poet-pair?
What if, in one point only, then and there
The otherwise all-unapproachable
Allowed impingement? Does the sphere pretend

To span the cube's breadth, cover end to end
The plane with its embrace? No, surely! Still,
Contact is contact, sphere's touch no whit less
Than cube's superimposure. Such success
Befell Smart only out of throngs between
Milton and Keats that donned the singing-dress—
Smart, solely of such songmen, pierced the screen
'Twixt thing and word, lit language straight from soul,—
Left no fine film-flake on the naked coal
Live from the censer—shapely or uncouth,
Fire-suffused through and through, one blaze of truth
Undeadened by a lie,—(you have my mind)—
For, think! this blaze outleapt with black behind
And blank before, when Hayley and the rest . . .
But let the dead successors worst and best
Bury their dead: with life be my concern—
Yours with the fire-flame: what I fain would learn
Is just—(suppose me haply ignorant
Down to the common knowledge, doctors vaunt)
Just this—why only once the fire-flame was:
No matter if the marvel came to pass
The way folks judged—if power too long suppressed
Broke loose and maddened, as the vulgar guessed,
Or simply brain-disorder (doctors said)
A turmoil of the particles disturbed
Brain's workaday performance in your head,
Spurred spirit to wild action health had curbed,
And so verse issued in a cataract
Whence prose, before and after, unperturbed
Was wont to wend its way. Concede the fact
That here a poet was who always could—
Never before did—never after would—
Achieve the feat: how were such fact explained?

VII

Was it that when, by rarest chance, there fell
Disguise from Nature, so that Truth remained
Naked, and whoso saw for once could tell
Us others of her majesty and might
In large, her lovelinesses infinite

In little,—straight you used the power wherewith
Sense, penetrating as through rind to pith
Each object, thoroughly revealed might view
And comprehend the old things thus made new,
So that while eye saw, soul to tongue could trust
Thing which struck word out, and once more adjust
Real vision to right language, till heaven's vault
Pompous with sunset, storm-stirred sea's assault
On the swilled rock-ridge, earth's embosomed brood
Of tree and flower and weed, with all the life
That flies or swims or crawls, in peace or strife,
Above, below,—each had its note and name
For Man to know by,—Man who, now—the same
As erst in Eden, needs that all he sees
Be named him ere he note by what degrees
Of strength and beauty to its end Design
Ever thus operates—(your thought and mine,
No matter for the many dissident)—
So did you sing your Song, so truth found vent
In words for once with you?

VIII

Then—back was furled
The robe thus thrown aside, and straight the world
Darkened into the old oft-catalogued
Repository of things that sky, wave, land,
Or show or hide, clear late, accretion-clogged
Now, just as long ago, by tellings and
Retellings to satiety, which strike
Muffled upon the ear's drum. Very like
None was so startled as yourself when friends
Came, hailed your fast-returning wits: "Health mends
Importantly, for—to be plain with you—
This scribble on the wall was done—in lieu
Of pen and paper—with—ha, ha!—your key
Denting it on the wainscot! Do you see
How wise our caution was? Thus much we stopped
Of babble that had else grown print: and lopped
From your trim bay-tree this unsightly bough—
Smart's who translated Horace! Write us now" . . .

Why, what Smart did write—never afterward
One line to show that he, who paced the sward,
Had reached the zenith from his madhouse cell.

IX

Was it because you judged (I know full well
You never had the fancy)—judged—as some—
That who makes poetry must reproduce
Thus ever and thus only, as they come,
Each strength, each beauty, everywhere diffuse
Throughout creation, so that eye and ear,
Seeing and hearing, straight shall recognize,
At touch of just a trait, the strength appear,—
Suggested by a line's lapse see arise
All evident the beauty,—fresh surprise
Startling at fresh achievement? "So, indeed,
Wallows the whale's bulk in the waste of brine,
Nor otherwise its feather-tufts make fine
Wild Virgin's Bower when stars faint off to seed!"
(My prose—your poetry I dare not give,
Purpling too much my mere grey argument.)
—Was it because you judged—when fugitive
Was glory found, and wholly gone and spent
Such power of startling up deaf ear, blind eye,
At truth's appearance,—that you humbly bent
The head and, bidding vivid work goodbye,
Doffed lyric dress and trod the world once more
A drab-clothed decent proseman as before?
Strengths, beauties, by one word's flash thus laid bare
—That was effectual service: made aware
Of strengths and beauties, Man but hears the text,
Awaits your teaching. Nature? What comes next?
Why all the strength and beauty?—to be shown
Thus in one word's flash, thenceforth let alone
By Man who needs must deal with aught that's known
Never so lately and so little? Friend,
First give us knowledge, then appoint its use!
Strength, beauty are the means: ignore their end?
As well you stopped at proving how profuse
Stones, sticks, nay stubble lie to left and right

Ready to help the builder,—careless quite
If he should take, or leave the same to strew
Earth idly,—as by word's flash bring in view
Strength, beauty, then bid who beholds the same
Go on beholding. Why gains unemployed?
Nature was made to be by Man enjoyed
First; followed duly by enjoyment's fruit,
Instruction—haply leaving joy behind:
And you, the instructor, would you slack pursuit
Of the main prize, as poet help mankind
Just to enjoy, there leave them? Play the fool,
Abjuring a superior privilege?
Please simply when your function is to rule—
By thought incite to deed? From edge to edge
Of earth's round, strength and beauty everywhere
Pullulate—and must you particularize
All, each and every apparition? Spare
Yourself and us the trouble! Ears and eyes
Want so much strength and beauty, and no less
Nor more, to learn life's lesson by. Oh, yes—
The other method's favoured in our day!
The end ere the beginning: as you may,
Master the heavens before you study earth,
Make you familiar with the meteor's birth
Ere you descend to scrutinize the rose!
I say, o'erstep no least one of the rows
That lead man from the bottom where he plants
Foot first of all, to life's last ladder-top:
Arrived there, vain enough will seem the vaunts
Of those who say—"We scale the skies, then drop
To earth—to find, how all things there are loth
To answer heavenly law: we understand
The meteor's course, and lo, the rose's growth—
How other than should be by law's command!"
Would not you tell such—"Friends, beware lest fume
Offuscate sense: learn earth first ere presume
To teach heaven legislation. Law must be
Active in earth or nowhere: earth you see,—
Or there or not at all, Will, Power and Love
Admit discovery,—as below, above

Seek next law's confirmation! But reverse
The order, where's the wonder things grow worse
Than, by the law your fancy formulates,
They should be? Cease from anger at the fates
Which thwart themselves so madly. Live and learn,
Not first learn and then live, is our concern."

FURINI SERMONIZES

I

AND, prayer done, painter—what if you should preach?
Not as of old when playing pulpiteer
To simple-witted country folk, but here
In actual London try your powers of speech
On us the cultured, therefore sceptical—
What would you? For, suppose he has his word
In faith's behalf, no matter how absurd,
This painter-theologian? One and all
We lend an ear—nay, Science takes thereto—
Encourages the meanest who has racked
Nature until he gains from her some fact,
To state what truth is from his point of view,
Mere pin-point though it be: since many such
Conduce to make a whole, she bids our friend
Come forward unabashed and haply lend
His little life-experience to our much
Of modern knowledge. Since she so insists,
Up stands Furini.

II

"Evolutionists!
At truth I glimpse from depths, you glance from heights,
Our stations for discovery opposites,—
How should ensue agreement? I explain:
'Tis the tip-top of things to which you strain
Your vision, until atoms, protoplasm,
And what and whence and how may be the spasm
Which sets all going, stop you: down perforce
Needs must your observation take its course,

Since there's no moving upwards: link by link
You drop to where the atoms somehow think,
Feel, know themselves to be: the world's begun,
Such as we recognize it. Have you done
Descending? Here's ourself,—Man, known to-day,
Duly evolved at last,—so far, you say,
The sum and seal of being's progress. Good!
Thus much at least is clearly understood—
Of power does Man possess no particle:
Of knowledge—just so much as shows that still
It ends in ignorance on every side:
But righteousness—ah, Man is deified
Thereby, for compensation! Make survey
Of Man's surroundings, try creation—nay,
Try emulation of the minimized
Minuteness fancy may conceive! Surprised
Reason becomes by two defeats for one—
Not only power at each phenomenon
Baffled, but knowledge also in default—
Asking what *is* minuteness—yonder vault
Speckled with suns, or this the millionth—thing,
How shall I call?—that on some insect's wing
Helps to make out in dyes the mimic star?
Weak, ignorant, accordingly we are:
What then? The worse for Nature! Where began
Righteousness, moral sense except in Man?
True, he makes nothing, understands no whit:
Had the initiator-spasm seen fit
Thus doubly to endow him, none the worse
And much the better were the universe.
What does Man see or feel or apprehend
Here, there, and everywhere, but faults to mend,
Omissions to supply,—one wide disease
Of things that are, which Man at once would ease
Had will but power and knowledge? failing both—
Things must take will for deed—Man, nowise loth,
Accepts pre-eminency: mere blind force—
Mere knowledge undirected in its course
By any care for what is made or marred
In either's operation—*these* award

The crown to? Rather let it deck thy brows,
Man, whom alone a righteousness endows
Would cure the wide world's ailing! Who disputes
Thy claim thereto? Had Spasm more attributes
Than power and knowledge in its gift, before
Man came to pass? The higher that we soar,
The less of moral sense like Man's we find:
No sign of such before,—what comes behind,
Who guesses? But until there crown our sight
The quite new—not the old mere infinite
Of changings,—some fresh kind of sun and moon,—
Then, not before, shall I expect a boon
Of intuition just as strange, which turns
Evil to good, and wrong to right, unlearns
All Man's experience learned since Man was he.
Accept in Man, advanced to this degree,
The Prime Mind, therefore! neither wise nor strong—
Whose fault? but were he both, then right, not wrong
As now, throughout the world were paramount
According to his will,—which I account
The qualifying faculty. He stands
Confessed supreme—the monarch whose commands
Could he enforce, how bettered were the world!
He's at the height this moment—to be hurled
Next moment to the bottom by rebound
Of his own peal of laughter. All around
Ignorance wraps him,—whence and how and why
Things are,—yet cloud breaks and lets blink the sky
Just overhead, not elsewhere! What assures
His optics that the very blue which lures
Comes not of black outside it, doubly dense?
Ignorance overwraps his moral sense,
Winds him about, relaxing, as it wraps,
So much and no more than lets through perhaps
The murmured knowledge—'Ignorance exists.'

III

"I at the bottom, Evolutionists,
Advise beginning, rather. I profess
To know just one fact—my self-consciousness,—

'Twixt ignorance and ignorance enisled,—
Knowledge: before me was my Cause—that's styled
God: after, in due course succeeds the rest,—
All that my knowledge comprehends—at best—
At worst, conceives about in mild despair.
Light needs must touch on either darkness: where?
Knowledge so far impinges on the Cause
Before me, that I know—by certain laws
Wholly unknown, whate'er I apprehend
Within, without me, had its rise: thus blend
I, and all things perceived, in one Effect.
How far can knowledge any ray project
On what comes after me—the universe?
Well, my attempt to make the cloud disperse
Begins—not from above but underneath:
I climb, you soar,—who soars soon loses breath
And sinks, who climbs keeps one foot firm on fact
Ere hazarding the next step: soul's first act
(Call consciousness the soul—some name we need)
Getting itself aware, through stuff decreed
Thereto (so call the body)—who has stept
So far, there let him stand, become adept
In body ere he shift his station thence
One single hair's breadth. Do I make pretence
To teach, myself unskilled in learning? Lo,
My life's work! Let my pictures prove I know
Somewhat of what this fleshly frame of ours
Or is or should be, how the soul empowers
The body to reveal its every mood
Of love and hate, pour forth its plenitude
Of passion. If my hand attained to give
Thus permanence to truth else fugitive,
Did not I also fix each fleeting grace
Of form and feature—save the beauteous face—
Arrest decay in transitory might
Of bone and muscle—cause the world to bless
For ever each transcendent nakedness
Of man and woman? Were such feats achieved
By sloth, or strenuous labour unrelieved,
—Yet lavished vainly? Ask that underground

(So may I speak) of all on surface found
Of flesh-perfection! Depths on depths to probe
Of all-inventive artifice, disrobe
Marvel at hiding under marvel, pluck
Veil after veil from Nature—were the luck
Ours to surprise the secret men so name,
That still eludes the searcher—all the same,
Repays his search with still fresh proof—'Externe,
Not inmost, is the Cause, fool! Look and learn!'
Thus teach my hundred pictures: firm and fast
There did I plant my first foot. And the next?
Nowhere! 'Twas put forth and withdrawn, perplexed
At touch of what seemed stable and proved stuff
Such as the coloured clouds are: plain enough
There lay the outside universe: try Man—
My most immediate! and the dip began
From safe and solid into that profound
Of ignorance I tell you surges round
My rock-spit of self-knowledge. Well and ill,
Evil and good irreconcilable
Above, beneath, about my every side,—
How did this wild confusion far and wide
Tally with my experience when my stamp—
So far from stirring—struck out, each a lamp,
Spark after spark of truth from where I stood—
Pedestalled triumph? Evil there was good,
Want was the promise of supply, defect
Ensured completion,—where and when and how?
Leave that to the first Cause! Enough that now,
Here where I stand, this moment's me and mine,
Shows me what is, permits me to divine
What shall be. Wherefore? Nay, how otherwise?
Look at my pictures! What so glorifies
The body that the permeating soul
Finds there no particle elude control
Direct, or fail of duty,—most obscure
When most subservient? Did that Cause ensure
The soul such raptures as its fancy stings
Body to furnish when, uplift by wings
Of passion, here and now, it leaves the earth,

Loses itself above, where bliss has birth—
(Heaven, be the phrase)—did that same Cause contrive
Such solace for the body, soul must dive
At drop of fancy's pinion, condescend
To bury both alike on earth, our friend
And fellow, where minutely exquisite
Low lie the pleasures, now and here—no herb
But hides its marvel, peace no doubts perturb
In each small mystery of insect life—
—Shall the soul's Cause thus gift the soul, yet strife
Continue still of fears with hopes,—for why?
What if the Cause, whereof we now descry
So far the wonder-working, lack at last
Will, power, benevolence—a protoplast,
No consummator, sealing up the sum
Of all things,—past and present and to come
Perfection? No, I have no doubt at all!
There's my amount of knowledge—great or small,
Sufficient for my needs: for see! advance
Its light now on that depth of ignorance
I shrank before from—yonder where the world
Lies wreck-strewn,—evil towering, prone good—
hurled
From pride of place, on every side. For me
(Patience, beseech you!) knowledge can but be
Of good by knowledge of good's opposite—
Evil,—since, to distinguish wrong from right,
Both must be known in each extreme, beside—
(Or what means knowledge—to aspire or bide
Content with half-attaining? Hardly so!)
Made to know on, know ever, I must know
All to be known at any halting-stage
Of my soul's progress, such as earth, where wage
War, just for soul's instruction, pain with joy,
Folly with wisdom, all that works annoy
With all that quiets and contents,—in brief,
Good strives with evil.
Now then for relief,
Friends, of your patience kindly curbed so long.
'What?' snarl you 'Is the fool's conceit thus strong—

Must the whole outside world in soul and sense
Suffer, that he grow sage at its expense?'
By no means! 'Tis by merest touch of toe
I try—not trench on—ignorance, just know—
And so keep steady footing: how you fare,
Caught in the whirlpool—that's the Cause's care,
Strong, wise, good,—this I know at any rate
In my own self,—but how may operate
With you—strength, wisdom, goodness—no least blink
Of knowledge breaks the darkness round me. Think!
Could I see plain, be somehow certified
All was illusion,—evil far and wide
Was good disguised,—why, out with one huge wipe
Goes knowledge from me. Type needs antitype:
As night needs day, as shine needs shade, so good
Needs evil: how were pity understood
Unless by pain? Make evident that pain
Permissibly masks pleasure—you abstain
From outstretch of the finger-tip that saves
A drowning fly. Who proffers help of hand
To weak Andromeda exposed on strand
At mercy of the monster? Were all true,
Help were not wanting: 'But 'tis false,' cry you,
'Mere fancy-work of paint and brush!' No less,
Were mine the skill, the magic, to impress
Beholders with a confidence they saw
Life,—veritable flesh and blood in awe
Of just as true a sea-beast,—would they stare
Simply as now, or cry out, curse and swear,
Or call the gods to help, or catch up stick
And stone, according as their hearts were quick
Or sluggish? Well, some old artificer
Could do as much,—at least, so books aver,—
Able to make-believe, while I, poor wight,
Make-fancy, nothing more. Though wrong were right,
Could we but know—still wrong must needs seem
  wrong
To do right's service, prove men weak or strong,
Choosers of evil or of good. 'No such
Illusion possible!' Ah, friends, you touch

Just here my solid standing-place amid
The wash and welter, whence all doubts are bid
Back to the ledge they break against in foam,
Futility: my soul, and my soul's home
This body,—how each operates on each,
And how things outside, fact or feigning, teach
What good is and what evil,—just the same,
Be feigning or be fact the teacher,—blame
Diffidence nowise if, from this I judge
My point of vantage, not an inch I budge.
All—for myself—seems ordered wise and well
Inside it,—what reigns outside, who can tell?
Contrariwise, who needs be told 'The space
Which yields thee knowledge,—do its bounds embrace
Well-willing and wise-working, each at height?
Enough: beyond thee lies the infinite—
Back to thy circumscription!'
Back indeed!
Ending where I began—thus: retrocede,
Who will,—what comes first, take first, I advise!
Acquaint you with the body ere your eyes
Look upward: this Andromeda of mine—
Gaze on the beauty, Art hangs out for sign
There's finer entertainment underneath.
Learn how they ministrate to life and death—
Those incommensurably marvellous
Contrivances which furnish forth the house
Where soul has sway! Though Master keep aloof,
Signs of His presence multiply from roof
To basement of the building. Look around,
Learn thoroughly,—no fear that you confound
Master with messuage! He's away, no doubt,
But what if, all at once, you come upon
A startling proof—not that the Master gone
Was present lately—but that something—whence
Light comes—has pushed Him into residence?
Was such the symbol's meaning,—old, uncouth—
That circle of the serpent, tail in mouth?
Only by looking low, ere looking high,
Comes penetration of the mystery."

ROUNDHEAD TUNE

Fife, trump, drum, sound! and singers then
Marching say "Pym, the man of men!"
Up, heads, your proudest—out, throats, your loudest—
"Somerset's Pym!"

Strafford from the block, Eliot from the den,
Foes, friends, shout "Pym, our citizen!"
Wail, the foes he quelled,—hail, the friends he held,
"Tavistock's Pym!"

Hearts prompt heads, hands that ply the pen
Teach babes unborn the where and when
—Tyrants, he braved them,—patriots, he saved them—
"Westminster's Pym!"

Asolando

FANCIES AND FACTS

1890

Asolando: Fancies and Facts. By Robert Browning. London: Smith, Elder, & Co., 15 Waterloo Place. 1890.

F'cap 8vo. Pp. viii + 160. Cloth boards.

Fourteen poems are here selected from the thirty in the first edition. Browning did not live to make any revision: he died in Venice on the day—12 December 1889—on which the book was published in London.

Asolando

PROLOGUE

"The Poet's age is sad: for why?
  In youth, the natural world could show
No common object but his eye
  At once involved with alien glow—
His own soul's iris-bow.

"And now a flower is just a flower:
  Man, bird, beast are but beast, bird, man—
Simply themselves, uncinct by dower
  Of dyes which, when life's day began,
Round each in glory ran."

Friend, did you need an optic glass,
  Which were your choice? A lens to drape
In ruby, emerald, chrysopras,
  Each object—or reveal its shape
Clear outlined, past escape,

The naked very thing?—so clear
  That, when you had the chance to gaze,
You found its inmost self appear
  Through outer seeming—truth ablaze,
Not falsehood's fancy-haze?

How many a year, my Asolo,
  Since—one step just from sea to land—
I found you, loved yet feared you so—
  For natural objects seemed to stand
Palpably fire-clothed! No—

No mastery of mine o'er these!
Terror with beauty, like the Bush
Burning but unconsumed. Bend knees,
Drop eyes to earthward! Language? Tush!
Silence 'tis awe decrees.

And now? The lambent flame is—where?
Lost from the naked world: earth, sky,
Hill, vale, tree, flower,—Italia's rare
O'er-running beauty crowds the eye—
But flame? The Bush is bare.

Hill, vale, tree, flower—they stand distinct,
Nature to know and name. What then?
A Voice spoke thence which straight unlinked
Fancy from fact: see, all's in ken:
Has once my eyelid winked?

No, for the purged ear apprehends
Earth's import, not the eye late dazed:
The Voice said "Call my works thy friends!
At Nature dost thou shrink amazed?
God is it who transcends."

DUBIETY

I WILL be happy if but for once:
Only help me, Autumn weather,
Me and my cares to screen, ensconce
In luxury's sofa-lap of leather!

Sleep? Nay, comfort—with just a cloud
Suffusing day too clear and bright:
Eve's essence, the single drop allowed
To sully, like milk, Noon's water-white.

Let gauziness shade, not shroud,—adjust,
Dim and not deaden,—somehow sheathe
Aught sharp in the rough world's busy thrust,
If it reach me through dreaming's vapour-wreath.

Be life so, all things ever the same!
  For, what has disarmed the world? Outside,
Quiet and peace: inside, nor blame
  Nor want, nor wish whate'er betide.

What is it like that has happened before?
  A dream? No dream, more real by much.
A vision? But fanciful days of yore
  Brought many: mere musing seems not such.

Perhaps but a memory, after all!
  —Of what came once when a woman leant
To feel for my brow where her kiss might fall.
  Truth ever, truth only the excellent!

NOW

Out of your whole life give but a moment!
All of your life that has gone before,
All to come after it,—so you ignore
So you make perfect the present,—condense,
In a rapture of rage, for perfection's endowment,
Thought and feeling and soul and sense—
Merged in a moment which gives me at last
You around me for once, you beneath me, above
    me—
Me—sure that despite of time future, time past,—
This tick of our life-time's one moment you love me!
How long such suspension may linger? Ah, Sweet—
The moment eternal—just that and no more—
When ecstasy's utmost we clutch at the core
While cheeks burn, arms open, eyes shut and lips
    meet!

HUMILITY

What girl but, having gathered flowers,
Stript the beds and spoilt the bowers,
From the lapful light she carries
Drops a careless bud?—nor tarries

To regain the waif and stray:
"Store enough for home"—she'll say.

So say I too: give your lover
Heaps of loving—under, over,
Whelm him—make the one the wealthy!
Am I all so poor who—stealthy
Work it was!—picked up what fell:
Not the worst bud—who can tell?

POETICS

"So say the foolish!" Say the foolish so, Love?
"Flower she is, my rose"—or else "My very swan is she"—
Or perhaps "Yon maid-moon, blessing earth below, Love,
That art thou!"—to them, belike: no such vain words from me.

"Hush, rose, blush! no balm like breath," I chide it:
"Bend thy neck its best, swan,—hers the whiter curve!"
Be the moon the moon: my Love I place beside it:
What is she? Her human self,—no lower word will serve.

SUMMUM BONUM

All the breath and the bloom of the year in the bag of one bee:
All the wonder and wealth of the mine in the heart of one gem:
In the core of one pearl all the shade and the shine of the sea:
Breath and bloom, shade and shine,—wonder, wealth, and—how far above them—
Truth, that's brighter than gem,
Trust, that's purer than pearl,—
Brightest truth, purest trust in the universe—all were for me
In the kiss of one girl.

SPECULATIVE

Others may need new life in Heaven—
Man, Nature, Art—made new, assume!
Man with new mind old sense to leaven,
Nature—new light to clear old gloom,
Art that breaks bounds, gets soaring-room.

I shall pray: "Fugitive as precious—
Minutes which passed,—return, remain!
Let earth's old life once more enmesh us,
You with old pleasure, me—old pain,
So we but meet nor part again!"

BAD DREAMS—I

Last night I saw you in my sleep:
And how your charm of face was changed!
I asked "Some love, some faith you keep?"
You answered "Faith gone, love estranged."

Whereat I woke—a twofold bliss:
Waking was one, but next there came
This other: "Though I felt, for this,
My heart break, I loved on the same."

BAD DREAMS—II

You in the flesh and here—
Your very self! Now, wait!
One word! May I hope or fear?
Must I speak in love or hate?
Stay while I ruminate!

The fact and each circumstance
Dare you disown? Not you!
That vast dome, that huge dance,
And the gloom which overgrew
A—possibly festive crew!

For why should men dance at all—
   Why women—a crowd of both—
Unless they are gay? Strange ball—
   Hands and feet plighting troth,
Yet partners enforced and loth!

Of who danced there, no shape
   Did I recognize: thwart, perverse,
Each grasped each, past escape
   In a whirl or weary or worse:
Man's sneer met woman's curse,

While he and she toiled as if
   Their guardian set galley-slaves
To supple chained limbs grown stiff:
   Unmanacled trulls and knaves—
The lash for who misbehaves!

And a gloom was, all the while,
   Deeper and deeper yet
O'ergrowing the rank and file
   Of that army of haters—set
To mimic love's fever-fret.

By the wall-side close I crept,
   Avoiding the livid maze,
And, safely so far, outstepped
   On a chamber—a chapel, says
My memory or betrays—

Closet-like, kept aloof
   From unseemly witnessing
What sport made floor and roof
   Of the Devil's palace ring
While his Damned amused their king.

Ay, for a low lamp burned,
   And a silence lay about
What I, in the midst, discerned
   Though dimly till, past doubt,
'Twas a sort of throne stood out—

High seat with steps, at least:
  And the topmost step was filled
By—whom? What vestured priest?
  A stranger to me,—his guild,
His cult, unreconciled

To my knowledge how guild and cult
  Are clothed in this world of ours:
I pondered, but no result
  Came to—unless that Giaours
So worship the Lower Powers.

When suddenly who entered?
  Who knelt—did you guess I saw?
Who—raising that face where centred
  Allegiance to love and law
So lately—off-casting awe,

Down-treading reserve, away
  Thrusting respect . . . but mine
Stands firm—firm still shall stay!
  Ask Satan! for I decline
To tell—what I saw, in fine!

Yet here in the flesh you come—
  Your same self, form and face,—
In the eyes, mirth still at home!
  On the lips, that commonplace
Perfection of honest grace!

Yet your errand is—needs must be—
  To palliate—well, explain,
Expurgate in some degree
  Your soul of its ugly stain.
Oh, you—the good in grain—

How was it your white took tinge?
  "A mere dream"—never object!
Sleep leaves a door on hinge
  Whence soul, ere our flesh suspect
Is off and away: detect

Her vagaries when loose, who can!
  Be she pranksome, be she prude,
Disguise with the day began:
  With the night—ah, what ensued
From draughts of a drink hell-brewed?

Then She: "What a queer wild dream!
  And perhaps the best fun is—
Myself had its fellow—I seem
  Scarce awake from yet. 'Twas this—
Shall I tell you? First, a kiss!

"For the fault was just your own,—
  'Tis myself expect apology:
You warned me to let alone
  (Since our studies were mere philology)
That ticklish (you said) Anthology.

"So, I dreamed that I passed *exam*
  Till a question posed me sore:
'Who translated this epigram
  By—an author we best ignore?'
And I answered 'Hannah More'!"

BAD DREAMS—III

THIS was my dream: I saw a Forest
  Old as the earth, no track nor trace
Of unmade man. Thou, Soul, explorest—
  Though in a trembling rapture—space
Immeasurable! Shrubs, turned trees,
Trees that touch heaven, support its frieze
Studded with sun and moon and star:
While—oh, the enormous growths that bar
Mine eye from penetrating past
  Their tangled twine where lurks—nay, lives
Royally lone, some brute-type cast
  I' the rough, time cancels, man forgives.

On, Soul! I saw a lucid City
  Of architectural device
Every way perfect. Pause for pity,
  Lightning! nor leave a cicatrice
On those bright marbles, dome and spire,
Structures palatial,—streets which mire
Dares not defile, paved all too fine
For human footstep's smirch, not thine—
Proud solitary traverser,
  My Soul, of silent lengths of way—
With what ecstatic dread, aver,
  Lest life start sanctioned by thy stay!

Ah, but the last sight was the hideous!
  A City, yes,—a Forest, true,—
But each devouring each. Perfidious
  Snake-plants had strangled what I knew
Was a pavilion once: each oak
Held on his horns some spoil he broke
By surreptitiously beneath
Upthrusting: pavements, as with teeth,
Griped huge weed widening crack and split
  In squares and circles stone-work erst.
Oh, Nature—good! Oh, Art—no whit
  Less worthy! Both in one—accurst!

BAD DREAMS—IV

It happened thus: my slab, though new,
  Was getting weather-stained,—beside,
Herbage, balm, peppermint o'ergrew
  Letter and letter: till you tried
Somewhat, the Name was scarce descried.

That strong stern man my lover came:
  —Was he my lover? Call him, pray,
My life's cold critic bent on blame
  Of all poor I could do or say
To make me worth his love one day—

One far day when, by diligent
  And dutiful amending faults,
Foibles, all weaknesses which went
  To challenge and excuse assaults
Of culture wronged by taste that halts—

Discrepancies should mar no plan
  Symmetric of the qualities
Claiming respect from—say—a man
  That's strong and stern. "Once more he pries
Into me with those critic eyes!"

No question! so—"Conclude, condemn
  Each failure my poor self avows!
Leave to its fate all you contemn!
  There's Solomon's selected spouse:
Earth needs must hold such maids—choose
    them!"

Why, he was weeping! Surely gone
  Sternness and strength: with eyes to ground
And voice a broken monotone—
  "Only be as you were! Abound
In foibles, faults,—laugh, robed and crowned

"As Folly's veriest queen,—care I
  One feather-fluff? Look pity, Love,
On prostrate me—your foot shall try
  This forehead's use—mount thence above,
And reach what Heaven you dignify!"

Now, what could bring such change about?
  The thought perplexed: till, following
His gaze upon the ground,—why, out
  Came all the secret! So, a thing
Thus simple has deposed my king!

For, spite of weeds that strove to spoil
  Plain reading on the lettered slab,
My name was clear enough—no soil
  Effaced the date when one chance stab
Of scorn . . . if only ghosts might blab!

INAPPREHENSIVENESS

We two stood simply friend-like side by side,
Viewing a twilight country far and wide,
Till she at length broke silence. "How it towers
Yonder, the ruin o'er this vale of ours!
The West's faint flare behind it so relieves
Its rugged outline—sight perhaps deceives,
Or I could almost fancy that I see
A branch wave plain—belike some wind-sown tree
Chance-rooted where a missing turret was.
What would I give for the perspective glass
At home, to make out if 'tis really so!
Has Ruskin noticed here at Asolo
That certain weed-growths on the ravaged wall
Seem" . . . something that I could not say at all,
My thought being rather—as absorbed she sent
Look onward after look from eyes distent
With longing to reach Heaven's gate left ajar—
"Oh, fancies that might be, oh, facts that are!
What of a wilding? By you stands, and may
So stand unnoticed till the Judgment Day,
One who, if once aware that your regard
Claimed what his heart holds,—woke, as from its sward
The flower, the dormant passion, so to speak—
Then what a rush of life would startling wreak
Revenge on your inapprehensive stare
While, from the ruin and the West's faint flare,
You let your eyes meet mine, touch what you term
Quietude—that's an universe in germ—
The dormant passion needing but a look
To burst into immense life!"

"No, the book
Which noticed how the wall-growths wave" said she
"Was not by Ruskin."

I said "Vernon Lee?"

"IMPERANTE AUGUSTO NATUS EST——"

What it was struck the terror into me?
This, Publius: closer! while we wait our turn
I'll tell you. Water's warm (they ring inside)
At the eighth hour, till when no use to bathe.

Here in the vestibule where now we sit,
One scarce stood yesterday, the throng was such
Of loyal gapers, folk all eye and ear
While Lucius Varius Rufus in their midst
Read out that long-planned late-completed piece,
His Panegyric on the Emperor.
"Nobody like him" little Flaccus laughed
"At leading forth an Epos with due pomp!
Only, when godlike Cæsar swells the theme,
How should mere mortals hope to praise aright?
Tell me, thou offshoot of Etruscan kings!"
Whereat Mæcenas smiling sighed assent.

I paid my quadrans, left the Thermæ's roar
Of rapture as the poet asked "What place
Among the godships Jove, for Cæsar's sake,
Would bid its actual occupant vacate
In favour of the new divinity?"
And got the expected answer "Yield thine own!"—
Jove thus dethroned, I somehow wanted air,
And found myself a-pacing street and street,
Letting the sunset, rosy over Rome,
Clear my head dizzy with the hubbub—say,
As if thought's dance therein had kicked up dust
By trampling on all else: the world lay prone,
As—poet-propped, in brave hexameters—
Their subject triumphed up from man to God.
Caius Octavius Cæsar the August—
Where was escape from his prepotency?
I judge I may have passed—how many piles
Of structure dropt like doles from his free hand
To Rome on every side? Why, right and left,
For temples you've the Thundering Jupiter,
Avenging Mars, Apollo Palatine:

How count Piazza, Forum—there's a third
All but completed. You've the Theatre
Named of Marcellus—all his work, such work!—
One thought still ending, dominating all—
With warrant Varius sang "Be Cæsar God!"
By what a hold arrests he Fortune's wheel,
Obtaining and retaining heaven and earth
Through Fortune, if you like, but favour—no!
For the great deeds flashed by me, fast and thick
As stars which storm the sky on autumn nights—
Those conquests! but peace crowned them,—so, of peace!
Count up his titles only—these, in few—
Ten years Triumvir, Consul thirteen times,
Emperor, nay—the glory topping all—
Hailed Father of his Country, last and best
Of titles, by himself accepted so:
And why not? See but feats achieved in Rome—
Not to say, Italy—he planted there
Some thirty colonies—but Rome itself
All new-built, "marble now, brick once," he boasts:
This Portico, that Circus. Would you sail?
He has drained Tiber for you: would you walk?
He straightened out the long Flaminian Way.
Poor? Profit by his score of donatives!
Rich—that is, mirthful? Half-a-hundred games
Challenge your choice! There's Rome—for you and me
Only? The centre of the world besides!
For, look the wide world over, where ends Rome?
To sunrise? There's Euphrates—all between!
To sunset? Ocean and immensity:
North,—stare till Danube stops you: South, see Nile,
The Desert and the earth-upholding Mount.
Well may the poet-people each with each
Vie in his praise, our company of swans,
Virgil and Horace, singers—in their way—
Nearly as good as Varius, though less famed:
Well may they cry, "No mortal, plainly God!"

Thus to myself myself said, while I walked:
Or would have said, could thought attain to speech,

Clean baffled by enormity of bliss
The while I strove to scale its heights and sound
Its depths—this masterdom o'er all the world
Of one who was but born,—like you, like me,
Like all the world he owns,—of flesh and blood.
But he—how grasp, how gauge his own conceit
Of bliss to me near inconceivable?
Or—since such flight too much makes reel the brain—
Let's sink—and so take refuge, as it were,
From life's excessive altitude—to life's
Breathable wayside shelter at its base!
If looms thus large this Cæsar to myself
—Of senatorial rank and somebody—
How must he strike the vulgar nameless crowd,
Innumerous swarm that's nobody at all?
Why,—for an instance,—much as yon gold shape
Crowned, sceptred, on the temple opposite—
Fulgurant Jupiter—must daze the sense
Of—say, yon outcast begging from its step!
What, anti-Cæsar, monarch in the mud,
As he is pinnacled above thy pate?
Ay, beg away! thy lot contrasts full well
With his whose bounty yields thee this support—
Our Holy and Inviolable One,
Cæsar, whose bounty built the fane above!
Dost read my thought? Thy garb, alack, displays
Sore usage truly in each rent and stain—
Faugh! Wash though in Suburra! 'Ware the dogs
Who may not so disdain a meal on thee!
What, stretchest forth a palm to catch my alms?
Aha, why yes: I must appear—who knows?—
I, in my toga, to thy rags and thee—
Quæstor—nay, Ædile, Censor—Pol! perhaps
The very City-Prætor's noble self!
As to me Cæsar, so to thee am I?
Good: nor in vain shall prove thy quest, poor rogue!
Hither—hold palm out—take this quarter-as!

And who did take it? As he raised his head,
(My gesture was a trifle—well, abrupt),

Back fell the broad flap of the peasant's-hat,
The homespun cloak that muffled half his cheek
Dropped somewhat, and I had a glimpse—just one!
One was enough. Whose—whose might be the face?
That unkempt careless hair—brown, yellowish—
Those sparkling eyes beneath their eyebrows' ridge
(Each meets each, and the hawk-nose rules between)
—That was enough, no glimpse was needed more!
And terrifyingly into my mind
Came that quick-hushed report was whispered us,
"They do say, once a year in sordid garb
He plays the mendicant, sits all day long,
Asking and taking alms of who may pass,
And so averting, if submission help,
Fate's envy, the dread chance and change of things
When Fortune—for a word, a look, a nought—
Turns spiteful and—the petted lioness—
Strikes with her sudden paw, and prone falls each
Who patted late her neck superiorly,
Or trifled with those claw-tips velvet-sheathed."
"He's God!" shouts Lucius Varius Rufus: "Man
And worms'-meat any moment!" mutters low
Some Power, admonishing the mortal-born.

Ay, do you mind? There's meaning in the fact
That whoso conquers, triumphs, enters Rome,
Climbing the Capitolian, soaring thus
To glory's summit,—Publius, do you mark—
Ever the same attendant who, behind,
Above the Conqueror's head supports the crown
All-too-demonstrative for human wear,
—One hand's employment—all the while reserves
Its fellow, backward flung, to point how, close
Appended from the car, beneath the foot
Of the up-borne exulting Conqueror,
Frown—half-descried—the instruments of shame,
The malefactor's due. Crown, now—Cross, when?

Who stands secure? Are even Gods so safe?
Jupiter that just now is dominant—

Are not there ancient dismal tales how once
A predecessor reigned ere Saturn came,
And who can say if Jupiter be last?
Was it for nothing the grey Sibyl wrote
"Cæsar Augustus regnant, shall be born
In blind Judæa"—one to master him,
Him and the universe? An old-wife's tale?

Bath-drudge! Here, slave! No cheating! Our turn next.
No loitering, or be sure you taste the lash!
Two strigils, two oil-drippers, each a sponge!

EPILOGUE

At the midnight in the silence of the sleep-time,
When you set your fancies free,
Will they pass to where—by death, fools think, imprisoned—
Low he lies who once so loved you, whom you loved so,
—Pity me?

Oh to love so, be so loved, yet so mistaken!
What had I on earth to do
With the slothful, with the mawkish, the unmanly?
Like the aimless, helpless, hopeless, did I drivel
—Being—who?

One who never turned his back but marched breast forward,
Never doubted clouds would break,
Never dreamed, though right were worsted, wrong would triumph,
Held we fall to rise, are baffled to fight better,
Sleep to wake.

No, at noonday in the bustle of man's work-time
Greet the unseen with a cheer!
Bid him forward, breast and back as either should be,
"Strive and thrive!" cry "Speed,—fight on, fare ever
There as here!"

PROSE

Essay on Shelley

1852

Letters of Percy Bysshe Shelley. With an introductory essay, by Robert Browning. London: Edward Moxon, Dover Street. 1852.

Royal 12mo. Pp. viii + 168. Cloth boards.

BROWNING'S essay occupies pages 1–44. The circumstances in which it was written, published and withdrawn are described on page xv above.

Essay on Shelley

An opportunity having presented itself for the acquisition of a series of unedited letters by Shelley, all more or less directly supplementary to and illustrative of the collection already published by Mr. Moxon, that gentleman has decided on securing them. They will prove an acceptable addition to a body of correspondence, the value of which towards a right understanding of its author's purpose and work, may be said to exceed that of any similar contribution exhibiting the worldly relations of a poet whose genius has operated by a different law.

Doubtless we accept gladly the biography of an objective poet, as the phrase now goes; one whose endeavour has been to reproduce things external (whether the phenomena of the scenic universe, or the manifested action of the human heart and brain) with an immediate reference, in every case, to the common eye and apprehension of his fellow men, assumed capable of receiving and profiting by this reproduction. It has been obtained through the poet's double faculty of seeing external objects more clearly, widely, and deeply, than is possible to the average mind, at the same time that he is so acquainted and in sympathy with its narrower comprehension as to be careful to supply it with no other materials than it can combine into an intelligible whole. The auditory of such a poet will include, not only the intelligences which, save for such assistance, would have missed the deeper meaning and enjoyment of the original objects, but also the spirits of a like endowment with his own, who, by means of his abstract, can forthwith pass to the reality it was made from, and either corroborate their impressions of things known already, or supply themselves with new from whatever shows in the inexhaustible variety of existence may have hitherto escaped their knowledge. Such a poet is properly the ποιήτης, the fashioner; and the thing fashioned, his poetry, will of necessity be substantive, projected from himself and distinct. We are ignorant what the inventor of "Othello" conceived of that fact as he beheld it in completeness, how he accounted for it, under what known law he registered its nature, or to what unknown law he traced its coincidence. We learn only what he intended we should learn by that particular exercise of his power,—the fact itself,—which, with its infinite significances, each of us receives for the first time as a creation, and is hereafter left to deal with, as, in proportion to his own intelligence, he best may. We are ignorant, and would fain be otherwise.

Doubtless, with respect to such a poet, we covet his biography. We desire to look back upon the process of gathering together in a lifetime, the materials of the work we behold entire; of elaborating, perhaps under difficulty and with hindrance, all that is familiar to our admiration in the apparent facility of success. And the inner impulse of this effort and operation, what induced it? Did a soul's delight in its own extended sphere of vision set it, for the gratification of an insuppressible power, on labour, as other men are set on rest? Or did a sense of duty or of love lead it to communicate its own sensations to mankind? Did an irresistible sympathy with men compel it to bring down and suit its own provision of knowledge and beauty to their narrow scope? Did the personality of such an one stand like an open watch-tower in the midst of the territory it is erected to gaze on, and were the storms and calms, the stars and meteors, its watchman was wont to report of, the habitual variegation of his every-day life, as they glanced across its open roof or lay reflected on its four-square parapet? Or did some sunken and darkened chamber of imagery witness, in the artificial illumination of every storied compartment we are permitted to contemplate, how rare and precious were the outlooks through here and there an embrasure upon a world beyond, and how blankly would have pressed on the artificer the boundary of his daily life, except for the amorous diligence with which he had rendered permanent by art whatever came to diversify the gloom? Still, fraught with instruction and interest as such details undoubtedly are, we can, if needs be, dispense with them. The man passes, the work remains. The work speaks for itself, as we say: and the biography of the worker is no more necessary to an understanding or enjoyment of it, than is a model or anatomy of some tropical tree, to the right tasting of the fruit we are familiar with on the market-stall,—or a geologist's map and stratification, to the prompt recognition of the hill-top, our land-mark of every day.

We turn with stronger needs to the genius of an opposite tendency—the subjective poet of modern classification. He, gifted like the objective poet with the fuller perception of nature and man, is impelled to embody the thing he perceives, not so much with reference to the many below as to the one above him, the supreme Intelligence which apprehends all things in their absolute truth,—an ultimate view ever aspired to, if but partially attained, by the poet's own soul. Not what man sees, but what God sees—the *Ideas* of Plato, seeds of creation lying burningly on the Divine Hand—it is toward these that he struggles. Not with the combination of humanity in action, but with the primal elements of humanity he has to do; and he digs where he stands,—preferring to seek them in his own soul as the nearest reflex of that absolute Mind, according to the intuitions of which he desires to perceive and speak. Such a poet does not deal habitually with the picturesque groupings and tempestuous tossings of the forest-trees, but with their roots and fibres naked to the chalk and stone. He does not paint pictures and hang them on the walls, but rather carries them on the retina of his own eyes: we must look deep into his human eyes, to see those pictures on them. He is rather a seer, accordingly, than a fashioner, and what he produces will be less a work than an effluence. That effluence cannot be easily considered in abstraction from his personality,—being indeed the very radiance and aroma of his personality, projected from it but not separated. Therefore, in our approach to the poetry, we necessarily approach the personality of the poet; in apprehending it we apprehend him, and certainly we cannot love it without loving him. Both for love's and for understanding's sake we desire to know him, and as readers of his poetry must be readers of his biography also.

I shall observe, in passing, that it seems not so much from any essential distinction in the faculty of the two poets or in the nature of the objects contemplated by either, as in the more immediate adaptability of these objects to the distinct purpose of each, that the objective poet, in his appeal to the aggregate human mind, chooses to deal with the doings of men, (the result of which dealing, in its pure form, when even description, as suggesting a describer, is dispensed with, is what we call dramatic poetry), while the subjective poet, whose study has been himself, appealing through himself to the absolute Divine mind, prefers to dwell upon those external scenic appearances which strike out most abundantly and uninterruptedly his inner light and power, selects that silence of the earth and sea in which he can best hear the beating of his individual heart, and leaves the noisy, complex, yet imperfect exhibitions of nature in the manifold experience of man around him, which serve only to distract and suppress the working of his brain. These opposite tendencies of genius will be more readily descried in their artistic effect than in their moral spring and cause. Pushed to an extreme and manifested as a deformity, they will be seen plainest of all in the fault of either artist, when subsidiarily to the human interest of his work his occasional illustrations from scenic nature are introduced as in the earlier works of the originative painters—men and women filling the foreground with consummate mastery, while mountain, grove and rivulet show like an anticipatory revenge on that succeeding race of landscape-painters whose "figures" disturb the perfection of their earth and sky. It would be idle to inquire, of these two kinds of poetic faculty in operation, which is the higher or even rarer endowment. If the subjective might seem to be the ultimate requirement of every age, the objective, in the strictest state, must still retain its original value. For it is with this world, as starting point and basis alike, that we shall always have to concern ourselves: the world is not to be learned and thrown aside, but reverted to and relearned. The spiritual comprehension may be infinitely subtilised, but the raw material it operates upon, must remain. There may be no end of the poets who communicate to us what they see in an object with reference to their own individuality; what it was before they saw it, in reference to the aggregate human mind, will be as desirable to know as ever. Nor is there any reason why these two modes of poetic faculty may not issue hereafter from the same poet in successive perfect works, examples of which, according to what are now considered the exigences of art, we have hitherto possessed in distinct individuals only. A mere running in of the one faculty upon the other, is, of course, the ordinary circumstance. Far more rarely it happens that either is found so decidedly prominent and superior, as to be pronounced comparatively pure: while of the perfect shield, with the gold and the silver side set up for all comers to challenge, there has as yet been no instance. Either faculty in its eminent state is doubtless conceded by Providence as a best gift to men, according to their especial want. There is a time when the general eye has, so to speak, absorbed its fill of the phenomena around it, whether spiritual or material, and desires rather to learn the exacter significance of what it possesses, than to receive any augmentation of what is possessed. Then is the opportunity for the poet of loftier vision, to lift his fellows, with their half-apprehensions, up to his own sphere, by intensifying the import of details and rounding the universal meaning. The influence of such an achievement will not soon die out. A tribe of successors (Homerides) working more or less in the same spirit, dwell on his discoveries and reinforce his doctrine; till, at unawares, the world is found to be subsisting wholly on the shadow of a reality, on sentiments diluted from passions, on the tradition of a fact, the convention of a moral, the straw of last year's harvest. Then is the imperative call for the appearance of another sort of poet, who shall at once replace this intellectual rumination of food swallowed long ago, by a supply of the fresh and living swathe; getting at new substance by breaking up the assumed wholes into parts of independent and unclassed value, careless of the unknown laws for recombining them (it will be the business of yet another poet to suggest those hereafter), prodigal of objects for men's outer and not inner sight, shaping for their uses a new and different creation from the last, which it replaces by the right of life over death,—to endure until, in the inevitable process, its very sufficiency to itself shall require, at length, an exposition of its affinity to something higher,—when the positive yet conflicting facts shall again precipitate themselves under an harmonising law, and one more degree will be apparent for a poet to climb in that mighty ladder, of which, however cloud-involved and undefined may glimmer the topmost step, the world dares no longer doubt that its gradations ascend.

Such being the two kinds of artists, it is naturally, as I have shown, with the biography of the subjective poet that we have the deeper concern. Apart from his recorded life altogether, we might fail to determine with satisfactory precision to what class his productions belong, and what amount of praise is assignable to the producer. Certainly, in the face of any conspicuous achievement of genius, philosophy, no less than sympathetic instinct, warrants our belief in a great moral purpose having mainly inspired even where it does not visibly look out of the same. Greatness in a work suggests an adequate instrumentality; and none of the lower incitements, however they may avail to initiate or even effect many considerable displays of power, simulating the nobler inspiration to which they are mistakenly referred, have been found able, under the ordinary conditions of humanity, to task themselves to the end of so exacting a performance as a poet's complete work. As soon will the galvanism that provokes to violent action the muscles of a corpse, induce it to cross the chamber steadily: sooner. The love of displaying power for the display's sake, the love of riches, of distinction, of notoriety,—the desire of a triumph over rivals, and the vanity in the applause of friends,—each and all of such whetted appetites grow intenser by exercise and increasingly sagacious as to the best and readiest means of self-appeasement,—while for any of their ends, whether the money, or the pointed finger of the crowd, or the flattery and hate to heart's content, there are cheaper prices to pay, they will all find soon enough, than the bestowment of a life upon a labour, hard slow, and not sure. Also, assuming the proper moral aim to have produced a work, there are many and various states of an aim: it may be more intense than clear-sighted, or too easily satisfied with a lower field of activity than a steadier aspiration would reach. All the bad poetry in the world (accounted poetry, that is, by its affinities) will be found to result from some one of the infinite degrees of discrepancy between the attributes of the poet's soul, occasioning a want of correspondency between his work and the verities of nature,—issuing in poetry, false under whatever form, which shows a thing not as it is to mankind generally, nor as it is to the particular describer, but as it is supposed to be for some unreal neutral mood, midway between both and of value to neither, and living its brief minute simply through the indolence of whoever accepts it or his incapacity to denounce a cheat. Although of such depths of failure there can be no question here, we must in every case betake ourselves to the review of a poet's life ere we determine some of the nicer questions concerning his poetry,—more especially if the performance we seek to estimate aright, has been obstructed and cut short of completion by circumstances,—a disastrous youth or a premature death. We may learn from the biography whether his spirit invariably saw and spoke from the last height to which it had attained. An absolute vision is not for this world, but we are permitted a continual approximation to it, every degree of which in the individual, provided it exceed the attainment of the masses, must procure him a clear advantage. Did the poet ever attain to a higher platform than where he rested and exhibited a result? Did he know more than he spoke of?

I concede however, in respect to the subject of our study as well as some few other illustrious examples, that the unmistakable quality of the verse would be evidence enough, under usual circumstances, not only of the kind and degree of the intellectual but of the moral constitution of Shelley: the whole personality of the poet shining forward from the poems, without much need of going further to seek it. The "Remains"—produced within a period of ten years, and at a season of life when other men of at all comparable genius have hardly done more than prepare the eye for future sight and the tongue for speech—present us with the complete enginery of a poet, as signal in the excellence of its several adaptitudes as transcendent in the combination of effects,—examples, in fact, of the whole poet's function of beholding with an understanding keenness the universe, nature and man, in their actual state of perfection in imperfection,—of the whole poet's virtue of being untempted by the manifold partial developments of beauty and good on every side, into leaving them the ultimates he found them,—induced by the facility of the gratification of his own sense of those qualities, or by the pleasure of acquiescence in the short-comings of his predecessors in art, and the pain of disturbing their conventionalisms,—the whole poet's virtue, I repeat, of looking higher than any manifestation yet made of both beauty and good, in order to suggest from the utmost actual realisation of the one a corresponding capability in the other, and out of the calm, purity and energy of nature, to reconstitute and store up for the forthcoming stage of man's being, a gift in repayment of that former gift, in which man's own thought and passion had been lavished by the poet on the else-incompleted magnificence of the sunrise, the else-uninterpreted mystery of the lake,—so drawing out, lifting up, and assimilating this ideal of a future man, thus descried as possible, to the present reality of the poet's soul already arrived at the higher state of development, and still aspirant to elevate and extend itself in conformity with its still-improving perceptions of, no longer the eventual Human, but the actual Divine. In conjunction with which noble and rare powers, came the subordinate power of delivering these attained results to the world in an embodiment of verse more closely answering to and indicative of the process of the informing spirit, (failing as it occasionally does, in art, only to succeed in highest art),—with a diction more adequate to the task in its natural and acquired richness, its material colour and spiritual transparency,—the whole being moved by and suffused with a music at once of the soul and the sense, expressive both of an external might of sincere passion and an internal fitness and consonancy,—than can be attributed to any other writer whose record is among us. Such was the spheric poetical faculty of Shelley, as its own self-sufficing central light, radiating equally through immaturity and accomplishment, through many fragments and occasional completion, reveals it to a competent judgement.

But the acceptance of this truth by the public, has been retarded by certain objections which cast us back on the evidence of biography, even with Shelley's poetry in our hands. Except for the particular character of these objections, indeed, the non-appreciation of his contemporaries would simply class, now that it is over, with a series of experiences which have necessarily happened and needlessly been wondered at, ever since the world began, and concerning which any present anger may well be moderated, no less in justice to our forerunners than in policy to ourselves. For the misapprehensiveness of his age is exactly what a poet is sent to remedy; and the interval between his operation and the generally perceptible effect of it, is no greater, less indeed, than in many other departments of the great human effort. The "E pur si muove" of the astronomer was as bitter a word as any uttered before or since by a poet over his rejected living work, in that depth of conviction which is so like despair.

But in this respect was the experience of Shelley peculiarly unfortunate that the disbelief in him as a man, even preceded the disbelief in him as a writer; the misconstruction of his moral nature preparing the way for the misappreciation of his intellectual labours. There existed from the beginning,—simultaneous with, indeed anterior to his earliest noticeable works, and not brought forward to counteract any impression they had succeeded in making,—certain charges against his private character and life, which, if substantiated to their whole breadth, would materially disturb, I do not attempt to deny, our reception and enjoyment of his works, however wonderful the artistic qualities of these. For we are not sufficiently supplied with instances of genius of his order, to be able to pronounce certainly how many of its constituent parts have been tasked and strained to the production of a given lie, and how high and pure a mood of the creative mind may be dramatically simulated as the poet's habitual and exclusive one. The doubts, therefore, arising from such a question, required to be set at rest, as they were effectually, by those early authentic notices of Shelley's career and the corrobative accompaniment of his letters, in which not only the main tenor and principal result of his life, but the purity and beauty of many of the processes which had conduced to them, were made apparent enough for the general reader's purpose,—whoever lightly condemned Shelley first, on the evidence of reviews and gossip, as lightly acquitting him now, on that of memoirs and correspondence. Still, it is advisable to lose no opportunity of strengthening and completing the chain of biographical testimony; much more, of course, for the sake of the poet's original lovers, whose volunteered sacrifice of particular principle in favour of absorbing sympathy we might desire to dispense with, than for the sake of his foolish haters, who have long since diverted upon other objects their obtuseness or malignancy. A full life of Shelley should be written at once, while the materials for it continue in reach; not to minister to the curiosity of the public, but to obliterate the last stain of that false life which was forced on the public's attention before it had any curiosity on the matter,—a biography, composed in harmony with the present general disposition to have faith in him, yet not shrinking from a candid statement of all ambiguous passages through a reasonable confidence that the most doubtful of them will be found consistent with a belief in the eventual perfection of his character, according to the poor limits of our humanity. Nor will men persist in confounding, any more than God confounds, with genuine infidelity and an atheism of the heart, those passionate, impatient struggles of a boy towards distant truth and love, made in the dark, and ended by one sweep of the natural seas before the full moral sunrise could shine out on him. Crude convictions of boyhood, conveyed in imperfect and inapt forms of speech,—for such things all boys have been pardoned. There are growing-pains, accompanied by temporary distortion, of the soul also. And it would be hard indeed upon this young Titan of genius, murmuring in divine music his human ignorances, through his very thirst for knowledge, and his rebellion, in mere aspiration to law, if the melody itself substantiated the error, and the tragic cutting short of life perpetuated into sins, such faults as, under happier circumstances, would have been left behind by the consent of the most arrogant moralist, forgotten on the lowest steps of youth.

The responsibility of presenting to the public a biography of Shelley, does not, however, lie with me: I have only to make it a little easier by arranging these few supplementary letters, with a recognition of the value of the whole collection. This value I take to consist in a most truthful conformity of the Correspondence, in its limited degree, with the moral and intellectual character of the writer as displayed in the highest manifestations of his genius. Letters and poems are obviously an act of the same mind, produced by the same law, only differing in the application to the individual or collective understanding. Letters and poems may be used indifferently as the basement of our opinion upon the writer's character; the finished expression of a sentiment in the poems, giving light and significance to the rudiments of the same in the letters, and these, again, in their incipiency and unripeness, authenticating the exalted mood and reattaching it to the personality of the writer. The musician speaks on the note he sings with; there is no change in the scale, as he diminishes the volume into familiar intercourse. There is nothing of that jarring between the man and the author, which has been found so amusing or so melancholy; no dropping of the tragic mask, as the crowd melts away; no mean discovery of the real motives of a life's achievement, often, in other lives, laid bare as pitifully as when, at the close of a holiday, we catch sight of the internal lead-pipes and wood-valves, to which, and not to the ostensible conch and dominant Triton of the fountain, we have owed our admired waterwork. No breaking out, in household privacy, of hatred, anger and scorn, incongruous with the higher mood and suppressed artistically in the book: no brutal return to self-delighting, when the audience of philanthropic schemes is out of hearing: no indecent stripping off the grander feeling and rule of life as too costly and cumbrous for every-day wear. Whatever Shelley was, he was with an admirable sincerity. It was not always truth that he thought and spoke; but in the purity of truth he spoke and thought always. Everywhere is apparent his belief in the existence of Good, to which Evil is an accident; his faithful holding by what he assumed to be the former, going everywhere in company with the tenderest pity for those acting or suffering on the opposite hypothesis. For he was tender, though tenderness is not always the characteristic of very sincere natures; he was eminently both tender and sincere. And not only do the same affection and yearning after the well-being of his kind, appear in the letters as in the poems, but they express themselves by the same theories and plans, however crude and unsound. There is no reservation of a subtler, less costly, more serviceable remedy for his own ill, than he has proposed for the general one; nor does he ever contemplate an object on his own account, from a less elevation than he uses in exhibiting it to the world. How shall we help believing Shelley to have been, in his ultimate attainment, the splendid spirit of his own best poetry, when we find even his carnal speech to agree faithfully, at faintest as at strongest, with the tone and rhythm of his most oracular utterances?

For the rest, these new letters are not offered as presenting any new feature of the poet's character. Regarded in themselves, and as the substantive productions of a man, their importance would be slight. But they possess interest beyond their limits, in confirming the evidence just dwelt on, of the poetical mood of Shelley being only the intensification of his habitual mood; the same tongue only speaking, for want of the special excitement to sing. The very first letter, as one instance for all, strikes the key-note of the predominating sentiment of Shelley throughout his whole life—his sympathy with the oppressed. And when we see him at so early an age, casting out, under the influence of such a sympathy, letters and pamphlets on every side, we accept it as the simple exemplification of the sincerity, with which, at the close of his life, he spoke of himself, as—

> One whose heart a stranger's tear might wear
> As water-drops the sandy fountain stone;
> Who loved and pitied all things, and could moan

For woes which others hear not, and could see
The absent with the glass of phantasy,
And near the poor and trampled sit and weep,
Following the captive to his dungeon deep—
One who was as a nerve o'er which do creep
The else-unfelt oppressions of this earth.

Such sympathy with his kind was evidently developed in him to an extraordinary and even morbid degree, at a period when the general intellectual powers it was impatient to put in motion, were immature or deficient.

I conjecture, from a review of the various publications of Shelley's youth, that one of the causes of his failure at the outset, was the peculiar *practicalness* of his mind, which was not without a determinate effect on his progress in theorising. An ordinary youth, who turns his attention to similar subjects, discovers falsities, incongruities, and various points for amendment, and, in the natural advance of the purely critical spirit unchecked by considerations of remedy, keeps up before his young eyes so many instances of the same error and wrong, that he finds himself unawares arrived at the startling conclusion, that all must be changed—or nothing: in the face of which plainly impossible achievement, he is apt (looking perhaps a little more serious by the time he touches at the decisive issue), to feel, either carelessly or considerately, that his own attempting a single piece of service would be worse than useless even, and to refer the whole task to another age and person—safe in proportion to his incapacity. Wanting words to speak, he has never made a fool of himself by speaking. But, in Shelley's case, the early fervour and power to *see*, was accompanied by as precocious a fertility to *contrive*: he endeavoured to realise as he went on idealising; every wrong had simultaneously its remedy, and, out of the strength of his hatred for the former, he took the strength of his confidence in the latter—till suddenly he stood pledged to the defence of a set of miserable little expedients, just as if they represented great principles, and to an attack upon various great principles, really so, without leaving himself time to examine whether, because they were antagonistical to the remedy he had suggested, they must therefore be identical or even essentially connected with the wrong he sought to cure,—playing with blind passion into the hands of his enemies, and dashing at whatever red cloak was held forth to him, as the cause of the fireball he had last been stung with—mistaking Churchdom for Christianity, and for marriage, "the sale of love" and the law of sexual oppression.

Gradually, however, he was leaving behind him this low practical dexterity, unable to keep up with his widening intellectual perception; and, in exact proportion as he did so, his true power strengthened and proved itself. Gradually he was raised above the contemplation of spots and the attempt at effacing them, to the great Abstract Light, and, through the discrepancy of the creation, to the sufficiency of the First Cause. Gradually he was learning that the best way of removing abuses is to stand fast by truth. Truth is one, as they are manifold; and innumerable negative effects are produced by the upholding of one positive principle. I shall say what I think,—had Shelley lived he would have finally ranged himself with the Christians; his very instinct for helping the weaker side (if numbers make strength), his very "hate of hate," which at first mistranslated itself into delirious Queen Mab notes and the like, would have got clearer-sighted by exercise. The preliminary step to following Christ, is the leaving the dead to bury their dead—not clamouring on His doctrine for an especial solution of difficulties which are referable to the general problem of the universe. Already he had attained to a profession of "a worship to the Spirit of good within, which requires (before it sends that inspiration forth, which impresses its likeness upon all it creates) devoted and disinterested homage," *as Coleridge says*,—and Paul likewise. And we find in one of his last exquisite fragments, avowedly a record of one of his own mornings and its experience, as it dawned on him at his soul and body's best in his boat on the Serchio—that as surely as

> The stars burnt out in the pale blue air,
> and the thin white moon lay withering there—
> Day had kindled the dewy woods,
> And the rocks above, and the streams below,
> And the vapours in their multitudes,

And the Appennine's shroud of summer snow—
Day had awakened all things that be;

just so surely, he tells us (stepping forward from this delicious dance-music, choragus-like, into the grander measure befitting the final enunciation),

All rose to do the task He set to each,
Who shaped us to His ends and not our own;
The million rose to learn, and One to teach
What none yet ever knew or can be known.

No more difference than this, from David's pregnant conclusion so long ago!

Meantime, as I call Shelley a moral man, because he was true, simple-hearted, and brave, and because what he acted corresponded to what he knew, so I call him a man of religious mind, because every audacious negative cast up by him against the Divine, was interpenetrated with a mood of reverence and adoration,—and because I find him everywhere taking for granted some of the capital dogmas of Christianity, while most vehemently denying their historical basement. There is such a thing as an efficacious knowledge of and belief in the politics of Junius, or the poetry of Rowley, though a man should at the same time dispute the title of Chatterton to the one, and consider the author of the other, as Byron wittily did, "really, truly, nobody at all."[1] There is even such a thing, we come to learn wonderingly in these few letters, as a profound sensibility and adaptitude for art, while the science of the percipient is so little advanced as to admit of his stronger admiration for Guido (and Carlo Dolce!) than for Michael Angelo. A Divine Being has Himself said, that "a word against the Son

[1] Or, to take our illustration from the writings of Shelley himself, there is such a thing as admirably appreciating a work by Andrea Verocchio,—and fancifully characterising the Pisan Torre Guelfa by the Ponte a Mare, black against the sunsets,—and consummately painting the islet of San Clemente with its penitentiary for rebellious priests, to the west between Venice and the Lido—while you believe the first to be a fragment of an antique sarcophagus,—the second, Ugolino's Tower of Famine (the vestiges of which should be sought for in the Piazza de' Cavalieri)—and the third (as I convinced myself last summer at Venice), San Servolo with its madhouse—which, far from being "windowless," is as full of windows as a barrack. [R. B.]

of man shall be forgiven to a man," while "a word against the spirit of God" (implying a general deliberate preference of perceived evil to perceived good) "shall not be forgiven to a man." Also, in religion, one earnest and unextorted assertion of belief should outweigh, as a matter of testimony, many assertions of unbelief. The fact that there is a gold-region is established by the finding of one lump, though you miss the vein never so often.

He died before his youth ended. In taking the measure of him as a man, he must be considered on the whole and at his ultimate spiritual stature, and not be judged of at the immaturity and by the mistakes of ten years before: that, indeed, would be to judge of the author of "Julian and Maddalo" by "Zastrozzi." Let the whole truth be told of his worst mistake. I believe, for my own part, that if anything could now shame or grieve Shelley, it would be an attempt to vindicate him at the expense of another.

In forming a judgement, I would, however, press on the reader the simple justice of considering tenderly his constitution of body as well as mind, and how unfavourable it was to the steady symmetries of conventional life; the body, in the torture of incurable disease, refusing to give repose to the bewildered soul, tossing in its hot fever of the fancy,—and the laudanum-bottle making but a perilous and pitiful truce between these two. He was constantly subject to "that state of mind" (I quote his own note to "Hellas") "in which ideas may be supposed to assume the force of sensation, through the confusion of thought with the objects of thought, and excess of passion animating the creations of the imagination:" in other words, he was liable to remarkable delusions and hallucinations. The nocturnal attack in Wales, for instance, was assuredly a delusion; and I venture to express my own conviction, derived from a little attention to the circumstances of either story, that the idea of the enamoured lady following him to Naples, and of the "man in the cloak" who struck him at the Pisan post-office, were equally illusory,—the mere projection, in fact, from himself, of the image of his own love and hate.

To thirst and find no fill—to wail and wander
With short unsteady steps—to pause and ponder—

To feel the blood run through the veins and tingle
When busy thought and blind sensation mingle,—
To nurse the image of *unfelt caresses*
Till dim imagination just possesses
The half-created shadow—

of unfelt caresses,—and of unfelt blows as well: to such conditions was his genius subject. It was not at Rome only (where he heard a mystic voice exclaiming, "Cenci, Cenci," in reference to the tragic theme which occupied him at the time),—it was not at Rome only that he mistook the cry of "old rags." The habit of somnambulism is said to have extended to the very last days of his life.

Let me conclude with a thought of Shelley as a poet. In the hierarchy of creative minds, it is the presence of the highest faculty that gives first rank, in virtue of its kind, not degree; no pretension of a lower nature, whatever the completeness of development or variety of effect, impeding the precedency of the rarer endowment though only in the germ. The contrary is sometimes maintained; it is attempted to make the lower gifts (which are potentially included in the higher faculty) of independent value, and equal to some excercise of the special function. For instance, should not a poet possess common sense? Then the possession of abundant common sense implies a step towards becoming a poet. Yes; such a step as the lapidary's, when, strong in the fact of carbon entering largely into the composition of the diamond, he heaps up a sack of charcoal in order to compete with the Koh-i-noor. I pass at once, therefore, from Shelley's minor excellences to his noblest and predominating characteristic.

This I call his simultaneous perception of Power and Love in the absolute, and of Beauty and Good in the concrete, while he throws, from his poet's station between both, swifter, subtler, and more numerous films for the connexion of each with each, than have been thrown by any modern artificer of whom I have knowedge; proving how, as he says,

The spirit of the worm within the sod,
In love and worship blends itself with God.

I would rather consider Shelley's poetry as a sublime fragmentary essay towards a presentment of the correspondency of the universe to Deity, of the natural to the spiritual, and of the actual to the ideal, than I would isolate and separately appraise the worth of many detachable portions which might be acknowledged as utterly perfect in a lower moral point of view, under the mere conditions of art. It would be easy to take my stand on successful instances of objectivity in Shelley: there is the unrivalled "Cenci;" there is the "Julian and Maddalo" too; there is the magnificent "Ode to Naples:" why not regard, it may be said, the less organised matter as the radiant elemental foam and solution, out of which would have been evolved, eventually, creations as perfect even as those? But I prefer to look for the highest attainment, not simply the high,—and, seeing it, I hold by it. There is surely enough of the work "Shelley" to be known enduringly among men, and, I believe, to be accepted of God, as human work may; and around the imperfect proportions of such, the most elaborated productions of ordinary art must arrange themselves as inferior illustrations.

It is because I have long held these opinions in assurance and gratitude that I catch at the opportunity offered to me of expressing them here; knowing that the alacrity to fulfil an humble office conveys more love than the acceptance of the honour of a higher one, and that better, therefore, than the signal service it was the dream of my boyhood to render to his fame and memory, may be the saying of a few inadequate words upon these scarcely more important supplementary letters of SHELLEY.

Letters

The Life and Work of John Ruskin, by W. G. Collingwood, two volumes, Methuen 1893.

Includes the letter from Browning to Ruskin printed on pages 751-4 below.

The Letters of Robert Browning and Elizabeth Barrett Barrett 1845–1846, two volumes, Smith Elder 1899.

Contains 284 letters from R. B. to E. B. B., and 287 from her to him. Twenty-eight of his letters are reprinted, in whole or part, below.

Robert Browning and Alfred Domett, edited by Frederic G. Kenyon, Smith Elder 1906.

Includes twenty-three letters from Browning to Domett, two of which are quoted below.

Letters of Robert Browning collected by Thomas J. Wise, edited by Thurman L. Hood, John Murray 1933.

Contains some 320 letters, of which nine are reprinted, in whole or part, below—namely those to Euphrasia Fanny Haworth and Isabella Blagden (previously published in Mrs. Sutherland Orr's *Life and Letters of Robert Browning* 1891); Leigh Hunt (partly printed in *The Correspondence of Leigh Hunt* edited by his eldest son 1862); Sarianna Browning (privately printed for T. J. Wise 1916); William G. Kingsland (in Kingsland's *Robert Browning Chief Poet of the Age* new edition 1890); A. B. Grosart (in Grosart's edition of *The Prose Works of William Wordsworth* 1876); F. J. Furnivall (in *Letters from Robert Browning to various correspondents* edited by T. J. Wise 1895); Edmund Yates (in William Sharp's *Life of Robert Browning* 1890); and Alfred Lord Tennyson (a fuller version in the *Memoir* of Tennyson by his son 1897).

From Robert and Elizabeth Browning, introduction by William Rose Benét, John Murray 1936.

Includes ten letters from Browning to Henrietta and Arabel Barrett, of which one is printed below.

Robert Browning and Julia Wedgwood, edited by Richard Curle, John Murray and Jonathan Cape 1937.

Includes thirty letters from Browning to Miss Wedgwood, of which two are quoted below.

Some slight changes have been made, for the sake of clarity, in the punctuation and paragraphing of certain of the letters. Browning's use of two "dots" (. .), which are often indistinguishable in manuscript from the more conventional "comma-dash" (,—) or "period-dash" (.—), has been eliminated. Three dots (. . .) are used to shew that part of a letter is omitted.

Eccentric and obsolete spellings (*e.g.* "sopha", "chymist") have been retained; but apparent slips of the pen (*e.g.* "haemorrage") have been corrected.

Letters

TO EUPHRASIA FANNY HAWORTH

[Written soon after Browning's return from his first visit to Italy, whither he had sailed, the sole passenger, in the *Norham Castle*. One object of his visit had been to complete *Sordello* "among the scenes it describes".]

[24 July 1838.]

. . . Do look at a Fuchsia in full bloom and notice the clear little honey-drop depending from every flower. I have but just found it out, to my no small satisfaction,—a bee's breakfast. I only answer for the *long* blossomed sort, though,—indeed, for this plant in my room. Taste and be Titania,—you can, that is. All this while, I forget that you will perhaps never guess the good of the discovery: I have, you are to know, such a love for flowers and leaves—some leaves—that I every now and then, in an impatience at being unable to possess myself of them thoroughly, to see them quite, satiate myself with their scent,—bite them to bits—so there will be some sense in that. How I remember the flowers—even grasses—of places I have seen!—some one flower or weed, I should say, that gets some strangehow connected with them. Snowdrops and Tilsit in Prussia go together; Cowslips and Windsor-park, for instance; flowering palm and some place or other in Holland.

Now to answer what can be answered in the letter I was happy to receive last week. I am quite well. I did not expect you would write; for none of your written reasons, however. You will see *Sordello* in a trice, if the fagging-fit holds. I did not write six lines while absent (except a scene in a play, jotted down as we sailed thro' the Straits of Gibraltar)—but I did hammer out some four, two of which are addressed to you, two to the Queen—the whole to go in Book 3, perhaps. I called you, "Eyebright"—meaning a simple and sad sort of translation of "Euphrasia" into my own language: folks would know who Euphrasia, or Fanny, was—and *I* should not know Ianthe or Clemanthe. Not that there is anything in them to care for, good or bad. Shall I say "Eyebright"? . . .

The story of the ship must have reached you "with a difference" as Ophelia says,—my sister told it to a Mr. Dow, who delivered it, I suppose, to Forster, who furnished Macready with it, who made it over &c. &c. &c. As short as I can tell, this way it happened: the Captain woke me one bright Sunday morning to say there was a ship floating keel uppermost half a mile off; they lowered a boat, made ropes fast to some floating canvass, and towed her towards our vessel. Both met half-way, and the little air that had risen an hour or two before sank at once. Our men made the wreck fast, and went to breakfast in high glee at the notion of having "new trousers out of the sails," and quite sure she was a French boat, broken from her moorings at Algiers, close by. Ropes were next hove (hang this sea-talk) round her stancheons, and after a quarter of an hour's pushing at the capstan, the vessel righted suddenly, one dead body floating out; five more were in the forecastle, and had probably been there a month—under a blazing African sun—don't imagine the wretched state of things. They were, these six, the "watch below"—(I give you the results of the day's observation)—the rest, some eight or ten, had been washed overboard at first. One or two were Algerines, the rest Spaniards. The vessel was a smuggler bound for Gibraltar; there were two stupidly-disproportionate guns, taking up the whole deck, which was convex and—nay, look you! [*a rough pen-and-ink sketch here*] these are the gun-rings, and the black square the place where the bodies lay. Well, the sailors covered up the hatchway, broke up the aft-deck, hauled up tobacco and cigars, good lord such heaps of them, and then bale after bale of prints and chintz, don't you call it, till the Captain was half frightened—he would get at the ship's papers, he said; so these poor fellows were pulled up, piecemeal, and pitched into the sea, the very sailors calling to each other to "cover the faces": no papers of importance were found, however, but fifteen swords, powder and ball enough for a dozen such boats, and bundles of cotton &c.

that would have taken a day to get out, but the Captain vowed that after five-o'clock she should be cut adrift: accordingly she was cast loose, not a third of her cargo having been touched; and you can hardly conceive the strange sight when the battered hulk turned round, actually, and looked at us, and then reeled off, like a mutilated creature from some scoundrel French surgeon's lecture-table, into the most gorgeous and lavish sunset in the world: there,—only, thank me for not taking you at your word and giving you the whole "story." "What I did"? I went to Trieste, then Venice—then thro' Treviso and Bassano to the mountains, delicious Asolo, all my places and castles, you will see. Then to Vicenza, Padua and Venice again. Then to Verona, Trent, Inspruck (the Tyrol), Munich, "Wurzburg in Franconia"! Frankfort and Mayence,—down the Rhine to Cologne, thence to Aix-la-Chapelle, Liége, and Antwerp—then home . . .

TO ALFRED DOMETT

31 July 1844.

. . . A very interesting young poet has flushed into bloom this season. I send you his "soul's child"—the contents were handed and bandied about, and Moxon was told by the knowing ones of the literary turf that Patmore was "safe to win"; so Moxon relented from his stern purpose of publishing no verse on his own account, and did publish this[1]—whereat he looks somewhat biliously just now, for the prôneurs and helping hands aforesaid have unaccountably hung back of a sudden, and poor Patmore is, in a manner, *planté là*—only, of course, in the detestable trade sense of the word, for "Lilian" could never be other than a great and—for a man of twenty—wonderful success under any circumstances. The imitation of Tennyson is, rather, a choosing Tennyson's "mode of the lyre," as who should say, hearing a mode was in favor, "I can adopt that, too"; but he will make more and meddle less in good time, it is to be hoped. In society he is all modesty and ingenuousness . . .

[1] *Poems* by Coventry Patmore, Moxon 1844. Moxon published Browning's *Sordello* and *Bells and Pomegranates* (and Elizabeth Barrett's *Poems* 1844) at the author's risk. For Domett see page 697 *n*.

TO THE SAME

23 February 1845.

. . . All you say about my poems greatly pleases me, and should profit. I do my best at all times—and really hope to be doing better already. The literary gossip you are benignant about, I can furnish but scantily—there is nothing doing, or announcing itself as to be done, except Carlyle's *Life of Cromwell*, of which he is going to publish the *prolegomena* in the shape of *Letters and Speeches*, with annotations—for, he says, if he can get people to read *them*, they will save him much trouble in telling them whether they have judged wisely of Cromwell or no. Himself seems to entertain a boundless admiration for the man. I spent this day fortnight's evening with Carlyle, and never remember him more delightful; the intensity of his Radicalism, too, is exquisite. He has a remarkable brother, Dr. C.—physician—whom I know also and who was there—a man like and unlike him.

What did you think of Patmore's little book? Some things were very beautiful—and yet, it seems that while I was away there appeared a brutal paper in *Blackwood*, of the old kind, which had the old almost-fabulous effect—the poor fellow despairs, and the sale of his book stops short, whereat Moxon smiles grimly with a super-*Ossianic* joy of grief, and says calmly, "I published *that* one book at my own risk—when I publish another . . ." The worst is, the *father* of Patmore it is, not himself, these critics want to hurt—he having been the second in a noted duel which ended in the death of Scott, the Editor of the *London Mag.*, about twenty years ago, or more, and probably before the son was born. Patmore, Senior, could have prevented the duel, they say—which is easily said. I wanted to introduce the son to an influential critic at a party one night, and "No," said he, "because of that bloody-minded father"—who stood by, silent in his white cravat, and grateful to me for speaking to "his boy." Are not these things fit to make an apostle swear?

But there have come out some divine things by Miss Barrett . . .

TO ELIZABETH BARRETT BARRETT

[Miss Barrett's *Poems in two volumes* had appeared in August 1844. One of the poems, *Lady Geraldine's Courtship*, contained the lines

> Or at times a modern volume, Wordsworth's solemn-thoughted idyl,
> Howitt's ballad-dew, or Tennyson's enchanted reverie,—
> Or from Browning some "Pomegranate", which, if cut deep down the middle,
> Shows a heart within blood-tinctured, of a veined humanity!

At the instigation of her cousin, John Kenyon, Browning wrote this first letter to her.]

[10 January 1845.][1]

I love your verses with all my heart, dear Miss Barrett,—and this is no off-hand complimentary letter that I shall write,—whatever else, no prompt matter-of-course recognition of your genius, and there a graceful and natural end of the thing. Since the day last week when I first read your poems, I quite laugh to remember how I have been turning and turning again in my mind what I should be able to tell you of their effect upon me, for in the first flush of delight I thought I would this once get out of my habit of purely passive enjoyment, when I do really enjoy, and thoroughly justify my admiration—perhaps even, as a loyal fellow-craftsman should, try and find fault and do you some little good to be proud of hereafter!—but nothing comes of it all—so into me has it gone, and part of me has it become, this great living poetry of yours, not a flower of which but took root and grew—oh, how different that is from lying to be dried and pressed flat and prized highly and put in a book with a proper account at top and bottom, and shut up and put away—and the book called a "Flora," besides! After all, I need not give up the thought of doing that, too, in time; because even now, talking with whoever is worthy, I can give a reason for my faith in one and another excellence, the fresh strange music, the affluent language, the exquisite pathos and true new brave thought; but in this addressing myself to you, your own self, and for the first time, my feeling rises altogether. I do, as I say, love these Books with all my

[1] Browning habitually wrote the day of the week, not the date, at the head of his letters to E. B. B. The dates here given in square brackets are those of the postmarks.

heart. And I love you too: do you know I was once not very far from seeing—really seeing you? Mr. Kenyon said to me one morning "Would you like to see Miss Barrett?" then he went to announce me,—then he returned—you were too unwell, and now it is years ago, and I feel as at some untoward passage in my travels, as if I had been close, so close, to some world's-wonder in chapel or crypt, only a screen to push and I might have entered, but there was some slight, so it now seems, slight and just-sufficient bar to admission, and the half-opened door shut, and I went home my thousands of miles, and the sight was never to be!

Well, these Poems were to be, and this true thankful joy and pride with which I feel myself,

Yours ever faithfully,

ROBERT BROWNING.

TO THE SAME

[11 February 1845.]

Dear Miss Barrett,—People would hardly ever tell falsehoods about a matter, if they had been let tell truth in the beginning, for it is hard to prophane one's very self, and nobody who has, for instance, used certain words and ways to a mother or a father *could*, even if by the devil's help he *would*, reproduce or mimic them with any effect to anybody else that was to be won over—and so, if "I love you" were always outspoken when it might be, there would, I suppose, be no fear of its desecration at any after time. But lo! only last night, I had to write, on the part of Mr. Carlyle, to a certain ungainly, foolish gentleman who keeps back from him, with all the fussy impotence of stupidity (not bad feeling, alas! for *that* we could deal with) a certain MS letter of Cromwell's which completes the collection now going to press; and this long-ears had to be "dear Sir'd and obedient servanted" till I *said* (to use a mild word) "commend me to the sincerities of this kind of thing."! When I spoke of you knowing little of me, one of the senses in which I meant so was this—that I would not well vowel-point my commonplace letters and syllables with a masoretic *other* sound and sense, make my "dear" something intenser than "dears" in ordinary, and "yours ever" a thought more significant than the run of its like. And all this came of your talking of "tiring me," "being too envious," &c. &c., which I should never have heard of had the plain truth looked out of my letter with its unmistakable eyes. *Now*, what you say of the "bowing," and convention that is to be, and *tant de façons* that are not to be, helps me once and for ever—for have I not a right to say simply that, for reasons I know, for other reasons I don't exactly know, but might if I chose to think a little, and for still other reasons, which, most likely, all the choosing and thinking in the world would not make me know, I had rather hear from you than see anybody else. Never you care, dear noble Carlyle, nor you, my own friend Alfred [1] over the sea, nor a troop of true lovers!—Are not their fates written? there! Don't you answer this, please, but, mind it is on record, and now then, with a lighter conscience I shall begin replying to your questions. But then—what I have printed gives *no* knowledge of me—it evidences abilities of various kinds, if you will—and a dramatic sympathy with certain modifications of passion—*that* I think.—But I never have begun, even, what I hope I was born to begin and end—"R. B. a poem"—and next, if I speak (and, God knows, feel), as if what you have read were sadly imperfect demonstrations of even mere ability, it is from no absurd vanity, though it might seem so—these scenes and song-scraps *are* such mere and very escapes of my inner power, which lives in me like the light in those crazy Mediterranean phares I have watched at sea, wherein the light is ever revolving in a dark gallery, bright and alive, and only after a weary interval leaps out, for a moment, from the one narrow chink, and then goes on with the blind wall between it and you; and, no doubt, *then*, precisely, does the poor drudge that carries the cresset set himself most busily to trim the wick—for don't think I want to say I have not worked hard—(this head of mine knows better)—but the work has been *inside*, and not when at stated times I held up my light to you—and, that there is no self-delusion here, I would

[1] Alfred Domett, the "Waring" of Browning's poem of that name and himself a minor poet. He was "over the sea"—in New Zealand—from 1842 to 1871.

prove to you (and nobody else), even by opening this desk I write on, and showing what stuff, in the way of wood, I *could* make a great bonfire with, if I might only knock the whole clumsy top off my tower! Of course, every writing body says the same, so I gain nothing by the avowal; but when I remember how I have done what was published, and half done what may never be, I say with some right, you can know but little of me. Still, I *hope* sometimes, though phrenologists will have it that I *cannot*, and am doing better with this darling *Luria*[1]—so safe in my head, and a tiny slip of paper I cover with my thumb!

Then you inquire about my "sensitiveness to criticism," and I shall be glad to tell you exactly, because I have, more than once, taken a course you might else not understand. I shall live always—that is for me—I am living here this 1845, that is for London. I write from a thorough conviction that it is the duty of me, and with the belief that, after every drawback and shortcoming, I do my best, all things considered—that is for *me*, and, so being, the not being listened to by one human creature would, I hope, in nowise affect me. But of course I must, if for merely scientific purposes, know all about this 1845, its ways and doings, and something I do know, as that for a dozen cabbages, if I pleased to grow them in the garden here, I might demand, say, a dozen pence at Covent Garden Market,—and that for a dozen scenes, of the average goodness, I may challenge as many plaudits at the theatre close by; and a dozen pages of verse, brought to the Rialto where verse-merchants most do congregate, ought to bring me a fair proportion of the Reviewers' gold currency, seeing the other traders pouch their winnings, as I do see. Well, when they won't pay me for my cabbages, nor praise me for my poems, I may, if I please, say "more's the shame," and bid both parties "decamp to the crows," in Greek phrase, and *yet* go very lighthearted back to a garden-full of rose-trees, and a soul-full of comforts. If they had bought my greens I should have been able to buy the last number of *Punch*, and go through the toll-gate of Waterloo Bridge, and give the blind clarionet-player a trifle, and all

[1] Browning's *Luria*, a tragedy in five acts, was not published until April 1846.

without changing my gold. If they had taken to my books, my father and mother would have been proud of this and the other "favourable critique," and—at least so folks hold—I should have to pay Mr. Moxon less by a few pounds, whereas—but you see! Indeed I force myself to say ever and anon, in the interest of the market-gardeners regular, and Keatses proper, "It's nothing to *you*, critics, hucksters, all of you, if I *have* this garden and this conscience—I might go die at Rome, or take to gin and the newspaper, for what *you* would care!" So I don't quite lay open my resources to everybody. But it does so happen, that I have met with much more than I could have expected in this matter of kindly and prompt recognition. I never wanted a real set of good hearty praisers—and no bad reviewers—I am quite content with my share. No—what I laughed at in my "gentle audience" is a sad trick the real admirers have of admiring at the wrong place—enough to make an apostle swear. *That* does make me savage—*never* the other kind of people; why, think now—take your own *Drama of Exile* and let *me* send it to the first twenty men and women that shall knock at your door to-day and after—of whom the first five are the Postman, the seller of cheap sealing-wax, Mr. Hawkins Junr, the Butcher for orders, and the Tax-gatherer—will you let me, by Cornelius Agrippa's assistance, force these five and these fellows to read, and report on, this *Drama*—and, when I have put these faithful reports into fair English, do you believe they would be better than, if as good as, the general run of Periodical criticisms? Not they, I will venture to affirm. But then—once again, I get these people together and give them your book, and persuade them, moreover, that by praising it, the Postman will be helping its author to divide Long Acre into two beats, one of which she will take with half the salary and all the red collar,—that a sealing-wax vendor will see red wafers brought into vogue, and so on with the rest—and won't you just wish for your *Spectators* and *Observers* and Newcastle-upon-Tyne Hebdomadal *Mercuries* back again! You see the inference—I do sincerely esteem it a perfectly providential and miraculous thing that they are so well-behaved in ordinary, these critics; and for Keats and Tennyson to "go softly all their days" for a gruff word or two is quite inexplicable to me, and always has been. Tennyson reads the *Quarterly* and does as they bid him, with the most solemn face in the world—out goes this, in goes that, all is changed and ranged. Oh me!

Out comes the sun, in comes the *Times* and eleven strikes (it *does*) already, and I have to go to Town, and I have no alternative but that this story of the Critic and Poet, "the Bear and the Fiddle," should "begin but break off in the middle"; yet I doubt—nor will you henceforth, I know, say, "I vex you, I am sure, by this lengthy writing." Mind that spring is coming, for all this snow; and know me for yours ever faithfully,

R. BROWNING.

TO THE SAME

[26 February 1845.]

. . . I know Tennyson "face to face,"—no more than that. I know Carlyle and love him—know him so well, that I would have told you had he shaken that grand head of his at "singing," so thoroughly does he love and live by it. When I last saw him, a fortnight ago, he turned, from I don't know what other talk, quite abruptly on me with, "Did you never try to write a *Song*? Of all things in the world, *that* I should be proudest to do." Then came his definition of a song—then, with an appealing look to Mrs. C., "I always say that some day in *spite of nature and my stars*, I shall burst into a song" (he is not mechanically "musical," he meant, and the music is the poetry, he holds, and should enwrap the thought as Donne says "an amber-drop enwraps a bee"), and then he began to recite an old Scotch song, stopping at the first rude couplet, "The beginning words are merely to set the tune, they tell me"—and then again at the couplet about —or, to the effect that—"give me" (but in broad Scotch) "give me but my lass, I care not for my cogie." "*He says*," quoth Carlyle magisterially, "that if you allow him the love of his lass, you may take away all else, even his cogie, his cup or can, and he cares not," just as a professor expounds Lycophron. And just before I left England, six months ago, did not I hear him croon, if not certainly sing, "Charlie is my darling" ("my *darling*" with an adoring emphasis), and then he stood back, as it were, from the song, to look at it better, and said "How must that notion of ideal wondrous perfection have impressed itself in this old Jacobite's 'young Cavalier'—('They go to save their land, and the *young Cavalier*!!')—when I who care nothing about such a rag of a man, cannot but feel as he felt, in speaking his words after him!" After saying which, he would be sure to counsel everybody to get their heads clear of all singing! . . .

And when I have said I like *Pippa* better than anything else I have done yet, I shall have answered all you bade me. And now may *I* begin questioning? No,—for it is all a pure delight to me, so that you do but write. I never was without good, kind, generous friends and lovers, so they say—so they were and are,—perhaps they came at the wrong time—I never wanted them—though that makes no difference in my gratitude I trust, but I know myself—surely—and always have done so, for is there not somewhere the little book [1] I first printed when a boy, with John Mill, the metaphysical head, *his* marginal note that "the writer possesses a deeper self-consciousness than I ever knew in a sane human being." So I never deceived myself much, nor called my feelings for people other than they were. And who has a right to say, if I have not, that I had, but I said that, supernatural or no. Pray tell me, too, of your present doings and projects, and never write yourself "grateful" to me, who *am* grateful, very grateful to you,—for none of your words but I take in earnest —and tell me if spring *be not* coming, come, and I will take to writing the gravest of letters, because this beginning is for gladness' sake, like Carlyle's song couplet. . . .

TO THE SAME

[On 20 May 1845 Browning met Elizabeth Barrett for the first time, in her father's house, 50 Wimpole Street. A day or two later he wrote a letter which drew from her this reply:

"I intended to write to you last night and this morning, and could not,—you do not know what pain you give me in speaking so wildly.

[1] *Pauline.* The copy containing Mill's criticisms and some comments by Browning is in the Forster collection in the Victoria and Albert Museum.

And if I disobey you, my dear friend, in speaking (I for my part) of your wild speaking, I do it, not to displease you, but to be in my own eyes, and before God, a little more worthy, or less unworthy, of a generosity from which I recoil by instinct and at the first glance, yet conclusively; and because my silence would be the most disloyal of all means of expression, in reference to it. Listen to me then in this. You have said some intemperate things—fancies,—which you will not say over again, nor unsay, but *forget at once*, and *for ever*, *having said at all*; and which (so) will die out between *you and me alone*, like a misprint between you and the printer. And this you will do *for my sake* who am your friend (and you have none truer)—and this I ask, because it is a condition necessary to our future liberty of intercourse. You remember—surely you do—that I am in the most exceptional of positions; and that, just *because of it*, I am able to receive you as I did on Tuesday; and that, for me to listen to 'unconscious exaggerations,' is as unbecoming to the humilities of my position, as unpropitious (which is of more consequence) to the prosperities of yours. Now, if there should be one word of answer attempted to this; or of reference; *I must not*—I *will not see you again*—and you will justify me later in your heart. . . ."

The offending letter was returned to Browning (as requested in the postscript to the letter printed below) and destroyed by him. It was the only one of the series not preserved.]

[24 May 1845.]

Don't you remember I told you, once on a time, that you "knew nothing of me"? whereat you demurred—but I meant what I said, and knew it was so. To be grand in a simile, for every poor speck of a Vesuvius or a Stromboli in my microcosm there are huge layers of ice and pits of black cold water—and I make the most of my two or three fire-eyes, because I know by experience, alas, how these tend to extinction—and the ice grows and grows—still this last is true part of me, most characteristic part, *best* part perhaps, and I disown nothing—only,—when you talked of "*knowing* me"! Still, I am [so] utterly unused, of these late years particularly, to dream of communicating anything about *that* to another person (all my writings are purely dramatic as I am always anxious to say) that when I make never so little an attempt, no wonder if I *bungle* notably—"language," too, is an organ that never studded this heavy heavy head of mine. Will you not think me very brutal if I tell you I could almost smile at your misapprehension of what I meant to write?—Yet I *will* tell you, because it will undo the bad effect of my thoughtlessness, and at the same time exemplify the point I have all along been honestly earnest to set you right upon—my real inferiority to you;

just that and no more. I wrote to you, in an unwise moment, on the spur of being again "thanked," and, unwisely writing just as if thinking to myself, said what must have looked absurd enough as seen apart from the horrible counter-balancing never-to-be-written *rest of me*—by the side of which, could it be written and put before you, my note would sink to its proper and relative place, and become a mere "thank you" for your good opinion—which I assure you is far too generous—for I really believe you to be my superior in many respects, and feel uncomfortable till *you* see that, too—since I hope for your sympathy and assistance, and frankness is everything in such a case. I do assure you, that had you read my note, *only* having "*known*" so much of me as is implied in having inspected, for instance, the contents, merely, of that fatal and often-referred-to "portfolio" there (*Dii meliora piis*!), you would see in it (the note not the portfolio) the blandest utterance ever mild gentleman gave birth to. But I forgot that one may make too much noise in a silent place by playing the few notes on the "ear-piercing fife" which in Othello's regimental band might have been thumped into decent subordination by his "spirit-stirring drum"—to say nothing of gong and ophicleide.

Will you forgive me, on promise to remember for the future, and be more considerate? Not that you must too much despise me, neither; nor, of all things, apprehend I am attitudinizing à la Byron, and giving you to understand unutterable somethings, longings for Lethe and all that—far from it! I never committed murders, and sleep the soundest of sleeps—but "the heart is desperately wicked," that is true, and though I dare not say "I know" mine, yet I have had signal opportunities, I who began life from the beginning, and can forget nothing (but names, and the date of the battle of Waterloo), and have known good and wicked men and women, gentle and simple, shaking hands with Edmund Kean and Father Mathew, you and—Ottima [1]! Then, I had a certain faculty of self-consciousness, years and years ago, at which John Mill wondered, and which ought

[1] Ottima, in *Pippa Passes,* murders her husband with the help of her lover.

to be improved by this time, if constant use helps at all—and, meaning, on the whole, to be a Poet, if not *the* Poet—for I am vain and ambitious some nights,—I do myself justice, and dare call things by their names to myself, and say boldly, this I love, this I hate, this I would do, this I would not do, under all kinds of circumstances,—and talking (thinking) in this style *to myself*, and beginning, however tremblingly, in spite of conviction, to write in this style *for myself*—on the top of the desk which contains my "Songs of the Poets—NO. 1 M.P.",[1] I wrote,—what you now forgive, I know! Because I am, from my heart, sorry that by a foolish fit of inconsideration I should have given pain for a minute to you, towards whom, on every account, I would rather soften and "sleeken every word as to a bird" (and, not such a bird as my black self that go screeching about the world for "dead horse"—corvus (picus)—mirandola!) I, too, who have been at such pains to acquire the reputation I enjoy in the world,—(ask Mr. Kenyon,) and who dine, and wine, and dance and enhance the company's pleasure till they make me ill and I keep house, as of late: Mr. Kenyon, (for I only quote where you may verify if you please) *he* says my common sense strikes him, and its contrast with my muddy metaphysical poetry! And so it shall strike you—for though I am glad that, since you *did* misunderstand me, you said so, and have given me an opportunity of doing by another way what I wished to do in *that*,—yet, if you had *not* alluded to my writing, as I meant you should not, you would have certainly understood *something* of its drift when you found me next Tuesday precisely the same quiet (no, for I feel I speak too loudly, in spite of your kind disclaimer, but—) the same mild man-about-town you were gracious to, the other morning—for, indeed, my own way of worldly life is marked out long ago, as precisely as yours can be, and I am set going with a hand, winker-wise, on each side of my head, and a directing finger before my eyes, to say nothing of an instinctive dread I have

[1] *M.P.*—Perhaps either *My Poem*, the "R. B. a poem" of page 697 *supra* and the "my own Poem" of a letter of 14 June; or *My Poet* = E. B. B., to whom on 30 April Browning had written "I think I will really write verse to you some day," and whom in a later letter (4 August) he addressed as "my poet" in quotation marks.

that a certain whip-lash is vibrating somewhere in the neighbourhood in playful readiness! So "I hope here be proofs," Dogberry's satisfaction, that, first, I am but a very poor creature compared to you and entitled by my wants to look up to you,—all I meant to say from the first of the first—and that, next, I shall be too much punished if, for this piece of mere inconsideration, you deprive me, more or less, or sooner or later, of the pleasure of seeing you,—a little over boisterous gratitude for which, perhaps, caused all the mischief!

The reasons you give for deferring my visits next week are too cogent for me to dispute—that is too true—and, being now and henceforward "on my good behaviour," I will at once cheerfully submit to them, if needs must—but should your mere kindness and forethought, as I half suspect, have induced you to take such a step, you will now smile, with me, at this new and very unnecessary addition to the "fears of me" I have got so triumphantly over in your case! Wise man, was I not, to clench my first favourable impression so adroitly—like a recent Cambridge worthy, my sister heard of; who, being on his theological (or rather, scripture-historical) examination, was asked by the Tutor, who wished to let him off easily, "who was the first King of Israel?"—"Saul" answered the trembling youth. "Good!" nodded approvingly the Tutor. "Otherwise called *Paul*," subjoined the youth in his elation! Now I have begged pardon, and blushingly assured you *that* was only a slip of the tongue, and that I did really *mean* all the while (Paul or no Paul) the veritable son of Kish, he that owned the asses, and found listening to the harp the best of all things for an evil spirit! Pray write me a line to say, "Oh—if *that's* all!" and remember me for good (which is very compatible with a moment's stupidity) and let me not for one fault, (and that the only one that shall be), lose *any pleasure*—for your friendship I am sure I have not lost—God bless you, my dear friend!

R. BROWNING.

And by the way, will it not be better, as co-operating with you more effectually in your kind promise to forget the "printer's error" in my blotted proof, to send me back that same "proof," if you have not inflicted proper and summary justice on it? When Mephistopheles last came to see us in this world outside here, he counselled sundry of us "never to write a letter,—and never to burn one"—do you know that? But I never mind what I am told! Seriously, I am ashamed. I shall next ask a servant for my paste in the "high fantastical" style of my own *Luria*.

TO THE SAME

[Miss Barrett had described "a storm of storms" that she had witnessed in her childhood, when a tree had been peeled bare by lightning, "and up that new whiteness of it ran the finger-mark of the lightning in a bright beautiful rose-colour." The poem to which Browning refers towards the end of this letter is *The Flight of the Duchess*.]

[14 July 1845.]

. . . What a grand sight your tree was—*is*, for I see it. My father has a print of a tree so struck—torn to ribbons, as you describe—but the rose-mark is striking and new to me. We had a good storm on our last voyage, but I went to bed at the end, as I thought—and only found there had been lightning next day by the bare poles under which we were riding: but the finest mountain fit of the kind I ever saw has an unfortunately ludicrous association. It was at Possagno, among the Euganean Hills, and I was at a poor house in the town—an old woman was before a little picture of the Virgin, and at every fresh clap she lighted, with the oddest sputtering muttering mouthful of prayer imaginable, an inch of guttery candle, which, the instant the last echo had rolled away, she as constantly blew out again for saving's sake—having, of course, to *light the smoke* of it, about an instant after that: the expenditure in wax at which the elements might be propitiated, you see, was a matter for curious calculation. I suppose I ought to have bought the whole taper for some four or five centesimi (100 of which make 8*d.* English) and so kept the countryside safe for about a century of bad weather. Leigh Hunt tells you a story he had from Byron, of kindred philosophy in a Jew who was surprised by a thunderstorm while he was dining on bacon—he tried to eat between-whiles, but the flashes were as pertinacious as he, so at last he pushed his plate away, just remarking with a compassionate shrug, "all this fuss about a piece of pork!"

By the way, what a characteristic of an Italian *late* evening is summer-lightning—it hangs in broad slow sheets, dropping from cloud to cloud, so long in dropping and dying off. The "bora," which you only get at Trieste, brings wonderful lightning—you are in glorious June-weather, fancy, of an evening, under green shock-headed acacias, so thick and green, with the cicalas stunning you above, and all about you men, women, rich and poor, sitting, standing and coming and going—and through all the laughter and screaming and singing, the loud clink of the spoons against the glasses, the way of calling for fresh "sorbetti"—for all the world is at open-coffee-house at such an hour—when suddenly there is a stop in the sunshine, a blackness drops down, then a great white column of dust drives straight on like a wedge, and you see the acacia heads snap off, now one, then another—and all the people scream "la bora, la bora!" and you are caught up in their whirl and landed in some interior, the man with the guitar on one side of you, and the boy with a cageful of little brown owls for sale, on the other—meanwhile, the thunder claps, claps, with such a persistence, and the rain, for a finale, falls in a mass, as if you had knocked out the whole bottom of a huge tank at once—then there is a second stop—out comes the sun—somebody clinks at his glass, all the world bursts out laughing, and prepares to pour out again,—but *you*, the stranger, *do* make the best of your way out, with no preparation at all; whereupon you infallibly put your foot (and half your leg) into a river, really that, of rainwater—that's a *Bora* (and that comment of yours, a justifiable pun!)

Such things you get in Italy, but better, better, the best of all things—you do not (*I* do not) get those. And I shall see you on Wednesday, please remember, and bring you the rest of the poem—that you should like it, gratifies me more than I will try to say, but then, do not you be tempted by that pleasure of pleasing which I think is your besetting sin—may it not be?—and so cut me off from the other pleasure of being profited. As I told you, I like so much to fancy that you see, and will see, what I do as *I* see it, while it is doing, as nobody else in the world should, certainly, even if they thought it worth while to want—but when I try and build a great building I shall want you to come with me and judge it and counsel me before the scaffolding is taken down, and while you have to make your way over hods and mortar and heaps of lime, and trembling tubs of size, and those thin broad whitewashing brushes I always had a desire to take up and bespatter with. And now goodbye—I am to see you on Wednesday I trust—and to hear you say you are better, still better, much better? God grant that, and all else good for you, dear friend, and so for R. B.

ever yours.

TO THE SAME

[Browning had confessed himself unable to distinguish Miss Barrett's sisters, Henrietta and Arabel: she had therefore sent him two descriptive sonnets, written in competition with her brother Alfred's pencil-drawings of them. She had also enclosed a letter from her brother George in which she was addressed by her family nickname, "Ba".

Miss Barrett, having been recommended by her doctor to winter in Pisa (a plan later vetoed by her father), had been reading, and had lent to Browning, Mary Shelley's *Rambles in Germany and Italy*, 1844. Mary Shelley had travelled with Samuel Rogers' *Italy* and Alexis François Rio's *De la Poésie chrétienne* (a work of art criticism).]

[11 September 1845.]

Here are your beautiful, and I am sure *true* sonnets; they look true—I remember the light hair, I find. And who paints, and dares exhibit, E. B. B.'s self? And surely "Alfred's" pencil has not foregone its best privilege, not left *the* face unsketched? Italians call such an "effect defective"—"l'andar a Roma senza vedere il Papa." He must have begun by seeing his Holiness, I know, and—*he* will not trust me with the result, that my sister may copy it for me, because we are strangers, he and I, and I could give him nothing, nothing like the proper price for it—but *you* would lend it to me, I think, nor need I do more than thank you in my usual effective and very eloquent way—for I have already been allowed to visit you seventeen times, do you know; and this last letter of yours, fiftieth is the same! So all my pride is gone, pride in that sense—and I mean to take of you for ever, and reconcile myself with my lot in this life. Could, and would, you give me such a sketch? It has been on my mind to ask you ever since I knew you if nothing in the way of *good* portrait existed—and this occasion bids me speak out, I dare believe: the more, that you have also quieted—have you not?—another old obstinate and very likely impertinent questioning of mine—as to the little name which was neither Orinda, nor Sacharissa (for which thank providence) and is never to appear in books, though you write them. Now I know it and write it—"Ba"—and thank you, and your brother George, and only burned his kind letter because you bade me who know best. So, wish by wish, one gets one's wishes—at least I do—for one instance, you will go to Italy . . .

Don't expect Neapolitan Scenery at Pisa, quite in the North, remember. Mrs. Shelley found Italy for the first time, real Italy, at Sorrento, she says. Oh that book—does one wake or sleep? The "Mary dear" with the brown eyes, and Godwin's daughter and Shelley's wife, and who surely was something better once upon a time—and to go through Rome and Florence and the rest, after what I suppose to be Lady Londonderry's fashion: the intrepidity of the commonplace quite astounds me. And then that way, when she and the like of her are put in a new place, with new flowers, new stones, faces, walls, all new—of looking wisely up at the sun, clouds, evening star, or mountain top and wisely saying "who shall describe *that* sight!"—Not *you*, we very well see—but why don't you tell us that at Rome they eat roasted chestnuts, and put the shells into their aprons, the women do, and calmly empty the whole on the heads of the passengers in the street below; and that at Padua when a man drives his waggon up to a house and stops, all the mouse-coloured oxen that pull it from a beam against their foreheads sit down in a heap and rest. But once she travelled the country with Shelley on arm; now she plods it, Rogers in hand—to such things and uses may we come at last! Her remarks on art, once she lets go of Rio's skirts, are amazing—Fra Angelico, for instance, only painted Martyrs, Virgins &c., she had no eyes for the divine *bon-bourgeoisie* of his pictures; the dear common folk of his crowds, those who sit and listen (spectacle at nose and bent into a comfortable heap to hear better) at the sermon of the Saint—and the children, and women,—divinely pure they all are, but fresh from the streets and market place—but she is wrong every where, that is, not right, not seeing what is to see, speaking what one expects to hear—I quarrel with her, for ever, I think. . . .

TO THE SAME

[13 September 1845.]

Now, dearest, I will try and write the little I shall be able, in reply to your letter of last week—and first of all I have to entreat you, now more than ever, to help me and understand from the few words the feelings behind them—(I should *speak* rather more easily, I think—but I dare not run the risk: and I know, after all, you will be just and kind where you can.) I have read your letter again and again. I will tell you—no, not *you*, but any imaginary other person, who should hear what I am going to avow; I would tell that person most sincerely there is not a particle of fatuity, shall I call it, in that avowal; cannot be, seeing that from the beginning and at this moment I never dreamed of winning your *love*. I can hardly write this word, so incongruous and impossible does it seem; such a change of our places does it imply—nor, next to that, though long after, *would* I, if I *could*, supplant one of any of the affections that I know to have taken root in you—*that* great and solemn one, for instance. I feel that if I could get myself *remade*, as if turned gold, I WOULD not even then desire to become more than the mere setting to *that* diamond you must always wear. The regard and esteem you now give me, in this letter, and which I press to my heart and bow my head upon, is all I can take and all too embarrassing, using *all* my gratitude. And yet, with that contented pride in being infinitely your debtor as it is, bound to you for ever as it is; when I read your letter with all the determination to be just to us both; I dare not so far withstand the light I am master of, as to refuse seeing that whatever is recorded as an objection to your disposing of that life of mine I would give you, has reference to some supposed good in that life which your accepting it would destroy (of which fancy I shall speak presently)—I say, wonder as I may at this, I cannot but find it there, surely there. I could no more "bind *you* by words," than you have bound me, as you say—but if I misunderstand you, one assurance to that effect will be but too intelligible to me—but, as it *is*, I have difficulty in imagining that while one of so many reasons, which I am not obliged to repeat to myself, but which any one easily conceives; while *any one* of those reasons would impose silence on me *for ever* (for, as I observed, I love you as you now are, and *would* not remove one affection that is already part of you,) —*would* you, being able to speak *so*, only say *that you* desire not to put "more sadness than I was born to," into my life? —that you "could give me only what it were ungenerous to give"?

Have I your meaning here? In so many words, is it on my account that you bid me "leave this subject"? I think if it were so, I would for once call my advantages round me. I am not what your generous self-forgetting appreciation would sometimes make me out—but it is not since yesterday, nor ten nor twenty years before, that I began to look into my own life, and study its end, and requirements, what would turn to its good or its loss—and I *know*, if one may know anything, that to make that life yours and increase it by union with yours, would render me *supremely happy*, as I said, and say, and feel. My whole suit to you is, in that sense, *selfish*—not that I am ignorant that *your* nature would most surely attain happiness in being conscious that it made another happy—but *that best, best end of all*, would, like the rest, come from yourself, be a reflection of your own gift.

Dearest, I will end here—words, persuasion, arguments, if they were at my service I would not use them—I believe in you, altogether have faith in you—in you. I will not think of insulting by trying to reassure you on one point which certain phrases in your letter might at first glance seem to imply—you do not understand me to be living and labouring and writing (and *not* writing) in order to be successful in the world's sense? I even convinced the people *here* what was my true "honourable position in society," &c. &c. therefore I shall not have to inform *you* that I desire to be very rich, very great; but not in reading Law gratis with dear foolish old Basil Montagu, as he ever and anon bothers me to do;—much less—enough of this nonsense.

"Tell me what I have a claim to hear": I can hear it, and be as grateful as I was before and am now—your friendship is my pride and happiness. If you told me your love was bestowed elsewhere, and that it was in my power to serve you *there*, to serve you there would still be my pride and happiness. I look on and on over the prospect of my love, it is all *on*wards—and all possible forms of unkindness—I quite laugh to think how they are *behind*—cannot be encountered in the route we are travelling! I submit to you and will obey you implicitly—obey what I am able to conceive of your least desire, much more of your expressed wish. But it was necessary to make this avowal, among other reasons, for one which the world would recognize too. My whole scheme of life (with its wants, material wants at least, closely cut down) was long ago calculated—and it supposed *you*, the finding such an one as you, utterly impossible—because in calculating one goes upon *chances*, not on providence—how could I expect you? So for my own future way in the world I have always refused to care—any one who can live a couple of years and more on bread and potatoes, as I did once on a time, and who prefers a blouse and a blue shirt (such as I now write in) to all manner of dress and gentlemanly appointment, and who can, if necessary, groom a horse not so badly, or at all events would rather do it all day long than succeed Mr. Fitzroy Kelly in the Solicitor-Generalship,—such an one need not very much concern himself beyond considering the lilies how they grow. But now I see you near this life, all changes—and at a word, I will do all that ought to be done, that every one used to say could be done, and let "all my powers find sweet employ" as Dr. Watts sings, in getting whatever is to be got—not very much, surely. I would print these things, get them away, and do this now, and go to you at Pisa with the news—at Pisa where one may live for some £100 a year—while, lo, I seem to remember, I *do* remember, that Charles Kean offered to give me 500 of those pounds for any play that might suit him—to say nothing of Mr. Colburn saying confidentially that he wanted more than his dinner "a novel on the subject of *Napoleon*"! So may one make money, if one does not live in a house in a row, and feel impelled to take the Princess's Theatre for a laudable development and exhibition of one's faculty.

Take the sense of all this, I beseech you, dearest—all you shall say will be best—I am yours—

Yes, Yours ever. God bless you for all you have been, and are, and will certainly be to me, come what He shall please!

R. B.

TO THE SAME

[18 September 1845.]

. . . I desire in this life (with very little fluctuation for a man and too weak a one) to live and just write out certain things which are in me, and so save my soul. I would endeavour to do this if I were forced to "live among lions" as you once said—but I should best do this if I lived quietly with myself and with you. That you cannot dance like Cerito does not materially disarrange this plan—nor that I might (beside the perpetual incentive and sustainment and consolation) get, over and above the main reward, the incidental, particular and unexpected happiness of being allowed when not working to rather occupy myself with watching you, than with certain other pursuits I might be otherwise addicted to—*this*, also, does not constitute an obstacle, as I see obstacles.

But *you* see them—and I see *you*, and know my first duty and do it resolutely if not cheerfully.

As for referring again, till leave by word or letter—you will see . . .

TO THE SAME

[23 October 1845.]

. . . I love you because I *love* you; I see you "once a week" because I cannot see you all day long; I think of you all day long, because I most certainly could not think of you once an hour less, if I tried, or went to Pisa, or "abroad" (in every sense) in order to "be happy"—a kind of adventure which you seem to suppose you have in some way interfered with. Do, for this once, think, and never after, on the impossibility of your ever (you know I must talk your own language, so I shall say—) hindering any scheme of mine, stopping any supposable advancement of mine. Do you really think that before I found you, I was going about the world seeking whom I might devour, that is, be devoured by, in the shape of a wife—do you suppose I ever dreamed of marrying? . . .

TO THE SAME

[17 January 1846.]

Did my own Ba, in the prosecution of her studies, get to a book on the forb—no, *un*forbidden shelf—wherein Voltaire pleases to say that "si Dieu n'existait pas, il faudrait l'inventer"? I feel, after reading these letters,—as ordinarily after seeing you, sweetest, or hearing from you,—that if *marriage* did not exist, I should infallibly *invent* it. I should say, no words, no *feelings* even, do justice to the whole conviction and *religion* of my soul—and though they may be suffered to represent some one minute's phase of it, yet, in their very fulness and passion they do injustice to the *unrepresented, other minutes'*, depth and breadth of love—which let my whole life (I would say) be devoted to telling and proving and exemplifying, if not in one, then in another way—let me have the plain palpable power of this; the assured time for this—something of the satisfaction (but for the fantasticalness of the illustration)—something like the earnestness of some suitor in Chancery if he could once get Lord Lyndhurst into a room with him, and lock the door on them both, and know that his whole story *must* be listened to now, and the "rights of it,"—dearest, the love unspoken now you are to hear "in all time of our tribulation, in all time of our wealth, at the hour of death, and"—

If I did not *know* this was so,—nothing would have been said, or sought for. Your friendship, the perfect pride in it, the wish for, and eager co-operation in, your welfare, all that is different, and, seen now, nothing.

I will care for it no more, dearest—I am wedded to you now. I believe no human being could love you more—that thought consoles me for my own imperfection—for when *that* does strike me, as so often it will, I turn round on my pursuing self, and ask "What if it were a claim then, what is in Her, demanded rationally, equitably, in return for what were in you—do you like *that* way!"—And I do *not*, Ba—you, even, might not—when people everyday buy improveable ground, and eligible sites for building, and don't want every inch filled up, covered over, done to their hands! So take me, and make me what you can and will—and though never to be *more* yours, yet more *like* you, I may and must be—Yes, indeed—best, only love! . . .

TO THE SAME

[Returning a letter of Harriet Martineau's]

[16 February 1846.]

Here is the letter again, dearest: I suppose it gives me the same pleasure, in reading, as you—and Mr. K[enyon] as me, and anybody else as him; if all the correspondence which was claimed again and burnt on some principle or other some years ago be at all of the nature of this sample, the measure seems questionable. Burn anybody's *real* letters, well and good: they move and live—the thoughts, feelings, and expressions even,—in a self-imposed circle limiting the experience of two persons only—*there* is the standard, and to *that* the appeal—how should a third person know? His presence breaks the line, so to speak, and lets in a whole tract of country on the originally inclosed spot—so that its trees, which were from side to side there, seem left alone and wondering at their sudden unimportance in the broad land; while its "ferns such as I never saw before" and which have been petted proportionably, look extravagant enough amid the new spread of good honest grey grass that is now the earth's general wear. So that the significance is lost at once, and whole value of such letters—the cypher changed, the vowel-points removed: but how can that affect clever writing like this? What do you, to whom it is addressed, see in it more than the world that wants to see it and shan't have it? One understands shutting an unprivileged eye to the ineffable mysteries of those "upper-rooms," now that the broom and dust pan, stocking-mending and gingerbread-making are invested with such unforeseen reverence; but the carriage-sweep and quarry, together with Jane and our baskets, and a pleasant shadow of Wordsworth's Sunday hat preceding his own rapid strides in the direction of Miss Fenwick's house—surely, "men's eyes were made to see, so let them gaze" at all *this*! And so I, gazing with a clear conscience, am very glad to hear so much good of a very good person and so well told. She plainly sees the proper use and advantage of a country-life; and *that* knowledge gets to seem a high point of attainment doubtless by the side of the Wordsworth she speaks of—for *mine* he shall not be as long as I am able! Was ever such a "*great*" poet before? Put one trait with the other—the theory of rural innocence—alternation of "vulgar trifles" with dissertating with style of "the utmost grandeur that *even you* can conceive" (speak for yourself, Miss M.!)—and that amiable transition from two o'clock's grief at the death of one's brother to three o'clock's happiness in the "extraordinary mesmeric discourse" of one's friend. All this, and the rest of the serene and happy inspired daily life which a piece of "unpunctuality" can ruin, and to which the guardian "angel" brings as crowning qualification the knack of poking the fire adroitly—of this—what can one say but that—no, best hold one's tongue and read the *Lyrical Ballads* with finger in ear. Did not Shelley say long ago "He had no more *imagination* than a pint-pot"—though in those days he used to walk about France and Flanders like a man? *Now*, he is "most comfortable in his worldly affairs" and just this comes of it! He lives the best twenty years of his life after the way of his own heart—and when one presses in to see the result of the rare experiment—what the *one* alchemist whom fortune has allowed to get all his coveted materials and set to work at last in earnest with fire and melting-pot—what *he* produces after all the talk of him and the like of him; why, you get *pulvis et cinis*—a man at the mercy of the tongs and shovel!

Well! Let us despair at nothing, but, wishing success to

the newer aspirant, expect better things from Miss M. when the "knoll," and "paradise," and their facilities, operate properly; and that she will make a truer estimate of the importance and responsibilities of "authorship" than she does at present, if I understand rightly the sense in which she describes her own life as it means to be; for in one sense it is all good and well, and quite natural that she should like "that sort of strenuous handwork" better than book-making; like the play better than the labour, as we are apt to do. If she realises a very ordinary scheme of literary life, planned under the eye of God not "the public," and prosecuted under the constant sense of the night's coming which ends it good or bad—then, she will be sure to "like" the rest and sport—teaching her maids and sewing her gloves and making delicate visitors comfortable—so much more rational a resource is the worst of them than gin-and-water, for instance. But if, as I rather suspect, these latter are to figure as a virtual *half* duty of the whole Man—as of equal importance (on the ground of the innocence and utility of such occupations) with the book-making aforesaid—always supposing *that* to be of the right kind—*then* I respect Miss M. just as I should an Archbishop of Canterbury whose business was the teaching A.B.C. at an infant-school—he who might set on the Tens to instruct the Hundreds how to convince the Thousands of the propriety of doing that and many other things. Of course one will respect him only the more if when *that* matter is off his mind he relaxes at such a school instead of over a chess-board; as it will increase our love for Miss M. to find that making "my good Jane (from Tyne-mouth)"—"happier and—I hope—wiser" is an amusement, or more, after the day's progress towards the "novel for next year" which is to inspire thousands, beyond computation, with the ardour of making innumerable other Janes and delicate relatives happier and wiser—who knows but as many as Burns did, and does, so make happier and wiser? Only, *his quarry* and after-solace was that "marble bowl often replenished with whiskey" on which Dr. Curry discourses mournfully. "Oh, be wiser Thou!"—and remember it was only *after* Lord Bacon had written to an end *his* Book—given us for ever the Art of Inventing—whether steam-engine or improved dust-pan—that he took on himself to do a little exemplary "hand work"; got out on that cold St. Alban's road to stuff a fowl with snow and so keep it fresh, and got into his bed and died of the cold in his hands ("strenuous *hand* work"—) before the snow had time to melt. He did not begin in his youth by saying—"I have a horror of merely writing 'Novum Organums' and shall give half my energies to the stuffing fowls"!

All this it is *my* amusement, of an indifferent kind, to put down solely on the pleasant assurance contained in that postscript, of the one way of never quarrelling with Miss M. —"by joining in her plan and practice of plain speaking"—could she but "get people to do it!" Well, she gets me for a beginner. . . .

TO THE SAME

[19 February 1846.]

. . . One thing vexed me in your letter—I will tell you, the praise of *my* letters. Now, one merit they have—in language mystical—that of having *no* merit. If I caught myself trying to write finely, graphically &c. &c., nay, if I found myself conscious of having, in my own opinion, so written, all would be over! yes, over! I should be respecting you inordinately, paying a proper tribute to your genius, summoning the necessary collectedness,—plenty of all that! But the feeling with which I write to you, not knowing that it is writing,—with *you*, face and mouth and hair and eyes opposite me, touching me, knowing that all *is* as I say, and helping out the imperfect phrases from your own intuition—*that* would be gone—and *what* in its place? "Let us eat and drink for to-morrow we write to Ambleside[1]." No, no, love, nor can it ever be so, nor should it ever be so if—even if, preserving all that intimate relation, with the carelessness, *still*, somehow, was obtained, with no effort in the world, graphic writing and philosophic and what you please—for I *will* be—*would* be, better than my works and words with an infinite stock beyond what I put into convenient circulation

[1] Miss Martineau's home.

whether in fine speeches fit to remember, or fine passages to quote. For the rest, I had meant to tell you before now, that you often put me "in a maze" when you particularize letters of mine—"such an one was kind" &c. I know, sometimes I seem to give the matter up in despair, I take out paper and fall thinking on you, and bless you with my whole heart and then begin: "What a fine day this is!" I distinctly remember having done that repeatedly—but the converse is not true by any means, that (when the expression may happen to fall more consentaneously to the mind's motion) that less is felt, oh no! But the particular thought at the time has not been of the *insufficiency* of expression, as in the other instance. . . .

TO THE SAME

[E. B. B. had written, concerning her father: "Dearest, it was plain to see yesterday evening when he came into this room for a moment at seven o'clock, before going to his own to dress for dinner—plain to see, that he was not altogether pleased at finding you here in the morning. There was no pretext for objecting gravely—but it was plain that he was not pleased. Do not let this make you uncomfortable, he will forget all about it, and I was not *scolded*, do you understand. It was more manner, but my sisters thought as I did of the significance:—and it was enough to prove to me (if I had not known) what a desperate game we should be playing if we depended on a yielding nerve *there*."]

[3 March 1846.]

. . . You tell me what was observed in the "moment's" visit; by you, and (after, I suppose) by your sisters. First, I *will* always see with your eyes *there*—next, what I see I will *never* speak, if it pain you; but just this much truth I ought to say, I think. I always give myself to you for the worst I am,—full of faults as you will find, if you have not found them. But I *will* not affect to be so bad, so wicked, as I count wickedness, as to call that conduct other than intolerable—*there*, in my conviction of *that*, is your real "security" and mine for the future as the present. That a father choosing to give out of his whole day some five minutes to a daughter, supposed to be prevented from participating in what he, probably, in common with the whole world of sensible men, as distinguished from poets and dreamers, considers *every* pleasure of life, by a complete foregoing of society—that he, after the Pisa business and the enforced continuance and, as he must believe, permanence of this state in which any other human being would go mad—I do dare say, for the justification of God, who gave the mind to be *used* in this world,—where it saves us, we are taught, or destroys us,—and not to be sunk quietly, overlooked, and forgotten; that, under these circumstances, finding—what, you say, unless he thinks he *does* find, he would close the door of his house instantly—a mere sympathizing man, of the same literary tastes, who comes good-naturedly, on a proper and unexceptionable introduction, to chat with and amuse a little that invalid daughter, once a month, so far as is known, for an hour perhaps,—that such a father should show himself "*not pleased* plainly," at such a circumstance—my Ba, it is SHOCKING! See, I go *wholly* on the supposition that the real relation is not imagined to exist between us. I so completely could understand a repugnance to trust you to me were the truth known, that, I will confess, I have several times been afraid the very reverse of this occurrence would befall; that your father would have at some time or other thought himself obliged, by the usual feeling of people in such cases, to see me for a few minutes and express some commonplace thanks after the customary mode (just as Capt. Domett sent a heap of unnecessary thanks to me not long ago for sending now a letter now a book to his son in New Zealand—keeping up the spirits of poor dear Alfred now he is cut off from the world at large)—and if *this* had been done, I shall not deny that my heart would have accused me—unreasonably I *know* but still, suppression, and reserve, and apprehension—the whole of *that is* horrible always! But this way of looking on the endeavour of anybody, however humble, to just preserve your life, remedy in some degree the first, if it *was* the first, unjustifiable measure,—this being "displeased"—is exactly what I did *not* calculate upon. Observe, that in this *only* instance I am able to do as I shall be done by; to take up the arms furnished by the world, the usages of society—this is monstrous on the *world's* showing! I say this now that I may never need recur to it—that you may understand why I keep *such* entire silence henceforth.

Get but well, keep but *as* well, and all is easy now. This

wonderful winter—the spring—the summer—you will take exercise, go up and down stairs, get strong. *I pray you, at your feet, to do this, dearest!* Then comes autumn, with the natural expectations, as after *rouge* one expects *noir*: the *likelihood* of a *severe* winter after this mild one, which to prevent, you reiterate your demand to go and save your life in Italy, ought you not to do that? And the matters brought to issue, (with even, if possible, less shadow of ground for a refusal than before, if you are *well*, plainly well enough to bear the voyage) *there* I *will* bid you "be mine in the obvious way"—if you shall preserve your belief in me—and you *may* in much, in all important to you. Mr. Kenyon's praise is undeserved enough, but yesterday Milnes said I was the only literary man he ever knew, *tenax propositi*, able to make out a life for himself and abide in it—"for," he went on, "you really do live without any of this *titillation* and fussy dependence upon adventitious excitement of all kinds, they all say they can't do without." That is *more* true—and I *intend* by God's help to live wholly for you; to spend my whole energies in reducing to practice the feeling which occupies me, and in the practical operation of which, the other work I had proposed to do will be found included, facilitated—I shall be able—but of this there is plenty time to speak hereafter—I shall, I believe, be able to do this without even allowing the world to *very much* misinterpret—against pure lying there is no defence, but all up to that I hope to hinder or render unimportant—as you shall know in time and place. . . .

TO THE SAME

[In what she later called a "*disagree* . . . able letter" E. B. B. had vehemently attacked the practice of duelling, which Browning, in conversation, had defended. She twitted him with inconsistency, in that he was opposed to capital punishment and war; and took her stand, not on "Christian principle", but on "the bare social rational ground".]

[8 April 1846.]

First of all, kiss me, dearest,—and again—and now, with the left arm round you, I will write what I think in as few words as possible. I think the fault of not carrying out principles is *yours*, here. Several principles would arrive at the result you desire—Christianity, Stoicism, Asceticism, Epicureanism (in the modern sense)—all these "carried out" stop the procedure you deprecate—but I fancy, as you state your principle, that it is an *eclecticism* from these and others; and presently one branch crosses its fellow, and we *stop*, arrive at nothing. Do you accept "life's warm-beating joy and dole," for an object of that life? Is "society" a thing to desire to participate in? not by the one exceptional case out of the million, but by men generally,—men who "live" only for living's sake, in the first instance; next, men who, having ulterior objects and aims of happiness, yet derive various degrees of sustainment and comfort from the social life round them; and so on, higher up, till you come to the half-dozen, for whom we need not be pressingly urgent to legislate just yet, having to attend to the world first. Well, is social life a good, generally, to these? If so,—go back to another principle which I suppose you to admit,—that "good" may be *lawfully* held, defended,—even to the death. Now see where the "cross" takes place. Something occurs which forces a man to *hold* this, defend this—he *must* do this, or *renounce* it. You let him do neither. Do not say he *needs* not renounce it,—we go avowedly on the vulgar broad ground of fact—you very well know it is a *fact* that by his refusing to accept a challenge, or send one, on conventionally sufficient ground, he will be infallibly excluded from a certain class of society thenceforth and forever. What society *should* do rather, is wholly out of the question—what *will* be done? And now, candidly, can you well fancy a more terrible wrong than this to the ordinary multitude of men? Alter the principles of your reasoning—say, Christianity forbids this,—and *that* will do—rational Simon renounces on his pillar more than the pleasures of society if so he may save his soul: say, society is not worth living in,—it is no wrong to be forced to quit it —*that* will do, also,—a man with *Paradise Lost* or *Othello* to write; or with a Ba to live beside for his one companion,—or many other compensations,—*he* may retire to his own world easily. Say, on the lowest possible ground, "out of society one eats, drinks, &c. excellently well; what loss is there?"—all these principles *avail*; but *mix* them—and they surely neutralize each other. A man *may* live, enjoy life, oppose an attempt to prevent his enjoying life,—yet not—you see! "The method is irrational, proves nothing &c."—what is that to the question? Is the *effect* disputable or no? Wordsworth decides he had better go to court—then he must buy or borrow a court-dress. He goes because of the poetry in him. What irrationality in the bag and sword—in the grey duffil gown yonder, he wrote—half through the exceeding ease and roominess of it—*The Excursion*; how proper he should go in it, therefore—beside it will wring his heartstrings to pay down the four pounds, ten and sixpence: good, Mr. Wordsworth! There's no compulsion; go back to the lakes and be entirely approved of by Miss Fenwick[1]. But, if you *do* choose to kiss hands (instead of cheeks "smackingly") why, you must even resolve to "grin and bear it" (a sea-phrase!)—and, Ba, your imaginary man, who is called "liar" before a large assembly, must decide for one or the other course.

"He makes his antagonist double the wrong"? Nay—*here* the wrong begins—the poor author of the outrage should have known his *word* was *nothing*—the sense of it, he and his like express abundantly every hour of the day, if they please, in language only a shade removed from this that causes all the harm,—and who does other than utterly, ineffably despise them? but he chooses, as the very phrase is, to *oblige* his adversary to act thus. *He* is nothing (I am going on your own case of a supposed futile cause of quarrel)—he may *think* just what he pleases—but having *said* this and *so,—it is entirely society's affair*—and what *is* society's present decision? Directly it relaxes a regulation, allows another outlet to the natural contempt for, and indifference to such men and their opinions spoken or unspoken, everybody avails himself of it directly. If the Lord Chamberlain issues an order this morning, "No swords need be worn at next levee"—who will appear with one? A politician is allowed to call his opponent a destructive &c. A critic may write that the author of such a book or such, is the poorest creature in the world—and who dreams of being angry? but society up to this time says, "if a man calls another &c. &c., *then* he must"— Will you renounce society? *I for one, could, easily: so therefore shall Mr.*

[1] Norwick *ed. princ.*

Kenyon! Beside, I on purpose depreciate the value of an admission into society—as if it were only for those who recognize no other value; and the wiser men might easily forego it. *Not so easily!* There are uses in it, great uses, for purposes quite beyond its limits—you pass through it, mix with it, to get something by it: you do *not* go in to the world to live on the breath of every fool there, but you reach something *out* of the world by being let go quietly, if not with a favourable welcome, among them. I leave *here* to go to Wimpole Street:—I want to have as little as possible to say to the people I find *between*—but, do you know, if I allow a foolish child to put the very smallest of fool's caps on my head instead of the hat I usually wear, though the comfort would be considerable in the change,—yet I shall be followed by an increasing crowd, say to Charing Cross, and thence pelted, perhaps, till I reach No 50—there, perhaps, to find the servant hesitate about opening the door to such an apparition,—and when Papa comes to hear how illustriously your visitor was attended through the streets! why he will specially set apart Easter Monday to testify in person his sense of the sublime philosophy, will he not? My Ba—I tell the child on the first symptom of such a wish on his part "Don't!" with all the eloquence in my power—if I can put it handsomely off my head, even, I will, and with pitying good nature—but if I *must* either wear the cap, and pay the penalty, or—slap his face, why—! "Ah," you say, "but he has got a pistol that you don't see and will shoot you dead like a foolish child as he is." That he may! Have I to be told that in this world men, foolish or wicked, do inflict tremendous injuries on their unoffending fellows? Let God look to it, I say with reverence, and do *you* look to this point, *where* the injury *is, begins*. The foolish man who throws some disfiguring liquid in your face, which to remove you must have recourse to some dangerous surgical operation,—perilling himself, too, by the consequent vengeance of the law, if you sink under knife or cauterizing iron,—shall I say "the fault is *yours*—why submit to the operation?" The fault is *his* that institutes the very fault—which begin by teaching him from his cradle in every possible shape! But don't, don't say—"the operation is *unnecessary*; your blistered face will look, *does* look just as usual, not merely to me who know you, perhaps love you,—but to the whole world—on whose opinion of its agreeableness, I confess that you are dependent for nearly every happy minute of your life."

In all this, I speak for the world, *not* for me—I have other, too many other sources of enjoyment—I could *easily*, I think, do what you require. I endeavour to care for others with none of these; as dear, dearest Ba, sitting in her room because of a dull day, would have *me* take a few miles' exercise. Has everybody a Ba? I had not last year—yet last year I had reasons, and still have, for, on occasion, renouncing society fifty times over: what I should do, therefore, is as improper to be held up for an example as the exemplary behaviour of Walpole's old French officer of ninety, who hearing some youths diverting themselves with some girls in a tent close by, asked, "Is this the example *I* set you, gentlemen?" But I shall be dishonoured however—Ba will "go and call the police"—why, so should I for your brother, in all but the extremest case!—because when I had told all the world, *with whom the concern solely* is, that, despite his uttermost endeavour, I had done this,—the world would be satisfied at once—and the whole procedure is *meant* to satisfy the world—even the foolishest know that the lion in a cage, through no fault of his, cannot snap at a fly outside the bars. The thing to know is, will Ba dictate to her husband "a refusal to fight," and then recommend him to go to a dinner-party? Say, "give up the dinner for my sake," if you like—one *or* the other it *must* be: you know, I hate and refuse dinner-parties. Does everybody?

But now in candour, hear me: I write all this to show the *not such irrationality* of the practice even on comparatively frivolous grounds, and that those individuals to whom you once admit society may be a legitimate enjoyment, must take such a course to retain the privileges they value—and that the painful consequences should be as unhesitatingly attributed to the first offence and its author,—as the explosion and horror to the fool who *would* put the match, in play perhaps, to the powder-barrel. And I excepted myself from the operation of this necessity. But I must confess that I can conceive of "combinations of circumstances" in which I see two things only—or a Third: a miscreant to be put out the world, my own arm and best will to do it; and, perhaps, God to excuse; which is, approve. My Ba, what is Evil, in its unmistakable shape, but a thing to suppress at any price? I *do* approve of judicial punishment to death under some circumstances—I think we may, *must* say: "When it comes to *that*, we will keep our pact of life, stand by God and put *that* out of us, our world—*it* shall not be endured, or *we* shall not be endured"! Dear Ba, is Life to become a child's game? A. is wronged, B. rights him, and is a hero as we say; B. is wronged again, by C.; but he must not right himself; *that* is D.'s proper part, who again is to let *E.* do the same kind office for *him*—and so on. "Defend the poor and fatherless" —and we all applaud—but if they could defend themselves, why not? I will not fancy cases—here's one that strikes me—a fact. Some soldiers were talking over a watch fire abroad —one said that once he was travelling in Scotland and knocked at a cottage-door—an old woman with one child let him in, gave him a supper and a bed—next morning he asked how they lived, and she said the cow, the milk of which he was then drinking, and the kale in the garden, such as he was eating—were all her "*mailien*" or sustenance —whereon, rising to go, he, for the fun, "killed the cow and destroyed the kale"—"the old witch crying out she should certainly be starved"—then he went his way. "And she *was* starved, of course," said a young man; "do you *rue* it?"—The other laughed "Rue aught like that!"—The young man said, "I was the boy, and that was my mother—now then!" In a minute or two the preparer of this "combination of circumstances" lay writhing with a sword through him up to the hilt. "If you had *rued* it," the youth said, "you should have answered it only to God!"

More than enough of this—but I was anxious to stand clearer in your dear eyes. "Vows and promises!"—I want to leave society for the Sirens' isle,—and *now,* I *often seriously reproach* myself with conduct quite the reverse of what you would guard against: I have too much *indifferentism* to the opinions of Mr. Smith and Mr. Brown—by no means am anxious to have his notions agree with mine. Smith thinks Cromwell a canting villain,—Brown believes no dissenter can be saved,—and I repeat Goethe's "Be it your unerring rule, ne'er to contradict a fool, for if folly choose to brave you, all your wisdom cannot save you!" And sometimes I help out their arguments by a touch or two, after Ogniben's fashion[1]—it all seems so wearisomely unprofitable; what comes of Smith's second thought if you change his first—out of *that* second will branch as great an error, you may be sure!

(11 o'clock) Here comes your letter! My own Ba! My dearest best, best beloved! *I*, angry! oh, how you misinterpret, misunderstand the motions of my mind! In all that I said, or write here, I speak of others—others, if you please, of limited natures: I say why *they* may be excused—that is all. "*You do not like pork*"? *But* those poor Irish Colliers whose only luxury is *bacon* once a month; you understand *them* liking it? I do not value society—others do: "*we are all His children*" says Euripides and quotes Paul.

Now, love, let this be a moot point to settle among the flowers one day—with Sir Thomas Browne's "other hard questions yet not impossible to be solved" ("What song the Sirens sang to Ulysses," is the first!) in which blessed hope let me leave off; for I confess to having written myself all-but-tired, headachy. But "vexed with you"! Ba, Ba; you perplex me, bewilder me; let me get right again; kiss me, dearest, and all is right—God bless you ever—

Your R.

TO THE SAME

[19 May 1846.]

With this day expires the first year since you have been yourself to me—putting aside the anticipations, and prognostications, and even assurances from all reasons short of absolute sight and hearing,—excluding the five or six months of these, there remains a year of this intimacy. You accuse me of talking extravagantly sometimes. I will be quiet here, —is the tone *too* subdued if I say, such a life—made up of such years—I would deliberately take rather than any other imaginable one in which fame and worldly prosperity and the love of the whole human race should combine, excluding

[1] Ogniben, the papal legate in Browning's *A Soul's Tragedy*.

"that of yours—to which I hearken"—only wishing the rest were there for a moment that you might see and know that I did turn from them to you. My dearest, inexpressibly dearest. How can I thank you? I feel sure you *need* not have been so kind to me, so perfectly kind and good,—I should have remained your own, gratefully, entirely your own, through the bare permission to love you, or even without it—seeing that I never dreamed of stipulating at the beginning for "a return," and "reward,"—but I also believe, joyfully, that no course but the course you have taken would have raised me above my very self, as I feel on looking back. I began by loving you in comparison with all the world,—now, I love you, my Ba, in the face of your past self, as I remember it.

All words are foolish—but I kiss your feet and offer you my heart and soul, dearest, dearest Ba. . . .

TO THE SAME

[1 June 1846.]

. . . Mrs. Jameson did tell me something about her intended journey to Italy—but not in detail as to you. Miss Bayley seems worthy to be your friend, dearest,—and it is satisfactory, very satisfactory to find her opinion thus confirming yours, of the good you will derive from travelling. You know I look on you with absolute awe, in a sense,—I don't understand how such a creature lives and breathes and moves and does *not* move into fine air altogether and leave us of the Etty-manufacture! I have solemnly set down in the tablets of my brain that Ba prefers morphine to pork, but can eat so much of a chicken as Flush[1] refuses—a chapter in my natural history quite as important as one in Pliny's (and Ælian's too)— "When the Lion is sick, nothing can cure him but to eat an Ape!"—though not so important as my great, greatest record of all— "A cup of coffee will generally cure Ba's headaches—"

As for Pisa or Florence, or Sorrento, or New Orleans,—*ubi* Ba, *ibi* R. B.! Florence, however, you describe exactly: the English there are intolerable,—even from a distance you

[1] Miss Barrett's spaniel.

see *that*. Indeed, I have heard here in England of a regular system of tactics by which *parvenus* manage to get among the privileged classes which at home would keep them off inexorably. Such go to Florence, make acquaintance as "travellers," keeping the native connexions in the farthest of back grounds, and after a year or two's expatriation, come back and go boldly to rejoice the friends they "passed those amusing days with" &c.

What you say of Lough[1] is right and true in one point of view—but I excuse him, knowing the way of life in London—what alternative has he? Even when you ask people by ones and twos, and think to be rational, what do you get for your pains? Not long ago somebody invited himself to dine with me—and got of course the plainest fare, and just hock and claret, because I like them better than heavier wines myself, and suppose others may. I had to dine in the same manner with my friend a week after, and he judiciously began by iced champagne, forced vegetables &c. What was that but telling me *such* was his notion of the duty of the giver of "just a chop" according to stipulation? It is all detestable—a mere pretext! there is simply a *fait accompli* in every such dinner,—it is an eternal record (to the seasons' end) that you witnessed (because you may let it alone for aught anybody cares, so long as you have eyes and can see)—*such* a succession of turbot, and spring-soup and—*basta!* I shall go and take tea with Carlyle before very long. Lough has asked me more than once, but I never went. I like him when he is not on the subject of himself or other artists. Of one particular in his liberality I can bear testimony, he promises at a great rate. Some three years ago he most preposterously signified his intention of giving me a cast of one of his busts—me who had neither claim on him, the slightest, nor much desire for the bust; but on this intimation I was bound to express as many thanks as if the bust had arrived in very plaster,—which it has not done to this day; so that I was too prodigal, you see, and instead of thanks ought to

[1] J. G. Lough, sculptor. Henrietta Barrett had been to a "splendid dinner" at his house, and E. B. B. had written: "Surely it *is* bad taste in a man like Mr. Lough who lives by his genius, to give ambitious dinners like a man who lives by his dinners . . ."

have contented myself with making over to him the whole profits of *Luria*—value received. But, jokes apart, he is a good, kind man I believe, so don't mention this absurdity to your sister—which I am sorry for having mentioned now that mentioned it is! . . .

TO THE SAME

[Browning and E. B. B. had for some time been anxiously considering which of their friends and relations they should tell of their intention to be secretly married. Browning had also proposed that he should take her to meet his parents; and she had replied "To keep all dear to you quite safe and away from all splashing of the mud which we cannot ourselves hope to escape, is the great object,—it does seem to me. Your father and mother would be blamed (in this house, I know, if not in others) for not apprizing my father of what they knew." Browning understood this—mistakenly, as appears from other letters—as an attempt to dissuade him from taking his parents into his confidence.]

[12 June 1846.]

When I am close to you, in your very room, I see through your eyes and feel what you feel—but after, the sight widens with the circle of outside things—I cannot fear for a moment what seemed redoubtable enough yesterday—nor do I believe that there will be two opinions anywhere in the world as to your perfect right to do as you please under the present circumstances. People are not quite so tolerant to other people's preposterousness, and that which yourself tell me exceeds anything I ever heard of or imagined—but, dearest, on twice thinking, one surely ought not to countenance it as you propose—why should not my father and mother know? What possible harm can follow from their knowing? Why should I wound them to the very soul and for ever, by as gratuitous a piece of unkindness as if,—no,—there is no comparison will do! Because, since I was a child I never looked for the least or greatest thing within the compass of their means to give, but given it was,—nor for liberty but it was conceded, nor confidence but it was bestowed. I dare say they would break their hearts at such an end of all. For in any case they will take my feeling for their own with implicit trust—and if I brought them a beggar, or a famous actress even, they would believe in her because of me,—if a Duchess or Miss Hudson,[1] or Lady Selina Huntingdon [2] rediviva—they would do just the same, sorrow to say! As to any harm or blame that can attach itself to *them*,—it is too absurd to think of! What earthly control can they have over me? They live here,—I go my own way, being of age and capability. How can they interfere?

And then, blame for *what*, in either God's or the devil's name? I believe you to be the one woman in the world I am able to marry because able to love. I wish, on some accounts, I had foreseen the contingency of such an one's crossing my path in this life—but I did not, and on all ordinary grounds preferred being free and poor, accordingly. All is altered now. Does anybody doubt that I can by application in proper quarters obtain quite enough to support us both in return for no extraordinary expenditure of such faculties as I have? If it *is* to be doubted, I have been greatly misinformed, that is all. Or, setting all friends and their proposals and the rest of the hatefulness aside—I should say that so simple a procedure as writing to anybody—Lord Monteagle, for instance, who reads and likes my works, as he said at Moxon's two days ago on calling there for a copy to give away—surely to write to him, "When you are minister next month, as is expected, will you give me for my utmost services about as much as you give Tennyson for nothing?"—*this* would be rational and as easy as all rationality. *Let me do so, and at once, my own* Ba! And do you, like the unutterably noble creature I know you, transfer your own advantages to your brothers or sisters—making if you please a proper reservation in the case of my own exertions failing, as failure comes everywhere. So shall the one possible occasion of calumny be removed and all other charges go for the simple absurdities they will be. I am entirely in earnest about this, and indeed had thought for a moment of putting my own share of the project into immediate execution—but on consideration,—no! *So* I will live and so die with you. I will not be poorly endeavouring to startle you with unforeseen generosities,

[1] The daughter of George Hudson the railway king (later Carlyle's "big swollen gambler") who in 1846 was at the zenith of his prosperity and fame.

[2] Selina Countess of Huntingdon, founder in the eighteenth century of a (still existing) Methodist "connexion".

catch you in pretty pitfalls of magnanimities, be always surprising you, or trying to do it. No, I resolve to do my best, *through* you—by your counsel, with your help, under your eye; the most strenuous endeavour will only approximate to an achievement of *that*,—and to suppose a superfluousness of devotion to you (as all these surprises do) would be miserably foolish. So, dear, dear Ba, understand and advise me. I took up the paper with ordinary feelings, but the absurdity and tyranny suddenly flashed upon me—it must not be borne—indeed its only safety in this instance is in its impotency. I am not without fear of some things in this world—but the "wrath of men," all the men living put together, I fear as I fear the fly I have just put out of the window; but I fear *God*—and am ready, he knows, to die this moment in taking his part against any piece of injustice and oppression, *so* I aspire to die!

See this long letter, and all about a tiny one, a plain palpable commonplace matter about which you agree with me, you the dear quiet Ba of my heart, with me that make all this unnecessary fuss! See what is behind all the "bated breath and whispered humbleness!"—but it is *right*, after all, to revolt against such monstrous tyranny. And I ought not, I feel, to have forgotten the feelings of my father and mother as I did—because I know as certainly as I know anything that if I could bring myself to ask them to give up everything in the world, they would do it and cheerfully.

So see, and forgive your own

R.

TO THE SAME

[30 June 1846.]

. . . I think my head is dizzy with reading the debates this morning—Peel's speech and farewell. How exquisitely absurd, it just strikes me, would be any measure after Miss Martineau's own heart, which should introduce women to Parliament as we understand its functions at present—how essentially retrograde a measure! Parliament seems no place for originating, creative minds—but for second-rate minds influenced by and bent on working out the results of these

—and the most efficient qualities for such a purpose are confessedly found oftener with men than with women—physical power having a great deal to do with it beside. So why shuffle the heaps together which, however arbitrarily divided at first, happen luckily to lie pretty much as one would desire, —here the great flint stones, here the pebbles—and diamonds too. The men of genius knew all this, said more than all this, in their way and proper place on the outside, where Miss M. is still saying something of the kind—to be taken up in its time by some other Mr. Cobden and talked about, and beleaguered. But such people cannot or will not see where their office begins and advantageously ends; and that there is such a thing as influencing the influencers, playing the Bentham to the Cobden, the Barry to a Commission for Public Works, the Lough to the three or four industrious men with square paper caps who get rules and plummets and dot the blocks of marble all over as his drawings indicate

TO THE SAME

[Benjamin Robert Haydon, the painter, had committed suicide on 22 June, bequeathing his literary property to Elizabeth Barrett whom he had never met but with whom he had carried on a correspondence.]

[9 July 1846.]

My own darling, my Ba, do you know when I read those letters (as soon as I remembered I had got them,—for you hold me long after both doors, up and down stairs, shut) when I looked through them, under a gateway, I was pricked at the heart to have thought so, and spoken so, of the poor writer. I will believe that he was good and even great when in communication with you—indeed all men are made, or make themselves, different in their approaches to different men—and the secret of goodness and greatness is in choosing *whom* you will approach, and live with, in memory or imagination, through the crowding obvious people who seem to live with you. That letter about the glory of being a painter "if only for the neglect" is most touching and admirable—there is the serene spot attained, the solid siren's isle amid the sea; and while *there*, he was safe and well—but he would put out to sea again, after a breathing time, I suppose? though even a smaller strip of land was enough to maintain Blake, for one instance, in power and glory through the poor, fleeting "sixty years"—then comes the rest from cartooning and exhibiting. But there is no standing, one foot on land and one on the waves, now with the high aim in view, now with the low aim,—and all the strange mistaken talk about "prestiges," "Youth and its luck," Napoleon and the world's surprise and interest. There comes the low aim between the other,—an organ grinds Mr. Jullien's newest dance-tune, and Camoens is vexed that the "choral singing which brought angels down," can't also draw street-passengers round.

I take your view of H.'s freedom, at that time, from the thoughts of what followed.

He was weak—a strong man would have borne what so many bear—what were his griefs, as grief *goes*? Do you remember I told you, when the news of Aliwal and the other battles came to England, of our gardener, and his son, a sergeant in one of the regiments engaged; how the father could learn nothing at first, of course; how they told him at the Horse Guards he should be duly informed in time, after his betters, whether this son was dead, or wounded. Since then, no news came—"which is *good* news" the father persuaded himself to think: so the apprehensions subside, and the hope confirms itself, more and more, while the old fellow digs and mows and rakes away, like a man painting historical pictures—only without the love of it. Well, this morning we had his daughter here to say "the letter" had arrived at last—her brother was killed in the first battle, so there's an end of the three months' sickness of heart,—and the poor fellow must bear his loss "like a man"—or like a woman—for I recollect another case, of an old woman whom my mother was in the habit of relieving, who brought a letter one day which she could hardly understand; it was from her son, a sailor, and went on for a couple of pages about his good health and expectations,—then, in a different handwriting, somebody, "your son's shipmate," "took up his pen to inform you that he fell from the masthead into the sea and was drowned yesterday,—which he therefore thought it right to put in the unfinished letter." All which the old woman bore somehow,—seeing she lives yet. . .

TO THE SAME

[3 August 1846.]

. . . How you have mistaken my words, whatever they may have been, about the "change" to be expected in my life! I have, most sincerely I tell you, no one habit nor manner to change or persevere in; if you once accept the general constitution of me as accordant to yours in a sufficient degree,—my incompleteness with your completeness, dearest,—there is no further difficulty. I want to be a Poet—to read books which make wise in their various ways, to see just so much of nature and the ways of men as seems necessary—and having done this already in some degree, I can easily and cheerfully afford to go without any or all of it for the future, if called upon, and so live on, and "use up," my past acquisitions such as they are. I will go to Pisa and learn,—or stay here and learn in another way putting, as I always have done, my whole pride, if that is the proper name, in the being able to work with the least possible materials. There is my scheme of life *without* you, *before* you existed for me; prosecuted hitherto with every sort of weakness, but always kept in view and believed in. Now then, please to introduce Ba, and say what is the habit she changes? But do not try to say what divinest confirmation she brings to "whatever is good and holy and true" in this scheme, because even She cannot say that! All the liberty and forbearance—most graceful, most characteristic of you, sweet! But why should I play with you, at taking what I mean to give again?—or rather, what it would be a horror to have to keep—why make fantastic stipulations only to have the glory of not abiding by them? If I may speak of my own desires for a moment unconnected with your happiness,—of what I want *for myself*, purely—what, I mean, by marrying you,—it is, that I may be with you forever. I cannot have enough of you in any other relation: why then should I pretend to make reservations and say "Yes, you shall deprive me of yourself (of your sympathy, of your knowledge, and good wishes, and counsel) on such and such occasions"? But I feel your entire goodness, dear angel of my life,—ever more I feel it, though all seems felt and recorded. . . .

TO THE SAME

[5 August 1846.]

If I had felt, as you pleased to feel yesterday, that it had been "only one hour" which my coming gained—I should richly deserve to find out to-day, as I do fully, what the precise value of such an hour is. But I never act so ungratefully and foolishly—you are more than ever you have been to me,—yet at any time I would have gone for the moment's sight of you,—one moment's—and returned happy. You never doubt this because I do not waylay you in your walks and rides? I consider your sisters, and your apprehension for them, and other reasons that make such a step objectionable. Do you remember what I said yesterday—what I have told myself so often? It is one proof how I love you that I am jealous of any conversation with you which should be too interesting *for itself*, apart from the joy of your presence—it is better to sit and see you, or hear you, or only say something which, in its insignificance, shall be obviously of no account beside the main and proper delight—as at wine-feasts you get the wine and a plate of thin dry tasteless biscuits—(observe, for instance, that this noble simile was not set before you yesterday—no, my Ba!)

And you *did* understand also why I left, on that mere chance of danger to you,—for it was not, do you think it was only the irksomeness to myself I sought to escape—though that would have been considerable. There is no unstable footing for me in the whole world except just in your house—which is *not* yours. I ought not to be in that one place—all I could do in any circumstances (were a meeting to happen) would be *wrong*, unfortunate. The certainty of misconception would spoil everything—so much of gentleness as is included in *gentle*manliness would pass for a very different quality—and the *manliness* which one observes there too, would look like whatever it is farthest from. This is a real avowal of weakness—because, being in the right, as I dare trust I am, so far as I can see through the involvement, I ought to be able to take my stand upon it,—and so, I shall be able, and easily—but not *here*, just here. With Mr. Kenyon, in spite of a few misgivings, I shall know what to say—I can justify myself, if not convince him. Never fancy, dearest, that he has any "clay" in his composition—he may show a drop of water at the heart of the else entire chrystal he is—did you ever see that pretty phenomenon—of which Claudian wrote so prettily? "Non potuit toto mentiri corpore gemmam, sed medio latuit proditor orbe latex." Our Druids used to make balls for divining out of such *all-but-solid* gems with the central weakness—I have had them in my hand. Such doubts and fears are infinitely more becoming in him, situated as he is, than their absence would be—if he said for instance, "Oh yes,—I am used to a certain style of living, which of course I do not change for *no* reason at all,—but who doubts that I *could* do so, without difficulty or regret? I shall hardly bestow any sympathy on what I am sure must be the easiest life in the world!" One would rather hear an epicure say frankly he cannot conceive how people can end a dinner without Tokay, than ask over his Tokay (as Sheridan's Abbot in the *Duenna*) of the poor starved wistful attendant monk, "Haven't you the chrystal spring?" . . .

Yesterday I was not in a mood to go quietly home—"for my soul kept up too much light under my eyelids for the night, and thus I *went* disquieted" till at Charing Cross it struck me that going home by water (to Greenwich, at least) would be a calmative—so I went on board a steamer. Close by me sate three elderly respectable men,—I could not help hearing them talk rationally about the prospects of the planters, the "compensation there is to be in the article of Rum,"—how we "get labour," which is the main thing, and may defy, with that, Cuba, the Brazils &c. One who talked thus was a fat genial fellow, ending every sentence in a laugh from pure good-nature—his companions somehow got to "the Church," then Puseyism, then Dissent—on all which this personage had his little opinion,—when one friend happened to ask "you think so?"—"I do," said the other "and indeed I *know* it." "How so?"—"Because it was revealed to me in a vision." "A . . . vision?"—"Yes, a vision"—and so he began to describe it, quite in earnest, but with the selfsame precision and assurance, with which he had been a little before describing the effect of the lightning on an iron steamboat at Woolwich as he witnessed it. In this vision he had seen the devil cast out of himself—which he took for an earnest of God's purposes for good to the world at large—I thought, "we mad poets,—and this very unpoetical person!" who had also previously been entering on the momentous question "why I grow fatter than of old, seeing that I eat no more." . . .

TO THE SAME

[25 August 1846.]

. . . You asked me about Ossian—now here is truth—the first book I ever bought in my life was Ossian—it is now in the next room. And years before that, the first *composition* I ever was guilty of was something in *imitation* of Ossian, whom I had not read, but *conceived*, through two or three scraps in other books—I never can recollect *not* writing rhymes, but I knew they were nonsense even then; *this*, however, I thought exceedingly well of, and laid up for posterity under the cushion of a great arm-chair. "And now my soul is satisfied"—so said one man after killing another, the death being suggested, in its height of honour, by stars and stars (* * * *). I could not have been five years old, that's one consolation. Years after, when I bought this book, I found a vile dissertation of Laing, all to prove Ossian was not Ossian. I would not read it, but could not help knowing the purpose of it, and the pith of the hatefully-irresistible arguments. The worst came in another shape, though—an after-gleaning of real Ossianic poems, by a firm believer whose name I forget—"if this is the *real*"—I thought! Well, to this day I believe in a nucleus for all that haze, a foundation of truth to Macpherson's fanciful superstructure—and I have been long intending to read once again those Fingals and Malvinas.

I remember that somewhere a chief cries "Come round me, my thousands!'—There is an Achilles! And another, complaining of old age remarks "*Now*—I feel the weight of my shield!" Nestor; and both beautifully perfect, are they not, *you* perfect Ba? . . .

TO THE SAME

[26 August 1846.]

. . . And now, dearest, I will revert, in as few words as I can, to the account you gave me, a short time since, of your income. At the beginning, if there had been the necessity I supposed, I should have proposed to myself the attainment of something like such an amount, by my utmost efforts, before we could marry. We could not under the circumstances begin with less—so as to be free from horrible contingencies,—not the least of which would be the application for assistance afterward. After we marry, nobody must hear of us. In spite of a few misgivings at first I am not proud, or rather, am proud in the right place. I am utterly, exclusively proud of you—and though I should have gloried in working myself to death to prove it, and shall be as ready to do so at any time a necessity shall exist, yet at present I shall best serve you, I think, by the life by your side, which we contemplate. I hope and believe, that by your side I shall accomplish something to justify God's goodness and yours—and, looking at the matter in a worldly light, I see not a few reasons for thinking that unproductive as the kind of literature may be, which I should aim at producing, yet, by judicious management, and profiting by certain favourable circumstances,—I shall be able to realise an annual sum quite sufficient for every purpose—at least in Italy.

As I never calculated on such a change in my life, I had the less repugnance to my father's generosity, that I knew that an effort at some time or other might furnish me with a few hundred pounds which would soon cover my very simple expenses. If we are poor, it is to my father's infinite glory, who, as my mother told me last night, as we sate alone, "conceived such a hatred to the slave-system in the West Indies," (where his mother was born, who died in his infancy), that he relinquished every prospect,—supported himself, while there, in some other capacity, and came back, while yet a boy, to his father's profound astonishment and rage—one proof of which was, that when he heard that his son was a suitor to *her*, my mother—he benevolently waited on her uncle to assure him that his niece would be thrown away on a man so evidently born to be hanged!—those were his words. My father on his return had the intention of devoting himself to art, for which he had many qualifications and abundant love—but the quarrel with his father,—who married again and continued to hate him till a few years before his death,—induced him to go at once and consume his life after a fashion he always detested. You may fancy, I am not ashamed of him.

I told my mother, who told *him*. They have never been used to interfere with, or act for me—and they trust me. If you care for any love, purely love,—you will have theirs—they give it you, whether you take it or no. You will understand, therefore, that I would not *accept* even the 100*l*. we shall want: I said "you shall lend it me—I will pay it back out of my first literary earnings—I take it, because I do not want to sell my copyrights, or engage myself to write a play, or any other nuisance. Surely I can get fifty pounds next year, and the other fifty in due course!"

So, dearest, we shall have plenty for the journey—and you have only to determine the when and the how. Oh, the time! Bless you, ever dearest! I love you with all my heart and soul—

R.

TO THE SAME

[31 August 1846.]

I wonder what I shall write to you, Ba—I could suppress my feelings here, as I do on other points, and say nothing of the hatefulness of this state of things which is prolonged so uselessly. There is the point—show me one good reason, or show of reason, why we gain anything by deferring our departure till next week instead of to-morrow, and I will bear to perform yesterday's part for the amusement of Mr. Kenyon a dozen times over without complaint. But if the cold plunge *must* be taken, all this shivering delay on the bank is hurtful as well as fruitless. I *do* understand your anxieties, dearest—I take your fears and make them mine, while I put my own natural feeling of quite another kind away from us both, succeeding in *that* beyond all expectation. There is no amount of patience of suffering I would not undergo to relieve you from these apprehensions. But if, on the whole, you really determine to act as we propose in spite of them,—why, a new leaf is turned over in our journal, an old part of our adventure done with, and a new one entered upon, altogether distinct from the other. Having once decided to go to Italy with me, the next thing to decide is on the best means of going—or rather, there is just this connection between the two measures, that by the success or failure of the last, the first will have to be justified or condemned. You tell me you have decided to go—then, dearest, you will be prepared to go earlier than you promised yesterday—by the end of September at very latest. In proportion to the too probable excitement and painful circumstances of the departure, the greater amount of advantages should be secured for the departure itself. How can I take you away in even the beginning of October? We shall be a fortnight on the journey—with the year, as everybody sees and says, a full month in advance,—cold mornings and dark evenings already. Everybody would cry out on such folly when it was found that we let the favourable weather escape, in full assurance that the autumn would come to us unattended by any one beneficial circumstance.

My own dearest, I am wholly your own, for ever, and under every determination of yours. If you find yourself unable, or unwilling to make this effort, tell me so and plainly and at once—I will not offer a word in objection,—I will continue our present life, if you please, so far as may be desirable, and wait till next autumn, and the next and the next, till providence end our waiting. It is clearly not for me to pretend to instruct you in your duties to God and yourself; enough, that I have long ago chosen to accept your decision. If, on the other hand, you make up your mind to leave England now, you will be prepared by the end of September.

I should think myself the most unworthy of human beings if I could employ any arguments with the remotest show of a tendency to *frighten* you into a compliance with any scheme of mine. Those methods are for people in another relation to you. But you love me, and, at lowest, shall I say, wish me well—and the fact is too obvious for me to commit any indelicacy in reminding you, that in any dreadful event to our journey of which I could accuse myself as the cause,—as of this undertaking to travel with you in the worst time of year when I could have taken the best,—in the case of your health being irretrievably shaken, for instance—the happiest fate I should pray for would be to live and die in some corner where I might never hear a word of the English language, much less a comment in it on my own wretched imbecility,—to disappear and be forgotten.

So that must not be, for all our sakes. My family will give me to you that we may be both of us happy,—but for such an end—no!

Dearest, do you think all this earnestness foolish and uncalled for?—that I might know you spoke yesterday in mere jest,—as yourself said, "only to hear what I would say"? Ah but consider, my own Ba, the way of our life, as it is, and is to be—a word, a simple word from you, is not as a word is counted in the world—the word between us is different—I am guided by your will, which a word shall signify to me. Consider that just such a word, so spoken, even with that lightness, would make me lay my life at your feet at any minute. Should we gain anything by my trying, if I could, to deaden the sense of hearing, dull the medium of communication between us; and procuring that, instead of this prompt rising of my will at the first intimation from yours, the same effect should only follow after fifty speeches, and as many protestations of complete serious desire for their success on your part, accompanied by all kinds of acts and deeds and other evidences of the same?

At all events, God knows I have said this in the deepest, truest love of you. . . .

TO THE SAME

[Flush, the spaniel, had been stolen by professional dog-thieves. "Two hours ago," E. B. B. wrote, "the chief of the Confederacy came to call on Henry and to tell him that the 'Society had the dog,' having done us the honour of tracking us into Bond Street and out of Bond Street into Vere Street where he was kidnapped. Now he is in Whitechapel (poor

Flush). And the great man was going down there at half past seven to meet other great men in council and hear the decision as to the ransom exacted, and would return with their *ultimatum*. Oh, the villainy of it is excellent, and then the humiliation of having to pay for your own vexations and anxieties! *Will* they have the insolence, now, to make me pay ten pounds, as they said they would? But I must have Flush, you know—I can't run any risk, and bargain and haggle. There is a dreadful tradition in this neighbourhood, of a lady who did *so* having her dog's head sent to her in a parcel. So I say to Henry—'Get Flush back, whatever you do'—for Henry is angry as he may well be, and as *I* should be if I was not too afraid, and talks police-officers against thieves, and finds it very hard to attend to my instructions and be civil and respectful to their captain. There he found him, smoking a cigar in a room with pictures! They make some three or four thousand a year by their honourable employment." The dog was restored to his mistress, but not until *after* the writing of the three following letters.]

Thursday [3 September 1846].

I am rejoiced that poor Flush is found again, dearest—altogether rejoiced.

And now that you probably have him by your side, I will tell you what I should have done in such a case, because it explains our two ways of seeing and meeting oppression lesser or greater. I would not have given five shillings on that fellow's application. I would have said,—and in entire earnestness "*You* are responsible for the proceedings of your gang, and *you* I mark—don't talk nonsense to me about cutting off heads or paws. Be as sure as that I stand here and tell you, I will spend my whole life in putting you down, the nuisance you declare yourself—and by every imaginable means I will be the death of you and as many of your accomplices as I can discover—but *you* I have discovered and will never lose sight of—now try my sincerity, by delaying to produce the dog by to-morrow. And for the ten pounds—see!" Whereupon I would give them to the first beggar in the street. You think I should receive Flush's head? Perhaps—*so* God allows matters to happen! on purpose, it may be, that I should vindicate him by the punishment I would exact.

Observe, Ba, this course ought not to be yours, because it *could* not be—it would not suit your other qualities. But all religion, right and justice, with me, seem implied in such a resistance to wickedness and refusal to multiply it a hundredfold—for from this prompt payment of ten pounds for a few minutes' act of the easiest villainy, there will be encouragement to—how many similar acts in the course of next month? And how will the poor owners fare who have not money enough for their dogs' redemption? I suppose the gentleman, properly disgusted with such obstinacy, will threaten roasting at a slow fire to test the sincerity of attachment! No—the world would grow too detestable a den of thieves and oppressors that way! . . .

TO THE SAME

Thursday Afternoon.

When I had finished that letter this morning, dearest dearest, before I could seal it, even, (my sister did it for me, and despatched it to the post at once) I became quite ill and so sick as to be forced to go up-stairs and throw myself on the bed. It is now six o'clock, and I feel better, and have some thoughts of breaking my fast to-day—but, first of all, did whatever it may have been I wrote seem *cross*—unnecessarily angry, to you, dearest Ba? Because, I confess to having felt indignant at this sample of the evils done under the sun every day—and as if it would be to no purpose though the whole world were peopled with Ba's instead of just Wimpole Street; as they would be just so many more soft cushions for the villainously-disposed to run pins into at their pleasure. Donne says that "Weakness invites, but silence *feasts* oppression." And it is horrible to fancy how all the oppressors in their several ranks may, if they choose, twitch back to them by the heartstrings after various modes the weak and silent whose secret they have found out. No one should profit by those qualities in me, at least. Having formed a resolution, I would keep it, I hope, through fire and water, and the threatener of any piece of rascality, who (as commonly happens) should be without the full heart to carry it into effect, should pay me exactly the same for the threat, which had determined my conduct once and for ever. But in this particular case, I ought to have told you (unless you divined it, as you might) that I would give all I am ever to be worth in the world to get back your Flush for you—for your interest is not *mine*, any more than the lake is the river that goes to feed it,—mine is only made to feed yours—I am yours, as we say—as I feel more and more every minute. . . .

TO THE SAME

Friday Morning [4 September 1846].

. . . Dear Ba, I wrote under the notion (as I said) that poor Flush was safe by your side; and only took that occasion to point at what I must still consider the wrongness of the whole system of giving way to, instead of opposing, such proceedings. I think it lamentable weakness—though I can quite understand and allow for it in you,—but weakness it essentially *is*, as *you* know perfectly. For see, you first put the matter in the gentlest possible light. "Who would give much time and trouble to the castigation of such a fellow as *that!*" you ask—and immediately after, for another purpose, you very rightly rank this crime with that other enormous one, of the Spanish banditti—nay, you confess that, in this very case, any such injury to Flush as you dread would give you inexpressible grief. Is the threatening this outrage then so little a matter? Am I to think it a less matter if the same miscreant should *strike* you in the street because you would probably suffer less than by this that he *has* done? There is the inevitable inconsistency of wrong reasoning in all this. Say, as I told you on another subject,—"I determine to resist no injury whatever, to be at the disposal of any villain in the world, trusting to God for protection here or recompense hereafter"—or take my course; *which* is the easier, and in the long run, however strangely it may seem, the more profitable, no one can doubt—but I take the harder—in all but the responsibility—which, without any cant, would be intolerable to me. Look at this "society" with its "four thousand a year"—which unless its members are perfect fools they will go on to double and treble—would this have existed if a proper stand had been made at the beginning? The first silly man, woman or child who consented to pay five shillings, beyond the mere expense of keeping the dog (on the supposition of its having been found, *not* stolen), is responsible for all the harm—

what could the thief do but go and steal another, and ask double for its ransom?

And see—dog-stealers so encouraged are the lowest of the vile—can neither write nor read, perhaps. One of the fraternity possesses this knowledge, however, and aims higher. Accordingly, instead of stealing your dog, he determines to steal your character; if a guinea (at the beginning) ransoms the one, ten pounds shall ransom the other; accordingly Mr. Barnard Gregory [1] takes pen in hand and writes to some timid man, in the first instance, that unless he receives that sum, his character will be blasted. The timid man takes your advice, says that the "love of an abstract principle" must not run him into "cruel hazards" "for the sake of a few guineas"—so he pays them—who would bother himself with such vermin as Gregory? So Gregory receives his pay for his five minutes' penmanship—takes down a directory, and writes five hundred such letters. Serjeant Talfourd told me, counting them on his fingers, "such and such (naming them) cut their throats after robbing their families, employers &c., such fled the country, such went mad—*that* was the commonest event." At last, even so poor a creature as the Duke of Brunswick, with his detestable character and painted face,—even *he* plucks up courage and turns on Gregory, grown by this time into a really formidable monster by these amiable victims to the other principle of easy virtue,—and the event is that this execrable "Abhorson's" trade is utterly destroyed—that form of atrocious persecution exists no longer. I am in no danger of being told, at next post delivery, that having been "tracked up Vere Street, down Bond Street, &c." into Wimpole Street my character and yours will be the subject of an article in the next *Satirist* "unless—"

To all of which you have a great answer—"What should I do if *you* were to be the victim?" That my note yesterday, the second one, told you. I sacrifice *myself*—all that belongs *to me*—but there are some interests which I belong to—I

[1] Owner-editor of *The Satirist, or Censor of the Times* (1831–49), already in 1846 convicted of several libels and soon to be driven out of his profession—that of the blackmailing journalist—by the persistence of ex-Duke Charles of Brunswick.

have no right, no more than inclination, in such a case, to think of myself if your safety is concerned, and as I could cut off a limb to save my head, so my head should fall most willingly to redeem yours—I would pay every farthing I had in the world, and shoot with my own hand the receiver of it after a chase of fifty years—esteeming *that* to be a very worthy recompense for the trouble.

But why write all this string of truisms about the plainest thing in the world? All reformers are met at the outset by such dissuasion from their efforts. "Better suffer the grievance and get off as cheaply as you [can]—You, Mahomet, —what if the Caaba *be* only a black stone? You need only bow your head as the others, and make any inward remark you like on the blindness of the people. You, Hampden, have you really so little wit as to contest payment of a paltry 20*s*. at such risk?"

Ah, but here all the fuss is just about stealing a dog—two or three words, and the matter becomes simply ludicrous—very easily got rid of! One cannot take vengeance on the "great man" with his cigar and room of pictures and burlesque dignities of mediation! Just so, when Robert was inclined to be sorry for the fate of Bertha's sister,[1] one can fancy what a relief and change would be operated in his feelings, if a good-natured friend send him a version of his mighty crime in Lord Rochester's funny account of "forsaken damsels"—with the motto "Women have died ere now and worms have eaten them—but not for love—" or "At lovers' perjuries Jove laughs"—why, Robert is a "lady-killer" like D'Orsay! Well, enough of sermonizing for the present; it is impossible for me to differ with you and treat *that* as a light matter—or, what on earth would have been so little to wonder at, as that, loving Flush, you should determine to save him at any price? If "Chiappino" [2] were to assure you, in terms that you could not disbelieve, that in the event of your marrying me he would destroy himself,—would you answer, as I should, "Do so, and take the consequences,"—and think no more about the matter? I should

[1] In E. B. B.'s poem *Bertha in the Lane*.

[2] Chiappino, the name of a character in Browning's *A Soul's Tragedy*, and E. B. B.'s private nickname for R. H. ("Orion") Horne.

absolutely leave it, as not my concern but God's—nor should blame myself any more than if the poor man, being uncertain what to do, had said "If a man first passes the window—yes—if a woman—no"—and I, a total stranger, had passed.

One word more—in all this, I labour against the execrable policy of the world's husbands, fathers, brothers, and domineerers in general. I am about to marry you: how wise, then, to encourage such a temper in you! such was that divine Griselda's—a word rules the gentle nature—"Do this, or—". . .

TO THE SAME

[Robert Browning and Elizabeth Barrett were married in St. Marylebone Church at 11 a.m. on 12 September 1846. One of the witnesses was Wilson, her maid. Browning's first letter to E. B. B. as his wife—she returned to Wimpole Street for a week before their elopement to Italy—was written two hours later.]

1 p.m. Saturday.

You will only expect a few words—what will those be? When the heart is full it may run over, but the real fulness stays within.

You asked me yesterday "if I should repent?" Yes—my own Ba,—I could wish all the past were to do over again, that in it I might somewhat more,—never so little more, conform in the outward homage to the inward feeling. What I have professed—(for I have performed nothing) seems to fall short of what my first love required even—and when I think of *this* moment's love—I could repent, as I say.

Words can never tell you, however,—form them, transform them any way,—how perfectly dear you are to me—perfectly dear to my heart and soul.

I look back, and in every one point, every word and gesture, every letter, every *silence*—you have been entirely perfect to me—I would not change one word, one look.

My hope and aim are to preserve this love, not to fall from it—for which I trust to God who procured it for me, and doubtlessly can preserve it.

Enough now, my dearest, dearest, own Ba! You have given me the highest, completest proof of love that ever one human being gave another. I am all gratitude—and all pride (under the proper feeling which ascribes pride to the right source) all pride that my life has been so crowned by you.

God bless you prays your very own R.

I will write to-morrow of course. Take every care of *my life* which is in that dearest little hand; try and be composed, my beloved.

Remember to thank Wilson for me.

TO HENRIETTA AND ARABEL BARRETT

[Browning's first letter to Wimpole Street after the elopement.]

Pisa, 24 November 1846.

Ba directs me to address this letter to "my sisters,"—or, even more familiar, to "Henrietta and Arabella"! If I could make up my mind to obey her, the liberty would be in some measure justified, perhaps, by the unaffected sincerity of the brotherly feeling with which I must ever regard them both—nor have I any right to doubt that they will kindly accept an assurance which their own letters drew forth. For I will say, my dear sisters, that I had not to wait for these letters, to know what your conduct has always been to Ba,—and whoever loves her as you do, must take my own love too, whether it be worth taking or not. But when I find that in addition to that constant love, continued under many trying circumstances, you further can afford to myself that generous sympathy which I never had the good fortune to be able to claim thro' a personal acquaintance,—what shall I say? Believe me thro' life, in all affectionate truth, your brother, as you have already proved yourselves the dearest of sisters—for which may God bless and reward you.

I am the better enabled to bear what is at least as much a surprise to me as a matter of concern—tho' it *does* concern me deeply—I mean, the light in which other members of your family, I am informed, look upon a step which your good sense must see to have been altogether unavoidable.

There is no need that I should reiterate what was, no doubt, sufficiently stated at the beginning, and, so far as I can find, is not disputed now. I will only say, that if, on a consideration of all the facts, your brothers can honestly come to the opinion that, by any of the ordinary methods applicable to any other case, I could have effected the same result,—that any amount of exertion on my part, any extent of sacrifice, would have availed to render extreme measures unnecessary,—*then,* I will express all the sorrow they can desire—tho' at the same time I shall expect some forgiveness for a very involuntary error, assuring them, as I do, that I believed—and believe—that their sister's life depended upon my acting as I acted.

Nor can I think that, if they saw her, as I have the happiness to see her, so changed as to be hardly recognizable, and with a fair prospect of life and enjoyment for many years to come—they could *not* be very angry I am sure! I can too easily understand the disappointment anyone must feel who has been accustomed to her society and is now deprived of it, but if I were convinced that her welfare was to be most effectually gained by her leaving me, she should leave me. This is a subject, as you feel, in which my tongue is tied—I could not help saying this much however. Now, let me speak of her.

There are very few to whom I can be at liberty so to speak—but you will understand, and forgive what may seem superfluous,—knowing her as you do. I, however, thought I knew her, while every day and hour reveals more and more to me the divine goodness and infinite tenderness of her heart,—while that wonderful mind of hers, with its inexhaustible affluence and power, continues unceasingly to impress me. I shall not attempt to tell you what she is to me. Her entire sweetness of temper makes it a delight to breathe the same air with her—and I cannot imagine any condition of life, however full of hardship, which her presence would not render not merely supportable but delicious. It is nothing to me that my whole life shall be devoted to such a woman,—its only happiness will consist in such a devotion. . . .

And now, may I ask you a favour? It is, that if anything

should strike you with respect to Ba's well-being—any suggestion that you may think of for her comfort—you will write of it to *me*—not to *her*, with her unselfish, generous disregard of what she fancies (most erroneously) to relate exclusively to herself—in all probability I should never hear of it—but for a hint, a word to *me*, directly, I shall be very grateful.

And now, my dear sisters, once more, God bless you for all your love and goodness. I thank you from my heart and shall never forget it—being ever most affectionately yours,

R. B.

TO JOHN RUSKIN

[In reply to criticism of the lately published *Men and Women.*]

Paris, 10 December 1855.

My dear Ruskin,—for so you let me begin, with the honest friendliness that befits.—You never were more in the wrong than when you professed to say "your unpleasant things" to me. This is pleasant and proper at all points, over-liberal of praise here and there, kindly and sympathetic everywhere, and with enough of yourself in even—what I fancy—the misjudging, to make the whole letter precious indeed. . . .

For the deepnesses you think you discern,—may they be more than mere blacknesses! For the hopes you entertain of what may come of subsequent readings,—all success to them! For your bewilderment more especially noted—how shall I help *that*? We don't read poetry the same way, by the same law; it is too clear. I cannot begin writing poetry till my imaginary reader has conceded licences to me which you demur at altogether. I *know* that I don't make out my conception by my language; all poetry being a putting the infinite within the finite. You would have me paint it all plain out, which can't be; but by various artifices I try to make shift with touches and bits of outlines which *succeed* if they bear the conception from me to you. You ought, I think, to keep pace with the thought tripping from ledge to ledge of my "glaciers," as you call them; not stand poking your alpenstock into the holes, and demonstrating that no foot could have stood there;—suppose it sprang over there? In *prose* you may criticize so—because that is the absolute representation of portions of truth, what chronicling is to history—but in asking for more *ultimates* you must accept less *mediates*, nor expect that a Druid stone-circle will be traced for you with as few breaks to the eye as the North Crescent and South Crescent that go together so cleverly in many a suburb. Why, you look at my little song [1] as if it were Hobbs' or Nobbs' lease of his house, or testament of his devisings, wherein, I grant you, not a "then and there," "to him and his heirs," "to have and to hold," and so on, would be superfluous; and so you begin:—"Stand still,—why?" For the reason indicated in the verse, to be sure—*to let me draw him*—and because he is at present going his way, and fancying nobody notices him,—and moreover, "going on" (as we say) against the injustice of that,—and lastly, inasmuch as one night he'll fail us, as a star is apt to drop out of heaven, in authentic astronomic records, and I want to make the most of my time. So much may be in "stand still." And how much more was (for instance) in that "stay!" of Samuel's (I. xv. 16). So could I twit you through the whole series of your objurgations, but the declaring my own notion of the law on the subject will do. And why,—I prithee, friend and fellow-student,—why, having told the Poet what you read, may I not turn to the bystanders, and tell them a bit of my own mind about their own stupid thanklessness and mistaking? Is the jump too much there? The whole is all but a simultaneous feeling with me.

The other hard measure you deal me I won't bear—about my requiring you to pronounce words short and long, exactly as I like. Nay, but exactly as the language likes, in this case. *Foldskirts* [2] not a trochee? A spondee possible in English? Two of the "longest monosyllables" continuing to be each of the old length when in junction? Sentence: let the delinquent be forced to supply the stone-cutter with a thousand companions to "Affliction sore—long time he bore," after the fashion of "He lost his life—

[1] *Popularity* ("Stand still, true poet that you are")—*supra*, p. 366.
[2] "Till I felt where the foldskirts fly open . . ."—*Saul* (*supra*, p. 338).

by a pen-knife," "He turned to clay—last Good Friday," "Departed hence—nor owed six-pence," and so on—so would pronounce a jury accustomed from the nipple to say lord and landlord, bridge and Cambridge, Gog and Magog, man and woman, house and workhouse, coal and charcoal, cloth and broadcloth, skirts and foldskirts, more and once more,—in short! Once *more* I prayed!—is the confession of a self-searching professor! "I stand here for law!"

The last charge I cannot answer, for you may be right in preferring it, however unwitting I am of the fact. I *may* put Robert Browning into Pippa and other men and maids. If so, *peccavi*: but I don't see myself in them, at all events.

Do you think poetry was ever generally understood—or can be? Is the business of it to tell people what they know already, as they know it, and so precisely that they shall be able to cry out—"Here you should supply *this—that* you evidently pass over, and I'll help you from my own stock?" It is all teaching, on the contrary, and the people hate to be taught. They say otherwise,—make foolish fables about Orpheus enchanting stocks and stones, poets standing up and being worshipped,—all nonsense and impossible dreaming. A poet's affair is with God, to whom he is accountable, and of whom is his reward: look elsewhere, and you find misery enough. Do you believe people understand *Hamlet*? The last time I saw it acted, the heartiest applause of the night went to a little by-play of the actor's own—who, to simulate madness in a hurry, plucked forth his handkerchief and flourished it hither and thither: certainly a third of the play, with no end of noble things, had been (as from time immemorial) suppressed, with the auditory's amplest acquiescence and benediction. Are these wasted, therefore? No—they act upon a very few, who react upon the rest: as Goldsmith says, "some lords, my acquaintance, that settle the nation, are pleased to be kind."

Don't let me lose *my* lord by any seeming self-sufficiency or petulance: I look on my own shortcomings too sorrowfully, try to remedy them too earnestly: but I shall never change my point of sight, or feel other than disconcerted and apprehensive when the public, critics and all, begin to understand and approve me. But what right have *you* to disconcert me in the other way? Why won't you ask the next perfumer for a packet of *orris*-root? Don't everybody know 'tis a corruption of *iris*-root—the Florentine lily, the *giaggolo*, of world-wide fame as a good savour? And because "iris" means so many objects already, and I use the old word, you blame me! But I write in the blind-dark and bitter cold, and past post-time as I fear. Take my truest thanks, and understand at least this rough writing, and, at all events, the real affection with which I venture to regard you. And "I" means my wife as well as—yours ever faithfully,

ROBERT BROWNING.

TO LEIGH HUNT

[In reply to a letter praising Mrs. Browning's *Aurora Leigh.*]

Bagni di Lucca, 6 October 1857.

. . . I will try and get one, at least, of the joys I came to find here, and really write to you from this place, as I meant to do—"*I*"—you know it is my wife that I write for,—though you entangle and distract either of us by the reverberations (so to speak) of pleasures over and above the main pleasure you give us. I intend to say, that you praise that poem, and mix it up with praise of her very self, and then give it to me, directly, and then give it to *her* with the pride you have just given me, and then it somehow comes back to me again increased so far, till the effect is—just as you probably intended. I wish my wife may know you more—I wish you may see and know her more—but you cannot live by her eleven years, as I have done: or, yes, what cannot you do, being the man, the poet you are? This last word I dare think I have a right to say; I *have* always venerated you as a poet; I believe your poetry to be sure of its eventual reward: other people, not unlikely, may feel like me that there has been no need of getting into feverish haste to cry out on what it is: yet you, who write it, can leave it and look at other poetry, and speak so of it: how well of you!

I am still too near the production of *Aurora Leigh* to be quite able to see it all: my wife used to write it, and lay it down to hear our child spell, or when a visitor came—it was thrust under the cushion then. At Paris, a year ago last March, she gave me the first six books to read—I having never seen a line before,—she then wrote the rest, and transcribed them in London, where I read them also. I wish, in one sense, that I had written, and she had read it, so: I should like also to tell you that I never suspected the existence of those *Sonnets from the Portuguese* till three years after they were written: they were shown to me at this very place eight years ago, in consequence of some word of mine, just as they had been suppressed thro' some mistaken word: it was I who would not bear that sacrifice, and thought of the subterfuge of a name. . . .

TO SARIANNA BROWNING

[Elizabeth Barrett Browning had died on 29 June. Browning had telegraphed the news to his sister.]

[Florence,] 30 June 1861.

Dearest, I know I have shocked you deeply, and perhaps more than was need, but you must forgive me and consider the need of doing something at once, as the news might have reached you even more abruptly,—and my own stupid state of mind yesterday. I can't even yet say of myself whether I was surprised or not, by this calamity; there is such a balance of reasons for fear (reasons for reassurance as they seemed then) that I don't know what I feel nor felt. She had been gravely affected by a series of misfortunes moral and physical,—or united, as they always were. The Villafranca Peace and the illness with it thro' the summer at Siena the year before last, last year's still worse trial for six months together, the daily waiting for news from Henrietta and the end (stopping as it did all chance of good and reparation from the summer) rendered her weaker—weaker—she did *nothing* at Rome, took some three or four little drives, never walked two paces out of the room, so could not but be in a worse state to meet an illness: yet, on the other hand, her cheerfulness, and the quick succeeding of good and quiet looks to the suffering, and the quiet of the last six months, made everyone say "how wonderfully she recovers,—she will soon be strong again, another *quiet* summer and *then*," &c. &c. Also her own impressions were in furtherance of this hope, and when I determined to forego the journey to Paris, in opposition to her expressed wishes, I not only knew but got her to confess candidly that for *herself* the reprieve from going and the trials it would entail on her would be an inestimable advantage—only, "still," "for my sake," &c., she would run the risk. *I* would not, however. We travelled, as I have told you, easily and with as little fatigue as possible, and on reaching here I let her repose at will, not asking her to go out, but take the air and exercise of the large rooms to begin with. She saw no one, two or three friends at most, had no one to tea (except when intimates looked in once or twice) and began to look well, everybody said. But the weather was suffocatingly hot, and she said to me "My cough has got well at once, as is always the way in such weather, but, curiously, it begins to affect me, as usual." I said "Let us *go* at once." We talked of places, the choice being with respect to her different requirements—when last Thursday week it seems that, while I was away at the newsroom, Miss Blagden came, say at six or seven in the evening: the windows which had been closely shut all day (as the only way of excluding the burning external air) were opened to the ground to admit the breeze which usually springs up after such days, and she placed her chair, I am told, in the doorway, between cross draughts of many windows—all the rooms opening into each other,—whereupon Isa B. remonstrated, but Ba said "Oh, the cushion at the back of the chair prevents my suffering." It was her constant way, besides. I came in and we had tea, and then she remarked "I think I have a sore throat."

Next day was past just as usual, only she told me she had a cold: at night she coughed much and sate up, restlessly, a good deal, and next morning took two Cooper's pills, I afterwards heard, with a view to staving off the attack she felt imminent: still, nothing happened unusual in the day, but toward night she felt so oppressed that she said, "I think you shall go and get me a blister and a little Ipecacuanha wine, to relieve the oppression: I find the medicine has acted inordinately,"—she rarely had recourse to it, but had taken this dose before with benefit—this time, the effects were beyond her expectation. I ran (at 10 p.m.) to the chemist's, got and applied the blister, and administered the wine, but she seemed little relieved till at 1 o'clock about or later she began to suffer distressingly from the accumulation of phlegm, which she had no power to cough up. I left her with Annunziata, dressed and knocked up (with difficulty) Dr. Wilson, a physician of great repute here, and specially conversant in maladies of the chest: he followed with me, and we found her worse, laboring most distressingly and ineffectually: Wilson prescribed promptly —got two prescriptions made up by two chymists (our porter and I got them), put on sinapisms to breast and back, and hot water with mustard to the feet. For a long while she continued unrelieved—he remained till nearly *five*. At last she recovered and we hoped all was over, but this was the second night she had passed in violent exertion without a minute's sleep. From this time things went on thus,—the symptoms were said to be always "a little better"; but Wilson examined carefully and reported, with a very serious face, that one lung was condensed (the right) and that he suspected an abscess in it; but he was aware of her long previous experience of the possibility of making shift with damaged lungs, and could not say how it might be— "it would require a long time to get well." I told part of this to Ba who repeatedly answered "It is the old story— they don't know my case—I have been tapped and sounded so, and condemned so, repeatedly: this time it is said the right is the affected lung while the left is free—Dr. Chambers said just the contrary. This is only one of my old attacks. I know all about it and I shall get better"—"It was not so bad an attack as that of two years ago," and so she continued: every day I carried her into the drawing-room where she sate only in her nightgown in her own chair, for the airiness of the room. She read newspapers, a little— saw nobody of course—going to bed about seven; I sate up most nights,—lay down by her only once, I think, or twice at most, when I was up so often that I discontinued it, which she seemed not to notice; for we brought a small bed into the drawingroom and placed her in it, and she began to doze very much, restlessly, and seemed unaware I was not in bed on a sopha behind: from the first the prescription was "nourishment, even wine, a little, often if in small quantities." But Ba never could or would try to take solid nourishment: she had strong brodo (clear soup) but would take nothing else.

So we went on, "rather better, but still with the unfavourable symptoms"—was I told twice a day. She was cheerful as ever, with voice all but extinct—still, "it would be nothing" she repeated. On Thursday night we tried asses' milk, with success—"had a better night decidedly"—always much expectoration however, and her feet swelled a little. I let Isa Blagden come and kiss her: she whispered "I am decidedly better," and gave that impression to Isa. On Friday she had asses' milk, broth twice, some bread and butter: we talked about our plans—about the house, Casa Guidi, which had suddenly grown distasteful to both of us, noisy, hot, close—poor place we have liked so for fourteen years! I said "it would be best to take a Villa—you decide on Rome for the winter, and properly,—what good of coming in the summer to a town house you cannot stay in?" She said "Ah, but I can't leave Florence, I like Florence,—you would like to establish ourselves in Rome." I said "no, there's Villa Niccolini, for instance—that would just suit." She said "that would suit—try, inquire"—and after seemed so interested about it that I said "There's no hurry,—we can get in there at once if you like, and it will be just as cool as Siena, with the convenience of being near the city." "Oh," she said, "that's not it—we must change the air now, that is my one chance. I meant, that if you take it for three years you can send up our furniture and we can enter at once in it when we return next spring." I observed a tendency to light headedness in all this—as she did—complaining of it to the doctor, and telling me how she had strange thoughts, about the windows, which "seemed to be hung in the Hungarian colours." And she smiled to Isa Blagden, at eight on Friday, as she took the glass, "Oh, I not only have asses' milk but asses' thoughts—I am so troubled with silly politics and nonsense." Isa told her something she had heard about the politics of Ricasoli which interested her so much that I interposed—"No talking, come, go Isa"—and I pushed her out; but Isa says that while my back was turned for a moment to pour out some medicine she whispered "Did you say Ricasoli said his politics were identical with those of Cavour, only they took different views of the best way of carrying them out?" —Yes—"Ah, so I thought." Isa left convinced she was better, the doctor came—"perhaps a little better." We talked over her aversion to food. I caused to be made a very strong fowl-jelly, placed in ice in readiness, and then asked if she would not try it during the night—"no". I did not know how little good it would do—the weakness came from other causes, and *these* were important, the other could be easily got rid of. I sat by her at night. She coughed little, took the emulgent duly, and another medicine, but dozed constantly: if I spoke she looked, knew me, smiled, said she was better, and relapsed. I continued this till past three in the morning, when the dozing made me very uneasy. She said "You did right not to wait—what a fine steamer—how comfortable!" I called Annunziata, bade her get hot water, as the Doctor had done, and send the porter for himself. I bade her sit up for the water. She did with little help—smiling, letting us act, and repeating "Well, you do make an exaggerated case of it!" "My hands too" she said and put them in another basin. I said you know me? "My Robert—my heavens, my beloved"—kissing me (but I can't tell you) she said "Our lives are held by God." I asked, "will you take jelly for my sake?" "Yes." I brought a saucerful and fed it by spoonfuls into her mouth. I then brought a second, and poured some into a glass—she took all. She put her arms round me—"God bless you" repeatedly—kissing me with such vehemence that when I laid her down she continued to kiss the air with her lips, and several times raised her own hands and kissed them; I said "Are you comfortable?" "Beautiful." I only put in a thing or two out of the many in my heart of hearts. Then she motioned to have her hands *sponged*—some of the jelly annoying her: this was done, and she began to sleep again—the *last*, I saw. I felt she must be raised, took her in my arms, I felt the struggle to cough begin, and end unavailingly—no pain, no sigh,—only a quiet *sight*. Her head fell on me. I thought she might have fainted, but presently there was the least knitting of the brows, and A. cried "Quest' anima benedetta è passata!"

It was so. She is with God, who takes from me the life of my life in one sense,—not so, in the truest. My life is fixed and sure now. I shall live out the remainder in her direct influence, endeavouring to complete mine, miserably imperfect now, but so as to take the good she was meant to give me. I go away from Italy at once, having no longer any business there: I have our child about whom I shall exclusively employ myself, doing her part by him. I shall live in the presence of her, in every sense, I hope and believe—so that so far my loss is not *irreparable*—but the future is nothing to me now, except inasmuch as it confirms and realizes the past. I cannot plan now, or at least talk about plans, but I shall leave Italy at once, only staying to take away the necessity of a return, for years at least. Pen has been perfect to me: he sate all yesterday with his arms round me; said things like her to me. I shall try and work hard, educate him, and live worthy of my past fifteen years' happiness. I do not feel paroxysms of grief, but as if the very blessing, she died giving me, insensible to all beside, had begun to work already. She will be buried tomorrow. Several times in writing this I have for a moment referred in my mind to her—"I will ask Ba about that." The grief of everybody is sincere, I am told. Everybody is kind in offers of help—all is done for me that can be; and it is not a little just now. Isa came at the early morning and stayed till night, taking away Pen. I shall now go in and sit with herself—my Ba, for ever. The service will be that of the Ch. of En., that I may hear those only words at the beginning. Bless you both, dearest papa and sis. I will write after tomorrow. Don't be in any concern for me, I have some of her strength, really, added to mine. Love to dear Milsand. Ever your own

R. BROWNING.

How she looks now—how perfectly beautiful!

TO JULIA WEDGWOOD

[November, 1864.]

. . . Yes, that was a strange, heavy crown, that wreath of Sonnets,[1] put on me one morning unawares, three years after it had been twined,—all this delay, because I happened early to say something against putting one's loves into verse: then again, I said something else on the other side, one evening at Lucca, and next morning she said hesitatingly "Do you know I once wrote some poems about *you*?"—and then "There they are, if you care to see them,"—and there was the little Book I have here—with the last sonnet dated two days before our marriage. How I see the gesture, and hear the tones,—and, for the matter of that, see the window at which I was standing, with the tall mimosa in front, and little church-court to the right. Afterward, the publishing them was through me. In the interest of the poet, I chose that they should be added to the other works, not minding the undue glory to me, if the fact should become transparent: there was a trial at covering it a little by leaving out one sonnet which had plainly a connexion with the former works: but it was put in afterwards when people chose to pull down the mask which, in old days, people used to respect at a masquerade. But I never cared. "The Portuguese"—purposely an ambiguous title—was that Caterina who left Camoens the riband from her hair . . . .

TO THE SAME

[Miss Wedgwood had written, "Please don't tell me the *Q(uarterly)* never killed Keats, I hate having old legends disturbed".]

[February 1865.]

. . . What you said about Keats is truer than as you say it: because I believe Keats *did* have death accelerated, if not induced, by that criticism. He did not put finger in eye, nor bully—but certainly felt strongly, what we feel strongly:

[1] Mrs. Browning's *Sonnets from the Portuguese*, first published among her collected *Poems* 1850. The "one sonnet" then left out of the sequence, *Future and Past*, was restored to it in the *Poems* of 1856.

don't believe a man of average sensibility is ever insulted by a blackguard without suffering enough: despise it? yes,—but you feel the slap in the face, too: and, in this case, to feel anything unduly was to spill the fast-lessening life: "the seeds of death were in him already," say the foolish people: why quicken them under a melon-glass then? Next, his personal discomforts were infinitely increased—that is, his death was hastened—by poverty: he had terrible fears, wanted to go abroad as ship-surgeon, to write reviews, anything to get money and keep off want and indebtedness: this came, or was not hindered coming, by the criticism which stopped the sale of his books—what poor fraction *could* have fallen to his share, when, at least six years after his death, I sent to his publisher and got a copy of each first edition?—no *second* having been called for even then [1]: lastly, from what Severn told me, his irritability at last almost amounted to madness,—don't suppose that joking about such a person's pestle and mortar, and so on, did not drop hell fire on the sore-place. . . .

TO ISABELLA BLAGDEN

20 June 1866.

My dearest Isa,—I was telegraphed for to Paris last week and arrived time enough to pass twenty-four hours more with my Father: he died on the 14th,—quite exhausted by internal hæmorrhage, which would have overcome a man of thirty. He retained all his faculties to the last—was utterly indifferent to death—asking with surprise what it was we were affected about, since he was perfectly happy?—and kept his old strange sweetness of soul to the end: nearly his last words to me, as I was fanning him, were "I am so afraid that I fatigue you, dear!"—this, while his sufferings were great; for the strength of his constitution seemed impossible to be subdued. He wanted three weeks exactly to complete his 85th year. So passed away this good, unworldly, kind hearted, religious man, whose powers natural

[1] Six years after Keats' death Browning was fifteen. Keats had been dead eight years when his poems were first reprinted—in Paris; and nineteen years before the first reprint in England.

and acquired would have so easily made him a notable man, had he known what vanity or ambition or the love of money or social influence meant. As it is, he was known by half a dozen friends. He was worthy of being Ba's father—out of the whole world, only he, so far as my experience goes. . .

TO W. G. KINGSLAND

27 November 1868.

My dear Sir,— . . . I am heartily glad I have your sympathy for what I write. Intelligence, by itself, is scarcely the thing with respect to a new book—as Wordsworth says (a little altered), "you must like it before it be worthy of your liking." In spite of your intelligence and sympathy, I can have but little doubt but that my writing has been, in the main, too hard for many I should have been pleased to communicate with, but I never designedly tried to puzzle people, as some of my critics have supposed. On the other hand, I never pretended to offer such literature as should be a substitute for a cigar, or a game of dominoes, to an idle man. So perhaps, on the whole, I get my deserts and something over,—not a crowd, but a few I value more. Let me remember gratefully that I may class you among these; while you, in turn, must remember me as—Yours very faithfully

ROBERT BROWNING.

TO ALEXANDER B. GROSART

[Grosart, preparing his edition of *The Prose Works of William Wordsworth* 1876, had written to ask whether Wordsworth had indeed been the original of Browning's *The Lost Leader*. Browning's poem is printed on page 133 above.]

24 February 1875.

Dear Mr. Grosart,—I have been asked the question you now address me with, and as duly answered it, I can't remember how many times: there is no sort of objection to one more assurance, or rather confession, on my part that I *did* in my hasty youth presume to use the great and venerated personality of Wordsworth as a sort of painter's model; one from which this or the other particular feature may be selected and turned to account: had I intended more, above all, such a boldness as portraying the entire man, I should not have talked about "handfuls of silver and bits of ribbon." These never influenced the change of politics in the great poet; whose defection, nevertheless, accompanied as it was by a regular face-about of his special party, was to my juvenile apprehension, and even mature consideration, an event to deplore. But just as in the tapestry on my wall I can recognize figures which have *struck out* a fancy, on occasion, that though truly enough thus derived, yet would be preposterous as a copy, so, though I dare not deny the original of my little poem, I altogether refuse to have it considered as the "very effigies" of such a moral and intellectual superiority. Faithfully yours,

ROBERT BROWNING.

TO F. J. FURNIVALL

[Furnivall, who at this date was in process of founding the Browning Society, had written one of the many letters in which he asked the poet questions relating to his writings and his beliefs.]

11 October 1881.

. . . Last, about my being "strongly against Darwin, rejecting the truths of science and regretting its advance"—you only do as I should hope and expect in disbelieving *that*. It came, I suppose, of Hohenstiel-Schwangau's[1] expressing the notion which was the popular one at the appearance of Darwin's book—and you might as well charge Shakespeare with holding that there were men whose heads grew beneath their shoulders, because Othello told Desdemona that he had seen such. In reality, all that seems *proved* in Darwin's scheme was a conception familiar to me from the beginning: see in *Paracelsus* the progressive development from senseless matter to organized, until man's appearance (Part V). Also in *Cleon*, see the order of "life's mechanics,"—and I daresay in many passages of my

[1] Of the writings referred to in this letter *Prince Hohenstiel-Schwangau* 1871 and *Luria* 1846 are not represented in the present volume. The relevant passage in *Paracelsus* will be found on page 41; *Cleon* on page 355; and *Mr Sludge "The Medium"* on page 440. Browning's last word on evolution was Francis Furini's sermon (*supra*; p. 639), published in 1887.

poetry: for how can one look at Nature as a whole and doubt that, wherever there is a gap, a "link" must be "missing"—through the limited power and opportunity of the looker? But go back and back, as you please, *at* the back, as Mr. Sludge is made to insist, you find (*my* faith is as constant) creative intelligence, acting on matter but not resulting from it. Once set the balls rolling, and ball may hit ball and send any number in any direction over the table; but I believe in the cue pushed by a hand. When one is taunted (as I notice is often fancied an easy method with the un-Darwinized)—taunted with thinking successive acts of creation credible, metaphysics have been stopped short at, however physics may fare: time and space being purely conceptions of our own, wholly inapplicable to intelligence of another kind—with whom, as I made Luria say, there is an "everlasting moment of creation," if one at all,—past, present, and future, one and the same state. This consideration does not affect Darwinism proper in any degree. But I do not consider that his case as to the changes in organization, brought about by desire and will in the creature, is proved. Tortoises never saw their own shells, top or bottom, nor those of their females, and are diversely variegated all over, each species after its own pattern. And the insects; this one is coloured to escape notice, this other to attract it, a third to frighten the foe—all out of one brood of caterpillars hatched in one day. No—I am incredulous—and *you*, dear patron and friend, are abundantly tired; so, thus much shall serve, scribbled as it has come to pass. . . .

TO EDMUND YATES

[? 1882.]

Dear Mr. Yates,—The Browning Society, I need not say, as well as Browning himself, are fair game for criticism. I had no more to do with the founding it than the babe unborn; and, as Wilkes was no Wilkeite, I am quite other than a Browningite. But I cannot wish harm to a society of, with a few exceptions, names unknown to me, who are busied about my books so disinterestedly. The exaggerations probably come of the fifty-years'-long charge of unintelligibility against my books; such reactions are possible, though I never looked for the beginning of one so soon. That there is a grotesque side to the thing is certain; but I have been surprised and touched by what cannot but have been well intentioned, I think. Anyhow, as I never felt inconvenienced by hard words, you will not expect me to wax bumptious because of undue compliment: so enough of "Browning,"—except that he is yours very truly, "while this machine is to him." Yours,

ROBERT BROWNING.

TO ALFRED LORD TENNYSON

[On the occasion of Tennyson's 80th birthday. Browning, who was 77, had only four more months to live: Tennyson survived him until 1892.]

5 August 1889.

My dear Tennyson,—To-morrow is your birthday—indeed a memorable one. Let me say I associate myself with the universal pride of our country in your glory, and in its hope that for many and many a year we may have your very self among us—secure that your poetry will be a wonder and delight to all those appointed to come after; and for my own part let me further say, I have loved you dearly. May God bless you and yours! . . . At no moment from first to last of my acquaintance with your works, or friendship with yourself, have I had any other feeling expressed or kept silent than this, which an opportunity allows me to utter—that I am and ever shall be, my dear Tennyson, admiringly and affectionately yours,

ROBERT BROWNING.

TENNYSON'S REPLY

August 1889.

My dear Browning,—I thank you with my whole heart and being for your noble and affectionate letter, and with my whole heart and being I return your friendship. To be loved and appreciated by so great and powerful a nature as yours will be a solace to me, and lighten my dark hours during the short time of life that is left to me. Ever yours,

TENNYSON.

INDEX OF TITLES AND FIRST LINES

INDEX OF TITLES AND FIRST LINES